THE ENCYCLOPAEDIA OF SPORTS

THE

ENCYCLOPAEDIA

OF

SPORTS

(in 4 vols.)

Edited By
HEDLEY PEEK
AND
F.G. AFLALO

Vol II

EL-LEO

GYAN PUBLISHING HOUSE

NEW DELHI-110 002

THE ENCYCLOPAEDIA OF SPORTS
(Sports, Physical Education)

ISBN: 81-212-0276-0 (Set)
ISBN : 81-212-0278-7

Published in 1997 in India
by Gyan Publishing House
5, Ansari Road
New Delhi-110002

Printed at Goyal Offset Printers, Delhi-110035

ELAND.—The Eland (*Oreas canna*), *Pofu* of the Bechuanas, *Mpofu* of the Matabele and Zulus, as well as of the Swahilis of East Africa, is the largest antelope in the world, and is found only in Africa. There are two varieties—the unstriped Eland, whose range seems never to have extended much north of Lake Ngami, and the striped or Derbian Eland (*Oreas derbianus*), discovered by Livingstone, which, towards the Zambesi and thence northward into the African continent, takes the place of the more southern, desert-loving, and unstriped Eland. The unstriped Eland attains greater dimensions than its striped congener, although it frequents by preference much more waterless and desert country.

At the present time, bull Elands may still be found in the northern portion of the Kalahari standing 6 feet at the shoulder and weighing 1,500 pounds or more. Instances are on record of these magnificent creatures measuring no less than 6 feet 6 inches (19½ hands) at the withers, and weighing 2,000 lbs. But, thanks to incessant persecution, Elands of the present day can seldom hope to attain such weight and measurement. The cows are considerably less in weight and height than the bulls. The colour of a herd of Elands varies greatly. The younger animals are of a rufous fawn; in the intermediate stages the colour is of a paler fawn or dun; while in the old bulls and cows the hair becomes much thinner with age, the skin shows through, and the body colouring is of a slaty blue. The coat is as smooth as that of an Alderney cow. The head, especially in the bulls, is small, neat, and game-like. The bulls are easily singled out by their much greater size and bulk, their shorter and more massive horns, and the thick bristly tuft of bright brown hair which stands out from the forehead just beneath the horns. The body is exceedingly massive, the shoulders are very deep, and a broad dewlap depends towards the knees. The legs are clean.

Although so frequently found in purely desert country, the Eland puts on flesh and fat in a quite amazing way. Even in the dry season of the South African winter the writer has hunted and killed these antelopes in the waterless recesses of the North Kalahari, and found them fat and in high condition. The flesh is excellent; tender, juicy, and partaking of the flavour of young, game-like beef—if such a combination can be imagined. The horns of a well-grown bull attain occasionally a length of 31 or 32 inches and are extremely massive at the base. The horns of a cow will sometimes reach a length of about 34 inches; but they are slimmer and less deeply marked in the twist than those of the male.

In the old days Elands must have been extraordinarily plentiful in every part of South Africa, down even to the shores of the Cape Peninsula. Their name yet lingers throughout the country, and Eland's Drift, Eland's Kopje, Eland's River, and Eland's Fontein, are amongst the commonest of South African place-names. But even in the days of the flint-lock the Eland was always one of the easiest of all game animals to shoot. Its flesh and skin were always in high demand; it was everywhere eagerly pursued; and at the present day, except in the difficult recesses of the Kalahari Desert, the old unstriped Eland of the Cape (*Oreas canna*) may now be looked upon as a vanished quadruped. In the Cape Colony, Great Namaqualand, Zululand, the Transvaal, the Orange Free State and Bechuanaland as far as the tropic of Capricorn it is extinct. Yet Cornwallis Harris in 1837 describes this noble beast as frequenting the

BULL ELAND.

Av. height, 72 in. Av. length of horns, 28 in.; Max. length, 34 in.

plains of the interior, *i.e.*, middle Bechuanaland, the Transvaal and Orange Free State, "in vast herds." A few are still preserved by the Natal Government in a corner of the Drakensberg Mountains between Natal and Basutoland. In the Kalahari, or desert portions of the Bakwena and Bamangwato countries—the territory of the chiefs Sebele and Khama—the Eland is now first encountered as the traveller passes north. In all this northern region of the Kalahari, and westward towards Lake Ngami, the unstriped Eland still roams in large herds. The writer has encountered them in recent years between Kanne and Inkouani in troops of between thirty and forty, and still larger herds exist. It is a fact that these desert-bred Elands can and do exist without water for seven months in the year, in common with the gemsbok, giraffe, duiker, and steinbok. In the Ovampo country, west of Lake Ngami, Elands are still found. Here and in Portuguese West Africa, however, they are striped. North of the Botletli River, and in Matabeleland, Mashonaland, and Portuguese South-East Africa, the striped variety of Eland is still to be found, occasionally in big troops. Thence into Africa, as far north as Senegambia on the West and British East Africa on the East, the Derbian Eland, distinguished by its white stripings, is to be found.

Of all African beasts of chase the Eland is the most readily killed. In South Africa, where game can be hunted on horseback, nothing is easier than to ride into a troop and turn out and shoot the fattest and most desirable specimen. Occasionally the Eland can be driven right up to the hunter's wagon and slain there. The Eland has no defensive powers whatever. Sometimes, however, in more hilly country, or where the animals are in low condition, the cows will give some trouble even to the mounted man. As a rule the hunter can, after five or ten minutes' gallop, ride right up to his quarry and shoot it without trouble from a saddle. Such is the writer's own experience. When thoroughly blown the Eland breaks from its gallop into a slinging trot, and the hunter may then easily know that the game is his. A Martini-Henry sporting rifle, a ·450, an Afrikander, or indeed any handy rifle, is sufficient to bring down an Eland, which is one of the softest and most easily killed of African game. In East Africa the Eland is principally stalked on foot, or driven by native beaters in the direction in which the sportsman lies concealed. The head of an Eland, especially of a good bull, forms an admirable trophy; yet these noble creatures are so easily shot, and are vanishing so rapidly, that the hunter may well content himself with a few good specimens.

At the present day in South Africa, the Eland is seldom encountered in wide open plains. It frequents by preference moderately bushed country or thin forest. In East Africa, however, it is still to be found on the open plains.

H. A. BRYDEN.

ELEPHANT, AFRICAN (*Elephas africanus*)—Though somewhat less in bulk and stature than either the Mastodon or the Mammoth—its vanished prototypes of prehistoric times—the African elephant is to-day the mightiest beast which yet exists upon our planet; and although we have unfortunately but scant data to go upon regarding the maximum size ever attained by the largest males of the species, I think I shall not be far wrong if I put the standing height of average sized animals at from ten feet to ten feet six inches. I have arrived at these figures not only from measurements taken by myself, but also from a study of what has been written on the subject by such practical sportsmen and naturalists as the late Colonel Sanderson and Sir Samuel Baker. According to the last-named eminent authority, the African elephant exceeds the Asiatic species in both sexes by about a foot in standing height at the shoulder, and as Colonel Sanderson has shown very clearly by an exhaustive series of measurements that the average standing height of the male Indian elephant is from nine feet to nine feet six inches, that of the African species should be from ten feet to ten feet six inches if Sir Samuel Baker's estimate of the average difference between the two be correct.

This accords exactly with my own experience, for of five ordinary full-grown bull African elephants whose standing height I carefully

HEAD OF AFRICAN ELEPHANT.

Av. height at shoulder, 10 ft. 3 in. Av. length of tusks, 7 ft. 6 in.; Max. length of tusks, 9 ft. 5 in.

measured by taking the distance in a straight line, between two poles placed exactly parallel to one another and fixed upright in the ground, the one at the sole of the forefoot, and the other at the top of the shoulder of the dead animal, one stood nine feet eleven inches, two exactly ten feet, one ten feet four inches, and one ten feet six inches.

But, just as in India some few elephants are known to have much exceeded the ordinary dimensions of the species, so also in Africa it may be supposed that animals occur from time to time of exceptional stature. The late William Cotton Oswell, in the account of his African hunting experiences contained in the volume on Big-game Shooting of the Badminton Library, says: "I have seen thousands of elephants, and shot the largest one I ever saw. I measured him, and he was twelve feet two inches."

I have also heard of other measurements of well over eleven feet taken by reliable men. Such exceptional animals must, I fancy have always been very rare in South Africa, for although in the earlier years of my hunting career I saw a large number of full-grown bull elephants in the aggregate, I never remember to have seen any one which towered above its fellows. My conclusion, therefore, is that although giants of the race undoubtedly occur, they are very exceptional, and that, speaking generally, the vertical standing height at the shoulder of the male elephant in South Africa may be taken to be from ten feet to ten feet six inches.

The size of the tusks in the African elephant varies very greatly, and is no criterion as to the stature of the animal. In the southern part of that continent a full-grown bull will seldom carry tusks weighing less than thirty pounds apiece, whilst tusks of over sixty pounds weight have, in my experience, always been exceptional. Thus, amongst considerably more than one hundred bull elephants which were shot in 1873 in the country between Matabeleland and the Zambesi River, there were only two animals whose tusks weighed over eighty pounds each, and not more than fifteen which weighed over sixty pounds.

In portions of Central and Eastern Africa I believe that the average size and weight of elephant tusks is greater than in the countries to the south of the Zambesi River. The largest tusk known is in the possession of Sir Edmund Loder. It was brought from Central Africa to Zanzibar, and is nine feet five inches long and twenty-two and a half inches in circumference at the thickest part, weighing 184 pounds now that it is thoroughly dried out, so that when freshly taken from the skull of the grand beast which carried it, it must have weighed over 200 pounds.

The largest tusk I have ever heard of in Southern Africa was bought by a Boer hunter, named Bernhard Bauer, from the natives near Lake N'gami, in 1873, I think. It was weighed in the presence of many people at the store of Messrs. Francis and Clark, traders in old Soshong, the former capital of Khama's country, and turned the scale at 174 pounds. What became of this remarkable tusk I have never heard. An elephant carrying a magnificent pair of tusks was killed in Matabeleland within seventy miles of the present township of Bulawayo, three or four years before my first visit to the country. Late one evening a young Boer hunter, named Potgieter, came across some elephant bulls in the thick bush between the Vungo and Gwelo rivers. Amongst them was an animal with tusks which protruded many feet from its head, and seemed almost to touch the ground. This elephant was severely wounded by young Potgieter, but, thanks to the thickness of the bush and the fast gathering darkness, it made its escape for the time being, only to die, however, shortly afterwards. The carcase was ultimately found by a native hunter, named Zwartboy, by whom the tusks were sold to a trader in Bulawayo. They were a very perfect pair, measuring over nine feet in length, and weighing upwards of 150 pounds each. Another very similar pair were bought from Umzila, the King of the Gaza Zulus, by Mr. Reuben Benningfield in 1874. This pair I saw myself in Durban in March, 1875. They were nearly nine feet in length measured over the curve, were a perfect pair, and together weighed just over 300 pounds. The late Mr. William Cotton Oswell also shot an elephant on the Botletli River about the year 1845 with tusks weighing between 230 and 240 pounds the pair—probably the largest pair of tusks, the original owner of which has ever been really shot by an Englishman, though larger have been obtained in barter from the natives. Personally I have been very unlucky in coming across elephants with abnormally large tusks, the largest pair I ever secured of my own shooting only weighing 166 pounds the pair, and I never saw larger tusks in the head of a living elephant.

In Africa, as is well known, female elephants as a rule carry tusks as well as the males. Ten to twelve pounds is the average weight of the tusk of a full grown elephant cow, and although a weight of fifteen or sixteen pounds is not uncommon, anything over twenty pounds is exceptionally fine. I once saw the tusks of a cow elephant shot in Matabeleland, one of which weighed thirty-nine pounds, and the other nearly as much. One of these tusks showed signs of having lain on the ground for a considerable time, as in one part the enamel was much dried and cracked, proving that the animal which once bore them had been found dead, having probably escaped from her pursuers when first wounded, only to die subsequently from her injuries. These abnormal cow tusks were about six feet in length, nearly straight, and almost solid, the hollows at their bases being singularly small. No one with any knowledge of elephant tusks could possibly have mistaken them for those of a male. Speaking generally, I should think that on the average the tusks of a full-grown African bull elephant weigh about four times as much as those of a full-grown cow, and I look upon a cow tusk weighing thirty-nine pounds as being as great a rarity as the largest bull tusk now in existence.

Amongst African elephants, tuskless animals of either sex are rare, though much more so amongst the bulls than the cows. Indeed, I only remember to have seen one bull elephant without tusks, though in every herd one or more tuskless cows are to be met with. I have seen and shot both bulls and cows with only one tusk, and in such cases have found the bone on the other side quite solid, and without any kind of rudimentary hollow where the missing tusk ought to have been set.

At the present day in South Africa, the elephant has ceased to exist in many parts of the country where it was once plentiful. In the Cape Colony it would in all probability have long since become extinct, had it not been strictly protected for many years by the Government. Thanks to this protection, wild elephants still roam the forests of the Knysma and the waste lands of the Addo bush in considerable and ever-increasing numbers, but save for these small remnants of a mighty host, not another individual of their race is to be found for many a hundred miles to the north and north-west.

In the interior of Eastern South Africa, however, elephants are not quite such a thing of the past, and from the eastern borders of the Transvaal to the Zambesi, they may still be found in districts where the country is uninhabited or very thinly peopled, and where at the same time the surroundings are suitable to their requirements. Through all the enormous expanse of low-lying forest-clad country, also, which lies between the habitable parts of Rhodesia and the Zambesi, to the east of the Victoria Falls, elephants still roam; but so cautious have these animals become, and so vast is the territory over which they perpetually wander, that they are very difficult to find.

Three things have saved the wild, unprotected elephant in Southern Africa from extinction. These are the extraordinary development of its sense of smell, its power of walking enormous distances without rest, and the vast extent of the country over which it can travel after having been disturbed. I can illustrate all three points.

Many years ago—in 1872—I was hunting elephants in company with an experienced Hottentot hunter in the forest country to the north of Matabeleland. One day we were ascending a small isolated hill in order to get a view over the surrounding country, when my companion espied a herd of elephants, and at once directed my attention to them. They were advancing rapidly through the forest in a long straggling line, and were heading in a direction that would have taken them across the line of march by which we had come to the hill. As soon as the old hunter at my side realised this fact, which he did at a glance, he said to me, "We must descend the hill at once and cut off the elephants before they reach our spoor, or they will assuredly scent it and take alarm." We therefore scrambled down the hill and ran back through the open forest as quickly as possible in the direction from which we had come. We were in time to intercept the elephants just as the foremost, an old cow, reached the line along which our feet had come in contact with the earth. I saw her stop dead and scent the ground rapidly with her outstretched trunk, the point of which was moved quickly to and fro close to the ground. That brief examination was sufficient, her delicate sense of smell having evidently conveyed to her brain the information that human beings, the dreaded enemies of her race, had lately passed that way, and might therefore still be near her. How she conveyed the information to her companions I do not know, but in another moment the whole herd had swung round, and were making off at a shambling trot in the opposite direction. Then followed a long and exhausting chase in the intense heat of an African sun, which, however, resulted in the death of several elephants.

On another occasion I remember following four enormous bulls which had come to drink one night in a lagoon formed by the overflow of the river Chobi. We took up the tracks at the first dawn of day, the elephants being not far ahead of us, and were in momentary expectation of coming up with them, when we suddenly found that they had become alarmed and had fled. An examination of the ground showed us that they had turned short round on reaching the track we had made when approaching the river on the previous day with a long retinue of Kaffirs. Their keenness of scent had at once enabled them to detect the taint left on the ground by human feet which had passed that way some twenty hours before, and, as we never caught them up, was the means of saving them for that day at least from the attentions of an elephant gun.

In the year 1885, some five years before the occupation of Mashunaland by Mr. Rhodes's pioneers, I was camped on the banks of the Umfuli river in company with a well-known Boer hunter, Cornelis van Rooyen. We had returned to camp after a good day's buffalo hunting, when two of the Kaffirs we had left at the carcase of one of the buffaloes reported that a herd of elephants had passed through the bush within sight of them, just as it was growing dusk. As the wind was favourable, they did not think the keen-scented animals had become aware of their presence, or taken alarm in any way, so we determined to follow them up the following day.

The next morning, therefore, at earliest dawn, we rode out and cut their spoor some two miles beyond the spot where the Kaffirs had seen them the preceding evening, and a glance at the tracks showed us that they had still been walking quietly here, and had evidently not scented any of the dead buffaloes. The elephants had a long start of about ten hours in front of us; but as they had been feeding to some extent, stripping a tree here and there of its bark, sometimes breaking off large branches, and even stopping now and then to dig up some succulent root, it looked as if they were altogether unsuspicious of danger, and might therefore be expected to halt as soon as the sun became uncomfortably warm, in order to enjoy a midday siesta in a shady spot, as lazy, sober-minded elephants always do in parts of the country where they have not been much hunted. There was, amongst the great round and oblong tracks of some twenty large elephants, the spoor of a tiny calf that could not have been many days old, and the fact that so young an animal was amongst the herd made us feel sure that we should come up with them in the course of the day; for we did not think such a baby elephant would be capable of travelling any very great distance without resting. We soon learned too, by a careful examination of the ground, that two bulls were with the herd, the one evidently an animal of the largest size, whilst the second was considerably smaller, but yet might be expected to carry tusks of about 20 to 25 lbs. weight each. The big bull, we feared, would prove to be a tuskless elephant, which both Van Rooyen and myself had lately seen in this district, the animal I have before mentioned as the only tuskless bull elephant I have ever seen.

We had ridden out from camp accompanied by some half dozen Kaffirs and a Masarwa Bushman. The former were Matabele and Mashunas, and were very much like any other ordinary specimens of their race, but the latter was one of the most sagacious hunters I have ever met even amongst men of his own wild race, and, although considerably past the prime of life, he was simply unsurpassable as a tracker and runner. It was, I should say, about 5.30 A.M. when old Marman the Bushman took up the spoor, and we stuck to it at a very fast walk till about 3 P.M., only twice taking the saddles off the horses for a few minutes at a time to ease their backs and allow them to stale.

By this time all the Kaffirs were very much fagged, as the heat of the sun had been intense for the last five hours, and when we saddled up our horses for the third time and old Marman announced his intention of running on the spoor, we told them to take a rest and follow quietly on the tracks of our horses. Old Marman now commenced to run, and in all my life I have never seen a more marvellous feat of endurance. He would run a mile at a good sharp trot, then walk very fast for a quarter or half a mile, then run again; and so he kept on for mile after mile and hour after hour. At length the burning sun sank from view, but still the elephants were far ahead of us, and still old Marman trotted doggedly on their tracks.

Soon after this time we came to where the elephants had rested during the fiercest heat of the day, possibly from two till four, and as on again moving they had scattered and commenced to feed in real earnest, breaking down trees and digging up roots in all directions, we might yet have come up with them had we been in a part of the world where the twilight is long drawn out. But within the tropics, some 20 degrees south of the equator, once the sun has set, night comes on apace. Nor could old Marman run without a check on the tracks of a herd of elephants that had now scattered about, thinking of nothing but appeasing their hunger, in the same way as he had done before when they kept travelling straight ahead, only breaking off branches occasionally and chewing them as they marched along. Darkness, therefore, soon forced us to abandon the pursuit till the following morning.

During the thirteen hours we had been on the elephants' tracks, I think we could not have covered less than fifty miles, as old Marman must have run nearly, if not quite, twenty after three o'clock, and allowing over an hour for the time lost while the horses were offsaddled, we had then already done about eight hours' very fast walking since first taking up the spoor in the early morning. The elephants had had twenty-four hours in which to accomplish this distance, but as they apparently had no particular cause for so long a journey, and were moreover accompanied by a very young calf, it would appear as if this were only their normal rate of travel during the twenty-four hours.

Even in districts where elephants have been but little molested, their tracks will often have to be followed for many hours before they can be overtaken, and where they have been constantly persecuted for many years, as is the case all over Matabeleland, and Mashunaland, they never seem to rest for more than a short time during the hottest portion of the day, but keep constantly moving forward, feeding as they walk. They do not confine themselves to any particular district, but roam over the whole of the enormous areas of uninhabited wilderness of which they were once the undisputed masters, but in which they are now never safe from the attacks of ivory hunters.

To return to the narrative of our pursuit, when it became so dark that we could no longer follow their tracks, we decided to pass the night at the nearest stream, and then take up the spoor again in the morning. Luckily, in this part of the country water was very plentiful, as we were in the midst of the many small streams which, rising on the northern face of Intaba Insimbi (the Hill of Iron), run down into the Umzweswe river. We soon reached one of these, a little rill of beautifully clear water, flowing down an open glade, carpeted with a short, succulent, red-seeded grass, which, springing up at the hottest time of year, affords excellent pasturage for horses and cattle, and which I have never seen anywhere else, but in the upland valleys of Rhodesia. As our horses had had no food at all during the day, we hobbled them and turned them loose, having first collected a large quantity of dry wood and kindled two large fires, one on each side of the little glade. This we did in order to scare away lions, and then, allowing the old Bushman to get a little well-earned sleep, Van Rooyen and I kept up the fires, and from time to time turned the horses whenever they strayed into the darkness. We had eaten nothing since the previous evening, nor had we brought any food with us; but to go a day without food and pass the night without a blanket is not looked upon as any very great hardship by an elephant hunter, and we should have felt quite happy had we been sure of overtaking our game on the morrow. Neither of us, I think, expected to do so, as the calf, on whose weakness we had reckoned to delay his seniors, was evidently a very strong little animal, and moreover, when day dawned, the elephants would again have had the whole night during which to increase their lead. However, we determined to follow them for another day and trust to fortune.

About midnight we tied the horses to a tree close behind one of our fires, and then lying down with our backs to the blaze, got what rest we could before daylight. As soon as we could see we saddled up, and once more took up the spoor of the elephants, which old Marman followed at a more sober pace than on the preceding evening, though he still got over the ground at a good sharp walk. For mile after mile we stuck to it, and with every mile the chance of ever overtaking them seemed to grow smaller. We had twice offsaddled the horses and were thinking of doing so for the third time. The cool of early dawn had gradually given place to a temperature which, culminating when the sun was at its zenith, seemed at length about to become more bearable, as the glowing orb was now dipping towards the west. And yet the elephants seemed further away from us than ever. Their dung, and the leaves of the branches which had been broken off and lay scattered on their track, were getting drier and drier, and I do not believe that at three in the afternoon of this second day of the pursuit we had yet reached the spot where they had passed at daybreak.

Suddenly old Marman stopped as we came to some tracks crossing the spoor we were following at right angles. After a quick, eager examination he said in the Matabele language, "Their familiar spirits (amaglosi) have deserted them," and then told us that the animals we were following were not far in front of us, as they had recrossed their own tracks but a short time ago. We soon satisfied ourselves that it was the same troop of elephants by noting that the footprints of the little calf and the big bull were amongst the fresh tracks.

Shortly after this we came up with the animals themselves in some very thick bush, and shot the two bulls, the biggest proving to be a tusker with teeth weighing slightly over 40 lbs. each, while the tusks of the smaller bull did not weigh quite 40 lbs. the pair. The Kaffirs we had left behind the previous day turned up, contrary to our expectation, before dark, and that night, after a forty-eight hours' fast, we all had a glorious meal of elephant's heart and trunk. The next day we chopped out the tusks and reached our camp on the Umfuli on the evening of the fourth day after we had left it. We should, however, never have overtaken these elephants had they not made a turn and recrossed their own spoor, unfortunately for them, just in front of us, for I believe that they had travelled just as far during the last day and night as they had done in the course of the previous twenty-four hours, and judging from my own experience on the foregoing and many other occasions, I am of opinion that when elephants have been much persecuted they travel continually during the whole year at the rate of from twenty to fifty miles every twenty-four hours.

The South African elephant, unlike any other animal with which I am acquainted, never, or at any rate very rarely, lies down to rest, though he will roll in mud or rub himself against the side of an ant-heap.[1] I make this statement advisedly, as I have seen altogether some thousands of elephants sleeping, but all have been standing, nor have I ever seen even the impression on the ground where one has been reposing. At night elephants travel and feed, taking their rest during the hottest hours of the day, at which time they stand in the shade of large trees, or in the recesses of the wait-a-bit thorn jungles for which they have such a strong predilection.

In proof of the assertion I have made that in South Africa elephants wander over enormous tracts of country, I will adduce the fact that in 1878 some friends of mine cut a bullet out of an elephant killed in Eastern Mashunaland that had been fired into it the year before, a long way to the west of the Gwai river. There was no mistaking the bullet, as it had retained its shape and the marks of the grooving perfectly, and could only have been fired out of a certain 12-bore Westley Richards rifle used the year before in the thorn jungles of the Linquasi district by an English hunter—Mr. Spencer Drake. The distance as the crow flies between the spot where this elephant was wounded in 1877 and where it was killed in 1878 is approximately some 250 miles.

I have seen it stated that in Africa full grown bull elephants are never found in company with cows, and as Dr. Livingstone has said that a picture representing bull and cow elephants mixed would at once stamp the artist who painted it as unfamiliar with the habits of the animals he depicted, the mixing of the sexes must be unusual, as the good doctor was a very careful observer, and few men have had better opportunities of observing the African elephant in its wild state. Nevertheless I have seen a good many exceptions to this rule, but such changes of habit may have been caused to a considerable extent by constant persecution, which would result in the breaking up of the small troops of bulls, until possibly single animals were left wandering alone, which were ready to consort with any others of their kind they happened to meet. On more than one occasion I have seen a small herd of bull elephants standing sleeping close to a large number of cows but in such cases the bulls were all together and not mixed with the females.

In South Africa, before the natives became possessed of firearms, the elephant was killed in various ways. Sometimes he was caught in a pitfall, though probably few but young and half-grown animals were the victims, and sometimes his death was compassed with heavy assegais, which were driven deep down between his shoulder blades by a savage seated in a tree waiting on his line of march. These long, broad-bladed assegais were fixed into heavy shafts, the weight of which worked them gradually into the vitals of the wounded animal.

In the country lying between Matabeleland and the Zambesi, even in my time, elephants were first hamstrung whilst standing asleep, by a blow from a thin, sharp, broad-bladed axe, which severed the "tendo Achillis," and then done to death with assegais. If the "tendo Achillis" was cut through, the poor brute was at the mercy of his assailants, being almost unable to move, but if the blow failed or was only partially successful, he was able to make good his escape, and in 1872 and 1873 I shot several elephants that had been wounded by blows dealt with axes in the endeavour to sever the "tendo Achillis," and in some cases found the wounds still unhealed and sloughing.

By Europeans elephants are, or rather have been, hunted (for I think there are now no professional elephant hunters left south of the Zambesi) both on foot and horseback. There is a considerable element of danger in either form of the sport, as, although elephants are in one way the most timid of animals, and will not allow a human being to approach them if they can possibly get out of his way, yet when interfered with, and when they discover that escape is hopeless, they are liable to become excessively vicious. Personally I rank the elephant as a more vicious animal than the buffalo; that is to say, taking an average of the considerable number of both animals I have shot, I have been charged by a larger proportion of elephants than of buffaloes.

As I have said, elephant hunting as a business has now become a thing of the past in South Africa, for the game is no longer worth the candle.

[1] In the interior of South Africa ant-heaps are sometimes twenty feet in height.

In the years 1872, 1873 and 1874, however, although I had to do an immense amount of hard work, I found it easy enough to pay all my expenses by elephant hunting in the country to the north and north-west of Matabeleland. During that period I hunted entirely on foot, using the commonest of old muzzle-loading trade guns, and cheap powder that was sold to the natives in 5lb. bags. My bag for the three years was seventy-eight elephants, but I cannot help thinking that had I then possessed a good breech-loading rifle I might have killed at least double that number.

Like every one else who has shot many elephants on foot, I have had some narrow escapes, and have owed my life many times to the fact that the African elephant can almost invariably be stopped in full charge by a shot in any part of the head or chest, even though the wound inflicted may not be mortal. When an African elephant charges he raises his head and spreads his enormous ears like two sails. When he first rushes out he often raises his trunk high in the air, trumpeting loudly the while. But such a demonstration is, I think, usually only meant to frighten his enemies, and he is not likely to come far with his trunk upraised before turning round and rejoining the herd. But when an elephant really means to charge home, he comes on (usually, at any rate) with his trunk held down between his tusks, and the point curled in towards his chest, keeping up a succession of short, sharp screams of rage all the time. It is useless then to try to kill him with a shot in the front of the head, as the angle at which his head is held makes it impossible for a bullet fired from the shoulder of the man he is charging, who is standing perhaps some twenty yards in front of him, to reach his brain (which lies low down in the back of the skull), without first passing through some 2ft. of trunk and a great deal of bone. The best shot under such circumstances is right through the trunk into the chest, as a powerful rifle or smooth bore gun will drive a bullet right through an elephant's trunk and then reach his heart. I have killed several in this way, and have hit many others in the head, trunk or chest on the side of the trunk when they were charging, but without exception every one, as soon as he was struck, immediately stopped screaming, and swerved off to one side. Once I remember I was charged by an elephant bull which I had wounded with a ·450 bore Metford rifle by Gibbs, of Bristol. As he came on, I wondered whether the small bore bullet would stop him, as it would have been all up with me had it not done so. He was screaming loudly, but immediately the little bullet struck him in the chest he swerved off, and became silent, and I killed him with another shot.

Elephant-hunting on horseback is very much pleasanter and infinitely less fatiguing than the same pursuit on foot, and, given a thoroughly trained horse and fairly open country to hunt in, there ought not to be much danger in the sport. But one cannot always have things one's own way, and, as a matter of fact, when you do come up with elephants, your horse will usually be pretty tired, and your game will be encountered very probably in dense thorny jungle, through which a charging elephant can crash in an almost straight line, whilst a horse has to pick his way amongst the trees and bushes. Under such circumstances a horse, which in open ground, and when fairly fresh, could give an elephant forty yards out of a hundred and then beat him, may very easily be caught by his bulky pursuer; and many cases have come within my own knowledge where horses and their riders have been overtaken by elephants, sometimes with fatal results. I myself once had a marvellous escape, as my tired horse was run into and thrown down by a wounded cow elephant, from under whose body I extricated myself, unhurt indeed, but covered with blood that was streaming from a wound in her chest.

I will now conclude this article with a few words as to the merits of various forms of rifles for elephant-shooting. Probably ninety per cent. of the enormous number of elephants which are now annually killed in Africa for the sake of their ivory are shot by the natives with 12-bore muzzle-loading muskets. Therefore a 12-bore rifle is quite capable of killing an elephant, and many indeed have been killed with rifles of a very much smaller bore than this. Indeed, I have killed ten elephants myself with a ·450-bore rifle by Gibbs, of Bristol.

However, although elephants can be killed with small-bore rifles pretty easily if picked shots can be taken, such rifles would not, in my opinion, be the best that could be used by a professional elephant hunter in dense bush, where a good view of the animal is not always or even often obtainable. A very good weapon to use under such conditions would, I think, be a double eight-bore for body shots, whilst the small-bore would often be found very useful for brain shots, if solid bullets were substituted for the hollow-pointed projectiles usually employed to kill antelope and all other soft-skinned animals.

Were I a young man to-day, and were I about to proceed to Central Africa with a view to making a living by elephant hunting, I would take with me two of Holland and Holland's double eight-bore paradox guns and a small-bore rifle; but were I going to Central Africa thinking that I might possibly get the chance of killing an elephant, but not for the special purpose of hunting elephants, I would not cumber myself with any heavy rifles at all, but trust to the chance of killing one or two of these animals by shots in the brain from a small-bore rifle, for I consider it most unprofitable to go to the trouble and expense of carrying heavy arms and heavier ammunition through the interior of Africa, unless such weapons are likely to be used frequently.

F. C. SELOUS.

Since writing the above my belief in the capability of small-bore rifles to kill such ponderous animals as African elephants has been much strengthened by a letter lately published in the *Field* newspaper by Mr. A. H. Neumann, who is a thoroughly practical hunter, and has had a wide experience of big game shooting in various portions of Southern and Eastern Africa.

Writing under date Jan. 2nd, Mr. Neumann says regarding elephant shooting: "I cannot say the exact number of elephants I have shot with the ·303 rifle, as during the first part of my trip I was using a 10-bore as well, but I killed a good many with it (chiefly body shots); and since I had the bad luck to get hurt by one, I have not dared to fire any other rifle for fear of the recoil, and then I killed five of my biggest bulls, none of which were shot in the brain. I have killed several elephants with a single bullet through the heart; and though, with such a tiny puncture, a big bull takes often (though not always) a little longer to die than from a large wound, I have never had to follow one far that had received a good shot. I always use the military cartridge with solid nickel-covered bullet."

F. C. S.

ELEPHANTS IN THE ADDO BUSH —Not far from Port Elizabeth, in the Eastern Province of the Cape Colony, is the small station of Addo, situated on the outskirts of the bush, in which elephants have thrived for many years. There are probably about one hundred elephants left, sometimes to be found in one troop, but more often split up in two or three smaller troops; they wander about from end to end, apparently never leaving the bush, except to visit the adjoining farms, where they break up fences, and otherwise do a vast amount of damage.

The bush is extremely thick, and in places almost impassable, except by following the elephant paths; there are no big trees, all being of about the same height as an elephant, thus affording him excellent cover, and food within easy reach.

Though there is a small river at the end of the bush, the elephants more often water at the few small vleis or water-holes, which are dotted here and there; at one or other of these vleis fresh spoor will often be found, and then the hard work commences. Should it be last night's spoor, it will often be necessary to follow as much as twelve or even twenty miles through thick scrub before coming up with the troop. It is well to have a "boy" who thoroughly knows the bush, as he will often save many miles of weary walking; platelayers, also, an other workmen can often give information as t where the troop has lately been seen. Ele phants sometimes trek great distances througl the night, but, unless disturbed, only sleep anc feed, moving slowly through the day. Very few seem to lie down, and the greater number of the troop sleep standing. This is perhaps advantageous to the hunter, as it affords a bettei opportunity of marking them down. It is most important to know roughly the relative positions of most of the elephants in a troop, for, should you walk into the middle of them, it is certain that some will wind you before you see them, and you will have little or no chance of a shot that day. Again, it is safer when shooting to choose an animal near the the outside, for I have constantly seen, on the report of a rifle, the whole troop rush round and round in a circle, congregate, and then make off in a straight line, carrying everything before them. There would be little chance for the sportsman who was in the centre of that circle.

By climbing up trees, and patiently watching, you may gradually work your way towards the outsiders, keeping down wind; they are very difficult to see, owing to the nature of the bush, but generally the flap of an ear in the sunlight, or some other movement, will discover their position. Having settled on your animal, it is, as a rule, simple to get up to the very bush behind which he is sleeping or feeding; once there, you should seize the first opportunity offered, and shoot quickly. Should he make off, in two or three strides he is hidden from view, and it is unlikely you will get another chance that day.

A little before midday is the best time to come up with them, as they are mostly sleeping then and easily approached; but towards evening it is more difficult, and they are beginning to get on the move.

During the day they are timid and will generally try to escape, though there are a few cases on record of men having been killed by elephants in the Addo Bush. In one of these cases, two brothers (Dutchmen) were followed by their dog, who ran forward and worried the elephants until they at last turned and chased him straight back to his masters, who, as a last resource, got up trees a little distance apart; one of them sat there, and saw his brother dragged down and trampled to death.

At night they are supposed to be "Kings of the Forest," and people say that after sunset they will more often charge than not. I remember one evening coming up with a troop just at sundown, after having had a long and disappointing day. We determined to try and get a shot while there was yet light, and in our hurry walked straight up to a tree, behind which one was standing. In a moment bang went the rifle on my right, for its owner had seen the head round the corner of the bush;

lmost simultaneously the other rifle rang out, nd I then saw the elephant in the centre of the ush making straight for us. There was no ime for careful aim, nor could I see her distinctly enough, so I fired at her point blank, nd dived through a "wait a bit" thorn bush, which stripped me of most of my clothing. She ell on the spot where we had been standing, but was up in a moment, and chased us for about half a mile, every now and again getting our wind and pressing us hard; it was too dark to try and tackle her again, and by this time the whole place was alive with the remainder of the troop. We were no doubt turned out of the bush that night, but then she was a cow elephant with her calf; and I think, had it been a bull, in all probability he would not have charged.

G. D. Wheeler.

ELEPHANT, INDIAN (*Elephas indicus*)—

Elephant shooting in India is now practically a thing of the past. Forty years ago, in the southern part of the Peninsula, and especially

Head of Indian Elephant.
Av. height at shoulder, 9 ft. 9 in. Av. length of tusk, 6 ft.; Max. length of tusk, 8 ft.

along the Western Ghats in the Wynaad, Malabar, Coimbatore, Madura, and Tinnevelly districts, wild elephants were so numerous and so troublesome to ryots and planters that the Government used to offer a reward for their destruction. In those days it was, therefore, not considered unsportsmanlike, as it would be now, to kill a female—although, of course, the male was more sought after by Europeans, for the sake of the trophy which his tusks afforded. Native shikaris, as well as many Europeans, who were glad of the Government reward to help to pay their shooting expenses, killed females as well as males, and the wild elephant was driven back into the more remote parts of the forests, and no longer molested the cultivator. The Government then ceased to offer the reward, and afterwards passed an order forbidding their destruction, and formed establishments for their capture alive. Now no one is allowed to shoot elephants without a special permit. This must be obtained direct from the Government, and is, as a general rule, restricted to one tusker or to a well-known rogue which has been attacking men.

It is a strange fact that whereas, in Ceylon, tuskers are exceedingly rare—the males, as a rule, being "Makhnas" carrying short stumps only—every herd in India, just across the narrow straits of Manaar, has one or more tuskers in it. There are also numbers of solitary males, but "Makhnas" are very uncommon.

In the northern part of British Burma, where elephants are numerous, I believe that no very hard and fast rule has been made against shooting them, and that permission to do so is readily obtained from the local civil authorities, and in the Native States of Travancore, Cochin, and Mysore permission to shoot a tusker may be obtained from the Maharajahs, through the influence of the British Resident.

Before attempting to shoot an elephant, it is wise to make a careful study of the head of a tame one in order to understand how a vital shot may be placed in the brain. It is well also to study a skull in a museum.

The head of the Asiatic elephant differs considerably in formation from that of the African; so, of course, it is the head of the former which must be studied. To kill him stone-dead with one ball the brain must be reached. It lies far back in the head, exactly between the orifices of the ears.

Supposing that a rod be passed in at one ear and out of the other, it would go right through the brain. It should be borne in mind that in order to kill the animal your ball must cut the middle of this imaginary rod. How to do this from various angles is the thing to be studied. I will endeavour to describe it.

(1) If the animal be directly facing you, with both eyes visible, and standing on the same level as yourself, or a little above you, plant your ball low in the rounded bump which is so conspicuous on an elephant's forehead just above the trunk. At that spot there is a convenient opening in the skull through which the bullet will pass, slightly upwards, direct to the brain.

(2) If he be facing you, with both eyes visible, but standing on a lower level than yourself, plant your ball in the concavity of the forehead just above the rounded bump, and it will crash through the crenelated bone, of which an elephant's head is composed, and will reach the brain.

(3) If the animal be standing at three-quarter face towards you, with only one eye visible, shoot into the hollow of the temple in a line between the eye and the orifice of the ear at such an

angle that the bullet may cut the middle of the imaginary rod passed through the ears.

(4) If he be standing exactly broadside on to you, shoot straight into the orifice of the ear.

(5) If he be standing with his head three-quarters turned away from you, and if you can still see one eye, shoot behind the ear, when he flaps it forward, at the level of the orifice. The ball will go forward into the brain. If his head be so much turned away from you that you cannot see his eye, do not fire, because if you do fire behind the ear the ball will go too much forward and miss the brain.

(6) Get as close as you possibly can; a golden rule. At twenty yards, or less, you are sure of hitting the exact spot at which you aim, and, moreover, at such close quarters the report, flash, and heavy blow inflicted will confuse the elephant so much that you are really safer than you would be at a greater distance. In case of failure to kill, he is nearly sure to turn tail.

It is unwise for a novice to approach elephants in high grass or in thick treeless jungle. A good tree handy, behind which you can dodge in case of a charge, is a wonderful steadier for the nerves. An elephant can be killed by shooting him behind the shoulder, and this is usually done in Africa, where they are found more in the open, and can be followed, fired at more than once, and kept in sight; but as an elephant hardly ever falls unless shot in the head, he may run for miles without stopping. In the dense jungle, in which they are usually found in India, you can seldom get more than one shot, and it is very difficult to track a wounded one, as his trail will probably cross and recross those of others and be lost. The shoulder shot should therefore never be tried. I have heard of its being attempted often, but I know of only one instance of the elephant falling dead.

I have great faith in the smooth bore gun and the spherical bullet for elephant shooting—an explosive or expanding ball is unsuitable; a round one gives a heavy blow and, if hardened, has great penetration. It is, I think, not so liable as a conical one to be diverted from its course in going through the eighteen inches of thick skin, flesh, and bone which it must traverse on its way to the brain. I have shot elephants dead, with one round ball, out of all sized guns from eight to sixteen bore. I would recommend Nos. 10 or 12. The gun should be strong in the breech, capable of carrying a good heavy charge of powder. The ball must be hardened. The best amalgam I know is one-third of block tin to two-thirds of lead, both by weight. The proper sort of tin can be procured in any Indian bazaar; in Tamul it is called *tŭtŭnāgŭm;* in Hindustani *rūpjās*. In casting these bullets, the tin should be put into the ladle first, as it melts at a lower temperature than lead; the latter can then be added, and when all is melted it should be stirred with an iron rod before it is poured into the mould. The ball is very nearly as heavy as a leaden one, and is exceedingly hard. I once shot a bull bison with a ball, thus hardened, out of a No. 10 two-grooved rifle; it went through both shoulder blades, and seeing it sticking just under the skin on the other side I cut it out and, finding it perfectly good, reloaded my right barrel with it. Shortly afterwards I walked unexpectedly up to within twenty yards of a sleeping tiger, and shot him through the head as he awoke and snarled at me. In skinning him I again found the ball at the back of his ear. It had gone right through the hard skull, but it was so little damaged that I could have used it again.

The season for forest shooting in Southern India is during the rains—*i.e.*, between July and December. The ground is then soft and moist, with no dry leaves lying about, so that one moves noiselessly through the jungle, and tracking is easier than when the ground is hard. The sportsman must be prepared to face a good deal of wet, but every now and then he will enjoy a week or ten days of a so-called "break in the monsoon," and then the southern forests are a very paradise—a pleasant, cool climate, beautiful, luxuriant vegetation, and plenty of shade.

At that time of year the forests are considered healthy, but just at the beginning of the rains, as well as just after they have ceased, there is great risk of malarious fever; miasma hardly exists as long as the ground remains thoroughly saturated.

After the monsoons are over, and the jungles are thoroughly dry, very heavy dews fall at night, sufficient to bring malaria out again, and accordingly the southern jungles should be then avoided. I believe it is just the reverse in the northern parts of India. The hot weather is safe and the rainy season unhealthy. At high elevations—5000 to 7000 feet, such as the Nilghiris, Palnis, Annamallies, and the Travancore hills—there is no malarious fever.

It is needless to say that dark clothes should be worn. "Khaki" or mud colour is the best. They should be of strong cotton material which will not tear readily in thorny or bamboo jungle. Jail cloth or workhouse sheeting, dyed brown, is the sort of thing, and very thin woollen vests and drawers can be worn underneath.

One very necessary article of clothing for the southern jungles needs description, namely, the "leech gaiter." Small and very voracious leeches abound in some places, which attack the legs and ankles. Their bite is not only irritable and unpleasant, but it is also very apt to fester. They will get through anything woollen, so the gaiter must be made of close cotton or linen material, shaped just like a fishing stocking, to be worn over the sock and inside the boot or shoe, with a running string to tie tight beneath the knee. Above that, leeches are easily seen and can be brushed off. Several pairs of these gaiters should be taken, as they fray or tear, and a leech will find his way through the smallest hole.

A light waterproof cape is necessary. Gun-covers should be very loose, because the guns must be nearly always carried in them during the rains, and I know of nothing so irritating as tugging frantically at a tight cover while a bull bison or a deer is standing gazing at you within shot, and the camp in want of meat.

A very portable kit is required for a trip into any of the remote forests where elephants, bison, &c., may be found. Everything must be carried on men's heads or backs; so, if a tent be taken, it must be of the lightest description—one or two squares of waterproof sheeting will be a great comfort, and a good *tente d'abri* can be made with them on emergency. Cooking utensils and food of all sorts must be taken, and as provisions for all the carriers and servants must be provided, the train of followers soon swells. It is very necessary to make definite arrangements before starting, through the district authorities, for supplies of rice, bread, fowls, curry stuffs, salt, &c., to be sent to the camp from the nearest villages. The jungle people are clever at building grass or bamboo huts. They are generally good trackers and indefatigable walkers, but they will seldom carry loads, and they require to be well fed and supplied with such luxuries as tobacco, betel nut, salt, &c., and although they have to be paid for their services in money, they expect and appreciate presents of cloths, beads, knives, &c., as a reward for successful shoots.

It is needless to say that these wild men must be kindly treated. Native servants are very apt to be rough and overbearing with them, and this should be carefully watched and deprecated —a blow from a servant may cause every one of the hill men to desert the camp with or without excuse.

Having arrived at your destination in the forest, and settled down in your camp, you may, possibly, get information from some of the neighbouring people that elephants have been seen or heard. They may then soon be found, but if not, you must confide yourself to a man who knows the forest well, and go out in search of a track. When one is found, which is judged to be only a few hours old, it should be steadily followed until you hear or see the elephants. This following up of a track is interesting and exciting, and by no means so easy as may be supposed, as in an elephant-frequented jungle old and new tracks cross and recross each other; and after rain it requires experience to keep to the fresh one. The sound of breaking branches or bamboos, and other signs, will generally give you timely notice when you are getting near, and then care must be taken to approach up wind. Elephants are accustomed to the noise of other animals moving in the forest, and are not very keen sighted, but their sense of smell is acute. If you have the wind, you may approach pretty close without fear of disturbing them, and if you are dealing with a herd, you may stand for any time behind a tree or bush, within fifty yards, and look them over in order to make out where the tusker is. When you have discovered him, if there be females or young ones between you and him, you must wait for your opportunity of getting within shot. It is not easy, at first, to refrain from firing a long shot on such occasions, but you must be patient if you wish to make sure of your tusker.

With a solitary elephant—and these generally carry the finest tusks—much more care must be taken in approaching. He is always on the alert, and he will stop feeding and listen if he hears a twig break under your foot; if you or your followers then move he will probably catch sight of you; and if he be a "rogue," he will charge—if not, he will hoist his tail and sail away through the jungle, carrying everything before him, and you will be lucky if you ever see him again, although you follow him till dark.

If he should charge, it becomes a mere matter of nerve. An elephant, as a general rule, coils his trunk when he means mischief, and does not lift it in the air. He thus presents you a capital front shot, and if you are cool and let him come near enough—say to within fifteen or twenty yards—the odds are against the elephant. Moreover, as I have already said, even if you do not kill him, the shot and the flash right in his face at such close quarters will generally confuse and turn him.

If an elephant should happen to charge with his trunk up, it covers the vulnerable spot, and the only thing to be done is to fire into his eye and step to one side. More than once I have had an elephant pass me so closely, under such circumstances, that I could have nearly touched him with my gun, but stopping and turning his head a few yards on, he has given me the chance of a shot behind his ear with the second barrel.

I may be pardoned for concluding with an instance of the value of patience and steadiness under exciting circumstances. On one occasion I had got close up to elephants feeding in a thick brake of thorny mimosa, and while listening to their movements and waiting till I could get sight of them, I became aware that some of the herd were coming towards me. I was well concealed behind some bushes when the two leading elephants appeared and I saw that they were both tuskers, one following the other. They walked slowly past me within about twenty yards and I was in the act of pulling trigger at the leading one when it flashed across me that, at the report of my gun, the other would see his friend fall and might turn his tail to me, so I shifted my aim to him, with exactly the result I anticipated. He fell dead to my right barrel, and the other one, seeing nothing, but hearing the shot, wheeled round and gazed at his prostrate companion. He also at once fell to my second barrel and the two lay dead with their trunks almost touching.

When an elephant is killed, his tusks, or, in the case of females, the pegs or tushes, may be cut out with an axe, a very laborious operation; or if the people around can be depended on, they may be left in the head for a week or so, till decomposition has taken place. They can then easily be drawn out.

The tip of the tail, which is more or less adorned with strong black bristles, like whalebone, may be cut off and dried, and makes a good memento. A capital footstool may be made with a forefoot cut off at the first joint and well cleaned out and dried.

The natives of Southern India do not eat the flesh of the elephant, but the Burmese do so. Once I had two friends coming to my camp to shoot, and being short of meat I had the tail of an old tusker I had killed that day made into soup, and very good soup we thought it, but perhaps that was because we were very hungry!

The rest of an elephant's carcase is absolutely useless.

J. MICHAEL.

ELEPHANT TRAPPING IN INDIA—Hog-hunting has been reckoned hitherto as the most exciting and dangerous sport in India, but I am not sure that noosing and running down elephants is not more trying to the nerves of the hunter, more fatiguing, and more dangerous.

The best caste female elephants are trained, exclusively for this work, almost as soon as caught, and are carefully fed on grain to give them endurance and wind. Only the fastest are retained as Koonkies, off whose backs the wild ones are noosed, but one or two good tuskers are employed to act as "chuckers-out," if their services are required.

The equipment of a Koonkie when arrayed for a hunt is as follows. A stout rope is passed twice round the body to act as a girth, then under the neck and tail like a breast-plate and crupper, and securely fastened close to the withers for the sling to be attached. The Mahout, who guides the elephant and throws the noose, must be a plucky fellow, specially trained to the work, and of course he must be at home on the beast's bare back. He has an assistant, who has also been trained, and on whom he can depend, and whose business it is to keep the Koonkie at full speed by striking it on a "raw" made on purpose near the root of the tail, and he has also to assist directly the lasso has been thrown and the wild elephant noosed. On falling in with a herd, the Mahout singles out one, generally a good-looking three-parts grown tusker, as they fetch the largest prices when broken, but, if no young male is present, a good female is selected. Occasionally a full grown tusker, or even a makhna is snared, but they give a great deal of trouble to catch, and to rear afterwards, as very many, from their stubborn resistance, get so badly cut by the rope forming the noose, that mortification sets in and destroys them. The large merchants who send out these hunters do not encourage the capture of any but half or three-quarter grown calves, but occasionally, when they obtain a prize, in the shape of a high caste male, they forgive the transgressors; yet, if their time has been wasted in catching useless animals, all the employees are heavily fined. As soon as a herd is sighted, the Mahout on his Koonkie rushes at full speed after the animal selected, and endeavours to separate it from the herd. The plain where the hunt takes place is covered with long grass, with trees scattered here and there, and the inequalities of the surface cannot be seen.

One moment it seems as if the elephant and its riders must go heels over head, the next that they must fall backwards. Whatever the dangers there must be no diminution of speed, and you must take the chances of breaking your own neck or of injuring your elephant. To bring your quarry to a standstill before it can recover its second wind, it must be pressed from the very first, and the superior training and condition of your elephant will enable you to do this in half or three-quarters of an hour, perhaps longer, if you meet an exceptionally fast antagonist. Unless your arms are muscular and well trained, and you hold on with the tenacity of a bull dog, you will soon be thrown off, and will see little or nothing of the chase and its results.

As soon as the wild elephant stops, the Koonkie ranges alongside, and the Mahout, who invariably stands up, holds on to a small rope fastened to the girth for that purpose with his left hand, whilst with his right he launches the lasso. The wild one, feeling the rope dangling about its face, curls up its trunk, and in so doing it assists in its own capture, as the noose then slips under the neck and is drawn tight The Koonkie now plants herself as firmly as possible, leaning her whole weight to the side opposite to its captive, with one foot advanced to meet the struggles of the one ensnared, who, having recovered a little breath and finding itself entangled, rushes off with great violence, dragging the Koonkie after it. But the noose tightens, the animal gets half suffocated, and has to pull up; another Koonkie then rushes along the other side, a second noose is thrown, and the captive is safe. The two assistants then jump off and tether the feet of their prize, which they do in a few minutes, being most expert from long practice. The Mahouts have now the dangerous task of loosening the slip knots and of fastening thick ropes round the necks of their victims, but all engaged in this sport—men and beasts—are so expert, that few or no accidents occur. Two or three tame elephants now close up and lavish attentions on the half-strangled captive, while the Mahouts attach a small rope to one end of the noose so as to loosen it, which is often a matter of difficulty, for the ropes sometimes cut deep into the flesh and cannot easily be extracted. Directly this has been accomplished, the prisoner is placed between two tame elephants, and marched off to a selected spot, where it is temporarily tethered with other *johnny raws*. Thence it is removed to a permanent camp, where it is broken in, and is generally fit for work under six months.

When a wild elephant is very violent, and proves too strong, the rope of the noose is cut, and it is allowed to go free. Now and then, but very rarely, a Koonkie is overthrown, and her riders killed in these encounters. So many thus caught died that the Government many years ago forbade this mode of hunting, but it is carried on in the remoter localities.

Capturing Elephants in a Keddah.—There are two descriptions of Keddahs in use. One is merely a ditch about nine feet deep, about the same breadth at top, but only a foot broad at bottom. The other a combination. Most Keddahs are constructed in forests where timber is plentiful. A narrow entrance is left, to be enclosed either by a portcullis or *abattis*, which is placed at the entrance after the herd has been driven in.

From this entrance two strong fences are made in a ∧ shape and carried to a considerable distance. If the herd once gets within this angle, and the beaters act vigorously together, it is not difficult to force the herd within the stockade. Every expedient is adopted to frighten the elephants, and to drive them forward; guns are fired, huge bonfires lighted, tom-toms beaten, cholera horns blown, and amidst the yelling of the beaters, the trumpeting of the bulls, the bellowing of the cows—in which the tame elephants join—an uproar is created sufficient to awaken the dead. Amid this overwhelming din a final exertion is made, the whole or the greater part of the herd is driven headlong into the Keddah, and the entrance is closed, while the wild animals, seeking in vain an exit, and finding themselves entrapped, set to work and create a row, to which that previous was as nothing. Every endeavour is made by the captives to pull down the sides of the stockade, but it is well guarded from the outside, and they are everywhere repulsed either with sharp spears or by blazing torches thrust into their faces. The scene is grand and animating, and continues without intermission for hours. The wild animals, finding escape impossible, abandon hope, and resign themselves to their fate. The next day a party of picked Koonkies and their attendants, usually as naked as at the time of their birth, enter the stockade and surround a captive. The legs are tethered in a moment, ropes as thick as hawsers are thrown round their necks, and they are removed one by one between two powerful elephants to some fixed spot where fodder and water are plentiful, and it is almost incredible how soon they become docile.

Catching Elephants in Pitfalls—This is now forbidden, but still men, in independent States and in our remoter districts, note the way elephants go to their feeding grounds, and dig pitfalls about nine feet deep, just sufficiently broad to hold the body of an elephant and so narrow at the bottom that his feet are jammed. These pits they cover over with boughs, bamboos, &c., scatter leaves, grass, and fresh elephant dung over the surface, and dig other pitfalls at right angles and along all paths in the vicinity.

I went once with a party. It was a dark night, the men lay in wait, and when the elephants entered the pathway, and were only a few yards from the first pit, they created such a din, firing guns and rockets, lighting fires, beating tom-toms, and rushing with lighted torches towards the affrighted herd, that a panic took place. The leader, a fine female, fell into the first pit; the others, on seeing her fate, scattered here and there, and, although there were perils in every direction, only three were caught.

In Upper Burma, in 1856, they had two enclosures close to the walls of Umrapoora. Well trained cow-elephants were let loose. These wandered into the jungles, allowed the males to make love to them, and then allured them into the enclosure. I was told that as many as twenty valuable males had thus been caught in one year. It cost nothing, as the females were let loose in the slack season, when not required for removing timber from the forest, and in almost every case they were found to be pregnant, and brought forth in due time.

F. T. POLLOK.

ELK (*Alces machlis*. Sweden and Norway, *Elg*)—The Elk was in old times, as we learn from early writers, abundant in the forests of ancient Germany, and is still found in the vast swampy tracts of the country once known as Lithuania or East Prussia. But it has in the main gradually retreated northward, and its range may be said to lie nowadays between 57° and 65° N. latitude. It thus inhabits nearly the whole of the Scandinavian Peninsula and Northern Russia, but is rare within the Arctic circle, and extends eastward through Siberia to northern China. Although, given both animals in their fullest development, it never quite attains the proportions of its congener, the Transatlantic Moose, it is, nevertheless, a magnificent beast, forming, as it were, a link between the present and pre-historic time.

Its huge size, its majestically uncouth appearance, its secluded existence and strange hoarse utterances amid the silence of the forest, all seem to indicate it as a representative of the gigantic and otherwise extinct fauna which afforded sport to the hunter of the palæolithic age.

These remarks of course apply chiefly to the full-grown bull, in the glory of his massive palmated antlers, shaggy neck, and enormous, long-nosed, bulbous-lipped head. The hornless cow is simply very big and very ugly, and an elk calf probably one of the most ungainly young creatures in the world. A first-class bull will stand 18 hands at the withers, weigh 90 stone, and possess antlers of from 45 to 50 inches spread, with a foot of palmation, and 20 to 24 tines or points, and these dimensions are sometimes exceeded. His hide is of a dark brownish grey, inclining to black, with a good deal of light colour on the belly and inner thighs; the latter often leads to his detection in the wood. Despite some recent and questionable assertions that the elk in Scandinavia are in danger of ultimate extinction by poaching and over slaughter during the brief legal season, it is an undoubted fact that in the last forty years—in Norway at least—their number has greatly increased, for in the fifties, as the writer can testify, they were seldom seen or heard of in many districts where they are now not infrequent. The truth is that the experience of most sportsmen does not go nearly so far back, and they are apt to overlook the fact that the perhaps frequent cases of poaching are a natural consequence of the great increase of elk. It cannot be denied that the huge deer is a very demoralising animal, tempting many an otherwise honest and law-abiding man to smother all scruples and shoot whenever he gets the chance.

In Norway it is forbidden, under a heavy penalty, to kill more than a single elk, bull, or cow on each farm or registered division of the land, and a return of all kills, with their locality, must be made to the local officials. The shooting of calves is strictly forbidden. As an annual blue-book is published, containing statistics of all the big game and beasts and birds of prey killed during the previous season, the authorities are kept fully posted on the subject. The legal season for elk-shooting is at present (1897) throughout Norway, with possibly an occasional local exception, just thirty days, namely, the month of September, and the returns show that during that time 1,200 deer are, on the average, killed annually in a legal manner.

To give statistics of a private forest, it may be noted that in the seasons from '91 to '96 about 400 elk, bulls, cows, and calves, or an average of over 66 per season, were sighted on the ground rented by the writer, and this in districts where the Lap hunter, born and bred on the place, allows that twenty-five years ago elk were scarce. Of the above number only 31, or an average of 5 per season, were shot, the best bag (to the writer's own rifle) being 9 elk in 1894.

In Sweden it has been hitherto lawful to slaughter bull, cow, and calf wherever they are met, without any restriction as to number or locality, and under this system far too many were killed—about double as many as in Norway. But the Swedish Government has shown itself sufficiently watchful in this direction. Last year it forbade the slaughter of calves, and limited the elk season to fourteen days, and now, by a recent enactment, a close time of three years' duration is to be accorded to the deer.

Now that all traps, spring-guns, pitfalls, and the like are abolished, there are three ways of dealing with the elk. It may be either driven, hunted with the loose dog and brought to bay, or stalked by the aid of a dog always kept in hand by a long leader or leash. In old days

ELK.
Av. height at shoulder, 72 in.; Av. spread at tips, 47 in.; Max. spread at tips, 52 in.

driving was practised in Sweden, chiefly in the royal forests, on a grand scale, and as late as 1885 a great "skall" of this kind was organized in honour of H.R.H. the Prince of Wales and other royal personages, when forty-nine elk were killed in the day, while in 1888, only three years later, a bag of sixty-three was obtained on the same ground! But in Norway the rule of "one farm, one elk," renders driving impossible except on an insignificant scale. Elk-hunting with the loose dog has always been a favourite sport in Sweden, and has been, and still is, practised to some extent in Norway, although it is in that country really illegal. This phase of the chase often demands great activity and endurance on the part of both man and dog, for an elk may travel some miles before he will stand. The shooter has then to judge from the baying of the hound how best to make his approach through the forest and get within the range. The old bulls are most easily brought to bay, as they disdain to run.

There can be no question as to this being a grand and exciting sport, but it has its disadvantages, inasmuch as it affords little scope for the science of woodcraft, disturbs a great extent of forest, and necessitates, as a rule—certainly, according to Swedish ideas—the shooting of whatever beast, be it young bull or cow, the dog has succeeded in stopping; otherwise he may continue the chase and not be recovered for half the day, or, if often baulked of blood, may lose his keenness.

The so-called elk-hound is clearly a descendant of the breed of dogs which have from time immemorial accompanied the nomad tribes, Esquimaux, Samoyeds, and Laps, of the North of Europe, and still retains all the characteristics of his race, a coat of thick hair, gray, brindled, foxy, black or white, with an undergrowth of wool, sharp ears and nose, and a bushy, tightly curled tail. There are two types of hound, the one smaller and less stoutly built than the other.

To become perfect at his work, the leash- or stalking-hound should never be loosed, and must be trained to precede the hunter at the length of his tether without straining, to select instinctively the easiest passage among the tree stems, to obey the gentlest motion of his master's hand, and above all to be temperate and mute even under the most exciting circumstances. He will, with a fair breeze and favourable lie of the land, often detect the presence of elk or of fresh spoor at the distance of a mile or considerably more. In advancing towards the quarter where elk are supposed to be, one cannot move too cautiously or noiselessly. The ground in front and on either side, and the depths of the foliage, should be repeatedly examined and penetrated with the field-glasses, and occasional halts be made for the purpose of both gazing and listening intently, inasmuch as the distant snapping, or, on calm days, when the task of the hound is most difficult, even the slight but visible shaking of a branch or young tree will often reveal the whereabouts of a feeding elk, as he crops the highest and tenderest shoots of the young birch, aspen, or mountain ash.

When at length the fresh spoor has been discovered, or, in default of this, when from the hound's eager movements it becomes clear that the elk is close at hand, then the hunter's experience and woodcraft come into play, and on these mainly depends the success of the ultimate approach.

Happily, the chase does not always plunge one in the dark recesses of the forest or the tangled swamp. It may be that the beat of the day will lead toward the uplands, where the elk, and especially the big solitary bulls, will be found scattered among the detached pine-woods, birchen thickets, and willow patches of the lower fjeld, or even on the open moor above. Here the field-glass is in constant requisition, and the sport assumes a strong resemblance to ordinary deer-stalking.

Small families of elk, consisting of bull, cow, and a calf or two, often keep together during the summer and early autumn, but when the rutting season commences about the middle of September, the bulls, who are really polygamous, begin to wander in search of the cows, and, to the satisfaction of the dog, become rankly odoriferous. Then, too, to the satisfaction of the hunter, they boldly betray their whereabouts by scraping conspicuous holes—also odoriferous—in the soil, and cutting young trees to ribbons with their horns, and above all by the hoarse love-call which resounds so impressively through the silence of the forest.

There is little use in following an elk, unless wounded, which has got the wind of man and been thoroughly scared; he will generally travel at a great pace in an enormous circle, and return nearly to the spot whence he started. But if only disturbed by sight or sound, he may relax his speed and be occasionally overtaken by a patient, quiet pursuit. Elk, when conscious that they are followed, resort to many cunning devices to baffle the pursuer, a favourite trick being to take to lake or river for a long distance, and then, on leaving the water, to double back at a sharp angle, thereby placing the hunter to windward of them. They generally lie down to leeward of their trail.

There is no better weapon for elk than a ·450 or ·500 express, and no deadlier shot than through the base of the broad neck. The writer is also able to state that a single soft-nosed bullet from a Lee-Metford ·303, placed in the right spot, will stop a good bull.

HENRY POTTINGER.

[*See also* MOOSE.]

ELK SHOOTING IN RUSSIA.—It may at once be stated that the splendid animals which form the subject of this note are not, in Russia and Finland, for the outsider or stranger. Elk are more tenderly protected in the country of the Tsar than any other creature, whether furred or feathered; the close time conceded to these favoured animals lasts, practically, throughout spring, summer and autumn, in Russia, while in the adjoining Grand Duchy of Finland it is illegal to shoot an elk at any time of the year. Moreover, so greatly is the pursuit of elk valued by the higher powers in the land that nearly all the best haunts of these beautiful creatures are strictly preserved by one or other of the relatives of the Tsar.

And yet, for any person who is so fortunate as to experience it, few things are more picturesque or more exciting than an elk battue, held, perhaps, thirty or forty miles from the nearest town, in the dead of a Russian winter, and in the midst of the forest. The elk being the shyest of creatures, as well as one of the acutest, it is rarely indeed that one is approached by accident, and shot by a favourable chance.

Occasionally, however, in the snow time, a family of elk will come from their sanctuary in Finland, and reach a Russian estate. In search of a change of air or food they come through the deep snow, most probably to the favourite haunts near Lake Ladoga, in the Erinofka district, or to Ostramanch. There they rest, and the keeper, who has been waiting for them, makes a wide circle around them in his snow-shoes, crossing their track but once. Then he makes a smaller circle. If he finds them still within, he places fifty or a hundred beaters around, and sends for his employers, who complete the battue.

FRED. WHISHAW.

EMU (*Dromaius ater*)—The large struthious bird of the Australian plains differs externally from the ostrich in the absence of the highly-developed tail feathers that render the latter so valuable. The emu is swift of foot, so that even in the days of natives and dingoes it managed to hold its own; since these factors have been practically removed, it is on the increase all over the continent. Its great strength, which tells on wire fences, whenever the two collide, renders it in some parts a serious trouble to the squatter, and the governments vote large sums in rewards for its slaughter. In the early days, before the great development of sheep-farming, this bird furnished sport in many ways. One way was to stalk it with rifle and shooting-pony, as colonials do at the present day when after bustards. But the most legitimate, as well as the most sporting method, was hunting it on horseback, with trained dogs that would hang on the bird's neck and bring it down. Nowadays, this amusement has its limitations, for the emus have the sagacity to keep to the sheep-country, and it is impossible to harm them without disturbing a mob of five or six thousand feeding sheep, which would entail more work than the venture is worth. As long as the emu does not come foul of the fences, or crop too much grass in bad times, it is better to leave it alone; and it is therefore only shot occasionally as a favour to a "new chum" who may wish to take a skin back with him.

Nevertheless, the writer has had many an enjoyable run with emus. We ran them with kangaroo-dogs, a powerful cross between the mastiff and greyhound, combining the strength and "stay" of the former with the pace of the latter. Nothing can be more deceptive than the jogging gait of the emu; it is like the apparently heavy flight of large birds, which proves so puzzling to the uninitiated. At the first, the emu seems to have no more pace than a turkey chick; somehow or other he keeps his distance, until, after your station hack has done his gallant best for a mile or so, the game grows monotonous. Should you happen to be in a "buggy" without dogs, the emu makes no move until you come within fifty or sixty yards, when he merely jogs a hundred yards or so off the track, and takes no more notice of the disturber. The writer has often been amused to notice the politeness with which the "old man" emu invariably waits until his wife and family have a start of a couple of hundred yards, when he ambles in leisurely fashion after them. Emus are generally to be seen from the railroad, especially in the summer months; and the writer when going by train to Bourke last November saw a pair of old birds every few

EMU.

minutes, usually accompanied by a family of eight or ten chicks the size of grown turkeys. One old male, indeed, started running parallel with the train, which, as there is no perceptible bend in the line in that part for close on two hundred miles, should have been making good time; yet he kept up bravely for quite three hundred yards before we left him.

The emu trusts to its keen sight to apprise it of danger; indeed, the blacks believed, though wrongly, that the bird was deaf. Among their curious laws was one, strictly adhered to, that only married elders might eat emu's flesh, doubtless a primitive method of preservation.

ARTHUR EDEN.

SPARROW HAWK IN WINTER PLUMAGE.

FALCONRY, or, as it is more commonly termed, *Hawking*, is the art of training birds for the chase, and of bringing them into such discipline and under such control that they will exert their marvellous powers at the pleasure of man. This is one of the oldest forms of sport that has ever been pursued by men of all nationalities. Sir A. Layard, in his work on Nineveh and Babylon, mentions that in a bas-relief found by him in the ruins of Khorsabad there was a figure depicted of a "falconer bearing a hawk upon his wrist." This would establish the fact that falconry existed as early as 1200 B.C. Colonel Delmie Radcliffe (Encyclopædia Britannica) states that it was known in China about 2000 B.C. and in Japan at least 600 B.C. It is certain that in almost all countries of Asia it is the most ancient, as it was, and in some countries is now, the most popular of all sports.

In Europe among the most ancient writers who mention the subject are Aristotle, Pliny, and Martial. Pliny says that "In a part of Thracia beyond Amphipolis men and hawks join in fellowship and catch birds together, for the men drive the woods and beat the bushes and reeds to spring the fowl; then the hawks, flying over their heads, seize upon them and either strike or bear them to the ground, fit for their hands. On the other side the hawkers and fowlers, when they have caught the fowl, divide the booty with the hawks, and, by report, let such birds fly again at liberty aloft in the air and then are the hawks ready to catch them for themselves. Moreover, when the time is of hawking, they will by their manner of cry and flying together give sign to the falconer that there is good game abroad, and so draw them forth to take the opportunities." Thus Pliny on falconry in his day; and if it does not quite well accord with the ideas of the present generation as to the proper management of the sport, yet it is a record that hawking of one kind or another was followed, and on a considerable scale, at that date.

To come to falconry in Great Britain, records are extant of its practice in early Saxon times. In a letter addressed by King Ethelbert, A.D. 748, to Saint Boniface, Archbishop of Mayence, the King asks for two falcons to fly at the crane. In Asser's life of Alfred the Great, the "incomparable felicity" of the king in hunting and hawking, as well as "in all the other gifts of God," is greatly enlarged upon. In the British Museum are numerous early manuscripts ranging from those above cited, through Saxon times (including one attributed to Edward the Confessor), into the Norman period. With the Conquest, falconry became not only the sport of the country gentleman, but also the appanage of the courtier. In the Bayeux tapestry Harold is depicted embarking for Normandy with a hawk, and after the Conquest the strictest regulations were made as to the class of hawk which each man in his rank or degree might keep. These ran as follows:—

The Eagle and the Vulture for an Emperor.
The Gerfalcon and Tiercel of the Gerfalcon for a King.
The Falcon gentle and Tiercel gentle for a Prince.
The Falcon of the Rock for a Duke.
The Falcon Peregrine for an Earl.
The Bastard for a Baron.
The Sacre and Sacret for a Knight.
The Lanner or Lanneret for an Esquire.
The Merlin for a lady.
The Hobby for a young man.
The Goshawk for a yeoman.
The Tiercel (? of the Goshawk) for a poor man.
The Sparrow-hawk for a priest.
The Musket for a holy-water clerk.
The Kestrel for a knave.

YOUNG FEMALE PEREGRINE.

Emperors, it may be concluded, would, except on state occasions, have no use for the birds allotted to them, while princes, dukes, and earls would carry the same bird under a different name. The list seems to be made out more to emphasise the various differences in rank than to prove that the hawks named were actually used by the several classes of men to whom they were allotted.

Throughout the Norman and Tudor periods falconry was the principal sport of the aristocracy. Apart from its superiority both as a pastime and a science, it afforded one of the principal means of supplying the table with delicacies. Herons were considered a choice dish, and these, with various sorts of game, were captured mainly with hawks in the days before "vile saltpetre" was introduced to make it easy to compass the death of any wild fowl.

In Professor Newton's *Notes on Hawking in Norfolk* (an appendix to Stevenson's *Birds of Norfolk*) we find an account of the visits of James I. to Thetford in the month of May for the purpose of hawking dotterels. The sparrow-hawk appears to have been used, and whether a net was also brought into requisition or not seems doubtful. At Royston, it is recorded how his Majesty partook of the sport of kite hawking, and how both kite and falcon soared to such a pitch that neither was seen again. The Grand Falconer of England was, during this reign, Sir Patrick Hume, who was afterwards succeeded by Sir Thomas Monson. The latter took so much trouble with his charge that Sir Anthony Weldon, in his *Court and Character of King James*, records that the "Master Falconer, Sir Thomas Monson, was in truth such an one as no Prince in Christendom had, for what flights other Princes had he would excel them for his Master, in which one was at the kite. . . . . Sir Thomas Monson desired to have that flight in all exquisiteness, and to that end was at £1,000 charge for falcons for that flight. In all that charge he never had but one cast would perform it, and those had killed nine kites and never missed one." The professional falconers under him were John Wood, with his brothers Robert and Luke Wood for assistants. Besides hawks they trained cormorants for fishing. Luke Wood was sent with three cormorants to Venice, but had his cormorants taken from him *en route* by the Duke of Savoy, "to his great loss and hindrance."

John Wood himself seems to have been a falconer of no little renown—one that, as was said of him, would "toss up a lure in a second that one might have taken for a partridge oneself," and "seemed to know what sort of relish to give their food by the very feel of their beaks under his finger." But from the days of this excellent falconer history takes a long stride before recording the name of another such professor of the art. The wars of the Commonwealth had intervened, and recreation had to play second fiddle to sterner pursuits. Gunpowder and fowling pieces had been introduced, and falconry was never again to take the place it had formerly held, both as a sport and as an appanage to the general establishment of the nobleman and the country squire. But about 1750 we find Lord Orford practising falconry in the highest style, with the aid, however, of Dutch falconers instead of the old English names. He was very successful in the flight at the kite, which must undoubtedly have been the highest form in which the sport of falconry could be carried on. This flight he pursued both on the warrens of Norfolk and Suffolk, and at Alconbury Hill in Huntingdonshire. Some twenty years later his establishment of hawks passed into the hands of a club known as the "Falconers' Society," later the Falconers' Club, and meetings were held every April for "kite and crow hawking." The establishment in 1783 consisted of "32 slight falcons (or peregrines), 13 German hawks (goshawks), and 7 Iceland falcons." About this period the notorious Colonel Thornton was manager, and controlled the destinies of the Club. From 1792 to 1838 the Club was under the control of Lord Berners, and the establishment was known as the High Ash Club—at this time they flew mainly at herons.

During these days there were doubtless many other establishments of hawks—a few of them large, but mostly small. In Scotland, many a gamekeeper had a knowledge of how to train falcons taken by himself on the ground in his charge. A more pretentious establishment was that of the Renfrewshire subscription hawks, under the control of the famous Scotch falconer John Anderson, and kept solely for game hawking at Barochan Castle. The Duke of Leeds, too, had a magnificent team of hawks flying on Deeside at game and woodcocks, with John Pells and Peter Ballantyne as his falconers. In 1839 the Falconers' Club, finding that kites were extinct and herons getting scarce on open ground in Norfolk, formed, under the auspices of the Royal Family of Holland, the Loo Hawking Club. These were the palmy days of modern falconry, and, under the management of the English-controlled Club and the falconers of the King of Holland, sport was shown such as has never been surpassed. In 1853 the Club came to an end, and hawking has never since been carried on in Holland on a large scale. After a brief interregnum the present "Old Hawking Club" was started, and, under the management of Mr. E. Clough Newcome, who had been for many years the chief guiding spirit of the Loo Hawking Club, fine sport was shown in rook hawking on the Wiltshire downs—the best substitute for heron hawking—and also at game of all kinds in Scotland and England. In 1871 Mr. Newcome died, and in 1872 the Club was re-organized on a larger basis under the auspices of the late Lord Lilford—one of the best of falconers, and the Hon. Cecil Duncombe, and was placed under the management of the Hon. Gerald Lascelles. Since that time it has continued to provide good sport for its members in every branch of falconry, besides training various young falconers, and providing hawks for a number of beginners whose efforts with an untrained bird could only result in failure.

Of private establishments in England may be named those of Major Fisher, one of the most successful of game hawkers; Mr. T. J. Mann, also a game hawker; Mr. W. H. St. Quintin, whose skilful training of peregrines to fly at the sea-gull, as well as his successes with game hawks, entitles him to rank among the best falconers of the century; Mr. Radcliffe, who hawks many peregrines annually in Dorsetshire; the Hon. C. W. Mills, who has chiefly cultivated the goshawk; and Mr. Arthur Newall, whose achievements with that variety of hawk are only rivalled by those of Sir Henry Boynton, of Burton Agnes. Mr. Riley, the Rev. G. E. Freeman, so well known as an able writer on falconry, the Rev. W. Willmott, and Mr. F. Salvin all bear names that are as household words among falconers, even if they no longer train hawks themselves; and there are many other gentlemen who have, with no mean success, taken up this difficult branch of sport.

A science so ancient, and for many centuries so popular as was falconry, has naturally both a language and a literature of its own. As to the former, a glossary of the terms used in falconry at the present time will be found at the end of this article. In former years such a glossary would have been far more comprehensive—every part of a hawk's body, and every action it could indulge in, was dignified by some special name. Many of these terms are obsolete now-a-days, but all those in general use will be found appended.

Of literature there exist books on falconry in every tongue that has been spoken since the days of Babel. The oldest of our English works is the well-known Boke of St. Albans, a treatise on *Hunting, Hawking and Coat Armour*, first edition, 1486. Various other editions followed, and works by different authors, but—to give only the principal and most serviceable thereof—the next work of importance is that of George Turbervile (which contains several very interesting woodcuts), first edition 1575, second 1611. This work is generally bound up with the same author's treatise on hunting, and is a most interesting and excellent work on both subjects.

The same period saw the publication of Symon Latham's *Falcons' Lure and Cure*, which is in many respects the best work on falconry published in the English language. It is, moreover, original, while the work of Turbervile is avowedly "collected," and is in fact a translation of sundry older works written in foreign languages.

The first edition of Latham was published in 1615, the *New and Second Booke on Faulconry* in 1618, and the second edition of both works in 1633. At this time, under the auspices of King James I., himself an able and active falconer, the literature and probably the sport of falconry flourished exceedingly. A year or two after the publication of the last named work, appeared *An Approved Treatise of Hawks and Hawking*, by Edmund Bert, Gentleman. This book deals entirely with the management of the short-winged hawks—the goshawk and sparrow-hawk. It is an original work, and apparently copied in no part from any previous writer, and is a most practical and excellent treatise. Except for the absurd physicking and doctoring of hawks which seems to have been the prevailing practice of the day, it may be said that any beginner who has mastered all that is contained in these two last cited books, and has the skill to put it in practice, is master of the art of falconry.

In 1674 appeared the first edition of the *Gentleman's Recreation*, by Nicholas Cox, a work dealing with sport of all kinds, but not containing much original matter; and the like may be said of a more magnificent folio, entitled *The Gentleman's Recreation*, by Richard Blome, published in 1686, with a series of copper-plate engravings (many of them highly interesting) depicting the manner of pursuing all kinds of sport at that period, and each dedicated to some one of the noblemen and gentlemen who were exponents of these various pursuits and were (presumably) subscribers to what must have been a costly work. We may pass from this period to the year 1773, when a treatise by James Campbell on "Modern Falconry," was published in Edinburgh. That part of the work which really treats of falconry is excellent and reliable, but a ridiculous preface is attached to it describing fabulous sports, which spoils a book otherwise worthy enough. Sir John Sebright's *Observations upon Hawking*, published in 1826, has only one fault, viz., that it is too concise; and in 1841 appeared an original work on falconry by James Belany, not very accurate or reliable.

In 1855 appeared what must be called the standard English work of modern times appertaining to falconry in England, viz., *Falconry in the British Isles*, by Messrs. Salvin and Brodrick, second edition (amended and added to), 1873. The illustrations to the work are excellent, and the letterpress is practical, and in the main reliable. This book is one that no falconer should omit to procure, if possible. *Falconry—its History, Claims, and Practice*, by G. E. Freeman and F. Salvin, appeared in 1895, and is a thoroughly practical treatise so far as the training of the eyas and the merlin is concerned. In 1892 was published the volume of the Badminton Library on Falconry (bound up with that on Coursing), and in this volume the literature of hawking and its modern practice was brought thoroughly up to date, and to its pages we may refer readers who desire the fullest information on these subjects. Space fails us to record the various works in foreign languages which treat of this subject. The earliest printed book on falconry is a German one, published at Augsburg in 1472. Of French works we may mention the ancient ones of Jean de Franchieres, first published in 1531, with subsequent additions ranging up to 1628. Especially should be noticed *La Fauconnerie*, by Charles d'Arcussia, first issue 1598, but published in successive parts until the complete volume was published in 1627. This is one of the most original and interesting works on falconry that has ever been written.

The most magnificent is perhaps the grand work of Schlegl and Wulverhorst—*Traité de Fauconnerie*, published at Leyden, 1844-53, and illustrated by J. Wolff. The accounts of the hawking at the Loo, by the Falconers' Club, referred to above, are most interesting, and the magnificent plates are unrivalled.

Some interesting modern Japanese works, profusely illustrated with pictures of hawking scenes, are in the possession of the author. A magnificent Persian manuscript on vellum, richly illuminated in the margins, is in the possession of the family of the late Prince Dhuleep Singh. At the sale of his various effects this volume was bought in by his family at the price of £410, up to which figure various collectors were willing to bid for its possession. For fuller details of hawking literature we may refer our readers to Mr. J. E. Harting's valuable *Bibliotheca Accipitraria*, wherein a most complete history of the works on this subject will be found.

The hawks used in falconry are of two groups (1) the true falcons or long-winged hawks;—distinguished by a tooth or indentation in the upper mandible; by the formation of the wing, in which the second feather is the longest; and by the iris of the eye, which is of so dark a brown as to give the effect of an eye full, bright, and of an uniform blackness. (2) The true or short-winged hawks;—these have rounded wings, the fourth feather being the longest; their tails are long in proportion to the wings, and the irides are yellow, changing with age to orange or deep red. They are the hawks of the woods and enclosed country, as the falcons are the lords of the open downs and wild moors. The habits of the two species are entirely different, and so, naturally, is their training. The first are termed "hawks of the lure," the second "hawks of the fist." Of the first, or nobler kind of falcon, those used in England are (1) the Peregrine: (2) the Northern falcons, viz., the Norwegian variety or *Falco gyr-falco;* the Iceland variety, *Falco islandicus;* and the Greenland variety, *Falco candicans*; for purposes of falconry these three varieties may be treated as one. (3) The Merlin; (4) The Hobby—rarely used. In India there are used, besides the peregrine, which in that country, as in all others, is the main "stand-by" of the falconer, the black shaheen—*Falco peregrinator;* the red-naped shaheen—*Falco babylonicus;* the lugger, the cherugh or sacre, used for flying kites, and a variety of the merlin, as well as the European merlin (*F. oesalon*).

Besides these, rarer species are occasionally trained, such as the lanner, the Barbary falcon, and the like; but the management of these varieties is but a *tour de force* on the part of the falconer who may chance to acquire them. Of the short winged hawks, only two varieties are in general use, viz., the Goshawk, *Astur palumbarius;* and the Sparrow-hawk, *Accipiter nisus.* In India two varieties of the latter are also used, termed respectively the Besra and the Shikra.

ADULT PEREGRINE.

In addition to these birds, regularly used in falconry, there are in some countries certain varieties of eagles used for purposes of sport. Of these, Bonelli's eagle is probably the principal one, and this variety has been successfully trained to take rabbits in Europe of late years by M. Paul Gervais. In Central Asia the golden eagle is said to be used and to be flown at both foxes and wolves, but neither of these birds can be said to be used in modern falconry except occasionally.

In this country, as in almost all others, the training of the peregrine is the principal business that is practised. It may be divided into two parts—the training of the eyas, or bird taken from the nest and reared in confinement or partially so, and the reclaiming of the "passage" or wild-caught falcon, entrapped during the migration or "passage" from north to south in the autumn. The first named of these—the eyas—is usually flown at game of all kinds—pigeons, blackbirds, and all the minor quarry. It is naturally more tractable, less easily lost, and more easily managed. A mistake as to condition or training will probably result in some little trouble in re-capturing the bird, but with the wild-caught hawk a similar error would cause the total loss of the falcon.

On the other hand, the wild-caught hawk is, as a rule, higher couraged, swifter, better tempered, and in the proper hands more efficient than any eyas except a peculiarly good one. It is generally used for the rook, the heron, the sea-gull, and similar quarry with which the eyas cannot, as a general rule, cope. When trained to "wait on" for game—especially grouse—the passage hawk flies in finer form, and is better than any but the very best eyases. To sum up the case: a good eyas is as good as a hawk need be, but only one in twenty is to be met with; while out of three passage hawks you may hope to find one that will be superior to nineteen eyases out of twenty, especially if you are aiming at *la haute volée.*

Eyases, or nestling peregrines, can be procured from the cliffs at most of the lofty headlands of the United Kingdom. They are also bred at many inland precipices in the deer forests of Scotland, in most of which they are well preserved. Great care must be exercised in taking them, for unless this be properly attended to the birds will never be worth their keep. They should never be removed from the nest until the white down which covers them in the early days of their existence is entirely replaced by brown feathers—in short, a few days only before they can fly. Hawks taken while in the down can be reared, sometimes, but they are very apt to be attacked by a disease called cramp, which is a contraction, apparently, of the muscles of the thighs and legs, so powerful as often to fracture the young and soft bones, and always to leave the limbs paralysed. It is incurable, and a hawk affected with it ever so slightly should be destroyed at once. Even if hawks thus taken should be reared, they invariably turn out bad tempered screaming brutes, not worth their railway carriage. Young peregrines well taken are well worth £1 apiece. Those that are ill-taken are dear at almost any price.

Should a nest of peregrines taken in proper order be received, the next step is to rear them properly. To do this they must be fed, and well fed, three times a day at first. Tender beef is the best food, rabbit once a day is permissible, and if warm pigeons, fowls, or even rooks or squirrels can be obtained, freshly killed, they make a good change. But regular and plentiful feeding is essential while the feathers are growing. A curious defect is often seen in the feathers of young hawks, called "hunger trace." It appears in the form of a mark in the web of the feather as though a knife had been drawn sharply across it, half severing the fibres. It will often be apparent right across the tail, every feather being affected. It also appears in the wing feathers, but not so often. Frequently it affects the quill of the feather, and may be felt as a little projecting ridge. In this case it is a serious matter, for the feather is sure to break at that point sooner or later. This defect is caused by irregular feeding, or possibly by a long journey when young. Sometimes, in wild hawks, the stronger nestlings have deprived the weaker of food, or from stress of weather, or the loss of one of the parent birds by the shot gun of some villainous "collector," the whole family has been reduced to short commons. But in either case, where a temporary starvation occurred, the growth of the feather is checked, and the "hunger trace" appears at the point where the feather was, at the time, "just in the blood." Hawks well taken, carefully transmitted, and well reared, do not often have "hunger traces."

The less that the young hawks see of their feeder the better at this period of their career. Eyases are easily made too tame and confidential, and generally show their familiarity by loud screaming and petulance. The first thing to do is to get a little native wildness into them before they are tamed or trained. An ideal place for rearing is a loft or outhouse, with a door opening on to some wild park or secluded ground. There the hawks should be fed by simply placing the food before them as quietly and as quickly as may be, and leaving them to themselves. As they get strong and able to fly, the door may be opened, and they may extend their flights to the neighbouring trees or rails. The pangs of hunger will bring them home to the accustomed board on which their food is placed, which may now be moved to some conspicuous place outside the original loft. By degrees the flight will be extended, but always the young hawks will return to their food, which may now be given to them twice a day only. Soon they will be seen soaring at vast heights, and will range to great distances; and when this state of things arrives—say, in a fortnight or three weeks—the time for catching the hawks has come. To explain this, we must describe some of the tackle which is in general use. Before the young hawk was allowed to fly at all, "jesses" were placed on her legs. These are two short strips of soft strong leather, such as soft horse-skin or well-tanned dog-skin. They are about a quarter of an inch wide for

FIG. 1.—JESS.

most of their length (which is about eight inches), and half an inch wide for about two inches at one end, where they encircle the hawk's leg (see Fig. 1). Two slits are made in this wider part, about an inch and a half apart, and, the jess being placed round the hawk's leg, the short end is passed through the slit nearest the middle of the jess; the longer end is brought through both slits and run down to its full length, by which means the jess is neatly knotted round the leg. At the long end of the jess, furthest from the hawk, is a slit about an inch long, which is passed over a swivel (Fig. 2) when the hawk is to be tied down. The end of the jess is passed through one ring of the swivel, and both rings then passed through the slit at the end of the jess. Through the lower ring of the swivel, which should be made of brass, is run the "leash," a thong of leather about a yard long, with a "button" at one end, by which the hawk can be fastened to the block or screen-perch. The latter is generally a pole about three inches in diameter (the plainer and rougher the better) that has had fastened to it a breadth of canvas about a yard wide, hanging loosely down from the under side of the pole to which it is nailed. The object of this canvas is to enable a hawk which has fluttered off the perch to regain its

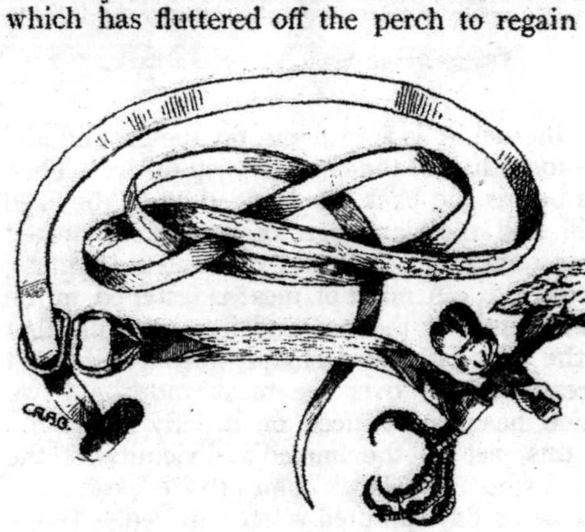

FIG. 2.—LEASH AND JESS ON HAWK'S FOOT, WITH SWIVEL.

position, and, at the same time, to ensure that it shall come up on the same side from which it fell, so that it cannot get twisted round the perch. Of blocks, the simplest are the best. A plain billet of hard wood, with the bark left on about a foot high, with an iron spike driven firmly into the lower end, which is to be driven into the ground to hold the block in position, and with a staple driven into the centre of the upper surface, is as good as anything. Various improvements for fastening the leash to running rings around the blocks have been devised, but only a few are effective. Bells, either one or two, according to size, should be placed on the hawk's legs. They are fastened on by short straps, called "bewits," on the same principle as the jesses are placed on the legs. The best bells are Indian made, and few others are now in use. Jesses and bells remain permanently on the hawk, and with these the young falcon was equipped before she left her rearing loft. They remain on her all the time she is at hack, and the instrument by which she is to be brought to hand is the bow-net. This is a circular net about three feet in diameter. One half of its circumference is fastened to a light hazel rod bent into a "bow" or semi-circular shape. To the centre of the bow is fastened a line, not less than fifty yards long. In order to

FIG. 3.—DUTCH HOOD, FRONT AND BACK.

set the net, it is spread out on the ground and the loose half of the circle pegged down. Then the bow is laid back, as if hinged on to the fixed half, and the slack part of the net is tucked away under the bow, and concealed by grass, leaves, &c. A piece of meat is fastened in the exact centre of the net, and it is obvious that if the bow be pulled sharply forward the net spreads exactly over the meat and the hawk which has come to feed on it. By such a net as this, set in the immediate vicinity of the board where the hawk comes to feed, each one can be readily captured when required. Jesses and bells are on its legs, the leash and swivel are readily applied, a hood is placed on its head, and it can be tied to a block and left to settle down at once.

Hoods are usually made in Holland, (Fig. 3). Attempts by the falconer to make them usually end in failure. Very good hoods are used of the Indian pattern (Fig. 4), which is in some ways superior to the Dutch pattern, being lighter and more comfortable, but easy for a hawk to get off, and therefore only suitable for use when the hawk is on hand. A third form of hood (Fig. 5) is the rufter hood, but this is only used for freshly caught wild hawks—it cannot

FIG. 4.—INDIAN HOOD, BACK AND FRONT.

be taken on and off, and though comfortable to the hawk is only suitable for use in the earlier stages of training.

Training the freshly caught eyas falcon consists, in the first place, of taking her on the fist hooded, and, by constant carriage and handling, gradually taming her. Ere long she can be induced to feed off a piece of meat held under her feet, after her attention is directed to it by stroking or pressing them. As soon as she will pull keenly at this meat through the hood, the meat is offered to her when she is bare-headed, at first, it may be, by candle-light (which has a taming and subduing effect upon all wild birds). In a short time she will, with care and patience, feed as readily bare-headed as she did through the hood. The next stage is to get her to jump to the hand from the perch for food, and this, as soon as she will feed keenly on the fist, she will do; at first a distance of a few inches, which may be gradually increased till she will come the whole length of the mews or outhouse, which may be converted to the use of the hawks.

As soon as the young falcon will feed readily on the fist and will jump to it for food, the "lure" (Fig. 6) must be introduced. This is the instrument by which the hawk is to be recalled to its

FIG. 5.—RUFTER HOOD, SIDE AND FRONT.

trainer from a distance when on the wing, and it must therefore be associated in the bird's mind with reward for obedience and with food. For training purposes, it is usually constructed of a bent piece of metal such as a horse-shoe,

well padded with tow and covered with leather, the object being to make the lure too heavy to be carried and so soft that a hawk cannot injure itself by stooping hard at it. This padded horse-shoe is then covered over with the wings of birds so as to resemble a dead quarry, and furnished with strings to which meat is fastened. For a day or two the hawk is fed on this lure. As soon as it is accustomed to it, the lure, well furnished with food, is tossed to a distance, and the hawk allowed to fly to it, and to "feed up." In a few days the pupil will hasten to it from as great a distance as it can be seen, and may then be termed a trained hawk. As soon as it will thus fly to the lure, the falconer, after calling it from a distance, will conceal the lure as the hawk approaches him. This will cause it to fly round him, ringing upwards, expectant of its food: after thus keeping it "waiting on," as it is termed, the lure is thrown out and the hawk rewarded. When a few lessons of the kind have been given, the hawk will wait on its master for a considerable time, never straying far from him; and yet, if a good one, rising higher and higher, the longer it is kept on the wing. A few live pigeons given from the hand will go far towards raising its pitch and imparting dash and keenness to the young hawk. When this stage has been reached, the young falcon is fit to fly at game. The first essay should be from a steady point at grouse or partridges in a good open country. The falcon should be "waiting on" as high as she will go, somewhat up-wind of the dog. The falconer should have "headed the point" and got the birds between himself and the setter. When the hawk is well placed he will flush the birds, and should the young falcon kill readily she may be considered as well "entered," and the rest of her career depends solely upon plenty of work and good chances.

With eyas falcons may be killed grouse, partridges, wild ducks, pheasants in the open,—game in fact of all sorts. Tiercels so trained will kill magpies and partridges well, and even give good sport at blackbirds, in certain places. For general purposes they may be termed the most useful description of hawk that can be employed.

The passage, or wild caught peregrine, is trained in precisely the same manner as the eyas, but, as it is far wilder and more shy, its education must proceed more gradually. The falconer must take infinitely more time and care, but the steps, though slower, are the same in character. More time and more patience are needed to induce the passage hawk to feed readily on the fist. When it will do this by candle-light, care and time will be required before the same degree of confidence is won by day-light. So also, in training to the lure, much time and care must be exercised in accustoming the hawk to that essential attraction while she is confined in a long string, and before she flies loose. But with patience and skill all shyness can be overcome. Starvation must never be resorted to. By its means the hawk can readily be reduced to subjection, but when so reduced it is but a worthless, and generally unhealthy, creature, useless for any purpose. The great object of the falconer must be to induce his timid pupil to feed well and keenly, and to rely on time and patience to effect its reclamation and to win its confidence. In all cases, the greatest care must be taken to accustom each hawk so completely to the use of the hood that she will allow herself to be hooded without trouble.

Passage hawks are generally, for their first season, flown "out of the hood," *i.e.*, straight at the quarry. This, generally, is the rook, heron, or some similar bird, according to the country where it is used. The higher training of "waiting on" is not always needed before the hawk is used, but it follows very rapidly when once

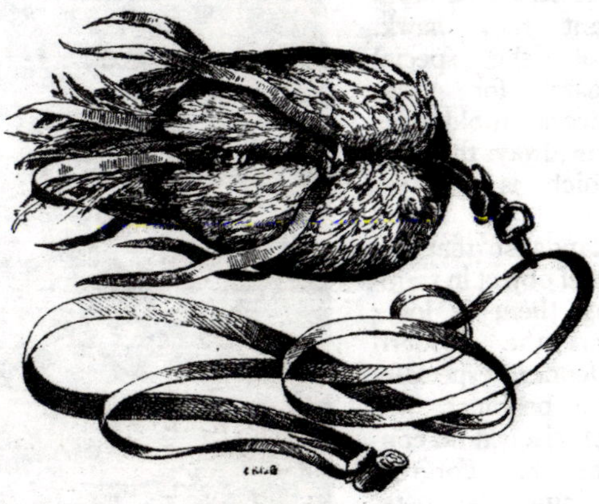

FIG. 6.—LURE.

the hawk is accustomed to look to her master for the lure. Once that is learned, there are no hawks steadier, more gentle, or more satisfactory to deal with than the wild caught ones. In ability they are, naturally, as professionals to amateurs. They have maintained themselves, and in some cases reared broods by the power of their flight, whereas the eyases have never flown at a wild bird, except one flushed for them by their master.

The Gerfalcon, in its three varieties, whether that of Greenland, Iceland, or Scandinavian, is the noblest falcon—in appearance at least—of all that are trained by man. In performance, however, it is apt to be somewhat disappointing. Most of the specimens used in this country are ship-caught birds or nestlings badly reared. In either case their plumage is so damaged and broken that they have to stand idle for a long time till the moulting season restores to them their powers of flight. Such hawks can hardly be said to have a fair chance. But in 1869, and again in 1876, falconers who were sent to Iceland and to Norway returned with consignments of these hawks in splendid order. Whether the art of training them is lost, or from what other causes failure arose, is uncertain, but only a few of these noble birds realised the expectations that were formed of them. Those that did were perhaps the finest hawks that have ever been flown in this country. But the damp climate was against them, the lungs of one hawk after another became affected, and before very long all the lot died. A very fine tiercel was caught in Holland in 1878, and was trained successfully by the falconer to the Old Hawking Club, eventually turning out to be a brilliant rook hawk. But the special quarry for these falcons in old days was always the kite, which is now extinct in these islands, so that the chief object in training them is lost; and the modern falconer, especially the beginner, will act wisely if he confines his efforts to training the peregrine.

The merlin is the smallest of the hawks used in falconry. It is a true falcon, though in some respects it is allied to the hawks. It possesses courage altogether out of proportion to its size, and, though not larger than a dove, will kill pigeons or partridges larger than itself. It is, however, best, and chiefly used for flying at larks—a beautiful form of falconry resembling heron hawking in miniature. Two merlins are generally used, and the lark in his efforts to escape will usually ring into the very clouds, often out-flying the hawks, which will follow him frequently till all three become lost as specks in the clear sky. Merlins are best kept loose in a large room, and called to hand when wanted for use. They are very delicate, and must be fed sparingly in the morning, and fully when the day's sport is over. It is the exception for them to be kept alive through their first winter, though some have been kept until the second.

GERFALCON.

The hobby is another miniature falcon, possessed of even more exquisite powers of flight than the merlin, but of less courage. It is hardier and more easily trained, but cannot be relied upon to follow its quarry with perseverance.

The merlin breeds freely on the moors in the northern counties of England and in Scotland. Its nest is on the ground and usually contains four young. The hobby, on the contrary, is a breeder in the southern and midland counties of England, and nests in trees.

Of the true hawks, as opposed to the falcons,—distinguished by having a smooth upper mandible instead of a tooth or festoon, by a yellow or orange iris to the eye, and by a long tail with short rounded wings, instead of long pointed ones—only two varieties are used, viz., the goshawk and the sparrowhawk. The goshawk breeds freely in France, Germany, and Scandinavia, but has been practically unknown in a wild state in this country for fifty years past. It is of larger size than the peregrine, and exceedingly powerful in its grip, so that it can take rabbits with ease. The stronger females can readily hold a full-grown hare. The male is flown at partridges in enclosed country—at pheasants, water-hens, and birds of slow flight, and the strongest will take rabbits well enough.

Short-winged hawks are only hooded when travelling. They require constant carriage at all times to accustom them to strange objects of every sort, and to keep them tame and in good heart. Training consists in thus taming them till they feed readily on the hand; then in accustoming them to jump to the hand for food. Gradually the distance is lengthened till the hawk will come to the falconer's fist, with or without food, as far as she can see him. As an old writer says: "She should know no perch but my fist, and when she goes to rest I will go with her." A hawk thus trained to regard the fist as her home, her feeding-place, and her resting-perch, will never give trouble by taking perch in trees and refusing to be called down; but such a result can only be gained by incessant care, patience, and perseverance. Bagged rabbits are necessary to enter the hawk with, and afterwards excellent sport may be obtained at wild ones sitting out in grass parks or fields. A goshawk intended for hares should be kept solely to them—if accustomed to an easier quarry they will cease to persevere at one that taxes them severely. Goshawks should be kept on a bow perch or on the screen-perch in the mews. They must never be allowed to be near other hawks or falcons, as they are very prone to "crab" or fight with them, and will inevitably kill them.

Sparrowhawks are trained in the same way as goshawks, but they are delicate and highly nervous little things, requiring care and gentleness in their management as well as infinite patience. They are usually flown at blackbirds and thrushes beaten out of hedgerows, and the best females take partridges well. Almost any number of small birds may be taken with a good sparrowhawk, as many as 327 having been caught in a single season, but they do not give the same sport as the larger birds named.

In the old English writers we find a great deal about the diseases of hawks and their treatment, and many of the prescriptions and modes of treatment are most complicated. Modern practice, however, does not follow the ancient lines in this respect, and medicines are few and sparingly used. In the East, however, the difficulties of a hot climate, and consequent disinclination of hawks to fly, are still overcome by the constant use of drugs. A few words as to the simpler remedies now in vogue and as to daily management are added here.

On each fine morning the hawks should be set out, each on its own block, bareheaded, on turf in some quiet field or garden, and so left for about two hours. A bath should be offered to each one (hawks are great bathers), and if not given this opportunity will often disappoint the falconer by raking off in search of water. Milk-pans make very fair baths, but a better one is made of the end of a large cask sawn off so as to be about seven inches deep. When hawks are bathing constantly, their jesses and leashes must be kept well greased. Good dog-skin is the best leather for these where it can be procured Calf leather or "kip" is good, and the toughest of all is horse-skin, which is good and durable, but must be kept well greased.

After about two hours of "weathering," the hawks may be hooded up, and either left on their blocks or removed to the mews until they are taken out to fly. Whatever training or discipline a hawk may be undergoing, a gorge, or full meal, must be given not less often than once a week; and the bigger in condition a hawk can be kept, so long as she be obedient, the better she will fly. "Castings" must be given regularly, if daily it is none the worse. They consist of several mouthfuls of fur or feathers with skin, which it is natural for all hawks to swallow while tearing up their prey. The skin of the head or neck of a pigeon makes a capital casting. In the morning these feathers or fur are ejected in the form of a pellet. By its condition the state of a hawk's health is surely indicated. If the casting is hard, firm, and dry all is well, but if it be soft and slimy, mixed up with mucus and undigested meat, something is wrong. A broken feather is a serious handicap to a hawk, and must be repaired or "imped" immediately, for if once a gap be

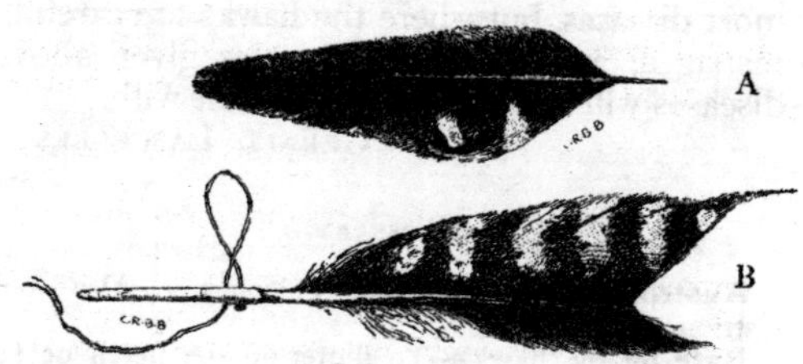

FIG. 7.—A, "IMPING" WITH NEEDLE. B, SEWING IN.

established in wings or tail, more feathers will become injured.

Imping is usually accomplished by means of a needle,—three-sided as to shape, sharp at both ends, and of a size to match the particular part of the feather that is broken. This feather is neatly cut with a sharp knife at an angle, and another feather, moulted by some hawk, or saved from a dead specimen, is cut at a corresponding angle and to the precise length that will supply the broken piece. The needle, dipped in a little brine or vinegar, is pushed half into the feather actually growing in the hawk's body and half into the new piece. When pushed close up the joint is hardly perceptible and the needle, rusting, will hold all firmly in place. (See Fig. 7, A.)

Sometimes the feather is broken actually in the quill, where no needle is available. In this case a whole feather from a dead bird is taken and the quill thereof cut into the shape of a pen, minus the nib. This pen-shaped quill is pushed carefully into the corresponding quill growing on the hawk, and secured by passing a waxed thread through both quills, lapping it around the joint and making fast. If care is taken to make the feather set at the right angle, this joint is almost impossible to detect. (See Fig. 7, B.)

Hawks, like other animals, suffer from cold,

and the form of the complaint takes that of a disease known as "*croaks*" or "*kecks*," from the incessant noise made by the hawk when exerting itself in any manner, as by bating or flying. It is the same as a bad cough in beasts, and is cured in the same manner, viz., by high feeding—and that on hot food, by keeping it warm, and avoiding risk of colds. Plenty of casting should be given.

Frounce is a canker or disease of the hawk's mouth and throat, difficult to cure, and in bad cases often fatal. The remedy is to dress the throat with burnt alum and vinegar, scraping off the canker as it forms with a quill or penknife before dressing.

Hawks often suffer from inflammation of the crop. The symptoms are green offensive mutes, and in bad cases a throwing up of the contents of the crop. The remedy is to give two or three doses of powdered Turkey rhubarb, about 4 grains to a dose. Light food should be given, warm and fresh killed, and in small quantities, frequently.

These simple remedies will meet the case in most diseases, but where the hawks are carefully managed, according to the rules given above, diseases will rarely have to be dealt with.

GERALD LASCELLES.

GLOSSARY.

Austringer—Old term for Falconer. Also spelt Ostringer.

Bate (of the hawk)—To flutter off the perch or fist owing to wildness or a fit of temper.

Bewits—Short leather straps by which bells are attached to the hawk's feet.

Bind (of the hawk)—To fasten on the quarry whilst in the air.

Block—The piece of wood on which falcons are placed when at rest.

Branchers—Young birds just able to fly from branch to branch. Also called *Boughers*.

Brail—A thong of soft leather with a small slit, through which is inserted the first joint of a hawk's wing, so as to confine it in its natural position and prevent the hawk from bating.

Cadge—A wooden frame with padded edges upon which hawks are taken into the field.

Canker—A tumour in a hawk's throat.

Carry (of the hawk)—To fly off with her quarry when the falconer comes to take her up.

Cast—(1) Two hawks; not necessarily a pair. (2) Verb: to hold a hawk above the pinions to keep her down when administering anything to her. Obs.

Casting—(1) The ejections of indigestible matter from a hawk's mouth. (2) The fur, feather, or tow given to them when in captivity in order to assist the process.

Check (of the hawk)—To leave her proper game and fly after something else that comes within view.

Cope—To trim or pare the beak and talons of a hawk.

Crab (of hawks)—To fight with each other.

Creance—A fine long line which is attached to the *leash* (*q. v.*) when extra liberty for the hawk is desired. It is chiefly used during the time of training.

Croaks—A sort of cough to which falcons, especially peregrines, are subject in this country. Also called Kecks.

Deck-Feathers—The two centre tail feathers.

Endew (of a hawk)—To digest its food thoroughly.

Enter—To give a new hawk the first sight of the game that it is to pursue.

Eyas—A hawk taken from the nest before it can fly, and brought up in captivity. Also spelt Eyess.

Eyrie—The nest of the hawk.

Falcon—(1) As used by falconers, the female of any hawk as opposed to the male. (2) As used by naturalists it denotes the long-winged members of the Falconidæ, which are further distinguished by a sharply defined tooth near the top of the upper mandible.

Falconer—The chief attendant in charge of the hawks.

Falcon-Gentle—The female of the peregrine falcon (*q.v.*).

Feak (of a hawk)—To clean the beak and feathers after feeding.

Flush—To put up game.

Foot (of the hawk)—To seize the game with the foot.

Frounce—A cancerous disease in the mouth and throat of hawks.

Gauntlet—The leather glove worn by a falconer.

Gentle—The special title of the peregrine, which could only be possessed by noblemen.

Ger-Falcon — *Falco gyrfalco*. The Scandinavian variety of the large Northern falcons. In plumage somewhat like the peregrine (*q.v.*), but bluer upon the flanks. It nests in Scandinavia.

Get in—To go up to the hawk when it has killed.

Gorge—(1) A full meal given to the hawks once or twice a week. (2) The crop. (3) Verb: to feed heavily.

Goshawk—*Falco palumbarius*. The largest of the short-winged hawks, or hawks proper. It is chiefly used for hawking pheasants and rabbits. The back is brown, the breast, of the adult bird, white, barred with brown: salmon colour streaked with dark brown in the young bird.

Greenland Falcon—*Falco candicans*. A variety of the ger-falcon. It may be distinguished by the greater preponderance of white in its plumage.

Gyr-Falcon—[*See* GER-FALCON].

Hack—The state of liberty in which young long-winged hawks are kept for a few weeks before pairing. They are loose to fly about, but are fed punctually at the hack-board every morning and later in the day. They are sometimes weighted with heavy hack-bells to prevent them from preying for themselves. Old falcons are sometimes put to "live at hack" if out of condition, but the hawks proper are rarely put out at any age.

Haggard—An adult bird taken wild.

Hawks Proper—Those members of the Falconidæ whose wings are shorter than the tail, and whose upper mandible lacks the sharp tooth. A further distinction is found in the iris, which in the hawk proper is yellow, but in the falcons very dark brown. Typical hawks proper are the goshawk and the sparrow-hawk.

Hunger-Trace—A line which appears across the feathers of a hawk that has been starved for a time when her feathers are growing down. It has the appearance of a knife mark drawn across the feather at the point where it, at the time of hunger, joined the flesh. The feathers often break off at the point where the line crosses the ribs.

Iceland Falcon—*Falco islandicus*. Another variety of the ger-falcon.

Imp—To mend the broken feathers of a hawk.

Intermewed—(1) A hawk is intermewed from the first exchange of her coat until she becomes a white hawk. (Latham and Campbell.) (2) Of a hawk that has been moulted in confinement (Lascelles and Salvin.)

Jack—Male of the merlin.

Jerkin—Male of the gerfalcon.

Jesses—The leather thongs (about six inches long) permanently attached to the legs of a hawk, and fastened to the swivel.

Jouk (of a hawk)—To sleep.

Kecks—[*See* CROAKS].

Leash—A leathern thong fastened by a swivel to the hawk's jesses in order to secure her to perch or block.

Long-Winged Hawk—[*See* HAWK and FALCON.]

Lure—A padded piece of wood or iron with feather

and meat attached to it by which the hawk is attracted to the falconer. The hawk is at first fed upon it, and taught to fly back to it when swung aloft in the air.

Mail—The breast feathers of a hawk.

Make in (of the falconer)—To go up to a hawk after it has killed.

Make a Hawk—To train a hawk. Also *Man* and *Reclaim.*

Make to the Hood—To accustom a hawk to the hood.

Man—In training a hawk; to accustom it to the sight of human beings.

Mantle (of a hawk)—(1) To stretch out wing and leg in order to gain relief by change of position. (2) To sit permanently with wings and tail spread. A sign of ill-temper. (Lascelles.)

Merlin—*Falco æsalon.* The smallest of the hawks, but a true long-winged falcon; has been known to kill a partridge. Chiefly used for larks and snipe.

Mew (of a hawk)—To moult.

Mews—The place where hawks are kept.

Mites—Parasites of the order Acarus, which infest the head and nostrils of a hawk.

Mount (of the hawk)—To wait on high.

Musket—Old term for the male of the sparrow-hawk.

Mutes and Mutings—The excrement of a hawk.

Nares—The nostrils of a hawk.

Pannel—The lower bowel of a hawk.

Passage—The regular flight of any quarry to or from its feeding ground, and the annual migration.

Passage Hawk—A bird taken during the migrations.

Pelt—The dead body of the quarry.

Perch—The pole or rail on which hawks are kept within doors.

Peregrine—*Falco peregrinus* or *gentilis.* The adult colouring is blue grey upon the back, ashen grey upon the breast barred with black. The young are brown on the back with longitudinal markings on the breast, which is pale buff. The length of the male is sixteen inches; of the female twenty-one and a half inches. Also known as Slight Falcon, Gentle Falcon, and *the* Falcon.

Petty Singles—The toes of a hawk.

Pitch—The highest point to which a hawk rises when waiting on.

Point—The perpendicular rising of a hawk over the place where its quarry has put in.

Pounces—The claws of a hawk.

Put in (of the quarry)—To take shelter in cover.

Put over (of the hawk)—To digest by passing the food from the crop to the pannel, or lower stomach.

Quarry—The object at which the hawk is flown.

Rake (of the hawk)—To fly wide of the quarry.

Ramage (of the hawk)—Wild and difficult to reclaim. Also called *Rammish.*

Ramage Hawk—Sometimes used for a hawk in its first year. Equivalent to *Soar-hawk.*

Rangle—Small stones given to a hawk to aid digestion.

Reclaim—[*See* MAKE and MAN.]

Red Plumage—The colouring of the young bird as contrasted with the blue of the adult. Hence Red Hawk.

Ring (of the hawk)—To mount in wide spiral circles.

Rouse (of the hawk)—To shake its feathers.

Ruff (of the hawk)—To strike the game without seizing it.

Rye—Old term for a cold in the head of the hawk. Also called Snurt. Obs.

Sacre and Sakeret—*Falco sacer.* A hawk largely used in the East, especially in India. Formerly found in Europe, but now extremely rare. It belongs to the group of desert falcons.

Sails—The wings of a hawk.

Screen—The perch, hung with canvas, on which hawks are set indoors.

Seel—To sew up the lower eyelids of a hawk, and tie the threads behind the head. An obsolete practice now superseded by the hood.

Serve (of the falconer)—To put out the quarry from the cover for the falcon waiting overhead.

Short-Winged Hawk—[*See* FALCON and HAWKS PROPER.]

Slight Falcon—[*See* PEREGRINE.]

Soar-Hawk—A hawk in its first year before it has moulted. Also called *Ramage-Hawk.*

Sparrow-Hawk—*Falco nisus.* A true short-winged hawk. The back of the adult male is blue-grey, and the breast a rusty white, barred with dark grey and red. The female and the young birds are brown, breast white barred with dark grey. The male is usually twelve and the female fifteen inches long, and the average weights are said by Montague to be five and nine ounces respectively.

Stoop—The rapid descent of a hawk from a height upon its quarry.

Summed (of a hawk)—Having all its feathers complete and ready for flying.

Swivel—The link attaching the jesses to the leash. It turns freely in order to prevent entanglement.

Talons—The claws of a hawk.

Tarsell, Tassell, Tiercel, Tercel—The male hawk as opposed to the female. Said to be derived from the fact of its being a third, or "tierce," smaller in size.

Tiring—A piece of tough food, such as the leg of a fowl with the flesh taken off, given to the hawk to afford it something to do.

Towering (of the hawk)—To soar above its quarry.

Train Bird—The bird at which the hawk is first practised by letting him fly at it when held in check by a fine cord.

Truss—To seize the quarry in the air, and fly off with it.

Varvels—Small rings of silver formerly attached to the jesses, on which the owner's name was engraved.

Wait on (of the hawk)—To soar above the falconer or dogs waiting for the game to be put up.

Wake or Watch (of the falconer)—To sit up all night with a newly-caught hawk in order to tame her.

Weather (of the falconer)—To place hawks unhooded upon their blocks in the open air.

Yarak—An Indian term, meaning a state of eagerness and expectancy which hawks reach when ready for flying. It is chiefly applied to the short-winged hawks. (Salvin.)

FALLOW DEER (*Cervus dama*)—A.S. *fealo*; German, *falb*, pale yellow.

Colour—The natural colour of the species in a wild state in summer is a bright fawn, with white spots irregularly distributed over the upper parts of the sides and haunches, the spotted tracts being bounded by indefinite white lines. In winter the spots disappear, the coat being changed in May and October.

Distribution—The Fallow Deer is believed to be not indigenous to England, but to have been introduced in Roman times, though it may have been later, from countries bordering the Mediterranean. In a wild state it is found at the present time in Southern Russia, Asia Minor, the island of Rhodes, parts of Greece, North Africa, Sardinia, Spain, the Cevennes Mountains, and the Alps of Dauphiné.

The Persian Fallow Deer (*Cervus mesopotamicus*) found also in Asia Minor, is regarded as a distinct species. Both *Cervus dama* and *C. mesopotamicus* are conspicuously distinguished from animals of the red deer type by having the antlers considerably palmated, instead of being entirely cylindrical, the palmation in the Persian form extending to the base of the horn, instead of being wholly above the main beam as in our Fallow Deer

In many parts of England, Fallow Deer formerly ranged in a wild state, unrestrained by any inclosure. This was notably the case in Cranbourne Chase, in the New Forest, and in Epping Forest, where, at the present day, there is a small herd of the dark brown variety, locally known as the "old forest breed." A noticeable peculiarity in this herd is the remarkable attenuation of the palmated portion of the antlers, resulting from isolation and deterioration through breeding in and in. Some interesting remarks by the Hon. G. Lascelles on the change of colour in the Fallow Deer as observed in the

FALLOW DEER.
Av. Ht. at shoulder, 36 in. Av. horn meas. 30 in. Max. horn meas. 36 in.

New Forest, will be found in the *Zoologist* for October, 1892.

Measurements—The Fallow buck usually stands about 3 feet at the shoulder, and measures about 5 feet in length, including the tail of 7 inches. The weight varies according to the feeding in different parks; the bucks averaging from 100 lbs. to 120 lbs., and the does from 50 lbs. to 60 lbs.

Habits—The pairing season begins in September, and the period of gestation is eight months. Usually one fawn is produced, sometimes two, more rarely three. They are dropped about the end of May or beginning of June, just as the fern is high enough to conceal them. Exceptionally they are dropped in autumn. The horns are shed in the spring, usually in April or beginning of May, the exact time depending upon age and temperature; a cold winter and protracted spring causes them to be shed later than would be otherwise the case. The younger animals retain their horns somewhat later than the older bucks. The shed horns are often picked up and eaten by the deer themselves, the saline flavour being relished by them. Bucks, if gelded after they have cast their horns, will never grow them again; if while growing, they will never shed them.

Fallow Deer venison is generally preferred to that of the red deer, being usually much fatter, though not so well flavoured. The bucks are killed in August, the does in January. Buck hunting begins on September 15th.

J. E. HARTING.

FENCE MONTHS—(*See* also GAME LAWS).

BRITISH ISLANDS—**Close time** or close season for fish is the time during which it is illegal to take, and not only to take, but to sell or have in possession for sale, the fish to which the close time applies.

Close time may be divided into three parts, concerning:—

I. Salmon and migratory trout.
II. Trout.
III. Freshwater coarse fish.

I. **Salmon**—In England and Wales the close time for salmon was fixed, by the Salmon Fishery Act 1861, from the 1st September to 1st February, both days inclusive, for all modes of fishing but rod and line, and for rod and line from the 1st November to 1st February. By the Salmon Fishery Act 1873, power was given to Boards of Conservators, with the consent of the central authority, to vary the close time in the districts; and, to the great injury not only of the fisheries in the district, but also of the fisheries generally, this power has been acted on to a considerable extent. In the report of the Inspector of Fisheries for each year, a list of the different close times in force in the different districts is given. If it is not varied, the time is, for rod, 1st October to 1st February, for all other modes, 1st September to 1st February. English salmon may only be legally sold if taken during the open season. Salmon taken by rod during the open season for rod cannot be sold. The fish seen in fishmongers' shops during the English close season are *said* to be Scotch fish or foreign, although often really poached English fish.

In addition to an annual close time, there is also a weekly close time for salmon from noon on Saturday to 6 A.M. on Monday. Power has been given to Fishery Boards to extend this, and in some cases (as on the Christchurch Fishery) it has been done. It only applies to fishing other than with rods.

In Scotland the close time is more variable than in England, and in some cases has been fixed by local acts. On the Tweed the rod fishing is open till the end of November.

In Ireland the close time is also very variable, but there it is fixed for the different districts by the Inspector of Fisheries.

The result is that the law as to salmon close time is in the most hopeless state of confusion, and, except the month of December, there is no time when, in some part of the United Kingdom by some means, salmon cannot be legally taken.

II. **Trout**—In England and Wales the close time for trout is from the 1st October to the 2nd February (for Thames trout 11th September to 31st March). There is also a power for Fishery Boards to vary this time, and in some cases the power has been exercised, usually by extending the close season to March. In Scotland there is no close time for trout.

III. **Freshwater (Coarse) Fish**—In 1878 a close time from the 15th March to the 15th June was introduced for freshwater fish, which are in effect all fish but trout and salmon. (In Norfolk and Suffolk the close time is 1st March to 30th June.) The close time, however, does not apply to landowners fishing in their own water or to persons to whom they give leave. It has also been altered by statute as to eels, and is now only applied to fishing for or taking eels with a rod and line. Presumably, all persons fishing between March and June are fishing for trout. Fishery Boards have power to except either the whole or part of the district from the close time, or any particular kind or kinds of fish, and orders under both these heads have been made by certain Fishery Boards.

On the whole, there is no subject which is more confused than that of the close time for fish; and except the general rules that the close time for salmon is from 1st September to 1st February, trout 1st October to 1st February, freshwater fish from 15th March to 15th June, unless locally varied, it is impossible within the limits of an article to state what the law is.

The Fishmonger's Company annually issue a table of the different close times in force, and the appendices to the reports of the inspectors in the three kingdoms contain the official notice of what the close times are in the different places.

J. WILLIS BUND.

CANADA, DOMINION OF—

Province of Ontario.

Trout	Sept. 15th to May 1st.
Black bass and Mascalonge .	April 15th to July 15th.

Province of Quebec.

Salmon	Aug. 15th to Feb. 1st.
No Sunday fishing.	
Trout	Oct. 1st to May 1st.
Ouananiche (land-locked salmon)	Sept. 15th to Dec. 1st.

FRANCE—

Salmon	Sept. 30th to Jan. 10th.
Trout	Oct. 20th to Jan. 31st.
Coarse fish	April 15th to June 15th.

[If June 15th should fall on a Sunday, or even Monday, it is usual to make the opening day on the Saturday preceding, so as to give the working men an extra Sunday, the chief day for angling in France.]

GERMANY—The fence-months for fish differ considerably in the various provinces, but the general system embraces a winter close time (October 15th to December 14th); a spring close time (Prussia, April 15th to June 14th; other provinces, April 10th to June 9th), and a weekly close time of at least twenty-four hours (from sunset on Saturday to sunset on Sunday). These restrictions, which are subject to local modifications, do not extend to closed waters. The most complicated regulations are those in force in the kingdom of Bavaria, where some nineteen fishes are specified in the act, each with a close time of its own, those for salmon (and sea-trout) and trout being respectively October 1st to December 31st, and October 20th to January 20th.

NORWAY and SWEDEN—

Salmon and sea-trout

(*a*) Rivers, estuaries, and lakes	Sept. 14th to Apr. 15th.
(*b*) Brooks, or on the sea coast	Sept. 14th to Feb. 14th.

UNITED STATES—All laws relating to fish and game in the States which constitute the United States are enacted by the legislatures of each state separately, and therefore what may be lawful in one state may be unlawful in another and adjoining state.

Each state may have general and special laws, *i.e.*, laws which relate to the state at large, except certain named counties of the state or even certain townships of a county. Some states have laws which forbid the shipment of fish or game within the state unless it is accompanied by its owner, and some have laws forbidding the shipment of fish or game beyond the borders of the state.

The close times for the same species of fish may differ in different states or even in different counties of a state—not a great difference, but enough to prove a snare to the uninformed—and so, altogether, the "game laws," the term usually applied to acts governing furred and feathered game and to fish as well, prove a labyrinth to the unwary.

Class legislation is dead. Broadly stated, it is the intention of the game laws of the United States to-day that all wild game and fish shall become the property of him who reduces them to possession, by killing or catching, with due regard to the laws of trespass on private property, be it land or water. Wild game and fish are not to be molested during the season of reproduction, and they must be allowed free and unobstructed passage to their breeding grounds or waters.

Changed conditions in recent years have made it necessary to elaborate these fundamental laws; to draw them more closely and define them more clearly until, as a whole, they have become multitudinous and almost hopelessly confusing to one who desires to fish or shoot in the different states of the Union, and who has not made a study of the laws from year to year as enacted. To add to the confusion, the states having annual sessions of the legislature (the law-making body) each year amend, repeal, make new laws, or change the open season for both fish and game. The tendency of the game laws in recent years is to shorten the close seasons and to increase the penalty for violating the laws; at the same time a constant warfare is waged by a body of thinking men on the one hand, to simplify the laws and make them less cumbersome by eliminating the special provisions which relate only to detached ponds or streams, and on the other hand by a horde of people who seek some personal advantage by excepting from the operation of the law waters in which they have a local interest.

The spread of civilisation; the destruction of the forests, drying up of the fountain heads of rivers and brooks; improved engines of destruction which thin out the fish and game; better means of transportation which carry devastation to the remoter habitats of this food supply; the sewage and refuse from towns, mills, and factories, which have made streams unfit for food fish; the increase of population, and the growing love of all that relates to sport and out-door life, have combined to make rigidly enforced game laws a necessity to preserve fish, birds, and animals from utter destruction. The lawless will always oppose the game laws, no matter how just or how necessary they may be, and the law-abiding must always strive for their enactment and enforcement.

In giving the close seasons (fence months of England) for fish in the principal states, I shall deal only with the so-called "game fishes," and refer alone to the general laws, omitting, except in special instances, the local laws which govern small bodies of water within the states. Any one who may desire to study the fish, bird, and animal laws of all the states in detail should procure the *Game Laws in Brief*, published at a nominal sum by the Forest and Stream Publishing Company, New York City. This "Brief" is amended annually, or oftener as occasion requires, and is a safe guide to any who desire to observe all the laws of all the states in the Union, and contains the laws of the Dominion of Canada as well.

Some fifty states and territories have enacted fish and game laws more or less elaborate and complicated, but fortunately not all of the states afford fishing to attract visitors from outside of the borders of the state.

New York State.

Kind of fish.	*Closed season.*
Trout	Sept. 1st to April 15th.
(This refers to brook, brown, rainbow, and Loch Leven trout).	
Lake Trout (*Salvelinus namaycush*)	Oct. 1st to April 30th.

Kind of Fish.	*Closed season.*
Land-locked salmon (the land-locked form of *Salmo salar*)	Oct. 1st to April 30th.
Black bass (*Micropterus salmondes* and *M. dolomieu*) .	Jan. 1st to May 30th.
Pike, pickerel, and pike-perch	Jan. 31st to May 1st.
Mascalonge	Last day of Feb. to May 30th.

There is a close season for salmon, *S. salar*, from August 15th to March 1st, but there is no fishing for this fish in the state to tempt an angler. The Hudson, a stocked stream, does not yet produce fish in numbers for fishing purposes.

There are limits to the length of fish which may be legally killed. For salmon it is 18 inches, for black bass 8 inches, except in the St. Lawrence River, where it is 10 inches. On Long Island the close season for trout of all kinds, except lake trout, is from August 31st to March 29th.

In the St. Lawrence River the close season for black bass, mascalonge, pike, pike-perch, and pickerel, is from January 1st to June 9th, and not more than twelve black bass shall be killed or possessed by one person in one day. The penalties for violating the provisions of the close season are from $10 to $100, besides being a misdemeanour which carries a fine with it.

Vermont.

Kind of fish.	*Closed season.*
Trout (*fontinalis*), lake trout (*namaycush*), and land-locked salmon	Sept. 1st to May 1st.
Black bass	Jan. 1st to June 15th.

Fish can only be taken by angling, and angling is defined to mean "not exceeding two rods or lines, with hooks attached, held in the hand."

New Hampshire.

Brook trout or lake trout . .	Sept. 18th to May 1st.
Land-locked salmon . .	Sept. 30th to Apr. 15th.
Black bass	April 30th to June 15th.
Mascalonge	April and May.

Not more than 10 lbs. of brook trout can be taken in one day by one person. Angling only permitted. Fish commissioners of the state have power to close any waters in the state for a term of years by publishing notice.

Maine.

Salmon (*Salar*) . . .	Sept. 15th to April 1st.

No salmon to be taken on Saturday and Sunday.

Brook trout, lake trout, and land-locked salmon . .	Oct. 1st to May 1st.
Black bass	April 1st to July 1st.

Angling confined to single hook and line or artificial flies. Not more than 50 lbs. of land-locked salmon, lake trout, or brook trout may be transported.

Delaware.

Black bass and trout . .	Nov. 1st to June 1st.

Connecticut.

Trout	July 1st to April 1st.
Black bass	May and June.

Massachusetts.

Trout of all kinds and land-locked salmon . . .	Sept. 1st to April 1st.
Black bass	Dec. 1st to June 1st.

Michigan.

Trout, grayling, land-locked salmon	Sept. 1st to May 1st.

Colorado.

Trout	Dec. 1st to June 1st.

South Dakota.

Trout	Sept. 1st to May 1st.

Unlawful to export trout.

Pennsylvania.

Kind of Fish.	*Closed season.*
Brook trout	July 15th to April 15th.
Lake trout	Oct., Nov., Dec.
Black bass	Jan. 1st. to May 30th.

Oregon.

Trout	Nov. 1st to April 1st.

Wyoming.

Trout	Oct. 1st to June 1st.

California.

Trout	Nov. 1st to April 1st.

Other states, Florida, Missouri, Louisiana, Kentucky, Nebraska, have no close season for fish, so far as hook and line fishing is concerned. The states I have given cover the lake and wilderness regions of the New England states, the Adirondacks of New York, the Rocky Mountains, and the Pacific coast. In the Eastern and Atlantic states, the "trout" or brook trout is the *fontinalis*; this is also true of the states about the Great Lakes. The Rocky Mountain states furnish the black spotted trout, *Salmo mykiss*, and the Pacific states the rainbow trout, *S. irideus*, there called mountain trout.

A. NELSON CHENEY.

FENCING—To hold a Foil—The thumb must be flat on the hilt (convex part) the forefinger grasping the under part and the two sides, and the other fingers lying flat along the left side. The four fingers should touch each other, and a small place should be left between the third phalanx of the little finger and the under part of the hilt. Lightness in the grip, holding the foil mostly with the thumb and forefinger, makes finger play possible.

First Position—The first position can be taken in two different ways:—

(A) Place both feet at right angles, both heels touching each other, the right foot in front and pointing towards the opponent,—the legs straight, the body upright without stiffness, and facing the opponent at three-quarters; both arms down, falling naturally along both sides of the body, the point of the foil in front touching or nearly touching the ground.

(B) The feet, the body, and left arm the same as above, the right hand holding the foil at the height of the head, knuckles upwards, and slightly to the right, the arm straight.

The first position (A) ought to be taken always by beginners before assuming the guard, and in assaults made in private. The first position (B) is used in public assaults and always when beginning an assault.

Second Position or Guard—When in the first position (A) with the right hand low, the second position is taken thus:—

Place the right foot at about two soles' length in front of the left heel, raise the left hand until on a level with the head, the arm half extended, rather backwards; raise the right hand until nearly at the height of the right breast, bending the arm, and keeping the elbow near the body, but not touching it, and the point of the foil at about the same height as the eye. Bend both knees, keeping the weight of the body well divided between the two legs. Keep the body upright, shoulders down without leaning either backwards or forwards, and always facing the opponent at three-quarters. The distance between both heels may vary according to the height of the fencer; when the legs are properly bent, the right knee must be perpendicular to the instep.

The second position, or guard, may be taken backwards, by placing the left foot behind, at about two soles' length from the right, the rest of the movement the same as above.

When in the first position (B) with the right hand high, to take the second position, lower the right hand, knuckles downwards, place it by the side of the left hip, and let the left hand take hold of the blade lightly as if it was in its sheath; raise both hands together to a level with the head, taking care to round the movement; let go the blade with the left hand, and place the left arm, half extended, rather backwards, keeping the hand at the same height. Place the right hand in front, slightly lower than the right breast, the arm bent, the elbow near the body, but not touching it, the point of the foil at about the same height as the eye. Place the right foot at about two soles' length in front of the left heel, and bend both knees as above.

Third Position or Lunge—From the second position, or guard, stretch out the right arm, without any jerk, on a level with the shoulder, finger nails turned upwards; advance the right foot about a sole and a half length, slightly raising the toes and allowing the heel almost to brush the ground; stretch the left leg and straighten the left knee, press in the loins and left hip, and lower the left hand towards the left thigh at a few inches above it. The right knee should be perpendicular to the instep, and the left foot kept flat on the ground. Great care must be taken not to drop forward, and the body should not be kept too upright, but in a slanting position, allowing a sufficiently long reach without compromising the retreat.

Observations on the Guard—Quickness and suddenness in the attack, readiness and firmness in the defence, and easiness in the retreat, depend on a good guard, therefore great care should be taken in assuming that position. Until late years most fencers thought it preferable to have the body well "effaced," *i.e.*, the body sideways, presenting the right side only, hoping to be exposed as little as possible to the thrust of the antagonist. This is an error which has been almost completely abandoned in France in the last few years.[1] The *Théorie pratique de*

FIG. 1.—THE GUARD.

[1] There are two *schools* or *methods* of fencing: the French and the Italian. In the lattter they have still kept the effaced position in the guard and lunge. The Italian foil is different to the French. There is a small iron bar (called *barrette*) across the handle; the foil is held with the forefinger and the middle finger round the barrette, the third and fourth grasping the handle, and the thumb lying close to the middle finger

l'Escrime and *L'Escrime et le Duel*, published in Paris, the first in 1886, the second in 1891, are mostly the cause of that progress.

The reasons that cause the effaced position to be wrong are the following. In regard to the defence, the effacement of the body makes it extremely difficult to keep a steady balance; it requires a constant muscular effort to turn the left shoulder and hip backwards towards the left. The right arm becomes stiff, and this stops finger play and causes the parries to be slower and wider. In regard to the attack, the effacement of the body, stiffening the right arm, makes its extension slower. The hip, being turned backwards, makes the left knee also turn backwards, and places it perpendicularly over the left toes; the left leg and thigh then are not in a favourable position to give quickness to the lunge; and the body is so placed that the action of the loins does not come into play. On guard, the left hand should always be placed as indicated, the left arm being a very useful counterbalance to the right.

It is most important that the body should be upright and its weight equally shared by both legs. If the fencer leans forward, he shortens his reach and exposes himself, and the weight of the body, bearing mostly on the right leg, prevents the right foot from moving properly forward in the lunge. If, on the other hand, the weight of the body is thrown on the left leg, the lunge becomes slow, as it cannot be done without a *jump*, or without a movement forward of the body before making use of the extension of the left leg.

FIG. 2.—THE LUNGE.

nail on the handle and barrette. Until about ten years ago, their blade was four or five inches longer than the French, and was heavy and whippy. Some Italian fencers, having been to Paris and having fenced with French fencers, understood that the exaggerated length and weight of their foil were a great disadvantage to them; they gradually shortened their blade, and have now adopted the French blade. They modified their way of fencing, and instead of keeping their arm stretched out on guard they bend it, and have taken most of the French parries, which they could not use before on account of the weight and length of their blades. They have also changed their way of attacking and lunging, *i.e.*, instead of making a sort of half lunge, keeping the body completely upright, always preceded by one or several little jumps forward, they make a longer lunge and slant the body forward, but they have not yet done away entirely with their jumps forward (the French advance one foot after the other, the right foot first; the Italians advance both feet at the same time with a jump). On account of their effaced position and their way of holding their foil or sword, their attacks are not so quick, and they are obliged to move a great deal more for their defence, and they require much more muscular strength.

Observations on the Lunge—A fencer must always bear in mind that quickness in the attack depends mostly on a supple and quick extension of the arm. The extension of the left leg must not begin the motion: the hand must start first, the right foot next, and the left leg must then push the body forward. These three parts of the lunge must follow each other so closely that they seem to be a single movement. To have a long reach, the body must certainly be *slanted forward*, but it is most important that it should not *drop forward*. The left hip must be well pressed in, and the loins tightened, or else the fencer will lose his balance and find the recovery extremely difficult. Care must be taken not to let the right knee overreach the foot; the knee must be just above the instep.

To Recover or Return on Guard—Just as the left leg pushes the body forward in the lunge, the right leg must, with the help of the loins, push it backwards in the recovery; simultaneously, the left hand must be raised, the right arm and the left leg bent, and the right foot placed at about two soles' length from the left, and the position of the guard assumed.

When the adversary has retired a certain distance to avoid the attack, and has put himself far out of reach, the guard may be regained forwards in the following manner. Keep the right knee bent, bring the left foot to about two soles' length from the right heel, bending the left leg; raise the left hand, bend the right arm and take the position of the guard. When, having attacked without success, the fencer is in danger and wishes to place himself immediately out of reach, he must, with a vigorous effort of the right leg and loins, throw the weight of the body on the left leg, which must be kept almost straight; place the right heel against the left, and assume the guard backwards. Beginners should not make use of these two latter ways of regaining the second position.

When on guard, the first position can be regained forwards by bringing the left foot close to the right, and backwards by placing the right heel near the left.

To Advance—When on guard, advance the right foot first a few inches, and let the left foot follow over an equal space.

To Retire or to Retreat—When on guard, step back a few inches with the left foot first, and bring the right foot the same distance from the left as before. If, for some special reason, it is necessary to get instantly out of reach, throw the weight of the body entirely on the left leg, bring the right foot against the left heel, or, if needed, behind the left foot, without keeping the legs quite so much bent, and fall on guard backwards. This way of retreating must only be used by fencers of some skill, and not by beginners.

The Lines—The space between the right or the left of the blade and the limit of the body on the corresponding side is called the *line*. There are four lines: two high and two low. The two high lines are: the *upper* line on the right of the blade when pointed high, and the *inside* line on the left of the blade when also pointed high. The two low lines are: the *lower* line on the left of the blade when pointed low, and the *outside* line on the right of the blade when also pointed low.[1] A line is either open or closed; it is open when the opponent's point can hit the fencer's body; it is closed when the point cannot touch it. The two high lines cannot be closed at the same time; if the inside line is closed, the upper line is bound to be open, and *vice versa*. The same for the two low lines.

Simple Parries—A *parry* is the action of warding off a thrust of the opponent's foil or sword. A simple parry is a direct parry which meets the opponent's blade in the line in which he thrusts. There are eight simple parries: four for the two high lines, four for the two low ones.

There names are: *Prime*, *Seconde*, *Tierce*, *Quarte*, *Quinte*, *Sixte*, *Septime*[2] and *Octave*.

Prime: The right hand opposite the left shoulder, the thumb turned downwards, the arm half bent, the foil pointed downwards.

Seconde: The hand opposite the right hip (slightly higher), the finger nails turned downwards, the arm straight without stiffness, the point very little lower than the hand, the blade almost horizontal.

Tierce: The hand on the right, the finger nails very slightly turned downwards, the elbow near the body, the point on a level with the eye a little outside the line on the right.

Quarte: The hand to the left, the thumb uppermost, the elbow near the body, the point on a level with the eye and a little to the left.

Quinte: The same as quarte, with the finger nails turned downwards and the point further to the left. The hand may be slightly lower.

Sixte: The same as tierce, with the finger nails turned upwards.

Septime: The hand opposite the right shoulder, the finger nails turned upwards, the arm half extended, elbow down, the blade horizontal, the point opposite the left shoulder. In the position of septime, the wrist must be slightly bent: the upper part convex, the inner part concave.

Octave: The same as seconde, with the finger nails turned upwards.

Theoretically there are eight parries, as described above, to protect four lines, two parries for each line, but this is a useless complication. Practically one parry for each line is sufficient; therefore, following the celebrated French master M. Bertrand's[3] example, we consider that four parries can be abandoned without any disadvantage, and they are the following:—

1. **Prime**, which is a dangerous parry. It

[1] Some masters give the same names to the lines and the parries; for instance, they name the *inside* line *quarte* line or *quinte* line, according to the position of the hand holding the foil, being with the finger nails turned upwards or downwards; and the upper line *tierce* line if the finger nails are turned downwards, or *sixte* line if they are upwards. According to that system there are two names to each line; therefore it complicates a demonstration when taken as a rule. Nevertheless, it may simplify or help an explanation when used exceptionally, and for this reason these expressions will be sometimes found in the course of this article.

[2] Septime has been called *semicircle* or *half-circle* for many years.

[3] M. Bertrand, born in 1797, died in 1876.

is slow and places the hand in such a position that, when deceived, the body is entirely uncovered. Septime protects the same line and is much more convenient. It is a much quicker parry, and the ripostes from it are more easily delivered and more rapid.

2. **Quinte,** which is a heavy and clumsy parry.

3. **Sixte,** because, the hand being turned finger nails upwards, the parry is made with the help of the ends of the fingers, while with tierce, which covers the same line, the parry is made with the help of the thumb, the finger nails being turned slightly downwards.

4. **Octave,** for the same reasons as sixte.

There are two ways of making the same parry: by an opposition, or by a smart or dry beat on the blade.

When the opponent presses on the blade while attacking, trying to force the stroke in notwithstanding the parry, the parry should be made by closing the line, thus pushing the point out of the direction of the body, and this is called "by opposition" (parade d'opposition).

If the blades are not joined in the attack, the opponent not weighing on the blade when the parry is being made, the parry should be, as the French name it, "parade sèche" or "parade detachée," that is, with a dry or smart beat sending the opponent's point out of the line. From this last parry the riposte called "du tac-au-tac" (explained further on) can be made.

In the parries of quarte and tierce, the point must be higher than in the ordinary engagement, so as to take the advantage of the fort of the blade on the feeble. As a rule it should be about on a level with the fencer's eye, and if the opponent weighs on the blade the point should be still higher.

The Engagement—The engagement is the junction of the blades. There are as many engagements as there are parries, and they take the same names, *i.e.*, the engagement in quarte, the engagement in tierce, &c. It may be either with or without opposition. It is with opposition when the opponent's blade cannot reach the body with a straight thrust, that is, when the line in which the blades are joined is closed. It is without opposition when the blades are placed so that the same line is open. The height of the point, when the blades are engaged in quarte or tierce (or sixte), should vary according to the opponent's size; if the antagonist is tall, it should be higher than if he is short. As a rule the point must be placed in the direction of his eyes, more to the left if in quarte, with opposition, or more to the right if in tierce.

FIG. 3.—THE PARRY IN SECONDE.

The Change of Engagement—To change the engagement in the upper lines is to quit an engagement in one high line, passing the point under the opponent's blade, and to take the engagement in the other high line: from quarte to tierce or from tierce to quarte In the changes of engagements from one low line to the other, that is, from septime to seconde, or from seconde to septime, the point must pass over the opponent's blade. Both fencers cannot have the opposition in the engagement, one of the two is fatally uncovered, and it is dangerous to attempt to get the opposition by forcing on the opponent's blade; therefore the changes of engagements are very useful, as they allow one to take the opposition in the other line without any effort.

Sometimes, when an adversary is preparing an attack, a change of engagement may oblige him to change his mind.

The Double Engagement—The double engagement is composed of two successive changes of engagement, rapidly done, the first very light, simply touching the blade, the second with opposition. It is only used in the high lines. It often allows opposition to be taken without forcing on the blade, and is very useful when advancing, as it renders a stop thrust (coup d'arrêt) very difficult. It may also disturb the adversary's plans. It requires light finger play the hilt; they must be in continual contact with it.

When parrying, the hand must be placed as explained for each parry, but when attacking, feinting, or riposting, the hand must be in supination, that is, with the finger nails turned upwards, this position of the hand being much more favourable for finger play; there are but very few exceptions, which will be explained in their proper place.

The great advantage of finger play over arm or wrist work in fencing is that it gives considerably more quickness in the movements of the blade. With it the feints are more effective and the opponent's parries deceived more surely

FIG. 4.—THE PARRY IN TIERCE.

to be well executed, and it is a very good exercise.

Finger Play (Doigté)—To have a good finger play is to be able to direct the point and move the blade in attacking, in parrying, and in executing all movements in fencing, with only the action of the fingers on the hilt.

The foil must be held mostly with the thumb and forefinger. These must act as a sort of pivot, the thumb giving the direction to the point, the three other fingers holding the hilt very lightly, giving momentary pressures when needed, either to move the blade properly in feints, attacks or ripostes, or to form the parries or "attacks on the blade," or to support any shock on it. It is a great mistake to hold the foil with force, but the fingers must never quit and safely; the parries are more rapid and made with more precision; and if a parry is deceived by the antagonist, a second parry is more easily and quickly done; and ripostes are quicker and neater.

Simple Attacks—Attacks which are not preceded by a feint are called simple attacks. There are four simple attacks and they can be executed in each line. Their names are: the straight thrust (coup droit), the disengagement, the cut-over (coupé), and the counter-disengagement (contre-dégagement).

A fencer must bear in mind that as the thrus is delivered with the foil or sword, the hand holding that weapon must move first in every attack, however quick the stroke may be. When a very good fencer makes a very quick straight thrust or a disengagement, the hand, foot and body all seem to move together at the same time, but, in fact, the hand begins the motion.

The Straight Thrust—This is the most simple of all the attacks. To make a straight thrust, straighten the arm, directing the point to the adversary's body in the line of engagement, and lunge. The direction must be given to the point with a pressure of the thumb while extending the arm. Some fencers direct the point first, placing the blade horizontally, and then straighten the arm; this is a mistake, because it involves loss of time, and the success of a straight thrust depends on quickness.

When disengaging from the engagement in quarte into the upper line, pass the point under the antagonist's hand while straightening the arm, and turn the hand knuckles up, keeping it opposite the right shoulder, and thrust in tierce. The turning of the hand in supination, while disengaging, helps finger play considerably. The same for disengaging from tierce into the inside (or quarte) line, only with the hand slightly to the left.

It is a mistake to try, as some fencers do, to pass the point as close as possible to the opponent's blade, because then the straightening of the arm can only take place when the point has passed into the opposite line; this makes

Fig. 5.—The Parry in Quarte.

The straight thrust can be made in each line with the fingers upwards or downwards, but a good direction is much more easily given to the point with the hand in supination. When engaged in tierce, if the opponent keeps his point too low, the straight thrust can be made thus: Place the fort of the blade on the feeble part of his, straighten the arm, and lunge, slightly forcing in the line, with the hand high, keeping opposition to the right.

The Disengagement (or **Disengage**)—To disengage is to quit the line in which the blades are placed and to thrust in another. In the high lines the disengage is made by passing the point under the opponent's hand; in the low lines, by passing it over the adversary's wrist.

two movements of one; it is absolutely necessary to extend the arm while disengaging and to pass the point round the antagonist's hand very closely, and, when disengaging into tierce, round the arm if possible.

To disengage from a high line into a low line, drop the point into the low line, on the corresponding side, while extending the arm, and lunge, and *vice versa* to disengage from a low line into a high line.

The Cut-over (**Coupé**)—When engaged in quarte, to cut-over into the upper line, raise the point by a movement of the thumb and forefinger, loosening the three other fingers, pass the blade over the adversary's, lower the point by a pressure of the last three fingers while straightening the arm, and lunge. The same when engaged in tierce to cut-over into quarte. The coupés are not used in the low lines.

The Counter - Disengagement — The counter-disengagement eludes a change of engagement or double engagement; or, when preceded by a feint, it deceives a parry.

The counter-disengagement is very much like a disengagement in appearance, but as it cannot be done if the opponent does not move his blade first, *ipso facto* it is quite different. The disengage goes from one line to another; the counter-disengage comes back into the same line.

When engaged in quarte, to counter-disengage, the instant the adversary quits the blade to change the engagement, let the point follow his blade, passing under his hand with a pressure of the thumb and forefinger, and lunge, thrusting in the inside line. The extension of the arm must take place while the point is passing under the hand. From the engagement in tierce, the counter-disengagement is the same, but in the reverse way.

The counter-disengage on a double engagement must take place on the second change, *i.e.*, when engaged in quarte, let the blade be touched by the other in tierce and avoid the second change by a counter-disengage in tierce. When in tierce, let the blade be touched in quarte and counter-disengage in quarte. Sometimes the counter-disengage may be abridged thus. From the engagement in tierce, to avoid the change of engagement, the instant the adversary's blade quits the engagement, drop the point into the lower line, and lunge. The same from the engagement in quarte, and thrust in the outside line.

In these two cases, although the thrust is not delivered in the line of engagement, the stroke is still called a counter-disengagement, and must not be mistaken for a disengage, as it is still made in the reverse way, following the opponent's blade.

How to protect oneself against the above Attacks with Simple Parries—Against a straight thrust that does not quit the blade, in whatever line the engagement may be, take the opposition. For instance, if engaged in quarte with the line open, and the adversary attacks with a straight thrust without quitting blades, raise the point slightly so as to take advantage of the fort of the blade on the feeble, and send the opponent's point out of the direction of the body by closing the line with a pressure of the fingers. The same in the other lines. Against a straight thrust with the blades not engaged, close the line with a smart beat, the fort of the blade on the feeble.

Against a disengage or a cut-over into the inside line, parry quarte, or septime (this last parry protecting the inside line as well as the lower line). Against a disengage or cut-over

FIG. 6.—THE PARRY IN SEPTIME.

into the upper line, parry tierce. Against a disengage into the lower line, parry septime; in the outside line, parry seconde.

Against a counter-disengage from the engagement in quarte into the inside line, parry quarte after the change of engagement: from the engagement of tierce into the upper line, parry tierce after the change of engagement. If the counter-disengagement is abridged and the thrust delivered in the outside line, parry seconde; in the lower line, parry septime.

Feints—A feint is a sham attack, or, rather, the threatening of an attack without lunging. Its object is to mislead the opponent, making him believe in a true attack, inducing him to form a parry which will be eluded by avoiding his blade, and thrusting in an open line. The feint takes the name of the simple attack it simulates.

Attacks made with one or more feints are called compound or composed attacks. Feints should be made with finger play and the extension of the arm, but great care must be taken not to straighten the arm with stiffness and not to move the shoulder forward, because then the finger play would become impossible. There must be no jerk in the extension of the arm.

When making a compound attack, the lunge must take place with the last movement. When making an attack with an advance, composed of one feint and the thrust, the step must be made rapidly with the feint and the lunge with the finale. When making an attack with an advance, composed of more than one feint, the step must be made with the first feint and the lunge with the finish; but as there should be no pause between the step and the lunge, their quickness must be moderated so as to accord with the movements of the blade, the step beginning with the first feint, and the lunge finishing with the finale.

When making composed attacks, it is most important to regulate one's speed by that of the opponent. Indeed, although a composed attack may be made with good judgment and well combined, if the feints are quicker or slower than the parries they are intended to deceive, the blades catch each other, and the attack cannot succeed.

Judgment is required to deceive parries; it is a mistake to rely on mere chance for the success of an attack; it may sometimes happen to be the right one, but very seldom; and generally causes what are called *parries by contraction*, and ugly fencing.

To foresee the opponent's parries is certainly not easy, but in the course of this article some advice will be given how to acquire judgment.

Some fencers very seldom engage the blades, and with others it is sometimes wiser to avoid joining blades. The reasons for so doing will be explained farther on; for the present it is simply useful to state the fact. In order to be more easily understood, all the attacks that will be described, to deceive parries, will be said to start from an engagement, but in practice, when there is no junction of blades, the same attacks can be made to deceive the same parries.

Counter-Parries — There is no English word equivalent to the French *contre*, but the French word *contre* is generally used with an English orthography and transformed into counter.

Counters are circular parries in which the blade follows that of the opponent, and meets it again where the former engagement was, sending the point out of the direction of the body.

There are as many counters as there are simple parries, and they are called counter-quarte, counter-tierce, &c., according to the engagement from which they are made. A counter can be correct only when the opponent's attack is either a disengagement or a cut-over in the line opposite that of the engagement; *e.g.*, from the engagement in quarte the counter-quarte can only be made against a disengage or a cut-over in the upper line (in tierce or sixte).

When engaged in quarte, to parry counter-quarte, the moment the adversary quits the blade to disengage into the upper line, let your blade follow his, and describe a circle with its point, passing under his hand or blade from left to right, thus bringing the blades in quarte again, and closing the line. The hand must not move while doing this; the thumb and forefinger must act as a pivot, slightly loosening the three other fingers at the first part of the movement, and tightening them at the finish to raise the point, and give a smart beat with the fort of the blade on the feeble of the adversary's.

The movement is the same against a cut-over.

When engaged in tierce, to parry counter-tierce, the moment the adversary quits the blade to disengage into the inside line, let your blade follow his and describe a circle with your point, passing under the hand from right to left, and close the line in tierce. The principles are the same as for counter-quarte.

The counter-tierce parry is not much used, and we do not recommend it; the parry of septime, as we have described it, is far superior, as it is much quicker (the point describing at least one-third less than a circle) and protects two lines, the lower and the inside lines.

When in seconde to parry counter-seconde, the moment the adversary quits the blade to disengage[1] into the lower line, let your blade follow his and describe a circle with your point, passing it over his hand from right to left, and bring the blades in seconde again, and close the line. Like the counter-quarte, it must be

[1] The disengagements, from one low line to the other, are made by passing the point over the wrist.

made with the forefinger and thumb, and finished with a pressure of all the fingers.

When in septime, to parry counter-septime, the moment the adversary quits the blade to disengage in the inside line, let the blade follow his and describe a circle with your point, passing it over his wrist from left to right, and close the line. The finger play is the same as for the other counters.

When the blades are not engaged, as often occurs, the counters are made in the same manner, and are named according to the line in which they are. For instance, when the point is directed high, and the blades are to the left of each other, that is, in the inside line, if the adversary attacks in the upper line with a simple disengagement or a cut-over, the circular parry is called counter-quarte. If the blades are in the upper line, and the attack made in the inside line, the circular parry is called counter-tierce. The same for the counters in the low lines.

Attacks on the Sword—An attack on the sword is intended to get the opponent's blade out of the way before making an attack at the body, to disarm him, to check his blade in a parry, to prevent him from timing, or to draw an attack.

The attacks on the blade are called: a pressure, a beat, a scrape, a twist disarmament, or a twist-and-thrust (pressions, battement, froissé, croisé, liement).

The *pressure* is the action of pressing on the blade in order to make an opening either for a direct attack or with the intention of deceiving a parry, &c.

The *beat* is a smart tap on the opponent's blade. Light beats are more advisable than heavy ones, but they must be done very suddenly and with finger play only; if they are done otherwise they are very easy to avoid. Their object is to get the opponent's blade slightly out of the way for a direct attack, or, when followed by a simple or compound attack, to check the blade and render the parry more difficult and slower.

The *scrape* (this is the nearest English word for the French *froissé*), is made only in the high lines and mostly in the upper line (tierce). It can only be used when the adversary keeps his point low; it is still more effective when his blade is horizontal and his arm straight.

It is meant either to disarm, or to send the other blade violently out of the line. It jars the hand considerably.

To execute a *scrape*, raise the point so as to place the fort of the blade against the feeble, the three last fingers loosened, and then with a vigorous pressure of the fingers, and especially of the thumb, and a three-quarter extension of the arm, bring the point violently down to the fort, near the hilt, sending the other blade away to the right, if in tierce, or to the left if in quarte. It must be quickly and suddenly done, otherwise it would be very easily deceived. It is intended either to disarm or to open a line widely for a simple attack, or, less violently done, and followed by a composed attack, to deceive a parry.

The *twist disarmament* (*croisé*) is to send the opponent's blade violently from a high line into and out of a low line; like the scrape it can only be effected if the opponent's point is low.

The twist disarmament is executed thus: when engaged in quarte, raise the point so as to bring the fort of the blade against the feeble, loosening the three last fingers, pass the point over the adversary's wrist and violently bring the blades into seconde with a powerful pressure of the thumb and fingers, but mostly of the thumb, and with full extension of the arm; at the end bring the point slightly higher than in the parry of seconde.

When engaged in tierce, raise the point as above, and with the fort against the feeble, bring the blades violently into septime.

If this does not completely disarm a fencer, it will at least loosen his grasp and jar his hand. The first described is the more telling of the two.

The *twist and thrust* is very much like the above, but is not intended to disarm, and for that reason is not so violent. It is an attack at the body as well as at the blade, with a continuous movement bringing the blades from a high line into a low one, or from a low one into a high one with a lunge.

Like the *croisé* it can only be attempted when the opponent keeps his point too low and is more easily executed when his arm is stretched out. It is delivered thus: place the fort of the blade against the feeble, and, if in quarte, pass the point over the opponent's hand and thrust in the outside line with the hand rather low and a strong opposition to the right. This is the stroke called the "Flanconnade."

The twist and thrusts from tierce to the lower line, and from seconde into the inside or quarte line are dangerous, and should not be resorted to as an attack, but may sometimes be used as a riposte.

From septime the twist and thrust is done by passing the point over the opponent's wrist and thrusting in the upper line, with opposition to the right. This is often used as a riposte after the parry of septime.

Attacks on the sword can be used after changes of engagement or double engagements. For instance, if in quarte, the opponent keeping his point too low, and seeming to be ready to straighten his arm with the intention of snatching a hit the moment you move, change the engagement, placing the fort of your blade on the feeble of his, and make a scrape, etc.

How to deceive or avoid Attacks on the Sword.—The pressure, the beat, and the scrape are deceived by disengaging into the other line. The twist disarmament from quarte to seconde is deceived by a disengage into the upper line. The twist disarmament from tierce to septime is deceived by yielding the blade at the beginning of the movement, and disengaging into the outside line.

The twist and thrust being both an attack on the sword and the body, should not be eluded, as it would occasion a simultaneous hit, but the finale should be parried thus: From the engagement in quarte, yield the blade completely until the point is quite to the left, lower the hand on the right side of the other blade, raising the point, and take the position of quarte with opposition to the left.

From septime: yield the blade at the beginning and parry tierce at the finish.

Principal Attacks to deceive the most Important Parries — When engaged in quarte, if the opponent keeps the inside line open (that is if the straight thrust can be attempted) to deceive the parry of quarte, feint a straight thrust, or make a beat or a pressure, and disengage or cut-over. When in tierce, the parry of tierce is deceived with the same attacks, in the reverse way. The same for septime and seconde, excepting the cut-over, which should not be made in the low lines.

From the Engagement in Quarte—To deceive the parry of seconde: disengage in the upper line.

To deceive the tierce parry:

(1) Feint a disengage in the upper line and a disengage in the inside line. This attack is called *one-two* and can be done also with the feint in the lower line and the finale in the inside line, or with the feint in the upper line and the finale in the outside line.

(2) Change the engagement with a pressure, a beat, or a scrape, and disengage.

To deceive septime: simulate a *one-two* and counter-disengage into the outside line; or beat and counter-disengage.

From the Engagement in Tierce—To deceive the seconde parry: one-two into the upper line, making the feint in the outside line.

To deceive the quarte parry: one-two in the upper line, the feint either in quarte or in outside line. Or change the engagement with a beat, or a pressure, and disengage.

To deceive the parry of septime: feint a disengage in the inside line and counter-disengage into the outside line. This is called a double disengagement, or by abbreviation a double. Or change the engagement with a beat and counter-disengage.

When engaged in quarte, to deceive counter-quarte:

(1) Feint a disengage in the upper line and counter-disengage into the upper line. This is called a double disengagement (or simply *double*) in the upper line.

(2) Feint a disengage in the upper line and counter-disengage into the lower line (double in the lower line). In this last attack the feint must be made with the thumb uppermost and the finale with the finger nails turned downwards and the hand low.

When engaged in tierce to deceive counter tierce: double into the inside line.

In the low lines the counter parries are deceived by double disengagements also.

There are several other ways of deceiving counter-parries, specially from the engagement in quarte, but they are a useless complication.

From quarte, to deceive the opposite counter (in tierce): simulate a one-two and counter-disengage, or beat and counter-disengage.

From tierce, to deceive the opposite counter (in quarte): simulate a one-two and counter-disengage in the upper line; or a beat or a scrape and counter-disengage in the upper line. If the parry is made with the hand high, let the finale of the attack be made in the lower line with the finger nails turned downwards, the same as in the double in the lower line to deceive counter quarte.

From quarte to deceive tierce and quarte: feint a disengage in tierce, a disengage in quarte, and disengage and thrust in tierce. This is called *one-two-three.*

From tierce to deceive quarte and tierce: reverse the same attack.

Every parry can be deceived, therefore the number of attacks is unlimited. Those above mentioned are the most important ones, and with them a fencer can find the others by himself. To do so he has to add a disengage to the feints he has already made to deceive a supplementary transversal parry, or a counter-disengage to deceive another counter parry. But here *time* and *stop thrusts* may come in to put an end to such protracted attacks.

How to protect Oneself against the Attacks above-mentioned — The feint straight thrust and disengage, the beat or pressure and disengage are parried in the same manner as the simple disengage, either by a simple parry or by a counter.

From tierce engagement the scrape and disengage is parried by quarte.

From quarte, against a one-two into quarte, parry tierce and quarte, or quarte only at the finale, or parry septime, or, if the feint is made in the upper line, parry seconde at once so as to meet the blade before it comes back in quarte.

Against a change with a pressure, a beat, or a scrape and disengage: parry quarte at the finale, or parry seconde.

Against a one-two and counter-disengage or a beat and counter-disengage: parry septime and seconde, or parry septime and counter-septime.

From the tierce engagement, against a one-two, or against a change with a beat or a pressure and disengage into tierce: parry quarte and tierce, or tierce at the finale, or the reverse counter (quarte and counter-quarte in one movement).

From tierce against a double, or a change with a beat and counter-disengage: parry septime and seconde, or septime and counter-septime.

From the engagement in quarte, against a double in the upper line: parry counter-quarte and tierce, or parry counter-quarte twice, which is called double counter-quarte. Against a double in the lower line: parry counter-quarte and seconde, or counter-quarte and septime, but then the point must only go half way in the counter-quarte in order to meet in time the other blade with septime.

When in tierce, against a one-two counter-disengage to the upper line, or a beat or a scrape and counter-disengage to the upper line: parry the opposite counter and tierce; or the double reverse counter. If these attacks are directed in the lower line: parry the opposite counter and seconde, or parry the reverse counter and septime, the point stopping half way in the reverse counter to be able to meet the other blade in time with septime.

Every attack can be parried, just as every parry can be deceived. If the parries above mentioned are deceived, add a supplementary one, and so on until the opponent's blade is met. But the best method is not to follow the antagonist's blade in all his feints, but wait for the finale

FIG. 7.—DIRECT RIPOSTE AFTER A PARRY IN QUARTE.

When engaged in quarte, against one-two-three in the upper line: parry tierce and the reverse counter (in quarte); or better, parry simply tierce at the finale or counter-quarte; but for this good judgment is required, as the attack must have been foreseen.

When engaged in tierce, against one-two-three in the inside line: parry quarte and septime or parry quarte and seconde, or parry septime at the finale only.

When in quarte, against a one-two counter-disengage to the inside line, or beat and counter-disengage into the inside line: parry the opposite counter and quarte, or the opposite counter and septime.

The Riposte—The riposte is a thrust delivered after a parry.[1]

The neatness of a riposte depends on the precision and smartness of the parry. Contraction of the muscles and too much force in the parry renders the riposte slow and heavy; but if the parry is well made, with the fingers, the riposte is the safest stroke.

Immediately after the parry, the fingers must

[1] A thrust or prod is not called riposte when delivered after the parry has been eluded; it is only so named when the parry has been effective and has cast off the antagonist's point.

be slightly loosened and the direction must be given to the point by a pressure of the thumb. The arm must not be straightened with a jerk, but more or less extended with suppleness according to distance.

Ripostes are of three kinds; direct, with a change of line or feints, and with a pause (in French—*à temps perdu*).

The direct riposte is delivered in the same line in which the parry has been effected.

There are two kinds of direct ripostes: the riposte quitting the blade, which is the best and the quickest; and the riposte by opposition or without quitting the blade (*riposte d'opposition*).

The direct riposte should reach the opponent while he is on the lunge; for that reason the right foot must not move forward, and sometimes the antagonist is so close that a complete extension of the arm is not needed.

After the parry in quarte [1], to deliver the direct riposte quitting blades (this riposte is called in French with happy onomatopœia, *riposte du tac-au-tac*): immediately after the click of the parry, bring the point down, in the direction of the opponent's body, with a pressure of the thumb on the hilt, turning the finger nails upwards, and straighten the arm more or less according to the distance and size of the fencer. In this riposte the point must describe a slight curve on the right so as to avoid the antagonist's hand. It is a great mistake to raise the hand higher than the shoulder while riposting, as some masters teach it, because the opponent being on the lunge, has his body low and slanted, and the raising of the hand makes the fencer who is riposting miss his aim. After the parry in quarte, if the adversary presses on the blade, so that the blades cannot quit each other lower the point and turn the finger nails upwards simultaneously, and advance the hand slightly higher than in the previous riposte, keeping a good opposition to the left.

After the parry in tierce, to deliver the direct riposte quitting blades: lower the point with a pressure of the thumb, turning the finger nails upwards, and extend the arm. In this riposte the hand must be slightly higher than in the riposte after quarte, as the stroke passes over the antagonist's arm or blade. The riposte, without quitting blades (by opposition), is made in the same manner, only with a stronger opposition to the right.

After the parry in seconde, to give the direct riposte, quitting blades or by opposition: loosen the three last fingers so as to bring the point into the direction of the opponent's body as if your blade sprang off his, keeping a strong opposition to the right.

After the parry in septime, to riposte in the direct line: drop the point immediately, as if your blade sprang off the other (loosening the fingers slightly) in order to clear the opponent's hand, and direct the point to his body, with a delicate pressure of all the fingers bringing the blade horizontal; if necessary, the hand must be slightly lowered, but never lower than the point.

How to Protect Oneself against the above Ripostes—When parrying a riposte the attacker should recover the guard. Unless he intends to give a counter-riposte (which will be described further on), to do this in most cases he may remain on the lunge, simply drawing his body slightly backward (*retraite de corps*) to help the parry.

Against the direct riposte, quitting blades after quarte: when remaining on the lunge, parry quarte with the hand higher than when on guard, the point very high, the blade almost vertical, and the arm half bent. When recovering the guard, parry quarte in the usual manner.

Against the riposte, without quitting blades after quarte: if the adversary presses heavily on the blade, trying to force the riposte in, notwithstanding the parry, raise the point quickly, the blade vertical, and bring the hand nearer to the body, bending the arm, and parry quarte with the fort of the blade against the feeble of his. Sometimes, when a fencer has parried with much force and weighs heavily on the blade when riposting, the best method is to yield completely, so as to give no support whatever to his blade; then the riposte is sure to miss the body, passing away from it.

Against the direct riposte after tierce; raise the point, bring the hand near the shoulder, bending the arm, and parry tierce; or parry the reverse counter in quarte while recovering. The last is rather slow, and with a quick fencer may not meet the blade in time to parry.

Against the direct riposte after seconde; yield the point completely to the left, lower the hand on the right side of the opponent's blade, raising the point, and take the position of quarte with opposition to the left. This parry is the same as the one against the twist and thrust (*flanconnade*) from the engagement in quarte.

Against the direct riposte from septime: parry septime or seconde while recovering, or parry quarte with the hand rather lower than in the usual quarte parry.

Ripostes changing Lines or with Feints, and how to Protect Oneself against them—These ripostes are used to elude or deceive one or more parries; judgment is required to make them with success, because the fencer must foresee the parry his antagonist intends making.

Ripostes changing lines or with feints are very numerous, but the principal ones are: with a disengage, a cut-over, a twist-and-thrust, a one-two, a cut-over and disengage or a double. There are as many composed ripostes as there

[1] When parrying quarte or tierce, as has been said before, the point must be on a level with the eye and sometimes still higher.

are composed attacks, but those above named are the only practical ones, the others being dangerous. When delivering a riposte with a feint, the arm must not be extended with the feint, as when attacking, because the opponent is on the lunge and therefore very close, and it would be impossible to pass the point properly under or over his hand. Sometimes, when the attacker recovers to make his parry, a half lunge is necessary, with the finale of the riposte, to be able to reach him.

After the parry in quarte: to deceive quarte made with the hand high, riposte with a disengage into the lower line, the finger-nails turned upwards, without raising the hand at all. This riposte is very much like the direct riposte quitting blades and is almost as rapid.

Against this riposte: parry septime or seconde, or to prevent it from being made, parry quarte with the hand lower.

To deceive the parry in quarte, made with the hand neither high nor low, disengage into the upper line. This requires good finger play, and must be done in the following manner: immediately after the parry, loosen the fingers (but keep them touching the hilt), and turn the finger-nails upwards. While this is being done, the point must pass under the opponent's hand or forearm. Then raise the point into the upper line with a light pressure of all the fingers, the upper part of the wrist slightly convexed.

While passing the point from quarte to the upper line, great care must be taken not to raise or advance the hand, and the arm must be extended only when the point is in the upper line, and opposition taken on the right.

To elude quarte made with the hand very low, riposte with a cut-over thus. Raise the point on the left, the hand slightly backwards towards the left breast, loosening the three last fingers so as to be able to pass your blade over the antagonist's point. Then lower your point into the upper line with a pressure of all the fingers, mostly of the thumb, finger-nails turned upwards.

Against ripostes with a disengage or a cut-over into the upper line: parry quarte and tierce, or parry counter-quarte, or, if the riposte has been foreseen, parry simply tierce.

To deceive septime quickly done, riposte with a counter-disengage.

Against this riposte, parry septime and seconde.

When the opponent takes a marked opposition to his left while attacking, or when, immediately the parry in quarte is made, he presses strongly on your blade to avoid a direct riposte, the riposte with a twist and thrust can be successfully made. But while delivering this riposte the hand must be kept on the left, and not on the right as when attacking, for the following reason. When attacking with a twist and thrust the opponent's point is in front of you, and it is necessary to push it away with an opposition to the right so as not to lunge against it. When riposting with a twist and thrust, the opponent is on the lunge and his point has been warded off to the left by the parry in quarte, therefore the opposition to the right would bring the point on the fencer's body.

Against this riposte yield the blade, turn the finger nails downwards, and take opposition in seconde.

To deceive tierce, riposte with a one-two, taking care not to move the hand forward or backwards with the feint.

Against this riposte, parry quarte on the finale. After the parry in tierce, to deceive tierce, riposte with a disengagement either into the inside or quarte line, or into the outside line. The latter is very successful against fencers who try to avoid the direct riposte by turning their body sideways and stooping forwards. It must then be directed at the ribs behind the elbow, but close to it, with the hand placed rather low and to the left, with the thumb uppermost.

Against the riposte with a disengage into the inside line, parry quarte; into the outside line, parry seconde or septime.

To deceive quarte or seconde, riposte with a one-two.

Against this riposte, parry quarte and tierce, or tierce only on the finale or the opposite counter.

After the parry in seconde, to deceive the quarte parry (as described against the direct riposte in seconde), riposte with a disengage into tierce line, turning the finger nails upwards; for this disengagement, the movement of the point must be a little wider, in order to pass round the opponent's arm without drawing your hand back. Against this riposte parry tierce.

After the Parry in Septime—When the opponent has attacked with his hand rather low, riposte with a twist and thrust, named in French *septime enveloppée*. To deliver this riposte, after the parry in septime, pass the point over the opponent's arm, without quitting blades into the upper line, keeping the hand high and on the right, finger nails turned upwards. It is a very telling riposte.

Against this riposte, raise the point very high, bend the arm, bringing the hand towards the right shoulder, and parry tierce.

To deceive the parry in quarte, riposte with a feint in the lower line and disengage into the upper line.

Against this riposte, parry quarte and tierce, or simply tierce on the finale.

To deceive the parry in septime, feint in the lower line and counter-disengage. This resembles a double disengagement.

Ripostes with a Pause—These ripostes are named in French "*ripostes à temps perdu*"; they are preceded by a pause, quitting blades, giving time to the opponent to begin a parry, with the intention of eluding it. Or, if the attacker has stooped forward so much that there is no place to hit with a sudden riposte, the pause enables a fencer to wait for the opponent to begin a retreat, or any other movement affording an opportunity for a riposte. If the parry made is right, the pause enables a fencer to regulate his own speed by his opponent's quickness. If the parry has not been made neatly enough to permit a rapid riposte, the pause allows the riposte to be made with precision. All the ripostes can be made with a pause, except those by opposition or with a twist and thrust.

A fencer must be very cautious when using ripostes with a pause, because they may draw *the remise.*

Counter Ripostes—When after having delivered an attack, which has been parried, a fencer has parried the riposte and thrusts again, this last thrust is called a *counter-riposte.*

All the ripostes named above can be made as counter-ripostes. When the first riposte has been parried while remaining on the lunge, the *counter-riposte* must be delivered still remaining on the lunge.

When the riposte has been parried with a recovery, the counter-riposte must be given with a second lunge.

If the opponent has retreated while parrying and is out of reach, recover the guard forwards, parry the riposte, and lunge again with the counter-riposte.

False Attacks—A false attack is an attack made with a half-lunge, and not intended to hit. It is meant to threaten the opponent without the attacker exposing himself, to induce him to believe in a real attack, either to make him parry and riposte, so as to parry his riposte more easily and deliver a counter-riposte, or a remise; or to draw a time-thrust in order to parry it, &c. It may be to make him form instinctive parries with the intention of deceiving them later on, or to try to discover what are his plans and to make him change them, and so on. False attacks are certainly very useful, but a fencer should not make use of them too often, because then they would lose their effect entirely and perhaps turn against him.

Attacks on Preparations—Some fencers are placed on guard so that they cannot attack without making some preparatory movement. They bend their legs more, bring their body forwards, or lengthen their foil by holding it by the pommel, &c. If an attack is suddenly made at this moment there are many chances for it to succeed, and then it is called an attack *on preparation.*

Renewed Attacks (*Reprises d'Attaque*)—A renewed attack is an attack delivered immediately after a phrase: for example, if after a succession of thrusts, attacks, ripostes, &c., which have all been parried or avoided, both fencers have regained the guard without having been hit, and one of the two immediately makes an attack, it is called a *renewed attack.*

The *reprise d'attaque* may be either simple or composed, and very often succeeds. It requires good execution, and firmness on the legs.

Stop Thrusts (*Coups d'Arrêt*)—A stop thrust is an attack made boldly with a full lunge as soon as the opponent moves forward to attack with an advance, stopping him before he can deliver his thrust. The least hesitation or preparation when executing a stop thrust would prevent it from succeeding, and occasion a most dangerous simultaneous hit. It is very useful against fencers who attack with a rush.

Time Thrusts—A time thrust is almost a parry and riposte undivided. It is a thrust delivered with opposition on a composed attack, barring or closing the line in which this composed attack is intended to finish.

Time thrusts require great knowledge in fencing, good judgment, and good execution. To make a time thrust, a fencer must have forecast the opponent's composed attack.

When engaged in quarte, to deliver the time thrust on a one-two: the instant the adversary quits the blade, making his feint in the upper line, drop your point in the outside line, as if making a counter-disengage, and thrust with a strong opposition to the right.

When in tierce, to deliver the time thrust on a one-two in the upper line: the instant the opponent quits the blade, thrust straight, keeping opposition to the right.

When in tierce, to deliver the time thrust on a double in the upper line: counter disengage with opposition to the right, closing the upper line.

When in tierce, to deliver the time thrust on a double: drop your point, as if beginning a parry in septime, and thrust in the outside line with opposition to the right and the hand low. This opposition to the right, closing the outside line, prevents the opponent's blade from passing into the inside line.

For every time thrust, except for the one on a one-two, a half lunge is necessary.

The opposition must always be taken to the right in time thrusts: *i.e.* in the outside line against composed attacks ending in the inside (quarte) line or outside (seconde or octave) line, and in the upper line against composed attacks ending in that line.

A fencer must be very cautious with time thrusts, and should not try them too often.

Parries against Time Thrusts—If you have forecast a time thrust, the way to parry it is the following: when making a composed attack, in the inside or outside line, transform the finale of the attack into seconde. When making a composed attack in the upper line, transform the finale into septime rather high.

Example: Being engaged in quarte, and having forecast a time on one-two: feint a disengage in the upper, half extending the arm, and instead of disengaging back into quarte, parry seconde.

The Remise—The remise is a thrust made on a riposte. It is somewhat like a time thrust made on a riposte, changing line or composed, without recovering.

Example: If the opponent has parried your attack in quarte and ripostes with a disengage in the upper line, the remise consists in thrusting again in the same line with opposition to the right, intercepting the upper line.

The remise can also be made on ripostes with a pause, during the pause, and must be delivered the instant the opponent quits the blade.

The remise is also a very good stroke against fencers who draw their hand back when riposting.

When the riposte hits, the remise is wrong; it is wrong even when the riposte misses the body from want of skill.

The Assault—The assault is a sham fight, It is the application of what has been described above and learnt with a master; it is impossible to learn fencing by one's self only with the help of a book. A master is required, and it is with his leave and with him that the first assaults must be made. The master must then moderate his quickness and not abuse his skill; he must allow the pupil to succeed with many of his strokes, and help him in every way.

Great care must be taken to follow the right principles, especially when beginning, because bad habits are very quickly acquired, and it is very hard to get rid of them. A fencer must always continue taking lessons, for that is the only way to improve. He could no more neglect to take lessons than a pianist could abandon practising scales and exercises.

A fencer should not be too anxious to hit his opponent, and should never try to hit anyhow; if a fencer wishes to make continual progress, he must consider a hit he gives as a reward for a stroke well executed and well combined.

The junction of the blades is a great help, it warns you when the opponent begins a movement, &c. If the opponent avoids joining blades, you must then not keep your blade too quiet in front of him, because it would favour his fencing. You must make use of false attacks, feints, &c., to draw an attack or find out his plans. If, on the contrary, the opponent has a heavy hand and weighs on the blade, then avoid joining blades and oppose lightness to his force, so as to give it no support.

One must vary strokes, and change plans, according to the opponent to be dealt with; practice of fencing depends on intellectual as well as on physical qualities, therefore it is not possible to give advice against every method or way of fencing.

We have described the principal movements and explained how to execute them, we have given advice on the most favourable positions; prudence, presence of mind, observation and experience must do the rest.

CAMILLE PREVOST.

FERRETS—Writers of works on natural history and books on the management of ferrets tell us that this animal is a native of Africa, but they are unable to indicate any part of that continent in which it may be found wild. There can be no doubt that the assertion is untenable, and the better opinion is that the ferret is nothing more than a domesticated variety of the polecat, with which it is frequently crossed for the purpose of improving the breed. There are positively no cranial, dental, or other structural characters by which they can be distinguished, and the brown variety of the ferret is so like a polecat that it might well be mistaken for one. Experience, moreover, has proved that they breed freely with one another.

Appearance and Weight—The appearance of the ferret is too well known to require any detailed description, and a cross-bred animal between a female brown ferret and a male wild polecat so closely resembles the latter as to be almost indistinguishable. With most wild animals the result of domestication is to increase their size and weight. With the ferret it is otherwise. The average weight of a male polecat is $2\frac{3}{4}$ lbs., and of a female $1\frac{3}{4}$ lbs.; no such weights have ever been recorded for ferrets. The reason for this, no doubt, is to be found in the different conditions of existence to which the two animals are subjected; confinement, want of fresh air, insufficient exercise, and want of warm animal food operate in the case of the ferret to produce an undersized, weakly, and spiritless progeny.

Treatment—The more the treatment of ferrets approximates to the natural conditions of life, the hardier and better they will be, and this is the secret of success in their management. Instead of keeping them in an outhouse in a small box with a bedding of musty straw, saturated with wet and dirt (so productive of "footrot," "sweat," and other diseases), with a small saucer of sour milk and a piece of tainted meat, on which to live or starve, they should be kept, at all events for the greater part of the year, as much as possible in the open air.

Ferret Courts—A writer who has been most successful in keeping ferrets in good health and working condition, thus describes his mode of treatment:—An enclosure is made with planks sufficiently high to restrain the ferrets, and sufficiently low to be stepped over by the owner. In these are put some well made, warmly constructed hutches, so placed as to be off the damp ground, and with small openings for the animals to go in and out, so that they are comfortable and warm during the night. They are thus enabled, during the whole of the summer, to gallop about the enclosure, bask in the sun, and breathe pure air, the result being that they are always lively and vigorous and altogether free from disease.

Another excellent plan has been thus described by R. A. Muntz:—"My court is about 12 ft. by 6 ft. in area, and several inches deep in turf and peat moss, the whole being thoroughly drained by placing tiles across one another so as to leave a passage for the water, which runs off at the lower end. This system allows of the sluicing of the entire court with 'sanitas,' or some other disinfectant. The sleeping hutch consists of a barrel cut in half longitudinally and placed on a plain wooden floor raised from the ground on a layer of bricks. The barrel can be lifted bodily up, and the sleeping place thoroughly cleaned with perfect ease, new bedding of fine deal shavings being substituted for the old."

Ferret Hutches—Where conditions like those above described are unattainable, and space for the accommodation of ferrets is limited, a roomy hutch must be contrived, and one of the most sensibly devised is that described by Capt. Darwin in his *Game-Preserver's Manual*. This hutch is made as follows:—The full inside length is 4 ft., the width 18 in., and the depth 22 in. The first partition is put in at 18 in. from the end, the second 18 in. also, thus leaving the third 12 in. The box itself is made of deal, $\frac{7}{8}$ in. thick; the partitions are $\frac{1}{2}$ in. thick, and slide down into their places between thin strips of wood. About 5 in. from the bottom of each, a round hole is cut, about 3 in. in diameter, to allow of the ferrets passing through, and each hole has a door working on a screw, with a piece of iron wire $\frac{1}{4}$ in. thick attached. These wires appear through the sides of the box in front, and are finished off with a ring to lay hold off. In the large division at the end of the box is a tray made of wood and lined with lead. The sides are 5 in. high, and the tray has two handles with which to lift it in and out. Each compartment has a separate coil. The two end lids, and also the sides of the compartments which they cover, are bored in a good many places with holes about $\frac{3}{4}$ in. in diameter; the centre compartment with four holes only, which must be in the lid and not in the sides. The tray must have about $\frac{1}{2}$ in. deep of dry sand or sawdust in it, which should be changed every day, and the tray washed out. This compartment is for the ferrets to retire to for a necessary purpose. The centre is for their sleeping place, and it should be filled three parts full of clean straw, and not be changed unless required. The third compartment is for a feeding place. The use of the separated lids and wires will be obvious. By drawing out the particular wire required, the ferrets can be confined in their sleeping place when it is necessary to clean or feed them.

Food—The staple food of ferrets should be bread and milk, or porridge, not too liquid, and occasionally fresh meat in the shape of small birds, mice, young rats, or a piece of freshly killed and warm rabbit. This should be tied by a bit of string to a staple, in order to prevent the ferrets from dragging it into their sleeping place and thus soiling their bedding.

They should never be fed in the morning of the day they are to be used, but on being brought home should have a good supper as soon as possible, and allowed to go to sleep.

Transport—The mode of carrying ferrets about is almost as important as the method of housing them. Nothing can be more objectionable than the time-honoured bag which most keepers and warreners use to save themselves trouble. Carried in this, a ferret is never at rest, and is so cramped and worried as to lose half his energy for work. Should the bag get wet, as is often the case, either from a downpour of rain or from being laid down on wet grass, the ferret is made thoroughly miserable, and will take an early opportunity of "laying up" in the first comfortable burrow it enters.

Breeding—Ferrets are often kept and bred under conditions which are entirely opposed to sanitary laws, with the result that they not only become weakly and diseased, but produce young which in course of time are practically worthless. It is of the utmost importance, therefore, to select healthy stock in the first instance, and to maintain them in a healthy condition as above indicated.

The tyro who, for want of experience, is no judge of "points," may be satisfied to get his stock in the first place from a good breeder. The sexes are distinguished as "hob" or "dog" and "jill," and should be kept apart except at pairing time, when they may run together for a day or two. Ferrets breed twice a year. The period of gestation lasts six weeks: and the young, usually six or seven in number, are born blind and do not open their eyes for a month. Within a week of their being expected, the sleeping compartment of the mother should be closed, after making up a fresh bed, and not be reopened for the next five or six weeks; for, if disturbed before then, the mother will probably destroy them. When they first show themselves outside their sleeping box and begin to feed with the "jill," they will require careful attention, and must be fed three or four times a day.

When about ten weeks old, if looking strong and well, they may be put in another hutch.

Crossing—As above stated, the ferret will breed readily with the wild polecat, and there can be no doubt that a cross with the latter improves the breed materially, for the young are stronger in constitution and work quicker and longer than ordinary ferrets, which after two years get slow and lazy. The half-bred progeny, while growing up, require more handling and more work than ordinary ferrets do, or they get shy of being picked up.

The second cross is perhaps the best for general purposes, although the first cross produces capital ratworkers round stacks, where agility is indispensable.

Diseases and Remedies — The chief point to be attended to in keeping ferrets is cleanliness. If this be neglected, they become a source of anxiety to their owner and a misery to themselves; for diseases are thereby engendered that are troublesome to get rid of, and become both infectious and contagious.

The disease in ferrets that answers to "distemper" in dogs is known as *sweat.* It is in the nature of a fever, which manifests itself by a dull listless manner, hot nose, high temperature, thirst, running from the nose and eyes, and loss of appetite followed by wasting. The malady being infectious, the animal affected should be isolated at once, and placed in a clean, dry hutch, free from draught. It should then be bathed in lukewarm water tinctured with Condy's fluid, rubbed dry, and replaced in the hutch in a warm bed. If the discharge from nose and eyes has become purulent, this must be carefully removed by washing, and the animal, in regard to diet, should be treated like a human patient in a fever, that is to say, kept for a time upon fresh, warm milk, arrowroot, and broth. As it improves, more solid food may be given, but not too much at a time. A good thing is a freshly killed sparrow or other small bird, given a limb at a time sprinkled with milk of sulphur. For ferrets this is much better than the ordinary sub-limed sulphur, as it is much milder. The dose, to be given once in twenty-four hours, should be as much as will lie on a threepenny bit. This treatment should be continued for a week, then discontinued for three or four days, when another week's treatment will complete the cure. It is not a bad plan, after washing the nose and eyes, to anoint them lightly with vaseline, and a vaseline pill given three times a day has been found to be very efficacious.

Foot-rot is a common complaint with ferrets, and generally arises from their being kept in a dirty condition or in a damp situation. An approved specific is spirit of tar, or creosote. This is a good application, too, when the hair comes off, and should be brushed on lightly with a feather. Perhaps the best treatment for "foot-rot" is to dress the feet once a day with nitrate of mercury ointment, one part ung. hydr. nit. to seven parts lard, without salt. This is better than the mild mercurial ointment, ung. hydr. mitius, which is apt to salivate. The other never does.

Red mange, or eczema, to which ferrets are liable, especially after distemper, is often troublesome to cure. Here, again, the necessity for cleanliness in the hutches is manifest. After washing with lukewarm water and Condy's fluid, and thoroughly drying, the affected parts should be treated with zinc lotion, or, in bad cases, dilute nitrate of silver. Ferrets will often set up an irritation of the skin by biting and scratching themselves to get rid of parasites. The remedy is washing in a solution of quassia wood. It is a good plan to examine the animals from time to time to free them from these insect pests, and to remove the ticks to which they are subject, and which cause them much annoyance.

To get rid of worms, a dose of powdered areca nut, preceded and followed by a dose of castor oil, will be found as efficacious with ferrets as it is with dogs.

While curing ferrets of these complaints, they should always be put in a fresh hutch, and the old one should be well scalded and dried before they are returned to it.

Muzzling and Working—Much difference of opinion prevails on the subject of muzzling and coping, and various patterns of both these methods of restraint have been recommended and advertised. In the opinion of the writer, a ferret should never be muzzled, and it is doubtful whether coping ought not also to be dispensed with, as it clearly should be when hunting rats. A coped ferret cannot kill a rabbit, but will scratch and worry it in the attempt to do so. A rabbit will bolt much sooner from a ferret that is free. If the ferret be worked on a line, care should be taken that there are no roots of trees or rocks underground, or the line will soon get fast and occasion much trouble.

It will not do to handle ferrets while they are quite young, or the old one will very likely destroy them. It will be time enough to handle them when half-grown, and it should then be done boldly, without snatching the hand away, or it will provoke them to bite. As already remarked under the head of "Transport," they should be carried about in a box, and not in a bag, by which means they will get rest and be much more lively. On coming home, they should always have their feet washed. In "entering" young ferrets it is a good plan to let them run with the mother, who will soon initiate them in working a rabbit-burrow. If they are slow to follow her down a hole, she can be used with a line, and pulled back from time to time to entice them forward. It is important to give a young ferret its first chance in a burrow where it will be sure to find a rabbit, as in a short, sandy hole, and to reward it with a kill. Nor should it be worked too long at first, but be allowed an occasional rest. If a rabbit is bolted and shot, it should be pegged down outside the hole, so that the ferret on coming out may find it at once and be rewarded. Should a ferret "lay up," or remain a long time in a hole, another ferret on a line should be run in, and the truant dug out; hence the desirability of choosing an easy place to begin with when entering young ferrets. A rabbit will sometimes decline to bolt, and will be killed in the burrow; the ferret then will have a gorge and "lay up." In that case the plan is to leave a boy to watch the burrow, or to set a trap just outside and visit it next morning. Strange to say, an old ferret that has been used constantly in the same neighbourhood, will learn to find its home like a dog. Instances of this "homing instinct," as it has been called, have been frequently commented upon and reported.

When rats form the "quarry" instead of rabbits, a ferret should never be muzzled or coped, or it will be unable to defend itself from the savage bites of a cornered rat, and may be badly injured. Should it get bitten, it is as well to attend to the wound as soon as possible, and, after washing in warm water, to dress it with an ointment made of carbolic acid and vaseline. In all cases where it becomes necessary to apply a remedy, the patient should be temporarily isolated from its fellows.

J. E. Harting.

FIRST AID—There is a measure of risk in most of our national sports, and some of the finest of them largely owe their popularity to the call they make on the pluck which the sportsman is proud to consider his characteristic. Doubtless, to the element of danger is due much of the value of sport in the training and development of the special senses—for hand, eye, and ear soon become quick to detect and to respond to its presence, but it is well that sportsmen should have some knowledge of the treatment of injury.

HÆMORRHAGE is a subject of such importance as to merit first place in the description of accidents. A broken limb can wait a surgeon's coming, but bleeding must be stopped at once.

The blood courses through the body in arteries, veins, and capillaries. The oozing which takes place from scratches, grazes, cuts, and small wounds generally, is from capillary vessels. Such bleeding is easily stopped by first washing the wound with cold water, and then tying it up with a pad and extemporised bandage. If an artery or vein be divided in the wound, the blood will flow more freely. From the artery it will come in a bright red pulsating jet, and from the vein in a steady stream of darker colour.

Serious venous bleeding may be met with in the accidental wounding or rupture of a varicose vein of the leg. The blood may well out with such rapidity as to endanger life. But it is fortunately easily checked if the sufferer be laid on the ground and the bleeding leg raised in the air. This simple manœuvre may alone be sufficient to stop the hæmorrhage. But the spot whence the blood comes should be found, a pad laid on it, and fixed by a couple of turns of a folded handkerchief round the limb.

The coats of the little blood tubes are elastic and will contract, in the case of a small severed artery, sufficiently almost to close the end of the vessel. The blood will then clot inside it and close it entirely. This is inadequate if a big artery be involved. Should the finger be placed on the point whence the blood is coming, a very little pressure will suffice to stop it; or the artery may be compressed at a spot between the wound and the heart, either digitally or by means of a tourniquet. The former method requires anatomical knowledge. The latter can be applied by any one after a little practice.

The simplest and best form of tourniquet consists of a strong elastic band, stretched and wrapped once or twice tightly round the limb above the wound and fastened. Such an arrangement may sometimes be improvised from a brace or belt, if it be sufficiently elastic. Another kind of tourniquet, and one which may be made from materials which are always to hand, is the "Garrot." A handkerchief or neckcloth, preferably of silk, is taken, folded into cravat form, and knotted *quite loosely* round the limb, the knot being on the outer side. A stick is then inserted between the limb and the knot and twisted round. The handkerchief is thus tightened round the limb to any required extent. When sufficient force has been employed to stop the bleeding, the stick is fastened to the limb and prevented from untwisting by a second folded handkerchief. A tourniquet should only be used to stop bleeding after other means have failed. It is often unnecessarily and quite inefficiently applied by amateurs. If too loosely applied, it actually increases bleeding by checking the return of the blood to the heart through the veins without checking the pumping of the blood into the wound from the arteries.

To sum up the treatment:—First, the patient should be laid flat on the ground, because this position is best in case of faintness, and faintness is likely to occur from loss of blood. Then, if the wounded part be a limb, it should be raised as high as possible in the air, for thus the circulation is lessened. The clothing should be cut away from the wound and the latter examined. It may be found full of blood clot which has stopped the bleeding. In this case the clot is by no means to be disturbed, but, if the bleeding be going on briskly, the finger should at once be pressed on the spot whence the blood comes, so as to check it, while pads, bandages, &c., are prepared. To make these, handkerchiefs, towels, or other available materials may be used. A strip from the tail of a shirt makes an excellent bandage in emergency. A good firm pad is now pressed on the wound and kept in position by tight bandages encircling it and the limb. Lastly, if these measures do not suffice to stop the bleeding, a tourniquet must be put on round the limb, between the wound and the trunk. This is best applied outside the clothing, and is tightened just sufficiently to check the blood-flow and no more. It is a dangerous practice to give brandy or other stimulant to a person who is bleeding, for the hæmorrhage is thereby increased. Stimulants in such cases are generally best avoided altogether, and certainly must never be given until the bleeding has been completely stopped.

Bleeding from the Nose—This commonly follows comparatively slight injuries, and may, as a rule, be easily stopped. But nose bleeding coming on after a severe head injury may be of grave indication and demands early medical attention. Position is the most important point in treatment. The patient must on no account be allowed to hang down his head or to blow his nose constantly. He must be seated with his head thrown back, and his clothes loosened round his neck. Ice, or, failing this, a cold wet cloth, should be applied to the bridge of the nose and the back of the neck.

Bleeding from a Scalp Wound—There is hardly any accidental injury more likely to occur than a wound in this situation. Thus a skating tumble often results in a scalp wound of the back of the head, or in a wound of the forehead above the eye. The blood vessels of the scalp are, however, easily closed by pressure against the skull, and all that is necessary to stop the most furious hæmorrhage is to put a thick hard pad on the wound and press it there by a bandage round the head. If the wound is on the top of the head the bandage should go under the chin, and may with advantage be crossed to prevent slipping.

Bleeding from the Hand or Wrist—This is often difficult to stop. If the wound is in the palm, put a tightly rolled handkerchief therein and bandage the fingers over it. In any case of difficulty, put a pad in the fold of the elbow, and, bending the fore-arm up to the arm, tie it there by an encircling bandage. This serves two purposes: it ensures that the bleeding point is well raised, and by the pressure of the pad, it checks the flow of blood through the main artery of the arm.

WOUNDS—Treatment of wounds may be summed up in two words: "Be clean." Unless the wound is trivial, a surgeon must attend to it as soon as possible, and all that is necessary in the meanwhile is to cleanse it and to keep it from contamination. The commonest wound is a "lacerated" one, with ragged torn edges, and more or less bruising or contusion of the soft tissues surrounding it. More rarely it will be a clean cut "incised" wound, such as is inflicted by a sharp knife. A "punctured" wound, caused by the piercing of a thin narrow weapon, may show but a trifling external opening, but, penetrating deeply, perhaps dangerously, may injure important internal structures or organs.

The treatment is the same in all cases,—wash the wound thoroughly with perfectly clean water, and thus remove as far as possible all grit and particles of foreign matter. If pure water cannot be obtained, it is better not to wash the wound at all, and soiled clothing must never be used for sponging purposes. The edges of the wound should be brought approximately together, and the whole covered with a moist compress made of clean linen wrung out of cold water. Paper, even if it has been written upon, crumpled up and softened by moisture, makes an efficient and fairly clean dressing in the absence of better material. Never use sticking plaster to close a wound bigger than a trifling domestic cut. It merely brings the skin edges together, and, leaving the deeper parts gaping, causes much delay in healing. Curious materials, such as tobacco, salt, cobwebs, onion leaves, and herbs of various sorts, are often applied to wounds, and are popularly supposed to help healing or stop bleeding. Avoid them all. Friar's balsam is also a thing not to be used except for very small cuts.

Dog Bites, and wounds in general inflicted by the teeth of animals, have no special danger if the animal is healthy. The wound is of the lacerated kind, and if washed, kept clean, and treated on the general principles before described, will usually heal readily. Dog bites are often cauterized with the erroneous idea that there is poison in the dog's tooth which must be destroyed. This proceeding is wholly unnecessary and even harmful, since a cauterized wound takes long to heal and leaves much scar. If the animal be mad, special precautions must be taken, and in this case far more than a superficial cauterization of the wound is needful.

In the course of big game shooting abroad very severe injuries are occasionally met with from the teeth of animals. An extensive lacerated wound may be complicated by crunching of the bone, and amputation may be necessary to save life. The first aid treatment should be directed to the arrest of arterial bleeding, which may be considerable.

Snake bites are treated like the bites of rabid animals, but, in addition to local measures, stimulants should be given freely to counteract the depression which invariably follows. [*See* SNAKEBITE, TREATMENT OF.]

Bruises, or "contusions," are best treated by cold water, which should be applied as soon as possible. The effect of cold is to contract the small vessels and so lessen the amount of blood poured out under the skin. This effused blood is the cause not only of the discolouration of a bruise, but of the swelling and pain also. Ice, if it can be obtained, or, failing this, a cold water pad, frequently changed, should be applied to the part. It is still better to mix with the water for damping the pad some spirit, such as eau de Cologne, brandy, or methylated spirit, because by evaporation it increases cold. After a day or so, gentle rubbing may be substituted for the cold water with advantage. The injured part should be kept at rest and raised, in a sling or otherwise, as far as possible.

FRACTURES—Broken bones are unfortunately common enough, and there is no form of accident in which a knowledge of what is best to be done on the spot is more really useful. Fractures are of two principal kinds, "simple" and "compound." A simple fracture is one in which there is no communication between the broken bone ends and the outer air. In a compound fracture, on the other hand, there is a wound of the skin which leads down to the fracture or through which even a jagged end of bone may protrude. This form of injury involves many risks from which a simple fracture is free, and is therefore very much more serious.

A broken limb must always be moved with the greatest caution lest the sharp bone ends be forced through the skin and a simple fracture converted into a compound one. The risk is very great in the case of the shin bone, which lies just under the skin, and a fracture in this situation demands especial care in handling.

To find out whether an injured limb is really broken or not it must be examined for the "signs of fracture." These are (1) shortening; (2) deformity; (3) unnatural mobility of the limb; (4) crepitus, or grating, felt when the broken bone ends are rubbed together. Of these facts the first three are determined by careful comparison of the injured limb with the sound one of the other side. The last one, if obtained, is proof positive of a fracture. But it is not wise to undertake any very elaborate investigations. Much harm may be done by the injudicious handling of a fractured member, and it is best to be content with enough evidence for suspicion of fracture, and then to treat the injury as such.

To begin with, the sufferer must be kept lying down. If he tries to stand on a broken leg, for example, he may do himself great harm. Yet to get him on his feet is generally the first wish of injudicious bystanders. If a doctor can be brought soon, nothing more need be done till he comes than to make the injured person comfortable where he is, resting the limb on some soft material. But very often it is necessary to convey the patient to a distance, and, to do this safely, measures must be taken to fix the limb so that no harm will come to the fracture in transit, and then some comfortable means of carriage must be found.

To fix a broken limb, extempore splints must be applied, and these will have to be manufactured from such materials as are to hand. Splints should always be strong and yet as light as possible, and long enough, whenever it can be managed, to fix the joint above and below the injury as well as the fracture itself. In the country it is seldom difficult to get suitable lengths of wood. Straight ash or hazel branches, bundles of osiers or reeds, strips of bark or pieces of fence wood serve excellently. Or use may be made of walking sticks, hunting crops, fishing rod lengths, or gun barrels, though the latter are rather heavy. In cases of fractured thigh, the entire gun may be utilized, with the stock in the armpit and the limb bandaged to the barrels.

As a general rule, if there is no bleeding, the fracture is a simple one, and the clothing need not be removed. If left, it makes good padding, and helps also to stiffen and support the limb. If, in order to get at the wound of a compound fracture, or for any other reason, the clothing is to be taken off, it must be cut away carefully and never dragged from the limb. When the splints are ready, they must be arranged round the injured part in such position as will give the greatest support to the broken bones, going beyond the joint above and below the fracture. Sufficient padding of soft material, such as hay or clothing, should be inserted under the splints to keep any painful pressure from the point of injury. Then, while an assistant pulls gently on the injured member below the fracture, pulling always in the direction of the limb, the splints must be rapidly fixed. Straps, borrowed from stirrups or skates, are useful for this purpose, or simple cravat bandages may be tied firmly round. Finally, in the case of the leg, it should be bandaged to its sound fellow, which thus assists in its support. Before the patient is moved it must be seen that the fracture is really efficiently fixed, and that the splints cause no unnecessary discomfort from pressure.

If the arm be the broken part, all that is now necessary is to put it in a sling, and the patient may safely get on his legs again. But if the leg be injured a safe means of transport must be devised. This question will be considered later, for it equally applies to serious injuries to the head or other parts, in which any attempt to walk is out of the question.

There are some special fractures which are not treated by splints. The following are worth mention.

Collar bone—This bone is more commonly broken than any other. The injury results from falls on the arm or shoulder, and is often met with on the ice, in the hunting field, or at football. The symptoms are pain, loss of power of raising the arm, and unevenness or perhaps grating, discovered by passing the finger along the bone. These symptoms are very characteristic, and the treatment is simple and effective. A pad the size of one's fist is put into the armpit, and the arm is held against the chest with the hand pointing upwards and across towards the opposite shoulder. The elbow is placed in the middle of a broad scarf, and is raised in the sling by fastening the two ends of it together over the opposite shoulder, one end going behind and the other in front of the chest. A second scarf encircling everything just above the elbow makes all secure and comfortable.

Broken Ribs—Severe pain on breathing is the most characteristic symptom. The only first aid treatment is to fix the chest by a tight bandage round it. This will prevent movement of the broken bones, and so relieve pain.

Spine—This is fortunately only endangered by very severe injury. Fractured spine has, however, been met with in the hunting field from such accidents as a fall on the back across a log of wood. The fracture is associated with injury to the delicate spinal cord, which shows itself by paralysis of the lower and perhaps upper limbs also. It is a most grave disaster and the patient should not, if it can be avoided, be moved until a medical man arrives, lest still more serious damage be done.

DISLOCATIONS—By dislocation is meant the displacement of a bone from its socket. A dislocation therefore always occurs at a joint. The signs of dislocation are markedly different from those of fracture. There is no crepitus felt, and, in place of increased mobility, there is loss of movement of the limb. There may be in different instances either shortening or lengthening.

The commonest joints dislocated are the shoulder and elbow. The treatment consists in reducing or replacing the bone in its socket. This must be attempted only by a medical man. Much harm has been done by amateur pulling at a dislocation in the vain hope of effecting reduction. Until a doctor sees it, a dislocation is to be left alone, except that the limb may be made more comfortable by support or relief of pressure of clothing.

SPRAINS are the commonest of accidents, and are met with constantly in the pursuit of sport. They may be trivial, but on the other hand they are often severe injuries, which may take long to recover from, and leave more lasting effects than fractures. Sprains are never to be trifled with. The injury is principally to the ligaments, which bind the bones of a joint together, and these are sometimes much torn by the sudden wrench given them. Sprains are exceedingly painful and are often followed by much swelling and bruising of the joint, due to escape of blood from tiny torn vessels.

For treatment, rest is the first thing, and no attempt to "walk it off" must be allowed. The injured man should be moved as though he had a fracture. The joint should be raised as high as possible to lessen pain and swelling, and cold and pressure must, during the first few hours, be applied to it. Wet cloths should be wrapped round the part and should be kept moist with spirit and water, allowing the air free access to encourage evaporation. It pays well to start the treatment of a sprain early, and if taken in hand at once serious results may often be prevented. Herein lies the advantage of intelligent first aid.

HEAD INJURIES—There are several severe injuries which may follow a fall on the head, or such an accident as a blow from a piece of falling rock on a climbing expedition. The important point is how much damage has been done to the brain. There may be concussion, laceration, or compression of this delicate organ, accompanied or not by a fracture of the skull. From a first aid point of view they may be classed together and call for the same treatment. Whenever unconsciousness, even if it is only transient, follows a head injury, the case must be regarded as serious, and other symptoms of grave indication are bleeding from the ear or nose, and twitching or paralysis of the limbs. The proper treatment is to lay the patient on his back with head a little raised and clothing loosened. If there is a scalp wound, the bleeding from this must be stopped. No attempt to raise the patient must be made, and he must be kept quiet and not be talked to or allowed to talk. Any necessary movement must be carried out with great care on a stretcher, and with as little jolting as possible.

TRANSPORT OF THE INJURED—The best way of conveying an injured person from place to place is a problem which has often to be faced. If he cannot or must not walk, he should, if possible, be carried on a stretcher. He will be far more comfortable conveyed thus than in any vehicle, except a properly equipped ambulance wagon. If a cart is used, four wheels should be chosen rather than two. A cab, and especially a hansom, is a bad form of conveyance, for it is impossible to stretch the patient out flat therein. A wagon may be made fairly comfortable if the floor be first covered with plenty of twigs and straw to diminish jolting, which is intolerable to one who is badly hurt.

But a stretcher is the best thing, and this may have to be extemporized. At a pinch, a hurdle or short ladder will do if well covered with soft litter. But a better stretcher can be made as follows:—Two saplings or other strong poles, such as pitchforks, oars, or boat hooks, should be obtained for the supports of the stretcher, which is completed by stretching between them empty sacks, rugs, or blankets. The sacks may have holes cut in the corners and the poles inserted in the loops thus made. Or a pole may be rolled tightly in each end of a blanket, which is fixed at the appropriate distance by nailing, or tying firmly to the pole. Even buttoned coats have been used with sleeves turned inside out and the poles inserted through them. Three at least will be required to make the stretcher long enough. Whatever material is employed, it should be stretched as tightly as possible, and this will be facilitated by binding cross-bars at each end. It is well to test an extemporized stretcher by putting the heaviest man of the party on it first. The patient must be lifted carefully from the ground on to the stretcher laid at his side. Two persons should stand facing one another on each side of him, and, stooping down, should pass their hands one under his shoulders and the other under his hips. The hands meeting beneath the patient should be locked together, and then, while a third person takes care of the injured part, he may be raised from the ground and then lowered on to the stretcher, or even carried a short distance in safety. The bearers should carry the poles in their hands and not on their shoulders, and, walking always out of step to avoid swinging the stretcher from side to side, should take short strides, never lifting their feet far from the ground.

SPORTS AND THEIR ACCIDENTS—Having gained a general idea of the proper treatment of accidents, it will be well to consider the special dangers of individual sports.

Angling—An accident which may occur is a hook catching in the flesh. If the barb is buried, it is a mistake to attempt to pull it straight out, but the point should be pushed through until it emerges from the skin. The hook can then either be pushed right through or the barb cut off before it is withdrawn.

Boxing—Serious accidents very seldom happen with the gloves. A black eye is of course common enough, and should be treated, like any other form of bruise, by the immediate application of cold to the part affected. The sooner a cold pad is applied after the injury, the less blood will escape from the vessels, and the less will be the resulting disfigurement. Raw beef steak is not a bad thing, but it is easy with ice or cold water to make a more effective and less unpleasant pack.

If a boxer gets a broken nose, he should put himself straightway in a surgeon's hands, for if the bones are not replaced in position an ugly deformity results.

A heavy blow on the lower jaw, even with a well padded glove, may occasionally fracture the bone. The pain of the injury is very great, and is best relieved by fixing the lower jaw to the upper by means of a folded handkerchief, the centre of which is placed under the chin with the two ends tied over the top of the head. The upper jaw then acts as a splint, and steadies the broken bone until such time as more effective measures can be taken for setting the fracture. Injury to the brain occasionally follows a blow on the jaw from transmission of the force through the hinge of the jaw at the base of the skull. Backward falls are dangerous when the head strikes a hard floor, for this may lead to concussion of the brain.

Cricket—Such accidents as occur in cricket are due to the ball. A knock on the head is a danger to which the batsman and wicket-keeper are especially exposed. Should insensibility follow for ever so short a time, the case should be treated as described under head injuries, with the greatest care, for fear of serious effects.

The knee-cap has sometimes been broken by a blow from a cricket ball on the bent knee, but injury more often follows a sudden muscular effort, such as is made in a violent attempt to recover lost balance while the knee is bent. Its effect is to disable the injured leg, which cannot be lifted from the ground. It should be temporarily treated by a splint on the back of the leg, which must reach from the knee to the hip.

A hot catch may result in a dislocation of one of the joints of the thumb or fingers. The deformity in such a case is very marked, the digit being bent backwards at the joint. It is important that the bones should be put back in their place as soon as possible, and if skilled help cannot be obtained, no harm can be done in attempting reduction by simply pulling steadily on the end of the thumb or the finger, as the case may be.

The sickening pain and faintness which follow a blow on the lower part of the person are well known. The best remedy is rest and the application of cold, which may be extemporized by a little ice in a tobacco pouch.

Cycling, with the introduction of the "Safety," has lost much of its danger. Accidents are now mostly due to inexperienced or careless riding, and are few in proportion to the enormous number of cyclists; but a rider thrown suddenly on to the road is liable to a variety of sprains, contusions, and lacerations. Among fractures, the most common are those of the collar-bone and of the bones of the wrist and ankle. (It may be worth remembering that the inner tube of a pneumatic tyre makes an admirable elastic band for a tourniquet.)

Football, it must be admitted, leads often to accident, but seldom to loss of life. The recorded fatalities are mostly from head injuries.

A severe muscular bruise, generally of the front of the thigh, well known to football players, is treated in the ordinary way, by rest and cold applications.

There is a certain skin eruption, known as "Football Impetigo," more popularly as Scrum Pox, which is observed on the face and neck of footballers, chiefly in the ranks of Rugby forwards. This affection has been epidemic in certain of the public schools and in the universities. Though not dangerous, it is very contagious and spreads from player to player. As soon, therefore, as it appears in a team, the member attacked should abstain from further play and put himself under medical care. Fortunately the disease soon yields to proper treatment.

Football players occasionally get damage to their ears, resulting in the formation of blood tumours, which should be taken in hand surgically, or an ugly deformity may remain.

Hunting.—The accidents are chiefly those which have been already described. The more serious are head injuries, fractures, and dislocations. Hunting is the only sport in which a fracture of the spine is likely to occur. The commonest fracture is that of the collar-bone, which results from falls on the outstretched hand. If the bone does not break, the accident may lead to a dislocation of the shoulder. As this injury is not uncommon in the hunting field, its signs, namely, pain, loss of power of movement of the arm, with deformity of the shoulder, but no crepitus, should be kept in mind.

In the application of temporary splints, the straps of the harness may often come in useful, and hunting-crops will in emergency do for short splints, though more suitable lengths of wood will generally be found in hedge or fence. Again, two or three girths stretched across a wooden frame will make an admirable foundation for a stretcher.

Riding men have a special injury of their own, the "Rider's Strain." It is due to a rupture of some of the fibres of the muscles on the inside of the thigh, and occurs in a violent effort to grip the saddle when the rider is slipping. It is generally seen in elderly riders or in those out of practice. Any attempt to remain on horseback after the accident will be extremely painful and must tend to aggravate the injury.

Lawn Tennis claims the dignity of naming at least two injuries, the "tennis elbow" and the "tennis leg." They exemplify the advantage of being in training, for they are far more likely to occur in players who are out of form, and are, therefore, most common at the beginning of the season. The precise injury is not the same in every case of "tennis elbow," but the effect is always an inflammation and swelling which prevent the use of the arm in play for a considerable time. The essential treatment is simple, namely, to rest the arm until it recovers. Tennis players should take it easy at the beginning of the season, and should especially avoid violent back-handed strokes until the muscles get trained to their work.

The "tennis leg" is due to the rupture of some of the muscle-fibres in the calf. The player, while running, feels as if he had received a sudden violent blow on the back of the leg, and can hardly stand; sometimes he actually falls. This is an injury most common in the middle-aged, and may be met with in other sports, when the muscle has to bear a sudden and unusual strain. Rest is the proper treatment, no attempt being made to stand on the leg until a doctor has seen it.

Mountaineering—The skilled climber reduces the dangers to a minimum by obeying certain rules of precaution, to forego which he would consider unsportsmanlike. In this connection it is significant that accidents are proportionately fewer among the members of the English Alpine Club than among other climbers. There are, however, certain risks which no amount of human forethought can always avoid, especially those arising from falling rock and snow. Mr. Wherry, in his *Alpine Notes*, points out another peril which comes unexpectedly, that of thunderstorms. Should a comrade be struck by lightning and lie unconscious, the best hope of restoring him to life is to resort at once to artificial respiration, as described in the rules for the restoration of the apparently drowned. (*See* LIFE SAVING.)

The so-called "Mountain Sickness" is a malady which is induced by the change in atmospheric conditions at high altitudes, and particularly the lack of a due proportion of oxygen in the air. In its worst form it is not seen in Europe, but its symptoms have been graphically reported by Mr. Whymper and Sir W. M. Conway from the Andes and the Himalayas. To avoid *mal de montagne* in climbing these lofty mountains it is necessary to postpone heroic ascents until lesser feats have trained the heart and lungs.

Of the conjunctivitis or inflammation of the eyes, which follows exposure to sunlight reflected from snow, it is unnecessary to say much, for every one who has been on a mountain knows how necessary it is to protect the eyes while on snow by smoked glasses. It is best treated by frequent bathing with warm water and keeping the eyes covered from the light by a large shade.

The intense cold met with on mountain tops offers a danger to the climber in the form of frost bite. The parts attacked are first blue and inflamed, and afterwards white and cold. This condition, if allowed to go on, may even lead to the loss of toes or fingers from gangrene. Friction is the proper treatment, and on no account should the return to warmth be too sudden. The patient should not be allowed near a fire until the circulation has returned.

Rowing—The remarkable diet a rowing man is induced to adopt when he trains for racing is chiefly responsible for the appearance of those troublesome boils from which he so frequently suffers. The sudden change in diet, and particularly the excessive amount of animal food taken, leads to an alteration of blood condition, of which boils are the outcome. They appear especially in parts exposed to friction, and are certainly less common with sliding than when fixed seats are used. The best thing to do when there is the least threatening of a boil, is to protect the inflamed spot from pressure and friction by a ring of thick felt-plaster. This often prevents the formation of matter, and the inflammation may subside. When once matter is formed, however, the boil should be opened without delay by a surgeon. The discharge from a boil, if rubbed into the surrounding skin, will readily produce a crop of others. For this reason poultices and fomentations should only be used with careful precaution under medical direction, and care should be taken to change the clothing frequently, and by strict cleanliness to lessen the chance of inoculation.

Shooting accidents are much more common than they ought to be. They almost invariably reveal a carelessness which is inexcusable, and almost criminal, in handling a weapon so dangerous as a loaded gun. The arch-offender is the young or untrained shooter. Gunshot wounds are often most disastrous in their results, and their prevention is infinitely easier than their cure. At a short range a shot gun will inflict a far worse injury than a rifle. The aperture of entrance of the wound is round and comparatively small, and its edges are blackened with unburnt powder. The shot, in passing through the tissue, quickly spread, tearing muscles and splintering bone in their passage. The exit of the charge leaves a huge lacerated hole. Such wounds are liable to bleed furiously from division of arteries, and to stop the bleeding at once is an urgent duty. To this end a tourniquet should, if possible, be applied. If the wound is in such a situation that this cannot be done, an attempt to check the blood by tight plugging and bandaging should be made.

At a long range less damage is done, for the clothes largely break the force of the shot, which spread considerably. The principal danger is to the unprotected face, where loss of sight may too easily follow the passage of a stray pellet into the eye.

Swimming—The question of the restoration of the apparently drowned will be dealt with under LIFE SAVING.

J. B. BYLES.
SAMUEL OSBORN.

FIVES—Nothing definite is known of the origin of the game of Fives. To hit a ball in turn with the hand above a line on a wall is Fives in its simplest form, and the game is played by boys who have never seen a Fives Court, nor heard the name of Fives. From this instinctive desire to hit a ball against a wall, the modern game—with rackets its "fairer daughter"—has been developed. At Eton a fortunate accident influenced the character of the game. The earliest Eton court was between the Chapel buttresses, and the end of the balustrade of the Chapel steps, projecting into the court, was the first "pepper-box" in the history of Fives. From this ancient court, too, were derived the step and the hole which, with the "pepper-box," have given the Eton game its special character. But elsewhere the game was played without these accidental obstacles and advantages, and the plain court, or Rugby game, as it is called, has as many adherents as the other. Of the great schools, Eton, Harrow, Westminster, Charterhouse, and Wellington play

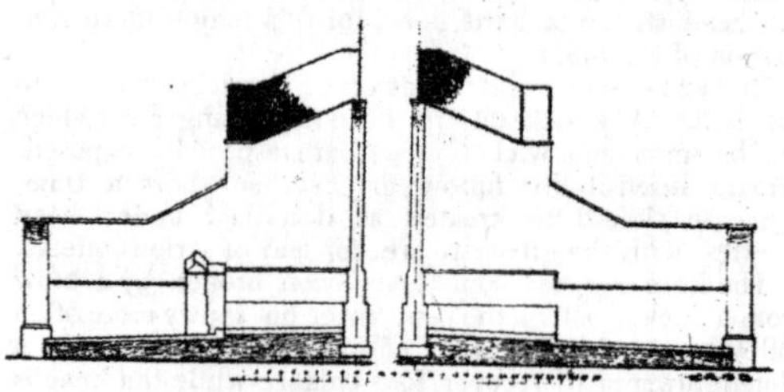

ETON FIVES COURT, RIGHT AND LEFT SIDES.

the one; Rugby, Winchester, Marlborough, Clifton, and Repton play the other.

In both games the aim of the players is to hit the ball above a line or ledge on the front wall, in such a way that their opponents shall not be able to hit it back again above the line before it has touched the floor of the court for the second time. The "bully" or "rally" begins by the server so tossing the ball against the walls, that it first hits the front wall above the line and then the right side wall; his opponent, on getting a service which suits him, returns it back to the front wall, hitting the right wall first; this is called "first-cut," and after it the ball is hit back to the front wall by either side in turn. In both games the laws and method of scoring are much the same, and in both the chief qualifications for success are skill in placing, a good eye for volleying, and a left hand which is "not afraid of work."

In the Eton court the line is twenty inches higher up than in the Rugby; there is no back wall, and the presence of the pepper-box, the hole, and the step, make the game in practice as different from Rugby Fives as in theory it is similar. The Eton court is almost invariably open, the Rugby court is generally covered in. The one has the advantage of better light and fresher air, the other makes Fives possible in wet and snowy weather when other exercise is hard to get. Both games afford most excellent exercise to all muscles of the body; so excellent, indeed, that it is a matter both for surprise and regret that few men continue to play after they have left school. The game costs little in time or money, and can still be played with success at an age when football has long ceased to be possible, and when cricket is beginning to lose some of its charm. A speculator might do worse than build Fives courts in our big towns. There are so many hundreds of Public School men in London who miss the opportunities for exercise which they have had at school, that the building of courts ought to be a remunerative investment. It is worthy of note that the Girls' Public Day School Company are building Rugby courts in some of their schools, but it is at present too early to say whether the game will ever be popular with girls.

The Rules—The Eton rules are the copyright of Mr. R. Ingalton Drake, of Eton College, to whose kindness we are indebted for permission to print them. The Rugby rules are not quite the same at all schools. Those printed here are the rules of the game as played at Winchester, and were drawn up by that famous Fives player, Mr. A. J. Toye, whose courtesy has allowed them to be reproduced here.

The Balls—In the Rugby game the ball weighs $1\frac{1}{8}$ oz.; the Eton balls are larger, and weigh $1\frac{1}{4}$ oz.; they vary greatly in quality, and much of the enjoyment of the game depends on getting good balls.

THE ETON GAME—A few hints may be useful to beginners on the position of the four players in a game in which A and B with first innings are playing C and D.

The Server—A, who begins serving, is bound to give C—who is said to be "in holes"—the sort of service which he prefers. Some players have eccentric preferences, but they must be humoured; otherwise time is wasted, and the enjoyment of the game, which depends greatly on the prevalence of good temper, may easily be lessened. In serving, and in serving only, A's aim should be to give C exactly what he wants. After serving, A has to decide where he will await "first-cut." If he has a good eye for volleying, and a left hand little inferior to his right, he should stand just in front of the pepper-box and about a yard from the left wall, prepared to volley the first-cut with either hand, or to move out of the way of a ball which will go to his partner in the outer court as a plain long-hop. If he has a weak left hand he should move forward and nearer the left wall. In this position he will be able to volley with his right many balls which in the other he would have missed with his left. Some players, whose weak point is volleying, move across to the left front corner and face the pepper-box, in order to get up on the bound

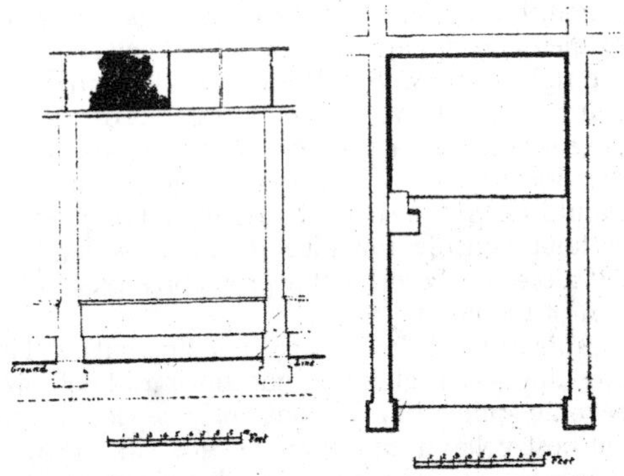

Eton Fives Court, Front Wall and Ground Plan.

the common first-cut which hits first the left wall and then the pepper-box. The innings of a player of this sort will not often add much to the score; but if he cannot volley, this course is probably his wisest, though, like "standing back" in wicket keeping, it is a confession of weakness, and such a player when serving fails to accomplish half his proper work.

First-Cut—C, on getting a service exactly to his mind, must above all avoid so returning it that it comes into the middle of the outer court as a long-hop; long-hops in the open are as easy in Fives as full pitches are in cricket. But if C's first-cut is of this kind, he must take great care, by moving forward at once, to get out of the way of B, his opponent in the back court. A "let" at this point of the game is justly irritating to B. C has made a bad stroke, and ought to give B the most ample opportunity to profit by it.

C in returning the service should, usually, hit hard at the right wall about a foot from the corner and a little above the line. Such a first-cut will, if not volleyed by A, hit first the left wall and then the pepper-box, and A in volleying will have to use his left and presumably weaker hand, unless he has moved nearer the left corner, as described above, in order to take it with his right. If C sees this forward movement of A in time, he should either aim a little higher and direct at the right corner, which may bring the ball out of reach of A's right, or else, by aiming about two yards to the right of the corner, he will give A a much more difficult volley at close quarters. If A has moved across to the right corner, it is best to hit rather gently at the corner, in order that the ball may go straight to the pepper-box without first hitting the left wall. Such a ball may either go into the hole, or run back along the left wall before A can get across, but the stroke should not be hard enough to let A eventually take it off the front wall.

If the server is conspicuously the stronger opponent, a very useful first-cut is the stroke which, hitting only the front wall—as described in the second part of Law VI.—keeps close to the right hand wall all the way to the end of the court. The stroke needs practice, or it will degenerate into a long hop in the open, or hit the side wall too soon and be quite easy. It should keep as near to the right wall as possible without actually touching it and look likely, if left alone by B, to hit the projecting pier at the end of the court.

Above all, C must vary his first-cuts. The one the server at first finds most difficult will become quite easy if constantly repeated, and the best volleyer can often be got rid of by a simple return which pitches before it reaches him.

The Server's Partner—B should stand near the right wall at the back of the outer court. He must expect *every* first-cut to be hit straight down to him, and only move forward when he sees it is not so hit. If he is too near the middle of the court or off his guard for a minute, a quite easy first-cut down the right wall will make him look foolish. But if he is in his place and ready, he will get some easy opportunities for good strokes from first-cuts which have gone round the three walls without hitting the pepper-box or have been hit down the right-hand wall with better intentions than results. These he should return hard and low into the pepper-box—unless A has stupidly put himself in front of it, or C is in a good position for volleying—or else he should hit them into the left hand corner of the outer court, where the pepper-box in front of him makes D's stroke an awkward one. The really difficult first-cut, which hugs the right wall, B had better take before it reaches the end of the court, where the projection will only add a new difficulty: if he is not too ambitious and is content to get behind the ball and half push, half hit it, he is more likely to get it up than if he hits hard at it or tries to do something brilliant with it. B's greatest difficulty will be when the walls are wet. Then, first-cuts aimed at the corner will, after hitting the right wall, come off the front at a much sharper angle than usual, direct to the left corner of the outer court. On such days, as B will have to look out for both corners at the same time, he must stand more to the left, and the server should stand a little more to the right than usual.

The Fourth Player—D at first has nothing to do except to prevent any first-cut from pitching out of court. He will naturally stand as far back as possible, but must remember that if he has to jump he must alight on the floor of the court.

The Bully—As soon as the first-cut has been got up, and the "bully" has commenced, all players alike will avoid hitting long-hops into the open or giving their opponents easy opportunities to volley. They should aim as much as possible at the hole and the pepper-box and at the corners of the outer court. A player in the inner court will volley whenever he gets a chance; he should keep near the left wall, but must leave his left arm room to work, and must be careful when his partner is hitting not to guard the pepper-box with his body. He should keep his head below the line, and, without turning his body, watch what is going on behind him, and when he gets an easy volley he should hit his very hardest, getting rather over the ball, and so aiming that the ball will come straight at the head of his opponent in the inner court, or go to whichever back corner is at the moment unguarded. A common fault is a want of agility in getting out of the way of an opponent; it must be remembered that a "let," in forcing the "bully" to begin again, is often unfair to one side or the other, and a player who is frequently in the way either annoys his opponents or irritates his partner by spoiling his winning strokes.

The players in the outer court must be always backing up, ready to take anything their partner cannot reach. The harder they hit the better, as the more difficult it will be for their opponents to volley, but they must aim low, or they will hit out of court. A soft, high stroke is usually bad, but it is useful if it brings the ball just behind the pepper-box, and often, when in the left back corner a hard stroke is difficult to place properly, a soft, high stroke brings the ball back to the same corner with a bound high enough to reach the ledge. A soft, low stroke only pays if your opponent is so far in the right front corner that your stroke hits the pepper-box before he can get across. All good judges agree that players in the outer court should hit at the front wall first.

THE RUGBY GAME—In discussing the Rugby game it must be remembered that all Rugby Courts are not the same. All alike differ from Eton Courts in having no pepper-box, hole, or step; they are generally covered in and have a back wall which makes slogging less dangerous. But at Oxford and Winchester there is a little buttress on the left hand wall, projecting at an angle of 135°, and at a distance of 9 ft. 9 in. from the front wall. This naturally divides the players into up and back pairs, but in a court with no buttress one partner takes everything on the left and the other on the right side. The buttress court is certainly a modification of the original court—probably the Eton pepper-box making itself felt beyond its legitimate sphere of influence—and at Rugby itself, Marlborough,

Clifton, and Repton, the courts are all without it. That the buttress improves the game most impartial players who have tried both kinds of court are agreed, but its presence or absence has by this time become a matter of tradition in public schools, and in matters of this sort changes are impossible.

The Stroke—The leg furthest from the hand which is making the stroke should be advanced, with the weight of the body thrown forward upon it. The best style of stroke at Rugby Fives closely resembles a jerk, the twist of the wrist putting on the cut.

The Server—In a double game the Server, if there is a buttress, is expected to take all balls in the front part of the court and to leave the back of the court to his partner. He should stand rather in front of the buttress and well away from the side wall. If there is no buttress—or, in a single game, even if there is—he must stand further back, ready to return any sort of first-cut and to take everything that pitches on the left side of the court. He must of course serve as his opponent may direct.

The Player who returns the Service should vary as much as he can the pace and angle at which his strokes come off the wall, and must notice the weak points of his opponent's play. First-cuts should usually be hard and low, and should hit the left wall before they pitch, but variety is the great thing to aim at, and a too frequent use of a favourite stroke has lost many a game. Many players ask for a service which falls close to the right wall, and then hit low and hard at the corner where the right wall joins the front wall. The ball, especially if it is new, comes off very fast, and with a great deal of cut, straight to the back left corner and is very difficult to get up.

Another favourite stroke which needs, and repays, practice, is made off a ball rather far out, by hitting the side wall so far from the corner that the ball comes on to the front wall to the left of its centre, just above the line, and falls at the very bottom of the left wall near the front corner. Such a ball will often not rise at all. In a single game a soft stroke is sometimes useful. It should hit the right wall very softly, not very near the corner, come on to the front wall to the right of its centre and fall very close to the front too softly to reach the left wall at all. But in the double game soft first-cuts are not very profitable; it is wiser to hit hard and low. If a first-cut is hit high, it should be hit very hard indeed. The ball will then hit the left wall more than half way up and come off the back on to the right in the back corner.

The Rally—When the rally has once begun, the beginner should try to watch his opponents. This not only aids him in placing his own strokes, but enables him to judge the direction in which his opponents are going to hit, so much so indeed that, while the poor player is always running after the ball, the good player seems to make the ball come to him. There is much less volleying than in Eton Fives. Low volleying pays well, but needs a good eye: high volleying the back wall makes of little use, for the rapidity of the volley which makes it so useful in the Eton game avails nothing when the ball can be waited for and taken off the back wall. With no pepper-box, and at best only a little buttress at which to aim, and with volleying difficult or useless, the beginner who wishes his strokes to score cannot pay too much attention to placing the ball. It is to his skill in placing he must chiefly look for success. Strokes into corners, or just falling short of corners, or hugging the side walls, or hitting the walls at their angle with the floor, can never be practised too much. Opponents who are elderly or in bad training, should be given plenty of running—*e.g.*, when both are at the back of the court a soft stroke into a front corner, hitting the side wall first, may, without affecting the result of the rally, still influence the result of the game.

In taking balls in back corners, beginners must not get too near the side wall, or the ball coming off it on to the back wall will prove difficult. Generally, in a corner, to be a little too far from the ball is a mistake more easy to remedy than the opposite one of being too near. A ball close to the front wall can be killed by a gentle low stroke so aimed that it will nick the side wall at its angle with the floor. In the course of the rally the beginner must expect to get many balls which it will take all his skill simply to get up; but, when he does get an easy return, he should try to do something definite with it. For instance, if he gets a ball in the middle of the right hand court, he may, with a hard low stroke at the left front corner, hitting the front wall first, bring the ball into the right back corner. To the practised fives player many other strokes will suggest themselves, and a beginner can learn more from watching good players than by any other means.

The Literature of the game is scanty, but all fives players may be referred to Mr. Arnan Tait's brilliant treatise on Fives in the All England Series, to the Badminton Fives, and to an article by Mr. G. C. Harrison, the old Oxford slow bowler, in the Fettes College Magazine for December, 1896. Mr. Ainger's interesting article in the Badminton Series deals mainly with Eton Fives. Mr. Harrison writes on the Rugby plain court game, but Mr. Tait's essay leaves no detail of either game untouched.

The Eton Rules.

The court is enclosed on three sides and open at the back. The "front" wall is the wall facing the player, and the "right-hand" and "left hand" walls are the walls on his right hand and left hand respectively. The "step" is a shallow step dividing the court into two portions, an inner and an outer court.

The vertical face of the "step" does not reckon as part of the floor of the court.

"On-wall" and "off-wall" denote the floors of the inner and outer court respectively.

The "pepper-box" is a buttress projecting from the left-hand wall. With the "step" it encloses a small square portion of the floor called the "hole."

The "line" is the ledge running across the front-wall at the height of 4 feet 6 inches.

A vertical line is marked on the front-wall at a distance o 3 feet 8 inches from the right-hand wall.

I. The ball must in every case be hit "up," *i.e.*, it must be returned against the front-wall on or above the lower angle of the "line." Any ball except "the service," which drops on the top of any of the walls of the inner court, or which, after going "up," touches the ground first outside the court, or touches any object or person outside the court, *invariably* counts against the striker, and is called a "good 'un."

II. The ball must be fairly hit with a single blow of the hand or wrist, and must not touch any other part of the striker's person under the penalty of losing a stroke. It must not be caught or held in any way except to "serve," or to stop a "blackguard" (see Rule VI.), or to save a "good 'un" (see Rule XIII.).

Position of the Players.

III. The game is usually played by four persons, two against two. Thus, if A and B (with first innings) play C and D, A, who goes in first, stands upon the "on-wall," near the "pepper-box"; B, his partner, on the "off-wall" near the right-hand outer corner; C stands near the middle of the "off-wall" ready to return the "service," and is said to be "in holes"; and D, his partner, on the "off-wall" near the left-hand outer corner.

Holes Innings.

IV. In the first innings of a game A (who goes in first) is said to have "holes innings," *i.e.*, when both A and B have been put out, A will be "in holes." This rule only applies to the side which goes in first at the beginning of a game; afterwards partners take it in turns to be "in holes." If in the first game A has "holes innings" and C is "in holes," then in the second game C has "holes innings" and A is "in holes," in the third game B has "holes innings" and D is "in holes," and in the fourth game D has "holes innings" and B is "in holes."

The Service.

V. The ball when served must hit first the front wall above the "line," and then the right-hand wall, and must fall on the "off-wall." The player "in holes" need not return the first or any "service" till he gets one to his mind, and if he fails to return the "service" above the "line" no stroke is counted. Serving a "good 'un" does not put a player out.

The First-Cut.

VI. The player "in holes" must not return the "service" before the first bound. This return is called the "first-cut." He must return it so that it should hit either (1) first the right-hand wall and then the front wall above the "line"; or (2) the front wall above the "line" between the right-hand side wall and the vertical line marked on the front wall. In both these cases the ball may afterwards hit any wall or walls, and may fall anywhere on the "on-wall" or "off-wall." Only the player "in holes" may return the service. A first-cut which is "up," but not in accordance with these conditions, is called a "blackguard." The player "in holes" or his partner may then touch or catch the ball before the first bound, and if this is done no stroke is counted. If the ball is not touched or caught, it may be returned or not by either of the opposite players at their option; and if it is not returned above the "line" no stroke is counted.

The Bully.

VII. After the "service" and the "first-cut" the ball is returned alternately by either side. It may be returned by either of the partners before the first or before the second bound, and may or may not hit the side walls. A "bully" is lost to his side by the player who fails to return the ball above the line or hits a "good 'un."

Lets.

VIII. A "let" may be claimed when the player is in any way prevented from returning, or impeded in his attempt to return the ball, by one of the opposite side. A stroke which would have hit the front wall above the "line," but is prevented from doing so by one of the opposite side, counts as a "let." A "let" cannot be claimed when a "good 'un" is hit, nor when a player is impeded by bystanders. In all cases of dispute the umpire's decision is final.

Note.—If there is no umpire a claim is generally allowed.

IX. If a ball while being returned first strikes one of the opposite side, and then the front wall above the "line," it counts as "up"; if it first strikes one of the same side it counts against the striker, whether it goes "up" or not.

X. If a ball returned by A or B strike A or B after going "up" before the second bound, it may be returned or not by C or D at their option, and *vice versâ*. If not returned it counts as a "let." If returned above the "line" no "let" can be claimed.

Scoring.

XI. The game consists of fifteen points. Only the "in" side can score points. When A is put out, B takes his place; when B is put out the side is out, and their opponents go in, the player "in holes" having first innings. The result of each "bully" (except in the case of a "let") is either to add one to the score of the "in" side, or to put one of them out, as the case may be.

Two Out.

XII. If C "in holes" loses one point to the opposite side, he is said to be "one out"; if he loses a second point, he is said to be "two out," and D takes his place; if D in his turn loses two points he is "two out" and C is "in holes" again, and so on till A and B are put out; provided that he who was "two out" first is then the first to go in; but if, through inadvertence or otherwise, he does not do so, the error cannot be corrected after the "service" has been returned. If the "out" side lose a point by failing to return a ball out of the "hole," it does not count as "one out" against the player "in holes.'

Note.—For the purposes of this rule all balls which fall on the "on-wall" belong to the player "in holes," and also all balls falling on the "off-wall" which he attempts to return.

Saving Good 'uns.

XIII. If the player "in holes" hit the "first-cut" in such a way that it will probably fall out of court and count as a "good 'un" he or his partner may, if they can, prevent it from doing so, by touching or catching the ball before it falls, provided that the player touching it have one or both feet on the floor of the court, or, if he jumps for the purpose, alights on the floor of the court with the foot which first touches the ground. If the ball is caught no stroke is counted; if only touched the opposite player may, if he pleases, return the ball as in Rule X; if he fail to do so, no stroke is counted. This rule only applies to "first-cut."

Blackguard Cut.

XIV. When the side "in" reaches fourteen points, the following rules must be observed:—(1) The player serving must stand quite close to the pepper-box with one foot on the "on-wall," and the other on the "off-wall," and he may not place both feet on the "on-wall" until the player "in holes" has hit the ball. If he forgets to stand thus, and serves the ball with both feet on the "on-wall," the player "in holes," or his partner, may try to be the first to touch the ball before it falls. If they succeed in this, the player serving is out. If the player serving or his partner touch the ball first, or if it hits the ground before being touched, it counts neither way. A player may remind his partner of this rule. (2) When the ball is properly served, the player "in holes" may return the "first-cut" against any part of the front wall above the "line," with or without hitting the side walls, and it is therefore called "blackguard cut." Rule VI., except the first sentence, is suspended at this point of the game.

Setting.

XV. If the players are "13 all," the game, as in rackets, may at the option of the out side be set to 5 or 3; if "14 all" to 3. Rule XIV. must then be observed at 1 and 2 respectively.

Single Wall Game.

XVI. When the game is played by two players only, no ball counts unless it fall upon the "on-wall," but a player may return a ball which falls on the "off-wall" if he pleases, except the "service." Of the two players, he who is "in" stands on the right-hand side of the court, and he who is "out" on the left-hand side. The "service" must hit first the right-hand wall and then the front wall above the "line." The "first-cut" must hit either (1) first the left-hand wall and then the front wall above the "line," or (2) first the front wall above the "line" and then the right-hand wall. Only so much of Rule XIV. need be observed as applies to the "out" player.

Laws of the Rugby Game as Played at Winchester.

The court is enclosed on four sides.

The buttress (if there be one) projects from the left-hand wall from 9½ to 10 inches, at an angle of 135°, and at a distance of 9 feet 9 inches from the front wall. In height it is co-extensive with the wall, which is flush with it at both angles, so that it is impossible to hit over or behind the buttress as it has but one face.

The "line," either simply painted on the wall, or better still set upon wood, runs across the front wall at a distance of 34 inches from the ground.

I. Each game shall consist of 14 points, or aces, and a game-ball; if both sides are at 13, the game may be set at 5, or at 3 if both have reached 14, at the option of the "out" side; provided that the "in" side at the time of setting shall only take one hand the first innings after the setting, and also that no false return of the game-ball shall be allowed.

II. The first innings of the first game shall be by lot; but, afterwards, the winner of the preceding game shall go in first.

III. The side going in first can only take one hand the first innings.

IV. In serving, the server must stand by or near the buttress, the player who returns the service standing in a line with him; the out-playing partner of the server stands behind the returner, and the out-playing partner of the returner stands behind the server.

V. The ball must be served to the front and right walls in that order, and returned on one of the side walls, and then on the front wall above the line, but if a ball be falsely served, it is at the option of the adversary to return it.

VI. The player who has to return the service may not, under any circumstances, change places with his partner.

VII. If a ball, after being struck by a player, touch his partner or himself, before one of his adversaries have touched it and before it has bounded a second time, it counts as an ace or hand-out against him, as the case may be.

Note.—The players shall be at liberty, before beginning to play, to agree that if the ball in returning from the wall hit the player or his partner it shall be a let instead of an ace or hand-out, but this shall only be allowed if the players are unanimous, and the marker is informed of it before the beginning of the game.

VIII. If a player strike at and miss a ball, his partner may play it, but he cannot claim a let if his adversary is in the way.

IX. If a ball strike the roof or gallery of a covered court, it is a hand-out.

X. Under no circumstances may kicking the ball be allowed.

XI. In returning the game-ball, the third successive false return counts against the striker. Only on the first occasion of game-ball being served need game-ball be called.

XII. Any service returned below the line counts against the striker.

XIII. The above rules apply to single as well as to double fives.

E. L. Fox.

FLOUNDER (*Pleuronectes flesus*).

Measurements, etc.—Length of head 4, of caudal fin 5⅔, height of body 2½, in the total length. *Eyes*—less than 1 diameter apart, and the lower slightly in advance of the upper. They are so prominent that they are capable of observing objects on both sides of the head. Lower jaw in advance of the upper. The length of the maxilla equals about ¼ that of the head, but does not reach to beneath the eyes. Anterior nostril tubular, having a small opening; posterior one oval, with wide lips. An obtuse ridge passes from the interorbital space to the lateral line. *Teeth*—conical, blunted, two rows in the upper, and one in the lower jaw: the outer row on the upper jaw of the blind side consists of 15 teeth, the corresponding row in the lower jaw of about 17. *Fins*—dorsal, commences opposite the middle of the upper eye, its longest rays in the posterior half of the body. Pectorals on the two sides similar, and about ½ as long as the head. Ventrals free. A strong spine, pointing forwards, exists before the base of the anal fin, which latter is similar to the dorsal. Caudal cut square. *Scales*—small, cycloid; rudimentary ones on the cheeks. A rounded and rough tubercle between the bases of the dorsal and anal rays. *Lateral line*—commencing opposite the angle of the mouth, curves round the lower eye, and having joined the interorbital ridge is continued to the centre of the base of the caudal fin. Coecal pylori short. *Colours*—vary very considerably, and depend upon that of the ground of the locality which they inhabit, but even then scarcely two will be found exactly similar. The colour of the upper side is generally olivaceous brown, with or without darker blotches. Occasionally examples are very dark, when they are termed sea-flounders. The under surface is white.

Day's *Fishes of Great Britain and Ireland*, vol. II. p. 34.

FLY-TYING—[*See* Salmon and Trout].

FOOTBALL—RUGBY FOOTBALL—

History of the game—I propose to devote this part of the article to a sketch of the various phases of development which the game has undergone from the period of twenty a side up to the present time.

When I was a school-boy at Clifton College, more than twenty years ago, the game played there was identical with that at Rugby School. The number on each side was twenty, and the arrangement of the field was as follows: two full backs, one three-quarter, and two halves. It was an act of high treason to put down one's head in the scrummage, and, if anybody did so, an opponent would promptly remind him of this breach of etiquette by raising his knee sharply against it. Hacking was permissible and, as there were no umpires to appeal to in the case of a breach of the rules, such as, for example, off-side play, the innocent party used to take the law into his own hands, and with a shout of "off-side, Sir," administer the orthodox punishment for the infringement by violently kicking the shin bone of the offender.

Hacking or tripping over were quite as much resorted to as tackling, and though it may in these more civilised days appear a rather brutal and crude method of stopping a runner, it required for success the greatest skill and accuracy. W. O. Moberley, the old Rugbeian and Gloucestershire cricketer, was a perfect master of the art. And not only was it legal to hack over the carrier of the ball, but also the first on side, and I have seen as many as four of the van brought to earth by this means.

There were extraordinary formalities to be gone through in taking the ball out for a place kick at goal. The kicker used to pick up the ball and make a mark at the place where the try was gained. He then went to the goal line, and, having made a second mark opposite the former one, he and the placer proceeded parallel with the goal line to as far away from the goal posts as they liked.

The defending sides were allowed to stretch forward to their utmost, provided they kept the hindmost foot on the second mark. The kicker, facing the placer and a few feet apart from him, gently punted the ball to him, and he made another mark as far inwards and towards the goal line as he could manage to do with safety.

The defending side endeavoured to frustrate this manœuvre, either by spoiling the catch, if they were able to reach the ball, or by seizing the leg of the placer while he was attempting to make, but before he had actually made, his mark. If they were successful in either, the kick at goal was lost. Mauls in goal were very frequent. I have seen as many as ten men in one, and there was no limit to their duration imposed by the laws.

The art of scrummaging consisted in straightforward propulsion. One of those in the front rank was expected to get the ball between his legs, and hold it there tight, while his forwards pushed on him might and main. The packs frequently lasted two or three minutes, with forwards equipoised; and, to show how times have altered, I have only to mention that in those days the longest scrummage was considered the best and that the spectators on the touch line often had their watches out, timing its duration.

The half-back, owing to the tight packing of the forwards, had a much easier task than he has now, and it sometimes occurred that he was right across the field before the scrummage had become dismembered.

When a ball was kicked into touch, both sides raced to touch it down, and it was legal for opponents to charge one another in the struggle for its possession.

The first step towards a faster game was the diminution in the number of players from twenty to fifteen. For a very long time after this, however, the original arrangement of the back players was preserved. By this change the forwards, now ten in number, found themselves able to break away from the scrummage, in which they had hitherto been boxed up, and to the art of dribbling, in consequence, there was imparted an enormous impetus. Heads down and watching the ball in the scrummage followed. Hacking in club games was abolished, though Rugby School retained it for some years later; a ball going into touch was declared by the rules to belong to the side other than the one which kicked it in, and two umpires and a referee made their *début* as adjuncts to the game, but the referee was only authorised to adjudicate when there was a diversity of opinion between the umpires. The maul in goal was retained even later than Vassall's day, but the preliminaries to a place kick, which I have described, were never in vogue in club football.

The next step in the same direction was a device known by the name of "Foiking," which emanated from Oxford. It consisted in a wing forward dexterously extricating the ball with his foot from the side of a scrummage. When the play had become very much faster, it was found that one man at three-quarter was no longer able to hold the field, and he was reinforced by a second, an addition which reduced the number of forwards to nine.

Next in order there was evolved a science which has had more to do with revolutionising the character of the game than any other innovation. I refer, of course, to "passing." To whom belongs the credit of the invention is a matter of much dispute, but its elaboration was unquestionably the work of the Blackheath team. It was at first entirely confined to the forwards, but by degrees spread to the halves. Who was the first half to pass out a ball is by no means clear. Many aver that J. Payne, of Lancashire, set the example, but Alan Rotherham was the first to reduce the art of feeding to a science, and remains to this day the pattern whom every half-back strives to imitate.

We come now to the addition of a third three-quarter. It happened in a somewhat peculiar manner. The South team, as originally selected, only contained two three-quarters. One of the forwards, P. Newton, however, could not play, and Harry Vassall wrote to the Committee from Oxford that they had a player there of extraordinary ability in the person of C. W.

Wade, and strongly urged his inclusion. Under the circumstances the Committee resolved to play him, though not without considerable misgiving. The brilliant success of the Southern trio, W. L. Bolton, A. M. Evanson, and C. W. Wade, on Richardson's field, settled this question for good.

The next development was the passing by the centre three-quarter to his wings, and in this the pioneer was Rawson Robertshaw, who, at centre, applied the same principles which Rotherham had demonstrated at half. Coincidently with the addition of a third three-quarter the backs were reduced from two to one.

It remained for the Welshmen to add yet another three-quarter, but for a long time the other countries did not adopt the alteration, nor indeed was this to be wondered at, seeing that Wales for a number of years was badly beaten by England, Scotland, and Ireland, who adhered to the three system.

But, just at the moment when the four three-quarter game appeared likely to die out, there came to its aid two most powerful allies in new methods of scrummaging, viz., heeling and wheeling, which very soon became the fashion, and superseded the time-honoured straightforward pushing game.

It is important here to note that up to this time the four three-quarter game had been a failure, because eight men were unable to hold their own against nine in the packs in the old style. By the introduction of heeling and wheeling this state of things was altered. The ninth man was no longer of the same value in a scrummage which was worked by the manœuvre of wheeling, or from which the ball was heeled back almost at the very moment of its insertion, as he was when the pack had to be carried by superior power and weight.

The device of wheeling originated in Yorkshire, and one of its earliest exponents was the then famous Bradford Club. Where the practice of heeling back first came from it is difficult to say. It is, of course, a clear breach of the rules of the game, but it was countenanced so long without the interference of the authorities that it ultimately came to be regarded as an unwritten law.

The last alteration up to date is in the relative position of the two halves. They no longer stand level with each other, but, with a view of facilitating the shortness, quickness, and accuracy of the passing, one of them takes the scrummage, the so-called "donkey-half," while the other stands back midway between his *confrère* and the three-quarters, transforming himself, as it were, into a quasi fifth three-quarter.

As the popularity of the game increased, and consequently partisanship became more violent, it was found impossible to get impartial umpires, and in their stead two linesmen were substituted, whose sole duty consisted in holding up a flag at the place where the ball went into touch, while the referee had the sole right of deciding on appeals made to him for breaches of the rules, and signified his allowance of them by blowing a whistle. Lastly, the right of appeal was abolished, and at the present time the referee is invested with an absolute discretion.

That the reduction of the number of players from twenty to fifteen, which brought about the introduction of dribbling and passing, effected a great improvement, is on all hands admitted, but whether the addition of a fourth three-quarter has been beneficial to the play is a matter which has been very hotly debated.

Hints on the Game—The first lesson to be appreciated is that the whole tendency of the modern game has been to convert the component parts of a football team into a well-regulated machine, and that it is on co-ordination, rather than individual excellence, that success depends.

The first step must be the choice of a definite style. You may elect to play a fast game or a slow one, a passing or a dribbling one, but, if your tactics are to be successful, your men must from the very first understand what the style is to be, and one and all must co-operate in carrying it out. Your selection will, no doubt, in a large measure be determined by the material at command, and you will have to consider whether your men are best adapted to a fast or slow game, or to a foot or hand one.

The Selection of Teams—I hold a very strong opinion that the fewer engaged in this task the better, and I have a firm belief in leaving the matter in the hands of the captain or secretary, if those officials are competent judges of play. The greater the power you vest in them, the more likely they are to realise their responsibility, and the greater the interest and work which they will devote to the management of the club. With a numerous selecting committee, on the other hand, you simply arrive at the resultant of divers opinions; and under such circumstances you are not likely to develop a homogeneous fifteen or unanimity of style.

It is always advisable, where possible, to keep a second fifteen in competition with the first. There is no such stimulus to a man's play as the knowledge that his place is not secure. This is year by year demonstrated by the University fifteens, who invariably play a very much harder game before the 'Varsity match, when each player is fighting for his blue, than they do after the Christmas vacation.

The Captain—On the shoulders of the captain falls the whole management of a team. The question of the selection of captain becomes, therefore, one of most vital importance. The custom prevails of electing to the post the oldest player. This I regard as a great mistake. In my opinion the man best qualified to discharge the duties of generalship ought to be selected, irrespective of any claims of seniority which another candidate may possess.

It goes without saying that he must be a popular man, but his popularity must not prevent his being a determined autocrat, whose word must be absolute law. He must possess a thorough knowledge of the game, insist on the observance of the strictest discipline, and never flag in his efforts to infuse enthusiasm and maintain vitality.

On the field his duties will be (1) to select the style of play, and see that its essential points are observed. (2) To correct mistakes. A man who indulges in a bad bit of play should be immediately reprimanded. (3) To keep his side together and at high pressure by continual exhortation, picking out the slackers for his censure, and rallying his side when it shows signs of going to pieces. (4) To preserve silence. All talking must be peremptorily stopped. It is a pure waste of energy, disorganises the game, and generally leads to wrangling. The captain is the only man who has a right to talk. (5) To watch most carefully the manœuvres of his adversaries, and endeavour to checkmate them by counter tactics. (6) To see that every player of the opposite side is marked by one of his own on the line out. This is most important.

From these suggestions it will be at once apparent that it is best to have as captain, if possible, a player outside the scrummage, inasmuch as in that position he has a better opportunity of seeing exactly how the game is going.

Method of Play—Passing—The whole tendency of modern play has been to make the game more fast and open, and the main factor in the transformation has been passing. But though this art has undoubtedly placed a very great premium on speed, it must not be forgotten that dribbling, though not so effective on a dry ground, or so attractive from a spectacular point of view, possesses nevertheless the advantage that it is practicable under any conditions of weather, whereas a greasy ground, a wet ball, or a boisterous wind render passing a matter of great difficulty, and sometimes an impossibility. Every club should be proficient in both schools of play.

The following are the axioms of passing:—

1. The one object is to transfer the ball to one of your own side who is in a more advantageous position than yourself.

2. It follows as a rider that, unless there is some one in such a position, you must on no account pass, but must stick to the ball yourself, inasmuch as passing at all times involves a risk, which, unless there is a palpable advantage to be gained—and in this case there is none whatever—ought not to be run.

3. For the same reason no one must ever pass *within his own* 25 *yards line*. N.B.—This golden rule is being continually transgressed, and I have often seen International players offend. A captain cannot be too severe on the transgressor.

4. You must pass at the most opportune moment, *i.e.*, when you have made the pass a certainty, and at the very moment when most can be gained by it.

5. The pass must be low, quick, clean and (where practicable) as short as possible. High slow passes are liable to be intercepted, while short ones are obviously very much more safe and accurate than long.

6. It follows from the above, that players should back up as nearly level and as close as possible to the carrier, and that the backing up should be done broadcast and towards the open. These remarks do not, of course, apply to a long pass by a half to a three-quarter back, and by a centre three-quarter to his wing.

7. Never call for a pass unless you are in a palpably better position than the carrier. At the present time a most pernicious practice exists of almost everybody in the vicinity of the carrier shouting for a pass. Now only one of this chorus can be the proper person to whom the pass should be made, and he is the player in the most advantageous position in relation to the runner. A captain ought to put his foot down at once on this silly abuse, which only bewilders the carrier, or brings him to a standstill in uncertainty as to what he ought to do.

8. The practice of feinting, which might be described as passing by not passing at all, is a most effective practice, but it requires the employment of great judgment as to when it should be resorted to, and a capacity to take in the situation in the twinkling of an eye. No definite law can be stated on the subject, which must be wholly governed by the circumstances attaching to the particular incident of play.

The carrier of the ball feints to pass, and so perplexes the would-be tackler and decoys him to the player to whom he imagines a pass has been made. In such a case the carrier secures an open field for himself.

It will be convenient here to consider what, under these circumstances, the tackler ought to do. He should most unquestionably invariably go for the carrier of the ball. It must be remembered that he is one against two. If he makes for the player who, he thinks, is about to receive the ball, he is bound to leave an open channel at the disposal of the runner, while he himself tackles nobody at all. If, on the other hand, he goes for the carrier, he at any rate forces his hand, and either tackles him with the ball, or compels him to make his pass. In this case he has rendered a service to his side, in the former to his adversaries.

Too much stress cannot be laid on this very

important point. I have constantly seen men wavering and hesitating as to which of the two they ought to make for and finally fall between two stools and go for neither. I would remark, moreover, that, even where there is no feinting done, it is the practice of the majority of centre three-quarters, when the opposite centre is running, immediately to deploy to the wing three-quarter, taking it for granted that the ball will be passed out. This is a very great error indeed, and it can be laid down as a hard and fast law *that it is the duty of every three-quarter to devote his attention primarily to his vis-à-vis.*

Lastly, passing is, in my opinion, greatly overdone, and in minor clubs the science is frequently burlesqued. A great many men appear to be imbued with the idea that they ought to get rid of the ball the moment they get it; so that one sees runners not sprinting or dodging, but going half speed, and looking first on one side and then on the other for some one to pass to. The consequence is that the ball very often passes through a dozen hands in a stationary position, and at the end of a pretty piece of legerdemain things are as they were, and the performers are no better off than when they started the manœuvre. I most strongly advise that a player receiving the ball should sprint ahead at full speed without hesitating or looking round, until he sees a risk of being tackled, and that then, and not till then, he should pass to the most advantageously placed player, who, if the backing up has been done in the proper manner, ought to be near him and on the open side.

Dribbling—Much that has been said about passing applies to dribbling. It is an art which can only be acquired by the most assiduous practice; and it must be recollected that what you want is combined and concentrated, and not isolated, dribbling, which is easily checked, and therefore not of great value.

The following are the most important rules :—

1. You must not be in too great a hurry in dribbling the ball, or you will be sure to overrun it. A Rugby ball does not roll with the accuracy of an Association one.

2. A player should thoroughly understand how to pass by the foot, and here the axioms enumerated with regard to passing by hand would apply to a very large extent.

3. A player should be able to use the outside as well as the inside of his foot, so that he may be able to pass right or left as occasion requires.

4. As in passing by hand, the forwards should back up the dribble broadcast, and on the side to which the ball can be most advantageously transferred.

5. When a half or three-quarter back is in a good position in the open to score, the dribbler, if he be sufficiently skilful to make a long pass, should shoot the ball across to him immediately.

6. A half-back should not make a practice of dribbling. It may pay occasionally, but you will generally find that the half-back who habitually dribbles is apt to neglect the feeding of his three-quarter backs, and cannot stop a rush of forwards, because he seldom picks up the ball, and cannot do it on an emergency.

The fact that there is not merely so much dribbling now as there used to be is probably due to the greater popularity of passing by hand. At the same time there is no saying what a team which had brought to perfection the art of combined dribbling might do.

In some clubs the catcher of the ball from the throw out immediately drops it, and starts a dribble, but this device, for success, requires

A Forward Dribble.

a previously understood concerted action amongst the forwards, and is by no means easy to accomplish successfully.

Judgment Kicking—I should mention that the Yorkshire forwards do not go in for dribbling, but for what is known as "judgment kicking." This consists in kicking the ball just hard enough to stop between themselves and the nearest half or three-quarter, and then following up at full speed, in order, if possible, to reach it first and to prevent their opponents from picking it up. Another variety of it is a long oblique kick to some unprotected part of the field with the same object. This device is all very well when it succeeds, but the kick must obviously be very well judged and directed, and is just as likely as not to go too far. On the whole, I think that dribbling is by far the soundest, and, in the long run, the most paying game.

Departments of Play—Forward Play—Pace, dash and skill, when combined with weight and physical power, are important attributes of a good forward, but the most valuable of all qualities is that of hard work, and you will do well, therefore, to impress continually upon your men that, whatever else they may be able to accomplish on the field of play, they must be able at any rate to play hard. It is very much wiser to have your team composed of men who play resolutely in any kind of game than of those who are brilliant and who figure conspicuously when they win, but fail when you have a beaten side.

One may take it as a hard and fast rule that one never should pick a loafer, no matter how brilliant a player he may be, for it must not be forgotten that his share of the hard work has to be done by the rest of the team, and that he is a source of weakness on defence.

There are two phases of play (1) play in the scrummage, (2) play in the open.

Scrummaging—The first great lesson to be appreciated is that all the pace and skill in the world are useless unless you hold the scrummage. This is, indeed, a golden axiom. Back players *must* have room, but if your forwards are routed, they are swamped and never have an opportunity of getting off, while the opposing phalanx sweeps all before it with the force of a torrent.

It follows that (1) You must have a sufficiency of scrummage work. (2) The best team is the one which combines this sufficiency with pace in the open.

The present fashionable methods of scrummaging are (1) wheeling or screwing, and (2) heeling out. The old practice of pushing straight ahead may be said to have fallen into disuse, for the time being, at any rate, if not for ever.

Wheeling—The means employed in wheeling are not strictly within the letter of the law, inasmuch as during the process the bulk of the scrummagers are off-side. The practice has, however, been admitted by tacit consent, and may be said to have become legitimate.

The essence of the science consists in your own forwards obtaining possession of the ball in the scrummage, and withdrawing it behind the first or second row of scrummagers, where it lies safe from the interference of your adversaries, who are thus prevented from executing a similar manœuvre. Here it is nursed by careful manipulation till it is seen in which direction the bias of the scrummage is tending, and an opinion can be formed whether it would be better to execute the wheel to the right or to the left. When this point has been ascertained, the wheel is made on the most favourable side by the back row bringing the ball round to the front, while the front row slide off their adversaries.

If you are going to wheel, then, (1) you must be the first to get possession of the ball in the scrummage. This is a *sine quâ non.* (2) You must immediately pull it back behind the front row of scrummagers, so that it will be safe from the interference of your adversaries, and you may execute your manœuvre in secrecy and unmolested. (3) You must nurse it skilfully, holding the scrummage at the same time, of course, till the moment for wheeling arrives. (4) You must wheel to the side on which you can best screw off your adversaries, and then rush ahead with the ball.

From the above it will be gathered that the manœuvre is by no means easy of execution, and as a matter of fact there are not many teams which can accomplish it with precision. With very few exceptions the International teams of the last few years have more often than not failed in their attempts to bring it into play. Like most other fanciful manœuvres it is very dangerous when it fails. The mistake which most sides make in attempts to employ it, is leaving the ball behind in their hurry to wheel. As a consequence, they make a present of the ball to their adversaries with a fair field in front of them, since they themselves, by screwing off their opponents, are now behind them, and off-side as far as the play is concerned. The greatest precaution must be taken to see that the ball is brought on by the wheelers, or the result is bound to be disastrous.

I am personally of opinion that a very much sounder method would be to pull the ball back, and then push straight ahead in the old-fashioned style. This possesses the advantage of being absolutely safe, and it is a surprise to me that no team as yet has adopted it. Any side which did so would meet with astonishing success in these days, when straight-ahead propulsion has become a dead letter.

Heeling Out—The art consists in this:—The heel out is not executed the moment the scrummage is formed. This would be too transparent a device. Possession of the ball must first of all be obtained as in wheeling, and the forwards must from the very commencement of the scrummage push their utmost in order to convey to their opponents the idea that they are trying to carry the pack and so mask the manœuvre. When they are actually pushing their opponents is the moment when heeling should be done.

Both wheeling and heeling are strategies which are distasteful to players of the old school, but they have without doubt become part and parcel of the game, and no side which is not versed in them would stand a ghost of a chance with one which is.

As regards scrummaging generally, the following points are of the highest importance. (1) Be the first to form the scrummage and pack quickly. This is half the battle. (2) Get the first push. The whole momentum should be applied the very instant the ball is put down. The above are the means by which what is termed "rushing" a scrummage is effected. (3) When you find yourself on your opponents' side of the scrummage and in front of the ball, get round immediately and reform. Too much stress cannot be laid on this last point. As a rule, forwards of the present day are apt to wait for the ball to overtake them instead of running round again immediately, and filling the breaches in the forward ranks. If under such circumstances the opposing side happen to get on a rush the result may be very serious. (4) Form a compact scrummage with the heads down. Long and straggling packs are easily broken through, and, moreover, do not admit of any of the manœuvres before detailed with reference to wheeling and heeling. (5) Never kick a ball forward in a scrummage. By so doing you lose it yourself, and hand it over to the control of

A TIGHT SCRUMMAGE.

your adversaries. (6) Always keep your eye on the ball in the fight, so as to detect the progress of your opponents' manœuvres. (7) The half backs should keep the forwards informed of the locality and movements of the ball in the pack.

Open Play—When once the scrummage is broken up, the first great secret of open play is to break away quickly and follow up at full speed. This should be sprinting, and not the trotting which we so often see. There is nothing more important than quick following up, and it should be done *en masse*, and not singly, so that five or six men, and not one only, are on the spot to tackle an adversary who gets the ball. Passing and dribbling I have already dealt with, so that I will say no more about them here, merely remarking that they are accomplishments essential to a good forward. Picking up by forwards should be discouraged, since it spoils the rushes.

One of the most important items of open forward play is the line out from touch, and I have found that in this it very much assists men to have their accustomed places, some near in, and some far out from the touch line.

Each of your forwards must mark one of the opposite side. Many a try is lost through leaving a man unmarked, and so allowing him to get away. This occurs over and over again even in the very best matches, and a captain should always keep a watchful eye on the line out.

Finally, a forward should be a sure and determined tackler, and recollect that even if he cannot nail his man, he is hampering his movements by going for him, and that by following him across the field after he has missed him he is narrowing his margin of open ground. If a forward misses his man, he should not give up, but follow in hot pursuit, for he may get him from behind at the next check.

Half-back Play—Imprimis, and above everything else, a half-back must realise that he is essentially a conduit pipe between the forwards and three-quarter backs, and that it is for the latter and not himself that he must mainly shape his play. This conception of his character originated the art of what is commonly known as "feeding," an innovation which has revolutionised the game. It is, therefore, necessary that a half-back should be intimately acquainted with this science; otherwise, he is wholly unfitted for the post.

There are two styles of "feeding": (1) stationary, *i.e.*, when the half passes the ball to the three-quarter the moment he receives it, without running himself; (2) when he runs himself, clears his *vis-à-vis*, gets his three-quarter on his legs, and nurses him till he gets an opportune moment to make his pass. The latter is undoubtedly the more efficacious way of proceeding, but it must be remembered that a half has not always time to carry it out, as for instance when his *vis-à-vis* is almost on the top of him, or when he is in front of his opponents' goal, and not a moment is to be lost. In these cases the half, if he passes at all, must do so immediately. To which of the three-quarters he will pass will depend on his judgment and the circumstances of the case, but it is best to pass to the centre, when possible, for he is in a better position to develop the game than a wing, whose field of operations is curtailed on one side by the touch line.

The most skilful passer, however, will be no good unless he is quick on the ball, for if he is not, his *vis-à-vis* will invariably get it before him. This opens up the question as to how far from the scrummage he ought to stand; and on this point, in my opinion, no hard and fast law can be laid down. Some great players have been in the habit of standing a long way off, while I have seen other famous ones stationed right on the fringe of the pack. Standing some distance off undoubtedly gives you more room when you get the ball, but on the other hand you are not so likely to get it as if you were standing nearer in, and, both in the matter of stopping rushes and getting on to your *vis-à-vis*, you are at a disadvantage. The precise spot should be that which a player finds best suited to his style.

A third essential for a half is a capacity to tackle and stop rushes. He must keep a vigilant eye on his *vis-à-vis*, and be ready to nail him the very instant the ball comes to him; and when his adversaries are making a dribbling rush he must throw himself fearlessly on the ball.

Fourthly, a half should be a good kicker, so that he can relieve his side by sending the ball

Stopping a Rush.

into touch when on defence. For this purpose screw-kicking is especially useful.

Fifthly, as the duty of throwing the ball out of touch devolves on the halves, every half ought to be a long and accurate thrower.

Co-operation of the two Half-backs—A most effective game can be played by the co-operation of the two halves in the employment of cross passing. For its accomplishment it is necessary that there should exist between the two a most complete understanding, and an intimate knowledge of each other's play, together with complete unselfishness. The method is this. When the ball comes out to a half on one side of the scrummage, he immediately throws across to his colleague, and *vice versa*. The essence of the theory, of course, is that it changes the tack of the game, and that the play is suddenly transposed from one side of the scrummage to the other, while the stream of players, who have brought the ball through, remain where they were. The *vis-à-vis* of the half-back who originally received the ball is thus prevented from tackling him, while his colleague, if the pass is a swift one, is probably not yet ready to tackle, or is possibly in ignorance of the fact that the pass has been made. The half, therefore, who has received the cross pass, is thus able to transfer to his three-quarter unmolested. It is a strategy most excellently employed when the play is near touch, and there is no margin between the scrummage and the touch-line in which to develop the game. Then, if the ball comes out to the half on the touch-line, he can, by throwing across to his colleague, immediately transfer the play to the open field. In point of defence, moreover, it is of very great value. When a half, for instance, gets the ball, and sees that there is no possible chance of his escaping being tackled by his *vis-à-vis*, who is close upon him, he can get out of the difficulty of the situation by a cross pass. The game of co-operation has come to be so generally recognised as the one to play that, in choosing half-backs for great matches, an inferior club couple are often preferred to two better individual players in order to preserve the combination.

Another innovation of recent years is the practice of one half taking the scrummage, while his colleague stands back between him and the three-quarters, an intermediary, as it were, between a half and three-quarters. The half who is on the open side of the play is the one to stand back, and the other takes the scrummage. The object in view is to facilitate the transit of the ball to the three-quarters by the agency of short passing. It is most important, however, to bear in mind that these tactics are only to be employed in offence. When on defence it is absolutely imperative that both halves should resume their usual position, *i.e.*, both take the scrummage for the purpose of stopping rushes and tackling their opponents.

Three-quarter-back Play—There are two systems of three-quarter-back play: (1) three three-quarters; (2) four three-quarters. Opinions have differed widely as to which is the better method, but after a prolonged controversy, throughout which England, Scotland and Ireland persevered with three three-quarters as against the four of Wales, the system of the latter has gradually made headway, and is now the more generally accepted.

It is important to note the fact that in the days of the old straightforward pushing the four three-quarter game was a failure, and year by year Wales paid the penalty for the innovation by disastrous defeats in International matches.

It has been contended (1) that eight forwards cannot hold their own against nine; (2) that the ground is not broad enough to give room to four three-quarters.

With regard to the first contention, I would remark that under the altered conditions of forward play, which heeling and wheeling have brought about, the theory that nine forwards are bound to rout eight is a fallacy. Nothing of the sort occurs. The fact is that the whole character of forward play has been altered by these innovations, and that scrummaging has become rather a question of finesse and manœuvre than of weight and physical power. Under these circumstances it is very obvious that the value of the ninth man in the scrummage is not what it used to be under the old régime. Then I admit that nine would have routed eight, but under the present method of scrummaging I am sure that they do not.

Assuming that eight men under the altered state of things can hold nine, is it not patent that an extra man at three-quarter is a manifest advantage both from an offensive and defensive point of view?

In the first place he strengthens the defence, for four men must of necessity be more difficult to get through than three—in fact I would go so far as to say that in the present state of things three are unable to hold four in check, unless the four three-quarter side are utterly broken down forward.

Secondly, it is clear that he contributes to your offence. His presence brings into play short passings, which is a great deal easier, and at the same time more precise than long, and his introduction admits of very delicate co-ordination, which, if brought to any degree of perfection, is difficult to break down.

In addition to this, whenever one of the four gets the ball, he is, *cæteris paribus*, at an advantage of two to one as regards his *vis-à-vis*, and it is, to my mind, an utter impossibility for one man to stop two. Supposing, we will say, one of the centres on the four side gets the ball, and that the centre of the three side goes, as he is bound to do, for him. He immediately, of course, passes to his fellow centre, for whom the wing on the three side must now make. The centre on the four side straightway passes to his wing, who has a clear field in front of him, for, the wing of the three side being already employed, there is no one left to stop him.

As regards the breadth of the ground, I would point out that the four game is a wholly different one from that of the three. In the former the three-quarters run straight, in the latter they run round, so that the four do not require an inch more latitude than the three.

Under the present phase of forward play, therefore, I am strongly of opinion that it is essential to play four. That the system substitutes machinery for individuality, and that it does not, and never will, produce players of the same ability as the three game I at once admit, and if you were to take some of the present famous four three-quarters and put them in a three game, you would find them most inferior players, because they have become accustomed to devote the whole of their attention to one department of the game only, *i.e.*, passing, in order that they may convert themselves into a component part of an elaborate machine, and are wholly devoid of resource.

If a radical change comes about in the forward play which will restore to weight and physical strength their premium,—a change which may occur any day,—then the three game will once more be universally adopted. There can be no question that the three game is an infinitely superior school wherein to train a young player, and it is a matter of congratulation to know that our great public schools, which are nurseries for the supply of our best talent, still adhere to the three game, except on the occasions of matches with outside clubs. The three game is, therefore, still very largely played, and I accordingly give the principles which govern it.

Three Three-quarters—The Centre—A centre is the correlative of the half-back, and as the latter has to play, not for himself, but for the men behind him, in the same way a centre has to make the game for his two wings. Every word which has been written about the opportune passing of a half to a three-quarter applies to the passing of a centre to his wings. Thus it will sometimes be his game to pass out at once without running himself, at other times he will be able to nurse his wings and get them well on their legs, passing at the exact moment when they will have the best chance of scoring, and again, at another time, he may resort to feinting, and, if he can secure a clear passage thereby, run in himself.

The other essentials of a centre are that he should be a sure kick and tackler, and a fearless stopper of rushes. These are most indispensable qualities, inasmuch as the burden of the defence will rest on his shoulders. The rushes, as a rule, fall to his share, and when in his own twenty-five, or at a moment when he cannot pass or make headway himself, he will be bound to kick. Though it may be safely said that all three-quarters ought to be good tacklers and kickers, this is essentially the case with the centre, so that efficient kicking in this position is absolutely necessary. And here I would remark—and this applies to kicking by halves and full backs—that every kick should reach touch. In this respect the modern generation has steadily deteriorated, for the reason that an enormous amount of attention is paid to passing, and kicking is consequently comparatively neglected—indeed, one might almost say that accurate kicking into touch is a lost art.

The centre will, of course, be on the look-out for a drop at goal, if he is an expert at this, but it is not good play to drop at goal when a judicious pass can make a try a certainty. When near his adversaries' goal, it is advisable for the centre to move up nearer to his halves, and to bring up his wings with him, so that he may be in a better position to take a pass and in quicker time.

The Wings—The modern game has placed a premium on speed, and it has consequently become the custom to place sprinters on the wing. By this I do not mean to say that other qualities, such as kicking and tackling, are not desirable, but only to point out that either speed or dodging powers are absolutely requisite in this position. All that has been written about the kicks of a centre reaching touch applies equally here.

When the centre is running and nursing the

wing, the latter must back him up in the position which will make the pass easiest for him. The dividing distance, however, must depend wholly on the situation.

The wings must be careful not to close in towards the scrummage, and so run the risk of being outflanked by their opponents; in fact, each three-quarter should keep exactly opposite his *vis-à-vis*, and on no account come nearer towards the scrummage than the latter does.

All three-quarters should go to the assistance of the full back in cases of emergency. This applies most particularly to cases where (1) a back has run in front of the three-quarter; or (2) has followed up his kick. In both these cases the post is undefended, and a three-quarter should drop back immediately.

Four Three-quarter Back Play—As previously remarked, the four three-quarter game is of a totally different character from the three. In the latter, as we have seen, the single centre nurses his wings and passes at the most opportune moment, but in the case of four we have two centres and the method employed is that of short passing. The running is not nearly to the same extent across the ground—in fact the field of play is not sufficiently broad to admit of this in the case of four—but very much straighter. The game is an elaboration, on a more precise scale, of the short passing of the forwards which occurs when they back up one another broadcast. The quartette, during a run by one of them, preserve their relative positions, advancing parallel.

The passing is done when the carrier is in full swing, and is of a to and fro character. The receiver of the ball, for instance, starts off at full pace; the other three back up symmetrically. The carrier, either when he finds himself menaced by an opponent, or when he sees an advantage to be gained thereby, makes his pass, and the receiver under similar circumstances re-transfers and sends the ball, if he be a centre, either back to his fellow centre or out to his wing, who, when he has exhausted his margin, and is hedged in on the touch line, once more returns it to the passer. Thus, by a series of short and machine-like passes and repasses, employed whenever an obstacle presents itself, each would-be tackler is outmanœuvred. Or, to take another case, a centre gets the ball and passes to the other centre. The impression probably prevails that this centre will pass to his wing, and the defending side deploy in that direction. Instead of this, however, the last carrier re-transfers to the first, who now has a clear field in front of him and runs down the unprotected channel.

It will be easily understood that this is a system which requires infinite practice, a thorough reciprocity of style, and a great deal of head work. The whole success depends on whether or not the passing is done at full speed. It is because English, Scotch, and Irish clubs have failed to appreciate this fact that they have so far been unable to master the art.

A manœuvre which has of late years been considerably employed by three-quarters, who are clever kickers, is the following. The three-quarter on receiving the ball drops or punts it obliquely across the ground to some unprotected part of the field, and then running straight ahead at full speed puts his forwards, who are on the side of the ground where the ball has landed, but who were off-side when he kicked, on-side. It is extremely effective, but it requires a very accurate kicker.

And, lastly, another bit of finesse employed with considerable success by some three-quarters is the practice, when they have run up close to the full back, of punting over his head with a very gentle kick and then racing for the ball. The back has, of course, to turn while the three-quarter is already moving at full speed, and consequently has a great disadvantage in starting.

Full Back Play—The post of full back in a four three-quarter game is the most difficult on the field. On his shoulder rests enormous responsibility, and it is not easy for him to decide where to take up his position. The first point to be considered is: where a full back ought to stand as regards his three-quarters. Practice alone will teach him the proper spot, and I can merely broadly state that it should be as near the three-quarters as the range of the opponents' kicks will permit, but it must on no account be so close in that these pass over his head. Next comes the question: what is he to do when the three-quarters, with a bout of passing, are bearing down upon him? All he can do is to watch for the final development of the passing, and then without hesitation go for the carrier. If the latter passes again this cannot be helped. What he must realise is that, if he shows the smallest hesitation, he is lost.

In the case of a dribbling rush he must on no account keep on retreating before the attacking phalanx, as is the custom with so many players, but he must rush in boldly, and either pick up (if he can) or fall upon the ball.

The essentials of a full back are that he should be (1) a good tackler; (2) a long and accurate kicker.

If a team does not possess a player endowed with both these qualities, and the question arises as to whether the tackler or kicker should play, preference should undoubtedly be given to the former, for not only is he more likely to be of service in the moment of extreme peril, but the three-quarters will play with a great deal more confidence when they know that they have a reliable tackler behind them.

It will be obvious that what has been said about kicks reaching touch applies to the full back more than to any other player, seeing that he is the last defender, and a kick by him into the open might lead to disastrous consequences. For this reason a full-back should be able to kick with either foot. If he can only use the right, he is in a dilemma when he gets the ball on the right side of the ground. Secondly, if he cannot make a certainty of his kick when surrounded by his adversaries near his own goal, he must hold on to the ball and be tackled.

The question of following up his own kick for the purpose of putting his players on-side is a vexed one. In my opinion it is a very hazardous proceeding, for if the ball happens to be returned immediately there is no one there to receive it, or, if an adversary gets by the three-quarters, there is no one there to tackle him, unless one of the three-quarters has dropped back to fill the vacant post, which, of course, it is his duty to do.

General Play—Tackling—No bettter advice can be given to a player, who is about to tackle, than that which one so often hears on the football field, *i.e.*, "go low." The ideal tackle is an octopus one, which holds both the player and the ball in an iron grasp and so prevents the possibility of a pass. If, however, a player is not an adept at this, and very few are, his next best plan will be to aim at the hips or knees and swoop on the adversary with sufficient impetus to bowl him over, and so prevent the pass. The whole secret in tackling, it should be remembered, is that it must be done with resolution and without the smallest hesitation.

Some General Hints—If you win the toss, always take the wind, which may drop at any time, and frequently does towards sunset; and, again, if you win the toss, always play with the slope to begin with. A score in the first half of a game inspires confidence in your side, and demoralises your opponents.

At kick-off and kick-out see that none of your own side get in front of the kicker. If they do, the advantage of the kick is lost, and a scrummage is formed midway between the touch-lines, either at the halfway or twenty-five yards' flag.

When your opponents kick off, draw out one of your forwards, who can drop-kick, and station him some fifteen yards behind your own forwards, so that he may frustrate the tactics of a short kick over your forwards' heads, which your opponents hope to reach before your halves or three-quarters can do so.

Select a regular place-kicker and placer. The placing of the ball is quite as important as the kicking. The placer must be acquainted with the kicker's taste with regard to the position of the ball on the ground.

In short kicks, the kicker should not rush at the ball. Two strides and a well-aimed kick are sufficient; in fact, it is often better to stand on one leg and lob the ball over the cross-bar with the other.

Many captains adopt the plan of pulling out a man from the scrummage for the purpose of defence, when the enemy is near the goal-line. This is a very great mistake. Forwards in their own twenty-five are always more or less demoralised. In this predicament you want, above all things, to strengthen your pack. If you weaken it, the enemy comes through pell-mell, and your back players are swamped. Withdrawing a forward is nothing less than detracting from the strength of your essential defence at a critical moment.

Always make your mark from a free catch, no matter how near you may be to your own goal, if your opponents are close upon you, and either take the kick yourself, or employ the best place kicker of your side to send the ball into touch out of danger.

CONVERTING A TRY.

It is better at kick-off or kick-out to kick high rather than long, so as to enable your forwards, by following up fast, either to reach the ball before their adversaries, or to tackle the catcher the moment he receives it.

A. BUDD.

ASSOCIATION FOOTBALL—**The Goalkeeper** is the last defensive resource on a side. By the rules of the Association game he is allowed to use his hands to play the ball anywhere in his own half of the ground. As, however, his duties are purely defensive, he, practically speaking, never uses his hands except in defence of his goal, *i.e.*, to prevent the ball passing between the two upright posts and under the cross-piece. The only case where a goalkeeper can be said to take part in the attack is when the ball has been considerably overkicked towards him by the opposing side; then he runs out, picks up the ball and punts it so as to place it as conveniently as possible for his forwards to carry it on towards the adversaries' goal.

The two chief duties of a goalkeeper are: (1) to prevent the ball passing through the goal; (2) to kick off the ball when it has been sent behind the goal-line by one of the opposing side.

Of these two duties the former is by far the more important; the second is frequently performed by one of the backs. But if the goalkeeper can kick off well, he saves the backs a somewhat tiresome duty and gives them a brief spell of rest which they often need.

In kicking off, low, long kicks are better than those that soar high in the air, because the former come more conveniently to the forwards, and the latter are more easily dealt with by the opposing half-backs and backs. When the wind is blowing against the kick it is essential to "loft" the ball as little as possible. Sometimes, when the wind is very strong, it pays to kick off right along the ground, provided always that one can see a space between the opposing forwards wide enough to allow of the kick travelling well down the ground. Usually, the best kick-off against the wind travels a fair distance without rising more than ten or twelve feet into the air. In order to bring off these difficult kicks, it is necessary to kick the ball as much as possible with the instep, and not with the toe, which should be pointed well down, and to get the body somewhat over the ball. Experiment will suggest the best method. It is probably more difficult to keep a long kick low, if the ball is stationary when kicked, so it sometimes pays for the goalkeeper merely to pass the ball to one of the backs. If this be done, care must be taken that none of the opposing forwards are lying up close to the back. The only occasion on which much is to be gained by this trick is when there is a wind against one, and it is precisely then that the opposing forwards are likely to stay rather near the goal. This method of kicking off should never be adopted except when the back is sure to be able to get the ball easily, and to have plenty of time. A mulled kick-off is dangerous to your charge, and exasperating to the rest of your side. One of the backs should take the kick-off if the goalkeeper is a weak or erratic kick.

It is somewhat difficult to place a long kick, especially when the ball is stationary before being kicked; but one should aim at sending the ball to a forward who is unmarked and in a good position for getting away. It will usually be found that it pays to kick out to the wings rather than towards the centre of the ground. The outside forwards generally have more room than the insides or centre, and it is more difficult for the opposing half-backs and backs to get the ball to their own forwards from the side of the ground.

To defend a space twenty-four feet broad and eight high against every conceivable kind of shot from all directions except from behind is not an easy task. Few can do it with even fair success.

A goalkeeper requires great quickness of eye and hand, and considerable activity and strength. He must be cool and full of resource. And if he is to be really great, he must have the instinct of knowing where the ball is coming.

Various shots have to be stopped in various ways as occasion demands. There are three ways of dealing with a shot successfully: (1) the ball may be *caught* and then got rid of by a throw or punt; (2) it may be *punched* away; (3) it may be *kicked*, the hands not being used.

The first way is by far the safest, and therefore best. Whenever possible, the ball, whether it come high or low, to the right hand, left hand, or straight, should be caught with both hands. When there is time, a long punt towards the side of the ground pays best, because it gains most ground and is likely to go out of the way of the opposing half-backs and backs. When pressed, a goalkeeper should throw, or rather sling, the ball away as far as he can, taking care to send it to the side rather than straight down the field, and to one of his own men. Sometimes a goalkeeper has time to catch the ball, but not to sling it deliberately; indeed, he often can do nothing but pop it over the head of an assailant and trust to some one of his own side getting to it and relieving the pressure. In order to be able to dispose of the ball advantageously on the spur of the moment the goalkeeper should get into the habit of observing exactly where the various players are, so that he can unhesitatingly send the ball where one of his own side is in a good position to receive it.

Some goalkeepers are in the habit of getting rid of the ball in another way. After catching it, they toss it slightly from them and *punch* it away with either an overhand or underhand swing of the hand. They find they can send the ball farther by this method than by throwing. But the throw is much safer. In punching a ball you can never be quite sure where it will go.

The second method of dealing with a shot, *i.e.*, by *punching* it as it comes, without catching it, is exceedingly brilliant, and must often be adopted when there is no time to catch the ball or when it cannot be reached with both hands. There have been very fine goalkeepers who always punched in preference to catching the ball. But for obvious reasons—principally because two hands are better than one—the latter method is by far the safer. It is particularly risky to punch at a slow dropping shot, especially when the wind is causing it to swerve or curl. A goalkeeper who punches at and misses such a shot looks very ridiculous. The only shot that should be punched away is one that cannot by any means be caught with both hands. Of course a punch is a quicker process of getting rid of the ball than a catch and throw, so, when the ball has to be cleared very rapidly for fear of the goalkeeper being rushed through the goal, ball and all, he may be justified in punching. But a clever goalkeeper can nearly always dodge the opposing forwards if he can get the ball fairly into his hands, especially now that it is illegal to impede or charge the goalkeeper before he touches the ball. Before the rule on this point was framed as it is now, the goalkeeper used often to have to wait for a dropping shot with several forwards hustling him; indeed, he was not unfrequently charged through the goal just a fraction of a second before he could reach the ball. Then was often a case of punch or nothing. Now a goalkeeper can take his time with long shots. Be careful never to punch a ball straight into an opponent who is charging you down.

The third method of clearing goal, *i.e.*, by *kicking* the ball without using the hands, should never be adopted unless the shot is so close and so fast and so low that it is impossible to bend down in time to use the hands. A long shot along the ground should always be gathered with both hands, and then punted or slung away. Nothing is more reprehensible in a goalkeeper than taking wild, flying kicks or, indeed, using his feet in any way when he can use his hands. Still, as occasions do arise when a kick is the only means of stopping the ball, a goalkeeper should practise kicking so as to be quick and sure with either foot. A low crossing shot into the corner of the goal may often be turned just outside the post by a deft "spread-eagle" kick.

In picking up a low shot, the best method is to face the direction from which the ball is coming, with the lines of the shoulders and hips *at right angles* to the line of flight of the ball. The feet should be kept close together. The goalkeeper should then stoop with his arms between his opened knees, and should field the ball as in cricket.

In a similar way, when the shot is higher from the ground, the safest method of taking it is facing square with the flight of the ball, so that some part of the body is behind the hands and arms when the ball is caught. Thus, when the shot comes from the side, the goalkeeper should be facing square towards the kicker, and not towards the other goal.

The safest way of dealing with a hard, high shot is to give it a tip up over the bar with both hands. This concedes a corner kick to the other side, but is better than risking a wild punch. However, a tall, active man can catch almost any shot that would go under the bar. A shot that is passing just under the bar can usually be jumped at and caught with safety if it is dropping at the time; but if it is still rising in its flight it is difficult to catch, and is more safely treated by being pushed up over the bar. A goalkeeper who has confidence and skill can punch away many high shots, but there is always the risk of missing the ball or sending it to one of the other side.

There should always be a complete understanding between the goalkeeper and the backs, so that he on his part and they on theirs know exactly what to do and what not to do. It is nearly always best for the goalkeeper to claim and take any long shot that is dropping into the mouth of goal, because he is at liberty to use his hands. When there is a crowd round goal, the backs are often unable to kick without sending the ball against an opponent; but the goalkeeper, if he can get hold of the ball, can throw it away over the heads of the attacking party. Round goal the goalkeeper should, therefore, try to get the backs to play to him and should shout to them decidedly whenever he sees he can deal with the ball.

When the ground is wet, most goalkeepers wear woollen gloves or mittens, in order the better to grasp the greasy ball. These gloves should not be too thick, or they are liable to be an impediment.

A goalkeeper should take care to keep warm when unemployed, as it is impossible to use the limbs with rapidity and certainty if they are chilled. Cold hands will not catch.

It is often very slippery in goal, so it is a mistake to be careless about the knobs or bars on the boots.

The Backs—The general practice nowadays is to have two backs, whose sphere of action is in front of the goalkeeper and behind the half-backs. But there is no rule to prescribe any particular arrangement of the eleven men on a side—except that only one goalkeeper is allowed. Sometimes, when a side is a goal or two ahead, and it is thought advisable to play a purely defensive game, a third back is added by diminishing the number of forwards. Experience, however, has proved that the division of the side into two backs, three half-backs, and five forwards works best. In the old days it was customary to have only one back; but this arrangement was found faulty, as one back could not cope with judicious passing or combined rushes. The only advantage gained by having only a single back is that the opposite forwards are liable to be off-side very frequently, unless they meet the circumstances by long passing across the ground, the receiving forward always taking care to be behind the passer at the moment the ball is kicked. These tactics would soon suggest themselves to anyone with a knowledge of Football. So, on the whole, there is not much to be said for the single back.

With regard to the shift of withdrawing a forward and putting an extra back, there is this much to be said: that three backs are extremely hard to get through. As a matter of fact, when a forward is withdrawn, he is generally put half-back and one of the half-backs put back. But unless the players thus moved are versatile and capable of performing satisfactorily the duties of their altered positions, it is a question whether the change really strengthens the defence. For by withdrawing a forward one of the opposing backs or half-backs is left comparatively free and unmarked, at liberty to do much more attacking work. The normal arrangement of a side seems the most telling and reliable. It is certainly unwise to play a third back, unless the extra man is a capable player in that position.

The best *type of man* for a back is a combination of weight, strength and activity. Very big, heavy men are liable to be rather too slow and clumsy, very small men to be too light and impressionable. A strong man rather above middle height, and fairly heavy, usually turns out the most serviceable. At the same time it must be confessed that a heavy, clumsy, slow man

THE FULL BACK.

does less harm at back than in any other position, and can use what powers he has to better advantage. There have been some very useful heavy backs who have been neither fast nor clever. Weight is certainly very telling at back, especially near goal. A light man is liable to be too easily brushed aside and hustled off the ball; but there have been players of very small stature who have been splendid backs, making up for their lack of weight by extraordinary nimbleness and activity. A light man who is neither fast nor clever had better be put anywhere else rather than back, for he does nothing much by his presence but keep the opposing forwards on-side.

The two essential and fundamental qualities in a back are—(1) sure, determined *tackling*; (2) sure, strong *kicking*.

A back has to *tackle* well in order to deprive the opposing forwards of the ball, and to *kick* well in order to transfer it from his own to the enemy's territory.

It is not easy to explain what tackling is, or to give instructions how to tackle successfully. Perhaps tackling may be roughly described as stopping an opponent who has possession of the ball and dispossessing him of it. Almost every player has his own particular way of tackling. But there are broadly speaking two methods which may be distinguished from one another.

In tackling the man with the ball you may (1) pay most attention to *the man;* charge or hustle him aside, and meanwhile, or just afterwards, secure the ball; practically you force the man off the ball, and then deal with it. Or (2) you may pay most attention to *the ball;* trusting to strength and cleverness of foot and leg to secure the ball without using the weight of your body against your opponent. Either you plant your foot firmly on one side of the ball and trust to being able to keep it so until the possessor staggers or overruns the ball, or you hook the ball away from his foot by a dexterous dive with your own.

The weakness in the first method is that you are liable to muddle the ball and fail to have it under your control even after dispossessing your adversary, and it may easily be secured by another man who is following up close behind, or beside the man with the ball. On the other hand, unless you bungle or are evaded, you at any rate stop the man for the time being, even if the ball is secured by one of his comrades; and you are probably in a position to prevent a pass back to him. In other words you put one man out of action temporarily.

The objection to the second method is that it is very difficult to get the foot so well planted beside the ball that your leg is not pushed away by your opponent's weight or impetus. On the other hand, if you do secure the ball thus, it is absolutely under your control.

Generally speaking, when your opponent is trying to rush through, or is dribbling fast, the first method is the better of the two. If he is going fast, he has less power to dodge, so you can generally block him with your body. Also, he is liable by his impetus to drive through a mere impeding leg.

But the second method is the better for stopping a deliberate, tricky piece of dribbling, because your opponent, not having much pace on, is not so likely to push your foot aside; and because, in meeting him thus, you need not make a dash or rush at him, which he can readily avoid, as at the pace he is going he can easily dodge to either side.

These are alternative methods of tackling, and most players are in the habit of using either one or the other exclusively. But there is a third method, which for general purposes is the best. It consists of a *combination* of the two above mentioned. Without distinctly charging your opponent you may contrive to put enough of your weight against him to stop or seriously impede him, preserving at the same time sufficient control over your own balance and movements to be able to use your legs and feet for extricating the ball from his possession. The difficulty is to apply sufficient weight to stop the man without losing the balance, which it is necessary to preserve in order to use the legs with firmness and accuracy. But the method is worth acquiring, because it is free from the drawbacks of pure charging and pure leg tackling. It does not entail a heavy rush which, if avoided by your opponent, carries you out of action for some, perhaps fatal, seconds: neither is it liable to be weak and ineffectual through your opponent's impetus. It is not only a pliable and versatile, but a strong and sufficiently forcible method.

The secrets of good tackling, by whatever method, are—(1) to *time* your tackle well; that is, to make your attempt to get the ball exactly at the right moment; (2) when you do make your effort, to make it with all *determination*, as if the whole match depended on your getting the ball. The great point, of course, is never to miss your tackle. Apart from this, the criterion of good tackling is whether, after failing in your attempt, you are able to renew it without any appreciable delay.

If the art of tackling is hard to explain on paper, that of *kicking* is even more so. It has already been said that strong, sound kicking is essential in a back. Certainly a weak, erratic, unsafe kick cannot be entrusted with the responsibility of defence.

There is little doubt that an Association ball should be kicked *not* with the point of the toe, but with the *instep*. When the ball is stationary, the instep cannot be applied to the ball, but the part of the foot between the instep and the toes can. In order to get force into a kick the leg should swing clean and free, and should follow through after the ball. The body should be so poised that the weight is brought to bear upon the ball much as it is in making a drive at cricket.

SAVED FROM TOUCH.

It is necessary to learn to kick in whatever position you may be, and however the ball happens to come to you. Sometimes the ball is on the ground, sometimes in the air, sometimes bouncing about. When the ball is kicked before it reaches the ground it is said to be volleyed. The *volley* is rather a difficult kick, and requires considerable practice. Some backs stand still to volley, and kick with a bent leg when the ball is about hip-high. Others run at the ball and kick it when it is about a foot off the ground, with a straight leg. The former method favours accuracy, the latter power. One of the secrets of safe back play is to make every kick as easy as possible, by always getting into the most suitable position in good time. In order to do this the attention must be kept closely upon the ball. Often a back has to kick in a hurry and as best he can, but the thing to aim at is to make each kick as easy as possible.

The ball is said to be *half-volleyed* when kicked the moment it touches the ground, or a fraction of a second afterwards. It is a brilliant, powerful kick when well-timed, but it is somewhat unsafe to attempt because, if mistimed, a "foozled" weak kick results. If you can, by all means use the half-volley; but remember that the volley is easier and surer than the half-volley, and the ordinary ground kick than either.

Often the best and safest way of dealing with the ball is to *head* it away. Instead of volleying the ball, the player receives it on the top of his head just above the forehead, where the skull is very thick, and makes it bounce forward. Impetus is given to the ball, partly by its own elasticity, and partly by force imparted by a movement of the neck, and sometimes by a semi-jump up towards the ball as it descends. Some players can head the ball an enormous distance. The art of heading is well worth cultivating. The difficulty is to meet the ball with the right part of the head.

For practice in kicking and heading, nothing is better than what is usually called a "punt-about." That is, three or four or more players go to a ground and kick the ball about to one another, taking it as it comes.

Combination—First of all, it is necessary to recognise that there is an attacking as well as a defensive side to back play. That is to say, a back should, as far as he can, help his side to get goals. His first duty is of course to defend his own goal, and that he must never forget. But it is a mistake for him to regard this as all that is expected of him. The way in which he can aid his side in attacking is by passing to, or, as it is called, feeding his forwards. Obviously huge lofty kicks are no good for this purpose. It is very common to see backs kicking as high and hard as ever they can on every possible occasion, but this is bad play. Low kicks of moderate length are the best. When there is room and time, a kick right along the ground is the best of all. Indeed, a back should regard accurate passing as no less necessary on his part than on that of a forward. A back should never kick without thinking where the ball is going. By continually trying to put the ball where desired, the power of placing may be gradually obtained.

It is most important to recognise the value of feeding the forwards. But it is even more important not to make the mistake of sacrificing soundness of defence in any way whatever. When a back is in difficulties, or is hard pressed near his own goal, he must kick as strongly and as quickly as he can. He must clear at all costs. Defence is the first point; then comes attack—in back-play.

Avoid, on the one hand, weak kicking and hesitation near your own goal, and, on the other, wild thoughtless kicking when you have the ball free somewhere down the field. Kick out to the wings when near your own goal; try to feed the centre and inside forwards when in your opponent's territory. Defend at all costs, but whenever possible feed your forwards. A back should never dribble—it serves no good purpose, and is sure to get him away from his proper place.

Combination in defence consists in playing, not alone, but together with the half-backs, the other back, and the goalkeeper. The backs and half-backs should one and all be in touch with one another. They should help one another in every possible way, and each one should allow himself to be helped. When one man is tackling, another should be ready to intercept the adversary's pass; when one man is kicking, another should try to keep him from being charged. Theoretically, each back and half-back should mark one of the five opposing forwards, but, as the game chops and changes almost every moment, no rigid, cut-and-dried system is much use. Near their own goal the backs should mark the two inside forwards. When half-way down the ground, they usually attend to the two outsides. They should never be so far from the half-backs as to be out of touch with them, nor so near up to them that the opposing side can over-kick with impunity.

In combining with one another, the backs should aim at mutual help. When one is rather forward, the other should be rather behind him. Sometimes it pays for one back to pass to the other, but a back should never pass when there is the least danger of the ball being intercepted.

Near goal, the backs should give the goalkeeper plenty of room, and, as far as possible, follow his directions. They should keep opponents from charging or hampering him. They should play to him; that is, give him every chance of getting the ball whenever he wants it.

The half-backs are the most important part of an Association side. They are the nucleus of the whole combination both for defence and attack. No matter how good the backs and forwards, a side cannot play a strong game if the half-backs are weak. In fact, one bad half-back is enough to handicap the other ten players considerably.

The old idea was that a side was divided into two parts: one, consisting of the goalkeeper, the backs, and the half-backs, for defence; the other, consisting of the forwards, for attack. That the backs, though their work is mainly defensive, share somewhat in the attack has been shown. Now the half-backs' work is neither purely defensive nor purely aggressive, but both in an equal degree. When the opponents are attacking, the half-backs must, equally with the backs, be defending, and, when their own side are attacking, they must help in the attack equally with the forwards. Near their own goal they are to all intents backs, near their adversaries' goal they are practically forwards. So a half-back has no rest. He is on the move and in the thick of the fight all the game through.

A half-back should be able to *tackle* as strongly and surely as a back, and kick nearly as hard and far: and at the same time should be able to *dribble* as skilfully and pass as accurately as a forward. He must have quickness and activity, is all the better with a turn of sheer speed, and certainly should be able to "head" the ball with certainty and effect. In addition, he should be a good shot at goal.

Three half-backs are played nowadays, except when such alteration as that described under "Backs" is made. They are called respectively the right, centre, and left half-back. The right and left half-backs have similar duties. The centre has to work in a way accommodated to his position, as the pivot upon which the whole side works.

The duties of the three half-backs may be summarised thus—(1) to defend like extra backs; (2) to attack like extra forwards; (3) to combine these two duties and accommodate their fulfilment to the varying circumstances of the game.

With regard to the *defensive part* of half-back play, when it is said that half-backs should defend like extra backs, it must not be forgotten that the circumstances wherein a half-back is called upon to act precisely as a back, do not occur frequently, and sometimes never during an entire game. A half-back is generally in an intermediate position, *i.e.*, he is generally half as near again to his forwards as is a back, and also, except in rare cases, he is not the last defensive resource between the opposing forwards and the goalkeeper, since the backs are behind him. Consequently, he is rarely called upon to make a very long kick or to clear as best he can without reference to where the ball goes; but sometimes the ball is taken into such a position that one of the backs has to leave the mouth of the goal and run out to the sides of the ground, and the nearest half-back has then to take up the vacated place. He is for the time being a back and must act as such and must be able to kick hard and far. Sure tackling is just as important in a half-back as in a back. There is a slight difference between the bulk of half-back and back tackling, due to the fact that the half-back, being nearer to the opposing forwards, can usually get at the man with the ball almost immediately, and before the man has got really

ROBBED OF THE BALL.

started. So the charging method of tackling is less, and leg-tackling more, needed in half-back play.

Directly an opponent gets the ball, a half-back must be upon him at once, so as either to tackle him or cause him to pass. If he tackles him and gets the ball, he should proceed to dispose of it to advantage. If he causes him to pass, the back may be able to intercept the ball. If he fails to tackle the man or cause him to pass, *i.e.*, misses him altogether, he must turn and be after him again with the least possible delay. It will be seen that rushing, headlong tactics are not suited for half-back tackling. It should be of the quick, clever, worrying order.

A half-back should be on the look out for *intercepting* passes, whether from the opposing backs, half-backs, or other forwards to the forwards or forward whom it is his place to watch. In order to do this, he must watch closely what the back, half-back, or other forward is doing, and must take steps to be in such a position that he can readily intercept the ball. But he must not get much out of his place, that is, he must be within easy reach of the forwards he ought to be watching, and in touch with the back behind him. If he gets out of his place, the ball may be kicked over his head by an opponent, and the back left to deal with two men, both unhampered.

The usual plan of defence is this. The centre half-back watches and deals with the opposing centre forward. The right back and the right half-back look after the opposing left wing forwards, the left back and left half-back attend to the opposing right wing forwards.

It is impossible to work out any hard and fast lines upon which half-backs should act. The usual plan is for the right half-back to work together with the right back in dealing with the opposing wing forwards, somewhat as follows. Provisionally the back watches the inside, and the half-back the outside forward, anywhere near the goal they are defending; down the field, the back takes the outside and the half-back the inside man. The reason for this is that near goal the back should be in the centre of the ground in order to block the mouth of goal as much as possible, and because the inside forward then is naturally nearer to him than the outside. Whereas, down the field, the outside forward is usually well in front of the inside and consequently nearer the back.

As a matter of practice, the best rule is for the half-back to go at once for the man who has the ball, and for the back to try to intercept the pass. Otherwise the back or half-back may go for the man with the ball, according to which of them is nearest to him. Convenience and expediency must be consulted and judgment used. But hesitation should at all costs be avoided.

The *left back* and *half-back* deal with the opposing right wing on similar lines.

Meanwhile the *centre half-back* is watching the opposing centre forward. He must do his best to prevent the centre forward from receiving a pass from either wing or from any of his comrades. Supposing the centre forward does get the ball, the centre half-back should go for him at once to tackle him. If he is successful, he disposes of the ball to the best advantage. If he misses his tackle, he must turn and be after the man with the ball at once. If, however, the ball is passed to the right or left wing by the centre forward, either the back or half-back should have intercepted the pass or be dealing with the man who received it. The centre half must in any case stick to the opposing centre forward, and hamper him as much as possible. Of course it frequently happens that the centre half-back is compelled by circumstances to tackle one of the inside forwards: in which case one of the wing half-backs has to deal with the unmarked centre forward as well as the other inside wing forward. The main idea is to prevent, as far as possible, combination between the opposing forwards. Each of the defenders looks after one of them, at the same time keeping within his own sphere. One essential point, with regard to the combination between backs and half-backs, is that the latter should subordinate their play entirely to that of the former. When it is a question as to which of the two should kick the ball and which take the man running for it, the proper thing is for the half-back to keep the opponent off and leave the back to deal with the ball. In other words, the half-backs should aim at providing the backs with freedom of action. The best half-backs are always entirely unselfish.

With regard to half-back play in the *attack*, whenever a half-back has possession of the ball, his duties may be said to be those of an extra forward. The only exception is when he is for the time being compelled to act as a back. Even near his own goal he rarely has occasion to kick blindly: there is generally a forward to whom he may with advantage send the ball.

In order to be successful in attacking, a half-back must be able (1) to *feed* his forwards; (2) to *dribble*; (3) to *shoot.*

Of these three qualifications the first is by far the most important. In fact it is, on the whole, the most important point in half-back play.

When a half-back has possession of the ball, and has not to kick in a hurry, he should take immediate note of the positions of his own forwards and his opponents', and proceed to pass the ball to that forward who is in the best position to receive. Sometimes the half-back is so placed that he cannot get the ball to the forwards without kicking in the air. But, whenever possible, he should pass along the ground precisely as one forward should to another. When he kicks in the air, he had better send the ball out to the wings, and, in any case, try to drop the ball just enough in front of his forwards for them to be able to get it before the opposing backs are upon them. In passing along the ground he should also aim at putting the ball rather in front of the forward, so that the latter can take the ball without having to stop still at all. When a forward has to wait for the ball to come to him there is more time for the opposing defenders to get at him. The usual practice is for the right half-back to feed the right wing, the left half the left wing, and the centre-half the centre-forward or one of the inside-forwards. But it often pays to send the ball right across the ground from left to right or *vice-versâ*. Certainly the centre half may often with great advantage send the ball to one of the outside-forwards. The half-back should particularly avoid so passing that the ball can be intercepted; he had better stick to the ball than send it to one of his opponents. A wild kick is better, on the whole, than a weak pass.

In order to learn how to pass, a half-back cannot do better than play forward occasionally in practice games. This will teach him not only how to pass cleverly, but what kind of passes from half-backs are easy for forwards to take. It is noticeable that forwards who take to half-back instead usually prove very skilful at passing. Converted backs are almost always inclined to kick needlessly hard.

The duty of *throwing-in* when the ball has gone over the touch-line falls to the lot of the

A THROW-IN.

two wing half-backs. As the rule is now framed, the player who throws in must do so with both hands on the ball and both feet upon the touch-line. The penalty for infringing the rule is a free kick to the other side.

It is usual for the wing half-back upon whose side it is to take the *corner-kick.* The ball must be placed a yard from the corner-flag. The best kick is one dropping from a fair height into the mouth of goal. It is a mistake to try to place the ball too near goal, as in nine cases out of ten such attempts end in the ball falling behind the goal-line. The outside forward sometimes takes the corner-kick.

It sometimes pays for a half-back to *dribble* the ball a few yards, either to make ground, or to draw one of the opposing half-backs away from watching a forward. But it is a mistake for a half-back to get far out of his place, as the ball may be returned at once to the gap his absence leaves. And it is very undesirable for a half-back to lose the ball to an opponent instead of passing it on to his forwards. A selfish half-back is an abomination, but, as a short dribble occasionally is very useful, all half-backs should learn the art of dribbling.

Half-backs should be good *shots at goal,* for they frequently have chances of scoring. It is often telling for a half-back to put in a high dropping shot or a long hard one into the corner of the goal. The centre half-back should certainly be a good shot, as he often gets a good opening when the ball comes out of a general muddle in the mouth of goal. As a rule, half-backs do not try shots nearly often enough. It is a mistake not to shoot when there is a fair chance of scoring.

The Forwards are the five players whose chief concern is to carry the ball down the field and put it through their opponents' goal. As an Association side is arranged nowadays, the five forwards are allotted places thus: the centre-forward is in the middle of the other four; the two on each side of him form the wings; one of the wing forwards plays outside, *i.e.*, near the touch-line; the other inside, *i.e.*, between the outside-forward and the centre-forward. Formerly six forwards were played, but the present system is better, because there is not room enough for more than five to work with full effect.

A forward should be a fast runner, a quick starter, and clever with his feet. Some who on a running track are comparatively slow seem to move quite rapidly on the football field. Sheer sprinting power is extremely useful in a forward, but quickness in starting and ability to dodge are even more valuable. Very few can sprint at full speed and control the ball at the same time, but the control is essential.

There have been first-rate forwards of almost every build. Before fair charging was, by a consensus of opinion among referees, turned into a punishable offence, weight sometimes stood a forward in good stead. As it is, a big forward is better than a small one, other things being equal: for the former can push his way through a scrummage with greater ease, and is less liable to be hustled off the ball. In a really hard-fought game, size and weight tell considerably; but small men seem to be the most effective when the ground is heavy with mud. Generally speaking, heavy men are most suited to be inside- and centre-forwards; light ones to be outsides.

The work a forward has to do requires him to be able (1) to *pass*; (2) to *dribble*; (3) to *shoot*.

The art of **passing** has been brought to mechanical perfection by the various professional teams. The theory of passing is that the forward who has the ball should, when in danger of being tackled, send it on to another who is for the time being unhampered. So it will be seen that a good pass depends upon the co-operation of two players. The one must get into a convenient position to receive the ball; the other must send it on to him accurately and conveniently. The former part of the co-operative process is often neglected, especially by beginners. That the effectiveness of a pass depends just as much upon the receiver as upon the kicker is, however, self-evident. It is useless to pass to a player who is not able to take the ball. One of the first points to grasp is that there is no merit or value in getting rid of the ball aimlessly. If the ball is sent to one of the opposing side, or even kicked so that an opponent has as good a chance of getting it as one of your own side, not much is gained.

Another point worth remembering is that the object of forward play, and of passing as part thereof, is to get the ball down the ground towards the adversaries' goal. Nothing but goals score in Association, so obtaining goals should be made the ultimate and only aim in forward play. It is quite useless for a set of forwards to play a clever passing game in the middle of the field if no progress is made towards goal. The best kind of pass is one which makes most ground towards goal; hence it pays to pass "through" and as much in front of you as possible. To pass sideways clearly gains less ground. The direction of a pass must depend upon where the prospective receiver is, and he ought to be as far forward as he can without getting out of touch with the passer, or infringing the off-side rule.

Again, it is not advisable to pass straight to where the receiving forward is, but a yard or two in front of him, in order that he may be able to take the ball on without stopping in his stride. Pass to where the man will be, and not to where he is. If the receiver has to stop he loses time and pace, and is likely to be tackled by an opponent before he can get started again. A pass which causes the receiver to face his own goal, or even go back a few feet to get the ball, is a bad one.

Sometimes it is necessary to pass back to a forward behind you; but this should never be done unless there is no way of getting rid of the ball to advantage in a forward direction. A few yards, it is true, do not make the difference in Association that they do in Rugby; still it is always advisable to make ground rather than lose it.

The forward with the ball should endeavour to draw one of his opponents on to him before passing, just as a three-quarter does in the Rugby game. When there is no danger of being tackled, the ball should be kept and not passed, unless there is some obvious advantage to be gained. The whole merit of a pass consists in its being well-timed and advancing matters; needless "piffling" passing is unprofitable. When drawing an opponent, care must be taken to get rid of the ball just in time; there need be no danger of losing the ball if the manœuvre is skilfully executed.

Most good forwards, in passing, kick the ball with the inside of the right foot when sending it to the left or in front, and with the outside of it when sending it to the right, and *vice versa* with the left foot.

Sometimes a short pass of a few yards, sometimes a long one right across the field, is suitable. The former game is liable to degenerate into mechanical "piffling" if carried too far, the latter into mere kick-and-rush. A side's passing should be versatile: both short and long passes should be used. Experience has proved that the short passing game can be broken up by a determined defence. For weak short passing nothing can be said. In exciting matches played at high pressure, long passing with plenty of individual dash seems to pay best. In ordinary club matches the "short" game is often successful, but, being mechanical, is not so well suited for cup-ties and such like.

For the very reason that passing can be carried to excess, the old art of **dribbling** must not be neglected by forwards, for, though combination is the foundation of a good forward

A Forward Dribbling.

game, an occasional individual effort is often very telling. In any case, when a man has the ball to himself and plenty of room in front of him, he should, in order to make ground as quickly as possible, be able to dribble. There is not much that can be said about dribbling. The great point is to go as fast as possible without losing control over the ball. A forward may be a good dribbler, and dribble often, and yet not be in any sense of the word a selfish player. The point is that a forward should pass the ball when a pass is required, and run with it himself when there is a proper opening for individual effort.

To be a good **shot at goal** is a great recommendation in a forward, and every forward should try to master the art of shooting. Many goals are got by combination and a shot that is merely a touch with the foot. But against a strong defence often the only chance of scoring is by smart, clever shooting. It is comparatively easy to shoot accurately in practice, but in a game, when you are being charged by a back or are in a difficult position, it is quite the reverse. Time after time one sees a side which can get the ball down to the goal, but cannot shoot. Such a side is often beaten by one which it outplays everywhere except in front of goal. Dash and determination at the last moment are requisite for goal-getting. It is no use passing and repassing in front of goal; such proceedings waste time, and allow the defenders to concentrate and pack the goal. Forwards should not shoot wildly and recklessly, but neither should they dally nor throw away fair opportunities. It is sound policy to shoot whenever there is a good chance of scoring, and certainly in this case *bis dat qui cito dat.* Low hard shots are the most effective; but the point is to get the ball through, no matter by what means. The more attention forwards give to practising shooting the better; good shooting wins, bad shooting loses matches. Of course it is more important for the centre and two insides than for the outsides to be able to shoot.

Forwards are all the better for being able to head the ball well; heading is especially useful for scoring goals from corner kicks. Some of the professionals can pass the ball almost as accurately with their heads as with their feet.

The **centre-forward** is the pivot on which the forward line works; his chief duty is to keep the other forwards together and feed them well. Sometimes he should pass right out to the outsides, sometimes keep the ball between himself and the insides. He should be able to pass accurately with either foot. In his own half he should aim at getting the ball to the outsides; nearer the opponents' goal he should keep it in the middle. He should be a good shot.

The two **inside-forwards** are the connecting links between the centre and the outsides. They should feed their outsides well and give them as many chances as possible of getting well away. After passing out they should get forward as fast as possible in order to be in a good position for receiving the ball back again.

The two **outside-forwards** should be fast runners, as they have frequent opportunities of getting away with the ball. But they should be ready, when necessary, to pass back to their inside men; they should send the ball across into the centre in good time. It is a mistake for an outside to run the ball too far down the ground before middling it. Long passes from wing to wing are very telling. Outside men should not attempt to shoot too often; it pays better to send the ball into the middle, for the centre- or inside-forwards to deal with it in front of goal. Usually the outsides should be rather in front of the other forwards, but they should avoid loafing and off-side tactics.

C. B. Fry.

AMERICAN FOOTBALL—The first mention of football in America refers to a time when, in New England, many years ago, unnumbered sides formed, and struggled for possession of an inflated bladder, much as in the earliest records of the English game; only, so far as we can learn, the first American football was more of a kicking game, whereas the very first English was more of a carrying or Rugby game. There were no rules, of course, except those of mere local application, and all disputes were settled on the field. Crude as it was, this game was taken up by schoolboys, and naturally found its way into the colleges. Yale University has the first authentic record of football in an annual Freshman-Sophomore match, which became an institution in 1840. The challenges and acceptances of these matches were publicly posted on the doors of Old Chapel. The game was by no means scientific, in fact it was a mere rough and tumble, and the ball was a round bladder in a leather case. These annual football scrambles were continued until 1858–59, when they were stopped by the order of the Faculty, and replaced by the annual rushes between the classes, which, after all, differed but little from the game as it had been played, except in the absence of a ball. These rushes were not governed by rules, but they were the means of suggesting later organisation. From 1859 until 1870 football was neglected in the United States; but with 1870 began an awakening which finally resulted, in 1873, in a convention, held in New York by Columbia, Princeton, Rutgers and Yale Universities, at which a set of rules was adopted, and the foundation laid for the intercollegiate matches. In 1872 Columbia played a match with Yale; there were twenty men on a side and the game was a species of Association. The men wore long trousers and jerseys. The few rules they had were very simple, and forbade anyone picking up, carrying or throwing the ball. There were no on-side and off-side rules, and goals were made by sending the ball under rather than over the cross bar. Fouls were penalised by compelling the erring player to throw the ball straight up in the air from the place where the foul was committed, and it was regarded unfair to touch the ball on its descent until it struck the ground. This rule developed some clever drop-kicking; the men practising kicking the ball just as it touched the ground. When a man was disabled and retired from the game, his place was not taken by a substitute, but conditions were evened by the other side dropping off a man.

In the year of the Convention, 1873, Yale played a game with eleven Englishmen, captained by an Eton boy named Allen, and beat them two goals to one. At about this time, 1874, Harvard had been playing matches with Canadian teams under the Rugby Union rules; Harvard and Yale had not met. In 1875 Harvard and Yale had a conference which resulted in an agreement for games to be played under compromise rules of the then existing American college game and the Rugby Union. The first Harvard-Yale game, in 1876, recorded the defeat of Yale by 4 goals and 2 touchdowns to nothing, and the result of the contest was a complete dissatisfaction with the compromise rules. This led to the adoption of the regular Rugby Union rules, and thence, from the Rugby Union of 1875, comes the American game.

With the adoption of the Rugby Union rules, there came an end to "shouldering"—a method pursued to put a man "off the ball,"—and hitting or batting the ball with the fist. In this latter practice, some men had grown so skilled that they could bat the ball almost as far as it is now kicked. The ball used at that time was the round black rubber one, and the system of play included a great deal of "babying" of the ball with the hand; this "babying" corresponded to the dribbling of the Association game, which early American players seemed unable to acquire to a very skilful degree.

When the Rugby Union rules were first adopted, American teams were made up of eleven men; subsequently they were increased to fifteen, continued at that number for several years, and finally changed back to eleven, at which number they have remained. When the sport was first introduced into America, the players were called "forwards," "half-backs" and "goal tends," and it was some time before the men received the specific titles by which they are at present known. One of the first to be particularly designated was the man who put down the ball in a scrimmage, namely, the "centre rush," or "snap-back." After the first game between Harvard and Yale in 1876, immediate effort was made to revise the rules to meet American ideas of the needs of American players. One of the features of the American game—perhaps the most distinctive one—is, and has always been since we first began rule revising, the outlet of the scrimmage. In the Rugby Union game, as it came to us, the man who chanced to have the ball when the down was made was the one to place it on the ground in the new line-up. Very little experience convinced Americans that some men were better calculated to put the ball in play than others, and so before long this play was given to one man, forthwith called the "snap-back." In English Rugby the ball may be rolled out by any man, and at no stated opening; in American Rugby one man has entire control of its coming and does not put it in play until signalled to do so by the quarter-back. In the English game the ball comes out in haphazard fashion, reaches the runner's hands, and off he goes with no especially preconceived plan of play. In the American game one man, the "snap-back," puts the ball in play; one man, the "quarter-back," gives the signal for putting it in play; the same man invariably receives it and gives it to the runner, and when the ball reaches the runner, the latter is only a part of a pre-arranged play in which the entire team performs a rehearsed and elaborate part. In an American game the ball never goes into play except by signal, and each play is the result of much theoretical study and long and careful practice. The American game is entirely strategic, and each season reveals new plays, the successful execution of which has taken weeks of preliminary work on the chess board as well as on the playing field. Originally the American game employed the English "scrum," but we shortly found it advantageous to let the other side do the kicking out of the ball; our side leaving an opening at the proper moment through which the ball could escape. This suggested one man behind the line (afterwards the quarter-back), whose business it would always be to receive the ball from the "scrum" and pass it to the backs. When the advantage derived from letting the other side in the "scrum" do the kicking became apparent, the rushers began rolling the ball sideways along between the two lines. Then we discovered that a man could snap the ball back with his toe, and hence started the first two divergencies from English play,—namely, the same man always to snap the ball out of the scrum and the same man always to receive it.

The next development was in specialising the work of the rushers. The centre rush or snap back was at first a light man, chosen for his activity, but it became apparent that heavy men were needed where the fight raged around the ball; hence, he became heavier. The next men who received attention were the end rushers. As the American game developed, it was discovered that the men on the end of the line had opportunities to make runs and free catches off short kicks; and so these positions became among the most important on the line. The next of the men named were the guards, who stood to the left and the right of the centre and protected the quarter-back when he passed the ball. The next two men on the line were called tackles, because more than to any other of the rushers it fell to them to get into and break up plays of the opponents.

With the designation of the players, which gave them specific duties, and the return to teams of eleven men, the American game may be said to have become fully established. In 1882, a system of play by which an inferior team was able to escape defeat through getting and keeping possession of the ball (making only a pretence of play), had become known as the "block system," and was so menacing to the interest of the game that the "five yard rule" was introduced. This is the rule that declares a side must advance the ball five, or retreat with it ten yards in three downs; a down being the end of each play, *i.e.*, when a runner is tackled and held. Ten yards has been increased of late years to twenty—otherwise the rule remains.

At first the attack was weak, and the question of how to protect the goal resulted in sending too many men up into the line. Gradually, however, experience taught us that the best defence was not to wait until a man got a good start for a goal, but to keep him, if possible, from getting free of the forward line,—in other words, to tackle the runner behind his line and not wait for him to get through it before tackling him. The tendency has been, therefore, in very recent years to lessen the number of men behind the line, and increase the number in the line, in order to crush the play of opponents before it is fairly started. This in its turn created the American interference. The more effort made to crush a play in its incipiency, the greater the effort to protect the runner: hence interference, which, in its American elaboration, is offside to English eyes. Interference, in a word, is protection of a runner, best assured by men going before him to tackle and get the opposing players out of the way. Interference did not spring full-fledged into the American game; it came by degrees. Once established, however, the query was immediately raised of how much aid the interferers could give the runner. At first the use of hands was permitted, but it was finally determined that the runner could be aided to any extent provided hands and arms were not used. The ultra-development of interference created in turn momentum and mass plays, which consisted of grouping a body of men some distance back of the line, and starting the mass before the ball was put in play, so that by the time it reached the line and the ball had been passed, the group had of course acquired great impetus, for the opponents were unable to go forward to meet it for fear of getting off-side. The momentum thus gained was almost impossible to check. This of course resulted in similar momentum tactics on the part of the defence, which for a couple of years—1893 and 1894—made brute strength a very objectionable feature of American football.

In 1895 began legislation against momentum, mass and push plays, and the undue development of interference. This has resulted in several football congresses of American experts under the auspices of the University Athletic Club of New York, with the result that some stringent and wholesome legislation has been passed against momentum and mass plays. The same Rules Committee of this Club made provision for the greater protection of a man on a fair catch, and for the encouragement of kicking and a more open game generally.

The history of American University football is the history of American football. It has always been said that baseball is the national game of the United States, and undoubtedly such is the case; but football has grown so enormously in popularity in the last ten years that it would be an interesting computation to cast up the number of men playing the newer game in America. It is safe to say, that practically every school large enough to support any form of athletics, every college, every university in this country has one or more football elevens, besides which a large majority of the athletic clubs and many other clubs devoted to sport of one kind or another have an annual football schedule. These all play the Americanised Rugby Union. During the last three years there have been spasmodic attempts to introduce Association football into parts of New England, especially in Massachusetts, where the mills furnish many young men who are eager for some kind of outdoor sport which does not demand the training of the Rugby game. One organization was perfected; but, although one occasionally sees incidental mention of it, Association has no place in American football, and the number of men who play it is comparatively insignificant.

Diagram of the American Rugby football field with arrangement of players. This shows the ordinary formation on the offensive. On the defensive the formation is more open, and the full-back near his goal:

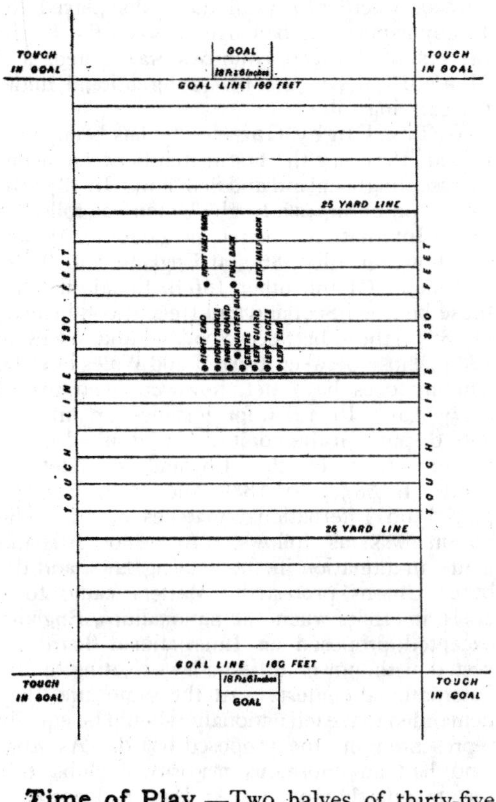

Time of Play.—Two halves of thirty-five minutes each, with ten minutes intermission.

A down.—The term used to indicate the number of attempts made to advance the ball. Each side has three tries in which to advance the ball five yards. The end of each try, *i.e.*, when the ball is held by the opposing side, is a down. As soon as the five yards have been gained it is first down again.

Officials.—One referee, who judges the position and the progress of the ball. One umpire, who judges the conduct of the players. Two linesmen, who mark the distance gained and lost, and are aids to the umpire.

CASPAR WHITNEY.

(AN ENGLISH VIEW OF THE AMERICAN GAME.)

When the history of the English game emerges from its somewhat nebulous and plebeian origins in the fourteenth century, which have great affinities to the primitive lacrosse, it may be traced at Rugby in the form which provided a nucleus for the play of the early Blackheath teams. But it was as late as 1849 before our Universities took it up, and it was not until 1873 that the first Oxford and Cambridge match was played. The dates are very similar in its history across the Atlantic. Football is known to have existed at Yale in 1840, but it was not till 1874 that that University beat Princeton, Columbia, and Rutgers; and not until 1876 that matches between Harvard, Yale, and Princeton are recorded, just five years after the formation of our own Rugby Union, and contemporaneously with the first International match in which, at the suggestion of Scotland, our sides were reduced to fifteen men. To increase the pace of the game, the Americans reduced the number on each side still further, to eleven; but there imitation of the Association rules came to an end.

The difficult question of what really constituted being "off-side" had soon been fairly settled by the early fifteens at our Universities, to whom omissions in the letter of their law mattered little in comparison with its accepted spirit. But as soon as the game was tried in the United States, it appeared that being "off-side," that is, playing ahead of the ball, was inevitable with all American teams. The illegality was not merely so often practised, but was also so difficult to detect that the authorities were obliged to legalise it. To the resulting invention of the "snap-back," with all that follows from it, are due most of the distinguishing characteristics of American football. This player stands in front of the "scrummage," holding the ball on the ground between his feet, and before "snapping" it back to his men he shouts a series of numbers (such as "39, 41, 26, 7"), which give the key to the evolutions that his own side are to make, as much to deceive the enemy as to benefit themselves. This system of "signals" is very carefully practised in the greatest secrecy, generally behind a high palisade, so that no hostile eye may watch the evolutions to be used in the coming battle.

The sense in which the word "scrummage" has just been used will be misleading to an English player, for by the reduction of the team, from fifteen to eleven, the original shoving mass of forwards has almost disappeared in American play. Attention has been concentrated on what is known as the "rush line." The arrangement of the men is almost entirely different; the snap-back (who is also called the "centre-rusher") has only the quarter-back, and the full-back directly behind him. The two half-backs are a little behind the quarter on each side. To the immediate right of the snap-back is the "right-guard," further on in the same line is the "right-tackle," outside is the "right end-rusher." The "left-guard," "left-tackle," and "left-end" complete the line upon the other side. The team which has the ball arranges, by means of the "signals" before described, for the massing of this line on one point of the enemy's defence, and the tactics which are employed to get through need careful description.

The influence of the snap-back will at once be realised from the consideration that the moment he puts the ball into play through his legs behind him, he also makes six men besides himself immediately off-side. The chief business of these men then becomes a general attack on some part of the enemy's line with the object, first, of clearing a path for the man who has to run with the ball, and, secondly, of keeping the opposing players from getting at the runner. This important part of the play is known as "interference"; and a comparison of Rules Nos. 21, 22, 23 in the English code with Nos. 24, 25 in the American, is advised to all who desire further information on a complicated point.

After the "snap-back" had been evolved, further alterations in the old rules followed thick and fast. Americans have very thoroughly convinced their law-makers of the inadequacy of legal language as a vehicle for legislation, and the struggle between the inventive player and the technical phrase-monger is still in active progress. Its details can be briefly sketched. To stop men holding their opponents firmly while their own side did what they pleased with the ball, the use of the arms and hands for this purpose was abolished. It was, however, an easy step to form an impassable barrier of bodies (for the rule had no mention of "bodies") round the ball, and thus prevent the other side from getting at it. Progress might be impossible, but so was defeat as well. A rule was at once made that the ball must advance at least five yards in three "downs," or be taken back ten yards and given to the other side. It was quite easy to avoid that; for if progress was essential, it should be made at any cost; and "flying wedges" were invented. Players were formed up some distance behind the line of play. At a given signal they dashed forward, and the momentum of their impact carried the man with the ball forward for the necessary distance. The other side never had a chance. This would plainly not do; so the rule was made that only three men might get in motion before the ball came into play; but it was rapidly discovered that a more accurate manipulation of the "scrummage" was all that was needed to produce almost the same effects. These tendencies need no further illustration. It will be seen at once that such a thing as a combined rush of the forwards down the field, dribbling the ball at their feet, is unknown; that the long, low passes which Vassall introduced with us are unappreciated; that for the pleasant uncertainty and all the sudden opportunities of independent brilliant play outside the scrummage, has been substituted a cut-and-dried system of "signals," "interference," and "mass-plays," which have utterly changed the aspect of the game.

THEODORE ANDREA COOK.

INTERNATIONAL FOOTBALL—In the winter of 1870 the first "International match" was played at the Oval. England and Scotland were the nations represented, and the Association code of rules was used. This naturally caused considerable indignation north of the Tweed, where nearly all the clubs played the Rugby game. A challenge between the Rugby players of the two countries was issued, and March 1871 saw the first International under the carrying rules.

I. The Rugby Game—As has been mentioned, 1871 saw the first match between teams representing England and Scotland. In 1875 the formation of an Irish Rugby Union was followed by an International match in London. It was not, however, till 1880 that England and Wales first met. Of the other International matches those between Scotland and Ireland commenced in 1877; those between Scotland and Wales in 1883; those between Ireland and Wales in 1882. The matches have not, however, been played every year. In 1884, for instance, an unfortunate dispute on the point of play resulted in the postponement of the England *v.* Scotland game of 1885. In 1888 and 1889 England played no International matches at all. The reason was as follows. In 1886 England made an alteration in the scoring laws, and the other Unions protested. Matters came to a crisis in 1887, when the nationalities, England excepted, proposed an International Board, invested with power to issue laws relating to the International contests. At the same time they demanded that each nationality should be equally represented on the proposed board. As England had an enormous majority of clubs, this was manifestly unfair. At last, in December 1889, Lord Kingsburgh and Major Marindin arbitrated on the whole question. From their award has sprung the present International Football Board. It consists of twelve members, six from England and two from each of the other nationalities. All International matches are played under rules that are subjected to its approval, although it has no jurisdiction over the game as played within the limits of the various Unions. A three-fourths majority is, however, necessary for any alteration in the laws of the game, while, in case of International disputes, a committee consisting of two representatives appointed by each Union shall arbitrate. Despite of these elaborate precautions a serious dispute between Wales and the International Board broke out in 1896. A proposed presentation to the celebrated Welsh three-quarter, A. J. Gould, was forbidden by the Board as savouring of professionalism. The quarrel is still proceeding, and owing to its evil influence, the Scotch and Irish matches with Wales fixed for January and March 1897 have not been played.

The method of selecting the members of the **International teams** differs in the various Unions. In England a system of trial matches allows the Selection Committee an opportunity of gauging the respective merits of the players. Up to the year 1890, the first trial match in the South was that between London and the Western Counties. This was followed by London and the West *v.* Oxford and Cambridge, a fixture which is still regularly played. From this game, and from the Oxford *v.* Cambridge match, the members who represent the South in the North *v.* South match are selected. The Northern players are chosen according to their display in the County matches, such as Yorkshire *v.* Lancashire and the like. After the North *v.* South match, two such games being now played a year, the English team is chosen.

In Scotland, as in England, a Committee of the Scotch Union is responsible for the selection of the Internationals. Big annual contests like the "Inter-City" enable members of this Committee to gather some idea of the merits of the players. Trial matches also exist, such as Edinburgh and Glasgow *v.* the Rest of Scotland, and Edinburgh or Glasgow *v.* the South of Scotland. In Ireland Inter-county matches practically decide the team. In Wales the fact that there are, comparatively speaking, few Clubs renders the trial game unnecessary, as the merits of the "crack" players are already known.

There is no special definition controlling the choice of a player as to the country for which he shall play. At the same time, the International Board decided at Leeds in 1894 that no player could in future play for more than one country.

The results of the International matches to date are here appended :—

ENGLAND *v.* SCOTLAND.

England, 9; Scotland, 8; Drawn, 7.

- 1871—Edinburgh. S, 1 g, 1 t—1 t
- 1872—Oval. E, 2 g, 2 t—1 g
- 1873—Glasgow. No score
- 1874—Oval. E, 1 g, 1 t—nil
- 1875—Edinburgh. No score
- 1876—Oval. E, 1 g, 1 t—nil
- 1877—Edinburgh. S, 1 g—nil
- 1878—Oval. No score
- 1879—Edinburgh. 1 g—1 g
- 1880—Manchester. E, 2g, 3t—1g
- 1881—Edinburgh. 1g, 1t—1g, 1t
- 1882—Manchester. S, 2 t—nil
- 1883—Edinburgh. E, 2 t—1 t
- 1884—Blackheath. E, 1 g—1 t
- 1886—Edinburgh. No score
- 1887—Manchester. 1 t—1 t
- 1890—Edinburgh. E, 1g, 1t—nil
- 1891—Richmond. S, 3 g—1 g
- 1892—Edinburgh, E, 1 g—nil
- 1893—Leeds. S, 2 g—nil
- 1894—Edinburgh. S, 2 t—nil
- 1895—Richmond. S, 1 g, 1 t—1 g
- 1896—Glasgow. S, 1 g, 2 t—nil
- 1897—Manchester. E, 2g, 1t—1t

ENGLAND *v.* IRELAND.

England, 16; Ireland, 4; Drawn, 1.

- 1875—London. E, 2 g, 1 t—nil
- 1876—Dublin. E, 1 g, 1 t—nil
- 1877—London. E, 2 g, 1 t—nil
- 1878—Dublin. E, 2 g, 1 t—nil
- 1879—London. E, 3 g, 2 t—nil
- 1880—Dublin. E, 1 g, 1 t—1 t
- 1881—Manchester. E, 2g, 2t—nil
- 1882—Dublin. 2 t—2 t
- 1883—Manchester. E, 1g, 3t—1t
- 1884—Dublin. E, 1 g—nil
- 1885—Manchester. E, 2 t—1 t
- 1886—Dublin. E, 1 t—nil
- 1887—Dublin. I, 2 g—nil
- 1890—Blackheath. E, 3 t—nil
- 1891—Dublin. E, 2 g, 3 t—nil
- 1892—Manchester. E, 1g, 1t—nil
- 1893—Dublin. E, 2 t—nil
- 1894—Blackheath. I, 1 g, 1 t—1 t
- 1895—Dublin. E, 2 t—1 t
- 1896—Leeds. I, 2 g—1 g
- 1897—Dublin. I, 1 g, 3 t—2 g, 1 t

ENGLAND *v.* WALES.

England, 10; Wales, 3; Drawn, 1.

- 1880-81—Blackheath. E, 8 g, 5 t—nil
- 1882-83—Swansea. E, 2 g, 4 t—nil
- 1883-84—Leeds. E, 1 g, 2 t—1 g
- 1884-85—Swansea. E, 1 g, 4 t—1 g, 1 t
- 1885-86—Blackheath. E, 1 g, 2 t—1 g
- 1886-87—Llanelly. No score
- 1889-90—Dewsbury. W, 1 t—nil
- 1890-91—Newport. E, 2 g, 1 t—1 g
- 1891-92—Blackheath. E, 3 g, 1 t—nil
- 1892-93—Cardiff. W, 2 g, 2 t—1 g, 3 t
- 1893-94—Birkenhead. E, 5 g—1 t
- 1894-95—Swansea. E, 1 g, 3 t—2 t
- 1895-96—Blackheath. E, 2 g, 5 t—nil
- 1896-97—Newport. W, 1 g, 2 t—nil

SCOTLAND *v.* IRELAND.

Scotland, 16; Ireland, 2; Drawn, 2.

- 1877—Belfast. S, 6 g, 2 t—nil
- 1879—S, 2 g, 1 t—nil
- 1880—Glasgow. S, 3 g, 2 t—nil
- 1881—Belfast. I, 1 g, 1 t—nil
- 1882—S, 2 t—nil
- 1883—S, 1 g, 1 t—nil
- 1884—S, 2 g, 2 t—1 t
- 1885—Edinburgh. S, 1 g, 2 t—nil
- 1886—S, 4 g, 2 t—nil
- 1887—S, 4 g—1 g
- 1888—Edinburgh. S, 1 g—nil
- 1889—S, 1 g—nil
- 1890—S, 1 d g, 1 t—nil
- 1891—Belfast. S, 4 g, 2 t—nil
- 1892—Edinburgh. S, 1 t—nil
- 1893—Belfast. No score
- 1894—Dublin. I, 1 g—nil
- 1895—Edinburgh. S, 2 t—1 t
- 1896—Dublin. No score
- 1897—Edinburgh. S, 2 g—1 t

SCOTLAND *v.* WALES.

Scotland, 9; Wales, 4; Drawn, 1.

- 1883—Edinburgh. S, 3 g—1 g
- 1884—Newport. S, 1 g, 1 t—nil
- 1885—Glasgow. No score
- 1886—Cardiff. S, 2 g, 1 t—nil
- 1887—Edinburgh. S, 4g, 8t—nil
- 1888—Newport. W, 1 t—nil
- 1889—Edinburgh. S, 2 t—nil
- 1890—Cardiff. S, 1 g, 2 t—1 t
- 1891—Edinburgh. S, 3 g, 6 t—nil
- 1892—Swansea. S, 1 g, 1 t—1 t
- 1893—Edinburgh. W, 1 g, 3 t—nil
- 1894—Newport. W, 1 g, 1 t—nil
- 1895—Edinburgh. S, 1 g—1 d g
- 1896—Cardiff. W, 2 t—nil

IRELAND *v.* WALES.

Ireland, 5; Wales, 6; Drawn, 1.

- 1882—Dublin. W, 2 g, 2 t—nil
- 1884—Cardiff. W, 1 g, 2 t—nil
- 1887—W, 1 g—3 t
- 1888—Dublin. I, 2 g, 1 t—nil
- 1889—Swansea. I, 2 t—nil
- 1890—Dublin. 1 g—1 g
- 1891—Llanelly. W, 2 g—1 g, 1 t
- 1892—Dublin. I, 1 g, 2 t—nil
- 1893—Llanelly. W, 1 t—nil
- 1894—Belfast. I, 1 g—nil
- 1895—Cardiff. W, 1 g—1 t
- 1896—Dublin. I, 1 g, 1 t—1 g

II. The Association Game—As in the Rugby game, matters affecting Association football in its International relations are under the control of an International Association Board. It is composed of eight members, two of whom represent the English, Scottish, Welsh and Irish Associations respectively. No alteration in the laws of the game can be made save by a unanimous vote of the members present. In International matches, the qualification is birth, or, in the case of British subjects born abroad, the nationality of their fathers. A Selection Committee of each Association is responsible for the team that is to represent the country in which that organisation is maintained. The following are the results of the International matches to date:—

ENGLAND *v.* SCOTLAND.

England, 7; Scotland, 13; Drawn, 6.

1872—Glasgow. 0—0
1873—Oval. E, 4—2
1874—Glasgow. S, 2—1
1875—Oval. 2—2
1876—Glasgow. S, 3—0
1877—Oval. S, 3—1
1878—Glasgow. S, 7—2
1879—Oval. E, 5—4
1880—Glasgow. S, 5—4
1881—Oval S, 6—1
1882—Glasgow. S, 5—4
1883—Sheffield. S, 3—2
1884—Glasgow. S, 1—0
1885—Oval. 1—1
1886—Glasgow. 1—1
1887—Blackburn. S, 3-2
1888—Glasgow, E, 5—0
1889—Oval. S, 3—2
1890—Glasgow. 1—1
1891—Blackburn. E, 2—1
1892—Glasgow. E, 4—1
1893—Richmond. E, 5—2
1894—Glasgow. 2-2
1895—Everton. E, 3—0
1896—Glasgow. S, 2—1
1897—Crystal Palace. S, 2—1

ENGLAND *v.* WALES.

England, 15; Wales, 2; Drawn, 2.

1878-79—Oval. E, 2—1
1879-80—Wrexham. E, 3—2
1880-81—Blackburn. W, 1—0
1881-82—Wrexham. W, 5—3
1882-83—Oval. E, 5—0
1883-84—Wrexham. E, 4—0
1884-85—Blackburn. 1—1
1885-86—Wrexham. E, 3—0
1886-87—Oval. E, 4—0
1887-88—Crewe. E, 5—1
1888-89—Stoke. E, 4—1
1889-90—Wrexham. E, 3—1
1890-91—Sunderland. E, 4—1
1891-92—Wrexham. E, 2—0
1892-93—Stoke. E, 6—0
1893-94—Wrexham, E, 5—1
1894-95 - Queen s Club. 1—1
1895-96—Cardiff. E, 9—1
1896-97—Sheffield. E, 4—0

ENGLAND *v.* IRELAND.

England, 15; Ireland, 0; Drawn, 1.

1881-82—Belfast. E, 13—0
1882-83—Liverpool. E, 7—0
1883-84—Belfast. E, 8—1
1884-85—Manchester. E, 4—0
1885-86—Belfast. E, 6—0
1886-87—Sheffield. E, 7—0
1887-88—Belfast. E, 5—1
1888-89—Liverpool. E, 6—1
1889-90—Belfast. E, 9—1
1890-91—Wolverhampton. E, 6-1
1891-92—Belfast. E, 2—0
1892-93—Birmingham. E, 6—1
1893-94—Belfast. 2—2
1894-95—Derby. E, 8—0
1895-96—Belfast. E, 2—0
1896-97—Nottingham. E, 6—0

SCOTLAND *v.* WALES.

Scotland, 19; Wales, 0; Drawn, 3.

1875-76—Glasgow. S, 4—0
1876-77—Wrexham. S, 2—0
1877-78—Glasgow. S, 9—0
1878-79—Wrexham. S, 3—0
1879-80—Glasgow. S, 5—1
1880-81—Wrexham. S, 5—1
1881-82—Glasgow. S, 5—0
1882-83—Wrexham. S, 3—0
1883-84—Glasgow. S, 4—1
1884-85—Wrexham. S, 8—1
1885-86—Glasgow. S, 4—1
1886-87—Wrexham. S, 2—1
1887-88—Edinburgh. S, 5—1
1888-89—Wrexham. 0—0
1889-90—Paisley. S, 5—1
1890-91—Wrexham. S, 4—3
1891-92—Edinburgh. S. 6—1
1893—Wrexham. S, 8—0
1894—Kilmarnock. S, 5—2
1895—Wrexham. 2—2
1896—Dundee. S, 4—0
1897—Wrexham. 2—2

SCOTLAND *v.* IRELAND.

Scotland, 13; Ireland, 0; Drawn, 1.

1883-84—Belfast. S, 5—0
1884-85—Glasgow. S, 8-2
1885-86—Belfast. S, 7—2
1886-87—Glasgow. S, 4—1
1887-88—Belfast. S, 10—2
1888-89—Glasgow. S, 7—0
1889-90—Belfast. S, 4—1
1890-91—Glasgow. S, 2—1
1891-92—Belfast. 3-2
1893—Glasgow. S, 6—1
1894—Belfast. S, 2—1
1895—Glasgow. S, 3—1
1896—Belfast. 3—3
1897—Glasgow. S, 5—1

IRELAND *v.* WALES.

Ireland, 4; Wales, 9; Drawn, 3.

1881-82—W, 7—1
1882-83—1—1
1883-84—W, 6—0
1884-85—W, 8—2
1885-86—W, 5—0
1886-87—I, 4—1
1887-88—W, 11—0
1888-89—W, 3—1
1889-90—W, 5—2
1890-91—I, 7—2
1891-92—1—1
1892-93—Belfast. I, 4—3
1894—Swansea. W, 4—2
1895—Belfast. 2—2
1896—Wrexham. W, 6—1
1897—Belfast. I, 4—3

B. F. ROBINSON.

[N.B.—For the Eton and Winchester forms of Football, see under PUBLIC SCHOOL GAMES.]

GLOSSARY.

All on side—(R.) If the ball, when kicked by a player, touches a member of the opposite side, the men upon his own, even though lying far in front of him, are put "all on side." The term is also heard when a man, after kicking, runs in front of men who previously lay before him, and thereby puts them "all on side." [*See also* OFF-SIDE.]

Association Football—That variety of football in which the arms are supposed to be non-existent, and any use of them whatever, except by the goal-keeper, involves the penalty of a free kick. The Football Association, which is formed by a federation of clubs observing this code, and controls their action, was founded in 1863, chiefly under the influence of Cambridge and old Public School men.

Back—(R.) The player who forms the last line of a team's defence, *i.e.*, plays alone and nearest to the goal line.

(A.) One of the two players who stand in front of the goal-keeper, and whose duties are mainly defensive.

Back up—To follow closely a man of one's own side who is in possession of the ball, in order to be in convenient position to take a pass from him, if he be too hard pressed, or to continue the dribbling if he should overrun the ball.

Ball—[*See* RULES 1 (R.) and 1 (A.).]

Behind—(A.) A ball is said to be behind when driven over the goal line by one of the attacking side. If by one of the defending side, a *corner-kick* (*q.v.*) is awarded.

Bully—(R.) Sometimes used for *scrummage* (*q.v.*).

(A.) Any confused play in which several men are very close together, and keep kicking the ball into one another. Especially used of such play when it occurs in front of goal, or when the referee throws up the ball on restarting a game after an accident.

Bye—(A.) A shot that crosses the goal line and goes behind, but fails to go between the goal posts.

Centre—(A.) The forward who plays with the two wing players on either side of him, combining and feeding them.

Charge—(A.) To throw one's weight against an opponent, using for the purpose any part of the body from shoulder to hip.

Clear—To kick or throw the ball well away when dangerously near to the goal.

Collar—(R.) To seize and retain hold of a player who is running with the ball. Also called TACKLE.

Come round—(R.) The exhortation addressed to the forwards when they have overrun the ball, or when the opposing forwards have come through them with the ball. They then have to turn and place themselves, if possible, once more between the opposing forwards and their goal line.

Convert—(R.) To turn a *try* (*q.v.*) into a *goal* (*q.v.*) by place kicking the ball over the bar and between the posts.

Corner—(A.) [*See* RULE 7 (A.).]

County Championship—(R.) The clubs competing for this honour are arranged in districts as follows: (*a*) *North-Western*, Lancashire, Cheshire, Cumberland, Westmoreland. (*b*) *North-Eastern*, Yorkshire, Durham, Northumberland. (*c*) *South-Eastern*. Senior group, Middlesex, Surrey, Kent, Midland Counties. Junior group, Hampshire, Sussex, Eastern Counties. (*d*) *South-Western*, Somerset, Devon, Cornwall. The winners in each group play one another, and the county obtaining the greatest number of points (two for a win, one for a draw) is declared the champion.

Dead Ball—The ball is dead whenever it is out of play, and in both games this is only when outside the field of play, or when the game is suspended for a moment to allow the infliction of a penalty kick, or the reward of a free kick for a *mark* (*q.v.*), &c.

Dead Ball Line—(R.) [*See* RULE 2 (R.).]

Dribbling—Propelling a ball by slight touches, so that, while the runner keeps at full speed, it never gets too far away for him to control it.

Drop-Kick—(R.) [*See* RULE 2 (R.).]

Drop Out—(R.) [*See* RULE 2 (R.).]

Dropped Goal—(R.) A goal obtained by a drop-kick, if it be not a free kick inflicted as a penalty for the breach of some rule. In such a case, even though from a drop-kick, it ranks as a penalty goal.

Fair Catch—(R.) [*See* RULE 2 (R.).]

Feed—To give to one of the same team a succession of convenient passes.

Five Yards—(R.) No man who lay in front of the kicker can interfere with a player waiting to receive the ball, or who has received it, until he has run "five yards" with the ball, or until he himself has been "put on side" by the kicker. Hence frequently heard as a cry of warning to an impetuous forward.

Follow Up—(R.) To run on after a high kick in order to reach the player who expects to receive it, and tackle him before he can return the kick.

Forward—(R.) [*See* THROWN FORWARD.]

Forwards—(R.) The eight or nine players who form the scrummage.

(A.) The five players who form the front line of a team, arranged as follows: left outside, left inside, centre, right inside, right outside.

Foul—(R.) Illegal obstruction of a player when not in possession of the ball.

(A.) Originally any deliberate unfairness in tackling a man, now often used for accidental illegality, *e.g.* a "foul throw," and also of hands ("to foul the ball") even though unintentionally.

Free Kick—(R.) [*See* RULE 10 (R.).]

(A.) [*See* DEFINITION 2 (A.).]

Full Back—[*See* BACK.]

Gate—(1) Money taken from the crowd that comes to see a football match or (2) persons composing the crowd.

Goal—(R.) [*See* RULES 1 (R.) and 1 (A.).]

Goal-keeper—(A.) The player who stands between the posts, who is allowed to use his hands in his own half of the field.

Goal-kick—(R.) The attempt to kick a goal from a try.

(A.) The kick-out when the ball has gone behind. It must be made from a spot within 6 yards of the nearest goal-post.

Goal-line—The line which runs from corner to corner of the ground under the cross-bar.

Goal-net—(A.) A network behind the goal, into which the ball passes if it goes through, and thereby assists the referee in determining disputes as to whether it went over or under the bar.

Ground—[*See* RULES 1 (R.) and 1 (A.).]

Hacking—Deliberately kicking at an opponent.

Half-back—(R.) One of the two players who stand behind the scrummage to intercept the ball if the opposing forwards bring it through, or the half bring it round, and themselves to pass it to the three-quarters.

(A.) One of the three players who keep between the full-backs and the forwards, feeding the latter and helping the former to keep back the opponents.

Handing-off—(R.) Pushing off an opponent who endeavours to impede a player running with the ball.

Handling, or Hands—(A.) Touching the ball with any part of the arm when in play. Only the goal-keeper can do so without a penalty. "*Hands*" is given against the offender.

Heeling-out—(R.) The practice of forwards in a scrummage pushing back the ball to their halves, in order that they may kick it into touch or pass to the three-quarters.

Held—(R.) A player is "held" when an opponent has both hands on the ball, or when he is neither able to go further himself nor to pass the ball to another.

Holding is the obstruction of a player by any part of hand or arm extending from the body. Illegal in Association football.

In-goal—(R.) [*See* RULE 2 (R.).]

Keep a man off—To obstruct an opponent from approaching a colleague who is about to play the ball. Illegal in Rugby Football.

Kick off—The kick taken at the centre of the ground when the game begins or is restarted after half-time, or after a goal has been scored. The side losing the toss commences the match; the side winning the toss kicks-off at half-time, and the side that loses the goal kicks off during the game.

Kick out or Drop out—[*See* RULE 2 (R.).]

Knock on—Legally equivalent to thrown forward, but more usually confined in practice to hitting the ball forward with hand or arms.

League System—The practice of selecting a definite number of clubs, and arranging for them all to play home and home matches with each other.

Leg up—(R.) The appeal against a forward lifting his leg in the scrummage before the ball is put in, so that he may scrape it back into his own half.

Line out—(R.) The arrangement of forwards opposite to one another when the ball is about to be thrown in from touch.

Linesman (A.) **or Touch-judge** (R.)—The official who stops the game when the ball goes out of the field of play, and decides whose is the right to throw it in.

Man down—(R.) The usual form of a request to the referee to stop the game on account of one or more forwards slipping down in the scrummage, and being unable to get up.

Mark—[*See* RULE 2 (R.)]

Marking a Man—Keeping close to an opponent in order to hamper him if he should receive the ball.

No charge—(R.) The decision of the referee not to allow the players of one side to rush at a man taking a free kick after the ball is down or after the man has started to run for the drop, on the ground that they had started the rush too early before.

No side—(R.) The form of the referee's announcement that the time allowed for the game, usually forty minutes each way, has expired.

Northern Union—(R.) An organisation formed almost entirely of clubs in Yorkshire and Lancashire, which left the Rugby Union in 1895, in order to be able to pay what they might think proper as compensation for the broken time of their members without incurring the punishment of suspension.

Off-side—[*See* RULES 7 and 8 (R.) and RULE 6 (A.).]

Pack—(R.) The forwards who compose one half of the scrummage. Frequently used of the scrummage itself, *e.g.*, "tight packs."

Pass—To kick or throw the ball deliberately to a colleague.

Penalty goal—(R.) A goal which is kicked from a free kick awarded by some breach of the rules.

Penalty kick—[*See* RULE 13 (A.).]

Picked up or Picked out—(R.) The appeal to a referee against a forward who has picked up the ball in a scrummage, or a half who has picked it out from the forwards' legs.

Place—(R.) To kick a ball successfully over the bar and between the posts after it has been placed upon the ground.

Place kick—[*See* RULE 2 (R.) and DEFINITION 1 (A.)]

Points—(R.) A try counts three points; a penalty goal three points; a goal from a try (in which case the try does not count) five points; any other goal, *e.g.*, a dropped goal, a goal from a mark, or one simply kicked from the ground, four points.

(A.) Each goal counts one point.

Poster—(R.) A place kick which, in the opinion of the referee, would have hit the posts produced upward and rebounded into the field of play.

Punch—(A.) To hit the ball away without catching it: of a goal-keeper.

Punt—[*See* RULE 2 (R.).]

Put on side—[*See* ALL ON SIDE.]

Referee—The official who is charged with the duty of starting the game, keeping time, and stopping, and penalising all unfair and illegal play. He is also charged with the keeping of the score.

Rugby Union—The Union, formed in 1871, is composed of those clubs which allow the use of the arms to carry the ball and to impede opponents.

Run-in—(R.) To carry the ball over an opponent's goal line and set it down upon the ground.

Scrag—(R.) To screw an opponent's neck under the arm in order to induce him to drop the ball.

Screw—(R.) [*See* WHEEL.]

Scrummage—(R.) A scrummage takes place when the ball is put down between players who have closed round it on their respective sides, and who must have both feet on the ground. Also called Scrimmage, Scrum, and Pack, and sometimes Bully.

Shin-guards—Short pads of cane and leather, sometimes worn down the front of the leg as a protection from accidental hacks.

Six yards' lines—(A.) Semicircles drawn on the field of play with goal posts for centre, six yards for radius and the goal line for diameter. From some point within these lines the goal kick should be taken.

Swing—(R.) [*See* WHEEL.]

Tackle—(R.) [*See* COLLAR.]

(A.) To put one's self in front of a player who is dribbling the ball, and either take it away or force him to get rid of it at a disadvantage.

Take the Man—(A.) To support a player of one's own side who is about to kick the ball by charging an opponent who is coming up with a view to kick it.

Taken over—(R.) No player may kick, pass, or knock on the ball across his own goal-line and there make it dead. Should he do so, an appeal is made for "taken over," and a scrummage must be formed five yards out.

Team—(R.) One side in a match, consisting of fifteen men, formerly of twenty.

(A.) One side in a match, consisting of eleven men.

Ten yards' circle—(A.) A circle of ten yards radius drawn around the centre of the field, upon which the ball is placed for the kick off. Within the circle no one is allowed to come of the side opposed to the kicker off.

Three-quarters—(R.) The players, formerly three, but now more often four in number, who stand between the half-backs and the full-back, waiting to take a pass from the former, or to save a rush of the opponents.

Throw-in—[*See* Rule 12 (R.) and Rule 5 (A.).]

Thrown forward, or Forward—(R.) The appeal against a pass which has been propelled by hand or arm in the direction of the opponents' goal-line.

Time—(R.) Usually 35 or 40 minutes each way.

(A.) Usually 45 minutes each way.

Touch—The space at the sides of the field of play, separated from it by the touch lines. In Rugby football the latter are a part of touch; in Association, of the field of play.

Touch-down—(R.) To settle the ball upon the ground between the goal-line and the dead ball-line. If this is done by one of the attacking side, it is usually called a run-in, and results in a *try* (*q v.*), and the term "touch-down" applied to the settling of the ball by a defender.

Touch in goal—[*See* RULE 2 (R.).]

Touch judge—[*See* LINESMAN.]

Try—(R.) A try is obtained when one of the attacking side grounds the ball over his opponents' goal-line.

Twelve yards' line—(A.) A line parallel to the goal-line, but 12 yards nearer the centre. Any intentionally unfair play between these two lines is punished with special severity. [*See* PENALTY KICK.]

Twenty-five—(R.) The space between the goal-lines and parallel lines drawn 25 yards nearer the centre.

Volley—To kick a ball before it bounces.

Wheel—(R.) When the forwards of one side, having obtained possession of the ball, go away to their left or right front with it, leaving the opponents on one side, they are said to wheel the scrummage. [*Also* SCREW and SWING.]

Wing-forward—(R.) A forward who comes late into the scrummage and devotes his attention rather to smart breaking away therefrom, and the interception of passes, than to hard shoving in the pack.

(A.) One of the pairs of forwards on either side of the Centre.

LAWS OF THE GAME

I. RUGBY.

I. Introduction—1. The Rugby Game of Football should be played by fifteen players on each side. (Any-one coming under the laws of professionalism shall not be allowed to take part in any game under this Union's jurisdiction.) The field of play shall not exceed 110 yards in length, nor 75 in breadth, and shall be as near these dimensions as practicable. The lines defining the boundary of the field of play shall be suitably marked, and shall be called the goal-lines at the ends and the touch-lines at the sides. On each goal-line, and equidistant from the touch-lines, shall be two upright posts, called goal posts, exceeding 11 feet in height, and placed 18 ft. 6 in. apart, and joined by a cross-bar 10 ft. from the ground; and the object of the game shall be to kick the ball over this cross-bar and between the posts. The game shall be played with an oval ball of as nearly as possible the following size and weight, namely:—

Length	11	to	$11\frac{1}{4}$ in.
Length circumference	30	,,	31 ,,
Width circumference	$25\frac{1}{2}$	,,	26 ,,
Weight	13	,,	$14\frac{1}{2}$ oz.

Hand sewn and not less than eight stitches to the inch.

II. Glossary—Duties of Officials—Scoring 2. The following terms occur in the laws, and have the respective meanings attached to each:—

Dead Ball Line—Not more than twenty-five yards behind and equidistant from each goal-line, and parallel thereto, shall be lines, which shall be called the dead-ball lines, and if the ball or player holding the ball touch or cross these lines the ball shall be dead and out of play.

In-Goal—Those portions of the ground immediately at the ends o the field of play and between the touch-lines, produced to the dead-ball lines, are called in-goal. The goal-lines are in-goal.

Touch—Those portions of the ground immediately at the sides of the field of play and between the goal-lines, if produced, are called touch. The touch-lines are in touch.

Touch-in-Goal—Those portions of the ground immediately at the four corners of the field of play, and between the goal and touch-lines, if respectively produced, are called touch-in-goal.

A Drop-kick is made by letting the ball fall from the hands, and kicking it the very instant it rises.

A Place-kick is made by kicking the ball after it has been placed on the ground.

A Punt is made by letting the ball fall from the hands and kicking it before it touches the ground.

A Tackle is when the holder of the ball is held by one or more players of the opposite side.

A Scrummage, which can only take place in the field of play, is when the ball is put down between players who have closed round on their respective sides, and who must have both feet on the ground.

A Try is gained by the player who first puts his hand on the ball on the ground in his opponents' in-goal.

A Touch-down is when a player touches down as above in his own in-goal.

A Goal is obtained by kicking the ball from the field of play, except from a punt, from a kick-off, or from a drop-out, direct (*i.e.*, without touching the ground or any player of either side) over the opponents' cross-bar, whether it touch such cross-bar or the goal-posts or not.

Knocking on and Throwing-forward are propelling the ball by the hand or arm in the direction of the opponents' in-goal; a throw out of touch cannot be claimed as a throw-forward.

A Fair-catch is a catch made direct from a kick or knock-on or throw-forward by one of the opposite side. The catcher must immediately claim the same by making a mark with his heel at the spot where he made the catch

Kick-off is a place-kick from the centre of the field of play; the opposite side may not stand within ten yards of the ball, nor charge until the ball be kicked, otherwise another kick-off shall be allowed. If the ball pitch in touch the opposite side may have it kicked off again.

Drop-out is a drop-kick from within 25 yards of the kicker's goal line; within which distance the opposite side may not charge, otherwise another drop-out shall be allowed. If the ball pitch in touch the opposite side may have it dropped out again.

At kick-off the ball must reach the limit of 10 yards, and at drop-out must reach the 25 yards line. If otherwise, the opposite side may have the ball re-kicked, or scrummaged, at the centre or in the middle of the 25 yards line, as the case may be.

Off-side—See LAWS 7 and 8.

3. In all matches a referee and two touch judges must be appointed, the former being mutually agreed upon.

Duties of Referee—The referee must carry a whistle, which he must blow in the following cases:—

(*a*) When he allows an appeal.

(*b*) When a player makes and claims a fair catch.

(*c*) On noticing rough or foul play or misconduct, when for the first offence he shall either caution the player or order him off the ground, but for the second offence he must order him off and afterwards report him to the union to which he belongs.

(*d*) When a player is down in a scrummage and he considers it dangerous.

(*e*) When the ball has been improperly put into a scrummage.
(*f*) When he allows a decision given by a touch judge.
(*g*) When wishing to stop the game for any purpose.
(*h*) If the ball or a player running with the ball touch him.
(*i*) At half-time and no-side, he being the sole timekeeper, having sole power to allow extra time for delays, but he shall not whistle for half-time or no-side until the ball be held or out of play.

Powers of Referee—The referee shall be sole judge in all matters of fact, but as to matters of law there shall be the right of appeal to the Rugby Union. All appeals must be made to him immediately, otherwise they cannot be entertained.

Duty of Touch-judges—The touch-judges shall carry flags, and shall each take one side of the ground, outside the field of play, and their duty shall be to hold up their flag when and where the ball goes into touch.

4. **Choice of Goals**—The captains of the respective sides shall toss for the choice of in-goals or the kick-off. Each side shall play an equal time from each in-goal, and a match shall be won by a majority of points; if no point be scored, or the number be equal, the match shall be drawn.

Scoring—The following shall be the mode of scoring:—

A try	equals	3 points
A penalty goal	,,	3 ,,
A goal from a try (in which case the try shall not count)	,,	5 ,,
Any other goal	,,	4 ,,

5. **Kick-off**—At the time of the kick-off all the kicker's side shall be behind the ball; if in front, the referee, on an appeal from the opposite side, shall order a scrummage where the kick-off took place. The game shall be re-started by a kick-off.

(*a*) After a goal, by the side losing such goal, and
(*b*) After half-time by the opposite side to that which started the game.

III. Mode of Play—Definitions—6. When once the game is started the ball may be kicked or picked up and run with by any player who is on-side, at any time; except that the ball may not be picked up—

(*a*) In a scrummage.
(*b*) When it has been put down after it has been fairly held.
(*c*) When it is on the ground after a player has been tackled.

It may be passed or knocked from one player to another provided it be not passed, knocked, or thrown forward. If a player while holding or running with the ball be tackled and the ball fairly held, he must at once put it down in front of him.

Off-side—7. A player is placed off-side if he enters a scrummage from his opponent's side, or if the ball has been kicked, touched, or is being run with by one of his own side behind him. A player can be off-side in his opponents' in-goal, but not in his own, except where one of his side takes a free kick behind his goal-line, in which case all of his side must be behind the ball when kicked.

8. An off-side player is placed on side:—

(*a*) When an opponent has run five yards with the ball.
(*b*) When the ball has been kicked by, or has touched an opponent.
(*c*) When one of his side has run in front of him with the ball.
(*d*) When one of his side has run in front of him having kicked the ball when behind him.

An off-side player shall not play the ball, nor during the time an opponent has the ball, run, tackle, or obstruct, nor may he approach within five yards of any player waiting for the ball; on any breach of this law, the opposite side, on an appeal by them, shall be awarded, at their option:—

(*e*) A free kick, the place of such breach being taken as the mark.
(*f*) A scrummage at the spot where the ball was last played by the offending side before such breach occurred.

Except in the case of unintentional off-side, when a scrummage shall be formed where such breach occurred.

9. **Fair Catch**—If a player makes a fair catch he shall be awarded a free kick, and he himself must either kick or place the ball.

10. **Free Kicks**—All free kicks may be place-kicks, drop-kicks, or punts, but must be in the direction of the opponents' goal line, and across the kicker's goal line, if kicked from behind the same. They may be taken at any spot behind the mark in a line parallel to the touch-lines. If taken by drop or punt the catcher must take the kick, if taken by a place-kick the catcher must place the ball. In all cases the kicker's side must be behind the ball when it is kicked, except the player who may be placing the ball for a place-kick. In case of any infringement of this law the referee shall, on a claim by the opposite side, order a scrummage at the mark. The opposite side may come up to, and charge from, anywhere on or behind a line drawn through the mark and parallel to the goal-lines, and may charge as soon as the catcher commences to run or offers to kick or places the ball on the ground for a place-kick, but in cases of a drop-kick or punt the kicker may always draw back, and unless he has dropped the ball or touched it with his foot, the opposite side must retire to the line of the mark. But if any of the opposite side charge before the player having the ball commences to run or offers to kick, or the ball has touched the ground for a place-kick (and this applies to tries at goal as well as free kicks), provided the kicker has not taken his kick, the charge may be disallowed on an appeal.

IV. Penalties—11. Free kicks by way of penalties shall be awarded on claims by the opposite side if any player—

(*a*) Intentionally either handles the ball or falls down in a scrummage, or picks the ball out of a scrummage.
(*b*) Having the ball, does not immediately put it down in front of him, on it being held.
(*c*) Being on the ground, does not immediately get up.
(*d*) Prevents an opponent getting up.
(*e*) Illegally tackles, charges, or obstructs, as in LAW 8.
(*f*) Wilfully puts the ball unfairly into a scrummage.
(*g*) Not himself running at the ball, charges or obstructs an opponent not holding the ball.
(*h*) When any player not in a scrummage wilfully obstructs his opponents' backs by standing on his opponents' side of the ball when it is in a scrummage.
(*i*) Being in a scrummage, lifts a foot from the ground before the ball has been put into such scrummage. In this case the referee must allow a free kick to the opposite side without any appeal.

The places of infringement shall be taken as the mark, and any one of the side granted the free kick may place or kick the ball.

V. General—Ball in Touch—12. The ball is in touch when it, or a player carrying it, touch or cross the touch-line; it shall then belong to the side opposite to that last touching it in the field of play, except when carried in. One of the side to whom the ball belongs shall bring it into play at the spot where it went into touch, by one of the following methods:—

(*a*) Bounding it on the field of play at right angles to the touch-line, and then run with it, kick it or pass it.
Throw-out—(*b*) Throwing it out so as to alight at right angles to the touch line, or
(*c*) Scrummaging it at any spot at right angles to the touch-line, between 5 and 15 yards from the place where it went into touch.

If the ball be not thrown out of touch so as to alight at right angles to the touch line the opposite side may at once claim to bring it out themselves as in (*c*).

13. **Try at Goal**—When a side has scored a try the ball shall be brought from the spot where the try was gained into the field of play in a line parallel to the touch-lines, such distance as the placer thinks proper, and there he shall place the ball for one of his side to try and kick a goal; this place kick is governed by law 10 as to charging, &c., the mark being taken as on the goal-line. It is the duty of the defending side to see that the ball is taken out straight.

Unfair Play—Allowing or Disallowing a Try—On an appeal the referee shall award a try if, in his opinion, one would undoubtedly have been obtained but for unfair play or interference of the defending side. Or he shall disallow a try and adjudge a touch-down if, in his opinion, a try would undoubtedly not have been gained but for unfair play or interference of the attacking side. In case of a try so allowed the kick at goal shall be taken at any point on a line parallel to the touch lines, and passing through the spot where the ball was when such unfair play or interference took place.

14. **Ball held in Goal**—If the ball, when over the goal-line and in possession of a player, be fairly held by an opposing player before it is grounded, it shall be scrummaged five yards from the goal-line, opposite the spot where the ball was held.

15. **Drop-out**—After an unsuccessful try or touch-down, or if the ball after crossing the goal-line go into touch-in-goal or touch or cross the dead-ball line, it shall be brought into play by means of a drop-out, when all the kicker's side must be behind the ball when kicked: in case any are in front, the referee shall, on an appeal from the opposite side, order a scrummage on the 25 yards line, and equidistant from the touch-lines.

16. **Knock-on, Throw-Forward**—In case of a throw forward or knock-on, the ball shall, on a claim by the opposite side, be at once brought back to where such infringement took place and there put down, unless a fair catch has been made and claimed. If the ball or a player running with the ball touches the referee it shall there be put down.

17. **Pass or carry back over own Goal-line**—If a player shall kick, pass, knock, or carry the ball back across his goal-line and it there be made dead, the opposite side may claim that the ball shall be brought back and a scrummage formed at the spot whence it was kicked, passed, knocked, or carried back. Under any other circumstances, a player may touch the ball down in his own in-goal.

18. **Hacking, Tripping**—No hacking, or hacking over, or tripping up, shall be allowed under any circumstances. No one wearing projecting nails, iron plates, or gutta percha, on any part of his boots or shoes shall be allowed to play in a match.

19. **Irregularities in In-goal not otherwise provided for**—In case of any law being infringed in in-goal by the attacking side, a touch-down shall be awarded, but where such breach is committed by the defending side, a scrummage shall be awarded five yards from the goal-line, opposite to the spot where the breach occurred.

Other Irregularities not provided for—But in the case of any law being broken, or any irregularity of play occurring on the part of either side not otherwise provided for, the opposite side may claim that the ball be taken back to the place where the breach of the law or irregularity of play occurred, and a scrummage formed there.

20. **Close Time**—There shall be an annual close time, during which it is illegal to play football where gate-money is taken, such close time being between April 20th and the third Saturday in September in each year.

At the Annual General Meeting held September 20th, 1893, the following resolution was adopted:—"That this meeting strongly approves of the principle that the referee shall have sole control over the game and may blow his whistle without waiting for any appeal, and recommends that it be acted upon in matches in which both sides consent."

Regulations authorised by the Rugby Union on County Qualifications

1. A man may play—

(*a*) For the county in which he was born; or

(*b*) For the county in which he has resided for the six months previous to the time of playing; or

(*c*) For the county in which he is residing at school or college, either as pupil or master, at the time of playing, provided his residence at the school or college be in the same county; or

(*d*) For the county for which he played in season 1887–1888.

2. A man shall still be qualified to play for a county, having previously qualified for and played for that county for three seasons, and not having subsequently played for any other county.

3. No man shall play for more than one county during the same season.

4. A man who is duly qualified and plays for a county in a certain season may continue to play for that county during the remainder of that season, even though he loses his other qualifications.

5. Should any question arise as to qualifications, the same shall be left to the decision of the Rugby Football Union Committee.

Rules as to Professionalism

1. Professionalism is illegal.

2. Acts of professionalism are

(1) by an individual—

(A) Asking, receiving, or relying on a promise, direct or implied, to receive any money consideration whatever, actual or prospective, any employment or advancement, any establishment in business, or any compensation whatever for playing football or rendering any service to a football organisation; training or loss of time connected therewith; time lost in playing football, or in travelling in connection with football; expenses in excess of the amount actually disbursed on account of reasonable hotel or travelling expenses.

(B) Transferring his services from one club to another in opposition to rule 6.

(C) Playing for a club while receiving, or after having received, from such club any consideration whatever for acting as secretary, treasurer, or in any other office, or for doing, or for having done any work or labour about the club's ground or in connection with the club's affairs.

(D) Remaining on tour at his club's expense longer than is reasonable.

(E) Giving or receiving any money testimonial, or giving or receiving any other testimonial, except under the authority of this union.

(F) Receiving any medal or other prize for any competition, except under the authority of this union.

(G) Playing on any ground where gate money is taken during the close season; in any match or contest where it is previously agreed that less than fifteen players on each side shall take part.

(H) Knowingly playing with or against any expelled or suspended player or club.

(I) Refusing to give evidence or otherwise assist in carrying out these rules when requested by this union to do so.

(J) Being registered as or declared a professional, or suspended by any national union, or by the Football Association.

(K) Playing within eight days of any accident for which he has claimed or received insurance compensation, if insured under these rules.

(L) Playing in any benefit match connected directly or indirectly with football.

(M) Knowingly playing or acting as referee or touch-judge on the ground of an expelled or suspended club.

(2) by a club or other organisation—

(A) Paying or promising payment, or giving, offering, or promising any inducement as to employment, advancement, or establishment in business, or any compensation whatever, to any player for playing for that club, training, or for travelling expenses to or from any training resort, or for loss of time in connection with training, loss of time while playing or travelling in connection with football, hotel or travelling expenses in excess of the sum actually and reasonably disbursed.

(B) Receiving as a member a member of another club in opposition to rule 6.

(C) Receiving or continuing as a member anyone it may pay or have paid for either regular or occasional services.

(D) Paying for any of its teams, players, officials, or members on tour longer than a reasonable time, or paying for more than a reasonable number.

(E) Giving from its funds, subscribing, or playing a match for any testimonial.

(F) Giving any medal or other prize for any competition except under the authority of this union.

(G) Taking gate money at any ground during the close season, at any match or contest where it is previously agreed that less than fifteen players on each side shall take part.

(H) Knowingly playing or allowing its members to play with or against any expelled or suspended player or club.

(I) Refusing to produce its books or documents, or to allow its officials or members to give evidence, or to assist in carrying out these rules when requested by the union to do so.

(J) Knowingly playing or admitting as a member without the consent of the union any member of an expelled or suspended club, or any expelled or suspended player, or any person registered as or declared a professional, or suspended by any National Rugby Union, or by the Football Association.

(K) Knowingly allowing a player to play in its matches within eight days of any accident for which he has received or claimed insurance compensation if insured under these rules.

(L) Playing or allowing its ground to be used for any benefit match connected directly or indirectly with football.

(M) Knowingly allowing its members or teams to play on the ground of any expelled or suspended club.

(N) Refusing to pay within one month any costs or expenses ordered by this union for inquiries held under these rules.

3. For offences under 2 (1), A, H, I, L, and M, an individual shall be expelled from all English clubs playing Rugby Football, and shall not be eligible for re-election or election to any club. For offences under 2 (1), B, C, D, E, F, G, J, and K, an individual shall be suspended during the pleasure of this union.

4. For offences under 2 (2), A, D, H, I, L, M, and N, a club shall be expelled from this union.

For offences under 2 (2), B, C, E, F, J, and K, a club shall be suspended during the pleasure of this union. Any club disregarding a sentence of suspension shall be liable to expulsion.

5. When this union is fully satisfied that any offence under 2 (2), A, D, H, I, L, and N was of an accidental, trivial, or technical character they may suspend instead of expel.

6. When a player wishes to join a new club he may do so. If this union request it, he shall produce a letter from his old club, stating that they have no objection. On receipt of such letter this union shall give the necessary permission, unless they believe there may have been collusion, or that illegal means have been employed to induce the player to join the new club, in which case they shall hold an inquiry.

In case any club or clubs refuse to give written permission this union must hold an inquiry at the request of the player or of the club he wishes to join. If from any cause an inquiry be held this union shall have full power to order the payment of the costs of such inquiry, and of the clubs and witnesses, as it may think fit. This union may grant power to recognised governing bodies to increase the stringency of this rule, provided such proposed alterations be submitted to and approved of by it.

7. A county or club may insure its players either through a recognised insurance company or a fund entirely set apart for insurance, the accounts of such fund to be yearly audited by a professional auditor. Such audit to be made at the close of each season, and to be concluded, and the auditor's certificate lodged with this union, not later than the 20th May in each year, provided that—

(A) Any injured player does not receive more than 6s. per week-day while injured.

(B) Payments are only made on the certificate of a registered medical practitioner.

(C) Any player does not play football within eight days of his accident. If he does so, no insurance compensation shall be paid.

(D) Proper books of account be kept.

8. This union may hold inquiries into any alleged breaches of these rules at its pleasure, and shall do so when requested by any club or member of a club provided any such club or member make a preliminary deposit of £10 or such smaller sum as this union may determine, to be accompanied by a preliminary written statement of the chief known facts. After any such an inquiry, this union may return the preliminary deposit wholly or in part, and may order the expenses of such inquiry, of clubs and members implicated, and of witnesses, to be paid as it may determine.

9. At all inquiries under rules 6 and 8, correct notes must be taken.

10. Any club, member, or player affected by any decision given by a county, union of counties, or university under the delegation of powers contained in rule 11, may appeal direct to this union. Such appeal must be made within ten days, and must be accompanied by a deposit of £50 and a written statement of the grounds of appeal. After any such appeal, this union may return such deposit wholly or in part, and may order the expenses of such inquiry, of clubs and members implicated, and of witnesses, to be paid as it may determine.

11. This union may delegate to recognised governing bodies, such as counties, union of counties, and universities, powers to act for it in such cases and under such regulations as it may determine. All powers so delegated, and the bodies to whom such delegation be made, shall be published annually in the official guide of this union.

12. This union may appoint a sub-committee or committees to act on its behalf in all cases arising under these rules, giving such powers as it may determine.

13. This union shall have power to deal with all cases arising out of these rules, and with all acts which it may consider as acts of professionalism, and which are not specially provided for.

14. Where the word union is used in these rules, the committee of this union for the time being shall be understood, and in the delegation of powers the committee of the recognised governing body shall be understood. In case any difference of opinion arises as to the meaning of any of these rules, such meaning shall be decided by the committee of this union, or if it occurs at a general meeting, by the chairman thereof. Any such decision shall be entered in the minutes, and shall be accepted as the true meaning until otherwise interpreted by a two-thirds majority at a general meeting of this union after due notice had been given.

II. Association

Revised June, 1896

1. The limits of the ground shall be—maximum length, 200 yards; minimum length, 100 yards; maximum breadth, 100 yards; minimum breadth, 50 yards. The length and breadth shall be marked off with four flags, with staffs not less than 5 feet high, and goal and touch lines; and lines defining 6 yards from the goal posts and 12 yards from the goal lines shall also be marked out. The centre of the ground shall be indicated by a suitable mark, and a circle with a 10 yards radius shall be made round it. The goals shall be upright posts, fixed on the goal lines, eight yards apart, equidistant from the corner flag staff, with a bar across them, 8 ft. from the ground. The maximum width of the goal posts and the maximum depth of the cross bar shall be 5 in. The circumference of the Association ball shall be not less than 27 in., nor more than 28 in.; and in International matches, at the commencement of the game the weight of the ball shall be from 13 to 15 ounces.

2. The winners of the toss shall have the option of kick-off, or choice of goals. The game shall be commenced by a place-kick from the centre of the ground in the direction of the opposite goal-line. The other side shall not approach within 10 yards of the ball until it is kicked off, nor shall any player on either side pass the centre of the ground in the direction of his opponents' goal until the ball is kicked off.

3. Ends shall only be changed at half-time. After a goal is won the losing side shall kick off, but after the change of ends at half-time the ball shall be kicked off by the opposite side from that which originally did so; and always as provided in Law 2.

4. A goal shall be won when the ball has passed between the goal posts under the bar, not being thrown, knocked on, or carried by any one of the attacking side. If from any cause during the progress of the game the bar should become displaced, the referee shall have power to award a goal if in his opinion the ball would have passed under the bar if it had not been displaced. The ball is in play if it rebounds from a goal-post, cross-bar, or a corner flag staff, into the field of play. The ball is in play if it touches the referee or a linesman when in the field of play. The ball crossing the goal or touch line, either on the ground or in the air, is out of play.

5. When the ball is in touch, a player of the opposite side to that which played it out shall throw it in from the point on the boundary line where it left the field of play. The player throwing the ball must stand on the touch line facing the field of play, and shall throw the ball in over his head with both hands in any direction, and it shall be in play when thrown in. The thrower shall not play until the ball has been played by another player. (Note.—This law is complied with if the player has any part of both feet on the line when he throws the ball.)

6. When a player plays the ball, or throws it in from touch, any one of the same side who at such moment of playing or throwing is nearer to the opponents' goal line is out of play, and may not touch the ball himself, or in any way whatever prevent any other player from doing so, until the ball has been played, unless there are at such moment of playing or throwing at least three of his opponents nearer their own goal-line; but no player is out of play in case of a corner-kick, or when the ball is kicked off from goal, or when it has been last played by an opponent.

7. When the ball is played behind the goal-line by one of the opposite side, it shall be kicked off by any one of the players behind whose goal-line it went, within six yards of the goal-post nearest the point where the ball left the field of play; but, if played behind by any one of the side whose goal-line it is, a player of the opposite side shall kick it from within one yard of the nearest corner flag-post. In either case no opponent shall be allowed within six yards of the ball until it is kicked off.

8. No player shall carry, knock on, or handle the ball under any pretence whatever, except in the case of the goalkeeper, who, within his own half of the ground, shall be allowed to use his hands in defence of his goal, either by knocking on or throwing, but not carrying the ball. The goalkeeper may be changed during the game, but not more than one player shall act as goalkeeper at the same time, and no second player shall step in and act during any period in which the regular goalkeeper may have vacated his position.

9. In no case shall a goal be scored from any free kick (except as provided in Law 13), nor shall the ball be again played by the kicker until it has been played by another player. The kick-off, corner-kick, and goal-kick shall be free kicks within the meaning of this rule.

10. Neither tripping, hacking, nor jumping at a player shall be allowed, and no player shall use his hands to hold or push his adversary, or play in any manner likely to cause injury. No player may charge an opponent from behind, unless such opponent be not

only facing his own goal, but is, in the opinion of the referee, wilfully impeding his adversary while in that position. The goalkeeper shall not be charged except he be in the act of playing the ball, or is obstructing an opponent. (Note.—In the act of playing the ball means actual contact with the ball.)

11. No player shall wear any nails, excepting such as have their heads driven in flush with the leather, or metal plates or projections, or gutta-percha, on the soles or heels of his boots, or on his shin-guards. If bars or studs on the soles or heels of the boots are used, they shall not project more than half an inch, and shall have all their fastenings driven in flush with the leather. Bars shall be transverse and flat, not less than one and a half inches in length, and half an inch in width. Studs shall be round in plan, not less than half an inch in diameter, and in no case conical or pointed. Any player discovered infringing this rule shall be prohibited from taking further part in the match.

12. A referee shall be appointed, whose duties shall be to enforce the rules and decide all disputed points; and his decision on points of fact connected with the play going on shall be final. He shall also keep a record of the game, and act as timekeeper; and, in the event of any ungentlemanly behaviour on the part of any of the contestants, the offender or offenders shall be cautioned, and if the offence is repeated, or, in case of violent conduct, without any previous caution, the referee shall have power to rule the offending player or players out of play, and shall transmit the name or names of such player or players to his or their (National) Association, in whom shall be solely vested the right of accepting an apology. The referee shall have power to terminate the game whenever, by reason of darkness, interference by spectators, or other cause, he shall think fit, and he shall report the same to the Association under whose jurisdiction the match was played, who shall have full power to deal with the matter. Two linesmen shall be appointed, whose duty (subject to the decision of the referee) shall be to decide when the ball is out of play, and which side is entitled to the corner-flag kick, goal kick, or throw in. Any undue interference by a linesman shall be reported by the referee to the National Association to which the linesman belongs, who shall deal with the matter in such manner as they may deem necessary. The referee shall have power to award a free kick, in any case where he thinks that the conduct of a player is dangerous, or likely to prove dangerous, but not sufficiently so as to justify him in putting in force the greater power vested in him as above.

13. If any player shall intentionally trip, charge from behind, push, or hold an opponent, or wilfully handle the ball, within 12 yards from his own goal-line, the referee shall award the opposing side a penalty kick, to be taken from any point 12 yards from the goal-line, under the following conditions:—All players, with the exception of the player taking the penalty kick and the opposing goalkeeper (who shall not advance more than six yards from the goal-line) shall stand at least six yards behind the ball. The ball must be kicked forward. The ball shall be in play when the kick is taken, and a goal may be scored from the penalty kick; but the ball shall not be again played by the kicker until it has been played by another player. If necessary, time of play shall be extended to admit of the penalty kick being taken.

14. In the event of a supposed infringement of the laws, the ball shall be in play until a decision has been given.

15. The referee shall have power to stop the game for such a time as he may think fit, whenever he may deem it necessary to do so.

16. In the event of any temporary suspension of play from any cause, the ball not having gone into touch, or behind the goal-line, the game shall be re-started by the referee throwing up the ball at the spot where the play was suspended, and the players on either side shall not play the ball until it has touched the ground.

17. In the event of any infringement of Laws 2, 5, 6, 8, 9, 10, or 16, a free kick shall be forfeited to the opposite side, from the spot where the infringement took place.

Definition of Terms

A Place Kick is a kick at the ball while it is on the ground, in the centre of the field of play.

A Free Kick is a kick at the ball in any direction that the player pleases, when it is lying on the ground, none of the kicker's opponents being allowed within six yards of the ball, unless they be standing on their own goal-line. The ball must at least be rolled over before it shall be considered played; *i.e.*, it must make a complete circuit or travel the distance of its circumference.

A Place Kick or a Free Kick must not be taken until the referee has given a signal for the same.

Hacking is kicking an adversary intentionally.

Tripping is throwing, or attempting to throw, an adversary by the use of the legs, or by stooping in front or behind him; unless in the opinion of a referee a trip is intentional, no punishment shall be imposed. Thus, within the twelve yards line, a referee must enforce law 13, and has no power to mitigate the penalty.

Knocking on is when a player strikes or propels the ball with his hands or arms.

Holding includes the obstruction of a player by the hand or any part of the arm extending from the body.

Handling is understood to be playing the ball with the hand or arm.

Touch is that part of the field, on either side of the ground, which is beyond the line of play.

Carrying is taking more than two steps while holding the ball.

Memorandum Issued by the Football Association

(*a*) Any player leaving the field during the progress of a game (except through accident), without the consent of the referee, will be deemed guilty of misconduct, and will render himself liable to be penalised.

(*b*) The scale of charges for officials appointed by the Association shall be one guinea and railway and cab fares actually paid. When necessary for officials to arrive the night before the match, hotel expenses will be allowed.

(*c*) A player cannot act as linesman or referee during suspension.

(*d*) Membership of any club having a name similar to one already affiliated with the Association shall not be recognised or accepted.

(*e*) Associations and clubs are recommended to grant free admission to soldiers and sailors wearing her Majesty's uniform to football matches, where practicable.

(*f*) Linesmen are not considered players for the purposes of Rule 34.

(*g*) It is the duty of members of the Council, officials of clubs, and referees to report to the Council all cases of misconduct likely to bring the game into disrepute; and officials of clubs must report to the Council any infringement of rules without delay.

(*h*) Any professional player whilst under suspension by the Council for breach of rules, shall not receive any wages or moneys from his club without the consent of the Council.

(*i*) All clubs connected with the Association must have bills printed and posted in their grounds, threatening with expulsion any person who is guilty of insulting or improper conduct towards the referee.

(*k*) Any misconduct towards a referee away from the field of play will be dealt with in the same way as if the offence had been committed on the field.

(*l*) Clubs are expected to provide a private way for players and officials from playing-ground to dressing-room wherever this is practicable.

(*m*) No player is entitled to take the proceeds of a benefit match until he has been registered a professional.

(*n*) Second or reserve teams must be known by the name of the club to which they belong, as S——O 2nd, or S——O Reserve.

(*o*) A professional transferred must be re-registered by the club to which he is transferred.

(*p*) Registration forms signed on Sundays are not valid.

(*q*) A professional must not practise with any club but the one for which he is registered.

(*r*) Clubs obtaining signatures on Sundays are liable to be penalised: also for taking a player's signature on a second form before the first form has been declared by the Council to be informal.

The Council of the Football Association have placed the following interpretations upon laws:—

(*a*) All reports by referees to be made within three days after occurrence.

(*b*) In important matches it is desirable that linesmen should be neutral. Linesmen, where neutral, must call the attention of the referee to rough play or ungentlemanly conduct, and generally assist him to carry out the game in a proper manner.

(*c*) A player putting his leg from behind another player in order to get the ball, and thus throwing his opponent, shall be penalised for tripping.

(*d*) Wearing soft india-rubber on the soles of boots is not a violation of Law 11.

(*e*) The corner flag must not be removed when a corner kick is taken.

(*f*) The whole of the ball must have passed over the goal line, or touch line, before it is out of play.

FOX—There is perhaps no better abused animal living than the Fox. Yet the sport he shows may atone for any trifling amount of roguery and retain for him the good name he deserves, whilst his beauty is beyond reproach. His head and eye are intelligent and he has well-formed shoulders, round and deep ribs, back, loin and thighs of the most muscular description, and the whole covered with a thick coating of fur, of the cleanest, brightest and best. All is set off by a handsome brush or tail, sometimes tipped with white; such an appendage, which no other animal can boast, places him quite in the front rank for looks, whilst the lines upon which he is built are so well calculated for speed as well as endurance, that he is perhaps, taking him all in all, as near perfection as is possible to be.

But that handsome brush was not given to him as a set off to his beauty alone, but is of the greatest service to him; using it as a rudder, he can twist and turn at any moment when going at full speed, as occasion may require, without over-running the mark an inch.

In jumping he also brings it into action. When approaching a high wall, the brush will be seen to revolve rapidly, when, the impetus being given, over he goes, for a wall seven, eight or nine feet high is nothing for a fox to jump.

The brush is no doubt used in the same way in climbing trees. Unassisted by claws like those of a cat (he has only the toe-nails of a dog to help him), pug will sometimes be found upon the butt of a tree eight feet or even more from the ground. In an elevated position of this kind, he undoubtedly feels himself secure, and rightly so, for he is not likely to be sought for there, unless by chance or ill fate his whereabouts becomes known.

I may here mention that the white "tag" frequently causes mistakes to be made as to the sex of the animal, for it is generally believed by the uninitiated that this is given to the male only. This is not the case; sex has but very little, if anything, to do with it, for very often a whole litter will be possessed of that mark of distinction, whilst in another case not one will show it, yet in each there may be about an equal number of males and females.

The fox is well aware of the fact that he is hunted by scent; as is proved by his methods of self-preservation, and by the different tactics he will sometimes pursue in trying to baffle and beat his enemies. He has been known, among other dodges, when hounds are upon his line, to mount and run along the top of a wall for three or four hundred yards at a stretch, by which, if he does not shake off the pack altogether, he is likely at any rate to cause a long check and to gain a considerable advantage. Perhaps one of the most peculiar and effectual things he has been known to do is to roll in manure. This once came to my knowledge in this way. Hounds had been running very fast for some twenty-five minutes and got to a small covert, when a gentleman, a well-known sportsman, galloped on to the end of it to try to get a view. To his astonishment, there was the quarry outside the covert, rolling over and over at the bottom of a manure heap; this, as may be imagined, so foiled the scent as almost to save his life, for hounds could hardly hunt him a yard after. He was, however, quite beat, and the hounds were so close that they scarcely lost sight of him again, and in the end they rolled him over. I have had an idea of such a thing happening upon other occasions, from the sudden way that scent would sometimes disappear, but have never been able clearly to prove it either before or since.

He is gifted with many other clever devices for the purpose of his own protection, and likes to know the whereabouts of his pursuers, for which reason he generally takes a down wind course. If he starts up wind his journey will be short in that direction, unless he has in view an earth or some other place of safety which he hopes to reach. His method of stopping to listen on the way, which may be often observed by whippers-in who are clever at what is called "telegraphing," clearly proves his object; and when the cry of the hounds comes floating down the breeze, he starts off again at best pace, and the chances are that he will shortly run them out of scent altogether.

Feeding at night—A rover by night, he turns out soon after the setting of the sun and embarks upon his usual rounds in search of food, rabbits, rats, mice, beetles, &c.; of rats and mice he is particularly fond, whilst the number of beetles he gets is astonishing. I have picked up handfuls of "billets" showing nothing but beetles' wings, and whence he could have obtained such a quantity has altogether puzzled me. I remember once witnessing a very pretty, and, as I venture to think, very peculiar sight, when the whereabouts is taken into consideration. A fox mouse-catching in a field, and within twenty yards of a kennel where a pack of hounds is kept, is a sight certainly not often to be met with: this I saw one summer evening just outside the Puckeridge Kennels during Mr. Parry's mastership. Perfectly healthy, and sleek as a mole, there was pug, with wonderful agility springing from tuft to tuft, driving his nose into the sedgy grass, and at times picking up the tiny morsel, which he seemed thoroughly to enjoy, notwithstanding that a note might occasionally be heard from one or more of the fifty couple who occupied the benches hard by. From evening to early morning he goes on the prowl, and the distance he will sometimes travel is great, especially when love-making commences, and this will go on generally through the months of

January, February and March. During this time long runs may be expected; for whenever a pack of hounds is fortunate enough to come across a traveller of this kind, he is sure to give them something to do, and may at the finish leave them baying outside an earth some ten or twelve miles distant.

Having returned from his midnight excursion, with contented mind and nothing indigestible in the stomach, he will curl himself up, lick his pads and, with brush around his nose, retire for rest, probably in a nice warm spot under a heap of briars, well sheltered from storm or wintry blast, and there wait the course of events by sleeping soundly. He may or may not be disturbed a little earlier than he anticipates, but at any rate he has a quick ear, and any enemy or intruder must be very gentle if he approach anywhere near the lair of the wily one, without putting him on the alert.

The huntsman's voice is as well known—if not so highly appreciated,—by the fox as it is by the very hounds which are cheered on to his destruction, and the moment he hears it he prepares for action by arousing himself from his lair, stretching his limbs, and giving himself a shake, when he listens again and steals away. On arriving at the edge of the covert, he will take a sly glance round to see if the course is clear. If so, and no voices are heard (gentlemen should never talk when standing at the corner of a covert), he will perhaps, if opportunity offer itself, for the sake of privacy choose a hedgerow to run beneath; then, with a whisk of the brush, dart off, and in all probability will give his pursuers something to do before the end comes, whatever the result may be.

Preserving—The best way of preserving foxes is to leave them alone; they require no other protection. Where they happen to be scarce, and it is necessary to import some, the best way is to get strong cubs, half-grown or more if possible (not things that have been kept up, but direct from their native home), put them into the earth at once, peg them in by driving stakes down at the mouth, and keep them there for a week or so. Feed them liberally on rabbits or rats, and at the end of the time pull up the stakes and leave them to their own resources; if they are strong they will be able to catch a rabbit for themselves and do well; the covert wil' be their play-ground, the earth their castle.

I have known foxes imported from Canada, but no good came of it; cubs from the Highlands of Scotland or the Welsh mountains are best and will be found an excellent change of blood.

Mange—The artificial way of rearing cubs which has come into existence during the last twenty years, is bad in the extreme, bad in every sense of the word; nearly every case of that dreadful disease, mange, springs from it.

The modern style, where the little red rover is not allowed at all times to roam at his leisure, is to keep up some cubs perhaps in a filthy dog-kennel, feed them on unnatural food, and, at a certain time, turn them down. Thereupon, or shortly after, mange is sure to break out.

As far as the hunt is concerned, it would be a thousand times better to find no fox at all. He cannot possibly do any good, but on the other hand must do an immense amount of harm. Mange is a terribly contagious disease, and any travelling fox from a distance may come in contact with it at any time, and so it quickly becomes spread over a wide space of country. There is no doubt that one mangy fox will do more harm among pheasants and poultry than a dozen healthy ones. The latter seek their food by night, when pheasants are at roost in the trees and out of reach, while the poultry are, or should be, locked up in safety; but both will fall an easy prey to the three-parts tame, hand-fed brute, who rests neither night nor day, the awful scourge which is upon him forbidding it. He is frequently seen by day moping about round "home," his only chance of gaining a livelihood; too weakly to go out at night and pounce upon rabbit or rat like his more healthy kinsmen, he crawls about in his agony by day into pheasantry or fowl-house, slaughtering whatever comes in the way. His natural instincts of obtaining a living have left him, and so he goes on growing weaker and weaker, until, if nothing else puts an end to his sufferings, he will in all probability be found eventually dead in or near some cart-hovel or other out-building, covered with scab from the nose to the tip of the tail, and near to the spot where he has been so mistakenly reared. To try to have foxes in the winter, and not in the summer, is to try for something which cannot be accomplished! The genuine article *or none* is best.

I have before now seen a good run with a mangy fox in the first stages of the disease, but let there be no mistake about it; this was not one of the hand-reared ones, but the traveller from a distance, who had unfortunately visited the haunts of the latter, and so contracted the disease. So much for mange and its dire effects.

Cubs at Play—There is no prettier sight to be seen on an evening in spring or early summer than a litter of cubs at play.

The activity displayed in skipping about, bouncing in the air, turning somersaults, playing hide and seek round a tree and cutting other capers is most amusing. For the purpose of observing this charming sight, it will be necessary to get on the down wind side of the earth where the cubs are known to be, making as little noise as possible in getting there, and then remaining perfectly silent; or a better way still is to climb a tree, perch yourself comfortably on one of its branches and there wait patiently their arrival. Presently the boldest of the litter will appear at the mouth of the earth, sniffing about on the ground and then darting back again. In a short time he will reappear with some of his brothers and sisters, a little more confidence is gained that all is right, and sports at once begin.

The chances are, too, that you may see the old vixen, who has gone out in the early evening to obtain something substantial in the way of food for her little ones; she returns with, most likely, a rabbit in her mouth, when the cubs will meet her, and a rare scuffle for the booty takes place. The rabbit will be taken, or rather dragged, into the earth, and probably in a few minutes the vixen will return to have a look round, taking a careful glance and winding in each direction: and if she obtains the smallest suspicion that you are in the neighbourhood, the odds are great that you will see, however much you may wish it, neither her nor her cubs again that night.

Mistakes are often made as regards the number of litters there are on a place, especially if there happen to be two or three earths in fairly close proximity. In such a case a fox with her cubs may not confine herself to one, but will perhaps use them all, keeping two or three homes going at one time, travelling backwards and forwards as she pleases, and the traffic that is made will give it the appearance of two or even three litters, when in reality there is but one.

Stub bred foxes—It is not always the case by any means that foxes are bred underground, and it is generally considered that stub bred foxes, as they are called, are the best, for the simple reason that they are not so much trouble to keep above ground when found by hounds, and every hole and drain is not so familiar to them as naturally it will be to others. In large woodlands, cubs will sometimes be found in hazel stub or root of tree, and the chances are, too, that they are as safe there as anywhere else, their greatest danger perhaps being from hounds in spring hunting. Not that I think one or two hounds would degrade themselves by swallowing up little cubs, but if several of them should by chance get down to the place at once, one might do it for fear another should. I was once a good way forward, looking down a ride in a wood, the huntsman being almost out of my hearing, but not of an old vixen fox, who came over the riding shortly after I arrived, with a cub in her mouth, stopping and turning her head to listen and then going on again. She evidently had her cubs above ground, and commenced to move them, as she thought, to a place of greater safety the moment she became aware of hounds in the neighbourhood. I at once informed the master of the fact, and hounds were taken to another covert without delay.

Earth-stopping and Badgers—It is very important that earth-stopping should be done thoroughly and well, and also at the proper time, or foxes may be stopped in the earths instead of outside. The easiest and best way, as a rule, is to have a faggot well tied (one end smaller than the other) for each opening; at night, when reynard is out on his rounds, the stopper should go and jam the faggot into the earth as tightly as possible; the next evening, when the hunt is over, all that is necessary is simply to withdraw it and lay it aside for future use. This is much better than the old-fashioned plan, of which we are sometimes reminded in pictures, where the venerable earth-stopper is seen marching off on his rounds, with candle and lantern, pick and spade.

Badgers are a great nuisance to an earth-stopper, for, with their long and strong claws, which are so well-shaped for the purpose, they can open out any earth at will, and in a very short time into the bargain; moreover they are deadly enemies to cubs. I know there are those who do not agree with me in this, but there are many who do; old George Carter of Tedworth fame, among others of great experience, always declared it, and I have myself on different occasions found dead cubs at the mouth of earths with tusk marks penetrating the brain, evidently from the chopping bite of the badger.

I do not intend to convey the idea that he would trouble himself to go out of his way for the purpose of killing a cub. He is too fat and lazy for that, and indeed there is no necessity for it, as it is well known that badgers and foxes will and do use the same earths, having separate compartments inside. But let the badger meet a cub either inside the earth or at the mouth of it, then the odds are great that that cub will never live to show a run over a country.

Fox Coverts—In countries not possessed of woodlands, it is sometimes necessary to make coverts, and when this has to be done there is nothing to beat the good old-fashioned gorse; this can be sown, or two or three year old plants put in; perhaps sowing is the best. In either case it is a mistake thoroughly to clean the ground. Some think differently, but the grass which springs up is a great protection to the young plant in winter, as well as forming a warm and comfortable lair for the fox.

Early in April is a good time for sowing the seed, and it should be drilled, not too thick, and with about fourteen or fifteen inches between the rows. A grass field is best for the purpose. Plough it up, put in the seed, harrow, and roll with Cambridge roller; the grass will soon come through, and, as before stated, will protect the young gorse in winter, and make a bed for the fox, who will be found there much earlier and more regularly than if there were nothing but the bare cold ground to lie upon.

Thorn or privet coverts are good in their way, and very hardy, but should not be planted too thickly, neither should they by any means be afterwards cut and "laird," as I have on some occasions seen, leaving only sufficient room for hounds to crawl through underneath. In the case of thorn coverts, with spikes sticking into them from every direction like porcupines' quills, they are totally unable to bustle a fox and drive him away. This is quite a mistake, as it is by no means necessary, for the purpose of holding, that coverts should be so desperately thick; besides, it has a tendency towards making bad foxes. With a bad scent inside, they are able to hang about, and much time may occasionally be spent there which would be better occupied in running over the open.

STOPPED.

Quiet is the thing which is absolutely necessary: coverts should remain undisturbed as much as possible except by hounds; and if the noble animal dwells in the neighbourhood, he is sure to make it his abode, and a find, once a fortnight at least, will be next to an absolute certainty.

A Good Fox—Naturally a good fox is he who shows the longest and straightest run, but unfortunately their number in most countries is small. One reason for this is that they do not travel such a great distance for their food, and become acquainted with so large an extent of country as we are told they did in years gone by. Another reason is, that the fox who has a tendency towards running straight, does not, as a rule, live to run many times; being so much easier to hunt, his chance of carrying off his brush in safety is much slighter than that of the dodging, twisting customer, who makes every available turn, running up one hedgerow, down another, &c., causing a check at almost every one, and thereby reaping so great an advantage.

Remarks may not infrequently be heard after a straight run,—"How splendidly they hunted him, no hounds ever deserved a fox more, &c.," when the fact is, their task has been made easy by the straight course taken; and although hounds always deserve blood after a persevering hunt, they deserve it much more with a bad fox than a good one, for their difficulties are far greater. When a bad, short-running fox goes to ground for instance, if he can be got out and despatched, so much the better, for he is the sort to blood hounds with. (It must be borne in mind that it is necessary to keep hounds well in blood.) On the other hand, if a fox makes a point of seven or eight miles, or as many more as you like, and goes to ground, cheer hounds at the earth to the very echo, rejoice over it as if you had him, but by all means leave him there. He is the sort you want for another day.

T. FIRR.

FRANCOLIN—These birds, nearly allied to the partridges of Europe, are found in most parts of Africa, often very abundantly. In South Africa alone there are some ten or eleven species. Some of these prefer thickly bushed localities, and roost on trees or bushes; these are always called by the colonists "pheasants." Other francolins, which inhabit more open country and at night remain upon the ground, are the best sporting birds, and are invariably known as "partridges." In Cape Colony excellent shooting is obtained with the "redwing" and "greywing" "partridges," known to scientists as *Francolinus levaillanti* and *Francolinus afer* respectively. Beyond the Orange River another "redwing," the Orange River francolin (*F. gariepensis*), and the beautiful little Coqui francolin (*F. subtorquatus*) afford the best sport, and very pretty shooting is often obtained with them. Pointers are usually employed for finding these birds; indeed, without the aid of a sporting dog but poor shooting would be obtained. A bag of from ten to twenty brace of these francolins can be secured by a couple of guns in localities where they are fairly numerous. Bechuanaland is one of the best grounds in South Africa for francolin shooting. The bush-frequenting francolins, or "pheasants," afford, from their running and perching habits, much poorer sport than the francolins found in open country. With the exception of the Coqui francolin (*Nswimpi* of the natives), all these birds exceed the English partridge in size and weight, the "pheasants" more especially. The flesh is fairly good eating, if somewhat dry.

One of the largest species (*F. jacksoni*) has been discovered in recent years by Mr. F. I. Jackson in Eastern Africa (*Masailand*). Another very fine species is Erckell's francolin, found in Abyssinia.

Although of the forty odd species of this game-bird at present known to scientists a large proportion are found in the African continent, some remarkable members of the family inhabit Asia. In parts of Asia and India, fair sport is occasionally to be obtained with various kinds of francolin. The Black Francolin (*F. vulgaris*) was formerly fairly abundant in Southern Europe, in Spain, Italy and Sicily, but is now to be found no nearer than Cyprus, whence its range extends to Palestine, Asia Minor, and as far East as Northern India.

This game-bird is well known in Southern Beluchistan and Afghanistan, upon the plains of Southern Persia, in Mesopotamia, and the region of the Caspian. In India, where it is known as the Black Partridge, it affects the river valleys and is found in high grass and tamarisk, often in the vicinity of cultivation. So lately as 1880, fifty brace of these birds have fallen in India to a single gun in a day's shooting; but, at the present time, it may be doubtful whether so good a bag could be made. Among the other well-known Asiatic francolins may be mentioned the Painted Francolin (*F. pictus*), familiar in India as the Painted Partridge. This bird is found in parts of Southern, Western, Central, and Northern India, in fairly open country, and affords good shooting. A steady pointer is very useful here, as in South Africa. Another well-known species is the Chinese Francolin (*F. chinensis*), found from the valley of the Irrawaddy as far East as Hong Kong, amid bushes, ferns, and bamboo-clad hills. This francolin is hard to flush, but has a strong flight

FRANCOLIN.

when roused. Phayre's Francolin (*F. phayrei*) is abundant in Upper Burmah. Nearly all the francolins are provided with sharp spurs, and the males fight fiercely in the mating season. Even the tiny Coqui francolin of Bechuanaland and the interior of South Africa is armed with strong and extremely sharp spurs, which, with the legs, are of a brilliant orange-yellow.

H. A. BRYDEN.

GAMEKEEPERS—Great changes have taken place in the duties of the gamekeeper during the last twenty years. Formerly the protection of game and the showing of a fair head on shooting days were practically all that was required. Any keeper, however ignorant, if sober and honest, was then, at least to some extent, competent to accomplish this. Now, however, when the rearing of game and the management of a shooting are reduced to a science, intelligence is indispensable to success. Poaching also, it must be noted, has been reduced to a science, and the nocturnal visits of the poacher with his stretches of nets and india-rubber shoes require skill, discrimination, and patient perseverance to be successfully dealt with. Even when there is a happy combination of all these, large quantities of both winged and ground game sometimes disappear in a single night.

The operation of the Ground Game Act has tended further to increase the difficulties of the keeper, and to render his position all the more embarrassing, for no amount of vigilant intelligence can subvert the drastic provisions of an ill-advised and disappointing legislative enactment. While an ignorant and indiscreet keeper is apt to bully and quarrel with farmers, the wise man, even when there is much provocation, will accept the inevitable and strive to exhibit a courteous demeanour towards them, so long as, in the exercise of their rights, they respect the statutes by which these are defined.

A keeper's books should be periodically examined by the estate auditor, but care should be taken to allow him the entire management of his own department. When he has the whole responsibility on his own shoulders, and knows what is expected of him, he feels it to be his interest to show good results and to compete in these respects with neighbouring keepers. Where there is a large consumption, a great saving can be effected in maize alone, in buying from honourable firms, who do not grant commissions (to the pecuniary injury of the proprietor and to the demoralisation of the keeper). Let the latter know that he is upon his honour and that his merits are appreciated, and this will go far to fortify him against giving way to temptation.

Pheasant-rearing—The rearing of pheasants is an important duty, and requires skill and patience alike to make it a uniform success. On most estates pheasants are captured and put in pens, in order that eggs may be secured for this purpose. There are so many devices for catching the birds—each one thinking his own the best—that it is unnecessary to refer to them here. The pens should be pretty long, with a door at each end, and a screen in the middle, in order that when a person goes in at one end the birds may run to the other and be out of sight, otherwise they are apt to fly and dash themselves against the wire. By careful and judicious feeding the number and fertility of eggs can be increased.

When the period of incubation has nearly expired, and the eggs are commencing to chip, they are sometimes removed from beneath the hen and put into an incubator. By this means the chicks are not trampled upon by the hen. If two eggs are left beneath a hen, the chances of loss by trampling are reduced to a minimum. But should a loss occur in this manner with only two chicks, it would be well to discard the hen at once from further service in pheasant-rearing. If, however, she appears to be a good mother, put her in a coop with the complement of chicks.

Turning down—Considerable difficulty is experienced in turning down pheasants in the cover which is to be their permanent home. Perhaps the best arrangement is to place the coops on a lorry which can carry a considerable number at once, convey them to the ridings in the woods, and put them in their respective positions. Up to this time the chicks are amenable to the call of their foster mother, and under her maternal care are soon reconciled to their new environment. They are now picking small maize, so that biscuit meal and other expensive foods may be more sparingly used. Prompted by nature, pheasants, before they are full grown, take to roosting in trees. The keeper then feels a sense of relief, as they are now practically safe, unless it be from vermin. Should a litter of fox cubs take up their abode in the woods, the destruction is incalculable. The intelligent keeper, however, knows at once if a stray cat, dog or fox, be in the wood. The warning cackle of a cock pheasant, the screeching of a jay, the excited piping of blackbirds and other birds, or the disturbed movements of any living thing, quickly notify to his practised ear that an enemy is abroad.

Foxes—Fox-hunters frequently assert that the fox does little damage to pheasants, and advance the most ingenious though unconvincing arguments in support of their assertions. From long experience in a hunting country, and having reared pheasants in the midst of foxes, I can here speak with confidence. On more than one occasion I have known a fox make a raid among the coops in the early morning, when the birds had commenced to sit out. Once, when watching in the rearing field on an estate in Berwickshire, and when partially asleep, I was aroused by a disturbed noise among the hens. On looking up, reynard was stealthily withdrawing from among the birds, but not until several had been destroyed, although none of them were carried off. The skilled keeper will on such occasions as these note the "airt o' the wind," as in no case will the fox approach from the lee side of the watcher.

Badgers—Badgers, although by no means so numerous as they once were in this country, must be classed among the enemies of the gamekeeper. While not indifferent to the luxury of a pheasant or partridge nest, or young brood, he is chiefly to be dreaded for his wholesale destruction of young rabbits. With unerring instinct he discovers the exact spot, although several feet below the surface, where the young rabbits have been deposited in their nest. It is to the badger a matter of no moment how many young the nest contains,—he makes a speedy clearance and renders a second visit unnecessary.

Vermin—The domestic cat, more especially when in close proximity to villages and agricultural steadings, proves a destructive pest to the keeper, and can only be kept in check by the free use of traps planted in and around the preserves.

Polecats, stoats, and weasels also claim the watchful attention of the gamekeeper. There is a ferocious and bloodthirsty instinct characteristic of these animals which is most hateful to the game preserver. They prosecute their work with a merciless persistency, which can only be satisfied by the blood of their victims. All of them seem positively to revel in the destruction of innocent and helpless birds and animals. They appear in some measure to possess the additional characteristic of being well-nigh ubiquitous. The keeper may have concluded, and that accurately, that he has cleared the entire estate of them, and yet within a few days thereafter he will be surprised to find the reappearance of one or more of the stoat species. This arises from their restless activity, for distance seems to be no obstacle to them. I have tracked the stoat for surprisingly long distances after a fresh fall of snow. A few years ago I was asked by a New Zealand Land Company to secure some hundreds of stoats and weasels in order to have them transported to that colony with the view of counteracting the rabbit plague. Within a short period it was discovered that some of them had travelled a distance of ninety miles in order to get round the head of a river and lake. Endowed as they are with such travelling powers, and with their bloodthirsty habits, it is easy to see that their presence cannot be tolerated in a game preserve.

The hedgehog is another enemy, and, from its habit of eating eggs, is much more destructive in the nesting season than most people imagine. Occasionally finding its way into coops among young pheasants in the dark, it does much mischief; and that old hens are killed and disembowelled by hedgehogs is a well attested fact, despite the sneers of acknowledged authorities on sport.

With the destructive habits of rats every one is familiar. Snaring instead of trapping has also afforded them opportunities for taking possession of rabbit holes. Nothing comes amiss to the rat; fish, flesh, fowl and vegetables are greedily devoured. When rats grow large they become very savage, and will kill every kind of young game they can get hold of.

Hawks—The hawk species, from the eagle down to the merlin, must ever engross the attention of the intelligent gamekeeper. There is an absolute pleasure in watching the habits of these winged marauders which affords to the naturalist a motive for the study of their peculiarities other than that which seeks to compass their destruction. The game preserver has chiefly to guard against the peregrine falcon, the sparrow-hawk, and the merlin, and, of the Corvidæ, carrion crows, ravens, and magpies. No mercy should be shown to any of these, but there are a number of others the destruction of which should be left to the good sense of the keeper. Among these may be mentioned rooks, jays, jackdaws, kestrels, and owls. The three first mentioned do damage chiefly to eggs, though very young game are by no means safe from their depredations. Kestrels in some cases are destructive to pheasants, partridges, and grouse. Owls may be included in the same category, although, when large quantities of mice are available, birds are not likely to suffer much. Indeed, mice would seem to be their normal food, as was strikingly illustrated in Scotland a few years ago, when the southern counties had a special visitation of a mice plague. It is a fact worthy of being remembered that owls were then to be found in immense numbers where the plague was most severely felt. Their arrival was almost simultaneous with the development of the plague, while it was noticed that they disappeared from the district with its abatement. It must not be supposed, however, that, where mice are not attainable, owls do not "harry" the nests of our singing birds. Tawny owls, in particular, during the nesting season, frequently feed the owlets with small birds and young game. Of this I have seen repeated examples.

Dogs—The efficient gamekeeper will ever be careful regarding his kennel, not merely seeing that the accommodation for his dogs is dry and comfortable, with an abundant supply of pure water, but that the conditions for the health and comfort of his dogs are such as he would like to provide for his own household. He will also see to the pure breed of his dogs, and that they receive a training which will afford to the sportsman enjoyment when they are shot over, altogether apart from that realised by the use of the gun. The positive torture arising from badly trained and untractable dogs partakes largely of the character of a nuisance. At the same time, however pure the breed, and however satisfactory the conditions in which dogs may be kept, perfection is neither to be secured nor expected except with considerable experience among game.

Tom Speedy.

Wages—A really good head-gamekeeper is invaluable to his master, and therefore he is not often overpaid, whatever the size of the manor may be. As for the underkeepers, they usually receive the maximum wages of agricultural labourers in the district, or a little more, and cottages and gardens rent free. A cow is often a useful help to a head man, if he has young children; but more than this is not advisable, as it is not well that keepers should be farmers.

Beaters had better be paid by the head keeper, and half-a-crown a day is a fair wage, with bread, cheese and beer, which the keeper may with advantage provide, as it saves friction with the house kitchen and pantry. While on this subject it may be well to suggest that the master should find out from the keeper whether the loaders, whose luncheon will doubtless be sent from the house with that of the shooters, have had food enough, for sometimes they do not fare very well. The subject of presents is cognate to that of wages, but it is a very delicate one; suffice it to say that a considerate guest is apt to give a little more to a man whose master only has a few days' shooting to which to invite his friends, than to the servant of the proprietor who has a party every other week throughout the season.

Game Production—In order to have a good supply of game on any ground, it is essential to keep it quiet, and to be able to keep away trespassers (and, of course, poachers) who have no business to be there at all, and also to be on good terms with those who must be present in order to follow their respective vocations in life, such as shepherds, labourers and farmers. Shepherds and farm-servants can help in the preservation of grouse and partridges in the most material way, and, if they are friendly, and if vermin is duly kept within bounds, a great deal is done towards a good stock of birds. In the case of grouse, if the control and judicious burning of the heather is added, little more is necessary. With partridges it is well to change the blood sometimes, either by turning out some imported birds at the end of a season, or by changing eggs with a neighbour, or from one side of a manor to another. There is no harm in rearing artificially eggs taken from nests disturbed in mowing, or otherwise in dangerous places; but the young ones are not easy to bring up, and afterwards do not afford very satisfactory sport, as they pack so readily, a great disadvantage if they are to be walked after, and also inconvenient for driving. In severe winters, when there is much snow, something may be done by a little judicious feeding of partridges in sheltered places, and the keepers' vigilance must then be doubled, as the coveys afford a tempting mark on the snow to the prowling gunner.

Shooting—It is not enough at the present time for a keeper to have woods full of pheasants, or fields full of partridges, but he must be clever enough to manage that they should be killed in a satisfactory way. To plan a large day's partridge-driving is as difficult a task as carrying out the plan when made. The keeper must know his men, be able to trust them when at a distance, especially when there are two sets of beaters out, and must be careful to judge accurately when to start the next drive, after one is over, so as to give reasonable time for picking up. He must not hurry the guns unnecessarily to their next station, nor keep them waiting too long when they have reached it. Then he must be sure to know whither the bulk of the birds have gone, and to vary his plan when necessary, so as to bring them back into the drives. The master can help materially in the management; but the most accomplished sportsman will usually find himself helpless, unless his keeper comprehends the various objects aimed at, and the right methods of attaining them.

The art of beating a covert may perhaps be less difficult than that of driving a country for partridges, but even here there is great scope for failure or success. The stops must be in their places long before the actual beating begins, and some trusty person must see that they do not leave their posts; for the result of a stop going away from where he has been ordered to stand is usually most disastrous. The beaters, too, must be under strict control, trained to keep line, to hold their tongues, to go through the thickest thorns and brambles, and to be always listening for orders and looking under their feet to see if they can pick up anything. But the most faithful stops and the most accomplished beaters are not enough; for even when all the pheasants are where they ought to be, it is most difficult to put them up satisfactorily, and this art many keepers, excellent in other ways, can never properly acquire. Some men can never help putting the greater part of a corner full of pheasants up in one flush, which is most distressing to all concerned, while others will never fail, even on ground where it would seem impossible, to send out their birds by tens and twenties at a time as long as there are any left in the thicket, though the process may last during an indefinite period.

Nor is this all. It is nowadays by no means thought enough to surround a corner with guns and drive out several hundred birds close to the heads of the shooters. They must be made to fly well; and to this end much skill and care must be directed; advantage must be taken of the slope of the ground, of the height of the trees, and of the way the pheasants would go by choice. It is far easier to make them fly properly if their heads are turned towards the place from which they have come than if they are being forced away from home on to unknown ground. To the modern shooter it makes all the difference whether the birds come well or not, and the day's sport is thought good, or the reverse, almost completely according to this test, so that it is absolutely necessary to attempt to make the birds fly well.

Picking Up—A good gamekeeper must have a good retriever. Walking up birds in line and driving them have banished pointers and setters to grouse-moors, and even on these they are being used less and less, but the retriever takes their place. It is unnecessary to say that he (or she) must be able to smell, be trained to obey, and have a soft mouth; but it may be useful to observe that, in addition to these indispensable attainments, quickness is a valuable quality to cultivate, especially for a keeper's dog, which need not be quite so perfectly broken as that of a gentleman. Indeed, in these days gentlemen's dogs are usually more ornamental than useful, and, except for grouse- and partridge-driving, had better be left at home. Not only the head keeper, but all his principal assistants, should have good dogs; and in covert shooting, whenever and wherever any guns are stationed away from the line of beaters, there should always be some one behind them with a dog, no matter whether it is an important stand or not. This is advisable in the interest of sport as well as of humanity, as it is very difficult and distracting for a gun and his loader to have to be thinking all the time where this or that bird fell, so as to be able to tell the keeper, when the line at last comes up. Good picking up is a most comforting thing to sportsmen, and it is not invariably attended to as well as it should be. After any ordinary day the ground must be hunted over by men and dogs as soon as possible, and it is for the master to see that this is done properly.

Too large a "pick up" means that the work was not properly done on the day itself, and too small a one often implies subsequent neglect. It has been observed that, as regards pheasants, about six or seven per cent. is a very common proportion under good ordinary management, so that much more or much less than this is a result which should be investigated.

Hares and Rabbits—Hitherto these remarks have been confined to the keeper's relations with feathered game, but there are such things as hares and rabbits, and it is hardly well to ignore them altogether. Hares are not good shooting at any time, and it is a pity, for the sake of good sport, to encourage them unduly anywhere; but a good keeper ought to do his very best to have an adequate number on any ground in his charge where they will exist at all, because a proper quantity of hares on any shooting is the surest proof that farmers are friendly and poachers absent.

Rabbits are not seldom a source of strife between master, keeper, agent, and tenant, and it is impossible to offer any general suggestions as to how the ideal keeper should deal with them. A rabbitless wood is a most delightful thing to its owner all the year round, except on the days when he shoots in it; but on those occasions it is apt to be voted dull, and then the difficult problem arises, of how to manage to have enough rabbits, and yet not too many.

It is quite easy to have none, it is easier to have swarms, but it is not at all easy to be able to make sure of killing a suitable number, and yet not to let them be a source of mischief. In spite of what people often say and believe, rabbits do far more harm inside a covert than outside it. Not much rabbiting can be done in a wood, where there are to be some pheasants as well, between March and the time when it is shot through in the following winter; but after that has been done once or, better still, twice, the keeper and his staff should kill rabbits there as hard as they can, till the spring is fairly started, not with guns, but with all other available engines; and if this is properly attended to year after year, there will not be much cause of complaint left either for the agriculturist or the lover of trees.

H.

GAME LAWS—Probably no set of laws have undergone so complete a change from their original purpose as the Game Laws. Denounced as relics of feudalism and barbarism, and as the means of oppression by landlords of tenants, they have become a valuable source of revenue to the country. Their abolition is often spoken of, but the tendency at the present day is rather to extend their operation than to repeal them. The whole of the Modern Wild Bird legislation shows this. For the purposes of this article the Game Laws may be grouped under four heads. 1. Who may kill game. 2. When game may be killed. 3. Where game may be killed. 4. How game may be killed.

Each of these requires separate consideration.

Who may Kill Game—Any of the Queen's subjects may kill game, provided he qualifies himself by taking out a proper license from the Inland Revenue. That is the only qualification now required. Before 1831 a person, to be entitled to kill game, had to possess a qualification; he had to be an esquire or person of higher degree. That was then abolished, and now a license is all that is necessary to enable a person to kill game. But every one must have a license, whether he kills game on his own land or on another person's. The licenses are of three kinds, and vary in price; they may be for the whole season, or for part of the season, or for gamekeepers. Those who take out licenses for the whole season are entitled to sell the game they kill, those who take it out for part of the season are not. Every one killing game legally must have one of these three licenses. Game is defined by the Game Act, 1831, as including hares, pheasants, partridges, grouse, heath or moor game, black game, and bustards; and this is the standard definition of game. There are other definitions which include other kinds of birds for the Night Poaching Acts, the Poaching Prevention Act, and the Excise Acts. By the Ground Game Act, hares and rabbits have been put into a class by themselves as ground game, and special rules apply to them. The confusion is made worse by some of these Acts applying to England only, others to England and Scotland, others to the United Kingdom. So the definition of game differs in England, Scotland, and Ireland. So far as killing game goes, the importance of the definition only relates to the sum to be paid for duty, as a gun can only be legally used if either a game or a gun license has been obtained; the holder of a game license does not require a gun license, but the holder of a gun license requires a game license. As distinguished from other animals and birds, special forms of protection are given to game, and the penalties are higher for illegally killing it; but as regards the question, "Who may kill Game?" the answer is, "A person who has taken out a proper license." It must not, however, be imagined that a properly licensed person has a right to kill game when, where, and as he pleases. There are certain modes of killing game that are illegal, and which no one may use. Game can only be killed at certain times of the year, and a licensed person cannot kill it except at these times; and no one has a right, however much he may have paid for license duty, to go on land and kill game, unless he has the right or permission to do so.

When Game can be Killed—The Game Act, 1831, fixes for England the times for killing game. No one may kill game on any Sunday in a year or a Christmas Day. Partridges may be killed on week days between September 1st and February 1st. Pheasants between October 1st and February 1st. Black game in Devon, Somerset, and the New Forest between September 1st and December 10th, elsewhere between August 20th and December 10th. Grouse between August 12th and December 10th. Bustard between September 1st and March 1st. For all birds not game, the time for killing is between August 1st and March 1st, unless in any particular county the time has been altered by the County Council. There is no close time for *eating* hares, but they may not be *sold* between March 1st and July 31st. Rabbits may be caught and sold all the year round. Substantially these times are the same throughout the United Kingdom, but there are some slight variations. Game and wild birds killed within the United Kingdom may not be sold during the times when they may not be taken, except that there is a short allowance at the beginning of the close time for clearing out stock. This does not apply to game and wild birds killed out of the United Kingdom, which may be sold at any time of the year. The proof that they were taken out of the United Kingdom lies on the person offering them for sale. The rule seems to apply to all British or Irish game sold during the close season, even to game kept in a cold store. The offence of killing game during close time is quite separate from the offence of selling game during close time; and the latter can be committed, even if the game has been killed in the open season. In addition to taking or selling game in close time, it is an offence for any one, unless he has the right or permission, to kill game on the land, to take the eggs of any bird, of game, or of any swan, wild duck, teal, or widgeon, or to have such eggs in possession. The taking of the eggs of birds other than game or those birds named is regulated by the different County Councils, which make byelaws prohibiting the taking of certain eggs, and these byelaws seem to differ almost in each county. If there is no byelaw, all eggs except those mentioned above may be legally taken. [*See* WILD BIRDS PROTECTION.]

Where Game may be Taken—The general rule is that neither game nor any other bird or beast can be taken without the leave of the *occupier* of the land.

The law in 1831 vested the right of killing game and of sporting in him, and, unless he has parted with the right, no one can kill game, or sport over land without the occupier's leave; if he has parted with it, the leave of the person who has acquired it must be obtained. The occupier usually parts with his right in two ways: he either gives it up to his landlord on taking the farm, which is the usual case when the game is reserved by the lease or agreement, or he lets it himself to some sporting tenant. Unless he has dealt with it in one or other of these two ways, it belongs to him. One part of sporting right the occupier cannot resign is the joint right, with the owner of the land, to kill ground game, hares, and rabbits. Whatever may be the reservation in the lease to the landlord, or in whatever terms the occupier has parted with his sporting rights to a tenant, the right to kill ground game remains in him, and he cannot divest himself of it.

Another restriction must be borne in mind. Unless the occupier either gives up to his landlord by some writing under seal, the right of sporting, or gives it to a tenant by some writing under seal, the right remains in the occupier. It is often forgotten that sporting rights of any nature can only be legally transferred by a document under seal. The neglect of this may cause great disappointment. A friend of the landlord goes shooting; if there is no leave under seal, the tenant can stop him. A sporting tenant summons a poacher; he fails to get a conviction, for he has no right to prosecute, there being no document under seal transferring the sporting right. Therefore, unless the occupier of lands has parted with the right of sporting by document under seal, he is the only person who can exercise such rights, or give leave to other persons to exercise such rights. In by far the larger number of cases the occupier has given up such right, either to his landlord or to some one else, but this has been by his own act. In law he is the owner and can deal with the right as he pleases.

There are certain exceptions to this rule, but they are of very rare occurrence, only being found in places to which formerly the Crown had granted special right. These places are Royal forests and chases and places where a right of free warren exists; but the number of such places is exceedingly limited, and the right to game may as a rule be safely dealt with on the footing that it is the occupier's, unless he has parted with it.

Very important questions have arisen as to the occupier's right when he has parted with the game. How far is he entitled to compensation for damage done by the game? If any special terms are made on his parting with it, either to the landlord or to the shooting tenant, those terms will regulate the bargain. It is a matter of contract like any other contract; and the occupier, by giving up for value his right to the game, cannot complain of any damage the game may do to him, provided the game is that naturally produced on the land. But, if the person who has the game is not content with the head of game produced on the land, and brings on the place game and turns it down, then he becomes liable for the damage that is done. The rule is that if a person brings anything on land that does damage to his neighbour he is liable for the consequence of his act. This has been decided as to his game, but the point has not as yet arisen how far a person who breeds pheasants from bought eggs is liable; it appears he would be, for there can be no real difference caused by the state in which the article causing the damage is brought on the land.

As to hares and rabbits, the occupier would have the right of killing them, and so of preventing any damage being done to him. But a neighbour would probably still be able to maintain an action for any damage caused by keeping an excessive quantity of ground game, the Act not having altered the law in this respect. The rights, therefore, of the occupier of land with his landlord and with the sporting tenant are now rights which are not so much regulated by Game Laws as by the special contract between the parties. If the landlord let the sporting which he has reserved, his tenant stands to the occupier of the land precisely in the landlord's place, and has the same rights as the landlord, neither more nor less; if the occupier let the sporting, the sporting tenant has the rights he has contracted for, and no more.

As might be expected, there are numberless points on the question of letting sporting rights that continually arise, and will be found in any book on the Law of Landlord and Tenant, or the Game Laws, but the rule is as here stated; the whole matter is a question of contract. Apart from the question of occupier, and persons deriving the rights from him, comes the next branch of the subject. Persons in pursuit of game without the permission of the occupier or holder of the sporting rights, trespass. In law, every one who has not the required permission authorising him to sport on each particular bit of land over which he goes is a trespasser, and is liable to be punished accordingly.

With the exception of the space between high and low water mark on the sea shore and on tidal navigable rivers, there is no place in the United Kingdom where every one can legally sport without permission. He must obtain permission from some one qualified to give it. It often happens that persons are allowed to sport in open or common lands, and are not interfered with, but still in law they are trespassers; they have no legal right there as members of the public. They cannot even go along roads for sporting, as the soil of the roads is supposed to belong to the owners of the adjoining land, or to some public body; and the public can only use it for the purpose of passing along, and for no other. Thus a man who shot a pheasant flying across a road was held liable to be convicted for unlawfully killing game, and a person who walked up and down a road for the purpose of obstructing a grouse drive was held liable in an action for damages.

So again, a person who walks along a road and sends a dog into the adjoining land to take the game would be liable. Indeed, it is almost impossible to put a case where one of the public can legally take game, except as above defined, unless he has permission. This restriction not only applies to game, but to all sporting, for any animal or bird, and is quite irrespective as to whether the person is or is not licensed.

While, on the one hand, a person who may have the legal right to kill game over half England cannot do it without a license, so, on the other, a person who is fully licensed cannot sport without the legal authority to go over some land.

As has been said, these rights are not pressed to the utmost extent, and so what is popularly known as "free shooting" exists in some places, but it has not any legal existence, and the person who is led to try it will probably find himself involved in a question of game trespass.

Apart from this class of case there are the cases of persons who deliberately break the law—poachers. Their offence is dealt with in different ways: (1) as to the time when it was done, day or night; (2) as to the number of persons who are engaged in it.

Trespassing in pursuit of game in the daytime is a matter which usually involves the trespassers in a summons before the justices in England, where the offence is dealt with summarily, and the trespasser finds his license. if he has one, forfeited, and, if he cannot pay the fine and has no goods on which a distress can be levied, he is liable to be imprisoned. If a trespasser refuse to [illegible] the owner, occupier, or gamekeeper his real na[illegible]nd address, he may be arrested, but, if so, must be brought before a justice within twelve hours. If the trespass be committed by five or more persons, the penalty is higher. These offences apply to any trespass on any land in pursuit of game; but if the trespass is on a special place, such as a rabbit warren, or in a deer park in pursuit of deer, or in a decoy or place where wildfowl are specially kept, the offence becomes one under the Larceny Act as well as under the Game Laws. The person can be proceeded against under either at the option of the owner, but the penalties are much more serious under the Larceny Act.

If the trespass take place at night, it is of a much more serious character, the first offence being punishable with imprisonment with hard labour for three months; and, if any violence is used to owner, occupier, or keeper, it becomes an indictable misdemeanour, liable to be punished with seven years' penal servitude.

If there are more persons on the land at night to catch game, armed with offensive weapons, it becomes a still more serious offence, punishable with penal servitude up to fourteen years. It will be seen that the poaching offence may be an ordinary trespass on land by an individual in the day, punishable with a fine; trespass on particular places, punished more severely; trespass at night still more so; and if by armed gangs at night, subject to a very heavy penalty.

In order to detect offences on the land, certain powers of search and seizure are given to gamekeepers, but these can only be exercised on the master's land. This limitation of powers led to the passing of the Poaching Prevention Act, which gave to the police power to stop and search any person on a highway whom they reasonably suspected of being in possession of game unlawfully taken. So, if a person is caught on land with recently killed game, it can be seized by the owner or his keeper. If a person suspected of having game unlawfully taken is met on a highway, he can be stopped and searched by a policeman; and if game is found on him, it can be seized, but the keeper has no power off his master's land, and the constable has no power off the highway. The powers of each are strictly limited as to the place where they may be exercised. They also differ in this, that the keeper cannot search on suspicion, but must see game recently killed; the constable has a right to search any one whom he reasonably suspects. Such are the main provisions against trespass in pursuit of game, and for stopping poaching.

One point must be borne in mind: the offences are cumulative—*e.g.*, a person enters another man's land and kills a partridge and refuses to give his name; he is liable for the trespass and also for another penalty for refusing to give his name.

There are numberless cases on the points as to what constitutes a trespass, such as whether an actual entry on the land is required; will it do if you fire over a hedge? This has been held sufficient. What is being armed? What is recently killed game? When do the rights of the keeper cease, and when do the rights of the police to search begin? For these, however, reference must be made to some work on the Game Laws.

Besides the penalties under the Game Laws, if the person trespassing in pursuit of game has not got a proper license (*e.g.*, if he killed a partridge when he had only a gun license), or had no license at all, or if he used a gun without a license, he would be liable to the excise penalties. These are quite distinct and independent from the Game Laws, and can be only sued for by the inspector of excise, not by any one who desires; and a conviction under the Game Acts would be no answer to an information by the excise, nor would the justice be justified in taking the proceedings under the Game Act into account in fixing the penalty. The whole of the excise rules are a separate and distinct code and proceed on quite distinct lines from the Game Acts. Much of the arbitrary procedure that is said to belong to the Game Laws really belongs to the excise, persons not taking the trouble to distinguish between the two classes of cases.

There is, and always has been, a good deal of difficulty as to who is entitled to the property in game. Strictly speaking, no one has any property in it until it is captured, the right of the occupier of the land being merely a qualified right. He can prevent any one going after it or disturbing it while on his land, but he has no real property in it. That is, he has no such property as would justify him in charging a person illegally taking it with stealing it. The Game Laws do not touch this point, and, so far as they are concerned, there is no difference in law in this respect between game and any other wild animal. The rule is that, to obtain property in game, it must be reduced into possession. A series of decisions, some of them dating back to the Middle Ages, have introduced into the English law some very curious and complicated rules as to when game or any other wild animal becomes property; and the rules are of practical importance. The first is that when wild animals are started and killed on a man's land they become the property of the owner of the land. But if, started on the land of one man, they are killed on the land of another, they become the property, not of either owner, but of the taker. He is liable to be proceeded against for illegally killing the animal, but he is the owner of it when killed. There have been several important cases on the subject as to when the property in dead game rested in the owner of the land, and when it did not. If the property rest in the owner of the land the taking it is larceny, and a different state of law arises with regard to it than if it merely comes under the Game Laws. It is a felony, and the rules as to felony prevail, while any offence against the Game Laws, however aggravated, is at best but a misdemeanour. It should, however, be borne in mind that, because certain offences against game and wild animals are dealt with under the Larceny Act, that does not make the larceny a felony. That Act merely relates to the procedure for the punishment of the offence; for instance, under that Act, killing rabbits in a warren is made highly penal, but it is not made larceny. This distinction as to when offences are merely offences against the Game Law and when they are offences against the general law, depending as it does on very refined and technical distinction, is one of the points that make it so difficult to state what the English law is on the subject.

Another point which has given rise to a good deal of discussion, and is not yet finally settled, is the question, what offence does a man commit, who, seeing a dead partridge or a dead pheasant or any dead bird in a field, goes into the field and picks it up? The general opinion is that it is larceny and a felony, and that the Game Laws have nothing to do with the case; but the point has not been expressly decided. The Game Laws only apply to the taking of live game. When it is dead, taking it from a field is in law the same as taking it from a shop. The rule that there is no property in wild animals until they are reduced into possession has the further limitation that it does not apply to game or other animals kept in confinement or semi-confinement. It has been decided that young partridges brought up by a hen can be stolen; the only question being when they cease to be property, and become so wild as to be outside the rule. In these days of artificial rearing and game farms, the point is one of some importance; the rule seems to be that the person who calls himself owner must be able to take them if and when he please; if he can do that they are his property, and the subject of larceny. The same question arises as to eggs. If the birds are reclaimed, or so far reclaimed that taking them would be larceny, then taking the eggs will be the same. If not, it is only the eggs of game birds that it is an offence to take or be in the possession of. The Game Act, 1831, provides that any one, without leave, taking or destroying the eggs of any game bird, or the eggs of any swan, wild duck, teal, or widgeon, or knowingly having them in possession, is liable to a penalty not exceeding five shillings for each egg. If, on the other hand, the eggs are the subject of larceny, the offence of taking them is punishable with penal servitude; and the receiving them, knowing them to have been stolen, is punishable with the same penalty. The eggs of other birds than game and those mentioned in the Game Act comes under the Wild Birds Acts, but the same rule applies to them; if taking the birds would be larceny, so will taking the eggs. But if the taking the bird is not larceny, the taking the eggs can only be punished under the Wild Birds Acts.

How Game may be Taken.—Even the owner or occupier of the land on which the game is, however much he may be entitled to it, and whatever license he may have, can only take the game in certain ways. (1) He may not use poison to kill the game; this is expressly provided for in the Game Act, but it has been extended by subsequent Acts to forbidding poison to be used for killing any animals or birds, and so far as game is concerned it is now only a part of the general law. (2) Under the Ground Game Act the occupier may not use spring traps in the open for taking ground game. Before the Game Act, 1831, there were a number of instruments by which it was illegal to take game, and certain ways of taking game—*e.g.*, tracking it in the snow, were also unlawful; but by that Act all these restrictions have been abolished, and, except by poison or spring traps, owners and occupiers can take game by any mode they please. A distinction here will be noticed between Game Laws and other laws where licenses are required, such as the Fishing Laws. With game, it is the *person* who is licensed, and he can use any engine or device he likes. In fishing matters it is the *instrument* that is licensed, and the person can only use an instrument of that kind and no other. One other restriction should be noticed: the Game Act makes it illegal to take game on Sunday or Christmas Day. It has been decided that this applies not only to the case of a person who goes in pursuit of game on any of those days, but also to a person who sets a trap on Saturday and leaves it down on Sunday. If a snare is placed for a hare on a Saturday and left over Sunday, and a hare or rabbit is caught on a Sunday, the person who set the snare, even if in his own garden, is liable to a penalty, and this even if he has a full game license. It is also unlawful for a person who is duly licensed to kill game, and on his own land, where he has full right to the game, to use any firearms for killing game at night—*i.e.*, between the expiration of the first hour after sunset and the beginning of the last hour before sunrise. This restriction, however, only applies to game and hares, and does not appear to include rabbits. It certainly does not include wildfowl.

Sale of Game.—There are very severe restrictions placed upon the sale of game. Previous to the Game Act, 1831, the sale of game was absolutely illegal, but that Act made a great change in the law and allowed game to be sold subject to certain restrictions. The chief of these are:—(1) The only persons who can legally sell game are:—(*a*) the holders of a full license to kill game; (*b*) a keeper duly licensed, who sells his master's game which he has killed on his master's land, for and on account of his master, and (*c*) a person entitled to ground game, selling it under the Ground Game Act. This would only apply to hares, and it would seem that, to come within the exemption, the hare must have been killed on the land in the occupation of the vendor; if a person sold a hare killed on another man's land he would be liable to a penalty. Every one else, however legally they may have obtained the game, if they sell it, are liable to a penalty. (2) The only persons to whom game can legally be sold are persons who are licensed to deal in game. The license used to be granted by justices at special sessions to such persons as applied for it as in the opinion of the justices were fit persons to hold it, the Act forbidding license to deal in game to be granted to certain persons, such as the keepers of public houses. Now the licenses are granted by the District Councils of the place in which the applicant resides, but the same restrictions apply as before to the person to whom they are to be granted. Every dealer who is licensed to deal in game should exhibit over his shop a board, with "Licensed to deal in game" on it. It is only from these licensed dealers that the public can legally buy; if they buy from any one else, they render themselves liable to a penalty. This restriction only applies to game as defined in the Game Act, 1831. Any one can sell rabbits, wood pigeons, and plovers, and they can be bought from any one; but grouse, partridges, and pheasants can only be purchased from licensed dealers. This is perhaps the one part of the Game Laws which, if rigidly enforced, would bear hardly on the public, as the onus of showing that the game was legally bought rests on the person in whose possession it is found. There is an exception in favour of the keepers of hotels, restaurants, and such places supplying game to their guests; but, except this, the prohibition is absolute, and there is a case reported of the conviction of an enthusiastic naturalist who bought from a labourer an old partridge, which the labourer said he found dead.

The number of exceptions that exist to any rule on game make it dangerous to try to state a rule. The whole subject is very special, and it by no means follows that the law is what it would be expected to be. One point the Game Law brings out clearly—the equality of all the Queen's subjects before the law. The wealthiest landowner in England can no more legally carry a gun without a license over his own fields than can the worst poacher. Neither the landowner nor poacher can legally take a partridge or pheasant, unless he has a license. If a landowner breed his own pheasants, he cannot sell one without a license. If he has not a license, and finds on his own ground a wounded partridge, he cannot catch it without incurring a penalty. It is not the landless man who alone feels the force of the Game Laws. They touch peer and peasant alike, and teach that it is not lawful for a man to do what he likes with his own, that he can only deal with this class of property subject to the restriction of the laws.

WILLIS BUND.

Game Defined—The Act 1 & 2 Will. IV. c. 32 is the principal Game Act now in force, but has been amended and supplemented by several Statutes passed during the present reign.

By this Act (sect. 2) "game" is defined to include "hares, pheasants, partridges, grouse, heath, or moor game, black game, and bustards." This definition has been slightly varied by other Acts (*e.g.*, the Night Poaching Act, 9 Geo. IV. c. 69, and the Act authorising constables to search suspected persons, 25 & 26 Vict. c. 114), while by the Game Licenses Act (23 & 24 Vict. c. 90) woodcocks, snipes, quails, landrails, conies, and deer, although not regarded as game strictly speaking, cannot be killed without a license. Nor can any of the birds named be killed during the breeding season or close time, which varies in England, Scotland, and Ireland.

The close time fixed for game birds is as follows:—for partridges from February 1 to September 1; pheasants, February 1 to October 1; black game, December 10 to August 20; grouse, December 10 to August 12; bustard, March 1 to September 1; and the possession of such game after ten days by dealers, and forty days by others, after the expiration of the season, is illegal.

By a recent decision of the Court of Queen's Bench, however, it has been held, on appeal in the case of *Guyer* v. *The Queen*, that this does not apply to game killed and received from abroad. (See report of this case in *The Field*, April 20, 1889.)

Close Time for Birds not Game—With regard to birds not included in the definition of "game," *sea birds* were in 1869 protected from April 1 to August 1 by 32 & 33 Vict. c. 17, and *wild fowl* between February 15 and August 1 by 39 & 40 Vict. c. 39 (1872). Now *all birds* are protected between March 1 and August 1 by the "Wild Birds Protection Acts," 1880–81 (43 & 44 Vict. c. 35, and 44 & 45 Vict. c. 51), under different penalties, according as the species of bird in question is included in the Schedule to the Act or not.

If the bird in question is *included in the Schedule* to the Act it may not be killed during the close time under a penalty not exceeding £1; if *not included* in the Schedule the penalty is, for a first offence, a reprimand and payment of costs, and for every subsequent offence a fine not exceeding 5*s*. in addition to costs. But any one may kill birds which are *not* in the Schedule to this Act *on his own land* during the close season, and authorise other persons to do so without incurring any penalty.

In 1894 a further Act was passed (57 & 58 Vict. c. 24), enabling a Secretary of State, upon application of a County Council, to prohibit by order the taking of eggs of any wild bird, either throughout the county or in certain specified areas within it, or the eggs of particular species, to be named in the order. Since the passing of this Act a number of orders have been made under its provisions, with the result that considerable confusion has been created by the variation in the provisions for different counties.

Ground Game—Hares and rabbits may be killed at any season of the year; but hares may not be killed on a Sunday, nor on Christmas Day, being game within the definition given in 3 & 4 Will. IV. c. 32.

Under the Ground Game Act (43 & 44 Vict. c. 47), every *occupier* of land has the right (of which he cannot divest himself) to take or kill hares and rabbits concurrently with the *owner* of the land, or his lessee of the shooting, certain provisions being made as to who may shoot on behalf of the occupier and as to the use of traps, no license to kill "ground game" being required under this Act.

The owner or occupier of land having the right to the game thereon may (except at night[1]) kill hares, or authorise another to do so, without taking out an excise license to kill game; and so may persons hunting or coursing. This privilege is given in England by 11 & 12 Vict. c. 29, and in Scotland by 11 & 12 Vict. c. 30. Ireland has no corresponding Act.

[1] The killing of game or rabbits by night is prohibited by 11 & 12 Vict. c. 29, sect. 5.

There is no close time for hares, that is to say, no period of the year in which they may not be *killed*; but by the provisions of the "Hares Preservation Act, 1872," it is illegal to *sell* a hare or expose one for sale during the months of March, April, May, June, and July.

Deer—Deer may not be killed in an *unenclosed* forest or . .ase under a penalty not exceeding £50 for a first offence, and imprisonment for a second; or in *enclosed* ground, or park, upon pain of imprisonment with or without hard labour, for a term not exceeding two years, under 24 & 25 Vict. c. 96; and a deer stealer in the commission of the offence may be arrested without warrant.

Since the passing of the Act 23 & 24 Vict. c. 90, an excise license is required for killing a deer as if it were game, except when pursued with hounds, or killed in a park, or other enclosure, by the owner or his agents. In Ireland there is a close season for deer under 10 Will. III. c. 8. But if a deer which has wandered from the forest, or escaped from a park, should take up its abode in another man's coverts, doing damage there, it may be killed by the owner of the covert, or his keeper or agent.

J. E. HARTING.

GAUR (*Bos gaurus*)—The Gaur, or Bison, as it is usually called by Indian sportsmen, ranges over Assam, Central Provinces, Mysore, and Travancore and the forests of Madras, &c.

My own experience of hunting this animal was confined to the forests of Mysore in 1892 and 1893, and in 1894 in the Central Provinces. The following remarks must be understood to apply exclusively to Mysore, as it was there that I had experience of tracking the gaur.

In several of the forests of Mysore, Keddah operations for the capture of wild elephants are established, and here I found the gaur pretty generally distributed. Being of a shy nature, he shuns civilisation, and roams through these vast forests.

The main advantage of this country consists in the fact that there exists a race of natives, Sholigas, Kurambas and others, who are many of them professional trackers, and, being brought up in these forests to forage for themselves, the art of tracking is second nature to them. Their powers in this respect appeared to me miraculous; they might often be compelled to give up a track in consequence of the beast getting too good a start, but I cannot recall an instance in which they ever lost it.

Very early rising is essential to this sport. The gaur, like others of the genus, wanders about during the night and early morning in search of food and water, lying quiet during the heat of the day under the shade of the jungles.

To be successful, it is therefore necessary that the sportsman should find a perfectly fresh track, almost as soon as it is light, for as the sun rises and the day advances, the quarry retires into the densest part of the jungle and lies down. Here, on account of the great difficulty of approaching without noise, it is impossible to get a shot. The reward of a long track may probably consist in hearing his snort of alarm and thundering rush as he dashes off.

The part of the gaur usually first seen is his head, but this is generally an uncertain chance, as (especially when alarmed) he carries it with his nose in the air, making it very difficult to hit the centre of the forehead. The most deadly spots are either the neck or behind the shoulder.

The best time of year for gaur tracking in the Mysore forests is in the early May rains, before the jungle is too thick and high. The ground is then softened by the wet, and tracking is easy. In the province of Mysore, the rainfall is earlier than in other of the more northern parts of India, and I remember that in the months of August and September, I was much handicapped by the dense growth consequent on early rains. The writer can recall being, in the month of August, within ten yards of a solitary gaur and being unable to see him, the animal making off. When tracking gaur, on their becoming alarmed and decamping, it is a good plan not to follow up too quickly, but give them time, and they will sometimes pull up after going a short distance.

A herd varies in number from about ten and upwards, the most I saw together being about fifteen. The solitary bull is usually considered to carry the best trophy. But I am inclined to think this not invariably true, although unquestionably the finest head in my possession is that of a solitary bull.

Sometimes a solitary gaur has his horns much chipped at the end, spoiling the grand curve which make the head so fine a trophy.

The weapons I used for the gaur were a ten-bore rifle and a twelve-bore rifle, firing respectively eight and seven drams of powder and hardened spherical balls.

The question often arises as to whether gaur shooting is a dangerous sport. The animal is usually harmless until wounded, and then he must be followed up with great caution, especially as he has a habit at times of turning back on his tracks and waiting for his pursuer. When charging, he carries his head bent down between his fore-legs.

GAUR.
Av. ht. at shoulder, 5 ft. 9 in. Av. horn meas., 2 ft. 7 in.; Max. horn meas., 3 ft. 3 in.

In August, 1892, I was tracking a solitary bull, and coming suddenly on him, as he presented a head shot, I fired at it. The shot, as I afterwards found, was not in the centre of the forehead. The gaur immediately, with head between his fore-legs, charged straight for me. He missed his point, and passing at about ten yards, received another in the shoulder which finished him.

In July, 1893, the writer and a friend happened

to be out together with only one tracker, the other being away. My friend fired at, and wounded, a gaur. Having hit off the tracks, we, accompanied by the shikari, followed it up. The tracks finally led into some dense bamboo jungle. It was so thick in places, that we had at times almost to crawl. We advanced cautiously, knowing it was not far ahead. Suddenly we heard it jump up, and in an instant the animal was on us. My friend had just time to fire from his hip, and the shot took effect in the gaur's head and dropped it. He was knocked down, but was not hurt, wonderful as it may seem.

A wounded gaur has wonderful vitality, and will at times travel considerable distances without lying down.

The writer can recall wounding a herd bull through the body, and following it for nearly four hours before he again came up with it and despatched it. I remember the advice given to me by a well-known sportsman in Mysore as follows. When a gaur has been wounded, do not follow him up at once, but sit down and wait: then in half an hour or more start on his tracks.

A. F. MACKENZIE.

GAYAL (*Bos frontalis*)—These wild kine are plentiful in parts of the Chittagong hilly districts, and extend into the interior to Munipore; a few exist in the northern and eastern parts of Assam, and probably extend to the north and east to the confines of China. They are numerous along the spurs of the Bhootan Hills, amongst the Dufflas, in Tipperah, amongst the Looshais, and are kept in herds, in a half-wild state, by the wild tribes which skirt Chittagong. They are domesticated extensively and easily. Very many of the young wild cattle are caught in nets and are soon tamed. The people scatter near their villages huge lumps of rock salt, which have an extraordinary fascination for the gayal. The herds are allowed to graze during the day in the adjoining forests, but are recalled towards dusk by the tinkling of bells or the striking of gongs.

The forehead of the gayal is not concave like a gaur's. It is quite straight and destitute of the semi-cylindrical crest. The horns grow straight out and then curve very slightly upwards, and now and then, in a very old bull, they are sometimes slightly truncated. The forehead is broad and, like a gaur's, covered with lightish coloured hair. It browses more than Bos gaurus, and has a small but distinct dewlap. The dorsal ridge is prominent, but not to the same extent as in the larger animal, though, at a distance in a forest, one might easily be mistaken for the other. Indeed, the Assamese called both the gaur and gayal "the Mithun," but, if pressed, say the former is the Asseel Mithun and the latter a Mithun only. Thus when that noted sportsman, Mr. Sanderson, shot a gaur on the confines of Assam, and heard it called by the aborigines a "Mithun," he jumped to the conclusion that the gayal does not exist in a feral state, but he is totally mistaken. These two wild cattle are, I believe, cousins many times removed. Not far from the confines of Arrakan Father Barbe found the gaur, gayal, and tsine; and I have heard Mahouts say that they had seen gayal not very far from the Wild Yak. Hybrids between the gayal and the humped cattle of India are common. Many have become feral, and are to be found near the Manass river in Baghdooar. I have seen them dead of the murrain, from which portions of Assam are never free. I have only shot two, and those were in the hills between Nowgong and Tipperah, but I have seen them several times elsewhere.

W. POLLOK.

GAZELLES—It has been shown in the article on ANTELOPES that the gazelles are widely distributed in Asia and Africa. Although some few of these animals, such as the so-called Ravine deer (*Gazella bennetti*), and the Thibetan Ravine deer (*Gazella picticaudata*), are, as their names imply, chiefly found in deep bushy valleys, among rocky hills and scrub, the great bulk of the gazelles are to be sought upon open plains, often far removed from water. Two north African forms, however, the Atlas gazelle and Loder's gazelle, are found well up among rocky hills. From the open character of their habitat, and the extremely wary and suspicious nature of the animals themselves, few game animals afford finer or more difficult stalking than the gazelles of the African and Asiatic plains. Successfully to accomplish the downfall of these fleet and most suspicious creatures, favoured as they usually are by the often hopelessly bare and open nature of the ground upon which they feed, the sportsman must be possessed of infinite patience, energy, and endurance. He must also be a good rifle shot, and employ the best and most accurate long-range weapon that modern science can offer to him. The heat and mirage of the hot plains form, after the early hours of the morning, another factor which tends to impede the gunner and to favour the gazelle. The novice at first often finds it very hard to overcome the difficulty of judging distances upon heated plains, and even practised gunners occasionally expend a large number of cartridges in proportion to the number of animals brought to bag. Undoubtedly, for all kinds of shooting, the very early hours of the morning are the best. The atmosphere is clear and refreshing, the game is usually at this time to be found quietly feeding, and the mirage has not yet made its appearance. On the other hand, such is the clearness of the atmosphere at sunrise that the game pursued often appears to be much closer than it is in reality. This difficulty, with practice, is however presently overcome, and due allowance is made for atmospheric peculiarities. Practice, indeed, and nothing but practice, will make a successful gazelle stalker. The gunner, even if he has been well known as a good rifle shot in Europe, will, no doubt, at first be horrified and discouraged at the amount of ammunition wasted. He must have patience. In gazelle shooting, as in all other pastimes, an apprenticeship has to be served.

In the heat of the midday, stalking on foot on hot open plains is extremely trying, and if the sportsman attempts crawling under a burning sun from one small patch of covert to another, he will find the experience a sufficiently distressing one. It is, however, true that in the hottest hours of afternoon game of all kinds are more inclined to rest and are less watchful than at early morning and late afternoon.

I have found the last two hours of daylight a pleasant time for stalking those active and beautiful gazelles, the springbok of South Africa. The light, it is true, is a trifle more difficult than at early morning, and the plains seem suffused with the glow of sunset; but the hour is full of charm, and I have seen many a good springbok successfully stalked between four and six o'clock in the evening. In South Africa springboks are stalked in a variety of ways. I have gone out on to the Karroo plains long before dawn upon a thick misty morning, and, so soon as the sun rose and the fog was dispersed, thus obtained a shot or two at fairly short range. I have seen these gazelles bagged by guns marching down-wind in carts or on horseback, spread out at long intervals, and thus obtaining long shots at the animals as they took, after their invariable custom, up-wind. Here and there upon the plains of Ngamiland I have been enabled to stalk springbok on foot from the edges of the plain, where some slight covert from grass or bush was afforded. Near the salt-pans of the South African interior, springbok may be found at daybreak in winter sheltering among the bush, where they have sought protection during the keen frosts and cold winds. At such times they may be occasionally shot within a hundred yards. As a general rule it may be laid down that few animals of the gazelle species suffer the gunner to approach in the ordinary way closer than four hundred yards. One of the most effectual modes of lessening this formidable distance is to drive a few cattle towards the game and so approach more closely. An excellent method is pursued in the interior of South Africa—*i.e.*, walking a shooting horse very quietly towards the game, always sheltering oneself as much as possible behind the animal. The springbok would, if the stalk were very carefully conducted, suffer the horse to approach sometimes as close as 250 yards. Nearer than this one can seldom hope to approach gazelles, except in the springbok country near Benguella—Portuguese South West Africa—where these animals have been little harried, and the hunter can often get his shot within 150 yards. If, when the sportsman, stalking behind a horse, misses his first shot, gunner and horse remain quiet, the game will not run very far. They retreat usually for a hundred yards or two, and stand again; and the sportsman, moving very quietly with his horse, may obtain a second and even a third shot. The plains of South Africa, scattered over as they are with large herds of springbok, afford more advantages to the gunner than plains where other species of gazelle are distributed in much smaller troops.

In North and East Africa, where gazelles of many species abound, driving by natives is sometimes employed. This method requires to be very carefully and very delicately conducted, or the game may be scared from the particular line of retreat, which they would under ordinary circumstances be likely to adopt. Since the introduction of the ·303 Lee-Metford rifle and the Mannlicher, the chances of the long range gunner have been immensely improved, and the gazelle stalker is now enabled to bring down his game at a distance which a few years since would have been deemed, with average shooting, almost impossible. The following are the gazelles to be found in Africa and Asia:—

Africa, *South:* Springbok (*Gazella euchore*). *East and North Africa:* Grant's gazelle (*G. granti*). Sœmmering's gazelle (*G. sœmmeringi*). Somali Plateau gazelle (*G. spekei*). Somali lowland gazelle (*G. pelzelni*). Dorcas gazelle (*G. dorcas*). Isabella gazelle (*G. isabella*). Dama gazelle (*G. dama*). Senegal gazelle (*G. rubrifrons*). Addra gazelle (*G. ruficollis*). Atlas gazelle (*G. cuvieri*). Loder's gazelle (*G. loderi*). Black-tailed gazelle (*G. tilonura*). Thomson's gazelle (*G. thomsoni*). Clarke's gazelle (*Ammodorcas clarkei*). Waller's gazelle (*Lithocranius walleri*).

Asia—Arabian gazelle (*G. arabica*). Dorcas gazelle (*G. dorcas*). Persian or Yarkand gazelle (*G. sub-gutturosa*). Gutturosa gazelle (*G. gutturosa*). Thibetan gazelle or Ravine deer (*G. picticaudata*). Indian gazelle or Ravine deer (*G. bennetti*).

This group of ruminants includes some of the fleetest, most beautiful, and most active creatures to be found in the wild state. The flesh of gazelles, if a little dry, is usually very well flavoured. That of the springbok affords the best venison to be found in South Africa. For further information on gazelles see *Records of Big Game*, Rowland Ward, 1896, and the *Book of the Antelope*, P. L. Sclater and Oldfield Thomas.

H. A. BRYDEN.

GIRAFFE (*Camelopardalis giraffa*), *Tūtla* of the Bechuanas, *Ntūtla* of the Matabele, *Nghabi* of the Masarwa Bushmen, *Kameel* (camel) of the Boers. This, the tallest of all animals, is now found only in the Continent of Africa, although fossil discoveries show that giraffe-like creatures roamed freely in the past in Southern Europe, Persia, and even as far East as the Siwalik Hills in Northern India, and in China.

From the days of Imperial Rome the giraffe was practically unknown to Europe until four hundred years back, when a single giraffe was shown at Florence by Lorenzo de Medici. After that period the giraffe again disappeared completely from the purview of Europeans, until towards the close of the last century, when it was re-discovered by Colonel Gordon, an officer in the Dutch service at the Cape, and by Lieutenant Paterson, an English officer. These gentlemen found and shot a specimen just north of the Orange River, then lately discovered. The skin of this animal was sent to the Leyden Museum. About 1835 four young giraffes, captured in North Africa, were acquired by the Zoological Society and exhibited in Regent's Park. These animals bred in confinement; and giraffes have since been familiar to the public for many years. Only one specimen of the giraffe, a female—an excellent example captured wild in South Africa some two years since—now remains to be seen alive in Great Britain, and as these animals grow rapidly scarce in Africa, and are year by year more difficult of capture, it is not likely that Europeans will for very long be able to enjoy the sight of these extraordinary mammals.

The giraffe forms a distinct family of its own (*Giraffidæ*), and, although provided with short horn-like processes, differs materially from all horned mammals. These false horns, which are covered with hair and tufted at the apex, are at first quite separate from the bones of the head. Later in life they become united with the skull. Rütimeyer has very well described the giraffe as "a most fantastic form of deer," which is perhaps as good a description as any one can invent for this animal. The giraffe owes its immense height mainly to the extreme length of its neck and limbs. A full-grown male will measure 19 feet from the hoofs to the horn tips. The writer measured very carefully an old bull giraffe, killed by his shooting companion, Mr. W. Dove, in the North Kalahari in 1890, which was but a bare quarter of an inch short of 19 feet. Full-grown females stand from 16 to 17 feet in height. A large cow shot by the writer during the same expedition, measured just over 16½ feet. The eyes of the giraffe, shaded by long lashes, are large, soft, melting, and extremely beautiful. The senses of smell and vision are extraordinarily acute, and the giraffe is an extremely shy and suspicious animal, hard to find and easily disturbed. As the animal attains maturity a curious osseous prominence in the middle of the forehead, between the eyes, is developed. The tongue is very long—some eighteen inches—slender and extremely flexible and prehensile. It is used for plucking down the leaves and branches of the acacia trees, on which these animals feed. The nostrils are long and slit-like, and, by a curious arrangement of the sphincter muscles, can be opened and closed tightly at will. I have little doubt that this arrangement is merely a provision against the sharp-pointed acacia thorns, amid which the giraffe gathers its food. For exactly the same reason, as I conceive, the prolonged and very prehensile upper lip, and the lower lip and chin, are provided with a thick, velvety, protective coating of hair.

GIRAFFE.

The colour of the giraffe varies greatly, from lemon-fawn to orange-tawny and dark chestnut. The old bulls and even old cows grow very dark—almost black—upon the back and upper parts. The patches of darker colouring are laid upon a ground of very pale fawn or cream. The lower parts and the insides of the legs are white. The hoofs are large—nearly a foot long in the old males—elongated and somewhat cow-like. There are no traces of false hoofs. In North-east Africa—Somaliland—Major Wood, an English officer, has discovered and shot within the last few years a new variety of giraffe, never before seen. In this variety the dark colouring is only separated by very fine lines of the paler hue, and at a short distance the animal would therefore appear as entirely of one dark colour. In the ordinary giraffe the blotches or mottling can be distinguished at a long distance. It is worthy of note that in the wild state giraffes are of much richer colouring than when kept in confinement. The skin of this animal is tough and extremely thick —nearly an inch upon the back in mature males—and has always been in great demand in South Africa for making sjamboks, or Colonial whips. The value of a skin varies from £2 10*s.* to £4 10*s.* or £5, and for this reward, unfortunately, very large numbers of giraffes are annually slain by native and Boer hunters.

In South Africa the giraffe is invariably hunted on horseback, a form of sport which has always had great attractions for English sportsmen. There is nothing finer in nature than the sight of a troop of giraffes in full flight, and the excitement of the find and the run up is intense. In its slower paces, the giraffe, with its curious gliding walk, is extremely deceptive. It is in reality travelling at a rapid rate. When thoroughly roused, these animals are capable of putting first-rate hunting horses to their utmost speed. It is well to remember that unless the hunter plies sjambok and spur, and rides his very hardest at the flying troop in the first two miles of chase, he may lose them altogether. At a steady, slinging gallop, giraffes will travel for hours and wear out a horse, but, if chased very hard and forced beyond their pace early in the run, the hunter will be enabled to ride close up to the particular beast he may single out, and put in his shots from the saddle. Some hunters prefer to get up within a hundred yards, jump off and fire. In the opinion of the writer and of many experienced African sportsmen, it is better to push one's horse close up to the stern of the giraffe, and, within a few yards, fire from the saddle. A good South African hunting pony needs little guiding in a run of this description, and the rider can drop his reins and safely use both hands. The best point to aim at, whether on foot or on horseback, is the root of the tail. The giraffe's body is very short, and a well-planted solid bullet travels right into the vitals of the animal and speedily brings it down. A broken limb will also effectually bring down a giraffe.

As the giraffe is possessed of a very thick skin, solid, and not hollow, bullets should invariably be used. The writer and his hunting companion used cartridges containing solid Martini-Henry lead bullets, and found them most efficacious. These cartridges (ordinary Government ammunition, which can be procured everywhere up-country in South Africa) were used in double Afrikander rifles, which are made specially for this ammunition (·450–·577), and are extremely useful weapons for this form of shooting. A single Martini-Henry sporting rifle, or a single or double ·450, ·500, or ·577 rifle would, however, be just as serviceable, provided solid bullets are used.

The giraffe is in South Africa nowadays seldom surprised in open country. Its chosen haunts are the open giraffe-acacia forests, or dense thorny jungles, in either of which the mounted man is a good deal handicapped. If the troop—usually from seven to a dozen, though the writer has encountered nineteen together—can be forced into a piece of open ground, the work is comparatively easy. If hunting in bush and forest, the sportsman may be well advised, despite the heat, to put on a strong cord coat, as the giraffe usually makes for the thickest part of the bush, through which it plunges, dodges, and ducks in a perfectly astonishing manner, quite regardless, thanks to its thick hide, of the terrible thorns which rip and tear the horse and rider. In East Africa, where these animals are usually stalked on foot, they are occasionally found in open country. In the North Kalahari region, where the best South African hunting grounds now lie, Masarwa Bushmen, perhaps the finest trackers in the world, are usually employed as spoorers. These people, whose services can be secured for a mere trifle, are intimately acquainted with the haunts and habits of this gigantic game.

For hunting in desert country—*e.g.*, the Kalahari—water-carts (barrels mounted on wheels) should be taken; the hunter has frequently to cut himself off from his wagons and water supply for two or three days at a time, when in pursuit of these animals.

The flesh of young giraffes, and especially of fat cows, is excellent. The old bulls are rank, and uneatable by Europeans. The immense marrow bones, roasted over the camp fire and sawn in half, are one of the greatest luxuries of the hunting veldt. The giraffe is voiceless and practically without means of defence, but, when run to a standstill, it will strike out dangerously with its fore-feet. At the present day the giraffe may be found in the North Kalahari, Khama's western and northern country, Ngamiland, Ovampoland, behind Benguella, in Portuguese South-west Africa, in Mashonaland, occasionally in Matabeleland, and in Portuguese South-east Africa. Thence northward, through Nyassaland, to German and British East Africa, the Soudan and Somaliland, it is to be found in localities suited to its habits. It is, curiously enough, extremely doubtful whether this animal ever ranged south of the Orange River. It seems to be unknown in West Africa, north of the Congo.

H. A. Bryden.

GNU—BRINDLED (*Connochætes taurinus*)—The **Blaauw Wildebeest** of the Boers, the blue wildebeest of British hunters, *Kokoon* of the Bechuanas, *Inkone-Kone* of the Matabele and Zulus, is, like its grotesque congener the white-tailed gnu, an antelope peculiar to the African continent. In the days when game was plentiful all over South Africa, the blue wildebeest was occasionally found in Cape Colony, just south of the Orange River. Northward it has a very wide distribution, being found in South Central Africa, and thence as far north as British East Africa, where a white-throated variety (*Connochætes taurinus albojubatus*), the *Nyumbo* of the Swahilis, has in recent years been plentifully discovered. The Brindled Gnu stands about four feet four inches at the shoulder. The body colouring is a dirty drab or dun, strongly marked on the fore part of the body and neck with the dark stripes or brindles from which it takes its name. The head is heavy and buffalo-like, and is covered upon the front and chin with thick, shaggy black hair. The long, upstanding, black mane, extending to the withers, and a quantity of black hair upon the dewlap and breast, add to the heavy-fronted, wild and cumbrous aspect of this antelope. The legs are slender and beautifully shaped. The tail is black and flowing, resembling that of a pony. The eyes are set very high in the head. The horns, which are somewhat buffalo-like in shape, are formidable, and a wounded blue wildebeest should be approached with caution. The flesh is poor and unpalatable, and, except as food for native servants or to supply trophies, there is no reason why the blue wildebeest should be remorselessly pursued and shot. These antelopes are gregarious, and run in troops numbering from a dozen to fifty. In the African winter season the bulls are frequently found ranging in herds apart from the cows and calves. I have encountered a troop of between thirty and forty, all of which were bulls, mostly full-grown. These wildebeests are found sometimes upon open plains, at others in thinly bushed country, and the more they are persecuted the more inclined they seem to seek the sanctuary of the bush. In South Africa they are always pursued on horseback. They are among the fleetest and most enduring of all game animals, and in a stern chase will often run clean away from a good African hunting pony. They can be turned, however, in full career by planting a bullet so as to strike up the dust in front of them; or, if the hunter can so manœuvre as to place himself between the bush and the plain upon which they feed, he can often render them utterly bewildered, and, jumping off his horse, can thus obtain easy shots. They are extremely tenacious of life, and with a bullet through the body, or a broken leg, will yet occasionally make good their escape. The blue wildebeest exhibits nothing like the antics of the white-tailed Gnu, but when first startled by the hunter, the herd usually execute a few kicks and flourishes and then, whisking their long black tails, speed across the plains or through

Brindled Gnu or Blue Wildebeest.

Av. height at shoulder, 52 in. Av. horn meas., 24 in.; Max. horn meas., 31¼ in.

the bush at what looks like a lumbering gallop, but is in reality a very fast pace. They are still fairly abundant in Khama's country, Ngamiland, Ovampoland, Matabeleland, and Mashonaland. In Portuguese South-east, and South-west Africa, and in parts of Central and Eastern Africa they range in very large numbers.

H. A. Bryden.

GNU—WHITE-TAILED (*Connochætes gnu*)—This, the **Zwart Wildebeest** of the Cape Boers, is best known in South Africa as the Black Wildebeest. The name Gnu or Gnoo is derived from the ancient Hottentot designation for this animal. Although a true antelope, the white-tailed gnu is one of the most strange and grotesque of nature's creations. Even among the myriads of wild animals to be found in Africa, it has always been remarkable. The head, stripped of the wild mane and shaggy hair with which it is adorned, is extremely ox-like; viewed at a short distance the muscular quarters are not unlike those of a pony. The legs are beautifully slender, terminating in neat hoofs. The tail is long, whitish, and flowing. The general colour of this gnu is dark brown. A full grown bull stands about 4 feet at the shoulder. The head, which is heavy and disproportioned to the size of the animal, is decked with bristling tufts of dark hair above the broad flat muzzle and under the eyes. The same shaggy hair is to be found under the throat, and upon the chest and part of the belly. On the upper lip, and surrounding the wild eyes, are long white bristles. A thick and full hog-mane of a lightish colour stands erect from the strong arched neck. The horns extend downward over the eyes, and then suddenly turn upwards in a sharp, formidable hook. The white-tailed gnu is a dangerous beast when wounded, and in captivity is extremely savage and treacherous.

This gnu is exceedingly fleet and active, and of a most suspicious nature. Yet, despite these qualities, the skin-hunting Boers of the Cape Colony, Griqualand West, and the Orange Free State have within these last thirty years almost succeeded in achieving its extermination. Forty or fifty years ago it thronged the plains of these territories—beyond which it was seldom or never to be found—in incredible numbers. Even thirty years ago or less, the Black Wildebeest was still distributed in large numbers in the Orange Free State. At the present day it is only to be found upon a few farms in the Free State, where it is preserved by Dutch pastoralists. A single small troop still existed on a farm near Victoria West, Cape Colony, a few years back. It is certain that the number of these grotesque and unique antelopes now left to South Africa is well below a thousand. And, unless the Boers now preserving the few remaining herds can succeed in perpetuating the species, the animal will, not long hence, be as extinct as the true Quagga. The white-tailed gnu is one of the most restless of all animals. Upon the approach of hunters or any strange object the herds exhibit the most astonishing pranks and oddities, wheeling, plunging, and fighting in every conceivable attitude, and then suddenly, with a fantastic kick of the heels, scouring across the plains with white tails streaming in the wind. Mr. J. G. Millais, in *A Breath from the Veldt* (H. Sotheran, 1895), gives the most recent and detailed account of these strange antelopes. They breed well in captivity, and are to be found in European Collections.

H. A. Bryden.

GOA (*Procapra picticaudata*) or **Tibetan Gazelle** — Stands between 22 inches and 24 inches on delicately formed limbs. Its general colour is a very pale kind of drab, tinged slightly with brown. A pure white disc bordered with brown surrounds a short brown tail. In most full-grown bucks there is a patch of longish white hair on the forehead between the large, lustrous eyes. Unlike almost all other Tibetan animals, including the dogs, the goa seems to have none of the soft, fine under-fur known as "Pushum." At any rate, the writer found not a vestige of it amongst the sleek hair of any specimens he shot. But its coat is said to grow longer in winter.

The buck's horns are black, and usually about a foot in length, though in extra fine specimens they may be an inch or two longer. They are closely annulated to within about two inches of their tips, which turn slightly upward, and as the horns spring up from the skull in a rather forward direction, and then curve much backward, they give the beautifully shaped little head a most jaunty appearance.

The doe almost exactly resembles the buck, but has no horns.

The goa is keen-sighted and wary, though, in the latter respect, perhaps less so than any other game animal of Tibet. It never herds in large numbers, two or more being usually found together, and a solitary animal is not infrequently met with.

Its habitat is on the bare, undulating and broken uplands extending all along, and far beyond, the base of the Himalayas on the Tibetan side, whilst certain localities there are more frequented by it than others. It is seldom, if ever, found at a lower altitude than about 14,000 feet, but often very much higher; consequently all the Himalayan approaches to goa land are, during winter, impracticable.

The howling blast of wind which comes sweeping almost incessantly over those bare Tibetan steppes often makes aiming there at so small a mark anything but steady. But as this characteristic wind of the country occasionally lulls for a few hours in the morning, that time of day, if windless, is the best for goa shooting. Few Tibetan sportsmen, however, hunt specially for goa, but take their chance, when searching for larger game, of coming across its more favoured haunts.

A double express rifle of ·450 bore is as suitable as any weapon for goa, because it is also quite capable of bringing down every other kind of Tibetan game animal, not excepting even the wild Yak.

Two things should always be borne in mind when aiming with the rifle on those high wastes, namely, that the strong gusty wind causes more or less deflection of the projectile, and that the very rarefied air at such high altitudes offers but little resistance to it, thereby lowering its trajectory. A powerful telescope with large field is an absolute necessity, for the goa so much resembles the colour of the ground it affects that often, if far out and stationary, its small form is almost indistinguishable from the stones around it, especially if the day be sunless. Cloudy or windless days are, however, exceptional in those high arid regions, where the sun, from the moment it tops the horizon, is scorching. The writer found a kind of mask of soft thin cloth, extending down over the nose, with apertures for the eyes, almost indispensable for alleviating the distressing effects of the broiling sun, combined with the piercing cold wind on his face. When traversing long tracts of glaring snow or ice on high Tibetan or Himalayan passes, a pair of green "goggles" may be added to the above as a precaution against snow-blindness.

DONALD MACINTYRE.

GOAT—NILGIRI (*Hemitragus hylocrius*)—This animal, better known in India by the name of Nilgiri Ibex, is the only goat found south of the North Temperate Zone, with the exception of an ibex on the higher mountains of Abyssinia. It is restricted to the south of India from the Nilgiris and Anamallays to Cape Comorin. It resembles the Tahr (*Hemitragus jemlaicus*) in some respects, but has short hair instead of the long coat, and its colour is different. The old males are nearly black, with a white space behind the shoulder, which gives them the name of saddlebacks. The horns are three-sided, fourteen inches long by eight in girth. It is considered a great prize for a sportsman to get an old saddleback, as they are hard to find and, when found, very difficult to stalk.

It still exists in the Nilgiris, where it was found in great numbers forty years ago. Now it is only found in those parts of Southern India that are difficult of access, and where the mountains are surrounded with dense malarious forests. The first I saw were on a low grassy hill, with very precipitous sides, that stood alone in a dense forest in the lower Anamallays, and it seemed strange for a goat to inhabit such a hot tropical region. Their favourite ground is the open grassy highlands adjoining the stupendous precipices that surround most of the mountains of Southern India. They are usually in herds of four or five up to sixty, and are very wary and sharpsighted. The old males, after feeding, retire into very safe hiding and inaccessible places, and are far less often met with than the herds. When looking for ibex, I once came unexpectedly upon a splendid tusker elephant, another day upon a solitary old bull bison, and twice happened upon black panthers, which shows the wild and sporting country into which the sportsman is led when in chase of the ibex. The best account of the country it occupies and adventures in its pursuit is to be found in *Records of Sport in Southern India*, by that grand sportsman and good naturalist, the late General Douglas Hamilton.

P. W. L'ESTRANGE.

GOAT — ROCKY MOUNTAIN, OR WHITE (A) (*Haploceros montanus*)—The white goat is not a goat at all, but a very peculiar mountain antelope, its nearest relatives being certain of the Himalayan antelopes. The fact that we call our only antelope a goat may, I suppose, be taken as an offset to the other fact that the prongbuck, which is universally called antelope by American hunters, is not one at all, standing among ruminants in a position as unique as that of the giraffe.

The white goat has certain peculiarities which mark it off from all other mountain game. It occasionally sits up on its haunches like a dog to look at something which strikes it as suspicious. It is extraordinarily tame or stupid, showing a bold self-confidence which no other animal of its size displays. Moreover, though it dwells by choice among appalling precipices, and is a marvellous climber, it utterly lacks the bounding agility, not only of the chamois, but even of such heavy beasts as the mountain sheep. It generally climbs with a sort of sturdy deliberation, and often lifts itself on a ledge by spreading its elbows apart and drawing the body up much as a man would. It is singularly intolerant of heat, and even on rather cold days will retire to a cave, with the temperature freezing, in order to get out of the sunlight.

There is a muskpod between the horn and ear which makes the flesh of all but young animals uneatable. The needle-pointed horns are from eight to ten inches long, and so do not offer much of a trophy. The pure white robe, which is very thick, long and woolly in winter, and which contrasts so vividly with the black hoofs, horns and muzzle, has some commercial value, but at present not very much. In consequence the beast is not much followed by the professional hunters, who can find more valuable game in less inaccessible places; for the chief protection of the white goat is the extraordinary roughness of its haunts.

Sportsmen have, within the last dozen years, begun to follow the white goat quite eagerly; but game is really never thinned out by true sportsmen, and the queer, musky self-confident beasts offer a striking contrast to other American game in the fact that they have hitherto decreased very little in numbers.

There is no game animal in America the pursuit of which entails such severe toil. In places where the mountains run down into little-frequented fiords, or great lonely lakes, it is possible to go right into the haunts of the white goat by canoe, and occasionally to surprise one near the water; but ordinarily the animals are to be found only after heart-breaking climbing. To get into the region where they are found it is sometimes possible to take a packtrain, and at other times a canoe. Often, however, the journey must be performed on foot from the beginning; and this is almost always the case when the edges of the hunting grounds themselves are reached, and it is desired to camp within reasonable distance of the range of the game. Only the barest necessities can be carried on a man's back. In my own experience I have usually gone after white goats with but one companion, some old mountaineer who knew the ranges; though in one instance I also took an Indian with me. The wooded lower slopes of the mountains throughout most of the white goats' range are so broken, and covered with such a tangled mass of forest and undergrowth, that the walking is difficult beyond belief. Every step is severe exertion. A walk is one perpetual scramble over fallen timber, through deep gullies, across boulder-strewn points up sheer cliff walls, through masses of twisted bushes, over windfalls where the down timber, amid the wildest confusion, lies sometimes thirty feet from the ground, with young spruce growing thickly between the logs—an added touch of discomfort being given where the country is burnt. After an hour's scramble over country like this a man will be so drenched with sweat that he will look as if he had fallen into water. His fare is of course but meagre, unless he can manage to shoot something, and this is very difficult in such a forest, because it is out of the question not to make a noise.

Camp is usually made in some glade by a stream, as near the upper edge of the timber as possible, for ordinarily the goats are found far above timber land. They can best be hunted in the evening and morning, although they feed at intervals all through the day. The start has to be made very early, because there is sure to be several hours' climbing before one finds the animal. They are by no means difficult to see, their white bodies being very conspicuous, and once seen the stalk itself is comparatively easy. All that is necessary is to get above them, for they seem to suspect danger only from below, and if surprised will almost always run up-hill. They are bold, pugnacious and stupid, and are so accustomed to the noise of falling rocks that they are not readily alarmed by a slip or a misstep on the part of the hunter. In consequence, there is little need to display the hunting craft absolutely necessary in the chase of the big horn, the moose and the wapiti. The qualities called for in the hunter are ability to endure the prolonged and extreme fatigue of climbing among the stupendous rock walls where the goat antelope dwells, and the nerve to cross the occasional bits of dangerous ground encountered. In other words, the demand is made upon the qualities called for in mountaineering rather than in ordinary hunting. Nevertheless, as the test of the highest sport is the display of manliness and hardihood, the chase of the white goat deserves fair rank; for the white goat hunter must be hardy and persevering, and must have a good head, good lungs, and good muscles.

THEODORE ROOSEVELT.

GOAT—ROCKY MOUNTAIN (B) (*Haploceros montanus*)—Some indefinite mention of the Rocky Mountain Goat is to be found in the narratives of the early Spanish explorers in California, but the first reliable information on the subject occurs in the account of Lewis and Clarke's overland journey in America (1814 edition, vol. ii., p. 169), in which the goat is described as "living in great numbers on the chain of mountains forming the commencement of the woody country on the coast," and as having been seen while the travellers were "passing the Columbia between the rapids and the falls."

Hamilton Smith, in a paper published in the *Linnæan Transactions*, 1822, states that he was assured that goats were found as far to the eastward as the "Lake of the Woods" in Manitoba. This statement was afterwards frequently copied, but is obviously incorrect, unless the goats have completely changed their habits since that time, as the country alluded to is and always has been utterly unsuited to their taste.

At the present time the march of civilisation is rapidly curtailing the range of the goat on the American side of the international boundary line, and Washington, Oregon, Idaho, and Montana are the only States which still afford the inaccessible mountain sanctuaries which this animal loves.

In Colorado, Wyoming, and Nevada, authentic instances of their occurrence have been noticed within the last twenty years, but it may be safely said that the present home of the mountain goat lies in the vast area of mountainous country contained by British Columbia and Alaska. In both these territories goats are extremely abundant, wherever high, rough mountains exist, from the waters of the Pacific to the Rocky Mountains, and from the boundary line to Peel's River, and possibly beyond to the point where the main range begins to slope down towards the Arctic Sea. Though spread over a very wide extent of country, the goat is, in a sense, local in its habits, and will haunt the particular mountain on which it was born until driven away by continual molestation.

Scientists have decided that this animal is really more allied to the antelopes than the goats, but to the ordinary sportsman and the miner of the West it must always remain a goat and nothing but a goat. Its clumsy external appearance, and close resemblance to the domestic goat, debar it from claiming a place among the antelopes, whose very name in Western America suggests the graceful, lively pronghorn of the prairies. Not that the goat is lacking in activity when jumping casually from ledge to ledge on the brink of awful precipices but he is slow of gait and ungainly of action, depending more on the inaccessibility of his haunts for his safety than on his own agility and keen observation. He is so absolutely stupid that a successful stalk brings little glory to the hunter, and the charm of the sport must always lie in the physical exertion necessary to force a way through the dense forest which clothes the sides of the mountains of British Columbia and Alaska, and the enjoyment of the natural beauties disclosed to the view of the hunter when once he has reached the rocky summits. Some of the Indians of the North-West Territories, especially the Stonies, frequenting the main range to the southward of the Canadian-Pacific Railway, hunt the goats with dogs, often exterminating a whole band held at bay in a narrow defile between two peaks. As a trophy the heads are insignificant; the horns of the female are usually the best, being longer and more sharply pointed than those of the male. The skins are of small commercial value, and the goat will therefore find a safe home for many years in the unexplored mountains of the farthest North-west.

WARBURTON PIKE.

[*See also* ANTELOPES, *p.* 39.]

ST. ANDREWS.

GOLF—The game of golf consists in playing a ball, in as few strokes as possible, from certain starting places, called teeing-grounds, with various clubs suited to the nature of the stroke, into a succession of holes cut in the ground at varying distances.

Golf may be played on any park or common, but its original home is the "Links" or common land which is found by the sea-shore, where the short close turf, the sandy subsoil, and the many natural obstacles in the shape of bents, whins, sand-holes and banks, supply the conditions which are essential to the proper pursuit of the game.

Eighteen is the usual number of holes in a golf course, and in arranging the succession of these holes, care should be taken that they are so placed that "parties playing to one hole" shall not be crossed or met by parties playing to another. If sufficient suitable ground be not available to admit of this being done, it is better to limit the number of holes to 15, 12 or 9.

The extent and nature of the ground available will determine the distances between the individual holes, and these should be placed so as to take advantage of any natural features in the shape of hillocks, hollows, ditches, or other obstacles, to test the skill of the golfer, and lend variety and interest to the play. As a general rule, a hole should not be much shorter than 100 yards, or longer than 500 yards, while the entire course, if made up of 18 holes and measured from hole to hole, should be from $2\frac{3}{4}$ to $3\frac{3}{4}$ or 4 miles in length. For each hole there is a starting point, called the teeing-ground. The first of these is usually marked out near the club-house, and the others are placed near the hole previously played but in such a position that parties playing from it will be out of the line of fire of those playing to the previous hole.

The game commences at the first teeing-ground, and the hole to which the ball is to be played is cut in a well-cared-for green, called the putting-green. The hole is round, $4\frac{1}{4}$ inches in diameter, and should be at least 4 inches in depth. To preserve its shape, it is usually lined with tin or iron, but this lining should be pressed down into the hole, so as to leave $\frac{1}{2}$ an inch of turf above its upper rim. If this is not done, and the metal rim is left flush with the surface of the grass, many balls that would otherwise go in, will either run round the rim or jump over the hole. A movable flag or disc, mounted on a stick or pin, is placed in the hole to indicate its position.

The putting-green, technically, is all ground within 20 yards of the hole (Rule 30), and all this space, if possible, should be of the closest and smoothest turf. It is not desirable to have the surface flat like a billiard-table, and an undulating surface, provided the turf be equal and true, will be found to make the putting more interesting and difficult.

Between the teeing-ground and the putting-green should be found, whether they be natural or artificially formed, various "hazards" in the shape of sand-pits or "bunkers," ditches, gorse, roads, or other obstacles, and these should be placed so as to catch and punish badly-played balls, while plenty of open space and good turf should be found between them to reward well-hit strokes.

Thus, supposing a hole be 250 yards in length measured from the teeing-ground, there should be a hazard of some sort extending right across the line of the hole, about 100 or 130 yards from the tee. Beyond this the ground should be good; but, guarding the hole again, and some 30 or 40 yards in front of it, there should be another hazard which the player would have to carry before reaching the putting-green. In addition, hazards may be placed on either side of the course to catch crooked balls, and also beyond the hole to punish those that are hit too strongly, but "blind" hazards—*i.e.*, hazards which are not visible to the player, such as sunk ditches or holes, should either be marked or filled up.

The Ball used in playing golf is made in various sizes, but that most in use measures about $1\frac{3}{4}$ inches in diameter. It is usually made of well-seasoned gutta-percha, grooved or notched on the surface, and painted white. Prior to the introduction of gutta-percha, golf-balls were made of feathers, forced into a case of leather, and the figures 27 and $27\frac{1}{2}$, &c., which are used to-day in differentiating the various sizes of balls, represent the weight in pennyweights of the old feather balls. Several kinds of composition balls, known generically as "putties," in contradistinction to the "gutties" or gutta-percha balls, though they have had a certain vogue, have failed to take the place of those made of the raw material. Balls made of fresh gutta-percha are properly seasoned and at their best about six months after being made and painted, but care should be taken that they

SET OF CLUBS.

are kept at an even and moderate temperature. If they are kept longer they are apt to become brittle, and, when struck, the paint will crack off.

There are many varieties of golf **Clubs**, but those most commonly in use, and all that are really necessary for the player, are as follows: **Driver, Brassy, Cleek, Mashie, Iron, Niblick, and Putter.**

All other golf clubs are either adaptations or modifications of these.

The driver and brassy are wooden clubs, and the putter may also be of the same material. The heads of the others are made of malleable iron. The heads of wooden clubs are usually made of well-seasoned beech-wood. Apple-wood is also used, but it is hard, and lacks the spring of beech-wood. The best shafts, both for wooden and iron clubs, are made of hickory, although good shafts are also made of ash, lance wood, greenheart, lemon tree, and a variety of other woods. The best heads for clubs are those in which the grain of the wood runs down the neck and along the head. If the grain runs across the neck, the club is sure to break in course of play. The finest shafts, though they are difficult to obtain, are made of split hickory—*i.e.*, hickory which is split from the wood with the grain, and not sawn off the plank.

The Driver—The driver is the club used from the tee if the hole be long, or if the ball lie well, whenever it is desired to play it as far as possible towards the hole. It is a wooden club with a long powerful shaft. The head should have plenty of wood in it and the face or hitting part of the head should be fairly deep. It should not be hollowed out in the middle, nor sloped back when the club head is laid on the ground.

The Brassy—The head of the brassy is smaller and shorter than that of the driver, and the sole is shod with brass, to preserve the wood when the ball has to be played from stony or hard ground. The face of the brassy is often "spooned" or sloped backward, so as to raise the ball in the air, and the smaller size of the head admits of its being used when the ball lies in a "cup" or indentation of the ground, which the driver head would be too large to enter.

The Cleek—The cleek is an iron-headed club with a straight and narrow face. The shaft is longer than that of other iron clubs, and it is chiefly used in playing full shots through the green, when the ball lies badly, or when a wooden club would take it too far.

The Iron—The iron has a deeper blade or face than the cleek and is shorter in the shaft. Irons are made of various weights and with various degrees of pitch or loft, and are chiefly used for approaching the hole, or for lifting the ball over hazards or out of sand.

The Mashie—The mashie is shorter in the head than the iron, and bears much the same relation to it that the brassy does to the driver. Like the iron, it is also made of various weights and degrees of loft, for particular strokes, and its uses are practically the same.

The Niblick—The niblick is used when the ball lies badly in sand, mud, whins or other hazards, or wherever it is necessary to use great force to extricate the ball from its position. The head is round, small and very heavy.

The Putter—The putter is used chiefly after the ball has been played on to the putting-green, to play the ball into the hole. The head is made either of wood or metal. It is more upright and the shaft is much shorter than that of any other club, and should be quite stiff. There are many varieties of metal putters, no one of which can be said to be better than another. The chief points to be looked to in a putter, its appearance and make being secondary considerations, are that it should be well balanced and not too heavy.

A Bulger is a wooden driver or brassy with a convex face instead of a straight one. It is claimed by its admirers, that a ball, struck on the heel or toe off this convex face, will still go straight, unlike a ball similarly struck from an ordinary club, which will fly to the right or left respectively. If, however, the club be drawn in towards the body, or thrown out from it in striking, as very commonly happens, the convex face will considerably augment the curve thus put upon the ball, so that any advantage it may possess in the one case is counterbalanced by its disadvantage in the other. It is generally conceded, however, that a ball, if struck truly with the apex of the convexity, will fly off quicker, and consequently travel farther, from the bulger than from a straight-faced club, where the area of contact is larger.

Spoons, or wooden clubs of different lengths, with their faces hollowed out at various angles, are now almost obsolete. The long spoon, mid spoon, short spoon and baffing spoon or baffy (the latter used for approaching the hole), are now rarely seen, having been supplanted by the brassy, and the modern irons and mashies.

Methods of Playing the Game.

The game is played by two or more sides, each playing its own ball (Rule 1), and the object of each side is to hole the ball in fewer strokes than the other.

There are two methods by which matches can be played, viz.: Match Play and Medal Play. In the former the players count by holes, and in the latter by strokes.

Match Play—In a match by **holes** the usual number of players is two, and the players begin at the first teeing-ground. The ball is placed on a small elevation, usually a pinch of sand, called a "tee." The player who strikes first, the order of starting being usually settled by agreement or by toss, is said to have the "honour," and this he retains until his opponent wins a hole. After both have struck from the tee, the player whose ball is farthest from the hole plays again, and so on until each player has played his ball into the hole. The player who has done the hole in the fewest strokes wins the hole, and if both have taken the same number, the hole is said to be "halved." At the end of the round, the player who has won most holes wins the match, and if both have won an equal number, the match is said to be "halved" or "drawn." It must be observed in "Match Play," that the total number of *strokes* taken to the various holes does not directly affect the result, as for instance, A may take 3 to the first hole and B 8, but A only wins 1 hole. At the second hole A may take 6 and B 5, which makes them "all square" or "all even" in holes, although A's total strokes are only 9, while B's are 13.

Should one of the players, A, find himself a number of holes to the good, equal to the number remaining to be played, or, in other words, in such a position that his opponent, B, even by winning all the remaining holes, could only tie with him, A is said to be "Dormy," and should A win the next hole, the match is over, as he must eventually win by 1 hole at least.

Supposing A were 3 holes to the good, with but 3 holes remaining to be played, he would be "dormy three," and should he win the next hole he would win by 4 holes and 2 to play.

The remaining holes in this case are only two, called the "bye," and A would be said to have won the "Long Match."

In Match Play the game is counted between the holes by the terms, "the odd," "the like," "2 more," "1 off 2," and so on. Thus when A has played one more than B, he is said to have played "the odd," and when B plays he has played "the like." If A has played two or three more strokes than B, B then plays one off 2 or 3, as the case may be, and so on.

A plays the "Long odds" to B, when B lies much nearer the hole in the same number of strokes.

Foursome—A match by holes is often played by four players, two against two, and is called a foursome. Only two balls are used, the partners striking alternately, both from the tees and throughout the green. A stroke exacted as a penalty under any of the rules does not affect the rotation of play. For example, if A and B are partners, and A plays their ball into water, from which it has to be lifted and dropped under a penalty of 1 stroke, the next stroke is played by B and not by A.

Three-ball Match.—Three-ball matches are played by three players, each playing his own ball, but if the play is by holes, the scoring becomes somewhat difficult and complicated, and, if the three players are all playing against each other, it makes a better game to count by strokes.

A good three-ball match can be made when one of the players plays what is called the "best ball" of the other two. This means that in order to win a hole, he must do it in fewer strokes than either of the other two. It is obvious that in this form of match, the conceder of odds must be superior to each of the other two players.

"Colonel Bogey."—A method of scoring by holes which has lately become popular, is for the players to compete against a score supposed to have been made by "Colonel Bogey." This gentleman is simply the committee's embodiment of a first-rate player, and his score represents approximately the number of strokes which ought to be taken to each hole without serious mistakes. The players play each hole, not directly against each other, but against the "Bogey" score for the hole, and they win, lose, or halve it with "Colonel Bogey," according as their respective scores are better or worse than, or equal to his. The player who is most holes up or least holes down to "Colonel Bogey" at the end of the round, wins the match.

Inter-Club Matches.—Inter-club matches are usually played by teams of varying numbers, representing the best players in each club. The individual members of each team play hole matches against each other, the players being pitted against each other, as far as possible, in order of merit. At the end, the total number of holes won by each side is added up, and the club having a balance in its favour wins the match. Another, and perhaps fairer, method of judging the result, is to count the number of individual matches won, instead of the number of holes. This latter method supplies a fairer test of the general strength of the teams. By the former method it frequently happens that the failure of one member of the team brings defeat to his side.

For example, suppose two clubs play a match with teams of six a-side with the following result:—

X		Z	
A	4	G	0
B	1	H	0
C	0	I	10
D	0	J	6
E	2	K	0
F	1	L	0
	8		16

It will be seen that though the X team won four of the six matches, they yet lost by eight holes, although the Z team only gained two matches of the six.

Club Tournaments are played on the same principle as the Amateur Championship competition. The competitors are drawn against each other in couples, and at the conclusion of the first round, the winner of the first couple plays against the winner of the second couple, for their places in the third round, and so on until the final stage is reached, the survivor of which is the ultimate winner.

In arranging a club tournament or match of this nature, it frequently happens that the number of entries is such, that by drawing the couples together in the usual way, it will not be possible to conclude the tournament without having byes right up to the final stages. This is rightly felt to be unfair, and in such a case the Bagnall-Wild system will ensure that no byes will occur after the first round.[1]

Medal Play.—(*See* special rules for Medal Play).

Medal Play is the method of playing a match, by counting the number of *strokes* required for the whole round, without reference to the number of individual *holes* lost or won. The player who completes the round in the fewest actual strokes, is the winner, if it be a scratch competition, and subject to his allowance or penalty if it be played under handicap. Ties are usually settled by playing another round.

A record score for a green, should be a score played under medal play, and not, as too often happens, a score compiled by a player playing a hole match.

Handicapping.—In order to enable an inferior player to make an even match with a superior, it is necessary that he should receive points, and there are various ways of doing this. In medal play, the weaker player simply receives a given number of strokes, which are deducted from his score at the end of the round. This same method is the usual one employed in match play, subject to certain regulations dealt with later.

Another method is for one player to concede the other a given number of strokes, which may be used singly or together at any hole or holes at the discretion of the receiver of the odds. These strokes are known as "bisques."

Still another method is, for the better player to allow the inferior a given number of holes to start with. For example, A gives B three holes of a start. B is then three holes up with eighteen to play, if the match is one of eighteen holes, but he has to play A level throughout the entire round. A has thus to beat B by four holes on the round to win the match.

Medal Play—For club competitions the handicaps of the members are settled by a committee, who usually proceed as follows: A score for the round is agreed upon as a good scratch score, say 80, and each player who is below scratch form, receives strokes sufficient to bring his average score down to this figure. It is usual to compel a new member of a club, or one whose play is not known, to hand in three or more scores for the information of the committee, before he is allowed to compete for a prize, and upon the average of these scores the committee decide what handicap he is to receive.

It is well to make the outside limit of all handicaps in club competitions 18 strokes. By this means overcrowding on competition days is avoided, and the absurdity of having a medal carried off by a beginner who is receiving, as sometimes happens, two strokes a hole from the scratch player is done away with.

When a player wins a prize, if his score be a good one, his handicap should be reduced immediately by one or two strokes, as the occasion may seem to demand, while, at the same time, the form of the other players must be watched by the committee, and their handicaps adjusted from time to time, irrespective of their winning prizes.

Should a scratch player be found to be winning too many handicap prizes, the best plan is to penalise him to the required extent by adding to his actual score. Thus, if he is penalised three strokes, and he hands in a card of 79, his score would read 79 + 3 = 82.

This saves the necessity of raising the handicaps of all the rest of the members.

Match Play—Reference has before been made to one or two methods of playing matches under handicap, but the one usually employed in club competitions is as follows:—

The handicaps for match play are based on the number of strokes received in medal play, but a smaller proportion is allowed in match play. The reason for this has been indicated above (*see* Match Play), viz., that an inferior player may take eight to a hole which his opponent does in three, but the latter thereby only gains one hole, and not five strokes, as he would in medal play.

It is impossible to settle absolutely what the proportionate difference should be in the handicaps of players for medal and match play respectively, as these would vary with every two players. For the purposes of club competitions, however, the table of match play odds adopted by the Royal Wimbledon Golf Club, and now in general use, which is here appended, will be found to work fairly satisfactorily.

Table of Match Play Odds.

In singles, three-fourths of difference between handicap allowances.

In foursomes, three-eighths of difference between the aggregate handicap allowances on either side. A half-stroke or over, both in singles and foursomes, shall count as one. Smaller fractions count as nothing.

	Strokes in			Strokes in			Strokes in	
Difference.	Singles.	Foursomes.	Difference.	Singles.	Foursomes.	Difference.	Singles.	Foursomes.
1	1	0	13	10	5	25	19	9
2	2	1	14	11	5	26	20	10
3	2	1	15	11	6	27	20	10
4	3	2	16	12	6	28	21	11
5	4	2	17	13	6	29	22	11
6	5	2	18	14	7	30	23	11
7	5	3	19	14	7	31	23	12
8	6	3	20	15	8	32	24	12
9	7	3	21	16	8	33	25	12
10	8	4	22	17	8	34	26	13
11	8	4	23	17	9	35	26	13
12	9	5	24	18	9	36	27	14

[1] By this system, after the competitors have been paired, the number of couples (counting the odd man, if there be one, as a couple), is subtracted from the nearest higher power of two, and the number forming the remainder is the number of byes.

Thus, in a single, if A's handicap is 2, and B's 9, the difference between them is 7, ¾ of seven is 5¼, or 5, as the quarter is not counted; 5 is thus the number of strokes B receives from A.

In a foursome A's handicap is 15, and B's 4, making 19, and their opponent's C and D + 2 and 14 respectively, making 12. The difference between them is 7, ⅜ of 7 is 2⅝, or three strokes, which is the allowance A and B receive.

The number of strokes being settled in the above manner, they are to be taken, should they exceed or be less than 18, at the holes specified in the club table, in which it is clearly set forth. If the strokes to be given are 18, one is, of course, taken at each hole. If more or less than 18, it is well to have the table arranged, so that as far as possible, strokes should be taken at the more difficult holes. It is usual to print this table for easy reference on the back of the club scoring card.

Style.

A sardonic observer has defined golf as consisting in striking a small ball into a succession of small holes with instruments very ill adapted for the purpose. Though this is but a limited definition, it is strictly true as far as it goes. The golf club is not a weapon of precision. The length of its shaft, the shortness of the head, and its exceedingly restricted hitting surface, the small size of the ball, the inequalities of the ground, and the state of the weather are all matters that make a successful stroke at golf most difficult of accomplishment. Moreover, it is not sufficient to hit the ball with the correct strength and direction, wherever it lies, on the proper part of its surface; it must also be hit with the proper part of the club. If both these things are not done, the result, unless favoured by luck, will be failure.

The part of the club used in accurate striking is the centre of the face, *i.e.*, half-way between the sole and the crown of the head, and half-way between the toe and the heel. The ball is hit correctly with the club when it is struck on the centre or a little below, at the back of the ball, and it is this spot, and not the top of the ball, that the aim should be taken from, and the eye kept on, in the process of striking. These two points, then, must be brought in contact, if the stroke is to be successful, no matter how the ball lies, except in the case of sand, &c., which will be dealt with later; and it is towards the consistent and harmonious accomplishment of this object that a golfer's style should be built up.

As the best players all exhibit differences more or less marked in the matter of style, it is impossible to say, except perhaps from the æsthetic point of view, that any one style is more correct than another. The measure of the excellence of any particular style is its consistent success, as consistent failure must point to some radical defect in its constitution. It must further be observed that the divergences in style amongst good players are the result, not of any essential difference in the force and accuracy with which the club head ultimately reaches the ball, but in the manner in which the club is handled to attain these objects. Individual idiosyncrasies of stature, strength, and temperament are sufficient to account for these differences, and the beginner, in trying to develop a good style of golf, will do well to observe the points where the styles of good players will be found to agree, and to pay no attention to the unimportant details where they differ. Style may be said to cover the player's grip, or grasp of the club, his stance, and his manner of swinging.

Grip—The grip of the club is a most important matter, as on it depends largely the command obtained over the club during the process of swinging.

Until recently, when golf became popular in England, there was, speaking generally, but one recognised way of holding and swinging a golf club. It is true that there were what have been called "the opposing schools of St. Andrews and Musselburgh," but the difference in their practice in this respect was practically nil, and any other differences that existed between them were the result either of the natural rivalry between two great golfing centres, or due to the different character of the two greens, each of which favoured the practice of certain kinds of shots more than others. But of late years in England a class of golfers has sprung up, born and bred

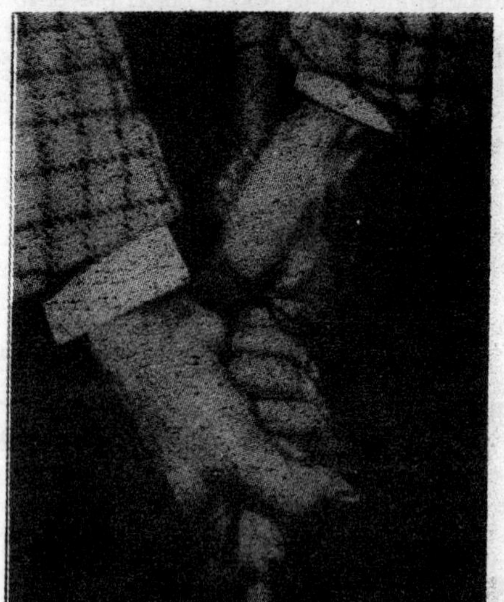

Cricket Grip.

altogether outside the old golfing traditions; men whose traditions are all of cricket, and to whom, perforce, a golf club is but a kind of bat wherewith to hit the ball. With this view of the matter, these players have developed a method of holding the club and hitting the ball which, while it has in a few cases met with success, is not one that can be recommended for the adoption of beginners. The grip for this hitting or

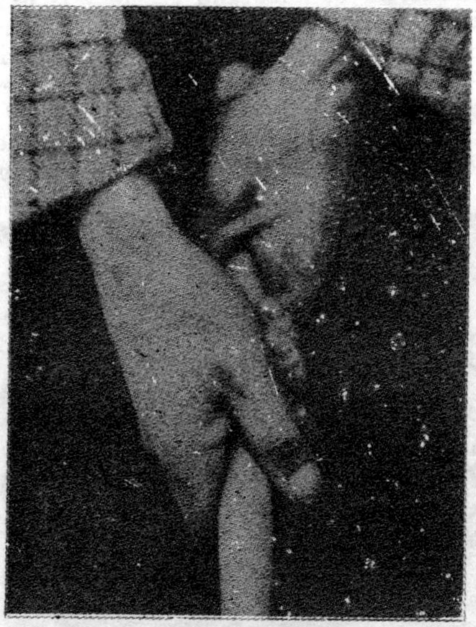

PROPER GRIP.

cricketing method of using a golf club may be dismissed shortly. It requires great strength of hand, wrist, and forearm, and the club is gripped tightly with the palms of the hands, the fingers holding firmly, the back of the right hand being kept well under, as shown in the illustration. For the proper or swinging method of using a golf club, a correct grip is of the first importance, and the hold is not so much a grip as a grasp. The club should be held firmly, but not tightly, with the fingers of both hands equally, the handle resting on the part of the palm just below the fingers, and not gripped with the hollow of the palms. The hands should touch each other, and the thumbs should lie over the handle of the club in an oblique direction, and not point down it. By this means the club will have the requisite play in the hands during the process of swinging; for it must be observed that, in swinging, the palms open out as the club is swung backward, so that it is gripped at the top of the swing practically by the fingers alone. As the club descends again, the palms close on it, and the stroke is delivered with the hands as shown in the illustration. To hold on tightly with the same immovable grip all through would check the swing, and prevent the club describing the true arc in the air which is essential to accurate and far hitting.

The grip, or the manner of it, should not vary with different strokes, and as a matter of style, a player should endeavour, as far as possible, to make all the various strokes in his play, in regard to grip, stance, and swing, in the same way. His half shot should be a part or segment of his full shot, his quarter shot like part of his half shot, and his putt but a smaller stroke in the same manner.

Nothing looks worse or is more fatal to good and consistent golf than for a player to have a different grip and stance for his various strokes; to play, for example, his full shots off the left leg and his quarter shots off the right, or to stand more or less erect for his full strokes and to huddle himself into a heap when playing an approach. The part of the handle to be gripped will depend entirely upon the manner of swinging adopted by the player. If the swing be long, more command will be obtained over the club by holding it near the top of the leather, if the swing be short, or, if the hitting or cricketing method be employed, it will be found that a shorter grip will be the more serviceable.

Stance—The position of the player's feet relative to each other, their distance apart, and the distance of the ball from each, depend on a variety of considerations, and it is impossible to lay down any hard and fast rule in these respects. The best players exhibit wide differences in the matter of stance, but these are entirely due to differences in stature, length of reach, and the length of club used. As a general rule, however, it will be found that the player has most command over the ball if he stand so that it lies opposite him at a point nearer his left foot than his right. The player should stand easily, facing the ball, his legs apart but not too much straddled, with his toes slightly pointed outwards. at such a distance from the ball that he can reach it comfortably by placing the club head

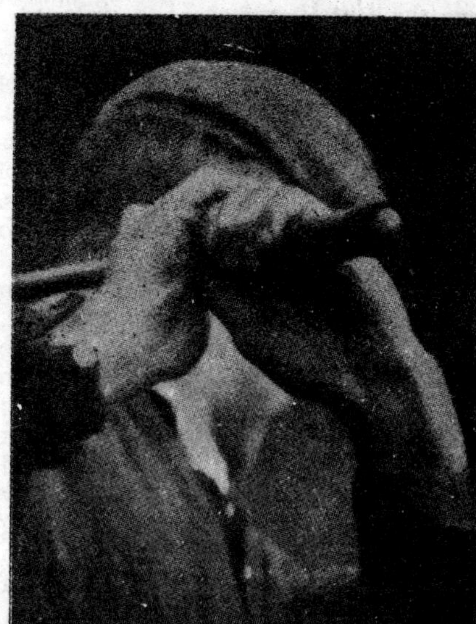

J. H. TAYLOR'S GRIP. TOP OF SWING.

behind the ball, and by holding the handle opposite the middle of his body, with the arms slightly bent outwards. His position should not be so far away from the ball that he has to reach forward in order to hit it, nor so close that his motions are cramped in the act of striking it. It is not of importance whether the feet are placed in a line with the ball or whether the right or left foot be slightly advanced, as the best players exhibit all these variations. The important matter is to take up, as far as the nature of the ground and the length of the club will permit, the same stance for each stroke. If a player is constantly changing his stance, it will have an absolutely fatal effect on his play, and will be the most fruitful cause of heeling, toeing, slicing and topping the ball.

Swing—For all balls that lie fairly on the turf, tee-shots of course included, the player will do well at the outset to think of the course to be described in the air by his club head during the stroke, as a circle or segment of a circle. It must not be supposed that it is meant that the club head must describe with geometrical accuracy a segment of a circle, if the stroke is to be a correct one; but simply that the course described by a club head, when the club is truly swung, more nearly resembles a circle than any other geometrical figure. With this view of his swing clearly in his mind, it will be obvious to the player that, to strike the ball fairly, the club face must reach it when the head is at the lowest point of its circumference; that is, after it has ceased to be describing its downward course and before it has commenced its upward. If this be not done, the stroke must be more or less missed, and the player must so arrange his stance as to ensure, if he swing accurately, that the club face will find the ball in the right place when it descends.

Addressing the Ball—In taking aim or addressing the ball, it is the almost invariable practice to pass or flourish the club head a few times backwards and forwards over the top of the ball, in the direction of the proposed stroke. This is called the "waggle," and has for its object the freeing of the wrists and arms, and of ensuring that the club lies properly in the hands. In addition, it is essential after the waggle to rest the club head for a moment on the ground close behind the ball, in the exact position in which the player wishes it to return on the ball. To do otherwise, as, for example, to place the toe or heel of the club opposite the ball, to place the club on the ground altogether clear of the ball, or not to ground it at all, is to court failure. If any of these eccentricities be indulged in, the difficulties of the stroke are enormously increased, as the player, after, as it were, leaving the rails to start with, has to find them again before reaching the ball, with consequent loss of force and great risk of inaccuracy.

The ball having been addressed in accordance with the foregoing instructions, the waggle, which must not be unduly prolonged, satisfactorily accomplished, and the aim taken, the next consideration is the swinging of the club.

As the swing is to be circular, the club head must be made to pursue the same orbit in the upward swing as in the downward, if the maximum of force and accuracy is to be attained, and all the motions of the hands, wrists, arms, and legs used in the upward swing will be simply reversed as the club comes downwards.

In commencing the upward swing there should be no swaying of the body to the right

John Ball, Junr. Full Swing.

side, nor should the swing of the club be commenced by pulling the hands to the right in advance of the club head, as this will throw the swing out of gear at its commencement. The club should be swept backwards and gradually upwards evenly and without jerk, the shoulders turning round as the club rises till it is well over the neck or right shoulder. The wrist and elbows will bend, following the upward motion of the club, and the grip open, as before indicated, as the club reaches the top of the swing. The backbone must be kept as rigid as possible and used as a pivot, round which the shoulders must work in making the swing. The head must also be kept steady, and the eye firmly fixed on the ball.

As the club is swung upwards the player will gradually transfer his weight, which in addressing the ball rests on both legs equally, to the right leg, his left knee turning inwards and his left heel rising in response to the turning of his shoulders as the club goes round. As has been said, the downward swing is an exact reversal of all these motions. There should be no pause at the top of the swing. The upward swing and the downward are one act and should be as harmonious and continuous as possible in every respect. A great deal of nonsense has been written and talked about the necessity of swinging "slow back," and the curious thing is that the very players who are responsible for the dictum are themselves notorious for the rapidity with which they swing the club both backwards and forwards. The truth is that, so long as it returns on the ball faster than it went up, and the balance is maintained, the club cannot be taken too fast back. This holds true with regard to all golfing strokes. Even on the putting-green, the backward movement of the club should be of the same nature as the forward, and the ball should not be struck with any sudden or jerky motion.

Up to a certain point, in a full shot, the longer the swing, the better, as the larger the circumference described by the club head the greater momentum will it gather before it reaches the ball; but care must be taken that the club is not swung so far round that the balance is lost and force expended uselessly in recovering it.

It must not be supposed that the stroke is finished when the club head has reached the ball, as both force and direction are imparted by what is technically known as the "follow through." The arms and shoulders following the direction of the swing are, as it were, thrown after the ball, and, the body turning round as the club descends, its weight is also thrown in, and the player at the end of the swing is facing the direction in which the ball has flown, the club going up over his left shoulder. The player should have the habit, so important is this "following through," of regarding the ball merely as a point *through* which the club head is to pass in the course of its circuit, and not a point where it is to be arrested. Another important matter to be noticed is that the club is swung at that angle round the shoulders, which gives the player most command over it both for direction and distance. It must not be swung at too upright an angle, which will be found to prevent the player getting the weight of his body into the stroke, nor must it be swung too low round the body, as this will cramp the player's motions and prevent the free use of his arms. Consistently with getting the weight of the body into the swing, a high or perpendicular swing is better than a low or more horizontal one.

Various Kinds of "Lies"—When a ball has been struck from the tee, the variety of places where it may ultimately rest awaiting the next stroke is infinite. If it be hit fairly and on the proper line it should lie fairly well, but if topped or hit to the right or left of the course, "grief," in the shape of a bunker or other hazard, will probably be its portion.

The method of hitting a ball that lies fairly on the turf, not being in any kind of hollow, is the same as for the tee stroke. There is no necessity to hit the ground with the club in striking the ball, as this can only check the force of the blow and most probably will have the effect of sending the ball in a contrary direction to what was intended. On the best of links, however, there are numerous small indentations on the sward, into which a golf ball frequently rolls, and a lie of this kind demands for its proper negotiation a considerable modification of the method used in hitting a fair lying ball. If the cup is only a slight one, the driver is the club to use,

JOHN BALL, JUNR. FULL SWING.

but if it be at all deep the brassy or cleek, with their slightly sloped faces, will be found of more service. The stand should be taken with the ball a shade nearer the right foot than usual, and the club gripped a little more firmly. It will be obvious that were the swing used in playing a fair lying ball to be employed, the ball would be either partially topped and driven into the far side of the cup, or the ground would be hit by the club head before it reached the ball, and its force checked. To avoid this, it is necessary to play the stroke with a more downward swing, so as to slip the club face in between the back of the cup and the ball. The "follow-through" in this case goes into the ground, but the ground is not touched by the club head till the ball is away. The slope on the face of the club, if the ball be truly hit, will raise it over the opposing slope of the cup, and a long shot will be the result. This stroke is called a "jerk."

A ball that lies fairly and not cupped on a slope towards the hole, is known as a "hanging-ball," and should be played in the same way with the exception, of course, that the club head does not strike the ground at all after the ball has been hit.

It frequently happens that a ball rests on a slope, either above or below the player. In both cases the sole of the club, in taking aim, must be grounded squarely with the slope. If the ball lies above the player, the club should be held shorter, and, if below him, allowance must be made for pulling the ball, which is in this case very difficult to avoid.

If a ball lies in thick bents, rushes, or long grass, a niblick or heavy mashie is the best club to use, as their weight enables them to cut through the grass better, and they present less surface for the grasses to catch on than the longer faced clubs.

Balls in Sand—When a ball lies in a sand bunker the first consideration for the player should be, "Shall I play it backwards, or sideways on to the grass, or try to get it over the face of the bunker nearer the hole?" and the nature of the lie, the width of the bunker, and the distance and height of the opposing face will decide his choice. If the ball lie close under or near the opposing face, he will have no alternative but to play it out to one side or the other. Unless it be very much buried, however, and if the face to be lofted over is not too near, the ball may be extricated in a forward direction. A firm downward and slightly forward stroke with a niblick or heavy mashie on the sand immediately behind the ball, on which spot, and not on the ball, the eye must be fixed, will cause the ball to spout upward and forward. Sometimes a ball is found actually teed in a bunker, in which case, of course, any club may be used that will take the ball the required distance. Great care must be taken with these shots, however, as to be successful the ball must be picked off quite clean, and it must also be remembered that it is not permissible to ground the club before striking.

When the ground is hard, a ball may sometimes lie close to, and in front of, a steep hazard, such as a hedge or fence, in a deep cup or heel mark. To loft such a ball over the hazard looks a hopeless task, but it may be very simply effected. It is only necessary to strike it sharply downwards against the opposing side of the cup with an iron putter, when it will jump upwards and forwards over the obstacle. The face of the putter must be held downwards and care must be taken that the ball, in rebounding, does not strike the player or his club.

Approaching and Putting—The term "approach" is applied to all shots with iron clubs that are intended to reach the putting green, and it need hardly be said that in playing an approach the player's object should be to lay the ball as near the hole as possible, and with luck, to hole it.

For approach shots of from 80 to 150 yards, or thereby, it used to be common to take what were known as half-shots with various clubs. A half-shot is a shot played with a half-swing. This, however, is an extremely difficult stroke to master or to play consistently, and nowadays, when cleeks, mashies, and irons are made with all degrees of loft, it is only an unnecessary complication of the game. A full approach shot with a lofted club is much more easy to play than a half-shot with a straighter faced club, for the reason that in the former the player is only concerned with hitting the ball clean and straight, whereas in the latter, he has also to think what strength he must use to reach the required distance. Once the art of hitting truly with an iron club is acquired, full shots with either cleek, mashie, or iron should present no difficulty, and it is only when the approach is shorter, say from 80 to 20 yards, and full strokes are no longer possible, that difficulty will be experienced. These shorter approaches are often called quarter-shots, on the same principle as half-shots, to indicate that a quarter-swing is used in playing them.

JOHN BALL, JUNR. APPROACHING.

The stance for an approach shot is of the same nature as for any other, though the ball may be a little more opposite the middle of the fork, and of course the shorter handle of the iron club will necessitate a stance somewhat nearer the ball.

The player must stand firmly on his feet, which, together with his legs, must on no account be moved, and the shot is played with the arms and wrists alone, the body being kept as steady as possible.

For wrist shots the player may permit himself a more exuberant waggle than for full shots, as this will ensure the wrists being kept free. The grip should be firm, so that the muscles of the forearm are taut, and the ball should be struck sharply. In this stroke, the right should be the master arm and the left only used to steady the club and help to bear its weight. If there be much pitch on the face of the iron or mashie, it will be almost necessary to take a little turf in making a quarter-stroke, even if the ball lie well, for it will be found that, unless this is done, the ball will be struck with the lower part of the face, and consequently will not be lofted sufficiently. Some of the best players invariably take a good deal of turf, no matter how the ball lies, but it must be pointed out that if this shot be played accurately, the piece of turf cut out by the iron is the piece immediately under and in front of the ball, and not the turf behind it, and that the ball is struck, if not first, at any rate simultaneously with the ground. It is of course evident that these shots can only be played where the ground is more or less soft.

It is sometimes desirable to make the ball stop as dead as possible after it reaches the ground, as, for instance, if the hole be close to the edge of a bunker; and this may be done in two ways, either by putting cut on it or by

JOHN BALL, JUNR. APPROACHING.

imparting a back-spin to it which will counteract its forward motion.

Cut is put on the ball by drawing the arms in, and the face of the club across the ball in the act of striking. This has the effect of putting a

JOHN BALL, JUNR. PUTTING.

right-hand spin or slice on the ball, and due allowance must be made for this in deciding the line to the hole. Back-spin is imparted in a similar way, but the swing is of a downward nature, and the ball is struck by the face of the iron as it crashes down into the turf. Both these strokes are of extreme difficulty, though the latter, as it permits the player to play straight at the hole, is perhaps the easier and more advisable. If the ground be at all hard and there are no hazards intervening, it is always better to play an approach by running the ball up with a straight-faced club, such as a cleek or putter. On hard ground, apart from the difficulty of hitting accurately with a lofted club, the ball is much more likely to be deflected from its course on alighting, than when it is run along the ground. There is an idea that it is not sportsmanlike to use a putter for these shots. Nothing could be more ridiculous. The object of an appproach is to get the ball as near the hole as possible, and the best club to use is the one that will achieve this most successfully and consistently.

Putting—It is commonly said that matches are won or lost on the putting-green, and experience certainly bears out the remark. It will not be contended that putting is more difficult than any other branch of the game, for there can be no doubt that, as a general rule, between good and bad players there is less difference on the putting-green than anywhere else. But probably the explanation lies in the fact that there is no part of his game in which a player goes off more completely than his putting.

He will consistently hole out two-yard putts one day, and the next as persistently miss those of a foot, and be quite unable to account for his failure.

Without an "infinite capacity for taking pains" a man will never be a good putter. A player cannot begin to study his putt too soon. Even for the approach shot, unless it is a very long one, he should first of all go forward and examine the ground, so as to select the spot for his ball to pitch on that will give him the best putt for the hole. The ball having been played on to the putting-green, if it is still some yards from the hole, it is well, before approaching the ball, to walk first to the hole and examine the geography in its immediate neighbourhood. A putting-green is not flat like a billiard table, and even the best of them have their differences of surface, one part being keen and smooth, and another stiff and rough, according to the nature of the grass. Then there are the undulations and slopes of the ground which will have their effect on the ball as it travels towards the hole. But more particularly, in a long putt, the ball will be travelling slowest, if it has strength to reach the hole, in the last yard or so, and it will consequently be then that it will be most affected by any inequalities or irregularities on the green. The line that the player will ultimately select to play the ball at the hole will therefore be determined chiefly by the character of this last crucial yard or thereby, and those few feet of turf ought to be the first object of his consideration in studying a putt. When this examination has been made, the player should walk slowly to his ball, removing any loose obstacles from the line likely to deflect it from its course, and taking a mental note of any other facts likely to influence it, but bearing in mind that the higher rate of speed at which the ball will be travelling at its start, will minimise considerably any inequalities of the green that may there exist.

Having arrived at his ball, the player should get behind it and survey the ground to be traversed from that position; for it is from the ball to the hole that the line must be taken, and not from the hole to the ball. The information gathered from his examination of the ground near the hole is only to be applied to modify his opinion of the line after he has arrived at his ball. If he has also studied the line from the hole to the ball, he will most probably only confuse his mind with two quite distinct lines. He will now determine the strength with which it will be necessary to hit the ball, to enable it to reach the hole, by travelling on the selected line, and thereafter address himself to the ball.

The stance for putting, as before indicated, should be of the same nature as for other strokes, except that as the putter is more upright and shorter in the shaft than other clubs, it will be necessary to stand more over the ball. The player should not stoop low over his putt nor straddle his legs too much. It is a good and useful plan to place the head of the putter in front of the ball, and then behind it, searching in this manner to get the head of the putter absolutely at right-angles to the projected line

J. H. TAYLOR. PUTTING.

of the putt, but in doing this, care must be taken that the ball be not moved. In a long putt, if there be any point half or three-quarters way to the hole, on the direct line, which is marked by a daisy or can otherwise be remarked from the ball, it will simplify matters very much if the player plays his ball for that point, giving the ball, of course, the requisite strength to reach the hole.

The club being firmly grasped in the usual way, the aim taken, and the eye firmly fixed on the back of the ball, it should not be allowed to wander off again to the hole before striking, but the club should immediately be drawn backwards, and returned on the ball at the same angle, and with the required strength. Great care must be taken to aim with the very centre of the putter. A ball struck on the toe or heel of the club, will not run straight any distance.

If the green be at all rough, a putter with its

face slightly set back will be found to keep the ball in a truer course. With an absolutely perpendicular face there is a tendency, unless the green be very smooth, for the ball to be deflected at its start. The lofted face enables the player to start the ball straight, as it will be slightly lofted for the first foot or so. In shorter putts, to which the line is straight, the ball should be played firmly for the back of the hole. If the player aims at the near lip, the chances are that the ball either "lingers shivering on the brink" and does not go in, or rolls off to one side or the other before reaching.

To take too long over a putt is as grave an error as to hurry it. Everything, however, should be done carefully and deliberately, and the player, having made up his mind as to the strength and direction, should hit the ball confidently, always bearing in mind the putter's golden maxim, "Never up, never in."

It sometimes happens that the player who is farthest from the hole plays his ball, which does not go in, but gets between the hole and his opponent's ball. If it rests less than six inches from the other ball, it has to be lifted till the other is played. If more than six inches, it is called a "Stymie," and there are two ways of negotiating it, viz., either by playing round the obstructing ball, or by lofting over it. To play round it, unless favoured by the lie of the ground, is extremely difficult, and must be done by putting on spin or cut, either with the toe or heel of the putter. The lofting shot is also a very delicate stroke. It must be played with a firm wrist, from a well-lofted mashie or iron, and not too strongly.

Topping, Duffing, Sclaffing, Heeling, Toeing, Pulling, and Slicing—Having considered heretofore the various ways of playing golf strokes correctly, it will now be necessary to deal with the various vices or faults into which players fall. With the exception of failing to hit the ball at all, or "missing the globe," as it is termed, the above list forms a complete catalogue of the seven deadly golfing sins.

Topping, as its name implies, consists in striking the ball on the top, with the lower edge of the club face, whereby an ugly gash is inflicted on the ball's surface, and it travels along the ground but a short distance. This is one of the most distressing maladies from which the golfer's game suffers, and its causes may be manifold. A firm determination to keep the eye on the back of the ball, and not on the top, and a little attention to stance, will usually correct it.

Duffing—The verb "to duff" does not mean, as might at first appear probable, to play as a "duffer" or hopelessly bad player, but simply to hit the ground first, behind the ball, so that the ball is struck with the upper edge of the face, and sent only a short way into the air. Here, again, a little attention to the stance will probably correct the fault, as duffing is very frequently caused by the player having his ball too near his right foot. It may also be caused by the player unconsciously ducking his body in the act of striking.

Sclaffing—Sclaffing is also the result of striking the ground behind the ball, but in this case the club head skids more over the surface of the ground and the ball may after all be hit perfectly truly and with little diminution of force. Sometimes a sclaffed ball travels a very long distance, as the club head comes off the ground in an upward direction, and seems to impart a forward spin to the ball, which takes great effect as soon as the ball touches the ground. Sclaffing, however, is a vice like duffing or topping, and must be corrected if a golfer's game is to become good and steady.

The terms "**Heeling**" and "**Toeing**" explain themselves, meaning as they do simply to hit the ball with the heel or near part of the face, or the toe or farther part. As the weight of the head is concentrated immediately behind the centre of the face, a ball struck anywhere outside this point will not travel so far as it would if hit exactly with the centre. If hit on the heel, the ball has a tendency to fly off to the right, and if on the toe, to the left. The usual cause of heeling is that the player is standing too near his ball, and of toeing, that he is too far away. If attention is paid to the stance, and if the player is careful to place the centre of the club face opposite his ball in addressing it, and before swinging, the tendency to heel or toe will probably disappear. As before pointed out, this correct aiming is a most important matter. It is quite common to see players who have contracted the habit of heeling the ball, endeavouring to cure it, by aiming with the toe, and *vice versâ*, in the hope that a compromise may be effected. The result of this can only be, that the player gets rid of one fault to contract the other, and however badly he may be playing, the golfer should never aim with any part of the face, except the part he desires to hit the ball with.

Slicing—A ball is sliced, when the club face is drawn more or less across it, by the player pulling his arms in towards him as the club descends, thereby imparting a right-hand spin to the ball, which robs it of much of its force and causes it to curl to the right. Though the cause of slicing is obvious, it is a very difficult vice to eradicate. It can only be cured by earnest endeavours to "follow through," by throwing the arms well out after the ball, and not checking the downward swing. It should be remembered that it is perfectly possible to slice with the toe as well as the heel, or indeed with any part of the club face.

Pulling—A pulled ball is one hit on the toe of the club, the left arm being pulled round at the finish of the swing, and the head of the club slightly hooked inward. The ball flies off with a left-hand curve on it, and sometimes travels a great distance. Pulling is not necessarily a vice, as many players habitually play for it. If the wind be blowing across the course from right to left, and a little behind the player, a pulled ball, if it be not hit too much on the toe, will travel farther than a clean hit one. The player plays his ball well to the right of the line, and more or less into the wind. As the ball begins to descend, the pull will take effect, and the ball will turn inwards towards the hole, so that the wind will blow directly behind it. It will thus travel farther than if played direct for the hole, as in that case the wind would be blowing across it during the whole course of its flight. Unless intentionally played for, however, pulling is as serious a vice as heeling, and both will land the player in endless difficulties.

Etiquette of Golf.

The following customs belong to the established Etiquette of Golf and should be observed by all players :—

1. No player, caddie, or onlooker should move or talk during a stroke.

Note.—When a stroke is being played, no person should move or stand behind the line of fire. The proper place for all onlookers is either behind the player's back at a safe distance or directly opposite him as he addresses the ball.

2. No player should play from the tee until the party in front have played their second strokes and are out of range, nor play to the putting-green till the party in front have holed out and moved away.

3. The player who leads from the tee should be allowed to play before his opponent tees his ball.

Note.—The object of this is to leave the player unhampered in his choice of tee and unobstructed in his movements by his opponent and his caddy. The player who leads from the tee, after playing his stroke, should at once step aside and remain quiet until his opponent has in turn teed and struck off. In playing throug h the green, a player should take care that he does not get in front of, or obstruct in any way, his opponent's play.

4. Players who have holed out should not try their putts over again when other players are following them.

5. Players looking for a lost ball must allow any other match coming up to pass them.

Note.—After giving permission for a match to pass, players should not play again, but remain where they are until the match has passed and gone out of range.

6. A party playing three or more balls must allow a two-ball match to pass them.

Note.—A player playing by himself has no status and must allow all matches to pass him if required.

7. A party playing a shorter round must allow a two-ball match playing the whole round to pass them.

8. A player should not putt at the hole when the flag is in it.

Note.—A player should be careful, in studying his putt, that he does not walk across or along the line of his putt. The penalty for this is the loss of the hole. (*See* Rule 34.)

9. The reckoning of the strokes is kept by the terms, "the odd," "two more," "three more," etc., and "one off three," "one off two," "the like." The reckoning of the holes is kept by the terms, so many "holes up" or "all even," and so many "to play."

10. Turf cut or displaced by a stroke in playing should be at once replaced.

Garden G. Smith.

LADIES' GOLF—One of the earliest references to Ladies' Golf (if we exclude the probably apocryphal story of Mary Queen of Scots as a golfer) says that in the eighteenth century "the women of Musselburgh often played Golf on holidays." And on the minutes of the Musselburgh Club is recorded, in 1810, the decision to present prizes ("a new creel, a shawl, and two silk handkerchiefs"), to be played for by the fish-wives of the town.

Leaving these earlier records, we find that some of the oldest Ladies' Golf Clubs are the Westward Ho! Club, which was originally founded in 1868 and reconstituted in 1893; the London Scottish, started in 1872 and reconstituted (as the Wimbledon Ladies' Golf Club) in 1890; the Pau Club, founded in 1874; and the Lytham and St. Anne's, in 1886. Several other clubs, notably the Royal Eastbourne, Blackheath, Ashdown Forest, and the Royal Belfast came into existence within the years 1887–1889. The Ladies' Links at St. Andrews is only a putting course, and this club can hardly be included among serious golf clubs.

The progress of ladies' golf can only be appreciated by those who have carefully watched the scores returned in club competitions, the records of inter-club matches, the championships, and, above all, the extraordinary improvement in style displayed by ladies on the links. This progress has only been attained by infinite perseverance and pluck, and in the face of many adverse criticisms by captious golfers of the other sex. At this point we may say, without undue conceit, that the form displayed in the Ladies' Championship this year (1897) at Gullane has done much to dispel the doubt, still lingering in the minds of older-fashioned golfers, of the ability of women to play golf well.

In many clubs where six or seven years ago

there were only two or three good players, there are now often eight or ten whose freedom and accuracy of play would hold their own on any links. As every year the tendency is to lengthen ladies' links, giving them more brassy and cleek play through the green, ladies' golf is sure to improve still more. This will make them stronger players, and induce greater steadiness of play, with those qualities of endurance and grit so necessary for a successful golfer. Even now, all the best lady-golfers play regularly over the full men's courses, where, in almost every instance, they are welcomed and encouraged by the members.

This desire of scratch lady-players for a longer course and one of eighteen holes is perfectly natural; for they know that if they are given longer carries, and many and more difficult hazards to negotiate, they will, with practice and determination, surmount these obstacles, and become longer drivers and more skilful in their approaching. Ladies will not be satisfied now with the drive from the tee and the short approach shot that have hitherto been their portion. True, there are still very few eighteen-hole courses, and not many long ladies' links, but it is safe to predict that this will not be the case a few years hence. The smallness of the greens on ladies' links is also a very real grievance, as the approach-putt becomes almost an unknown quantity. There is certainly too great an element of luck in approaching on to a small green, as any inequality in the surrounding ground may unduly punish a good approach, which if played to a really large green, would pitch *on* it, and of course, stay there.

In speaking of the leading qualities of ladies' play, one does not intend to draw any comparison with that of men, but simply to discuss as shortly as possible the points in which the average player shines or fails. So, while freely acknowledging her many excellent qualities, one is bound to say that it is more often in the lack of nerve or the fault of judgment, than in any actual defect of play, that her mistakes are made. And yet a woman's natural quickness of perception and rapidity of thought should stand her in good stead at critical moments in a match. Having found this one fault, it is difficult to speak too highly of the quality of a really scratch lady-golfer's play. Her easy full-swing in driving, her accurate approaching and her marvellous putting compel admiration from the coldest critic. Perhaps the most striking feature of her play is her accuracy. She may not be an enormously long driver, but the ball is driven as straight as a die, and no distance is wasted by driving out of the course. And this straightness is what scores so heavily in her favour in the long run. For where a long and somewhat wild driver may drive some excellent balls from the tee, or through the green, many of the other drives will probably land the ball in hopeless trouble, far out of the course. Her accuracy in approaching is remarkable, whether in the short chop stroke on to the green, or in the far prettier and more scientific wrist shot. It is this neatly played wrist stroke which puts the hall-mark of excellence on any golfer. Her accuracy on the green is often wonderful, and perhaps needs less comment than other points of her game. But here it must be frankly confessed that, on the green, many indifferent lady players, who at other points of the game take a very humble position, come well to the front, and putt with consistent excellence. Both in the long approach putt from the far edge of the green, and also in the deadly yard-long putt which is the undoing of so many players, she holds her own with the best. Indeed one is often much disconcerted by the play *on* the green of a lady who has excited sincere pity by her efforts to reach it.

The golf-clubs used by ladies are in almost every case rather lighter in weight than men's clubs, and, of course, shorter, in proportion to the height of the player. All good professionals advise ladies to use light clubs, especially light drivers and brassies, and in very many instances this advice is followed with complete success.

In these up-to-date times it is hardly necessary to say anything about the suitable dress for lady golfers. For though at any open meeting one still sees a few grotesque figures, either aping man's attire, or limply trailing about in frilled petticoats and flower-trimmed hats, the bulk of the players are neatly and serviceably dressed in plain tailor-made coats and skirts, sailor-hats and strong nailed boots.

With the numerous golfers' annuals, guides, &c., giving particulars of the eighty or ninety ladies' golf clubs in the United Kingdom (fifty-four of which are in England) it is, perhaps, rather invidious to single out any club for special notice. It is enough to say that, of the London clubs, Prince's (Mitcham) is perhaps the best, or very soon will be so, when the new eighteen-hole course has been put into thorough order. Of the provincial clubs, the West Lancashire (eighteen holes) is quite one of the best. Other good links are the Ashdown Forest, which is a very sporting course of nine holes, and immensely improved lately; the Mid-Surrey (in Richmond Park) which is a long course but somewhat monotonous; and Wimbledon, which is short and tricky, and most unhappily hedged in by the restrictions of the Conservators of the Common.

In the management of their club affairs women succeed all along the line. Many clubs that one could name are excellently carried on, the tact, energy and resource displayed by the secretaries being truly admirable. It takes all those qualities, and more, successfully to carry through the work of a large open meeting of players from all parts, to say nothing of the everyday work of the club itself. Very careful financing is also needed in managing the funds of ladies' clubs, as in many cases the subscription is a moderate, not to say an insignificant one, and much is expected by the members in the up-keep of the green, and in many other ways.

The Ladies' Golf Union, which was founded in 1893, has done much in bringing together the various clubs belonging to it, and in trying to institute some approximately uniform system of handicapping. To the Union's excellent hon. secretary, Miss Pearson, is due practically all its success. The Union also inaugurated the Ladies' Championship, which was held first at Lytham and St. Anne's in 1893; then at Littlestone-on-Sea in 1894; at Portrush in 1895; at Hoylake in 1896, and at Gullane (N.B.) in 1897. The winners of their respective years were, in 1893, 1894 and 1895, Lady Margaret Scott; in 1896, Miss Pascoe; and in 1897, Miss E. C. Orr. This year's championship was of very special interest for several reasons. The entries (over 100) were more numerous than ever before; the championship was held for the first time in Scotland; and last, but certainly not least, the Scotch representatives came splendidly to the front.

If women will only strive to keep up the steady progress in the royal and ancient game which they have shown during the last few years, they may face their golfing fate with a light heart.

LOUIE MACKERN.

GLOSSARY

Addressing the ball—The player's method of standing and handling the club preparatory to striking the ball.

All Even—An expression used to describe the position or result of a match when neither side has gained any advantage. *See* HALVED.

All Square—Synonymous with *All Even*.

Approach—The stroke by which the ball is played on to the putting-green.

Baff—To play a ball high into the air with a backward spin.

Baffing Spoon or Baffy—A short wooden club with a deeply lofted face, formerly used for playing approaches.

Bents—The long wiry grasses found on sea-shore links.

Bisque—A point taken by the receiver of odds at any period during the game.

Blind hole or Hazard—A Blind hole is one of which the putting-green is not visible to the player as he plays his shot. A Blind hazard is also a hazard which is hidden from his view.

Bogey—*See* p. 460. A method of scoring by holes against an imaginary opponent. The number of strokes which ought to be taken to each hole without serious mistakes.

Bone—The piece of horn, vulcanite, or other material let into the sole of wooden clubs to protect the lower edge of the face.

Borrow—To play a ball up a hill or slope, instead of straight across it, so that the slope will cause the ball to return towards the hole.

Brassy—A wooden club soled with brass.

Break Club—Any hard object lying near the ball, which might break the club in the act of striking.

Bulger—A convex-faced club.

Bunker—Originally a natural sand hole on the golf course. Now used also of artificially made hazards with built-up faces.

Bye—The hole or holes of the stipulated course that remain unplayed, after a match is finished.

Caddie—The boy or man who carries the players' clubs, tees his ball, and from whom he takes advice.

Carry—The distance which a ball travels from the club face to the spot where it first alights on the ground.

Cleek—An iron club with a long and narrow face—used for long shots through the green when a ball lies badly or when a wooden club would take it too far.

Club—Any legitimate implement used in striking the ball.

Course—The ground within the limits of which the game is played.

Cup—Any small indentation on the ground.

Cut—To put right-hand or backward spin on the ball so as to check its rolling forward after its fall.

Dead—A ball is said to lie dead when it lies so near the hole that the player is certain to hole it in the next stroke. A ball is also said to "fall dead" when it does not roll after reaching the ground.

Divot—The slice of turf cut out by the club in playing a stroke.

Dormy—A player is said to be dormy when he is as many holes up as there remain to be played, so that he cannot be beaten, and at the worst must halve the match.

Down—A player is said to be down when his opponent has won one or more holes than he has.

Draw—Synonymous with *Pull*.

Driver—The wooden club used for playing the longest strokes.

Duff—To hit the ground so far or so deep behind the ball that the ball only travels a short distance.

Face—The hitting surface of a club head.

Fog—Thick mossy grass.

Follow-through—The forward following of the club after hitting the ball.

Foozle—Any thoroughly bad stroke short of missing the ball altogether.

Fore!—The word shouted by the golfer when about to strike to give warning to parties in front.

Fore-caddie—The boy who precedes the players to show the line to the hole and to mark where the balls lie.

Full shot—A shot played with a full swing, and intended to travel as far as possible

Gobble—A ball played too hard at the hole which nevertheless goes in.

Green—Synonymous with *Links* or *Course*; also used as a contraction for *putting-green*.

Grief—When a player has played his ball into a hazard of any description he is said to be in *grief*.

Grip—First, the upper part of the club shaft gripped by the player; second, the manner of gripping the club; third, a narrow ditch on the course used as a drain.

Gutty—A gutta-percha golf ball.

Half-one—A handicap of one stroke at every second hole.

Half-shot—A shot played with a half swing, and not intended to go as far as a full shot.

Halved—A halved hole is one to which both sides have taken the same number of strokes. A match is halved when no advantage has been gained on either side.

Hanging ball—A ball which lies on a downward slope in the direction in which it has to be driven.

Hazard—Any kind of difficulty, not being the ordinary grass of the course, into which a golf ball may get, with the exceptions mentioned in Rule 15.

Heel—First, the part of the face or hitting surface of the club head nearest the shaft; second, to hit the ball with the heel so as to cause it to fly to the right.

Hole—First, the entire space of ground between the teeing ground and the hole; second, the hole itself; third, to play the ball into the hole.

Hole High—A ball is said to be hole high when it is played on to the putting green from a distance.

Honour—The privilege of playing first from the tee.

Hook—To pull the ball round to the left with the toe of the club. Synonymous with *Pull* and *Draw.*

Horn—*See* BONE.

Hose—The hose or socket is that part of the head of an iron club into which the shaft is fitted.

Iron—A club with an iron head, used chiefly for approaching the hole and for lifting the ball over obstacles.

Jerk—To play a ball so that the club head strikes into the ground after hitting the ball.

Lie—The position of a ball anywhere on the course after it has been played.

Lift—To take a ball out of a hazard and drop it or tee it according to the Rules.

Like—To play the like at a given hole is to play a stroke which equalises the number played by the opposite side.

Links—The ground on which the game is played.

Loft—To raise a ball into the air.

Lofter—An iron club used to loft the ball.

Made—A player is said to be made when he is within a full shot of the green.

Mashie—An iron club which is shorter in the head than the iron.

Match play—The method of playing a game of golf by counting the number of holes gained or lost by each side.

Medal play—The method of playing a game of golf by counting the number of strokes taken to the round by each side.

Miss the globe—An expression used to describe the failure of a player to move the ball at all, after striking at it.

Neck—The curved part of the head next the shaft.

Niblick—An iron club with a round, small, and very heavy head, used when great force is necessary to extract a ball from its position.

Nose—The end of the head farthest from the shaft.

Odds—To play the odds, at a given hole, is to play one stroke more than the opposite side.

One off two, one off three, &c.—When the opposite side has played two or three strokes more, the other side plays "one off two" or "one off three" as the case may be.

Par—The par of a hole or round is the total number of strokes which should be required for them without mistakes.

Press—To put an extra amount of force into the swing.

Pull—Synonymous with *Draw* or *Hook.*

Putt—A stroke played with a putter on the putting-green with the object of playing the ball into the hole.

Putter—A club with either a wooden or metal head, used on the putting-green to play the ball into the hole.

Putty—A golf-ball made of composition.

Quarter shot—A shot played with a quarter swing from the wrists.

Round—A term used to describe a game over the whole course.

Run—First, the distance a ball travels after alighting on the ground; second, to make the ball travel along the ground instead of lofting it.

Scare—The part of the club where the head and shaft are joined.

Sclaff—To scrape the surface of the ground with the sole of the club head before striking the ball.

Scratch player—A good player, who receives neither handicap nor penalty.

Set—The players' equipment of clubs.

Shaft—The handle of the club.

Short Game—Approaching and putting.

Slice—To draw the face of the club across the ball so that it curves to the right.

Socket—*See* HOSE.

Sole—The flat part of the club-head which rests on the ground.

Spoon—A wooden club with a lofted face.

Spring—The elasticity of the club shaft.

Stance—The position of the player's feet in playing a stroke.

Steal—A long putt holed unexpectedly.

Stymie—A stymie occurs on the putting-green when one of the balls lies directly in front of the other on the line to the hole, and the balls are more than six inches apart.

Swing—The method in which the club is swung in the act of striking.

Swipe—A full shot.

Tee—The small elevation, usually a pinch of sand, from which the ball is struck for the first stroke to each hole.

Teeing-ground—The marked-out space from which the ball must be struck at the commencement of each hole.

Third—A handicap of one stroke given at every third hole.

Toe—Synonymous with *Nose.*

Top—To hit the ball above its centre.

Up—A player is said to be up when he has gained one or more holes upon his opponent.

Wrist Shot—A short stroke played with the wrists.

GARDEN G. SMITH.

RULES.

1. The Game of Golf is played by two or more sides, each playing its own ball. A side may consist of one o: more persons.

2. The game consists in each side playing a bal from a tee into a hole by successive strokes, and th hole is won by the side holing its ball in the fewe: strokes, except as otherwise provided for in the rules.] two sides hole out in the same number of strokes, th hole is halved.

3. The teeing ground shall be indicated by twc mark placed in a line at right angles to the course, and th player shall not tee in front of, nor on either side o these marks, nor more than two club lengths behin them. A ball played from outside the limits of the te ing ground, as thus defined, may be recalled by th opposite side.

The hole shall be $4\frac{1}{4}$ inches in diameter, and at lea 4 inches deep.

4. The ball must be fairly struck at, and not pushe scraped, or spooned, under penalty of the loss of th hole. Any movement of the club which is intended t strike the ball is a stroke.

5. The game commences by each side playing a bal from the first teeing ground. In a match with two o more on a side, the partners shall strike off alternatel from the tees, and shall strike alternately during the play of the hole.

The players who are to strike against each other shall be named at starting, and shall continue in the same order during the match.

The player who shall play first on each side shall be named by his own side.

In case of failure to agree, it shall be settled by lot or toss which side shall have the option of leading.

6. If a player shall play when his partner should have done so, his side shall lose the hole, except in the case of the tee shot, when the stroke may be recalled at the option of the opponents.

7. The side winning a hole shall lead in starting for the next hole, and may recall the opponent's stroke should he play out of order. This privilege is called the "honour." On starting for a new match, the winner of the long match in the previous round is entitled to the "honour." Should the first match have been halved, the winner of the last hole gained is entitled to the "honour."

8. One round of the Links—generally 18 holes—is a match, unless otherwise agreed upon. The match is won by the side which gets more holes ahead than there remain holes to be played, or by the side winning the last hole when the match was all even at the second last

hole. If both sides have won the same number, it is a halved match.

9. After the balls are struck from the tee, the ball furthest from the hole to which the parties are playing shall be played first, except as otherwise provided for in the rules. Should the wrong side play first, the opponent may recall the stroke before his side has played.

10. Unless with the opponent's consent, a ball struck from the tee shall not be changed, touched, or moved before the hole is played out, under the penalty of one stroke, except as otherwise provided for in the rules.

11. In playing through the green, all *loose* impediments, within a club length of a ball which is not lying in or touching a hazard, may be removed, but loose impediments which are more than a club length from the ball shall not be removed under the penalty of one stroke.

12. Before striking at the ball, the player shall not move, bend, or break anything fixed or growing near the ball, except in the act of placing his feet on the ground for the purpose of addressing the ball, and in soling his club to address the ball, under the penalty of the loss of the hole, except as provided for in Rule 18.

13. A ball stuck fast in wet ground or sand may be taken out and replaced loosely in the hole which it has made.

14. When a ball lies in or touches a hazard, the club shall not touch the ground, nor shall anything be touched or moved before the player strikes at the ball, except that the player may place his feet firmly on the ground for the purpose of addressing the ball, under the penalty of the loss of the hole. But if in the backward or in the downward swing, any grass, bent, whin, or other growing substance, or the side of a bunker, a wall, paling, or other immovable obstacle be touched, no penalty shall be incurred.

15. A "hazard" shall be any bunker of whatever nature:—water, sand, loose earth, mole hills, paths, roads or railways, whins, bushes, rushes, rabbit scrapes, fences, ditches, or anything which is not the ordinary green of the course, except sand blown on to the grass by wind, or sprinkled on grass for the preservation of the Links, or snow or ice, or bare patches on the course.

16. A player or a player's caddie shall not press down or remove any irregularities of surface near the ball, except at the teeing ground, under the penalty of the loss of the hole.

17. If any vessel, wheelbarrow, tool, roller, grass-cutter, box, or other similar obstruction has been placed upon the course, such obstruction may be removed. A ball lying on or touching such obstruction, or on clothes, or nets, or on ground under repair or temporarily covered up or opened, may be lifted and dropped at the nearest point of the course, but a ball lifted in a hazard shall be dropped in the hazard. A ball lying in a golf hole or flag hole may be lifted and dropped not more than a club length behind such hole.

18. When a ball is completely covered with fog, bent, whins, &c., only so much thereof shall be set aside as that the player shall have a view of his ball before he plays, whether in a line with the hole or otherwise.

19. When a ball is to be dropped, the player shall drop it. He shall front the hole, stand erect behind the hazard, keep the spot from which the ball was lifted (or in the case of running water, the spot at which it entered) in a line between him and the hole, and drop the ball behind him from his head, standing as far behind the hazard as he may please.

20. When the balls in play lie within six inches of each other—measured from their nearest points—the ball nearer the hole shall be lifted until the other is played, and shall then be replaced as nearly as possible in its original position. Should the ball further from the hole be accidentally moved in so doing, it shall be replaced. Should the lie of the lifted ball be altered by the opponent in playing, it may be placed in a lie near to, and as nearly as possible similar to, that from which it was lifted.

21. If the ball lie or be lost in water, the player may drop a ball, under the penalty of one stroke.

22. Whatever happens by accident to a ball *in motion*, such as its being deflected or stopped by any agency outside the match, or by the fore caddie, is a "rub of the green," and the ball shall be played from where it lies. Should a ball lodge in anything moving, such ball, or, if it cannot be recovered, another ball shall be dropped as nearly as possible at the spot where the object was when the ball lodged in it. But if a ball *at rest* be displaced by any agency outside the match, the player shall drop it or another ball as nearly as possible at the spot where it lay. On the Putting Green the ball may be replaced by hand.

23. If the player's ball strike, or be accidentally moved by an opponent or an opponent's caddie or clubs, the opponent loses the hole.

24. If the player's ball strike, or be stopped by himself or his partner, or either of their caddies or clubs, or if, while in the act of playing, the player strike the ball twice, his side loses the hole.

25. If the player when not making a stroke, or his partner or either of their caddies touch their side's ball, except at the tee, so as to move it, or by touching anything cause it to move, the penalty is one stroke.

26. A ball is considered to have been moved if it leave its original position in the least degree and stop in another; but if a player touches his ball and thereby cause it to oscillate, without causing it to leave its original position, it is not moved in the sense of Rule 25.

27. A player's side loses a stroke if he play the opponent's ball, unless (1) the opponent then play the player's ball, whereby the penalty is cancelled, and the hole must be played out with the balls thus exchanged, or (2) the mistake occur through wrong information given by the opponent, in which case the mistake, if discovered before the opponent has played, must be rectified by placing a ball as nearly as possible where the opponent's ball lay.

If it be discovered before either side has struck off at the tee that one side has played out the previous hole with the ball of a party not engaged in the match, that side loses that hole.

28. If a ball be lost, the player's side loses the hole. A ball shall be held as lost if it be not found within five minutes after the search is begun.

29. A ball must be played wherever it lies, or the hole be given up, except as otherwise provided for in the Rules.

30. The term "putting green" shall mean the ground within 20 yards of the hole, excepting hazards.

31. All loose impediments may be removed from the putting green, except the opponent's ball when at a greater distance from the player's than six inches.

32. In a match of three or more sides, a ball in any degree lying between the player and the hole must be lifted, or, if on the putting green, holed out.

33. When the ball is on the putting green, no mark shall be placed, nor line drawn as a guide. The line to the hole may be pointed out, but the person doing so may not touch the ground with the hand or club.

The player may have his own or his partner's caddie to stand at the hole, but none of the players or their caddies may move so as to shield the ball from, or expose it to, the wind.

The penalty for any breach of this rule is the loss of the hole.

34. The player or his caddie may remove (but not press down) sand, earth, worm casts or snow lying around the hole or on the line of his put. This shall be done by brushing lightly with the hand only across the put and not along it. Dung may be removed to a side by an iron club, but the club must not be laid with more than its own weight upon the ground. The putting line must not be touched by club, hand, or foot, except as above authorised, or immediately in front of the ball in the act of addressing it, under the penalty of the loss of the hole.

35. Either side is entitled to have the flag-stick removed when approaching the hole. If the ball rest against the flag-stick when in the hole, the player shall be entitled to remove the stick, and, if the ball fall in, it shall be considered as holed out in the previous stroke.

36. A player shall not play until the opponent's ball shall have ceased to roll, under the penalty of one stroke. Should the player's ball knock in the opponent's ball, the latter shall be counted as holed out in the previous stroke. If, in playing, the player's ball displace the opponent's ball, the opponent shall have the option of replacing it.

37. A player shall not ask for advice, nor be knowingly advised about the game by word, look, or gesture from any one except his own caddie, or his partner or partner's caddie, under the penalty of the loss of the hole.

38. If a ball split into separate pieces, another ball may be put down where the largest portion lies, or if two pieces are apparently of equal size, it may be put where either piece lies, at the option of the player. If a ball crack or become unplayable, the player may change it, on intimating to his opponent his intention to do so.

39. A penalty stroke shall not be counted the stroke of a player, and shall not affect the rotation of play.

40. Should any dispute arise on any point, the players have the right of determining the party or parties to whom the dispute shall be referred; but should they not agree, either party may refer it to the Green Committee of the green where the dispute occurs, and their decision shall be final. Should the dispute not be covered by the Rules of Golf, the arbiters must decide it by equity.

Special Rules for Medal Play.

1. In Club competitions, the competitor doing the stipulated course in fewest strokes shall be the winner.

2. If the lowest score be made by two or more competitors, the ties shall be decided by another round to be played either on the same or on any other day as the Captain, or, in his absence, the Secretary shall direct.

3. New holes shall be made for the Medal Round, and thereafter no member shall play any stroke on a putting green before competing.

4. The scores shall be kept by a special marker, or by the competitors noting each other's scores. The scores marked shall be checked at the finish of each hole. On completion of the course, the score of the player shall be signed by the person keeping the score and handed to the Secretary.

5. If a ball be lost, the player shall return as nearly as possible to the spot where the ball was struck, tee another ball, and lose a stroke. If the lost ball be found before he has struck the other ball, the first shall continue in play.

6. If the player's ball strike himself, or his clubs or caddie, or if, in the act of playing, the player strike the ball twice, the penalty shall be one stroke.

7. If a competitor's ball strike the other player, or his clubs or caddie, it is a "rub of the green," and the ball shall be played from where it lies.

8. A ball may, under a penalty of two strokes, be lifted out of a difficulty of any description, and be teed behind same.

9. All balls shall be holed out, and when play is on the putting green, the flag shall be removed, and the competitor whose ball is nearest the hole shall have the option of holing out first, or of lifting his ball, if it be in such a position that it might, if left, give an advantage to the other competitor. Throughout the green a competitor can have the other competitor's ball lifted, if he find that it interferes with his stroke.

10. A competitor may not play with a professional, and he may not receive advice from any one but his caddie.

A fore caddie may be employed.

11. Competitors may not discontinue play because of bad weather.

12. The penalty for a breach of any rule shall be disqualification.

13. Any dispute regarding the play shall be determined by the Green Committee.

14. The ordinary Rules of Golf, so far as they are not at variance with these special rules, shall apply to medal play.

GOORAL or **GORAL** (*Nemorhædus goral*) —By naturalists the Gooral is said to be one of the connecting links between the goat and antelope tribes. A full-grown buck stands from 27 inches to 28 inches on sturdy, goat-like limbs. The colour of its short, rough pile is a dark brownish-grey, with a distinct white patch on the throat. Both sexes carry short, black horns; those of a good buck are about 7 inches long, with a slight curve backwards, and nearly 4 inches base circumference. They are rather irregularly annulated up to about half their

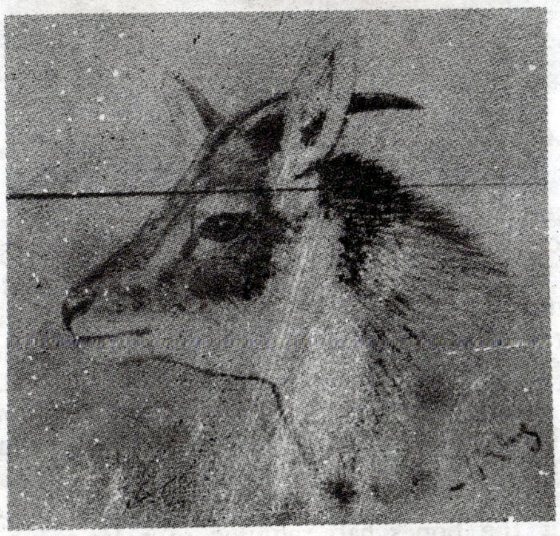

Gooral (Doe).

length. The doe's horns are thinner, more indistinctly annulated, and usually shorter.

The gooral always affects craggy and precipitous heights, which may or may not be forest-clad. During the day it usually lies up in some secluded nook, but it feeds on steep grassy slopes among the crags until late in the morning, and again towards evening. The writer has shot gooral as low, if not lower, than 4,000 feet in the outer ranges, including the higher crests of the Sewaliks; and as high as about 10,000 feet in the higher ones, not very far below the perpetual snow-line, and on the same ground with the Tahr (*Hemitragus jemlaicus*). It is more or less common all along the Himalayan ranges from Cashmere to Nepal.

Its powers of sight, scent, and hearing are acute, and its disposition suspicious, wary, and timid. Yet, after being disturbed, or even shot at, and missed, it will frequently perch itself on some prominent crag, emitting at short regular intervals its note of alarm, which may be compared to a word spelt "tschick"—pronounced short and sharp. It usually returns, in course of

GOORAL (BUCK).
Av. height at shoulder, 27½ in. Av. horn meas. 7 in.; Max. horn meas. 8½ in.

time, to its favourite haunts, after being driven from them by being fired at or even wounded.

One November morning the writer wounded one of a small band of gooral. It went off with its companions, but the telescope showed that a fore-leg was broken at the knee. In November of the following year a similar band of gooral was found on almost exactly the same spot and one was killed out of it. This animal had a stiff knee-joint, evidently the work of a bullet, but the bones had reunited in a long lump, and the writer had no doubt it was the identical animal he had wounded there the previous year.

As regards its characteristics, the gooral may be said to take the same place in the Himalayas as the chamois does in the Alps. And gooral-hunting on the precipitous and craggy heights of the middle and outer ranges, where there is enough hard climbing to give it zest, is most charming sport. Moreover, the sportsman has seldom to score the blank days which are so common when after grander game on the higher ranges and in Tibet.

A double express rifle of ·450 bore is about the best for gooral, as well as for all other Himalayan game animals.

A. F. MACKENZIE.

GOOSE, WILD.—Six species of wild geese are more or less commonly met with in the British Islands. These are the Grey Lag, the Bean, the Pink-footed, the White-fronted, the Bernicle, and the Brent goose. In addition to the half-dozen enumerated, there are some others which may be looked upon as rare or occasional visitors, and in this class may be placed the Red-breasted and the Snow goose; whilst two sub-species, the Lesser White-fronted and the White-bellied form of the Brent goose, may also be regarded as of this class. Others might perhaps be deemed to have the right to inclusion in the list of British geese, but as some of them—notably the Canadian and Egyptian geese—are now kept in a state of semi-domestication in various parts of the country, the occurrence of really wild visitors is always difficult to determine.

The Grey Lag Goose (*Anser cinereus*) is our only resident wild goose. It breeds in the north of Scotland, in the counties of Ross, Sutherland and Caithness, but is, notwithstanding, the scarcest of our wild geese. This perhaps may be partly accounted for by the fact that it prefers a more temperate climate than the rest of the British geese, its breeding haunts and winter quarters being generally situated further to the south than are theirs.

Professor Newton divides the grey geese into two groups: in the first the "nail" at the tip of the bill is white, or of a very pale flesh colour, and in the second this nail is black. To the white-nailed division belong the Grey Lag and the White-fronted goose, and to the black-nailed group the Bean and Pink-footed goose.

The bill of the Grey Lag has a white tip or nail, the other portions, and also the legs, being pale pink or flesh-coloured. A light ashen coloured patch of feathers on the shoulder is a

GREY LAG GOOSE.

distinguishing feature of the plumage, and by this means alone the bird may be recognised at some little distance. The breast of this bird, usually of a plain grey colour, has sometimes dark feathers, as the White-fronted goose. The Grey Lag measures some thirty-three to thirty-five inches from tip of bill to end of tail, and weighs up to about 10 lbs.

The White-fronted Goose (*Anser albifrons*) comes to us in winter, but is not perhaps quite so regular in its visits as the other grey geese. In both appearance and general characteristics this goose is more nearly allied to the Grey Lag than either the Bean or the Pink-footed goose. It is generally to be found in the vicinity of marshes. The breast in adult birds of this species is barred with dark feathers, and the bird takes its name from the white frontal margin of feathers at the base of the bill. The nail of the bill is white, the rest being orange, as also are the legs and feet. The White-fronted goose is the smallest of our grey geese; it measures only 27 inches or so in length, and weighs about $5\frac{3}{4}$ lbs. The Rev. H. A. Macpherson says the heaviest he ever weighed scaled $6\frac{1}{2}$ lbs., and this is the heaviest weight that I have seen recorded for this species.

The Lesser White-fronted Goose (*Anser erythropus*) is a diminutive form of the White-fronted goose. It is an extremely rare straggler to the British Islands, and, so far as I am aware, the only authenticated example of a British-killed specimen is one shot on the coast of Northumberland some few years ago by the late Mr. Alfred C. Chapman.

The Bean Goose (*Anser segetum*), another winter visitor, is a hardier species than the Grey Lag, its breeding haunts, and also its general winter habitat, being much farther to the North. In my experience the Bean goose generally prefers the marshland grasses to the uplands, and does not take such extended inland flights as its greyer relative the Pink-footed goose. In England it may usually be found grazing upon the young clovers and growing corn not far away from the coast line. In Ireland it is the commonest grey goose, and this fact goes to prove that it is more a marsh-feeding species than the Pink-footed goose. We have been frequently told that this bird congregates in vast numbers to feed upon the scattered grain left in the fields far inland. This, however, has been proved to be a mistake in one or two instances, and from personal observation of the habits of the Bean and the Pink-footed goose, extending over a number of years, I am inclined to think that it is a case of mis-identification in some other instances also. Seven and a half to 8 lbs. is a good weight for a Bean goose, but in open winters, when food is plentiful, they have been killed weighing 9 lbs. and upwards. Length about 33 inches. The nail and basal portion of the bill are black, the rest orange, as also are the legs and feet.

The Pink-footed Goose (*Anser brachyrhynchus*), as its name signifies, has a bill somewhat shorter than the rest of the grey geese. The nail of the bill in this goose is black, the middle portion as well as the legs and feet being pink—vermilion-pink, one writer has described it. Occasionally adult birds are found to have a white band of feathers at the base of the bill, similar to, although not generally quite so deep as, that on *A. albifrons.* The light shoulder patch is present in old birds, but it is not so

PINK-FOOTED GOOSE.

pronounced as in the Grey Lag. Of all our migratory birds, summer or winter, none are more regular in the date of their arrival than the Pink-footed geese. In East Yorkshire I have noticed that they arrive on or about September 25th, with unvarying punctuality. By that date the harvest is usually completed, and the geese visit the stubbles day by day to feed upon the scattered corn. Pink-footed geese are remarkably local in their distribution, confining their visits to certain circumscribed areas where peaceable possession of the food they most desire is to be obtained. Barley is their favourite grain, and so long as this is obtainable they will not leave the stubbles; on its exhaustion they turn to the young clover and the tender blades of the autumn sown wheat, with marsh or other grasses as a change. Pink-footed geese usually weigh about $1\frac{1}{2}$ lbs. less than Bean geese, and they measure 30 inches from bill to tail.

The Snow Goose (*Anser hyperboreus*) is a rare visitor to this country. As this goose is more numerous in North America than elsewhere, it is not singular that it should have been observed more frequently in Ireland than in Great Britain. It is not mentioned as having occurred in England until the hard weather of January 1891, when, on the fifteenth of that month, I saw three Snow geese in East Yorkshire, the incident being recorded in the *Field* newspaper at the time. These birds appeared very large and swan-like, and it is possible they might be referred to *A. hyperboreus*, the larger form of Snow goose, instead of to *Anser albatus*, the lesser Snow goose. In the same month, the Rev. H. A. Macpherson saw four Snow geese in Cumberland. The plumage of this bird, white with black quill feathers, is sufficiently conspicuous to attract attention to it wherever it goes. It may, therefore, be taken for granted that it occurs very sparingly in this country.

The Bernicle Goose (*Bernicla leucopsis*) visits this country in considerable numbers, but it evinces a strong partiality for certain districts,

BERNICLE GOOSE.

notably the west coast of Scotland and some parts of Ireland, and seldom strays far from those haunts, save under exceptional circumstances. With respect to habit, the Bernicle goose may be said to form a connecting link between the grey geese and the Brent geese, for it is seldom to be found far away from salt water, although not so strictly marine in its tastes as the black goose. The Rev. H. A. Macpherson has given an interesting description of the habits of Bernicle geese on the Cumberland coast in his *Fauna of Lakeland.* This goose weighs about 5½ lbs. and measures 25 inches in total length.

The Brent Goose (*Bernicla brenta*) is best of all the geese from both the gastronomist's and

BRENT GOOSE.

the punt-gunner's points of view. It is very rarely seen inland, being strictly marine in its tastes; but in extremely rough and snowy weather these birds occasionally get blown out of their course. Brent geese commence to arrive about the end of September or beginning of October in the north of Scotland, but the majority of the black geese do not reach these shores until November. They depart for circumpolar breeding haunts about the end of March or beginning of April. A white-bellied form of the Brent goose (*Bernicla brenta glaucogaster*) is sometimes, though rarely, met with. Thousands of Brent geese are to be found in winter in various suitable localities around our coasts. Their numbers are invariably considerably augmented during any protracted spell of hard weather by fresh arrivals of geese from Northern Europe. The principal food of the Brent goose whilst here is the grass wrack (*Zostera marina*), which grows upon the mudbanks in certain estuaries and along the open coast. When the tide leaves these mudbanks the geese alight to feed upon this weed, and, where they are not subjected to much persecution at the hands of punt-gunners, the operation may be continued upon the rising of the tide until the long waving blades of grass can be no longer reached. Even then the meal is not always at an end, for the geese, when on the muds or shallows, instinctively pull up much more of the weed than can be devoured at the time, and this, floating away on the tide, provides food for them at those times when the *zostera* beds are deeply submerged. The Brent measures 22 in. to 25 in. in length and weighs from 3½ to 4½ lbs.

The Red-breasted Goose (*Bernicla ruficollis*) has only been obtained a dozen times in the British Islands. The plumage of adult birds is strikingly handsome, black, white, and rich chestnut predominating. According to Seebohm the Red-breasted goose, so far as is known, is confined during the breeding season to the tundras in some parts of Northern Siberia. This goose would seem to be equally exclusive in its choice of winter quarters, for up to the present it is known to spend the winter only on the large Asiatic inland sea, the Caspian. Length about 22 inches.

GOOSE-SHOOTING—Wild-goose chasing has sometimes been mentioned slightingly. This perhaps springs as much from ignorance as from want of appreciation, for few true sportsmen who have once indulged to the full in the sport of wild-goose shooting will vote it either slow or void of interest. One reason why this sport is so inspiriting arises from the fact that it has an accompaniment seldom found in other branches of sport in which the gun has a part. This is the wild music of the quarry. The clamour of a large "gaggle" of geese, heard from a distance, has been likened by some old writers to the sound emitted by a pack of hounds in full cry. Certainly, the ringing chorus of a good-sized skein of Pink-footed geese,

uttered as they sweep along through the air, strikes the ear quite as pleasantly, and is a sound just as exhilarating to the senses of the wild-fowler and of all who love wild nature, as hound-music to the fox-hunter.

In order the more readily to discuss the question of wild-goose shooting, it will be as well to place the six commoner species of British geese in two divisions, the grey and the black. The first division includes the Grey Lag, Bean, Pink-footed and White-fronted, and these in a general way may be looked upon as inland-feeders; the second division, Bernicle and Brent geese, are coast-feeders.

The grey geese usually rest at night upon mud and sandbanks, or higher saltings in the wider estuaries or along the open coast, or upon islands on the larger inland sheets of water, as well as in secluded spots upon the moors. From thence, in open weather, they take daily flights of greater or less extent to feed inland. Of all the grey geese the Pink-footed goose is perhaps the greatest lover of corn, *i.e.*, corn in the ear, and to obtain this particular food these birds will fly many miles out and home, morning and evening. The Grey Lag and the Bean goose prefer the vicinity of the coast, and the White-fronted goose is even more particularly a marsh-haunting bird. The Bernicle, also, has a preference for the marshes, spending his time chiefly by the sea. Brent geese are essentially sea-going fowl; seldom, indeed, are they to be found out of sight of salt water. The favourite food of Brent geese is the sea-grass (*Zostera marina*), and where this is abundant, and its quiet enjoyment may be obtained, on our eastern coasts at all events, the black geese are usually to be found.

Judged by the nature of their surroundings and habits, it seems but natural that a considerable percentage of the grey geese killed in this country should fall to the shoulder gun. With Brent geese, however, it is different, for, as these fowl must in a general way be approached by water, it happens that by far the greater number are killed by the punt-gun. Where they are much followed, the Brent geese will not be found to incur many risks by moving over the saltings, their farthest landward flights seldom extending beyond the mud flats uncovered at low water. By digging a hole, or sinking a cask well out upon the mud flats, the shoulder-gunner may have some sport in stormy weather or, what is equally good, in a thick fog. When one is properly equipped in long wading boots and suitable clothing, the discomforts attending this method of shooting are not great, and, certainly, the exciting nature of the pursuit well repays the fowler for any extra trouble in suitably fixing his position.

In **punting** to geese, the gunner proceeds in either a single or a double-handed punt. For this purpose the latter is, all things considered, the best; as one then embarks in a roomier and more seaworthy boat. This is of first importance on the open coast, where a heavy sea may spring up quickly. In the more sheltered situations the narrower single-handed punt answers well, and is better to get about in. It is usually extremely difficult to approach within gun-shot of Brent geese in mild weather, and in this pursuit, as in nearly all shooting with the punt gun, success is best attained during prolonged frosts.

Grey geese will seldom allow a punt to approach them when on the water in the daytime. Seasoned punt-gunners seldom trouble after them in daylight, well knowing such pursuit to be futile. In the grey dawn or evening twilight they may be occasionally outwitted by stealing upon them as they rest on the sand or mudbanks of their night haunt. But the heaviest shots at grey geese are usually made on dark nights, when carefully-laid plans and a well-timed shot into the dense black mass of geese, as they rise in the dark with a sound like thunder, will often fill the punt with dead birds. On these occasions a goodly proportion of the birds falling to the shot cannot be secured in the gloom, and they should be searched for in likely situations, according to set of tide and direction of wind, at daybreak the following morning. This method of shooting more or less by sound—for very little can be discerned in the darkness necessary to secure a close approach to these wary birds—is, however, usually pursued by gunners who shoot for a living; the amateur prefers to note the result of each shot, and the shooting by guesswork in the dark certainly robs the sport of half its pleasure.

For full particulars as to dimensions and style of punts, double and single-handed, I may refer my readers to Col. Hawker's well-known work, and also to some recently-published works on wild-fowling named below. This remark applies also to punt-guns, of which, both muzzle and breech-loading, there are many varieties, as well as several ingenious methods of fixing them up so as to ease the gunner of all recoil on firing.

In districts much frequented by grey geese excellent sport may at times be obtained with the shoulder gun. By waylaying them as they take morning and evening flights to and from the feeding ground, some geese may now and again be killed, particularly when a head wind keeps them near to the ground. In still weather they usually fly at a good altitude, taking care to keep well up out of gunshot. Another and more successful method of obtaining sport with grey geese is to conceal one's self on the night haunt of the game. When too often followed, this will, of course, cause the geese to seek quiet in other quarters, but an occasional night spent with the geese in this way is often prolific of sport of a most exciting character. Now and again a skilful stalker may approach within shot of grey geese as they feed on the fields; but as the stalking of wild geese needs a combination of favouring circumstances not always obtainable, it cannot be relied upon as a means whereby sport may be obtained.

Driving, all things considered, is the most successful plan to adopt when following grey geese inland. Properly followed this is most exciting sport, for both gunner and driver will, perforce, have to undertake many long and arduous stalks. Geese, like other fowl, fly against wind on rising; and, knowing this, the sportsman endeavours to conceal himself within shot of the line they will take on being disturbed by the driver. As this place of concealment must be to windward of the geese, it follows that the utmost caution must be observed in securing such positions. The approach must be carefully planned, as must that of the driver, and the planning and execution of these strategical movements is not by any means the least exciting part of the business. An Irish servant I once had proved himself an invaluable aid as a driver. He entered into the sport heart and soul, and enjoyed the successes quite as much as I did. I shall never forget his delight when on one occasion he very skilfully drove a nice gaggle of Pink-footed geese past my stand, and five were secured as the result of a shot from a big 4-bore.

Guns and Ammunition—It is sometimes found that heavy shoulder guns of large calibre are absolutely essential to success in goose-shooting. In a wild, open country, geese are not easily approached, and in such situation a powerful 8- or 4-bore gun will prove most effective. In these guns weight, to a certain extent, means power; and as they have not to be carried far as a rule, a single 4-bore for goose-shooting may well weigh as much as 18 lb. From a fully choked gun of this weight 3½ oz. of large shot will be delivered with deadly force at 80 to 100 yards, up to which distance geese may regularly be killed. If an 8-bore is chosen, this may be a double-barrel, weighing 15 lbs. or so. From a gun of this weight 2½ oz. of large shot may be fired from each barrel with comfort. The large shot known as A.A., counting 40 pellets to the ounce, is a suitable size to use for goose-shooting, at ranges of from 80 to 100 yards. At shorter distances B.B., of 58 pellets to the ounce, will answer. Many people pin their faith to the use of coarse-grained black powder in heavy shoulder guns, but in suitable cartridge cases the nitro-powders, Schultze, E.C., and Amberite, answer admirably. They are not nearly so noisy as black powder, and the report of the heavy gun has a much less disturbing effect upon the fowl. A stout double 12-bore is a very handy weapon to use in some situations, particularly when visiting the night haunts of the geese. A gun of this sort, weighing 7½ to 8 lbs., will carry up to 1½ oz. of No. 1 or B.B. shot, and may be used with deadly effect upon geese at fifty yards.

Clothing is a matter of first importance, for to the improperly-clad sportsman the pursuit lacks half its pleasure, to say nothing of the needless risks to health incurred by reason of a faulty system. In the sport of wildfowl shooting much waiting about in the cold is often necessary. We may take a hint from nature in deciding that for warmth, health, and comfort, nothing beats pure wool for wear next the skin. Let the foundation at all events be wool; and if the weather is very cold, and two or three layers of clothing are worn, the lower strata should be of wool also. The outer covering, too, may be of wool in fine weather, but for wet work gabardine is excellent wear, and, being very light, does not impede one's movements so much as a thicker material. This is a matter of much importance where a gun has to be handled. In bitterly cold weather, particularly when icy winds pierce one to the marrow, a leather jacket may be worn as an overall with an infinite degree of comfort. On other occasions the latter form of clothing is superfluous, and perhaps also unhealthy. Ordinary shooting boots may be worn on most occasions when following geese inland. But proper wildfowling rig must be donned for shooting upon the mud flats. In such situations long leather wading boots may be worn two sizes too large, to enable an extra pair or two of thick woollen stockings to be put on, without which the gunner would suffer much from cold feet.

Bibliography—Those who desire to learn more as to the habits and general characteristics of the geese may turn to one or other of the following works: *A History of British Birds*, Henry Seebohm (Porter); Yarrell's *British Birds*, 4th edition; *A Manual of British Birds*, Howard Saunders; *A Hand-book of British Birds*, J. E. Harting; *A Dictionary of Birds*, Professor A. Newton.

For more complete directions as to the sport of wild-goose shooting much information will be gathered from the following: *Instructions to Young Sportsmen*, Col. Hawker, several editions of which were published by Messrs. Longman fifty and more years ago, but much of which is still applicable. *The Wildfowler*, by H. C. Folkard (Longmans), a work that is quite unsurpassed as a history of wildfowling; *The Fowler in Ireland*, by Sir R. Payne-Gallwey, Bart. (Gurney and Jackson), an excellent work; in his *Letters to Young Shooters* the same author, in the section on *Wildfowling*, imparts valuable instruction. Then we have *The Art of Wildfowling*, by Mr. Abel Chapman, a thoroughly reliable work (Horace Cox), and, by the present writer, *Practical Wildfowling* (L. Upcott Gill).

HENRY SHARP.

GRASMERE SPORTS—The origin of these now famous sports is the subject of keen discussion amongst men who were not young in the early fifties of the now decaying century. Whether, as they now exist, the Sports are the direct lineal descendants of the old Fair-day

Athletic gatherings which were held in Grasmere after the sheep and cattle bargains had been concluded, or are a survival of the village Rush-bearing Competitions, or whether they are the growth and outcome of Sports initiated in the year 1852 by certain gentlemen who, at that time, were prominent sportsmen in the district, is an extremely difficult question to decide. That Grasmere has long been the home of the famous Westmorland and Cumberland style of wrestling is certain, and it is primarily to wrestling that the sports owe the position they hold to-day in the Athletic world.

WRESTLING.

It is certain, from documentary evidence which the writer has seen, that, in 1852, several of the more prominent sporting gentlemen of the district (of whom now only a few survive) formed themselves into a committee to keep the wrestling fame of Grasmere alive, and from that date up to the present—with the exception of the year of the Crimean war, when, owing to the military demands of the day, the chief supporters were called from home and no sports were held—the Grasmere Gathering has a practically unbroken record. In 1852 the Sports occupied two days and included steeple-chasing; now the fixture is for one day only and the horse element has long been eliminated from the programme. The events during the last thirty years have comprised Heavy Weight and Light Weight Wrestling, Guides' Race, Pole and High Leaping, and a Hound Trail.

Wrestling is the *pièce de résistance* of the day. The light-weight Competition is restricted to men under 11 stone 3 lbs., whilst the heavy-weight is open to the world.

The present heavy-weight champion is George Steadman, of Whitehaven. Steadman is now 51 years of age, but, when he carried away the belt from the Grasmere ring in 1896 for the thirteenth time, he was as good, both in attack and defence, as when he first claimed the girdle in 1872. To give some slight idea of what manner of man this champion is, the following facts concerning him may be interesting. He made his first public appearance as a wrestler in 1862; he can wrestle in any and every recognised style, and has met and thrown the thin French Champion Le Boeuf, at Lillie Bridge, in the Frenchman's own style, and at

WRESTLING.

the Alexandra Palace, he served Boulanger in the same way; whilst in three successive years, 1880, 1881, and 1882, he carried away Sir John Astley's belt from Lillie Bridge. He measures 47 inches round the chest, stands 5 feet 4½ inches in height, and draws the scales at 18 stone 3 lbs. Without a doubt, Steadman is a worthy upholder of the best traditions of Westmorland and Cumberland wrestling, and is an honourable successor to such men as Noble Ewbank, Adam Walker, of Troutbeck, and Tom Longmire, of Windermere.

The **Guides' Race** is one of the most important and attractive events in the Grasmere programme, and certainly it is one of the severest struggles to which an athlete could be put. The race, an open one, is from a field in the valley round a flag-post on one of the peaks of Sölva How, and down into the valley again. There is a level field to cross at the start, preceded by a high stone wall, and afterwards one long, steep, craggy climb to the summit, a height of 1100 feet from the valley, and 1300 feet above sea-level. The ground is either of the very roughest, or, what is almost worse, of slippery bracken-grown screes, and the stiffness of the race may be imagined. The average number of competitors for this race is fifteen, and the sight of these men leaping over the first stone wall, galloping across the level field, winding their devious ways through the single pine wood, again appearing in the open and racing over moor and fell, crag and torrent, until the leader rounds the post and hands his ticket to the official stationed there, is an exciting and picturesque one. The race down is almost incredible, for the speed at which the men descend is terrific, and, oftener than not, the race is won on the homeward journey. The runners appear to be driven down by some unseen irresistible force; to the spectators, in the valley below, each man resembles a huge boulder that has been disturbed from its balance and rolls and bounds along, gaining impetus as it proceeds. A few years ago, a certain Mungo Park won the race and, in his downward course, he came across a little precipice, but, nothing daunted, he made the jump which was, then and there, officially measured as 22 feet. The record time for the race was broken in 1896, when T. Conchie, of Shap, ran it in 14 min. 26 4-5 sec. He is the best man who hitherto has run the race, and his uphill work especially is admirable. He is 23 years of age, weighs 11½ stone, and stands 5 feet 10½ inches in height. He earns his livelihood as a labourer, at the famous Shap granite works, and his training is of the simplest.

When the guides have come safely home, the **Hound Trail** is started. It is a pretty sight to watch the dozen or fifteen dogs as they are held in their leashes, giving loud mouth and awaiting impatiently the signal to go. The trail is laid by a man running over the course, and dragging behind him a rag steeped in a mixture of train oil and oil of aniseed. There are several trails in Westmorland, but the Grasmere course is admittedly the roughest and most testing. The trail starts from the Sports' field, runs along the breast of Sölva How by Red Bank, along Loughrigg Terrace, crosses by White Moss along by Forrest Side, over the old turnpike road above the Travellers' Rest, along the breast of Helm Crag, across by Easedale Head, along the opposite breast, and so into the field again by Allan Bank, a circuit covering something between nine and ten miles of ground. The course varies every year, though not to any extent, either in distance or direction, and only sufficiently to prevent hounds from being previously trained to run the special trail selected for the day. The circuit indicated above embraces the whole village of Grasmere, and, from first to last, the ground lies over the hills and moun-

GUIDES' RACE.

tains, and the going throughout is as rough as loose stones and rocky boulders can make it. Obstacles in the shape of high stone walls, wooden palings, and mountain streams intersect the trail at every point. So soon as the trailer has come in, the hounds are loosed, and, for the next half hour, the fleeting specks are watched through the field glasses, a pack in full view of game which they are never fated to kill, and yet as keen as though the brush was whisking their tongues. As mile is added to mile, the pack begins to scatter and the line grows thinner. Sometimes the leader loses his place by reason of a loose stone on the top of a difficult wall toppling over, sometimes a stream offers an irresistible temptation for delay, whilst a favourite has been known to lose the run through waiting for a companion in distress behind him. The astonishing pace is always maintained by the majority, and often it is a nose and nose race home between the first couple, and not until a certain line has been passed, and the number appears on the board, and the band strikes up the old Cumberland air, "D'ye ken, John Peel?" does even the owner of the gallant little animal know the winner. The official time for the race in 1896, won by Mr. Rayner's "Ruler," was 30 minutes 28 seconds. The dogs are clean, thoroughbred foxhounds, and are most carefully trained for months before the sports. It is an exception for them to belong to a hunting pack, though "Wyndham," one of the best hounds that ever ran a trail, was also one of the hardest working members of the Rev. E. M. Reynolds's Coniston pack. Every precaution is taken as to what the hound is fed upon, and one of the most successful trainers, John Lancaster, for a fortnight before a trail, feeds his dogs upon a diet consisting of the white of two hard-boiled eggs finely pulped together with two raw eggs, mixed with a quantity of bread, specially made with eggs, without yeast or salt, but with plenty of sugar-candy and fruits; a certain quantity of good sherry is added to this, which, together with half a pound of a roast leg of mutton, is given to each dog twice a day. Lancaster has also a special mixture of his own preparation which he gives to the hound the moment before running, the object of which is to keep the animal cool and so minimise the chance of his staying to drink at cooling streams when heated in the chase. Hound-trailing has become a fashionable form of sport in Westmorland, and many gentlemen own, train, and enter their own hounds at Grasmere, and a good prize-winning trailer has become a valuable possession.

TRAIL RACE.

After the hound-trail follows the pole and high leaping, and these events, always capitally contested, bring the programme to a close.

The Grasmere Sports are held at Pavement End, on the Thursday nearest to the 21st of August. Every event is open, and the best talent is year by year seen here. With the single exception which has been mentioned, the programme is identical with what it was in 1852, and it is to be hoped that, so long as the Sports continue to be held, it will remain what it is to-day. Round after round of wrestling may possibly prove, towards the end of the day, monotonous to the uninitiated, but it is the great feature of the meeting, and of the £250 distributed in prizes, no less than £120 is devoted to this competition. Wrestling is the form of sport indigenous to the soil, and has played its part in forming the splendid physique of Westmorland and Cumberland men.

Very pleasant features of the gathering are the large number of downright Cumberland and Westmorland people who annually attend, the entire absence of rowdyism, and the total prohibition of betting.

J. C. SHEPHERD.

GRAYLING—(*Salmo thymallus*, Lin.; *Thymallus vulgaris*, Cuvier, Yarrell and others).

Name and Origin—The contentions associated with the name of the grayling are interesting rather than important, and the good St. Ambrose of Milan was both safe and happy in pronouncing it the flower of fishes, apparently in reference to its manifold tints and to the odour which is supposed to have induced Ausonius to dub it *Thymallus*. Few men can be found to agree as to the specific perfume which is discernible in handling a newly caught grayling in normal condition, and the fact is that in very large or very small specimens it is less strong than in a grayling of the herring size, which is the average upon many rivers. The smelt

GRAYLING.

yields precisely such a faint suggestion of cucumber, or thyme, as that which the majority of observers claim for the grayling, and as a rule it is unmistakable, if not easily defined. The suggestion has been thrown out that the odour of the grayling varies with its diet. The French call the grayling *L'Ombre Commune*, and Umber, or its corruption Oumer, is an old English local name. As to the word "Grayling," it has been referred to the gray lines along the sides of the fish. The prevailing hue of *Salmo thymallus*, as it appears in the water, is grey. The observer who, looking over the parapet of a bridge, has the opportunity of seeing a trout and a grayling lying on a shallow not far apart, will be struck with this distinguishing tone, by contrast with the rich ruddy brown of the former; and when the grayling moves away, it is like the fading of a pale shadow, very different from the brisk dart into cover of its darker-hued companion.

There appears to be no sound foundation for the belief that the grayling was originally introduced into England from the Continent. Until the early part of the present century it was not widely distributed, but even in Walton's lifetime the Dove, Trent, and the Wiltshire rivers were known to be grayling rivers. In our own time the fish has been introduced with every promise of success in the Clyde and Ayr, and is found in numbers in the Tweed. It is further to be observed that the grayling is not the only British fish of merely partial distribution. The burbot, the gwyniad, the vendace, and the chars may be classed with the grayling in this respect, and there is on the whole no justification for the assumption that the fish is not indigenous.

Appearance and Habits—The grayling resembles certain of the coarse fishes in form rather than the *Salmonidæ* of the more orthodox type, and the small, unarmed, square mouth, suggesting suction, is formed somewhat like that of the ground-feeders, the protrusion of the upper jaw being sufficient to give it character without constituting deformity, as in the barbel. Its most striking peculiarities are the huge dorsal fin and the lozenge or pear-shaped eye. The bright red, shading to violet, of the edges of the fin, and the red and black of the sides, with purple streaks irregularly marked, have warranted comparison with the wing of a butterfly. In repose, the delicate upper fringes of this fin lap curiously over, betraying the identity of the fish should the other characters be indistinct. The tail is forked and powerfully formed. The scales are small and clearly defined, and the grey longitudinal lines are peculiar to this species. The colouring of the fish varies greatly according to age. Few descriptions of the grayling agree in detail, and indeed the difference between the fish of different ages, and different districts is very marked. A pound grayling from a Derbyshire or Yorkshire river is probably a type of the best, while one of the big two-and-a-half- or three-pounders from the Southern chalk streams is almost invariably a dull presentment, the purpling of the grey vesture having changed to brown, and the rainbow hues having practically disappeared.

The grayling differs considerably in size according to the rivers which it inhabits. A pound fish in Derbyshire, Yorkshire, or Worcestershire is considered worthy of special regard, and a panier of a dozen and half will often have but one of such respectable bulk. Occasionally larger fish will be taken. In the Hampshire rivers, to which the species has been introduced during the present century, two-pounders are common, and the largest known specimen of recent years was a superbly proportioned fish of 3 lbs. 9 oz., caught by Mr. F. M. Walbran, in a hatch-hole on the Test near Houghton Mill, and duly shown at the Imperial Institute Exhibition of 1897.

The habits of the grayling differ in some

important respects from those of the trout, and in balancing the one against the other, it is essential to bear this in mind. The grayling, for example, is a spring spawner, moving to the breeding-shallows towards the end of March, or even as late as the beginning of May. It is said that the grayling, being free from domestic concerns in mid-winter when the trout spawn, works havoc upon the ova of trout, and to some extent no doubt this does occur. The grayling, however, are, at that period, in the deep, slow running water, while the trout have pushed up to the rapid streams flowing over the gravel. The extent of damage, therefore, done to trout eggs is very inconsiderable, though, when spawners are busy, some few grayling and coarse fish may be seen in the neighbourhood of the redds waiting for the few unburied eggs which may be brought down by the stream. Another important consideration is that the grayling is a fish of quick growth, but not so rapid perhaps, as Sir Humphry Davy believed when he wrote that fish hatched in May or June grew to nine or ten inches in length by September. Although the fry of the grayling, when early hatched, is so minute that a purchaser who had received a consignment is said to have imagined that the can contained nothing but water, within little more than a couple of months they are four or five inches long.

The grayling also produces a larger number of eggs than the trout, so that in a stream favourable for the fish, the increase is likely to be proportionately greater.

As a Game Fish—The merits of the grayling as a game fish may not be quite equal to those of the trout, but, all points considered, they come so near that there is little margin for dispute. The trout fights fiercely and with a dash peculiar to its breed, but the grayling fights, in its way, just as strenuously and as perseveringly. The slower movements after the first rush lead some critics into the mistake of supposing that the fish is chicken-hearted, and a remark of Walton (who probably had no large experience of its character) has given the cue for that verdict. The grayling is, in fact, the next best game fish to the trout amongst our British non-migratory fresh-water species, and it may take even longer to bring to the net than a trout of the same size. It leaps out of the water occasionally, and if its charges into the stream are not so swift, it has an artful and dangerous habit of rolling and twisting, and of boring downwards, that is very trying to tackle and nerves.

It must also be placed to the credit of the grayling that it rises freely, and is not easily "put down." It is an axiom of the dry-fly angler that a trout rises but once to the artificial fly; as long, however, as the grayling continues to rise, so long may the artificial fly be cast, and it is no uncommon result to kill your fish at the eighth or ninth time of presentation. There is nothing more full of concentrated sport than to kneel to a grayling which refuses again and again, yet is taken at last. It must be added, however, to this tribute to the grayling's generous spirit that the fish often makes ostentatious movement at the lure, without intending to take it. The grayling is a master of short rising. On all but the very "shy" chalk streams, it may be risen, if such a term is permissible, against its will. The best baskets are often made by the wet-fly fisherman on days when there is no visible sign of a rising fish, and the order of procedure is under any and every circumstance to fish the stream methodically. This is especially successful on the stone-bedded North Country rivers, where the absence of aquatic vegetation signifies dearth of insect food. Otherwise the grayling is as much a dry-fly fish as the trout, and should be treated in a similar manner.

The strongest plea for the grayling is that it keeps the fly-rod going months after the end of the trout season. The grayling may be caught from the middle of July to the middle of February; but a secure and unexceptionable limit would be August 1st to New Year's Day. It seems strange that some anglers do not place these absolute advantages—namely, three months of additional sport, and a possible dish of great excellence for the table when salmon and trout are "off"—against drawbacks that are mostly theoretical.

Tackle—"Fine and far off" is the rule with grayling as with trout. The same rod, line, and fine gut collar go with the same waders and other items of equipment. It is the fly-box that must be slightly refurnished. Practically, the 00 and 000 sizes of the best trout patterns are admirable for grayling, and to them are added a few fancy flies which imitate no insect known to entomology. The red tag is indispensable, though it is beginning to be discussed in doubtful terms, and variations are ventured upon because the original dressing, so many years infallible, is supposed to have been found out by the grayling on Itchen and Test. It may be laid down as a rule that the selection of artificial flies which are pronounced best by local authorities is sound, and that the floating duns of the South, the bumbles and wet flies of the Midlands, and the spidery hackles of Yorkshire have their distinctive functions. Among the books indicated at the end of this article are representative pronouncements as to flies—Halford for the Southern dry-fly waters, Pritt and Walbran for the North, Foster for the Midlands.

The special grayling flies which may be here described are not numerous, and they are generally patterns characterised by the bit of tinsel or glitter by which the indigo-blue eye of the grayling is attracted; and almost without exception they will serve either wet or dry, and in most waters. The best tags are the red, the orange, and the macaw; the claret, yellow, orange-claret, and furnace bumble are of almost equal value, but should be tied on, at the most, oo hooks; and flies of the little chap order, the curses, black gnats, Hammond's adopted, Wickham's fancy, silver sedge, red and claret spinners, and at all times the hare's ear with gold or silver twist, should be in use. The grayling seldom rises, as trout do, in the evening, and the best fishing will be found between eleven and five o'clock in and after September.

The grayling does not forage in solitary determination, but ever wanders in company. The fish move from the deep pools at varying times to the adjacent shallows, and it is never very certain where they may be, except that they are not in rough ripples. The rise of a grayling is so often a mere dimpling of the surface that it is never wise to be contemptuous of the sign, and abandon a position on the supposition that the game is not worth the trouble of tempting. A two-pound grayling frequently makes no more fuss than a dace. Fortunately for the angler, the grayling generally makes his first rush up stream, and there is little fear of his making direct for the weeds. The fish should be firmly held, turned, and kept moving down stream until his powers are exhausted. Grayling are frequently lost by allowing them either to bore to the bottom, rolling and gyrating the while, or to work below the angler and bring fins and tail to bear against the stream. The outer edges of the mouth are tender, and no doubt less calculated to retain the hook than the hard interior of a trout's jaws, but the large number of breakages is not due so much to this cause as to the short rising propensities of the fish, and the consequent light hooking in the weaker portion of the mouth. When the barb is well struck into the solid flesh, the hold is really of the firmest kind, and there is no abnormal danger of breaking away.

It seems wicked to angle for a generously rising fish like the grayling with any other lure than the artificial fly, but it is often done, and there is the somewhat especial excuse in this instance, that, upon many rivers where fly-fishing would be useless in the winter, weeks and months of sport are afforded by certain methods of bottom-fishing. Some of these are purely local, others are more widespread.

"Grasshopper" Fishing — The most singular instance of a local bait in all angling is probably the so-called "grasshopper" of the West Country. In Herefordshire, Shropshire, and Worcestershire, perhaps one of our best grayling districts, this so-called "grasshopper" is still used, and has been used from time immemorial. It is not a grasshopper at all, though originally it may have been intended to imitate that summer insect. A large hook is used (No. 5 or 6), weighted with lead wrapped around the shank. This is in turn overlaid with Berlin wool of primary colours, green predominating, with yellow bands, until the affair resembles a gaudy and clumsy chrysalis. Upon the hook five or six maggots are impaled, and the game is to "sink and draw" as it is technically termed. The lure, such as it is, is allowed to dive to the bottom, and is then slightly jerked up and down as the stream bears it onwards. It is, for grayling, what the old-fashioned trolling bait was for pike, and very clever some of the West Country anglers of the old type are at this primitive method. The largest and best fish are taken in this way, but on well-preserved waters, it need scarcely be said, it is prohibited. Such baskets are not made nowadays, as those recorded by Francis in his Book on Angling, when a single rod could fill a 25-lb. or 30-lb. basket two or three times in one day. This grotesque "grasshopper" has fortunately been found wanting when experimented upon in the north or south, and it is not regarded with respect by the true angler. Why the grayling should take it is not very apparent, but the fish is rather erratic in its tastes. It is not by any means fitted with mouth or teeth to indulge in fish food, but instances have been known of grayling following and being caught fairly in the mouth by artificial minnows, and upon the Costa, which is one of the well-known grayling streams of Yorkshire, a fly dressed on the pattern of the Alexandra, but on a small hook, is often more killing than the correct grayling flies.

Swimming the Worm—The most sporting method of winter bait-fishing is probably that of swimming the worm, as described by Mr. F. M. Walbran, who is its leading exponent on the Ure and Wharfe, and by the late Mr. Pritt, whose *Book of the Grayling* was the first monograph on the subject. Grayling love to lie in herds along the gently sloping sandy shelf of a fairly strong stream, and in about four or five feet of water. The angler is equipped with a rod slightly stiffer than that used for fly-fishing; a short collar of drawn gut, attached to a freely running fine line, and a tiny pear-shaped float affixed two or three feet from the hook. A small red worm is used for bait, and the angler, wading along the edge of the stream, allows his lure to swim so as to touch and go upon the clean bottom of the aforesaid shelf. It is a method requiring much caution and skill, and although the fish will not always bite, this style is found amply to repay the fisherman for the wintry weather to which he is exposed. December seems to be the favourite month for this form of sport, and the angler prefers hard and bright frosty weather. The grayling thus treated bites very gently, seldom taking the float under, and the expert fishermen recognise the slightest slant of the painted cork as an indication for striking. It is necessary to keep out of sight while this swimming process is carried on, and a quick strike and firm hand are essential to success. When the fish are feeding greedily, the float disappears wholly, but the only indication is frequently the abrupt stopping of the float, as if it had been caught in a weed. All these movements are to be explained by the habits of the fish. If the small red worm is travelling close to the bottom, the sucking mouth of the grayling arrests it, and it is then that the float merely halts. The fish will rise, however, to the worm as it is floating overhead, and it is tolerably certain that its sudden disappearance is the result of a grayling forced to rise a foot or so upwards to seize the morsel on its passage. The grayling will also take gentles, wasp-grubs and caddis bait, and, in the waters where these methods are possible, the best baskets are made on these occasional days of mid-winter fishing, and the grayling then are in their best condition. Fly-fishing is the only method permitted on all well-ordered grayling waters.

Range—The grayling, with a few structural differences, occurs in many of the Continental rivers, and in nearly all the lakes and rivers of Northern Europe. It is found in the United States, and in parts of Canada. In England it has been introduced into numerous trout rivers, for some of which it is not suited. Typical grayling streams are the Test, Itchen (below Winchester), Wiltshire Avon and the tributary Wylie; the Dove, Derwent, Wye, and Manifold in Derbyshire, and the higher waters of the Trent; the streams of Worcestershire, Shropshire and Herefordshire, some of which, such as the Lugg, Teme, and Arrow, are associated with grayling fishers of a past generation; the Clyde, Tweed, Ayr, and Tay in Scotland; the Dee in Wales. The rivers in which the grayling are still in the experimental stage are the Thames, Lea, Colne, and Kennet. In the more rapid streams of the Midlands and West Country, where the alternating pools and rough streams are frequent, the grayling loves the gliding heads, tails, and sides of strong currents, and so sharp is its vision, and so adapted to such movements are its air-bladder and fins, that it will rise almost perpendicularly from a depth of five or six feet and secure the passing fly.

MEASUREMENTS, ETC.—Length of head 5¼ to 6, of caudal fin 6, height of body 4¾ to 5 in the total length. *Eyes*—diameter of each 4 in the length of the head, 1¼ diameters from the end of the snout, and about the same distance apart. Upper jaw very slightly the longer; the posterior extremity of the maxilla reaches to beneath the anterior edge or first-third of the orbit. *Teeth*—fine ones in the jaws near the head of the vomer, and on the anterior portion of the palatines; none on the tongue. *Fins*—these vary with the sex, the last dorsal rays are somewhat produced in adults. The first dorsal fin commences midway between the end of the snout and on a line above the front edge of the anal fin, the height of its rays being about two-thirds of that of the body below it. Pectoral inserted in the lower fourth of the height, and as long as the head excluding the snout. Ventrals situated beneath the middle of the rayed dorsal fin, and comparatively small, terminating on a line below the hind edge of the adipose dorsal. Caudal forked. *Scales*—in regular rows, some small ones being present over the basal portion of the caudal fin. The chest, or that portion of it as far as the pectoral fin, may be entirely destitute of scales or else scaled. *Colours*—these during life are beautifully changeable; head of a bluish-purple and a golden tinge along the back, while the horizontal lines along the body are dark, and each of the scales has a golden tinge. Dorsal fins with purplish bands and ocelli, which have a purplish red centre, and there are likewise some purplish streaks along the courses of the rays, while the outer edge is likewise purplish. Occasionally there are some black spots on the fins, also scattered over the body. The brighter colours decrease with age, and grey lines show themselves along each row of scales; while the young have transverse bars or bands.

Day's *British Fishes*, vol. ii. pp. 131.

Bibliography—*Grayling and how to catch them*, F. M. Walbran (Angler Co., Scarborough); *Fly-fishing for Salmon, Trout, and Grayling*, Ed. Hamilton, M.D. (Sampson Low and Co.); *A Book on Angling*, Francis Francis (Longmans, Green and Co.); *Dry Fly Fishing in Theory and Practice*, F. M. Halford (Sampson Low and Co.); *Making a Fishery*, F. M. Halford (Horace Cox); *Book of the All-round Angler*, John Bickerdyke (L. Upcott Gill); *The Compleat Angler*, Izaak Walton (Part 2); *The Book of the Dry Fly*, G. A. B. Dewar (Lawrence and Bullen); *The Badminton Library* (*Salmon and Trout*) (Longmans, Green and Co.); *Salmonia* (7th day), Sir Humphry Davy (John Murray); *The Rod and the Line*, Wheatley (Longmans, Green and Co.): *The Scientific Angler*, David Foster (Bemrose and Son); *The Sporting Fish of Great Britain*, Cholmondeley Pennell (Sampson Low and Co.); *British and Irish Salmoniæ*, Dr. Day (Horace Cox); *The Book of the Grayling*, T. E. Pritt (Goodall and Suddick, Leeds); *North Country Flies*, T. E. Pritt (Sampson Low and Co.); *British Angling Flies*, Michael Theakston, revised and annotated by F. M. Walbran (Sampson Low and Co.); *The Yorkshire Angler's Guide*, Tom Bradley (Tom Bradley, Leeds).

WILLIAM SENIOR.

GROUSE—The Grouse (*Tetrao scoticus*) is found in parts of Scotland, Wales, Ireland and England. In Scotland it is pretty general wherever heather exists. In Ireland it is by no means as numerous as in Scotland, owing partly to the system of steady poaching which obtains in that singularly improvident country. In Wales it is spread over a comparatively small area, while in England at the present time the great bulk of grouse-bearing grounds are the northern counties and Derbyshire.

Attempts have been made from time to time to introduce this bird into other parts of England where the surroundings seemed to be suitable, but little success has attended these endeavours. The Hon. Gerald Lascelles, Ranger of the New Forest, informs me that, previous to his tenure of office there, experiments were made to further this object by putting grouse eggs into the nests of black game, of which a certain number still are to be found in the New Forest. But no satisfactory results ensued.

Natural History—The "Red Grouse" is a singularly handsome and attractive bird. His weight is about 19 oz.; but one may be found to weigh as much as 29 or even 30 oz.; the length is about 15 inches. The general colour is, in the cock-bird, deep reddish-brown, while the hen is somewhat less conspicuous in hue, and the tone of her plumage quieter and more sombre. A brilliant scarlet patch is arched over each eye, and the throat is of a reddish colour. Considering this bird from every point of view—of sport, of culinary excellence, of appearance, and of the charm of the scenery amongst which it lives—it very properly occupies a special and eminent position among the game birds of these islands.

The average number of eggs laid by a grouse is seven, though fourteen or fifteen have been found in a nest, and possibly even more. The colour of the eggs is a pale olive, blotched thickly with dark reddish-brown. The hen sits on the eggs, and I am not aware that a cock-bird has ever been known to relieve his mate in her onerous duties in this respect. The early part of April is the period when grouse commence to lay, and the eggs take about three weeks to hatch.

A dry season is the best for nesting purposes, so long as there is a good supply of young heather. The winter of 1895 was one which proved singularly fatal to grouse both young and old. On many moors the intense frost and prolonged snow so damaged the heather that portions of the moors did not recover till the following year. The young heather either failed to come up at all, or not till many weeks after the usual time, thus depriving sitting hens, and young when hatched, of their customary and necessary food. The old heather plants were also in many instances so killed down as to be of little use to the grouse. For these reasons hundreds of birds died on some of the English moors. This also happened in Scotland and elsewhere. Grouse are largely dependent on a sufficient water supply existing on a moor. A *very* dry moor is rarely a good one.

There are curious exceptions to the rule that there *must* be plenty of heather if grouse are to exist in any numbers. In certain parts of Lancashire and Yorkshire, near the great centres of industry, there are tracts of country on which grouse flourish in numbers, and where they breed well, although there is practically no heather at all on them. With much trouble, a single plant might perhaps be found in one or two situations, but, to all intents and purposes, these moors consist entirely of various kinds of grasses and a certain quantity of bilberry plants. Though there is not a great amount of grouse on moors such as these, yet good and sufficient sport is to be obtained; and the birds continue to breed well, and seem strong and healthy.

Shooting—The legitimate methods of killing grouse are two:—

(1) Shooting them over dogs, and
(2) Driving them to the guns.

In Scotland the system usually followed is the one first mentioned; and the reason for this is easily comprehended, as the steep nature of much of the ground on which grouse are to be found in that country renders driving them a difficult and comparatively unproductive process, and one which it is often almost impossible to carry out satisfactorily in consequence of the difficulty of obtaining, in the sparsely inhabited districts of the Highlands, an adequate quantity of men to act as drivers. There are, however, an increasing number of Scotch moors on which driving is now regularly resorted to, and on which large bags are obtained. The moors belonging to the Mackintosh at Moy; those in the valley of the Don; at Drumour, in Perthshire, and many other moors, both in the Highlands and the Lowlands, have been carefully shot in this manner for some years past, with steadily improving results. These, of course, are tracts of country of a comparatively level nature.

Driving—It should be said, however, that most excellent and exciting sport may be obtained by driving moors which do not apparently lend themselves naturally to such a proceeding. That is, instead of being flattish in their conformation, they consist of the sides of steep hills, narrow corries, and generally broken and uneven ground. Under circumstances such as these, grouse come over the guns at every kind of height and at every sort of angle, thereby affording far more difficult and sporting shots than can as a rule be obtained when driving a reasonably level stretch of moorland. In fact, a day's driving on wild, steep, and mountainous Highland ground, which produces some fifty to seventy brace to five or six guns, is, or should be, as gratifying to the sportsman as a day of 250 or 300 brace on an easily managed and flat moor in one of the more southern counties.

In England, on the other hand, driving is nowadays the almost invariable practice; and this is so for various reasons. In the first place, English grouse are as a rule hatched somewhat earlier than are those in the bleak North, and are therefore stronger on the wing when the 12th of August arrives.

Fewer coveys, in consequence, lie well to the dogs when walking after them. This is partly due to their precocity, and possibly, also, to the relatively larger number of birds on an English moor, the latter fact tending to increase wildness. It is a very difficult matter to get a decent bag of grouse when shooting over dogs on an English moor after the 20th of August, even if it can be done so late as that, and this makes the upkeep of a kennel of pointers and setters an exaggerated and undue expense, in which few sportsmen care to indulge.

Again, the great majority of English moors lend themselves so admirably to grouse driving that those who shoot over them avail themselves at once of the good fortune thus placed to their hand.

More grouse are killed by driving than by any other method of shooting; grand sport is obtained; and, what is very important, the number of birds is largely increased, and the health of the stock maintained and improved. It seems an odd and inconsequential thing to say that the more grouse you kill by driving, the more you improve and increase the breed; but it is so, and this is why. In walking grouse, should the weather be favourable, and the birds lying well, whole coveys are sometimes entirely destroyed, the great improvement both in guns and shooting, which has of late years taken place, being largely responsible for this; whereas, in driving, the older birds are usually the pioneers of the packs, and are therefore most liable to suffer should the shooting be accurate. The younger birds are in this way to a certain extent spared, at any rate till they are stronger and more able to take care of themselves.

Furthermore, by killing a considerably larger number of the old birds than would be possible were the moor only to be walked, one of the breeding difficulties which beset grouse is largely obviated. The interference with the nesting arrangements of the younger birds by the older ones is diminished. And this is important, as old grouse are most quarrelsome and pugnacious, and drive off from their proposed nesting-grounds many of the younger birds which are desirous of breeding and multiplying in peace and quiet. Moors which have been regularly and carefully driven for the last thirty or forty years now present such a wonderful difference in their game records that it must be evident to all that this system of shooting is very advantageous to any moor to which it is adaptable.

The game books of a well known English moor are now before me, and, as far as I can discover, the earliest mention of grouse-driving in them is in 1849. In September of that year a note is made that "on this day (September 11th) the birds were unmanageable, and at three o'clock we took station by a wall and killed a few birds out of packs which were driven past." This is by no means, I believe, the earliest record of driving, shooting in this manner having been attempted on other moors as early as 1842, if not before then; but it gives an approximate date as regards the commencement of that system which is now so prevalent on most English and many Scotch moors.

While dealing with this branch of grouse-shooting, a few suggestions may not be out of place with respect to the best method of laying out a moor for driving purposes, and the most necessary points to be observed for the attainment of sport, when the ground has been decided on. Should the moor never have been regularly driven before, two or three men should walk those portions of it which seem most promising, towards the ground on which it is proposed to build the butts, or batteries, as they are indifferently called. The usual flight of the birds can then be noticed and the necessary arrangements determined for placing the butts in the most favourable positions.

The batteries should, if possible, be erected toward the centre of the moor, as then the grouse will not be driven off it: but of course all moors vary much, and the local peculiarities must in every instance be carefully considered. The butts themselves ought to consist of blocks of turf, and should be about five feet high, and from six feet six inches to seven feet across the opening.

If it is intended that they should be used for drives both from the front and rear, then their shape should be either oblong or almost circular, with the entrance at the side; in fact I think this, where practicable, is in any case the best plan. They should always be made large enough to hold three persons and a dog or two.

The plan of the internal arrangements of a butt must be left to the fancy of the owner of the shooting: some like a small piece of wood inserted as a shelf, to put spare cartridges or anything else on. A built-up seat of turf in the corner is advisable, and a trench should be cut outside to drain the battery. Sometimes a few pieces of planking on the floor are almost essential if, as is often the unavoidable necessity, the butts have to be placed on swampy ground. Opinions vary greatly as to the proper distance that one battery should be from another. To a certain extent, this must depend on the breadth of ground to be covered by the guns; but, as a rule, fifty yards is a "workable" distance. If the guns are much nearer to one another than this, not only is the danger increased, but the picking up after a drive is more confusing, and natural jealousy comes out in a strongly developed manner, which does not tend to enhance the pleasure of a day's sport.

Sometimes, where the front of the drive is very broad, eighty or even ninety yards must be allowed between the butts, and a false battery, consisting of a couple of turf walls just higher than the butts themselves, with a man to separate and turn the packs of grouse which may come straight towards him, should be constructed equidistant between them. By this means, the great majority of the birds will fly over the adjacent guns.

Having arranged the batteries and the direction of the drives, the next thing is to see how the general plan of action with regard to the management and carrying out of the drive is to be effected.

For an ordinary sized moor, twenty men in addition to keepers and "flankers" are sufficient. They should be divided into two parties, so that one may be ready to commence another drive as soon as the previous one has ended, the killed grouse been picked up, and the guns placed in their new positions.

Both drivers and flankers should carry flags, white in colour for choice, with a conspicuous one for the centre man, who must control the proceedings. Opinions vary as to the best colour for flags, but, as a generality, white is the safest and best. The line of drivers should be slightly horseshoe in shape, but, with a strong cross wind blowing, the *down*-wind flank ought to be strongly advanced.

Allusion has been made to flankers: they are most important, and should be men with an intimate knowledge of the moors and of the usual flight of the grouse. Their duties are to act in advance of the driving-line on either side, and to prevent the grouse from breaking away, and thus not going over the guns. A good "flanker" will not put his flag up till the exact moment arrives, as otherwise he might head the birds back instead of sending them forward, or turn them so much that they would break away over the flankers on the far side.

GROUSE.

There are, needless almost to say, many occasions when grouse will go where they please, even straight back over the drivers, and then no flankers in the world can turn them. The earlier drives of the day should be down-wind, if practicable; for, later in the day, the birds can be brought back, aided by their natural inclination, to their original ground, and will carry with them the grouse from the other drive.

Shooting over Dogs—Turning to the older branch of grouse shooting, namely, that of walking them over dogs, the points to be insisted on are:

(1) The importance of procuring well-broken dogs, whether pointers or setters.

(2) The necessity of the sportsman getting himself into some sort of "condition" before attempting to go through the hard work entailed by this method of shooting; and

(3) The advisability of working the outside higher ground of the beats early in the day.

With regard to the question of dogs, so much of the pleasure of a day's grouse-shooting depends on them that it is needless to add much on this subject. It will suffice to say that if dogs are headstrong and badly broken, they not only spoil the ground over which they range, and by this means destroy all chance of a good bag, but they also completely demoralise the temper of the sportsman, thereby minimising the probability of his killing whatever grouse may, notwithstanding the conduct of the dogs, come within range.

As to the "condition" of the sportsman, there is undoubtedly not only much inconvenience, but a certain amount of danger, in any one's attempting a hard day's grouse shooting over dogs, if he comes straight to it from office, or House of Commons, or any occupation or business of a sedentary nature. I have myself known of two or three persons who did themselves irreparable harm by coming straight from a compulsorily inactive life in London to Scotch moors, which require really hard walking, and who, by attempting too much during the first few days of the season, seriously injured their hearts.

The wisdom of working round the outside of the beat in the early part of the day must be patent to all. It is partly by this means that the grouse are induced to move towards the better feeding-grounds near the burns and the lower parts of the beat, and then they may be more satisfactorily attacked in the afternoon, when, as a general rule, they lie better than at any other time. (I am premising that the beat has, as is usually the case, the low flat grounds in the centre, and that the higher, wilder ground is on the outside.) If this manœuvre is carefully executed, the sportsman will probably be rewarded for all the hard walking of the morning by a successful afternoon on the easier ground on the lower portion of the moor.

Guns—One word as to guns and cartridges in connection with grouse-shooting, whether walking or driving. Every one has his own views on this subject. But I do not think that any better "all-round" charge can be recommended than 3 *drs. full*, of whatever powder the sportsman may prefer, and $1\frac{1}{8}$ ounces of No. 6 shot.

As regards the gun, the only advice to be given is, go to a good gunmaker and he will sell you a good gun.

If, with a weapon thus supplied, 12-bore, slightly choked in the left barrel only, and with the above-mentioned charge, a man cannot kill grouse, then the fault lies, humanly speaking, behind the gun and not in it.

GRANBY.

GROUSE, DISEASES OF—The Grouse disease *par excellence* is an acute infectious pneumonia associated with the presence of Bacteria in certain parts of the blood system. The Bacteria are oval or coccus-like, more rarely rod-shaped with rounded ends, and belong to that group of microbes known as Bacilli. Examination of the body of diseased grouse shows that the Bacilli are not freely disseminated through the blood, but are collected in small plugs or masses in the capillaries of the lungs and liver. The microbes can be cultivated outside the body in suitable media, and in this state, when examined with high powers of the microscope, usually present the appearance of an oval or a cylinder with rounded ends. Frequently, two remain in juxtaposition, giving rise to the "dumb-bell" appearance. The majority of the cultivated germs are motionless, but a few are actively mobile, and similar organisms provided with flagella are found, though not very numerously, in the fresh blood of the grouse in the late summer and autumn. The oval forms are about ·6 μ[1] long and ·4 broad, the rod-shaped are ·8–1·6 μ long and as thick as the oval. No spores are formed.

The more severe attacks of the disease amongst grouse usually occur in May and June, but there is also an autumn attack, as a rule less frequent and less virulent. The affected birds lose their activity and seek for water. Flight is slow and limited in extent. The "call" becomes hoarse and feeble, the feathers of the back and throat lose their lustre and become ruffled. The eye is dimmed. On opening the body, one or both of the lungs is found to be congested, and the wind-pipe dark in colour; the air-spaces inside the lungs may be full of blood or some granular exudation which points to some rupture of the smaller blood vessels. The liver is congested and soft; the kidneys are also, to some extent, congested, and there may be exudation on the peritoneum.

Owing to the reluctance of the owners of grouse moors to permit experiments on their game, and owing to the difficulty of keeping the birds in confinement, we have little direct proof that the epidemics which have decimated the moors are due to the Bacillus in question, especially since the latter is, so far as we know, identical with the *Bacillus coli*, an organism which is widely distributed and frequently found under conditions which exclude disease, and which always occurs in the digestive track.

How the Bacillus gains entrance into the body of the bird is not known. If it be identical with the *Bacillus coli*, it enters the intestinal track with the food. On the other hand, experiments on susceptible mice and birds, made by mixing the cultivated microbes with their food, show that it is improbable that it reaches the vascular system through the alimentary canal. In all cases the Bacilli were digested. It may gain access through the respiratory organs, and the disease seems to spread readily from bird to bird. An infected Yellow-hammer communicated the disease to two others in the same cage, and even to six healthy birds in another cage placed close to its own, but covered by one cloth. All died within three days. It seems probable that the disease is carried on from spring to autumn and from autumn to spring by the lingering on of some lightly diseased birds, but it may also be that the microbes, after a period of sickness, may remain in the soil under the heather and grass, ready to start the disease at any moment.

The existence of the less virulent autumn disease, and the ease with which the Bacillus is cultivated outside the body, encourages the belief that a protective vaccine could be prepared which, if inoculated, would produce a transitory attack and render the birds immune from further infection. Whether it would be practical to undertake the vaccination of young birds is for the owners of the grouse-moors to determine. Up to the present time they have shown little or no inclination to make the experiment.

Two species of larger parasites are found in the Grouse: (1) a tape-worm (Cestoda), *Taenia calva*, which Baird found in the intestines, and (2) a thread-worm (Nematoda), *Strongylus pergracilis*, which Cobbold found in the intestinal cæca. The former is from 4 to 10 inches in length: the head is provided with four suckers and a small rostellum bearing a double crown of minute hooks. The segments increase in length towards the hinder end, but the largest never become longer than they are broad. Unfortunately, the short descriptions of the external appearance of this tape-worm is all we know about this parasite. Its second host, in which the larva develops, is unknown, and its effect on the Grouse can only be conjectured. It may weaken the individual, but, as far as we can judge at present, it cannot be held responsible for any serious or widely-distributed disease.

The Nematoda, *Strongylus pergracilis*, is

[1] μ = ·001 millimetre, or about $\frac{1}{25000}$ of an inch.

probably the cause of more serious disturbance. It is a minute thread-worm, the male measuring $\frac{1}{3}$ inch in length, the female being very slightly longer. As is usual in the genus *Strongylus*, the tail of the male is expanded into an umbrella-shaped bursa, each half of which is supported by four rays. Cobbold states that these worms occupied the whole length of the intestinal cæca; they are much more commonly found than the tape-worms, and exist in very great numbers. At present, we are entirely ignorant of the life-history of this parasite, and the data we have are insufficient for making any estimate as to the amount of damage it causes.

ARTHUR E. SHIPLEY.

GUDGEON—

MEASUREMENTS, ETC.—Length of head $4\frac{1}{2}$ to 5, of caudal fin $5\frac{1}{2}$, height of body $4\frac{1}{2}$ to $5\frac{1}{4}$ or even 6 times in the total length. *Eye*—high up, in or slightly behind the middle of the length of the head, diameter $4\frac{3}{4}$ to 5 in the length of the head, $1\frac{3}{4}$ to 2 diameters from the end of the snout, and $1\frac{1}{2}$ apart: interorbital space flattened. Dorsal profile much more convex than that of the abdomen, which is nearly horizontal. Body compressed, becoming more so in its caudal portion. Snout somewhat obtuse. Upper jaw the longer, the maxilla does not extend so far posteriorly as to beneath the front edge of the orbit. *Barbels*—one at the maxilla usually reaching to below the middle of the eye, but liable to variations in length. *Fins*—dorsal commences about the centre of the length of the fish, excluding the caudal fin: the length of its base nearly equals half its height; its first ray minute, its third, which is undivided, $\frac{4}{5}$ the height of the body below it. Pectoral inserted in the lower fourth of the body, as long as the head without the snout, and rounded at its extremity: it does not extend to so far as the ventral, which latter is still slightly shorter and does not reach the anal. Caudal deeply forked, with pointed lobes. *Scales*—large, and the exposed portion angular. *Lateral line*—continuous to the middle of the base of the caudal fin. *Colours*—olive along the upper portion of the head and back, becoming silvery on the sides and beneath. Upper portion of the body with numerous irregular brown spots and dark edgings to the scales, and in the young a row of dark spots cross the lateral line; but in large specimens a wide silvery band runs along the side of the body, mostly above the lateral line: a dark mark under the eye and a few black spots in the pectoral region. Dorsal fin with several irregular rows of black spots, and similar ones exist on the lobes of the caudal fin most distinct externally. Young examples are darker than adults, and more blotched and spotted: a line of spots runs across the anal fin, while the ventral is dark tipped: opercle nearly black.

Day's *British Fishes*, vol. ii. p. 172.

GUNS—BUYING A GUN—No man can confidently choose a gun for another. Nevertheless, modern improvements have made it possible for the experienced looker-on not only to detect the faults in a brother sportsman's shooting, but also their cause, whether they be attributable to the gun itself or to the action and methods of the person using it. Amongst the chief factors in remedying such defects are, first, the broken stock which most gunmakers now employ in order to ascertain the bend and cast necessary to suit the purchaser's shape and muscular development, and, secondly, the new shooting schools. As to the broken stock, it may be taken for granted that, given an experienced gunmaker and a customer more or less in the habit of handling a gun, a very close idea will be obtained of the weapon required, because the gun will be put up quickly and naturally at the object of aim—the gunmaker's eye, for instance—and he will at once see where the fault lies and correct it. For many years this has been the only guide of the gunmaker, but it is far from infallible when an adult, who has never before handled a gun, takes it into his head that he will begin shooting, for he never puts up his gun twice alike, and, when shooting seriously, he generally describes an arc with it from the hip to the shoulder, which arc varies according to his equilibrium. Thus he not only shoots wide of his object, but is proportionately dangerous to his neighbours, to whom, not less than to the neophyte, the shooting schools have become a positive boon.

The large white walls crossed with wires, over which imitation partridges are propelled, form an excellent means of ascertaining the truth, and it is somewhat startling to see the black bouquet made by the shot on the white surface—feet, even yards, wide of the very visible bird.

To all beginners these schools cannot be too highly recommended as an easy means of acquiring a fixed habit of shooting, *i.e.* to make use of a regular movement of the arms and head in firing, and, as far as possible, to plant the legs firmly in such a position that the body can be turned sharply to right or left without rolling. To attain this result it is easy to see how necessary must be the perfect fit and adjustment of the gun to the shooter's formation.

Even to trained shots these schools are of the greatest use for the purpose of trying guns before they are quite finished off.

When the would-be purchaser has availed himself of the above two methods of testing his fire-arm, should he be a sportsman with experience acquired early in life, he will probably succeed in getting a gun that suits him. He will have gone through a careful examination of barrels, lock, action and stock, and will as nearly as possible obtain his money's worth. But how to instruct the novice in his purchase? It may be that, once having satisfied himself that a gun suits him as to balance and bend, he will ask an expert friend to investigate its soundness. He will thus be able to make sure that the stock is of walnut; that no creak foreboding a probable rupture in hot shooting is to be heard in the neck; that no flaw is visible in the barrels, and that the locks are properly fixed. But how can even the most experienced tell for anybody else whether the triggers have the right pull, or even that they are the proper distance apart? This is a most essential point, for it often happens in heavy shooting that the recoil of the second barrel causes the front trigger to cut the first joint of the fore-finger. Again, there is the setting of the trigger guard, which so often causes a swelling of the middle joint of the middle finger; either or both of these faults may put a man off his shooting for weeks. The novice must to a great extent buy his experience in this as in other pursuits. One season he will have to devote to shooting with the nearest approach obtainable to what suits him, and, as there are plenty of faddists who think it necessary to have new guns nearly every year, he should have no difficulty in getting a choice of second-hand articles at a reasonable price. From them he may pick out a pair fit to teach him what he needs, and open his eyes to the little miseries above enumerated, and perhaps many more. After this period of probation he may spend the next summer in obtaining his idea of perfection from one of the many excellent gunmakers to be found in London and other towns. He can then sell his trial guns, thus probably paying a less price for his experience than if he had begun by ordering a new pair.

As an instance of what good bargains may occasionally be picked up, I may mention that a friend of mine once imparted to me the longing of his heart for a good pair of guns, he having up to that time been shooting really well with a converted family gun which he had inherited. Asked how much he was prepared to give, he said he might go as far as £50, but could barely afford that sum. I took the measure of his stock and promised to see what could be done. In the course of the summer I found an excellent pair, and bought them—price £25 down and the other £25 on the first day of March following. Ten seasons afterwards I saw my friend heading the score, partridge-driving, with these same guns. This, however, was all pure luck; as the only alteration required was a slight paring away of the stock, especially at the toe.

Now as to ammunition. For a beginner, there can be no doubt that the first consideration is a minimum of recoil and smoke. There is no powder which need be unduly extolled above its fellows, for there is none with which *no* fault can be found; but, in my opinion, the best for regularity of shooting is the black powder, though it has the great drawback of heavy smoke and a greater recoil than any other. It is, however, less affected than others by temperature and by shaking about in cartridge-bags. But now that we have been fairly initiated in the "Nitros," a sportsman must indeed be conservative who will use black powder in covert where there are rabbits, or even on the moors in damp muggy weather.

Speaking for myself, I have great confidence in Schulze, but have also used E.C. and Cannonite, and killed with them whenever the gun was held straight. But I have found *old* Schulze cartridges reliable, whereas the contrary has occasionally been the case with the other compounds when they have been lying by for any time, as they become affected with changes of temperature. A good gunmaker will have tested all powders and be in a position to recommend the good "brand" of the year. By his advice the novice had better be guided.

W. G. CRAVEN.

MECHANICAL—The present century has witnessed many important changes both in the form and in the mechanism of the shot gun. At its commencement, single guns were commonly used, and the clumsy and uncertain flint was the only recognised agent for igniting the powder charge within the barrel. The utility of guns with two barrels placed side by side came gradually to be recognised, the need for a reserve fire doubtless making itself felt more acutely by reason of the frequency of the miss-fires with the flint ignition. The efficacy of fulminating powder as an ignitive agent was discovered, and detonating guns of various forms were introduced. In 1807, the Rev. A. J. Forsyth took out a patent for the first percussion gun; but the principle met with so much opposition from many influential gunners of the period, Colonel Hawker foremost amongst the number, that something like a third of a century had run its course before detonating guns were at all extensively used. This system, as applied to muzzle-loading guns, had but a comparatively brief reign; for about 1836 the first practical method of loading guns at the breech instead of at the muzzle was invented. This idea originated in France, and was the invention of M. Lefaucheux, and was introduced in this country by Joseph Lang in 1857. The cartridges employed were termed pin-fire, from the awkward device used for firing. A pin projected from the side of the cartridge at its base, one end of which, reaching into the cap, touched the fulminate; the blow dealt by the hammer of the gun on the outer end of the pin caused the explosion. The breech-loading system had to contend with much opposition at its inception. One contention constantly reiterated was that breech-loaders did not shoot so hard as muzzle-loaders; and, truly, there was much to be urged against the crude idea of the pin-fire cartridge, which at first was far from gas-tight, besides being dangerous and awkward. It was dangerous, because a slight tap or a fall might at any time explode a loaded cartridge, and awkward because the pins were uncomfortable to handle and had a knack of boring holes in pocket or cartridge bag. The introduction of the central fire cartridge removed these objections, and did much to popularise the method of loading guns at the breech. From 1853 onwards British gunmakers have given increased attention to the improvement of the breech-loading shot gun, and many important changes and valuable additions have been made. The outward form of the gun remains much the same, save for the removal of the hammers; but the mechanism has been so altered and added to that, in respect of ease and rapidity of fire, a gain of at least 50 per cent. has been attained. This has in great part been accomplished by the introduction of the, so-called, hammerless system, by which method of construction the hammers or strikers are placed within the lock, instead of on the outside of the lock-plate. In this way a much more compact gun is made up, and as the hammers are automatically raised to the firing position by the drop of the barrels on the opening of the gun, a great saving of time is effected as compared with the old form of lock in which the hammers were raised by hand alone. The conditions of sport were so altered by the introduction of the system of driving game to the gun that greater rapidity of fire had become an imperative necessity, and the improvement was much appreciated. The idea next arose that exploded cases could be expelled from the gun with far greater celerity and certainty by mechanical means than by the thumb and forefinger of the loader, and this brought about the invention of the automatic cartridge-ejecting apparatus. The most recent movement towards perfecting the shot-gun consists of the device by which both locks are fired by a single trigger. Several practical and workable forms of single-trigger guns have been invented, and, judging this comparatively new idea by the persistency with which it is advocated by several prominent gunmakers, and by men of great experience, it would seem as though it too may have a prolonged period of usefulness before it.

These, briefly, are the most important changes wrought in the shot-gun, and some of the more widely used types will now be described and illustrated.

Game Guns—The game gun, being far more extensively used than any other kind, first claims attention. The general consensus of opinion is that the 12-bore hammerless ejector, with 28 in. or 30 in. barrels, and weighing about 6½ lbs., is the best gun to employ for the purpose of shooting the furred and feathered game of this country. The patterns given with 1⅛ oz. No. 6 shot in a circle 30 inches in diameter at a range of 40 yards may be about 130 pellets with the right barrel and 160 with the left. Patterns such as these will be found to be sufficiently close in practice, for a very large percentage of game is killed at a less distance than 30 yards. The accompanying illustrations will convey an idea as to the form and outward appearance of the modern game gun.

PURDEY'S GAME GUN.

"HOLLAND'S" GAME GUN.

The *Vena Contracta* is another type of game gun that is rapidly coming into favour in consequence of its extreme handiness, strength and lightness. It was introduced by Joseph Lang and Son in 1893. This gun has been designed with a view to secure greater immunity from accident with modern explosives. To effect this, there has been a remodelling of the shot gun in such way that those parts which have to bear the intensity of the strain set up on explosion of the charge are fortified, whilst in other directions there is a reduction of unnecessary strength and weight of metal. A large proportion of the total weight of metal in the barrels is placed around the cartridge chambers, where it is necessary tc resist the enormous pressures sometimes given off by the more violent nitro powders. The breech action is exceptionally strong and heavy, weighing about 4 ounces more than usual, with the result that weight and strength are concentrated in the vicinity of the explosion. The barrels are 28 or 30 inches in length and, for about 2 feet from the muzzle, are exactly the same, inside and out, as those for a gun of 18-gauge. At 6 inches from the breech a curved conical portion, of a form known in the scientific gun-making world as a "Vena Contracta," commences; this joins the 18-gauge barrel to the 12-gauge cartridge chamber. Ordinary 12-bore cartridges are used, and although it might be imagined that great force would be necessary to drive the shot charge through the constricted portion of the bore, this is not the case. It is found in practice that the pellets flow through the long easy cone in much the same way as water would do. The recoil and the pressure in the chamber of this gun are practically the same as are set up with an ordinary 12-bore firing the same cartridges; but the vibration set up in the stock of an ordinary gun —which is the chief factor in producing gun-headache—is almost entirely absent in the "Vena Contracta," the vibrations being absorbed by the mass of metal surrounding the breech of the gun.

The accompanying illustration will convey an idea as to the form and distribution of the metal in the barrels :—

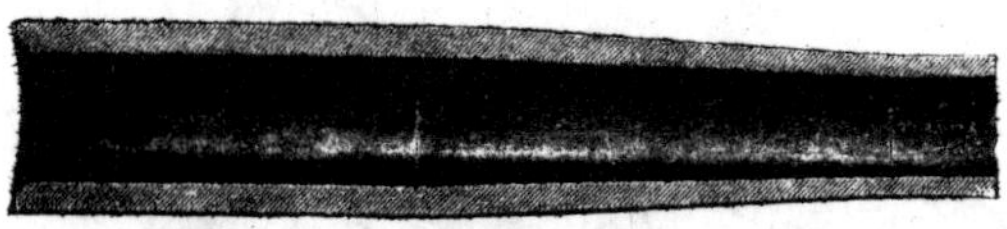

"VENA CONTRACTA," SHOWING SECTION OF BORE.

The "Vena Contracta" weighs about 6 lbs., and excellent results have been obtained with it both at the target and in the field. The tables given herewith were published by the Editor of the *Field* in October 1890, as the result of his trial, and sufficiently illustrate the remarkable regularity of pattern, height of velocity, and low recoil attained in the shooting of these guns :—

"VENA-CONTRACTA" GUN (12-18 Bore), with 1⅛ oz. shot.

Barometer, 29·83 ; Thermometer—Dry 61°, Wet 61°. Weight 6 lbs. 9 oz. ; barrels, 30 in.

Right Barrel—Powder (Shot-gun Rifleite), 37 grs. ; shot, 1⅛ oz. No. 6 (304 pellets). Gas pressure, average 1·82 tons per sq. inch.

Round.	40 yards pattern.						Total		Velocity (10 yds.)	Recoil.
	1st ring	2nd ring	3rd ring	4th ring	5th ring	6th ring	In 30 in. circle.	Outside 30 in.	Ft. sec.	Ft. lb
1	64	49	33	20	17	18	166	138	1181	27·4
2	76	51	28	22	19	13	177	127	1167	27 2
3	62	55	30	17	18	15	164	140	1172	28·0
4	67	50	32	21	15	13	170	134	1149	26·0
5	73	46	35	20	19	17	174	130	1167	27·0
6	58	50	38	22	14	14	168	136	1154	26·8
7	70	52	26	18	16	13	166	138	1176	27·6
8	75	47	31	21	18	11	174	130	1158	26·4
9	52	41	23	24	25	23	140	164	1172	28·3
10	58	44	31	14	20	16	147	157	1186	28·2
Aver.	66	48	31	20	18	15	165	139	1168	27·3

Left Barrel—Powder, 37 grs. ; 1⅛ oz. ; No. 6 shot (304 pellets).

Round.	40 yards pattern.						Total		Velocity (10 yds.)	Recoil
	1st ring	2nd ring	3rd ring	4th ring	5th ring	6th ring	In 30 in. circle.	Outside 30 in.	Ft. sec.	Ft. lb.
1	46	42	30	26	24	12	144	160	(As above)	
2	59	41	39	23	18	16	162	142		
3	65	48	35	17	16	12	165	139		
4	60	43	37	24	18	19	164	140		
5	55	40	38	21	19	16	151	150		
6	63	46	35	20	15	12	164	140		
7	56	40	40	27	16	20	163	141		
8	54	47	37	25	19	17	163	141		
9	66	45	33	26	20	14	170	134		
10	58	42	36	29	22	16	165	139		
Aver.	58	43	36	24	19	15	161	143		

Small Bores—Many sportsmen pin their faith to 16-bores and 20-bores for game shooting, and no doubt very good shooting is obtained from these sizes when made by gunmakers who have paid particular attention to small bores. Mr. W. R. Leeson, of Ashford, in Kent, is a gunmaker who has made a study of 16- and 20-bore guns, and with considerable success, as the following results of the trials of a 20-bore made by the Editor of the *Field* newspaper in 1896 sufficiently testify.

W. R. LEESON'S 20-BORE NO. 1012.

Weight, 5 lbs. 13½ oz. ; barrels, 29 in. ; 30 grs. powder ; ⅞ oz. shot (236 pellets) ; gas pressure, 2·14 tons per square inch.

Patterns of the Left Barrel in 30-in. Circle.

40 Yards.	30 Yards.	20 Yards.
137	197	189
150	224	223
146	205	207
127	218	219
130	205	214
142	187	215
173	202	208
140	210	223
168	224	219
144	202	222
Average 146	Average 207	Average 214

Average velocity, 1,177 ft. per second.
Average recoil, 21·2 ft. lbs.

Patterns of the Right Barrel in 30-in. Circle.

40 Yards.	30 Yards.	20 Yards.
135	154	215
110	182	210
122	173	214
121	144	218
118	157	211
128	91	218
139	180	209
126	163	220
145	174	206
114	181	205
Average 126	Average 160	Average 213

Average velocity, 1,177 ft. per second.
Average recoil, 21·2 ft. lbs.

Mr. Leeson asserts that it is a fallacy to suppose, as many sportsmen have hitherto done, that 20-bores throw the shot like a bullet at short distances, or that properly bored guns of this calibre smash game more than 12-bores. In this contention he is certainly supported by the comparisons of the shooting of the two sizes given below. These were made by the Editor of the *Field*, at the request of several sportsmen who desired to be informed on the point :—

12-BORES, SLIGHT CHOKE.

	20 Yards.	30 Yards.	40 Yards.
Pattern . . .	230	186	130
Killing Circle .	30 inches.	32 inches.	35 inches.

LEESON 20-BORE, GAME-BORING.

	20 Yards.	30 Yards.	40 Yards.
Pattern . . .	213	160	126
Killing Circle .	30 inches.	36 inches.	33 inches.

12-BORES, FULLER CHOKE.

	20 Yards.	30 Yards.	40 Yards.
Pattern . . .	229	203	152
Killing Circle .	25 inches.	31 inches.	35 inches.

LEESON 20-BORE, SLIGHT CHOKE.

	20 Yards.	30 Yards.	40 Yards.
Pattern . . .	214	207	146
Killing Circle .	26 inches.	30 inches.	33 inches.

From the above it will be clearly seen that although both 12- and 20-bore guns gave nearly the same pattern at 40 yards, the number of pellets at 20 yards in the 30 in. circle was less with the 20-bore than with the 12-bore; and yet the killing circle of the small bore was no smaller, at 30 yards it was even greater, and at 40 yards only two inches less than that of the 12-bore.

Ejectors— Messrs. Westley Richard and Co.'s ejector mechanism for throwing out the spent cartridge is contained in a box fastened upon the fore-end of the gun by a small screw. The ejector hammers are cocked by the forward movement of the extractor leg, when the latter is pushed inwards on the closing of the gun, and is held in that position by the scear. A sliding rod, fitted into the body of the gun, is driven forward by the fall of the firing hammer and placed under the tail of the scear. When the gun is opened after discharge, the end of the sliding rod, coming in contact with the scear, takes it out of the bend and releases the ejector hammer, which forcibly strikes the extractor leg and thus effects the ejection of the fired cartridge case. From the illustration it will be

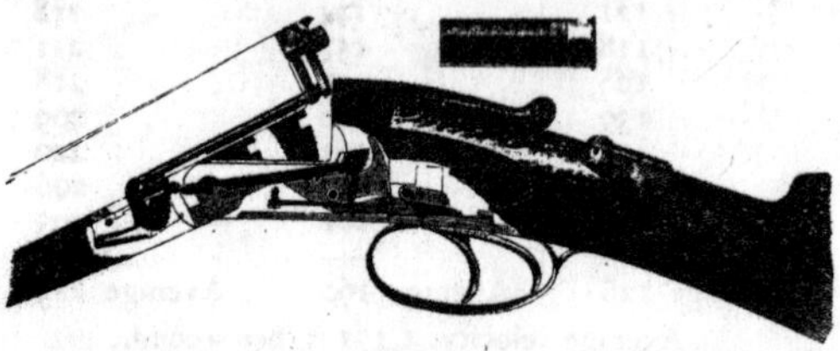

MESSRS. WESTLEY RICHARD AND CO.'S EJECTOR.

gathered that the end of the sliding rod cannot be in a position to move the ejector until after the fall of the firing hammer.

Another excellent system is that employed by Messrs. Cogswell and Harrison, the working of which is as follows. On the firing of the gun, the mainspring moves a retainer or scear into the line of outward travel of the extractor, so that on the gun being opened for reloading, the extractor, which is actuated by the ejector spring, partially withdraws the spent cartridge. In this position the outward travel of the extractor is retained until the gun is fully opened. At this point the retainer is reversed to its original position by coming into contact with the body of the gun; the pent-up force of the ejector spring then comes into play and completes the throwing out of the cartridge case. In the event of a sticking cartridge the lever or lugger forces out the cartridge for extraction. In this system of ejection the only parts are the retainer or scear,

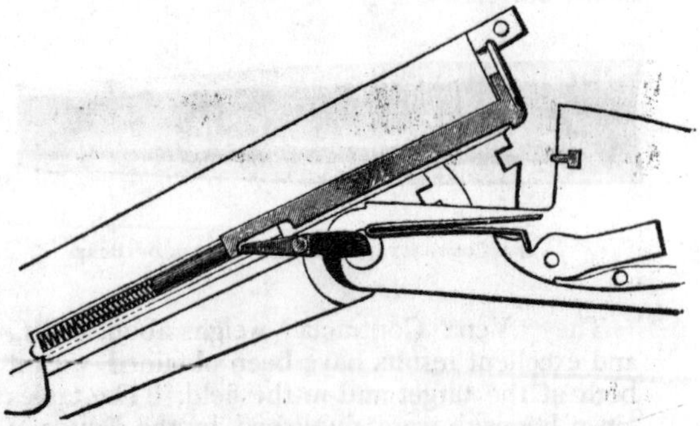

MESSRS. COGSWELL AND HARRISON'S EJECTOR.

and the ejector spring, which latter is placed in the ordinary fore-part loop on the barrels, an exceedingly neat arrangement.

Compared with the Greener ejector of 1880, the essential difference in the W. W. Greener "Unique" ejector gun consists in the tumblers, which, instead of being each in one piece, are jointed; the forearms by which they are raised to cock are pivoted in the tumblers instead of being solid with them. The parts are adjusted so that the action of each lock is as follows: On the gun being opened after firing, the tumbler is raised, both parts moving substantially together until the scear nose is beyond the bent, the gun at that time being opened to its full extent; at this moment the point of the fore-arm slips past the tripping point on the cocking swivel and, by the power of the mainspring, is driven down upon the projecting end of the ejector lever, and the fired case is thrown out. This action is most sharply brought about, owing to the great strength of the mainspring and the sudden stop to the blow by the forearm of the tumbler driving the lower end of the ejecting lever until it is stopped by

W. W. GREENER'S "UNIQUE" EJECTOR.

abutting against the cocking swivel. The gun may then be loaded without any further opening of the barrels. As it is closed the back or striking part of the tumbler descends until retained in bent by the scear, and remains there at full cock until the scear is releasea ; the forearm, carried down on its pivot, becomes shorter as it descends. When the upper part of the tumbler falls to fire the cartridge, the forearm is thrust forward until its extremity again engages with the tripping stud on the cocking swivel, and is ready to perform again the like motions of cocking and ejecting upon the gun being re-opened.

Gunmakers have for many years been striving to reduce the number of parts and to strengthen the limbs of the ejector work in double-barrelled guns, and this has been gradually accomplished, so that there is now much less risk of ejector guns breaking down. The general tendency has been towards dispensing with the scears and scear-springs and to adopt the push over centre system. One of the best and simplest forms of this arrangement is that in Messrs. Holland and Holland's "Royal" A. B. ejector gun. Here there are but two limbs in the ejector lock, as will be gathered from the accompanying illustration, A

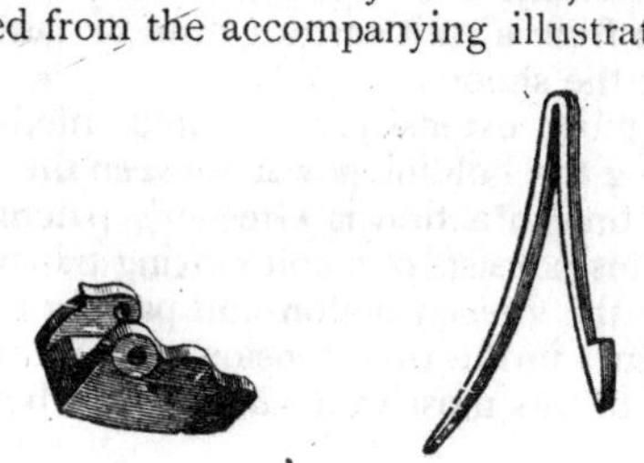

A B

HOLLAND'S "A. B." EJECTOR.

being the kicker and B the actuating spring. The former is raised to its cocked position by the end of the extractor when the gun is closed, and is pushed over centre by a projection on the end of the ordinary cocking lever. These two parts are very strong, and it is improbable that any further simplification of ejector mechanism can be made.

The foregoing may be considered as the four leading types of ejector.

Single-Trigger Double Guns—Quite recently there has been a decided movement in favour of double guns, with one trigger to actuate both locks. One of the most reliable single-trigger double guns is that made by Messrs. Green and Son, of Cheltenham, an illustration of which is here given.

The mechanism of this gun consists of a longitudinal sliding bar, provided with studs for firing both barrels, mounted on the trigger plate. This bar is held in its normal position by a bolting catch, which also acts as the trigger safety. The involuntary or second pull is effectually prevented, either by the toe of the guard (which has a sliding motion engaging with the trigger) or by a movable tongue mounted in the rear of the trigger—both being actuated by the recoil of the gun. The simple device for altering the order of firing is a most important feature of Messrs. Green's invention. The ordinary thumb safety slide is utilised for this purpose; so that, when required, by moving the slide from "safe" to "optional" the left

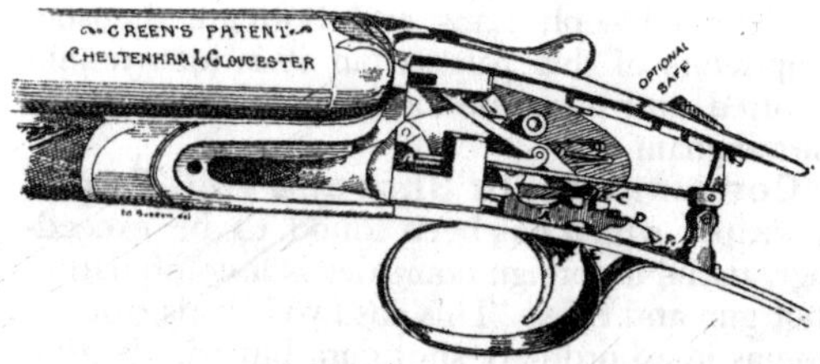

GREEN'S SINGLE-TRIGGER GUN.

barrel can be fired first, followed by the right, or *vice versa*.

The principal movement is obtained by a neatly-arranged switching trigger actuated mainly by the tumbler of the lock, the blade of the trigger being switched from one scear to the other by a simple but effective combination of a pivoted lever and its spring. To prevent the recoil of one barrel discharging the other almost simultaneously, there is fitted what may be termed a "timer," whereby the action of the switching trigger upon the scear of the other lock is delayed for an instant, but sufficiently long to prevent its touching the scear until all recoil and consequent movement of the gun after the first discharge has ceased, when the trigger can be pulled a second time to discharge the second barrel. There is no gunmaker so enthusiastic on the subject of single-triggers for double guns as Mr. Charles Lancaster; he has gone so far as to fit them as double rifles.

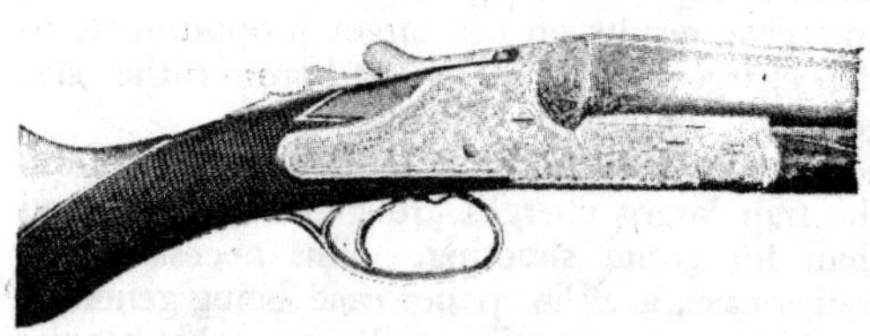

C. LANCASTER'S SINGLE-TRIGGER.

Twin-triggers—In these guns the two finger pieces or pulls are placed one under, or

LANG'S TWIN-TRIGGER GUN.

nearly under, the other, so that they are in the arc of a circle described from the knuckle of the fore-finger. By arranging the triggers in this way either the right or left barrel may be fired without relaxing the grip on the hand of the stock. This system is applicable to double guns or rifles of all types.

Messrs. Joseph Lang and Son are the sole proprietors of this patent, but it is also manufactured under license by Mr. W. P. Jones, of Birmingham.

Combination, or Shot and Ball Gun—A weapon which has been found to be exceedingly useful in foreign countries is a combination shot gun and rifle. This has two barrels side by side as in an ordinary shot gun, but with a rifle barrel on the top taking the place of the usual top rib. This rifle barrel is useful for shooting deer and other small game. The weight of this weapon ranges from 7 lbs. upward, according to the size and power of the cartridges to be used. The firing arrangements are simple and not liable to get out of order. The following is a good example of a gun of the kind.

W. P. JONES'S THREE-BARRELLED GUN.

A gun of another type is the "Paradox," which is a double gun bored to shoot shot or ball. With $1\frac{1}{8}$ oz. No. 6 shot this gun makes the pattern of a modified choke—140 to 160 on the 30 in. circle at 40 yds. These guns are made in the following sizes, 8, 10, 12 and 16, and give results on the target proportionate to the charges used. The 12-bore is the size generally employed.

Pigeon Guns—In shooting pigeons from the trap larger charges are generally employed than for game shooting. This necessitates a longer case, a $2\frac{3}{4}$ in. paper case being generally used for pigeon shooting, and a somewhat heavier gun, 7 lbs. to $7\frac{1}{4}$ lbs. being the usual weight for guns of this class.

Messrs. James Purdey and Sons, Stephen Grant and Sons, and E. J. Churchill are well known for the successes of their pigeon shooting guns, as well as for the excellence of their game guns.

Ford's special gun for pigeon or wildfowl shooting has a solid bar action (not cut away to admit the springs), and is fitted either with side or under lever. This gun weighs from $9\frac{1}{4}$ lbs. upwards, according to length of barrel, and is made to take No. 12, $3\frac{1}{4}$ in. "perfect" cases. Thus a charge of 2 ounces of shot can be used with splendid results at 60 yards range. In the face of the action is a recess into which the barrels are drawn by a double grip eccentric lever. After the barrels are fairly home the last push of the lever places another bolt across the extension, making the gun perfectly solid. The bottom lump extends beyond the end of the barrels, and, on the closing of the gun, this extension acts as an additional fastening. This gun has the equivalent of seven grips, and, from

FORD'S MULTIGRIP GUN.

the form of the action body, it is impossible for the flash from a split cartridge rim or faulty cap to affect the shooter.

The most extensively adopted method of increasing the holding power between the barrels and the breech action is Greener's patent cross bolt. This consists of a bolt moving transversely through the breech action and passing through an aperture in the rib extension. An illustration is given of this most valuable auxiliary bolt.

GREENER'S CROSSBOLT.

The Screw Grip Action—This is a patent that has been adopted by Mr. W. R. Leeson for use in his hammerless guns for a number of years and with eminently satisfactory results. The screw grip arrangement is applied in the following manner:—The barrels are jointed to the breech with an extension of the upper rib, firmly binds them to the action at the point most calculated to resist all tendency to spring apart at the moment of firing. They are held down, first by the ordinary Purdey bolt system operated by a vertical shaft through the head of action; this shaft carries upon it the "screw grip" of tempered steel working in a square-threaded screw cut in the solid portion of the breech; this grip has an enlarged head, which engages with the extension of the rib, firmly drawing the barrels home in the act of closing. The entire arrangement is worked by an ordinary top lever attached soundly to the bolt shaft and the screw grip. A gap cut in the head of the latter allows the barrel to pass in opening the gun, the lever having been moved to the right. When closing, the gun is locked by means of a spiral spring, mounted on a rod actuating both the locking apparatus and the safety bolt. The soundness and holding down power obtained by this introduction of the screw principle, applied as it is to the most effective point (the farthest from the barrel's centre of motion), is unquestionable, and the working is characterised by perfect smoothness and freedom. Another important feature is the insertion of the strikers from the face of the action, a method that effectually prevents wet or a flash from the cap entering the lockwork. Guns with this action have had from fifty to sixty thousand shots fired from them without becoming shaky or loose at the breech.

Shooting Schools—A description of the shot-gun would be incomplete without some mention of the modern shooting school. A good example of the out-door school of gunnery for sportsmen, several of which have sprung up around London and in one or two places elsewhere in recent years. Notably those of Messrs. Holland and Holland, at Cricklewood, Middlesex, of Messrs. Lang and Son, at Wimbledon Park, Surrey, and of Messrs. Cogswell and Harrison, at Blaydon, Surrey. The two latter are on the London and South-Western Railway, and of easy access. All possess beautifully wooded grounds, and are fitted with every convenience for visitors.

A tower 50 feet in height, having several platforms, from which inanimate birds are thrown in every direction, affords practice in shooting at objects overhead. For gun-measuring purposes there are mechanically driven birds, some rising vertically and others at a steep angle.

WILDFOWL GUNS—In the sport of wildfowl shooting the conditions are totally different to those of game shooting, and therefore another class of weapon is required. In game shooting the sportsman selects one object to fire at; the shooter who "browns" his birds, *i.e.* habitually fires at and bags more than one head of game for each shot, is dubbed a pot-hunter by all true sportsmen. Wildfowl shooting is governed by a different code of rules, the killing of a number of ducks or geese at one shot being accounted unto the fowler for cleverness. This, doubtless, is owing to the fact that wildfowl are both strictly gregarious in habit and much more difficult to approach than are game birds.

12-Bores—There can remain no doubt in the mind of practical wildfowlers at the present time respecting the all-round utility of the 12-bore gun for general purposes of wildfowl shooting, provided this is made slightly heavier and stouter than the gun ordinarily employed for game shooting. The wildfowling 12-bore may be bored for the long paper cases or for the thin brass cases known as "perfects," which are exclusively manufactured by the originators, Messrs. Kynoch and Co., of Birmingham. These thin metallic cases, being thoroughly waterproof, have much to recommend them for use in a sport so humid as that of wildfowling.

10-Bores—This size appears to be less used now than formerly; and this, doubtless, may in great measure be accounted for by the fact that the long-case 12-bores, with their increased load, now trench closely upon the power and attributes of the ordinary 10-bore. Modern gunners, therefore, appear to overlook the 10-bore, preferring to take to the 8-bore whenever an increase of power is found to be requisite.

8-Bores—This is by far the commonest size in use of the largest shoulder duck guns. Under certain conditions of sport the 8-bore will be found extremely useful; for, with a gun of this weight and power, wildfowl may be killed at much greater distances than with lighter weapons. The increased range and killing power of the 8-bore—and this applies also to larger guns in proportionate degree—is derived principally from the increase both in size and weight of pellets and of shot charge. A pellet of No. 1 shot is more than twice as heavy as a pellet of No. 4 shot, and it will readily be perceived that a 2¼ oz. load of No. 1 from an 8-bore will be killing fowl handsomely when the 1¼ oz. of No. 4 from a 12-bore simply rattles harmlessly upon their feathers. For boat-work and for shore shooting at large gatherings of fowl, the 8-bore is at times particularly useful. Some wildfowl gunmakers have recently given much attention to the production of light double 8-bores, and these have been turned out weighing little more than 10 lbs., to carry a charge of 2 oz. shot with a proportionate powder load. The average weight for a double 8-bore would seem to be about 12 lbs. to 13 lbs., and such guns carry 2¼ oz. of shot. Heavier double and single 8-bores have been made, and these carry from 7 drs. powder and 2½ oz. shot up to what is practically a 4-bore charge.

4-Bores—This is the biggest calibre shoulder duck gun made in a general way. Some few 2-bores have been made by two of our wildfowl gunmakers, probably not a dozen in all; but as these guns shoot the paper cases, there is not so much difference as regards charge and power between this size and the gun bored specially for the No. 4 "perfect" case. The ordinary weight of a 4-bore paper case gun is about 13 lbs. to 14 lbs., and for such guns the charge is about 9 drs. powder to 3 oz. lead. A good weight for a gun bored for the thin brass cases is 15 lbs. to 16 lbs., and in such guns an extra ½ oz. of shot and a drachm and a half of powder may be used with comfort. Brass case guns of about 18 lbs. are built, and in these 12 drs. powder and 4 oz. of shot may be used, but a quarter of a pound of shot is about as much as most wildfowlers care to fire from the shoulder. The weights given are for single guns. Few double 4-bores are made, such guns proving unmanageable save in the hands of persons of quite exceptional physique. But few hammerless wildfowl guns are seen; and this is singular, for it cannot for one moment be doubted that the hammerless system is by far the safest, quickest, and best for all purposes of wildfowl shooting.

The Care of Guns—A few hints on the care of guns will appropriately close this article. At the end of a day's shooting, the barrels should be removed from the stock and thoroughly cleaned with paraffin oil. After the superfluous oil has been removed, they should be coated inside and out with pure vaseline. The main-springs should be released and the breech-action wiped over with a little vaseline, and the stock rubbed with an oily rag, linseed oil for preference. Webley's anti-corrosive lubricant, "Semper Idem," may be used instead of vaseline.

At the end of the season, the gun should be taken entirely to pieces and thoroughly cleaned and lubricated, special care being taken to remove all traces of lead from the interior of the barrels. This may be done by placing a cork in one end and filling the bore with spirits of turpentine. When practicable, it is far better, on account of the complications of modern guns, to entrust the maker of the gun with the final cleaning, before putting it away until the next season.

H. F. Phillips.

[*See also* Rifles.]

GYMNASTICS—**Gymnos (nude)** defines the condition in which the Greek athlete practised his physical training, but modern usage has diverted this derivation, and the term is now generally accepted as implying the practice of physical exercises, as usually taught in a gymnasium. The word is frequently used also to discriminate between the physical exercises practised indoors, and those practised in the open air, such as running, cycling, throwing the hammer, and other similar pastimes which are generally understood as belonging to athletics.

Greek Gymnastics have at the present time no place or influence in the gymnastic world, and though an attempt has recently been made to revive them, they were modernised in details, and would more properly come under the designation of athletics. Although the decadence of Greek gymnastics is in itself a matter of regret, it may be said that it is not entirely lost to the present generation, for the principal teachers of gymnastics generally choose as their physical conception the graceful model of the antique Greek school.

Educational Gymnastics is a term given to physical exercises which are usually taught in schools, and which are specially adapted to the requirements of pupils of both sexes, and the facilities afforded by the schools in the matter of space and equipment. This branch of gymnastics is sub-divided into various systems, which are named after the respective countries from which they originate. The partisans of these systems claim for their respective methods special advantages.

Swedish Gymnastics comprise exercises without apparatus, and are sometimes known as "free movements." These motions are divided into groups for developing the various parts of the body, such as the ankle, feet, legs, trunk, arms, neck, etc.

German Gymnastics may be considered as involving the opposite principle to Swedish gymnastics, for although they include "free movements," or exercises without apparatus, these are only practised as a rudimentary preparation to more serious work. Various and complicated apparatus is in constant use in every town, village, and school in Germany. Indeed, its great feature is the universality of its indulgence, and it undoubtedly takes the place occupied in England by athletics. The State not only recognises its usefulness, but has official control of its practice, making it compulsory for every child and adult to undergo a prescribed amount of such physical training. That this has had a beneficial result upon the health, character, and practical ability of the German race is recognised by all. German gymnasts are very expert upon apparatus, and at their festivals some very clever feats, which have a useful aim, may be seen. This is particularly the case with their Escalading Tableaux.

Danish Gymnastics are symbolical of what we should expect from such a race, full of agility, nimbleness, and daring, with a liking for anything of a warlike character, such as the lance, dagger, sabre, or foil. Indeed, they combine the variety of the German school with the vivacity of the French. Their particular forte is perhaps tumbling and rope-climbing.

Russian Gymnastics appear to aim at the art of the development of the body rather than the acquisition of skill in performing difficult feats. Nevertheless, even from this scientific standpoint, they are necessarily thrown upon the expedient, as in other countries, of largely introducing the principle of variety into their movements. The cold climate which they are compelled to endure, for a lengthened period of the year, forces them into movements of activity, rather than the slower feats of strength. One of their favourite methods is to jump through a double line, a feat which requires a considerable amount of judgment, combined with looseness of limb and abdominal contraction.

French Gymnastics have recently had the advantage of being taken in hand by the State, and English ideals seem to be their favourite model. The movements are conducted to musical accompaniment, and must be performed unanimously to ensure success.

Swiss Gymnastics are very similar to those practised in Germany. They have the same liking for *fêtes*, and the feats which are witnessed there are of an extraordinary character. The gymnastics in the schools are also very picturesque, and are often accompanied by Tyrolean choruses.

Italian Gymnastics are not of the active character of the more Northern Countries. They have, however, one or two features essentially their own, such as the Floor Movements with a pair of dumb-bells resembling the English flat-iron. In these exercises they go through many attitudes, resting on the irons and feet only. Another is the practice of marching with baskets poised upon their heads, in order to exercise the muscles of the spine and neck, thus ensuring a straight and graceful carriage.

Spanish Gymnastics on account of the climatic conditions of the country, are necessarily of a slow and deliberate type. Their principal feature is their power of equilibrium.

American Gymnastics present no special feature of originality, if we except the wonderful progress they have made in the manufacture of appliances suitable for physical exercises. By means of their pulley-apparatus, physical training at home is made easy. Americans are also very thorough in their methods of partaking of exercise. They have evidently searched the old world, and culled the best points, which they have endeavoured to improve for their special requirements.

English Gymnastics are very similar to the American system. They have made use of the best features of exercise, as taught in other countries, and adapted them to their special requirements. They have wisely introduced music and recreation into their work, and made light and cheerful that which is sometimes in danger of becoming dull and monotonous. Variety has not been lost sight of, and for this reason English Gymnastics compare very favourably with the systems of other countries.

Finn Gymnastics—Although Finland is now a province of Russia, the Finns have a system of Gymnastics which is essentially their own, and which possesses so many elements of originality, dash, vigour and grace, that no notice of Educational Gymnastics would be complete without some particulars of it. As in Russia, the climatic conditions of Finland render it imperative that the influences of a cold and rigorous season should be resisted by recourse to such active physical exercises as will tend to keep the blood at a proper temperature and the muscles and organs of the body in a proper and healthy condition.

Games are not always possible in Finland, the winter being long and severe. In accepting the alternative of Gymnastic exercises under a covered roof, the Finns very naturally evade monotony of cut and dried systems by introducing as much variety as possible into their exercises, as well as in the shape of their apparatus. The beneficial effect of this is at once seen in their sturdy, muscular figures. Their Gymnastic movements possess all, if they do not excel, the precision of the Swedish drill, while it has none of the latter's jerky and ungraceful style. One of the best features of Finland Gymnastics is a set of movements which they perform with a bar of steel, measuring about 4 feet 6 inches long, and $\frac{3}{4}$ inch in diameter, and weighing about 5 lbs. Some of the attitudes of a squad of men with this implement are most graceful, while the effect upon the physique cannot fail to be of the most beneficial character. Nor are the women of Finland less experts at Gymnastics than the men, for both single and married women join systematically in these exercises. Indeed, we have seen an exhibition upon the parallel bars by married women in Finland which would be considered very creditable to any ordinary class of men in other countries. Taken altogether, Finland Gymnastics are of high merit, and they are entitled to much praise for their enthusiasm and skill.

Recreative Gymnastics embrace all physical exercises which are undertaken from a recreative point of view. These do not necessarily debar those movements described under the heading of Educational Gymnastics, but would include them in an intricate form, or when exhibited by large numbers of gymnasts. Indeed, we know of no more novel, exhilarating, and pleasing sight than to see a musical drill performed by a large number of school children, with an occasional vocal chorus. Such a sight can now be happily seen at any of our large Board Schools, or a similar sight may be witnessed at any of our large gymnasia, or with some of our regiments at Aldershot and other camps. Recreative Gymnastics of this kind are more common in England than in other countries, and the beneficial results cannot be overestimated, for they not only possess the fascination of dancing, but from their more varied character, they secure a greater amount of physical benefit, and the musical accompaniment enables the pupil to partake of a greater amount of exercise, as in marching. Swedish Gymnasts and other opponents of Recreative Gymnastics argue that, by the introduction of music, precision and correctness of detail are sacrificed, but this need not necessarily be the case, for naturally the pupils are first taught without the music. Although the English gymnasts base their Recreative Gymnastics largely upon musical drill, they frequently pursue the more complicated forms of practising intricate gymnastic feats upon horizontal and parallel bars, rings, trapeze, vaulting-horse, and other kinds of apparatus, but physical results in these cases are not so satisfactory as in the musical drill. At the same time a greater amount of muscular strength, activity, and resource are secured, which prove of great utility in many walks of life, and for this reason, the practice, if not pursued to extremes, is to be commended.

Recreative Gymnastics on the Continent are conducted in quite a different fashion. They have drills performed by large bodies of gymnasts, but they are unaccompanied by music. The orders are given by leaders, who are placed over sections, and who in turn take their orders from a chief leader. It is, in fact, conducted on the military system of issuing orders. It is a very fine sight to see, at one of their great gymnastic *fêtes*, several thousands of gymnasts performing in this way simultaneous movements. In another form, however, Continental gymnasts have quite a speciality in Recreative Gymnastics. In this "simultaneous squad" practice, several thousand gymnasts are divided into groups. To each group are allotted various pieces of apparatus, and at a given signal each member of a group performs a stipulated exercise.

Acrobatic Gymnastics may be described as an advanced stage of Recreative Gymnastics. They are useful as showing the marvellous degree of perfection to which the body can be trained, and the wonderful powers which such a physique possesses. It must, however, be pointed out that such a training is not advisable, as often, after the great strain to which the valvular and arterial system is exposed, collapse of the side walls of the blood vessels takes place, and an aneurism results.

Medical Gymnastics is the name given to movements which, scientifically based upon physiological conditions, are calculated to improve weak and delicate physiques. For this work an accurate knowledge of the muscles and their functions is required of the teacher. By relaxing one, and contracting another, group of muscles, the bones can often be corrected out of crooked into straight lines. The thorax and abdominal walls can be enlarged, and thus, by giving more room to the organs, greater comfort can be experienced, and very often ailments of the chest and liver, and other physical and organic defects absolutely remedied.

A. ALEXANDER.

GLOSSARY.

Bar-bell—Two large metal balls connected by an iron rod about 5 feet long and 1 inch in diameter. The weight varies largely, the heaviest being about 200 lbs. For exercise a light bell of wood is frequently substituted.

Dumb-bell—Two masses of metal joined by a handle, which is usually covered with leather. The weight varies from 1 lb. to about 16 lbs. a pair, according to the age and strength of the user.

English Board—A spring board about 5 feet by 3 feet 6 inches, resting at either end upon bars, which are inserted into rings upon four stands, each about a foot high. The rings must clutch the bars loosely so as to give the springs free play.

Flying Rings—Rings suspended from ropes usually from 9 to 12 feet long, the rings themselves being about 9 inches in diameter. They should hang about 3 feet from one another, and ought to be covered with leather.

Horizontal Bar—A bar of wood about 6 or 8 feet long, with a core of steel inserted down its whole length. The diameter is usually about 1½ inches, and the ends are inserted into posts by pegs whose height can be graduated.

Indian Clubs—Wooden clubs, in shape like a champagne bottle, but tapering rapidly at the end furthest from the thin neck which the hand grasps. They usually weigh about 4 to 7 lbs. each, and vary in length from 18 to 24 inches.

Parallel Bars—Two bars of wood of equal height from the ground supported at their extremities by stout posts. Usually about 8 feet long and from 4 to 5 feet high.

Trapeze—Consists of a bar of wood from 2 to 3 feet long, joining the ends of two ropes which swing freely from the roof.

Vaulting Horse or Wooden Horse—Consists of a solid block of wood, shaped somewhat after the manner of a horse's body, standing on four legs or props some 4½ feet above the ground.

HARE—The genus *Lepus* includes about twenty species, which are restricted chiefly to the Palæarctic and Nearctic regions, although one (*Lepus brasiliensis*) is found in South America. The common brown hare (*Lepus timidus*) may be regarded as typical of the genus, and is characterised chiefly by the great length of the ears and hind-limbs.

Distribution—It occurs throughout Europe, except in the north of Russia and in Scandinavia, although found in Denmark and East Finland. Its absence from Scandinavia renders it possible that the name *timidus* was applied by Linnæus to the mountain hare, and some writers accordingly employ the specific name *Europæus* in preference. The hare of Sardinia has been described as a distinct species, *Lepus mediterraneus*.

Colour—Its fur is usually of a sandy colour, greyer in winter, interspersed with long black hairs which, being set close along the dorsal surface, cause it to look blacker on the back than elsewhere, the upper surface of the short tail and the tips of the ears being also black. The under parts are pure white. The colour of the fur differs, however, in different latitudes and at different seasons of the year; showing a tendency to become white in winter in northern latitudes, while assuming a reddish-yellow hue in the more genial climate of South Europe, where in winter its prevailing tint is grey.

Varieties—Beyond the change which takes place in summer and winter, it may be said that the common brown hare is not subject to much variation in colour, although at rare intervals grey, sandy (or yellow, without any black hairs), parti-coloured, white, and even black varieties have been seen and procured.

At Tillyfour in Aberdeenshire and in the Isle of Mull a large yellow variety with hazel eyes, and weighing about 10 lbs. has been noticed. (*The Field*, October 31 and November 21, 1896.)

A grey variety of the common hare has been occasionally noticed in Norfolk, examples of which have been shot at Burnham, Sutton near Wells, near Cromer, and near Scole (*Zoologist*, 1865, p. 9646; 1866, p. 385; see also Gurney, *Trans. Norf. Nat. Hist. Soc.*, vol. i. p. 26, who mentions a variety of the ordinary colour with the face white).

In January, 1865, a parti-coloured hare was killed near Salisbury. It was unusually white all over the face, and its hind-quarters were of a silvery grey. Its pale colour could not be attributed to age, for it was a young animal, weighing about $5\frac{1}{2}$ lbs. On March 5, 1866, a hare was killed at Stalham, Norfolk, which was peculiarly marked by having a large patch of white on the forehead, extending from the tip of the nose to the base of the ears, the remainder of the fur being of the usual colour. In October, 1882, Mr. J. Whitaker, of Rainworth, near Mansfield, shot a hare which had three of her legs white as far up as the first joint, the fourth (a hind one) being white up to the body. She had also a white stripe on her side.

Daniel, in his *Rural Sports* (vol. i. p. 446, and Suppl. p. 6?4), mentions several instances of white hares; and Scott, in his *British Field Sports* (p. 361), gives an account of a coursed hare which was said to have become white from fright!

In December, 1854, an albino hare was shot at Trebarrow, near Dolsdown, Cornwall, by Mr. Southby, of Cambridge Terrace, Hyde Park, who had it preserved as a curiosity. Another albino was shot by Mr. H. M. Spurling, in North Devon, and was preserved by Rowland Ward, in October, 1884.

In January, 1875, a white variety of the common hare was killed at Kintore, in Aberdeenshire, but this animal had a light-brown tinge down the back. It was reported by Mr. W. E. May, of Kintore, in the *Field* of January 16, 1875.

In October, 1888, the Earl of Burford, at Bestwood Park, Notts, shot a full-grown white hare, with eyes of a pale blue; and in the same neighbourhood a white leveret was caught in the previous April. These are both preserved in the curious collection of varieties belonging to Mr. Whitaker, of Rainworth. In December, 1888, a white hare was shot at Rufford; and it is curious that these should all have occurred in one year in a district where hares are now by no means plentiful. So recently as September, 1890, Mr. Alfred Turner, of Kington, Herefordshire, while beating a potato field near that town, found and bagged a pure white hare with pink eyes, as mentioned in the *Field* of September 20, 1890.

Black hares are apparently of much rarer occurrence, though several have been reported at intervals in different years. So long ago as 1828, Dr. Fleming, in his *History of British Animals* (p. 21), noticed a black hare which was "lately killed at Netley, in Shropshire, by his respected friend, the Rev. F. W. Hope." And some years ago one was shot at Blake Hall, in Essex.

In November, 1853, a black hare was coursed and killed at Enville, the seat of Lord Stamford. A perfectly black hare shot at Denham, in Suffolk, is preserved in the possession of Sir Edward Kerrison, Bart. Another, full-grown, was shot at Firle by General Gage. In 1885 one was shot near Lutterworth by Mr. Joshua Harrison, of Parlton Field, and another about the same time by Mr. J. Cross, of Althorp Towers, near Rugby.

Weight—The average weight of a full-grown brown hare may be put down at about 8 lbs., but this weight has occasionally been considerably exceeded, particularly in Lincolnshire, where the hares are unusually fine and heavy. Thus, in October, 1877, a hare was shot on the farm of Mr. Tupholme, of Eastville, near Boston, which weighed 11 lbs. 3 oz.; and in the *Field* of November 10, 1877, others are reported to have been killed in Lincolnshire, weighing respectively 11 lbs. 3 oz. and $11\frac{3}{4}$ lbs. Perhaps the heaviest on record is one which was shot in October, 1876, by Mr. Robert Henderson, on the Longwitten estate, near Morpeth (the *Field*, October 28, 1876). It is said to have weighed $13\frac{1}{4}$ lbs.

Russian hares are considerably larger than English ones, and are much more thickly furred. Two shot in October, 1893, weighed 12 lbs. and $14\frac{1}{2}$ lbs. respectively. (*The Field*, November 18, 1893).

Habits—The mischievous operation of the Ground Game Act for the past seventeen years, and the neglect on the part of the Legislature to provide a close time for hares,[1] have caused a woeful diminution in many parts of the country of this most useful animal. It is no exaggeration to say that in some counties, more particularly in the south of England, the number of hares now to be met with is about one-fifth of what it was before the Ground Game Act was passed in 1880.

[1] The so-called Hares Preservation Act of 1892 imposes no penalty for killing hares out of season in England. It merely provides that they are not to be sold or exposed for sale during the months of March, April, May, June, and July. In Ireland, however, by 42 and 43 Vict. c. 23, no one may kill or take a hare between April 20 and August 12 under a penalty of 20*s*.

Hares have suffered reduction more than rabbits for several reasons. Their larger size renders it more difficult for them to escape observation; they do not as a rule go to ground, unless hard pressed by a dog; they breed less frequently in the year and have fewer young at a birth. Added to this, they are inconsiderately coursed so late in the spring that many does in young are killed, and are then utterly unfit for food. Under this disastrous process of reduction, it is no wonder that English hares are getting scarcer every year.

The champions of sport and the advocates of humanity and common sense have alike failed to convince their unreasonable opponents of the wisdom of enforcing a close time. One would have supposed that the vested interests of masters of harriers, owners of greyhounds, game preservers, and game shooters, to say nothing of game dealers and game consumers, would have long since operated to secure the passing of such a Bill as is needed, and it is difficult to understand on what grounds so reasonable a measure has been so persistently opposed.

Hares breed when twelve months old, and the female, after thirty days' gestation, brings off from two to five young. Adult hares will breed two or three times in a year.

Unlike the rabbit, which is born under ground naked and blind, young hares at birth are deposited in a "form," are clothed with fur, and have the eyes open. They are thus sooner enabled to shift for themselves and escape their enemies. In time of danger they are often transported from their place of birth by the parent, which carries them one by one in her mouth as a cat carries her kittens, to be concealed in a place of greater safety. Hares swim well, not only when pressed by hounds, but also when in search of a mate, or seeking fresh feeding grounds across a river. This is especially the case on saltings near the sea, when to escape the incoming tide a hare which has been surrounded by the water is compelled to swim to reach dry land.

The amount of sport which this animal provides, in the shape of hunting, coursing, and shooting, surely demands some effort for its proper protection (say from March 1 to August 12, the first day of grouse shooting), and preservers would do well to bear in mind that food without shelter is not sufficient to ensure the maintenance of a proper stock. In times of much rain and heavy snow, hares leave the open country and betake themselves to thick hedgerows and coverts. Hence the more accommodation there is of this kind the better for the interests of sportsmen, since the fewer plantations there are upon a sporting estate the fewer will be the number of hares. They will undoubtedly seek shelter elsewhere.

Diseases—Hares are occasionally subject to a parasitic disease, a sort of pulmonary tuberculosis, caused by the presence in the lungs and air passages of thread-worm, *Filaria pulmonalis* (*Strongylus commutatus* of some authors). A few years ago, on the Walton Hall Estate, in Yorkshire, the writer remarked that the hares were suffering from a peculiar malady which seemed to be due to an unusually wet summer. The wet "seat" attracted the flies when the animal moved, and they deposited their eggs *in ano*. Maggots were engendered, which found their way into the intestine, and caused a lingering and painful death. Numbers of hares thus affected were picked up that summer in a dead and dying condition.

The Scotch, Blue, White, or Mountain Hare (*Lepus variabilis*)—It was at one time supposed that there were three distinct species of hare in the British Islands, and in the first edition of Bell's *British Quadrupeds*, the so-called Irish hare was described and figured as differing in certain respects from the English and Scottish animals. The chief distinctions relied on were that it differed from the English hare in its shorter and rounder head, shorter ears and limbs, and in the texture of the fur, which is without the long black hairs with which the fur of the latter is in parts interspersed; while from the Scotch hare it was said to differ in never turning white in winter. This has now been proved to be a fallacy, for in the points in which it differs from the English hare it resembles the Scotch one, and the testimony of numerous observers in different parts of Ireland goes to prove that if the majority of the hares in that country do not turn wholly white in winter, as many do, they at least become partially so. In other words, the Scotch hare and the Irish hare are specifically identical. The geographical appellation, moreover, no longer holds good; for English hares have been introduced into Ireland, and hares both from Ireland and Scotland have been imported into England. In North Wales (Carnarvonshire) representatives from the three countries may be seen and shot on the same day.

The reason we do not see so many white hares in the market (except after Christmas, when more are killed and have to be got rid of) is that they are not so saleable as brown hares. Being much inferior in size and flavour, they do not command the same price, and the dealers consequently prefer to take those which are as brown as possible, that they may pass muster amongst those of the more esteemed species.

Description—Many people then would not know the difference, especially if told that some allowance must be made for individual variation. They should notice, however, the smaller size, rounder head, shorter ears and hind-limbs, and the soft woolly nature of the fur.

Colour—The variation in colour which takes place in the Scotch hare is considerable.

This depends wholly upon season; and as the change proceeds from the summer to the winter garb, every variety may be seen between blue grey and pure white.

Weight—The average weight of a Scotch hare may be set down as between 5 lbs. and 6 lbs. The heaviest ever noticed by the writer, shot in Caithness, weighed 7½ lbs. The largest Irish hare weighed 9 lbs. Good ones will weigh 8 lbs.; but a great many, probably, are little over half that size (see Harvie Brown, *Fauna of Argyll*, p. 43, footnote). It is, therefore, far behind the common hare in size and weight, for the latter has, as stated above, been recorded to the weight of over 13 lbs.

Habits—As might be supposed from the nature of its haunts, the mountain hare differs in its habits from the brown hare of the lowlands. It is given to skulking amongst boulders on the hillsides, and when pursued seldom goes far before retreating into some hole or cranny, in this respect seeking safety in hiding like a rabbit, rather than by swift flight like a brown hare. On this account it affords but little sport for the gun, and were it not for the fact that it makes excellent soup, it would probably not often be shot by those who, in pursuit of grouse or ptarmigan, have an object in reducing the weight they have to carry when climbing a steep hillside. Moreover, when a "hare drive" is resorted to, the Scotch animal affords but poor sport by comparison with "grouse driving," for, on account of its conspicuous colour and slow rate of speed, it is by no means difficult to shoot. Scotch and Irish grouse shooters, however, if they happen to be naturalists, will regard white hares with some favour, since they afford food

MOUNTAIN HARE.

for the eagles and hill-foxes, which, were it not for their existence, would take heavier toll of the grouse.

Interbreeding—Whether the brown and the white hare ever interbreed is a question that is sometimes asked, and generally answered in the negative. There are, however, cases on record which tend to prove that they occasionally do so. (See Cordeaux, *The Field*, Sept. 23, 1876, McNicol and Colquhoun, *The Field*, Oct. 7, 1876, Lumsden, *Zoologist*, 1877, p. 101, and Harting, *Proc. Linn. Soc.*, 1897.) Mr.

COMMON HARE.

J. G. Millais has come across several such hybrids in Perthshire, and is convinced that on the ground to which the blue hares descend from the hills and meet the lowland brown hares, such interbreeding is not so uncommon as is usually supposed. Their general similarity to one or other parent causes them to be overlooked.

J. E. HARTING.

HARTEBEEST (*Bubalis caama*); *Rooi hartebeest* (red hartebeest), of the Transvaal Boers; *Khama* of the Bechuanas; *Mthluzele* of the Zulus; *Ingama* of the Makalakas; *Khama* (with a click) of the Masarwa Bushmen. This fine antelope is one of the fastest and most enduring in all Africa; its near relative the Tsesseby being probably the only antelope that can excel it in these respects. The **Cape Hartebeest**, as this animal may for convenience be called to distinguish it from several near congeners in various parts of Africa, was formerly to be found in great abundance throughout most of South Africa from the Cape Peninsula to Lake Ngami. It has never been found, curiously enough, in Matabeleland or Mashunaland. It is described by Cornwallis Harris as frequenting the plains beyond the Orange River, in his time (1837) "in immense herds," but, chiefly owing to the wasteful slaughter of the great game-slaying period—1837 to 1890—its numbers have been much reduced in many parts of the country. Still, thanks to its vigilance, wariness, and extraordinary powers of flight, the hartebeest may be found in large herds in portions of Bechuanaland, Ngamiland, and the Kalahari Desert. A few linger here and there in the parched and desolate Bushmanland country, to the north-west of the Cape Colony, just south of the Orange river. In parts of Griqualand West they still exist, and there enjoy some slight measure of protection. They are also preserved in small numbers in Natal, and a few still remain in Zululand. To the westward of British Bechuanaland, and thence into the adjacent Kalahari, fair troops may still be found occasionally in the park-like, open forest and grass country so often to be met with in those regions. Throughout the Bechuanaland Protectorate, towards the Kalahari, and thence into Khama's country, hartebeests may yet be encountered in respectable numbers. In the more desert, westerly portion of Khama's country, in the open giraffe-acacia forests south of the Botletli River, near the various salt pans of the Ngamiland region and throughout much of the Northern Kalahari, large herds of these antelopes still roam freely. Ngamiland and the northern portion of the Kalahari desert may

Cape Hartebeest.
Av. height at shoulder, 48 in.; Max. horn meas. 25 in.

indeed be said to be now the principal head-quarters of the Cape hartebeest. Its northern range seems rarely to extend north of the great Makarrikarri salt-pan, north of the Botletli River. The writer has within recent years found these antelopes running in large troops in the waterless "Thirstland" between Palachwe (Khama's Town) and the Botletli river, also between Khama's and the Makarrikarri salt-pan. In both cases they were to be found at no great distance from the wagon roads. In the waterless Kalahari forests, some twenty miles south of the Botletli River, they were also fairly abundant. The Cape hartebeest shares, with the giraffe, the gemsbuck, the eland, and one or two other antelopes, the faculty of being able to subsist without water, during the period of African winter, for several months at a time. This peculiarity will, without doubt, serve to postpone its extinction for many years to come.

This antelope is one of the most difficult of all African game animals to bring to bag. One seldom hears even of Boer hunters shooting many of these animals during a hunting expedition. It is found nowadays usually upon open grass plains in the vicinity of thin bush or forest, or, as in so many parts of Bechuanaland and the Kalahari, in flat grassy country amid open forests of giraffe-acacia. As a rule hartebeests will be found at the present day in troops of from a dozen to five and twenty or thirty. But, in country where they have been little disturbed, herds numbering fifty and upwards may yet be found.

The Cape hartebeest is quite one of the most remarkable of all the South African antelopes. It is a quaint, old-fashioned-looking quadruped, rather what a racing man would call "a three-cornered brute," standing high at the shoulders and sloping considerably towards the rump. An average specimen will stand four feet high at the withers, but instances have been known where the measurement has reached five feet. The legs are slender, hard as iron, clean and shapely. The general colour is a rich, bright brown-bay, varied by the black face, by dark markings upon the fore and hind legs, and by patches of yellowish-white upon the rump and quarters. The head is long and awkward-looking, the face narrow and strongly marked with black. The strong rugged horns, corrugated up to the backward curve, after rising upward, bend back suddenly, almost at a right angle; they are set upon a singularly high frontal bone. Both male and female carry horns, those of the cows being somewhat thinner and less robust than are the bulls'. The eyes, planted high up in the head, are of a reddish hue. The flesh of the hartebeest is very fair eating, and makes good "*bültong*," *i.e.* salted and sun-dried venison, much in favour among the Boers. The handsome skin of this antelope is much prized by the Bechuanas, as well as by the Vaalpens and Masarwa bushmen of the Kalahari, all of whom use it, when tanned in native fashion, with the hair partly left on, as a cloak. The bushy tail-tuft, which is of a curious reddish-black tint, is retained on the cloak and allowed to fall down the back of the wearer, just below the neck.

As a beast of chase the hartebeest stands almost unrivalled. Some of the larger South African antelopes, as the eland, koodoo, sable antelope and others, may be run down with a good horse in favourable country. Not so with the hartebeest, which, as the writer can personally testify, can show its heels to the best Cape hunting horse ever foaled. Nor is it of the slightest use to persist in a long tail-on-end chase with the idea of wearing out these most fleet and enduring animals if they have really taken alarm and mean to go. In its slower paces the hartebeest looks heavy and lumbering, and the novice will probably regard it as a beast not very difficult to run down. Once begin to push it, however, and the animal stretches itself out, gets its hind legs well under its belly, and covers mile after mile of veldt in wonderfully smooth, machine-like fashion. This strong and untiring gallop it seems capable of keeping up indefinitely, to the despair of the mounted hunter. I have seen hartebeests chased hard for seven miles; by which time the horses had been ridden to a standstill, while the antelopes were as fresh as ever.

If it were not for certain rather foolish traits possessed by this animal, few hartebeests, indeed, would fall to the rifle. But occasionally they will afford comparatively easy shots. These antelopes are extremely curious, and will not infrequently wheel round, if not chased too hard at first, and so afford the gunner a fair chance at reasonable distance. I have seen this happen two or three times in a single run. Or, if the leader of the troop, usually some cunning old bull, can be wounded and turned out, the rest of the herd become flustered and will run in circles and can be thus cut off. Again, if a bullet or two is planted so as to strike up the sand in front of the troop, the hartebeests will sometimes turn short back and give the hunter a fair shot. In the pleasant forest country of West Bechuanaland and the Kalahari, in which these antelopes are often found, the mounted hunter, riding quietly, is sometimes enabled, thanks to the bush and covert often afforded, to get within easy distance of them. In such country they are far more readily approached and cut off than upon the broad, open plains which they affect in parts of Khama's country and Ngamiland. The writer has headed a troop in such country in British Bechuanaland and been enabled to cut the herd right in half. The antelopes seemed confounded, and stood staring for some seconds within less than 150 yards, thus affording two easy shots. It is to be remembered, however, that the hartebeest is one of the most tenacious of life among all South African antelopes—a proverbially tough family—and that even when severely and even mortally wounded it is still capable of distancing its pursuers and making good its escape.

For shooting these antelopes a Martini-Henri sporting rifle, a ·303 Lee-Metford, a Mannlicher, or any other good modern long-range sporting rifle will be found sufficient. Very few hartebeests are ever stalked on foot, and the hunter may be strongly advised, if he is desirous of saving time and trouble, to follow the usual practice and take the field mounted on a good reliable South African hunting horse. It may be mentioned, however, that a good many of these antelopes are shot, especially by the Boers, by night, at brack or salt-pans, of which hartebeests are extremely fond, and to which they come, with other game, to lick.

In addition to the Cape hartebeest, a number of other hartebeests, not distantly connected with this antelope, are to be found in various parts of the African continent. These are Lichtenstein's hartebeest, found in South Eastern and South Central Africa; Jackson's hartebeest, found in Central Africa; the Tora or Tetel, found in the Soudan and North East Africa;

LICHTENSTEIN'S HARTEBEEST.

Av. height at shoulder, 50 in.; Max. horn meas. 21 in.

the Tiang hartebeest, Soudan; Swayne's hartebeest, Somaliland; the Topi hartebeest, East Africa; Coke's hartebeest, East Africa; the West African hartebeest, found in the Gambia, Niger, Cameroons and other western regions; and the Senegal hartebeest, which frequents Senegambia and West Central Africa. Besides these forms, the Tsesseby of South Africa (*Damaliscus lunatus*), often called by the Boers, the Bastard hartebeest or Zulu hartebeest, is obviously nearly allied to the Cape hartebeest. For further information on all these animals, their horn measurements, and habitats, &c., the reader may be referred to the *Book of the Antelope*, by Oldfield Thomas and P. L. Sclater, and *Records of Big Game*, by Rowland Ward.

H. A. BRYDEN.

HERON—As an object of sport the great grey heron (*Ardea cinerea*) has come to be almost forgotten. There was a time, and that within memory of those still living, when heron-hawking was practised by an English falconer, who died in his sixty-second year no longer ago than 1871. This was the late Edward Clough Newcome, of Hockwold in the county of Norfolk. His hawking career commenced about 1827 or 1828, when, as a boy of 17 or 18, he used to go out with Colonel Wilson of Didlington, who succeeded Lord Orford as chief of the Norfolk falconers. The heron-hawks were then kept at High Ash in charge of some Dutch falconers, and the "meets" were, according to the wind, at High Ash, Mundford, Cranwich Barn, Northwold Field, and Methwold Field. The heronry at Didlington was in those days surrounded by open country on every side, and the herons used to go out in the morning to the fens as well as to rivers and ponds at a considerable distance in search of food, returning to the heronry towards evening. It was at this time (as described by Sir John Sebright) that the falconers placed themselves down wind of the heronry, so that when the herons were intercepted on their return home, they were obliged to fly against the wind to gain their place of retreat, and a fine ringing flight was then usually obtained. If the heron flew down wind, it was seldom taken; the hawks were in danger of being lost; and, as the flight was in a straight line, it afforded little sport.

HERON.

In 1838, after the death of Colonel Wilson (who in 1832 had become Lord Berners), Mr. Newcome, with the Duke of Leeds, Mr. Stuart Wortley and Baron d'Offémont, helped to found the celebrated Loo Hawking Club, whose head-quarters were at the Loo near Apeldoorn, the summer palace of the King of Holland, under whose patronage and with whose consent the members met every summer for about six weeks' heron hawking. The following extract from the archives of the club shows the number of hawks (peregrines and gerfalcons) maintained by the members, and the number of herons captured by them between 1840 and 1852:—

Year	Falcons	Herons
1840	22 Falcons	138 Herons
1841	44 "	287 "
1842	44 "	148 "
1843	40 "	200 "
1844	36 "	100 "
1849	14 "	128 "
1850	16 "	138 "
1851	18 "	130 "
1852	36 "	297 "

When taken uninjured, the herons were often liberated, after having a brass ring fastened on one leg inscribed with the name of the club and the date of capture. They were sometimes retaken at long intervals at a considerable distance from the Loo. In 1856 one of them was killed near Perpignan, having a ring on its leg which it had carried for seven years.

Mr. Newcome was the last falconer who kept heron-hawks in England, and an interesting account of two remarkable birds which he possessed, named "Sultan" and "De Ruyter," will be found in Freeman and Salvin's *Falconry* (1859). They were brought from Holland by the Dutch falconer Jan Pells, and in their first year took fifty-four herons, and in the following season fifty-seven.

But although the heron from various causes no longer serves as a quarry for trained falcons, it is still an object of some solicitude on the part of wildfowlers, not because it is reckoned of much account for the table—although formerly it was held in some estimation and was served up at city feasts together with cranes, bustards, and shovelards—but on account of its extreme wariness. Its long neck and long legs enable it to keep so sharp a look-out above the sedges or other aquatic herbage amongst which its great body is often partially or entirely concealed, that it usually requires all the skill of a deer-stalker to approach it within gunshot, the difficulty being of course increased when the bird is out on an open marsh, on the seashore, or fishing on the extensive mudflats of a tidal harbour.

By anglers the heron is regarded as a deadly foe, though it would be fairer to regard it merely as a rival. It has to get its living chiefly, though not entirely, by fishing, and its instinct naturally prompts it to seek the fish where it has the best chance of capturing it, namely, in shallow water. For this reason it is not surprising that it should visit the shallows of a trout stream, or the bed of a pool which is not too deep for wading. In such places no doubt the heron takes certain toll of such fish as come within reach of its long-pointed beak, but it varies its fish diet with frogs, water-rats, and the young of water-fowl, such as moorhens, coots and wild ducks, to an extent which should relieve it from the objurgations of anglers. When we consider the extraordinary fecundity of most fishes, the extreme rapidity of their movements in their own element, and the comparative infrequency with which they can be struck by the bird's beak (we have repeatedly seen a heron miss its mark) we should not be disposed to grudge it the meal which eventually rewards its skill and patience.

Considering its large size, most apparent when on the wing, at which time it looks fully as large as a wild goose, its weight is insignificant. An adult heron will weigh $3\frac{1}{2}$ lbs., a bean-goose $7\frac{1}{2}$ to 8 lbs., and a grey lag 9 to 10 lbs.

NESTING TIME (WANSTEAD PARK)

The length of an adult heron is about 3 feet 4 inches to the end of the tail. One of the most remarkable points in its life history is the circumstance of its congregating in the breeding season to nest in colonies, like the rook, on the tops of tall trees, or in cliffs overhanging a river, as is the case on the Findhorn. That so large a bird, with such long legs, and toes formed for wading rather than for grasping, should select the slender branches of an oak or wych elm, on which to construct a ponderous nest of twigs, is sufficiently curious; but the habit is no doubt a precautionary one for safety during the time the young are helpless in the nest. Where tall trees are absent and the herons are not molested, they sometimes make them on or near the ground, at times on dwarf bushes—as on a small island in Lough Clinn, co. Kerry, where the nests, on hollies and mountain ash, are built so low down that they may be almost reached by standing up in a boat—or amongst reeds as at Tollesbury, in Essex, where they were formerly numerous.

Occasionally, when seeking to establish a new colony, herons will attempt to take forcible possession of a rookery, and pitched battles between the two species will last for several days. A notable instance of this occurred at Dallam Tower, Westmorland, where a grove in which herons built having been cut down, the herons endeavoured to effect a settlement in a neighbouring rookery. The rooks opposed this invasion, and desperate battles ensued. Many of the rooks were killed and some of the herons lost their lives; but the latter succeeded in holding some of the trees, and harmony was at length restored.

Modern statistics seem to show that heronries in Great Britain, instead of decreasing in number as some writers suppose, are really on the increase, and this in spite of the persecution to which the birds are subjected at the hands of the fish preservers and holders of a ten shilling gun license.

In James the First's time an Act of Parliament (1 Jac. I. cap. 27. sec. 7) made it illegal to shoot with any gun within 600 paces of a heronry; no one beyond his own ground might kill or take a heron except by hawking or with the long bow under a penalty of 6*s.* 8*d.* for every bird so killed or taken, and no one might take a young heron from the nest under a penalty of 10*s.* (19 Hen. VII. cap. 11. sec. 1). The eggs of herons, bitterns, and spoonbills (shovelard) were protected (25 Hen. VIII. cap. 11. sec. 5), and it is worthy of note that in those days there was a heronry in the Bishop of London's park at Fulham in which spoonbills were also nesting. For a full account of this interesting circumstance the reader may be referred to the *Zoologist* for 1886, pp. 81–88. But these statutes were repealed by what is now known as the principal Game Act of William IV. (1 and 2 Will. IV. cap. 32), and while the legal protection once afforded to these birds was withdrawn, the means for their destruction increased by the improvement in guns, which added to the number of shooters. Notwithstanding these facts the birds themselves have not (like the crane and the bustard) ceased to breed in the British Islands, nor have our British heronries materially decreased. This is probably due to the fact that although many more people use shot guns than was formerly the case, they use them for fowl which are better worth their notice, and, in the case of professional gunners, command a higher market value.

Some years ago, by means of a published circular, the writer collected a considerable mass of information relating to heronries existing in the British Islands (*Zoologist*, 1872). No less than 130 were noted for England and Wales, seventy for Scotland, and forty-nine for Ireland. In a subsequently published appendix (*Zoologist*, 1873), twenty more were added for England and Wales, two for Scotland, and three for Ireland, and twenty-six further additions in subsequent numbers of that journal made a total of about 300 in the United Kingdom.

From these statistics the list of British heronries given in Yarrell's *British Birds* was revised, and omitting the details which had been collected as to the kind of tree on which the nests were built, the number of nests, ownership, and so forth, the following list will serve to show approximately the present distribution of heronries throughout the country.

BERKSHIRE—Windsor Great Park; Coley Park, Reading.

BRECONSHIRE—Senny Bridge; Hay.

CAERMARTHENSHIRE—Neuadd-fawr, Cilcwn, near Llandovery.

CAMBRIDGESHIRE—Chippenham Park.

CARDIGANSHIRE—Gorgerddan.

CARNARVONSHIRE—Vaynol Park, near Bangor.

CHESHIRE—Aston Hall, near Frodsham; Tabley Park, Hooton-on-the-Mersey; Eaton Hall, near Chester, and Burton Hall.

CORNWALL—Lamorran, near Truro; Fowey; Trenant Wood.

CUMBERLAND—Greystoke; Wythrop Woods, near Bassenthwaite; Gobay Park, and Edenhall, near Penrith; Eamont River, below Ulleswater; Muncaster Castle.

DENBIGHSHIRE—Vorlas Hall.

DERBYSHIRE—Kedleston, near Derby; Eaton Wood, near Uttoxeter; Sutton Scarsdale, near Chesterfield.

DEVONSHIRE—Powderham Castle, near Exeter; Sharpham, on the Dart; Warleigh, on the Tamar; Bellever, Dartmoor; Fremington, near Barnstaple; Shute Park, near Axminster; Pixton Park, near Dulverton.

DORSETSHIRE—Brownsea Island, near Poole; Upton, near Wimborne; Bryanstone Park; Admiston Hall, Kingston Lacy; Sherborne Park.

DURHAM—Ravensworth Castle; Sands, near Sedgefield; Gainford; Wycliffe.

ESSEX—Wanstead Park; Lieut.-Col. Tufnell-Tyrrell's, near Chelmsford: Chest Wood, Layer de la Haye; St. Osyth Priory.

FLINTSHIRE—Bodryddan, by St. Asaph,

GLAMORGANSHIRE—Hensol Castle; Margam Abbey Penrice Castle.

HAMPSHIRE—Heron Court; Vinney Ridge, New Forest; Wolmer Forest.

KENT—Cobham Hall; Penshurst Park; Chilham Park, near Canterbury.

LANCASHIRE—Ashton Hall, near Lancaster; Claughton Hall, Garstang; Rigg's Wood, near Garstang; Scarisbrick Hall, near Ormskirk.

LINCOLNSHIRE—Skillingthorpe Wood, near Lincoln; Swanpool; Evedon Wood, Haverholme Priory, near Sleaford; Manby, near Brigg.

MERIONETHSHIRE—Talgarth Hall, Machynlleth: Rûg, near Corwen; Glyn Hall.

MIDDLESEX—Osterley Park.

MONMOUTHSHIRE—Pantygoitre; Court Blethyn; Treowen, near Monmouth.

MONTGOMERYSHIRE—Peniarth.

NORFOLK—Gunton; Didlington; Earlham; Mautby; Wolferton Wood, near Castle Rising; Kimberley; Old Buckenham; Burnham Overy; East Walton; Taverham Hall, near Norwich; Stokesby, near Acle; Westacre; Billingford; Holkam, Strumpshaw, near Brundall.

NORTHAMPTON—Althorpe; Milton, near Peterborough; Bulwick.

NORTHUMBERLAND—Chillingham Park; Harbottle Castle, Upper Coquetdale; Bolam Lake, near Wallington; Redewater; Unthank, South Tyne.

NOTTINGHAM—Clumber Park; Colwick Park; Thoresby Park.

OXFORDSHIRE—Far Wood, Southleigh.

SHROPSHIRE—Altingham; Ellesmere; Plowden; Halston; Oakley.

SOMERSETSHIRE—Picton; Knowle House, near Dunster; Halsewell, near Bridgwater.

STAFFORDSHIRE—Swithamley; Trentham; Betley.

SUFFOLK—Cavenham; Chippenham; Henham Hall; Friston, on the Orwell; Orwell Park.

SURREY—Cobham Park; Ashley Park, Walton-on-Thames; Richmond Park.

SUSSEX—Windmill Hill, Hurstmonceaux; Sowden's Wood, Brede, Parham Park.

WARWICKSHIRE—Warwick Castle; Coombe Abbey; Ragley Park, near Alcester.

WESTMORLAND—Dalham Tower; Rydal Lake; Ingmire Hall.

WILTSHIRE—Bowood, near Melksham; Longleat, near Bath; Longford Park, near Salisbury.

WORCESTERSHIRE—Wedgwood Park, near Droitwich.

YORKSHIRE—Kildale-in-Cleveland; Newton Hall, near Malton; Harewood Park, near Leeds; Eshton Hall, near Gargrave; Browsholme Hall, near Clitheroe; Nostell Priory; Morby Park, near York.

In Scotland there are comparatively few large heronries, but the small ones are so numerous, that for a list of them the reader must be referred to the sources of information above indicated, where also will be found particulars respecting many of the colonies in Ireland.

In the case of a species so generally distributed there should be surely no excuse for not "knowing a hawk from a hernshaw!"

J. E. HARTING

HIGHLAND GATHERINGS AND GAMES

HIGHLAND GATHERINGS AND GAMES—Highland games are often held in the midst of most romantic scenery, and offer a very pretty contrast to the sombre and business-like surroundings of a town athletic meeting. What matter if the running path in the North is often only a moderately level grass-grown spot of irregular shape, with sudden acute-angled corners that would fill the heart of an Oxford or Cambridge president with a sense of the liveliest dismay? One such is at Glenisla, held under the shadow of Mount Blair, 2,400 feet high, with the river Isla meandering in front, where the "going" is indifferent, and where a mile in 5 min. 5 sec. is really fast time. But at local countryside gatherings there is not much interest taken in the running competitions, unless there is a hill-race—such as we have also in Cumberland and Westmorland—where local stalkers, shepherds, keepers, and the like have a better prospect of victory than the professional sprinter.

It is where the features peculiarly Scottish have been preserved that the interest and excitement come in, and the men with rough plaids on their shoulders, and the lasses with gay tartan shawls, that do double duty both for umbrella and cloak, flock to witness with absorbing attention the "foursome" reel dancing, or the Highland "fling," the bagpipe-playing, "tossing the caber," and the award of the prizes for the best-dressed "Hielandman" on the ground.

Amongst these events peculiarly Scottish, **Tossing the Caber** certainly requires a few words of explanation to southern ears. A "caber" in the Gaelic is a straight rod or wand. So a "caber slait" stag has a head without the bristling points and cups that adorn his fellows; *his* horns go up straight and plain above his brow antlers, for all the world like those of a big cow. The "caber" in the present juncture is a straight, tapering pine tree, 16 to 20 feet long, with all its branches lopped off close to the trunk, in appearance not unlike a telegraph pole, though more roughly trimmed and more unkempt. The "tosser" has the caber raised for him by others into an upright position—thin end downwards and resting on the turf. Stooping down, with his shoulder and one foot firmly against the caber, he raises it gingerly from the ground with the thin end between his two hands until it is nearly, if not quite, level with his elbows, and proceeds forward. At first he goes quietly, feeling cautiously for his balance. Gradually getting his pace up, as he feels that it is now balanced, with the weight well and properly set against his shoulder, he takes a good run forward and tosses the caber upward, forward, and away from him. It should turn a complete "Catherine wheel," striking the ground truly with the thick end, not falling quaveringly away to the right hand or to the left, but turning right over so that it may lie with the heavy end nearest him and the thin end right away.

The caber is often too good for the performers: in fact, it is the custom at many gatherings to bring it on to the ground too large at first for successful operations, and cut it down in length gradually till it comes within the range of practical politics. It is, of course, essentially a strong man's feat, though long practice and great dexterity too are required to get the balance right, as the forward movement is being initiated. No one could touch the great Donald Dinnie at his best in this particular sport. His height—6 ft. ½ in.—was much in his favour.

Bagpipe-playing—The name of great pipers is legion. The post of piper to the chief of a clan has long been a most honourable position, and in some cases the place has descended for generations from father to son. The Macrimmons, hereditary pipers to Macleod of Macleod, and the MacArthurs, pipers to MacDonald of the Isles, are historic instances. The last of a long line of Macrimmons died in 1822.

Reel Dancing, Highland Flings, and Sword Dance—The national dances, accompanied as they are by the national music, form the most picturesque feature of a Scottish gathering. Prize dancing, to be good, should not show the laborious, affected, and machine-like regularity of a music-hall clog dancer. The more graceful, natural, and easy the movement is, the more do our sympathies go out with the dancer. Drilling and practice are good, but natural aptitude is more. Lissom grace, with natural aptitude, is able to conceal the real strain and stress of the movement. A spectator should not be able to judge of the exertion actually involved, either by the agonised countenances, the muscular contortions, or the heavy, cow-like capers of the performers.

John MacNeill, sen., of Edinburgh, was the best all-round dancer of his time, whether in reels or flings. James Paton, the great athlete, was, for a big man, the most graceful of his fellows in the dance. John Cumming, Tarland, may be quoted as a model reel dancer. These and many more were public characters, but it often happens that a really first-class dancer does not travel beyond his own country and his own local gathering.

Putting the Stone and **Throwing the Hammer** are more interesting to Scottish athletes than to English. They have taken great pains with these feats, and have arrived at great results. Unfortunately, in Scotland there are three different styles of "putting" practised—the ordinary, the Braemar, and the Border style. So that when we come to test good individual performances, and endeavour to place them in order of merit, we are confronted with this difficulty, that they were not, and are not, undertaken under the same conditions. The curious should consult a capital little book, *The Athletes and Athletic Sports of Scotland*, by W. McCombie Smith, Esq. (F.S.A., Scotland), published by A. Gardner, 26 Paternoster Square, London. It is written by the acknowledged authority on these sports in the North, and the writer of this article is deeply indebted to him for putting all his abundant materials in the kindest manner at his disposal.

The standard weights of the stone are 22 and 16 lbs. The hop or run is generally limited to 7 ft. 6 ins., and the ground is most indifferently level. Of the weapon used, the stone itself, Mr. Smith writes: "A smooth round stone at Inverness, a rough-surfaced iron ball at Luss, and a lead ball, with indentations for the fingers, at Aboyne." This triple description alone opens out a wide field for variety of performances.

Famous "putters" up to date are Donald Dinnie, G. Davidson, O. Duffy, James Fleming, J. George, K. Macrae, J. D. MacPherson, J. and W. Tait, and G. Perrie, Lanark. Donald Dinnie has the following records with the stone of 22 lbs. weight—42 ft. 3 ins. at Dunkeld; 39 ft. 9 ins. at Coupar Angus, 1868. With the 16 lb. stone 45 ft. 7 ins. at Aboyne, 1867; and 49 ft. 6 ins. Perth, 1868 (private practice) while James Fleming has 44 ft. 9 ins. with 22 lbs. at Dunkeld. The Dunkeld ground is allowed, even by its admirers, to have been "far from level," which, being translated, doubtless means "sadly downhill." The best genuine and authentic "putts" last year were made at Pitlochry, September 5, on a ground above suspicion. G. Perrie, Lanark, put the 22 lbs. ball 37 ft. 5 ins., and the 16 lbs. do. 44 ft. 8 ins.

Throwing the 56 lb. Weight is not much practised, but is perhaps just worthy of mention. D. Dinnie, George Davidson, and G. M. Ross have all thrown it over 28 ft.; Ross, at Pitlochry, September 10, 1892, threw it 29 ft. 1 in.

Throwing the Hammer—Here again there are differences of Scottish style, and undoubted discrepancies in the weight of the hammer, and in the length and flexibility of the handle. At the standing, or Scottish style, Donald Dinnie was the best thrower on record. After him came George Davidson and Kenneth Macrae, who were hard pressed by G. Johnstone and Alexander McCulloch. In 1896 G. Johnstone was *facile princeps.* Donald Dinnie threw a 16 lbs. hammer, standing style, at Coupar Angus on level ground 132 ft. 8 ins., but it had an abnormally long handle. George Johnstone, with the improved 1890 handles, has the best on record at Aboyne, 83 ft. 4 ins. with $24\frac{3}{4}$ lbs. hammer, and 111 ft. 3 ins. with $16\frac{1}{2}$ lbs. hammer. The same athlete at Pitlochry, September 5, 1896, threw the 22 lbs. standard hammer 92 ft. 2 ins., and the 16 lbs. hammer at Stirling 119 ft. $\frac{1}{2}$ ins. Kenneth Macrae has thrown 120 ft. 6 ins. with the Inverness "light" hammer.

Running—Of course on rough grass-tracks, like Glenisla, fast times are not to be expected. At town meetings, not "gatherings," W. Cummings, Paisley, has held the mile record for a while, and still holds the ten mile record, 51 min. $6\frac{3}{5}$ sec., without ever having been driven along to do his best. P. Cannon, Stirling, has the four mile record with 19 min. $25\frac{2}{5}$ sec., and the three mile record 14 min. $19\frac{1}{5}$ sec.

High Leaping and Long Leaping—On ground nearly, if not absolutely level, the following have cleared 5 ft. 11 ins.: Donald Dinnie, James Methven, Fife, and Andrew Milne, Forfarshire. Tivendale, Fife, claims 6 ft. 1 in. at Cupar, 1861, and Hugh Andrews the same at Alva, 1881. J. W. Parsons, the Scottish amateur, has 6 ft. put to his credit.

Long Leaping—Here, too, authentic records are spoiled by the gathering grounds being seldom level. On Leven Links, with the run obviously downhill, Carruthers has cleared 23 ft. 6 ins. J. W. Parsons, again (amateur), did 23 ft. ¼ inch, L.A.C. Meeting, 1886.

Hop, Step, and Leap—This, like tossing the caber, is distinctly a Scottish feat. Great performers, such as S. Muir and A. Bower of Old Meldrum, do 45 to 48 ft.

Scotch wrestling is in a heterogeneous and disorganised condition.

In conclusion, so far as competitions and careful arrangements go, Bridge of Allan, Luss, and Aboyne are perhaps the best conducted of the gatherings.

E. LENNOX PEEL.

HIPPOPOTAMUS.
Av. height at shoulder, 44 *ins.*

HIPPOPOTAMUS (*Hippopotamus africus*)—Huge unwieldy beast as he is, slow of movement, and without special means of defence or a superabundance of intelligence, the Hippopotamus has yet held his own against his human foes during the present century—terribly destructive as that period has been to animal life in every quarter of the globe—better than any other beast whose hide or flesh is useful to man. Even the last thirty years, which have witnessed the complete extermination of the millions of shaggy bisons which once roamed the great prairies of North America, and which have changed into a dead world (zoologically speaking) the vast wastes of Southern Africa, which, when first visited by Europeans, were tenanted by innumerable herds of wild animals, have made but little difference to the range of the Hippopotamus, whose loud trumpeting bellow may still be heard on every lake or river of any size from the upper waters of the Nile to the bay of St. Lucia in Zululand. A few yet linger in the lower reaches of the Orange river, and also in the St. John's river in Pondoland, whilst a small herd, which is now protected, finds an asylum in an inland lake not far from the Ungeni river, in the colony of Natal. In the lower Limpopo the Hippopotamus is plentiful, and it is to be found also in greater or lesser numbers in every stream, where the conditions are favourable to its existence, between that river and the Zambesi, and from thence throughout the whole of Central, Eastern, and Western Africa, ranging northwards on the west to the confines of the waterless Sahara, and on the east to the upper cataracts of the Nile. Thus the Hippopotamus seems likely to be able to maintain itself for centuries to come in the vast rivers and swamps of Africa, and bids fair to outlive as a wild animal both the elephant and the rhinoceros.

In 1893 a considerable number of Hippopotami inhabited the deep pools of the upper Umzingwani river, some forty miles south of Bulawayo. These animals had been protected for many years, both by Lo Bengula and his father Umziligazi before him, but, to the shame of our race be it said, no sooner were the Matabele conquered and their country thrown open to Europeans, than certain white men destroyed nearly all these animals, which had been rendered tame by long protection, for the sake of their hides. A small herd was also protected by Lo Bengula in the Umzuza river, within twenty miles of Bulawayo, and these animals are strictly preserved.

Although the African and Asiatic elephants and rhinoceroses differ considerably from their prototypes of pleistocene times, the Hippopotamus of the present day appears to be identical in structure with the animal whose fossil bones have been discovered in the caves and river beds of Southern Britain, and which must have been an inhabitant of that country at a very remote period of the world's history, probably anterior to the glacial period, for during and subsequent to that time the English climate would hardly have been suitable to his requirements.

In Africa itself the Hippopotamus must have existed for countless ages of time, for I have seen places in the lower Umfuli river, in northern Mashunaland where these uncouth beasts have worn paths some three or four inches deep in the solid bed of rock, through the centre of which the river has worn a deep channel. Over these beds of rock the Hippopotami have walked night after night, always on the same trail, until little by little their soft spongy feet have worn a deep track in the hard metamorphic rock. A fresh Hippopotamus track made in soft muddy ground is some two feet in width with a little ridge in the centre, as, unlike other animals, Hippopotami do not cross their feet in walking, but move the front and hind foot on each side in parallel lines, thus producing two paths, or rather one broad path with a slight ridge in the centre. The paths cut in the rock beds of the Umfuli river show the ridge in the centre as plainly as paths made but yesterday in soft ground.

In following the course of a river in a wild uninhabited part of Africa, the European traveller will often have reason to thank the Hippopotami for the broad paths they have tramped for him to walk along. These paths will sometimes lead right across country for several miles from one bend of a river to another, and in broken country will be found winding up and down steep hill sides, or piercing dense jungles or beds of reeds on the level ground. The same paths are kept open and used year after year, and it may be fairly said that the Hippopotamus is the only animal capable of making a track that it is comfortable to walk along in the interior of Africa; as his only rival, the native, makes a path which exasperates a European, being not only so zigzag, that in a jungle you very often cannot see a man three yards in front of you, but also so narrow that you cannot walk in it without crossing your feet.

Hippopotami are strictly nocturnal in their habits, never leaving the water to feed until after dark. Their food consists of reeds and grass, and as their huge stomachs can hold a good part of a haystack, they often wander far to obtain the requisite amount of nourishment; more especially during the rainy season, at which time I have seen their tracks more than a mile away from the water.

Before daylight they are all back again in the river they frequent, and during the daytime they lie lazily floating about in the water, or else bask like huge pigs on the tail of some island; some lying on the dry sand, others half immersed in the water, and others again with just their heads showing above the surface.

Hippopotami consort together in herds or families of from four or five to twenty or thirty in number, and in one portion of the Lower Zambesi below the gorge of Kariba, I once saw over 100 of these animals in several distinct herds, but scattered over a distance of less than a mile of river. The old bulls are often met with by themselves, and these old fellows, as well as cows with very young calves, are sometimes very savage, and will on occasion attack with great fury a boat or canoe which incautiously approaches them. Once, when travelling on the Upper Zambesi, I had a canoe capsized in deep water by a Hippopotamus cow with a small calf, and lost ivory and other things to the value of £60 through the accident.

It is by no means easy to shoot Hippopotami in a large river like the Zambesi, as not only are they in all probability pretty wary, through having been more or less molested by the natives, but the great breadth of the river enables them to keep out of the hunter's way. Again, it is by no means easy to hit the small mark presented by the vulnerable portion of a Hippopotamus's head (which is only shown above the water during the few seconds of time during which the animal is taking breath) from a rickety native canoe. Should the poor animals be found, as is often the case, in the pools of a small and narrow river, where they are always well within shot from either bank, they are easily destroyed, and in such cases, unless their flesh is required for food, to kill them is mere slaughter with no element of sport in it.

African natives who possess firearms seldom attack Hippopotami in the daytime, as experience has taught them that they cannot shoot accurately enough to hit so small a mark as the vital part of a Hippopotamus's head, which is usually all that can be seen of these animals when they are in the water, as they almost always are in the daytime. They therefore lie in wait for them at nights, and as the unsuspecting animals graze past them, put a heavy bullet into their great round bodies at close range. If the bullet is well placed and reaches the heart or penetrates both lungs, the stricken beast rushes back to the river, but only to die, and his carcase is found floating on the surface of the water the following morning. Should the bullet not be well placed, the wounded animal will probably recover, and for every Hippopotamus that is killed by the natives by night shooting, a good many doubtless escape with wounds which do not prove fatal. Where the natives have no guns, Hippopotami are usually either attacked in the water with harpoons to which long lines are attached, or caught in pitfalls; but the most deadly method which I have ever heard of to compass the destruction of these animals was one which I saw practised many years ago in Northern Mashunaland, when a whole herd was starved to death in a pool of the Umniati river.

To accomplish their object, a whole tribe of Mashunas, men, women, and children, had cooperated, and having found a herd of Hippopotami in a deep reach of the river some 150 yards in breadth by 300 in length, they had fenced it in—the river both above and below the pool running in shallow channels amongst large rocks—and by keeping up fires all night and beating tom-toms had prevented the animals coming out to feed.

When I arrived on the scene there were eight starving animals lying huddled together on a submerged sandbank in the centre of the pool, and two swimming about vainly seeking a place of exit, with assegais in their backs, whilst two which had died of starvation or of assegai wounds, were being cut up on the edge of the pool, and the meat of many others hung drying in festoons on the trees around. In a few more days the survivors must all have died, as the natives said that they had not eaten anything but water for three weeks, and thus a herd of nearly twenty Hippopotami were done to death. The destruction of these animals, however, supplied a whole tribe with a quantity of much required food, and was to my mind not so reprehensible as the slaughter of the Hippopotami in the Umzingwani river near Bulawayo by white men for the sake of their hides alone in 1894.

The meat of the Hippopotamus is most excellent, at least in those parts of Africa where the altitude above the sea level renders the climate rather temperate than tropical, and where the winter nights are cold and frosty. It has a flavour of its own something between beef and pork.

During the rainy season, when the feeding is rich and plentiful, Hippopotami get into high condition, and besides developing much inside fat, put on a layer of blubber between the skin and the flesh, which sometimes covers the whole body to a thickness of an inch or even more. When in this condition I would rather have a piece of meat cut from the ribs of a young Hippopotamus cow, and roasted on a forked stick over the camp fire, than the best piece of meat that England could offer me. Good, however, as is the meat of a fat Hippopotamus cow, an old bull is to be avoided as an article of diet, should any other kind of meat be obtainable, as he is sure to be both lean and tough.

As Hippopotami are almost always killed by Europeans by brain shots, no rifle could be more suitable for their destruction than the newly invented small-bore military rifles, with solid bullets; and the most deadly spot to hit is the root of the ear, if the animal is either facing sideways or looking half away. Should a Hippopotamus be facing directly towards one, it will be found easier to hit than kill him, and it will therefore be advisable to wait for a better chance. In conclusion, let me say that although the African traveller or hunter may often find it necessary to kill Hippopotami to supply himself and his large native following with meat, he will, I think, soon realise that there is little sport to be got out of killing them, and will therefore soon learn not to molest unnecessarily these usually inoffensive beasts; for, once they have disappeared from an African river, the scenery has lost one of its greatest charms for every lover of nature.

F. C. SELOUS.

HOCKEY—History of the Game—The game of hockey as now played may be considered to have originated in the year 1883, the first attempt to establish the game under a definite code of rules being successfully undertaken by the Wimbledon Club in that year. The game had of course existed in various forms for a very long time, but how long no one can well say, as there do not appear to be any records preserved. In Ireland it was long known as Hurley, and in Scotland as Shinty. In England it was played a good deal round London in the seventies, but seems to have died out for some years before the Wimbledon Club was formed in 1883. Since that date it has prospered and developed to such an extent both in the number of clubs all over the country and in the skill displayed in the game, that players of twelve or fourteen years ago, who have given up their interest in the game, would scarcely recognise it now. Combination was then a thing unknown. The side consisted, it is true, of the same number of players, viz., eleven, but of these eight were forwards, two so-called half-backs, and a goalkeeper. The disproportion between attack and defence seems absurd, but the game then consisted almost entirely of scrimmages between the two sets of forwards varied by occasional individual dribbling which the half-backs generally proved equal to checking. As the idea of combination developed, the number of backs was increased, making the proportions more equal. First a third half-back was introduced. After that one of these three was placed behind the other two as a back. Next the forwards were reduced to six, the half-backs again numbering three, and finally a second back was added, making the numbers of attack and defence practically equal, the forwards numbering five, with three half-backs, two backs and a goalkeeper. This arrangement of the side did not become general until the season of 1889–90, so it will be seen that the changes mentioned were only gradually introduced, but they have undoubtedly conduced to the improvement and development of the game.

The Hockey Association was formed in 1886 and from that date has been the recognised authority for the control of the game. In the North of England the game was not taken up until the year 1887, and for some years it was confined to Manchester and Liverpool and the neighbourhood. At the present time, however, it is spreading fast in Yorkshire and the other Northern counties. The Northern Counties Hockey Association was formed in the winter of 1889–90, but has always been under the control of the Hockey Association. Most of the counties in which the game is played have their own associations, which are affiliated to the Hockey Association, but they exist for little more than the arrangement and control of inter-county matches, and the details connected with them. Ireland has taken up the game in the last few years, as well as Wales, and international matches first took place in the season 1894–95, Ireland playing England and Wales. These matches have now become regular fixtures. Wales has not yet encountered England, as the game has not yet made enough progress in the Principality. The oldest clubs in the South of England are Wimbledon, Molesey, Surbiton, Teddington, and Ealing, and in the North, the Western (Eccles), Didsbury, Bowdon, and Kersal.

Conditions of Play—The game is played on a ground 100 yards long and 60 yards wide. The width may vary from 50 to 60 yards, but it has been found that the full width allowed conduces to the best game. The goals are 12 ft. wide and 7 ft. high, and should always be fitted with goal nets, which prevent any disputes as to whether a shot has gone between or outside the posts. Fifteen yards in front of the goal a line parallel to the goal-line is marked, also 12 ft. long, and from each extremity of this line, taking each goal post as a centre, is described a segment of a circle terminating at the goal-line. This constitutes what is, roughly speaking, a semicircle in front of the goal, and the attacking side cannot score a goal unless the ball was last hit by one of them inside this line. The object of this is to prevent a goal being scored by indiscriminate hitting from any part of the field. The game is started by what is called a bully in the centre of the ground. The centre forward on each side strikes with his stick, first the ground, then his opponent's stick thrice, after which proceeding the ball is in play. When the ball is driven over the goal-line by one of the attacking side, a bully takes place 25 yards from the goal-line in a direct line from where the ball passed over it. When a defending player hits the ball over his own goal-line, or the ball glances off him or his stick and

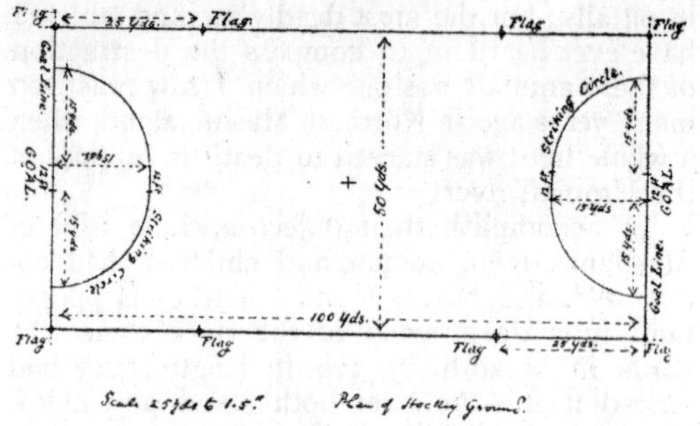

goes behind the line, the penalty is a corner hit. This is a free hit by the attacking side from the corner flag, usually hit by the outside forward or a half-back, whilst the other forwards range round the circle line. The defending side must stand with feet and sticks behind the goal-line until the ball is hit, when they may run out. The attacking side cannot score a goal from a corner hit, unless the ball has been first stopped dead on the ground, or been touched by one of the defending side. A penalty bully is given for deliberately unfair play by the defending side in their own circle. It consists of a bully between the offender and any one player of the attacking side. The rest of the defending side must stand behind their goal-line, and the rest of the attacking side may range round the circle, but neither side may enter the circle or play the ball until it has been hit outside the circle again by one of the players taking part in the bully.

The Players—Of the five *forwards* the most important is of course the centre forward. He is the connecting link between the two sets of wing players, and is responsible for the combination of the front rank as a whole. He should be a fast and thoroughly unselfish player and a first-rate shot at goal. He must always be careful to keep his place, or he will interfere with his wings. His passes to the other forwards are of two kinds, the short pass to either of the inside wing players, or the long pass well forward to the outside men. He must use his discretion which to employ, but he is always safer in passing out hard to the outside man when near his own goal. On the other hand he should not do so when approaching his opponents' circle, the only exception being when the inside forwards cannot get an opening and the outside men are left unguarded. In shooting at goal he should be able to put in a good shot from a pass, without waiting to stop it first. The shot will go harder, and the goalkeeper has less time to note the direction from which the ball comes. This rule will apply to all the forwards, and countless goals are lost by stopping the ball first, and then trying to shoot. By that time it is more likely than not the backs will have deprived the forward of the ball. These flying shots may not always be accurate, but more opportunities are gained for scoring, and some of the shots are sure to be successful. The inside wing players should be considered as partners of the outside men, and are responsible for their getting proper opportunities. Nothing is prettier than a combined run of two wing players passing and re-passing to each other. The inside men should always try to pass well forward to the outsides so as to allow the latter, who should always be fast men, to get well into their stride before taking the ball. They should try and draw the opposing half-back away from the outside men before passing, and if they are successful in this, the way is cleared for a good run down the ground. Inside forwards should not pass out too much near their opponents' circle, unless both they and the centre are unable to get an opening for a shot. When the ball is thrown in from touch they have to try to get possession of it, and should generally pass it back to the outside man. This is a comparatively easy task for inside right, but by no means so for inside left, who cannot reach out to hit the ball as it is rolled in. All he can do as a rule is to hamper his opponent by hooking or knocking up his stick before he can reach the ball. Of the two outside forwards, he on the right has much the easier position in which to play. Unless the half-back opposed to him keeps out near the line, he can nearly always slip past him on the outside. He can middle the ball with ease while going at a good pace, which is an impossibility for outside left, who has either to get slightly in front of the ball as it is running, and then try and middle it, with a good chance of missing it altogether, or else stop it first with his foot or stick, and then get in his stroke. The outside forwards should make a point of passing into the centre as soon as they have got beyond the twenty-five yard line, though outside left may go a little further than outside right, for his passes always come more at right angles to the side line than those from outside right. The outside forwards have to throw the ball in from touch, and must remember not to throw in hard near their own goal, but when near their opponents' to get the ball well into the centre if possible. All the forwards should make a point of taking passes with their sticks, and not waste time by stopping the ball with their hands or feet before hitting it. Individual play is quite useless, and no team with selfish forwards can expect to meet with much success.

Half-backs are perhaps the most important element in the team. Three good halves certainly go further towards making a good team than any other three players. Both backs and forwards are dependent on them. A good set of forwards will lose half their opportunities with weak half-backs behind them. Half-back is without doubt the position in the field that entails the hardest work, and, of the three, centre half has the most to do. Their duty is to support their forwards when they have the ball, and to break up the passing of the opposing forwards, and when they have done this, to feed their own forwards. They must assist the backs by falling back at once directly they have themselves failed to stop a run, taking care not to get in their way. They must never deprive a back of the ball when he is in a position to get in a good hit, as he is much better able to clear his lines than a half-back rushing towards his own goal. Centre half is perhaps the most difficult position of the three. He has practically to look after all the three inside forwards, whilst the wing half has at the most two forwards to mark and should devote his chief attention to the outside forward. In feeding the forwards, the centre half has much more scope, as he is in a position to pass to any of the five, and must be able to see at a glance which of them is in the most favourable position to start an effective run. A long pass to either of the outside forwards is a possibility for which he must always be on the look out, as this frequently proves very advantageous, particularly when the opposing wing halves are not keeping as near the touch line as they should do. A half-back must be full of resource for every emergency, and so needs to be quick and accurate with hands, feet, and stick. Short passing is best broken up by using the feet or the stick, as the half-back can then get the ball at once, whereas if the hands are used the stick has to be gripped again before hitting the ball. The hands should only be used for fielding the ball when it is in the air, and when there is plenty of time to get rid of the ball before the opposing forwards can get up to it. Half-backs must never dribble, but get rid of the ball as soon as possible to their forwards and then follow them up closely. It will thus be seen that half-backs need to be fast and to have plenty of staying power. They must be able to hit hard when near their own goal. Their passes to their forwards must be cleanly hit and go sharp and straight. If he cannot get in a hit to his forwards, a half-back can sometimes pass back to one of the backs; but it is obvious that this pass must always be very accurate, or it may prove disastrous. If the forwards have got past them, they can often hinder their progress by hooking their sticks and so help their backs to get the ball. One other point should be noted, and that is that no one-handed play should ever be indulged in by half-backs. It is nearly always ineffective in forwards, but is quite out of the question in defensive play.

The position of *back* is one in which a mistake may at any time prove fatal, so that a cool and steady player is absolutely essential for this post. He must be able to hit hard, but must not hit wildly and in any direction, and should always feed his forwards like a half-back whenever possible. When a half-back in front of him compels a forward to pass, he must be ready to intercept the pass and then get rid of the ball at once. If he is fast, he can play close up behind his half-backs, and smother passing before it becomes dangerous. If not he must keep further back, and rely on the half-back catching up the forward again, or hampering his play so that he is easily tackled. He must have a thorough understanding with the half-backs in front of him, or they will constantly be running into one another. Inside the circle he must see that the half-backs keep well out of his way, or they will prevent his getting the ball away, and he in turn must always be careful to give the goal-keeper plenty of room and not obstruct his view of the ball. He should avoid as much as he can getting out to the side of the ground to tackle an outside forward, particularly in his own half of the ground, as this is likely to leave an opening in the centre and weaken the defence. In hitting the ball he should, whenever he has time, stop it first and then get in his hit. This will lessen the chance of a mis-hit or of missing the ball altogether, but of course there is not always time when forwards are rushing down on him. Being able to hit the ball on the run with accuracy is therefore a valuable quality in a back. A brilliant but erratic player is not the man for back, but rather the cautious man who will leave nothing to chance.

A good *goalkeeper* is a treasure that few clubs are fortunate enough to possess, and he makes an enormous difference to his side, not only by the actual number of goals he saves, but by the confidence imparted to backs and half-backs when they know they have a safe man behind them. He has a thankless task, and his position affords very little enjoyment and a large amount of responsibility. He needs to have an accurate eye, and to be very quick with hands, feet, and stick. His stick should be held in both hands, so that he can quickly have either hand free to stop a shot in the air. He should rely on his feet to stop shots along the ground, only using his stick as a forlorn hope for shots he could not otherwise reach He should always hit the ball away if possible rather than kick it, as it takes a long kick to get the ball out of the circle, but frequently all he can do is to scrape the ball away with his feet. He should never hesitate to concede a corner when he can see no other opening, as he must get the ball away at all risks. To stop side shots he should move towards that side of the goal from which direction the shot is coming, as he will thus cover more of the space available for shooting at. The only occasion on which he should run out of goal is when a forward has got away and has hit the ball so hard that the goalkeeper can easily get to it first, or when a forward has broken through and is likely to get in a shot before he can be overtaken by the backs. In this latter case the goalkeeper should run forward right out of the circle so as to attempt to tackle him before he can get within shooting range, as this will be his only chance of saving his goal. There is very little likelihood of his stopping any fairly hard shot from a forward who can take his aim unmolested. Goalkeepers are divided in their opinions as to whether cricket pads or shin guards are the most effective to keep goal in. The former afford more protection to the feet and knees, but some say the ball bounces further off them than from shin guards, which is a great objection if correct, as a shot rebounding from the goalkeeper often affords a second opportunity to a forward and generally a very easy one. This matter must be left to the taste of the individual.

Outfit—All other players should always wear shin guards. They are no encumbrance, and, though a hard hit hurts nearly as much through a guard as without it, they prevent the skin from being broken, saving many nasty wounds. Gloves of some sort are worn by most players, as the knuckles are very liable to get knocked about by one stick glancing up another. Ordinary batting gloves are very convenient, as they leave the fingers comparatively free for a good grip of the stick. It is hardly necessary to add that boots should always have bars or studs on the soles and heels to prevent slipping. Rubber soles are sometimes worn, but they are not very effective on a wet ground. The choice of a stick, which must be capable of passing through a two-inch ring, must be left to the player's taste. He will soon find out what weight and shape suits him best. Forwards will find it convenient to play with a fairly short stick, which should not weigh more than 22 ozs. Backs and half-backs need a stick two or three inches longer than a forward, as they require a longer reach. This extra length, and the fact that they require to hit harder, entails a heavier stick, but 25 ozs. is quite heavy enough for any player. It has been found by experience that sticks of 26 and 28 ozs., or even more, which some players formerly used, are no more effective for such hard hitting as is necessary, and their weight prevents their being freely handled. Hard slogging is not the correct game, and the lighter the stick

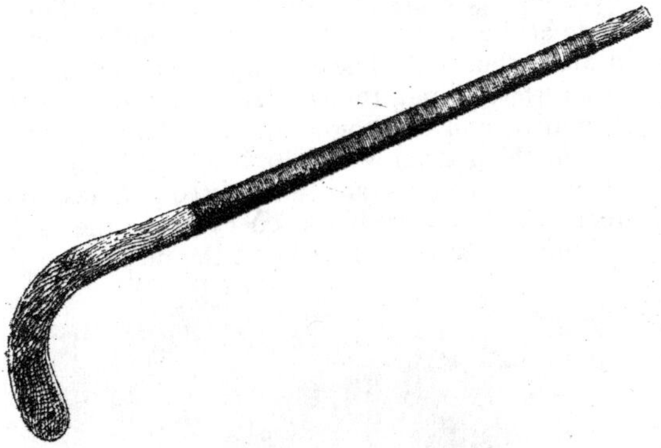

HOCKEY STICK.

a player can use efficiently the better. The ball is an ordinary cricket ball painted white. Attempts have been made to find another more suitable ball, the idea being that a cricket ball is too hard, but nothing better has yet been discovered.

Umpires—The umpires are as a rule two in number, with occasionally, but very seldom, a referee. The game is too fast for one man to take entire charge as at football, so each umpire takes one half of the ground. They are on either side of the ground, so that each can control one touchline for the whole length of the ground. They should always try to keep level with the ball while it is in their own half, as they are then less likely to make mistakes in the case of appeals for offside. The ball travels at such a great pace that umpiring is no easy matter at hockey. A series of hints to umpires has been drawn up by the Hockey Association and is published at the end of the official book of the rules of the game.

Matches—Of representative matches the annual game between North and South is always looked forward to with great interest and never fails to afford a good exhibition of the game. The match first took place in 1890, when hockey had only been played for two or three seasons in the North and naturally resulted in an easy victory for the South. Each year saw a reduction in the score against the North, until in 1894 the match was a draw, but the South have won the three matches since then, though each game has been a close fight. England has played three matches with Ireland, winning in 1895 by 5-0, in 1896 by 1-0 after a hard game at Dublin, while in 1897 the result has been another win for England by 8-3. Ireland has played Wales three times and won easily on each occasion.

County matches have taken place for years between Surrey and Middlesex, and latterly each of these counties has played Kent. These matches do not excite much interest in the South, as club matches are considered far more important, and a great struggle takes place every year for the position of premier club. For the first six seasons after hockey was revived, Molesey was undoubtedly the strongest club, but from 1891 to 1896 Wimbledon was top of the list. The season of 1896—97 saw both Wimbledon and Molesey ousted from the position by Bromley, a comparatively young club in Kent. The last two seasons have witnessed a general levelling up of the clubs as regards form, and there is very little to choose between the four or five best teams. More interest is taken in county matches in the North, and Lancashire and Cheshire have frequently beaten the Southern Counties.

The game has so far been kept entirely free from any suspicion of professionalism, thanks to the efforts of the Hockey Association.

E. L. CLAPHAM.

RULES OF THE GAME

1. A hockey team shall number eleven players, unless otherwise agreed by the respective captains.

2. The ground shall be 100 yards long and 50 yards wide, marked with white lines, and with a flag at each corner. The longer sides to be called the "side lines," and the shorter sides the "goal lines."

3. The goals shall be in the centre of each goal line, and shall consist of two uprights 12 feet apart, with a horizontal bar 7 feet from the ground.

4. In front of each goal shall be drawn a line 12 feet long, parallel to the goal line, and 15 yards from it. The ends of this line shall be curved round to the goal lines by quarter circles, of which the goal posts form the centres. This line to be called the "striking circle."

5. The ball shall be an ordinary cricket ball, painted white.

6. The sticks shall have no metal fittings whatever, and no sharp edges, and they must be able to pass through a ring 2 inches in diameter.

7. No player is to have any metal spikes or projecting nails in his boots or shoes.

8. The choice of goals shall be tossed for at the beginning of the game, and the goals shall be changed at half-time.

9. The game shall be started by one player of each side bullying the ball in the centre of the ground, and after each goal and after half-time there shall be a bully in the centre of the ground. The bully shall be played as follows: Each player is to strike the ground on his own side of the ball, and his opponent's stick over the ball three times alternately; after which either of the two players shall be at liberty to strike the ball.

10. In all cases of a bully, every player shall be between the ball and his own goal line.

11. A goal is scored when the ball has been driven between the goal posts under the bar. No goal can be scored unless the ball be hit from a point within the striking circle. A ball struck from without the striking circle, and touching or glancing off the person or stick of a player on the defending side, cannot score a goal.

12. When a player hits the ball, any player of the same side who at the moment of hitting is nearer his opponent's goal line is off side, and may not touch the ball himself, nor in any way whatever prevent any other player from doing so, unless there are at least three of

his opponents nearer their own goal line, and a player once off side cannot be in play again until the ball has touched or been hit by another player.

13. The ball may be caught (but must be at once dropped) or stopped with any part of the body; but it must not be carried, kicked, or knocked on, except with the stick. The ball shall be played from right to left only, and no left or backhanded play, charging, kicking, collaring, shinning, or tripping, shall be allowed. Fencing or hooking sticks shall not be allowed, unless one of the players is on the ball. A player shall not run in between his opponent and the ball so as to obstruct him, nor cross him from the left so as to foul him. The goal-keeper shall, however, be allowed to kick the ball away in defence of goal.

14. When a player strikes at the ball, his stick must not during any portion of the stroke rise above his shoulder. And no player may interfere in any way with the game unless his stick be in his hand.

15. On the occasion of a free hit, no member of the offending side shall be within 5 yards of the spot where such hit is made, and the striker must not play the ball again until it has touched or been hit by another player.

16. The penalty for any breach of Rules 12, 13, 14 and 15, committed outside the striking circles, shall be a "free hit" by one of the opposite side, on the spot where the rule was broken. For any breach of Rules 12, 13, 14 and 15, by the attacking side, committed inside the striking circle, a free hit may be claimed by the defending side. For any breach of Rules 12, 13, 14 and 15, committed by the defending side inside the striking circle, the attacking side can only claim a "bully."

17. When a ball passes the "side line," it shall be rolled out along the ground from the spot where it crossed the line by one of the opposite side to that of the player who last touched it in any direction except forward. No other player shall stand within five yards of the side line. The ball may be rolled out at once, and the player who rolls it out must not touch the ball again until it has touched or been hit by another player.

18. If the ball is hit behind the goal line by the attacking side, it shall be brought out 25 yards in a direction at right angles to the goal line from a point where it crossed the line and there "bullied;" but if the ball glance off, or is hit behind by any player of the defending side, a player of the attacking side shall hit it out from a point on the side or base line within a yard of the nearest corner flag, and at the moment the ball is so "hit out," all the defending side must be behind their goal line, and all the attacking side must be outside the striking circle.

19. Should there be no umpire or umpires appointed by the two captains, the captains shall be arbitrators in all disputes, and should two umpires or arbitrators fail to agree, they must appoint a referee, whose decision shall be final.

NOTE.—The game is usually played for one hour and ten minutes, half-time being called after thirty-five minutes.

HOMING PIGEONS—Homing pigeons, under various disguises, such as Antwerps, Skinnums, Longfaced Beards, Horsemen, &c., have been known, in this country at any rate, since the publication of Moore's Columbarium early in the eighteenth century. The homing instinct is common to all the varieties of the pigeon, and goes right back to the fountain head, the half domesticated blue rock. In the fancy varieties, the breeding for points purely has tended to decrease the homing instinct, whereas the homing fancier heeds not the colour of the eye or shape of bill or wattle; his one idea has been to intensify "the homing qualities" of the parents, and in this way only the best performers have been used for stock purposes. It has been a game of the "survival of the fittest," and the homing pigeon, with its muscular shoulders, deep chest, and "vanishing keel," has been produced. The flight feathers are long and wide, the webs of the feathers overlapping, while the skull is moderately short, wide at the base and across, and furnished with a strong short bill. The eye may be of any shade, from white to red, though deep red is the most common, and the colour of the plumage may be anything from white to black, though the prevailing colours are undoubtedly blues, or reds with blue or black checkering, the self colours of white or black being the rarest.

HOMING PIGEON.

The homing pigeon, like all the other varieties, is a product of human patience and skill, and, it has been said, derives its strength of wing from the dragon, and its height of flight from the tumbler, but it is curious how very soon the tumbling propensity which distinguishes the pigeons of that name vanishes from a loft of pigeons kept for racing purposes. In Belgium, the home undoubtedly of the homing pigeon, it may be stated that there are two great divisions of the breed. These are the Antwerp type, which is the one above described, with the size throughout exaggerated, and the Liège type, which is finer in build generally, save that the wing power is retained, while the skull is shorter and rounder. Some of the finest long distance performances have been

accomplished by these little "messengers of Liege," and the British fancier has for some time been importing the Liege type as a cross with what may be called, for want of a better term, the Antwerp type. The result is apparent, for the homing pigeon of to-day is finer in body form than it was ten years ago. It may be said that the Belgium fancier has proceeded on the same lines, and we think the result has been to produce a bird distinct in itself as a variety, more pleasing to the eye than formerly, and without sacrifice of stamina or speed.

The history of long distance flying in this country may be soon told. Before the introduction of the telegraph, the pigeon was used almost exclusively as a messenger for conveying commercial intelligence, and many of the large houses had lofts especially devoted to bringing news of the ebb and flow of the markets. The distances over which these messages were conveyed did not exceed fifty miles, though some of the firms had birds capable of flying from London to Lancashire, which was considered a notable fly thirty years ago. It is a historical fact that the news of the victory of Waterloo was, by means of a pigeon post, in the hands of a private firm many hours before the Government knew the result of the battle. The telegraph killed the homing pigeon as a messenger for commercial purposes, though it is interesting to record that the progeny of these birds are doing good work in the races of to-day. It was, however, through the Siege of Paris, when the city was shut in on every side, that the world at large became really aware of what the homing pigeon was capable. Mr. J. W. Logan, M.P., may be credited with the Fatherhood of the Fancy, for he first organised races on almost a national scale, and was one of the first to import, for stock purposes, the very cream of the Belgium lofts. The United Counties Club was formed about 1880, under which the larger part of England was divided into competing districts, and the era of long distance racing began. It is interesting to record that the south-eastern was the route first adopted, *vià* Dover and Arras to Paris.

There are now clubs in every town and village in the United Kingdom flying long races, and the number of birds in training amounts to hundreds of thousands. The Homing Pigeon Fancy, as it exists to-day, is not in any way associated with public house sweeps of, say, one mile to three miles; the shortest race of the majority of clubs is about seventy miles, extending, with intermediate races, up to a final point of 400 to 550 miles. The four clubs in this country with the largest membership are the Manchester Flying Club, the Central Counties Flying Club, Airdale Flying Club, and New Mills Flying Club. London and Liverpool have each three clubs of recognised standing. The Central Counties Flying Club, of which H.R.H. the Duke of York is a member, has a double programme, and flies races from Marennes on the south, and Thurso on the north route. The La Rochelle Club has one race only, which must be for a distance over 500 miles for all members. The best routes to fly are the northerly or southerly, and experience has proved that easterly winds are to be avoided as far as possible. In addition to the club races, several clubs band themselves together under the name of federations, and thus we find from one to three

KEY TO PLATE.
1, Light Mealy; 2, Common Antwerp; 3, Dark, Long-faced Antwerp (short distance swift flyer) 4, Mottled Homer; 5, Short-faced Antwerp; 6, Blue Antwerp; 7, Dark Mottled (long distance flyer).

thousand birds competing in a race. There is a Homing Pigeon Protection Society, which undertakes the prosecution of persons shooting or detaining pigeons the property of members. In addition to this there are two weekly papers devoted to pigeon flying, *The Homing News* and *The Fanciers' Gazette*.

So unwieldy has the Fancy grown that it has been found necessary to have a governing body at the head of affairs, and hence at the end of 1896 the National Homing Union was formed, of which Mr. J. W. Logan, M.P., is president, and Mr. Plackett is the secretary. The rules of the Union have been drawn on the lines of those of the Jockey Club, and in fact the Union is the Jockey Club of pigeon flying. There are 114 clubs enrolled under the Union representing an individual membership of over 3,000. The Homing Pigeon has also found its way into most of our Colonies.

In dealing with the instinct of the homing pigeon, little can be given in explanation. It is an enigma which possibly will never be unriddled. It has been put down to a mysterious sixth sense, to a love of home, to marvellous sight, &c., but the fact stands out that if a number of birds were taken without having been previously trained at intermediate stages and tossed at, say, 100 miles, not a bird would find its loft again; whereas, if carefully trained up to about 250 miles, the birds may safely be jumped another 250 miles over strange country. If the weather is favourable, a large percentage will be in their lofts again the same day. This would point to the fact that education plays the important part, but, over and above all, the pigeon possesses some unexplained power of orienting itself, and so striking on the line for home.

This leads to the speed of the homing pigeon, and a moment's consideration will show that the speed of flight must depend on the direction and the force of the wind. It is quite a common occurrence for pigeons to fly over a mile a minute for long distances with a strong favouring wind, and the season of 1897 stands out prominent in the many velocities recorded of over 1,800 yards a minute. The races, however, that want winning are those flown against a head wind, the winning bird flying 700 to 800 yards a minute. These are the races that bring out stamina, and in which blood and condition tell a tale, and these undoubtedly are the birds that will become the Hermits and the Herchells of the Pigeon Stud Book.

The ambition of the Fancy is to fly over 500 miles in the day, but it is apparent, if this is to be done, that wind and weather must be favourable for the entire journey. It is therefore much easier to fly 550 miles on a favourable day than 200 against a head wind on a bad day. The 500 miles in the day has often been accomplished on the Continent and in America, and in 1896 several birds flew from Thurso to London in the day, the winner actually covering 1,454 yards per minute for the entire journey of 501 miles. In 1897 the La Rochelle and one or two other Clubs, flying on the same day, flew from Marennes, in the south-west of France, about 550 miles in the day, many birds accomplishing from 1,000 to 1,300 yards a minute. These two performances stand out as high water marks over ten years of as many attempts and as many dreary failures, and we have no hesitation in saying the Fancy would have been a great gainer if these 500 mile races had never been attempted.

The Fancy, we think, should finish its season at about 400 miles. This distance has been, and can be, accomplished in the day against a head wind, and it is doubtful if 500 ever will. The conclusion of the matter is, that no distance should be attempted that cannot be accomplished in the day against a head wind. Pigeons have returned from a 1,000 miles, but this is not sport but cruelty; the moment the bird has to drop for the night it becomes a mere chance whether it reaches home or not. We are not pessimists by any means, and, whatever we say, the Fancy will go on throwing birds away in the attempt; but it is a mere question of dividing miles into minutes, and you cannot lengthen out time. We grant that much may yet be accomplished in improving the stamina of the birds, and the Fancy at present knows very little of what is condition or fitness, or, in other words, of the circumstances under which birds do their best work.

It is simply astounding to see the lethargy of the Government in not recognising at once the value of the homing pigeon as an accessory to military and naval operations. On the Continent we find France, Germany, Belgium, Spain, Italy, and other countries with hundreds of military lofts and thousands of trained birds. It was recorded in the summer of 1897 that the German Government had liberated 2,000 birds at Dover.

For short distances, say from thirty to fifty miles, the pigeon may be considered as reliable as the telegraph, and a pigeon can accompany a ship out to sea, and we cannot, at any rate at present, carry the telegraph in our pocket.

A few words in answer to the question, "How to start a loft?" There is no need whatever to go on importing birds from Belgium. We have as good birds in England as ever flew in Belgium, and, given Continental weather, there is no doubt whatever that our performances in the 500 miles races would compare favourably with anything done in Belgium. We should advise purchasing half a dozen pairs or so of squeakers of the best blood. If these are taken away early enough, they may be easily used to a new loft. As regards the loft, any room will answer the purpose provided it is dry, sweet, and free from draught. The homer is of the hardiest nature, and does not want coddling in any way. There must, however, be no overcrowding, and cleanliness of water fountains, food, and loft are essentials. The food varies according to the season. Good sound barley is the best food during the moulting season and to the end of January. The birds may then be put on to a mixture of maize, peas, dari, &c., and this may be continued to the end of April, when they go into the training baskets, after which old peas and tic beans are the strongest and most sustaining food. The life of a homing pigeon as regards racing may be briefly put as follows :—At twelve weeks old it may be taken a mile from home, and this may be increased to three miles the next day, and so by stages of six, twelve, twenty-five, fifty, and seventy-four miles. The last would be about the first race point. The birds should not be sent on every day, but allowed a day or so to rest, especially if they should have met with bad weather. From the seventy-four miles it would be jumped to the next race point, say, in seven days after to ninety-six miles, and so to 124, 154, and 200 miles. It will seem by this that a bird under twenty weeks old would have flown over 600 miles in races alone. This is what many birds do, but it is perhaps forcing matters too far. The racing season is then over for the year, and the following year the bird will go over the same ground again and on to, say, 250 miles; though some few birds go through to 350. In the fast race from Marennes several yearlings flew over 520 miles and were well up in the prizes. For long distance work, the third to fifth season is undoubtedly the best, though birds have been known to work well for nine or ten years, and in some rare cases to much older.

In conclusion, the training of the homing pigeon is a most fascinating pastime, and, granted a real love of animals to begin with, and sufficient time to study the birds and to attend to their training and feeding, there is no reason why success should not follow one's efforts.

W. BANCROFT.

HORSE—THE ARABIAN—The Arabian horse—in Arabic *Kehailan*—is probably the most ancient of existing domestic breeds. He is also the original "thoroughbred" horse of the East, from whose exemplar all Western ideas of thorough breeding in horseflesh were derived. He has been held in repute as of "noble" blood for at least 1,300 years, and has been bred with fanatical reverence and pure from all foreign admixture in peninsular Arabia as far back as the records of that country go; that is to say, till the second century before Mohammed, the sixth of our era.

It is a matter of considerable dispute in modern science whether or not the Kehailan was indigenous to Arabia as an original wild breed. The common Mohammedan tradition would make him a gift from Solomon to the Arabs, or, again, descended from mares ridden by the prophet; but Western criticism rightly rejects these tales, nor are they, in truth, real Bedouin traditions local to Arabia itself. The local tradition is that the Kehailan is a separate wild breed kept pure in the desert from the time of his first capture and domestication; that his habitat was Nejd and the high plateaux of Yemen, and that he owes his distinguishing qualities to the fact that his original blood has never been mixed with that of breeds of inferior type. In physical science there is as yet nothing positively ascertained which would show this to be improbable. The high plateaux of Arabia, though all of them desert land—in the sense that they contain no district where crops can be grown in full dependence on the rainfall—are neither without pasture nor without water. It is unquestionable that the wild ass existed, if he does not still exist, in Yemen, and the wild horse too may have there existed. In the sandy tracts there is a certain fine grass called *nossi*, which grows freely, especially within range of the occasional monsoon rains, and it is excellent pasture for horses, so that it is quite conceivable that in the gradual drying up of the peninsula, of which we have geological proof, a section of the wild species may have found itself cut off in the South from the rest of its kind, and have developed there in isolation the special qualities we find in the Kehailan. This is Professor Ewart's opinion, and, in the absence of evidence contradicting it, may be provisionally accepted as true. On the other hand, what historical evidence does exist is adverse to the idea of a very early possession of the horse as a tame animal in Arabia. The Bedouins, certainly of Northern Arabia, would seem during the ages immediately preceding Christ to have been, as indeed many of them are still, exclusively camel-riders, and there is a significant absence of all mention of the horse in lists which have been preserved of the then products of the country. Strabo, on the authority of his friend Ælius Gallus, Prefect of Egypt, who made an armed expedition into Western Arabia in the year A.D. 24, says of Arabia Felix (Yemen): "The products of the soil are good. Much honey is made and much cattle reared, amongst which, it is true, are seen neither horses nor mules"; and again of the land of the Nabatheans (Hejaz): "the land does not produce horses, but camels take their place."

The monumental French work of M. Piètrement, *Les Chevaux préhistoriques et historiques*, should be consulted on this point, his opinion being, that the Arabs did not become horse riders till the third century after Christ. In English our best authority on the subject, though perhaps rather out of date, Colonel Hamilton Smith, is of a similar opinion; and on historic grounds alone the balance of evidence would seem to be in favour of a comparatively late date for the domestication of the Kehailan. All that we know positively is that in the fifth and sixth centuries of our era the Bedouins of Nejd and Yemen were already possessed of a special breed of horses of which they boasted as an "ancestral possession." "Are not these," says their poets of that date, "an inheritance from our fathers? Shall not we to our sons in turn bequeath them?" It is clear too from their descriptions that the horse then possessed by them was identical in his chief characteristics

"AZREK," AGED TEN YEARS.

A pure Anazeh horse, bred in the desert.

with the modern Kehailan, as were the ideas of his owners concerning him. There is a description in one of the Abu Zeyd cycle of romances of a Bedouin mare, which is precise in its details and which might have been written yesterday:—

"*Spare is her head and lean, her ears pricked close together,*
Her forelock is a net, her forehead a lamp lighted,
Illumining the tribe, *her neck curved like a palm branch,*
Her wither sharp and clean. Upon her chest and throttle
An amulet hangs of gold. Her forelegs are twin lances.
Her hoofs fly forward faster ever than flies the whirlwind,
Her tail bone borne aloft, yet the hairs sweep the gravel."

Nor are prose writers silent. Ockley, in his *History of the Saracens*, quotes from the Arab historian, El Wakidi, a decree of the Caliph Omar, A.D. 633, which shows the value already set in Arabia on this special breed. "After the battle of Yermuk," El Wakidi says, "Abu Obeidah, the Arabian commander, divided the spoil thus: 'To a horseman he gave thrice as much as to a footman, and made a further difference between those horses which were *of the right Arabian breed* (which they looked upon to be far the best) and those that were not, allowing twice as much to the former as to the latter. And when they were not satisfied with the distribution Abu Obeidah told them that the Prophet had done the same after the battle of Khaibar, which upon appeal to Omar was by him confirmed.'"

Of European authors the oldest I can find mentioning the Arabian horse as a special and valued breed is Marco Polo. He, writing about the year 1290, says of Arabia and the Port of Aden: "It is from this Port of Aden that the merchants obtain the fine Arabian destriers of which they make such great profit in India, for you must know that they sell in India a good horse for well one hundred marks of silver and more."

It is certain, however, that long before this the Kehailan must have made his way into Europe, for the first time doubtless in the van of the Arab invasions of the eighth and ninth centuries, which having swept across North Africa, passed over into Spain, and through Spain into France. Here he left his trace permanently in the Barb and the Andalusian, and, as is locally believed, in the French Limousin. The great value however of the Kehailan blood does not seem to have been fully recognised in Europe until the practice of wearing heavy armour in war was well on the decline, and it was then introduced rather through Turkey and the Barbary States than directly from Arabia. Leo Africanus, a Moor of the sixteenth century, who had travelled through the whole of North Africa and of the Arabian deserts from Timbuctoo as far as the Persian Gulf and allowed himself to be converted to Christianity at Rome, makes an interesting mention in his description of Africa of the Arabian horses, which, under the name of Barbs, began at that time to be renowned in Europe, and which is of especial value as showing the close connection between the Barb and the Arab. "This name (of Barb)," he says, "is given unto the Barbarie horses throughout Italy and all Europe, because they come foorth of Barbarie and are a kind of horses that are bred in those regions, but they which thinke so are deceived, for the horses of Barbarie differ not in any respect from other horses; but horses of the same swiftness and agilitie are in the Arabian toong called throughout all Egypt, Syria, Asia, Arabia Felix, and Deserta by the name of Arabian horses. Historiographers affirme that this kind of wild horse ranging up and down the Arabian deserts ever since the time of Ismael have so exceedingly multiplied and increased that they have replenished the most part of Africa; which opinion savoureth of truth, for even at this present there are great store of wilde horses founde both in the African and Arabian deserts. And I myself saw in the Numidian Desert a wilde colte of a white colour and having a curled maine. The most certain triall of these horses is when they can overtake the beast called lant or the ostrich in a race; which if they be able to performe they are esteemed woorth a thousand ducats or an hundred camels." The *lant* (eland?), he explains, "is so exceeding swift that no beast can overtake him, but only the Barbarie horse as is beforesaid." He also affirms that "the Arabians of the desert take the wilde horse and eate him, but he will hardly be taken with either horses or dogs. In the waters where this beast keepeth they lay certain snares, covering them over with sand, wherein his foot being caught he is entangled and slaine." The writer of this monograph quite recently received identically the same account as this of Leo's from a negro of Wadai, who spoke of the wild horses still captured there as Kehail. He described the method of snaring them, and declared that when tamed they could go ten days without water. The Arabs of Wadai used them as sires with their tame mares.

In England we first hear of "Barbs" in Charles II.'s time, when the "Royal Mares" were brought for the King from Tangiers, and about the same time of "Turks," captured in the wars in Hungary. It was not however till the beginning of the eighteenth century that the great success of the "Darley Arabian," a horse of undoubted Kehailan blood and purchased direct from the Arabs of Northern Arabia by Mr. Darley, our Consul at Aleppo, revealed to English breeders the true source of excellence in Eastern blood. From this date the importations registered in the Stud Book show a constantly increasing preponderance of "Arabians," as against Barbs or Turks. They were, I imagine, obtained direct from the Syrian Ports or the Persian Gulf; and there is every probability, judging from such portraits of them as remain to us, that they were pure Kehailans, though of the Darley Arabian alone we know the particular strain of blood, Mánaki, to which he belonged.

Captain Upton, in his interesting book *Newmarket and Arabia*, enumerates 101 Arabian stallions, 44 Barbs, and 28 Turks, as having been registered first and last in our Stud Book. The importation was well maintained until near the close of the eighteenth century, when it seems to have been interrupted by the great war which then began and which made communication with the Levant difficult.

It would be an interesting speculation to calculate the amount of true Kehailan blood flowing in the veins of our modern English racehorse, but it is one on which I dare not enter here, beyond hazarding the opinion that it amounts to at least three-quarters, perhaps to seven-eighths, of the whole. It may well be that even the unknown English mares figuring at the head of most pedigrees were in fact partly of this blood, either through Barb or Turk or Spanish ancestors—while in the male line the blood of the Darley and Godolphin Arabians is everywhere preponderant. The Godolphin, though reaching Europe through Tunis, was almost certainly an Arabian, as his original name, "Scham" (Damascus), would seem to indicate.

The price of Arab horses in the seventeenth and eighteenth centuries seems to have been high. Henry Blount, 1634, says that in Egypt in his day as much as 1,000 pieces of eight was paid for a three-year-old of the true breed; Hamilton, 1720, mentions £50 and £60 as being a small price for one at Moccha, and Niebuhr, 1762, says: "The English sometimes purchase their horses at the price of 800 or 1,000 crowns each." An English merchant was offered at Bengal twice the purchase money for one of their horses, but he sent him to England, where he hoped that he would draw four times the original price (say £800). The *Sporting Gentleman's Dictionary*, 1735, mentions still higher sums "£500, £1,000, £2,000, and even £3,000;" as "the intolerable price" demanded for the "right Arabian horses" exported from Scanderoon, pricing at the same time the Turkish horses at £100 to £150 and the Barbs at but £30 in their own countries. In 1782 Arthur Young records that at the Royal Stud of Pompadour in France three Arab horses had just been acquired at a cost to the King of 72,000 livres (£3,149).

In former days the Kehailan was bred in most Arabic speaking lands with more or less purity. Egypt, Syria, and South-Western Persia, to say nothing of the Barbary States, had their own breeds, which boasted of pure Arab origin; but at present the area of his distribution has been restricted even in Arabia itself within comparatively narrow limits, and there are indications of a decline of the race which seems to be becoming general. Egypt, with the exception of the single stud of Ali Pasha Sherif, possesses no pure blood, nor is it to be found in Tunis, Tripoli, or Algeria. In southern Morocco the tradition of pure breeding, if preserved at all, is so only among the remote desert tribes beyond the Atlas—who still boast of possessing strains of blood brought with them in their migrations from Nejd in the thirteenth and fourteenth centuries. Syria is almost stripped of its authentic breeds, once numerous in the Lebanon; and although a considerable sprinkling of pure mares is still to be found in Homs, Hama, and Aleppo, and in the villages of the Euphrates, their quality is far from what it used to be; so much so that the horse-buying commissions sent by the French and other European Governments find it yearly more difficult to acquire stallions of standard merit. In Mesopotamia the breed is becoming more and more mixed, and in all the Bagdad district it has long been a by-word. A few good mares are still to be found in Persian

Arabistan but the great studs of the Bakhtiari chiefs are gone, and it is very doubtful whether any pure blood at all is to be found now in Persia proper. Pure Kehailan blood may therefore be considered as confined in the present day strictly to Arabia, and even there within ever narrowing limits.

"MESAOUD," A PURE BRED SEGLAUR; TEN YEARS OLD.

The reasons of this general decline are, first, the ever-increasing military pressure of the Ottoman Government, which has broken the independence of the tribes on the Arabian frontier and limited their areas of summer pasture. Secondly, the gradual adoption of firearms by the Bedouins in their inter-tribal wars, and thirdly, the more systematic "combing" of the desert for stallions for the Indian market. It has been found that, wherever firearms take the place of the lance, there the tribesmen care less about their horses and revert to their original camel-riding in their raids. It is certain too that for many years past the handsomest and strongest colts have been taken away more and more unsparingly from the strength of the breeding stock, while the tribes have contented themselves with less and less perfect stallions for their stud use. The blood has remained the same, but the stock has declined in vigour, in beauty, and in excellence.

The following is a list of all the tribes of whom it can safely be affirmed at the present moment, 1897, that they are possessed of the true Kehailan blood stock.

Sebaa, Fedaan, Ibn Haddal } Anazeh

Kahtan	Montefik
Muteyr	Oteybeh
Ajman	Harb (a few)
Shammar	Beni Suleiman (a few)
Rowala	Daffiri.

There are also in Arabia certain studs still flourishing in the hands of princes and individuals which are recognised as authentic. The chief of these are the studs of the Emir Ibn Rashid at Hail, of Eid et Temimi at Oneyzeh, of the Emir Ibn Khalifa at Bahreyn, and of the Sultan of Muscat. Outside Arabia the only Eastern stud of any importance recognised by the Arabs as authentic is that of Ali Pasha Sherif, at Cairo, which is held in great respect by them, as descended from the mares and horses collected, at the expense, it is said, of a million sterling, fifty years ago in Nejd by Abbas I., Viceroy of Egypt. The Ottoman Sultan's stud at Constantinople is of recent growth and of no special value. It is a collection of some 800 stallions, many of them of great beauty, but of which the pedigrees have been lost, and of some 40 mares, few of them "*mazbutat*" (of known pedigree) or of the first quality. In India fine horses abound in the stables of the native princes, especially at Jodpore, and in the hands of the rich Bombay merchants, but few mares; and I do not know of any Indian stud exclusively managed on the Arabian principles of breeding. The Indian Government in 1893 had 147 Arab stallions in stud use in Bombay and the Northern provinces. These had been purchased at from 1,200 to 2,000 rupees, but the price has since risen. In Europe the oldest Arab studs are those of Prince Sanguscko and Count Joseph Potocki, in Poland, both of high quality, which date from the end of the last century, and of the Branicki family in the Ukraine. Although the pedigrees in these are imperfect from an Arab point of view, they all contain mares of fine Arabian type, especially Prince Sanguscko's, and supply magnificent chargers to the Russian Imperial cavalry. Next to these come the Royal Stud of Wurtemberg and the Austro-Hungarian Imperial Studs at Libitza and Babolna, at all which establishments great care has been taken in the acquisition of Kehailan mares as well as horses. In Italy there was in the time of King Victor Emmanuel a truly magnificent stud, containing as it did half of Abbas Pasha's famous collection. But it was unfortunately sold and dispersed at the King's death in 1878; while in France, though Arab stallions are largely used for cross breeding, there is still no pure Kehailan "Haras." Prussia has quite recently been endowed by the Emperor William with a pure stud at Neustadt; but Spain, Portugal, and the rest of the European States are still unrepresented. In England the first attempt to breed from pure Arabian mares as well as horses was made by Mr. Chaplin in 1875, who sent Captain Upton, an enthusiast on the subject, to Aleppo, where with the help of Mr. Skene, H.M. Consul, he purchaased some authentic stock. But ill luck attended the venture. The best stallion died, and one or two of the best mares proving barren, the project was shortly after abandoned. It was revived, however, in 1877 by the writer of this monograph on a larger scale and with better results. The Crabbet Park Stud, established in the autumn of that year, now numbers some thirty brood mares of the most authentic strains of blood, the produce of which are sold yearly by auction and realise good prices. The average of all sales during the last fifteen years from the stud stands as high as 110 guineas. It is carried on on strict Arabian principles, and as there is no attempt at increasing the height of the stock, the Kehailan type has been well preserved. It has supplied breeding stallions to nearly every part of the globe, including North and South America, South Africa, Australia, India, and even Turkey. The Honourable Miss Dillon's stud at Pudlicote, started in 1884, has won many prizes in open jumping competitions.[1]

In America Arab breeding was commenced some twenty years ago by Mr. Huntington, and has subsequently been taken up, but on no large scale, by others. Several small studs exist in Australia, and Arab stallions and mares have lately been imported by Mr. Cecil Rhodes into South Africa. It may be hoped, therefore that any falling off there may be in his original home is being compensated to the Kehailan elsewhere.

The total census of the Arabian horse cannot be large. Of quite pure authentic blood there are probably not 2,000 brood mares left in Peninsular Arabia, with perhaps as many more among the northern tribes—5,000, let us say, the world through, all counted.

The Bedouin system of breeding is one rigid in its principles. The noble tribes divide their mares into three categories. 1. The *Mazbutat* (authentic) mares, of absolutely certain pedigree, their ancestors having been from time immemorial in the tribe. From these alone colts are chosen as stallions for the tribe, all others being sold away as yearlings. 2. Mares taken from other noble tribes and their descendants. These are often authentic, their pedigree being known. But their colt produce is disqualified, and even one of their own Mazbutat mares, if lost and bred from away from the tribe, remains on her return disclassed. 3. Mares of unknown pedigree. These in the best tribes are used for riding only, and are not bred from. They go by the name of *Shimalieh*, Northerners, or Kadisheh, mares of no breed, the Mazbutat mares being sometimes called *Nejdieh*, of Nejd, in distinction, though there is no such thing as a "Nejd" breed.

All authentic mares claim to be descended from certain original strains of Kehailan blood. The most notable are the Seglawi, Managhi, Abeyan, Hamdani, Dahman, Hadban, Jilfan, Toweysan, Saadan, and Wadnan. The five first are generally known as the "Khamsa." The pedigrees are chiefly remembered through the dams, the blood of the sire being taken for granted as always beyond question. These are not written in the desert, but kept by oral tradition. Within the tribe the blood of each mare is of common notoriety and so is not a subject for deception, but strangers need to be on their guard.

The single object for which the Kehailan is bred by the Bedouins is service in their wars. For this the qualities necessary are great powers of endurance, the capacity of making long marches, of 300 or 400 miles, without flagging, an extreme sobriety in the matter of food and drink, and a sufficient turn of speed at the end of the raid to overtake the enemy or elude pursuit. Mere speed over a short distance is not encouraged by any system of racing or trials. The sole practical test is in the raid ("ghazu," Italianised "razzia"). What is of at least equal importance with speed, inasmuch as all fighting is done with the lance, is perfect shoulder action, facility in turning, a light mouth, intelligence and courage. All these qualities are conspicuous in the true Kehailan, and seem inherent in his blood. The rigorous conditions of his desert life ensure a certain hardihood of constitution; his feet are of iron. He stands unsheltered night and day; he is hardened against hot sunshine and bitter winds. The Bedouin camp is a perpetual turmoil of noise: he is bold and cool-headed. From his foalhood the children have crawled among his feet in the tents: he has the temper of a lamb. He is made for the vicissitudes of campaigning life, and is thus the most complete light cavalry horse imaginable for all countries where hard work and short commons, especially under a burning sun, are the rule of the campaign.

As a racehorse, the Kehailan, though not scientifically bred for the purpose, would seem to have in him a natural quality of speed superior to any other natural breed. Neither the Tartar of Eastern Asia, nor the Cossack, nor any of the unimproved European breeds, can at all compare with him on this head; and it is only his own illegitimate descendant, the English thoroughbred, that has at length distanced him. For over a hundred years he figured victorious against all comers on the Indian turf, and until quite recently he held his own there even against English blood. Latterly, however, he has become less in fashion in India, and has had to give place on most racecourses to the improved Waler, who, thoroughbred or nearly thoroughbred, has been found able to beat him at an allowance. At the present time Arab racing proper is nearly confined to the Bombay Presidency, where the horses arriving from the Persian Gulf are first landed. Here the general price given for a Kehailan of the best strains is from 1,500

1 The Duke of Bedford, Lord Warwick, Mr. Vidal and Mr. Stephens, M.P., are also breeders of the pure stock.

to 2,000 rupees before he has been tried for racing, or 2,500 to 3,000 when tried successfully. In the rest of India, Arabs figure mainly as polo ponies, and are run in races of that class when under the standard height. In the palmy days of Arab racing in India, the performances of the best horses were very nearly on a time level with those of our own thoroughbreds.

On the English turf it is rather as a sire of racehorses than as himself a racehorse that the Kehailan is honoured. Few of the imported Arabs, even of the eighteenth century, distinguished themselves as winners; and in the present century, no pure Kehailan has carried off an important race. The last Eastern horse entered for any of our classic contests was in 1863, when the Duke of Beaufort's Barb "Mazagan" ran for the Goodwood Cup, high hopes being entertained of him by his owner and trainer; but in the event he was easily beaten. In 1883, through the exertions of Lord Calthorpe, Lord Bradford, Prince Batthyani, Mr. Edward Weatherby and others, the Jockey Club, in the interests of horse breeding, consented to the establishment of a special race for Arabs, to be run at Newmarket yearly at their July meeting; and a single contest took place in accordance with their decision in the following year. Fifteen Arabians were entered and eight of them appeared at the post, including two that had run well on the Indian turf, with the result that Admiral Tryon's "Asil," a three-year-old colt, bred in England from an Anazeh mare imported in foal from Aleppo, proved the winner. The same colt however was shortly afterwards beaten in a match by "Jambic," an English thoroughbred of inferior class; and this was considered so discouraging that the Arab race has not since been renewed. The superiority of the English thoroughbred on the flat cannot indeed be contested. At the same time it is by no means proved that a new infusion of Kehailan blood would not be an advantage to breeders for our turf; and Lord Bradford's experience is encouraging. From Arab mares mated with Bend Or and Chippendale he has had produce in the second and even in the first generation which have proved winners of good English races, notably of the Dee Stakes at Chester, and he is continuing the experiment.

The practical value however of the Kehailan lies undoubtedly in his *rôle* of sire to half-bred stocks, especially for all such countries as suffer from extremes of heat and cold, drought, poverty of pasture and general hard conditions of life. For this purpose he is inestimable, for he has the power of transmitting to his half-bred offspring his own enduring qualities, with much of his speed, action and courage, and no little of his beauty. In this he is superior to any but the very highest class of our English thoroughbreds, and has been successful wherever he has been fairly tried. Certain rules however are very necessary to be laid down in the choice of Arabians as stallions, the neglect of which will lead to failure; and, as it is a subject not well understood, I think I cannot do better than close this monograph with a few practical suggestions in the interest of breeders.

The first point in choosing an Arab stallion, as indeed any other, for stud use is to be certain of his blood. Unless the horse chosen can show a clean Kehailan pedigree it will always be a matter of chance whether his stock proves satisfactory. Many a stout horse on the Indian turf has proved a despicable sire, and many an unconsidered slug a good one. Apart however from pedigree, and where this cannot be ascertained, there are certain characteristics of shape and figure which very seldom mislead, and a certain ideal type without an approximation to which no Arabian ever yet proved of value as a stock getter. The Arabian points are not very different from those of our English thoroughbred sires of eighty and a hundred years ago; and there are half-a-dozen representations in the collection of *Portraits of Celebrated Race-horses*, which might stand for those of Kehailans of the highest type. Such are "Flying Childers" (the portrait without the saddle), "Sedbury" 1734, "Dungannon" 1780, his grandson "Walton" 1792, his great grandson "Partizan" 1811, and above all, "Sultan" 1816, an almost perfect type of the pure Kehailan. "Actaeon" 1822, and "Venison" 1833, are the latest that show any strong Arabian character in this collection, all the recent portraits having diverged widely from the type. If the reader wishes to contrast the Arab points with those of the modern thoroughbred, he cannot do better than set the portrait of "Sultan" side by side with that of the great modern racehorse Fisherman. Of living "English" sires "Petrarch" and "Bend Or" come nearest to the Kehailan type.

The best Arabian sires are about 14 hands 2 inches high, of great thickness through, depth and substance, but very short on the leg and with the shortest possible cannon bones, the feet large, deep and perfectly round; the legs clean and flat, with a fair amount of bone, say 7½ to 8 inches below the knee; powerful forearms and second thighs; broad knees and hocks; but a greater development of bone than 8 inches seldom goes with the highest quality. The horse should cover a deal of ground, but should have a short back, with just sufficient space between the wither and the rise of the loins for a short saddle. The wither should be high (this is an original Kehailan characteristic found in no other natural breed), but not exaggerated, and the highest point of the croup should be nearly level with it. It is a great point of breeding that the tail should be set on high and that it should rise at an angle of about 45 degs. from the point of insertion, curving however sharply downwards so as just to clear the hocks in walking. It is no defect that the tail should hang a little sideways, that being often the effect of a twist given it at the foal's birth by the Bedouin breeder for luck. Both mane and tail should be fine as silk and fairly abundant, never heavy. The shoulder should be well sloped, but without the exaggeration of the English hunter's. It should have, however, the freest possible action, and there is no better test of quality than to turn a colt loose in a paddock and take note of how he moves his shoulders and fore-arms. There should be little high knee-action, but the whole limb should be thrown forward and the hoof "dwell" a second in the air before it is put down. This, with corresponding action behind—like that of a deer trotting through fern—is most important in a sire and a great test of quality. The most characteristic point however of all in the Kehailan is his head. It is difficult to describe this intelligibly. It should be very broad between the eyes, the forehead high and slightly convex, but with a sudden upward turn of the profile, such as is seen in the gazelle. This can hardly be too exaggerated. The muzzle should be extremely fine, the lips delicately compressed, the nostrils set somewhat high and on a plane with the face in repose, but capable of great expansion when excited; great depth of the cheek bones and width at the throttle; great distance between the eyes and the ears, the head well set on and the neck arched. The following are the exact measurements of "Mesaoud," bred by Ali Pasha Sherif, the most successful stallion of the Crabbet Park Stud, also of the head of "Sherifa," a Nejd mare bred by the Emir Feysul Ibn Saoud, both admirable types.

Measurements of "Mesaoud" at ten years of age:—Height, 14 hands 2 inches; girth, 69 inches; from summit of skull to wither, 38 inches; from wither to root of tail, 41 inches; tail bone, 18 inches; from summit of skull to point of muzzle, $23\frac{3}{4}$ inches; round jowl and forehead, 37 inches; round muzzle, $19\frac{1}{2}$ inches; wither to knee, 45 inches; knee to pastern, $11\frac{1}{2}$ inches; point of hip to point of hock, 40 inches; point of hock to fetlock joint, $17\frac{1}{2}$ inches; round forearm, 19 inches; round cannon bone, $7\frac{3}{4}$ inches; round hoof, 16 inches; length of ear from junction with skull, $5\frac{3}{4}$ inches.

Measurements of the head of "Sherifa":—From summit of skull to point of muzzle, 24 inches; round jowl and forehead, 36 inches; round muzzle, $14\frac{1}{2}$ inches; width between cheeks $5\frac{1}{2}$ inches.

The best Kehailan colours are—1. Bay with black points. This would seem to have been the original wild colour, and is that principally esteemed by the Bedouins, especially a dark full bay with the black markings well above the knees and hocks. 2. Chestnut, a strong bright chestnut with mane and tail of the same shade, accompanied generally with three or four white feet and a blaze. These markings are commoner among the Anazeh tribes than in Nejd. Pale shades of chestnut should be avoided, but a sprinkling of white hair is no disadvantage. 3. White. This, when quite pure, is perhaps the best as it is the most beautiful of all colours. It is the "fortunate" colour with Mohammedans, and for this reason has been more carefully bred for than any other. The most perfect Kehailan types I have seen have been white, or in advancing years flea-bitten. No Kehailan however is ever foaled white, and

"Bint Nure," Brood Mare.

for the first five years colts go through many changes of coat, from bay, chestnut or nearly black to rose-roan, iron grey and grey. A white stallion should not be used as sire, says Guarmani, till he attains his full white colour at eight years old. White is the favourite colour in Nejd; and all the great collections have been mainly white, notably Ibn Saoud's at Riad, described by Palgrave, Abbas Pasha's in Egypt, and Ibn Rashid's at Haïl. Except in the Sultan's stables at Yildiz, I have never seen a quite black Arabian, and I doubt black being a true Kehailan colour, though Bedouins say it occasionally occurs. Dun, blue-roan, and piebald certainly are not. The skin, where clear of hair, especially round the eyes, should be in all cases of a deep slaty blue. The eyes should be large and prominent, and shaped like the human eye, the white showing well round the cornea. This is very characteristic of the true Kehailan.

The chief modern works to be consulted on the subject are:—

Piétremont's *Chevaux Préhistoriques et Historiques.*
Doughty's *Travels in Arabia Deserta.*
Naturalist's Library, Section by Colonel Hamilton Smith.
Upton's *Newmarket and Arabia.*

Lieut.-Colonel Hallen's *Reports to the Indian Government*, 1892-3.
Palgrave, *Travels in Central Arabia.*
Lady Anne Blunt's *Bedovins of the Euphrates.*
" " " *Pilgrimage to Nejd.*
General Tweedie's *Arabian Horse.*
Sidney's *Book of the Horse.*

WILFRED BLUNT.

HORSES—THE BRITISH THOROUGHBRED—**British Ancestry**—What combination of causes produced the British thoroughbred it would be almost futile to inquire, for the combination was in most cases more or less fortuitous, and the extraordinary result must have been, in the last century, quite unexpected. It is not intended here to deal in detail with the origin of our horses, but it may be stated with absolute confidence that while vitality, quality and stamina were gained from Eastern sources, speed was in the first instance derived from the native English breed. This proposition can have its truth on the one part demonstrated to-day by the fact that not the highest caste Arab, however admirable for other purposes, can gallop even as against a polo pony of its own size, while on the other hand we know from Gervase Markham that the native English-bred horses did excel in speed, long before the stud-book was thought of. Thus, he writes :

"Again, for swiftness, what nation hath brought forth a horse which hath exceeded the English ?—when the best Barbaries that ever were in their prime, I saw them overrunne by a black hobbie at Salisbury ; yet that hobbie was more overrunne by a horse called Valentine, which Valentine, neither in hunting or running was ever equalled, yet was a plain bred English horse both by syre and dam."

The incident referred to was described as above in the reign of James I, and it may be further gathered that during that reign the public races were contested by a breed distinct from, and more speedy than, Arabs ; that is to say, a native breed, including "hobbies," which had preserved the native distinctions of form and head, but had never been surpassed by the very best Arabs ever raced against them.

"In other words," writes that veteran authority, Mr. Joseph Osborne, "the breed was British because it was Britain that produced its excellence, and it retained the native characteristics in a paramount degree despite any Eastern crosses that may have been in it." The Arab blood exercised a purifying, refining influence which has, by luck rather than design, built up on the native British foundation the extraordinary thoroughbred which we now know ; but it is clear that, without such a foundation, that result could never have been achieved. Many nations have had greater facilities than England for using Eastern blood, but none have succeeded in producing horses of anything like such character, insomuch that the British thoroughbred has to be imported, not merely for racing, but for the production of cavalry remounts and other active horses, to all parts of the world, and without constant recurrence to the parent stock the breed, save in Great Britain and Ireland, can nowhere be maintained without degeneration.

Arabian Blood—Without going further into the origin of the British thoroughbred, it may be stated that every such animal in the stud book of the present day, in this country or in any other, descends in tail male from one of three original Eastern sires, the Darley Arabian, the Byerly Turk, or the Godolphin Arabian, or, to earmark them more clearly by their respective and responsible representatives, from Eclipse, Herod, or Matchem. Of course, in the composition of the horses of that day, a vast number of strains of blood, Eastern and otherwise, was involved, but the prepotency of the strongest lines in tail male gradually asserted itself, till only three families, as above stated, remained. Whereas the Godolphin and Byerly Turk lines were in the late days of the last century and the earlier ones of the present most strongly supported, the descendants of Eclipse have ever since been swamping the others, not only in this country, but all over the world. The extraordinary character of this phenomenon may be proved from the winning statistics of any recent year. Taking at random the season of 1893, we find there were in this country 709 tail male descendants of Eclipse who won 1,298 races, value £384,197, whereas there were but 41 winners claiming descent from the Godolphin Arabian, with 78 races, worth, in all, £19,116 to their credit ; and, from the Byerly Turk, 85 winners of 146 races, worth £33,280. Such a result as this cannot be explained away by the doctrine of mere chance, more especially when it is found that such Godolphin or Byerly Turk winners as exist are built up in almost every line of their pedigrees except the top one by the Darley Arabian.

Original Mares—Rightly to understand this remarkable situation, we have also to analyse descent in tail female, and here the eminent Australian authority, the late Mr. Bruce Lowe, whose *Breeding Racehorses by the Figure System* has already become a classic, renders invaluable assistance. He carries us back, not to the original sires, but to the original mares, and though these are more numerously represented in tail female at the present day than are the original sires in tail male, we none the less find an almost similar phenomenon—that a very few of them monopolise all the important winners of the past and present. Mr. Bruce Lowe based his figure system on the plain common-sense idea of judgment by results, and placed the original mares in order, 1, 2, 3, &c., in accordance with the number of classic winners (counting only Derby, Oaks, and Leger) which had descended in the female line from each of them. He also dealt with the further attribute of sire potency, inherent in certain of these families and due to robust native blood. These families he classed as "sire families," and attached to them an importance altogether apart from the order of merit by winning results, though number 3 family comes out successful under either test. and is, by consequence, perhaps the best family of all. To present a reasonable idea of this system, we give a list of the original mares placed in order according to classic results, the "sire families" being printed in black letters, and a sample or two of her descendants being given after each mare. The first five families are classed by Mr. Bruce Lowe as "running families," and are printed in italics, except No. 3, which, being also a sire family, is printed in black type.

THE ALLOTMENT OF FIGURES.

No.	*Original Mares.*	*Descendants.*
1	Tregonwell's Natural Barb mare	Whalebone, Minting.
2	Burton's Barb mare	Voltigeur, Blacklock.
3	The Dam of Two True Blues	Stockwell, Sir Peter.
4	Layton Barb mare	Matchem, Thormanby.
5	Dau. of Massey's Black Barb	Gladiateur, Hermit.
6	Old Bald Peg	Priam, Diomed.
7	Darcy's Black Legged Royal mare	W. Australian, Donovan.
8	Bustler mare (dam of Byerly Turk mare)	Marske, Newminster, Sultan.
9	Old Wintner mare	Mercury, Bendigo, Peter.
10	Dau. of Gower's stallion	Blair Athol, Hampton.
11	Sedbury Royal mare	Regulus, Birdcatcher, St. Simon.
12	A Royal mare (Montagu mare)	Eclipse, Sterling, Prince Rudolph.
13	A Royal mare (dam of Turk mare)	Highflyer, Orlando.
14	The Oldfield mare	Touchstone, Macaroni.
15	Royal mare (dam of Old Whynot)	Soothsayer, Jerry, Coxhall.
16	Sister to Stripling by Hutton's Spot	Ormonde and Agnes family.
17	Byerly Turk mare	Pantaloon, Yattendon.
18	Old Woodcock mare (dam of Old Spot mare)	Waxy, Trenton (Aus.)
19	Dau. of Davill's Old Woodcock	Isonomy, Sir Hugo.
20	Dau. of Gascoigne's Foreign horse	Citadel, Traducer (N.Z.), Ghuznee.
21	Moonah Barb mare	Sweetmeat, Lonely.
22	Belgrade Turk mare	Gladiator, St. Blaise.
23	Piping Peg	Ossian, Barcaldine.
24	Helmsley Turk mare	Camel, The Baron, Hindoo (Am.)
25	Brimmer mare	Y. Melbourne, Comus, Sefton.
26	Merlin mare	Herod, Promised Land.
27	Spanker mare	Saunterer, Pero Gomez.
28	Dau. of Place's White Turk	Emilius, Dalesman.
29	Natural Barb mare (dam of Bosset Arab mare)	Landscape, Ashton.
30	Dau. of Duc de Chartres' Hawker	Paris, Delpini, Stamford.
31	Dick Barton's Barb mare	Ruler, Fazzoletto.
32	Barb mare (Dodsworth's dam)	Nike, Fitz Gladiator.

No.	*Original Mares.*	*Descendants.*
33	Sister to Honeycombe Punch	Sergeant, Dungannon.
34	Hautboy mare	Antonio, Birmingham.
35	Dau. of Bustler	Haphazard, Bustard (Castrel).
36	Dau. of Curwen's Bay Barb	Economist, Old Engineer.
37	Sister to Old Merlin	Dr. Syntax, Little Red Rover.
38	Thwait's Dun Mare	Pot-8-os.
39	Bonny Black	Dagworth (Aus.).
40	Royal mare (dam of Brimmer)	Boston (Am.).
41	Grasshopper mare	Bagot, Portrait.
42	Spanker mare	Oiseau, Cestus.
43	Natural Barb mare (Emperor of Morocco's gift)	Balfe, Underhand.

It would be absurd to produce here any mere theories, but results render the figure system incontrovertible. To put it in a nutshell, there have been 358 winners of the Derby, Oaks, and Leger, and the original mares still represented number 43, or rather more; but of the 358 winners no fewer than 202 trace in tail female to those *five* original mares whom Mr. Bruce Lowe numbered as the "running families."

A remarkable confirmation of this position has been furnished by the eminent German authority, Mr. Hermann Goos, who for some years past has published pedigree tables tracing all horses that are or have been of note in England or on the Continent to their original female sources. He has in his last edition adopted Mr. Bruce Lowe's figures, which, as already explained, are based only on the results of the English Derby, Oaks, and Leger, but the record of these original mares based on all the other big races in England and on the Continent comes out substantially the same; and of the 50 original mares from which Mr. Goos traces descendants of some note, there are no fewer than 11,618 representatives indexed and accounted for in his tables. These are animals that have won in France, Germany, Austria, and elsewhere, besides England, from the last century until now, and of these no fewer than 4,622—a really amazing proportion, all things considered—descend from the first five mares out of the fifty; in other words, from the "running" families.

It follows almost as a necessary consequence of the above facts that a prudent breeder of bloodstock will, so far as tail male representation goes, secure as much of the Darley Arabian as possible in any proposed pedigree, and in the tail female line at all points will follow without hesitation Mr. Bruce Lowe's figures, which simply show "form at a glance," and are no matter of mere scientific theory. To make the application of the figure system perfectly plain, a brief statement of a pedigree is here given, viz., St. Simon (11) by Galopin (3) out of St. Angela by King Tom (3). The figures indicate that St. Simon himself belongs to the No. 11

family (The Sedbury Royal Mare), and the same figure would of course attach to his dam and every other ancestress in tail female up to the original. Galopin, the sire of St. Simon, is of the No. 3 family (the dam of the two True Blues), as also is King Tom, the sire of St. Angela; and so the pedigree may be extended, the figure being added to each fresh horse in the combination, and showing at once how much of the most successful blood is represented.

The Stud Book—The first edition of the first volume of the *General Stud Book* was published in 1793, and the eighteenth volume has recently been issued by Messrs. Weatherby, whose firm has throughout maintained a high standard of accuracy in the work. No animal can be unconditionally admitted to the book whose pedigree cannot be traced at all points of it to the first volume; but as a question has arisen over the admission of Australasian and American bred race horses, which in some cases take in strains native to their own countries, their inclusion in the English stud book is subject in each instance to a note of reference to the Australian or American stud book, as the case may be. In France, Germany, and throughout the Continent, the race horses are purely English in blood.

The result of the last hundred years of careful breeding and development has been a distinct and continuous improvement of the breed both in size, power, and quality. It is thought by many that the prevalence of short distance racing and the early forcing of yearlings for sale and two-year-olds for racing has to some extent impaired constitution, soundness and stamina, and there may be a certain amount of truth in this view, more especially as the Irish bred horses, reared under more natural conditions, have of late been carrying all before them on the English turf; but there can be no real doubt that such horses as Isinglass, Persimmon and Galtee More—to mention only three of the best of recent years—can challenge comparison with any that have gone before them, both as commanding specimens of the horse in his highest development, and for first-class racing capacity over any distance.

Eclipse, Matchem, Herod—At the present day the descendants of Eclipse enormously outnumber the other two lines. Of Eclipse's three grandsons that survive in their descendants, Waxy is far the most numerously represented, as from his sons, Whalebone and Whisker, we get the great houses of Birdcatcher, Touchstone and Harkaway. Of these, Birdcatcher has asserted and is asserting supremacy, mainly through Stockwell, the most extraordinary sire of all time, whose blood is coming more than ever to the front this year through Kendal and others of his tail male descendants. The advent of Galopin, however, revived the Blacklock or King Fergus branch of Eclipse; and the Joe Andrews branch still lives pretty vigorously through the sons and grandsons of Beadsman. All these various branches of Eclipse, as now represented, differ widely in character, the Stockwells being remarkable for size, power and bone, the Galopins for light, wiry, bloodlike frames and fiery, excitable courage, the Beadsmans for truth of symmetry in a medium scale of size.

Matchem lives to-day only through Melbourne, and he again would all but have died out but for Solon. The characteristics of the family are well known. A typical member of it is heavy, very lengthy, lop-eared and short of quality; yet there have been brilliant horses among them, such as West Australian and Barcaldine. These however were very strongly fortified with Eclipse blood. Mares of Melbourne blood have been very successful, and Persimmon, no doubt, owes his size, bone and power to his dam having two Melbourne crosses.

The Herod line is but feebly represented to-day through descendants of Sweetmeat, Ion, Thormanby, the Flying Dutchman, and Lexington, the last-named of whom had three native American crosses. The characteristics of the family (not including Lexington) are neatness and quality rather than size or bone, though this cannot be said of the Wild Dayrells. Here again the blood has proved valuable in the making of brood mares, those by Macaroni at the present day being remarkably successful, while it was a Flying Dutchman mare that produced Galopin.

Breeders and Sales—In the last volume of the *Stud Book* 5,239 brood mares are accounted for in the year 1896. It is therefore apparent that the breeding of bloodstock is conducted on a very large scale in this country. The age of the thoroughbred horse dates in England and on the Continent from the 1st of January; in Australia it dates from the 1st of August, and this fact alone renders any weight for age comparison between English and Australian horses almost impossible. In England thoroughbred stock is largely bred for sale as yearlings, but a number of the leading supporters of the Turf, such as the Prince of Wales, the Duke of Westminster, the Duke of Portland, the Marquis of Zetland, the Earl of Durham, Sir J. Blundell Maple, Bart., the Earl of Rosebery, Mr. Leopold de Rothschild, Mr. Douglas Baird, &c., breed their own racing stock, and have this advantage over public breeders that they have not to make up their yearlings for sale, and are also able to place them all in the charge of first-rate trainers, so that each one gets a fair chance of showing any merit it may possess.

The principal sales of yearlings are held at Ascot, the Cobham Stud, the Newmarket July

Meetings, and at Doncaster, when very high prices are often realised, 6,000 guineas paid by Sir J. Blundell Maple for Childwick being the highest up to date. The December sales at Newmarket consist mostly of brood mares, foals, horses in training, and stallions. There is scarcely any limit to the value of the thoroughbred horse now that the stakes to be won are of such immense value, and a stallion like St. Simon can command a 500 guineas fee. Ormonde was actually sold for 30,000 guineas, and a similar sum was refused for Galtee More. Offers of 20,000 guineas each made by the late Colonel W. P. Thompson, of Brookdale, U.S.A., for Orme and Ladas were also refused, and Mr. J. E. Platt gave the equivalent of 20,000 guineas for Kendal. Sir J. Blundell Maple paid 15,000 guineas for Common.

THOROUGHBRED.

Yearlings, according to their growth and development, go into the trainer's charge at an early or late period of the second half of the year, and they are very commonly tried before the season is out. The merits of Bend Or were ascertained by Mr. Robert Peck in the September of that great horse's yearling days.

General Character of the Thoroughbred—Thoroughbred horses are mostly bay, brown or chestnut in colour. There are also greys, roans, and blacks, but never piebalds or (in these days) duns. Bred primarily for racing purposes, they have long since been found to be of almost inestimable value for the improvement of the breed of horses at large, excepting of course those devoted to heavy draught work. The severe test of training and racing proves better than anything else could do what really are the soundest and best constitutioned animals to breed from. The blood horse is infinitely superior to all half-breeds and commoners in the matter of courage and endurance. Even when degraded to the shafts of a hansom he thoroughly vindicates his class. The distinction was never more clearly marked than when the R.H.A. horses were returning from Egypt after Tel El Kebir, and some came in for shocking weather. On one transport they were overbalanced by the rolling of the vessel, and something over seventy of them simply lay and died. These were the commoners. But a thoroughbred Rosicrucian mare, though she was down at least a dozen times one night, always struggled up again and reached England fit and well. The value of a troop horse or hunter depends almost entirely on the number of crosses of blood that he has in him, no matter how good-looking he may be; and an actually thoroughbred hunter or charger is far away the best of all, but when up to weight is too valuable to suit average purses.

If it be asked wherein consists the individual character of the British thoroughbred, the answer is by no means a ready one; but it may be stated with confidence that the general conformation is one tending alike to speed and endurance — lengthy, oblique shoulders, deep brisket without width of chest, and yet plenty of heart room through the fore-ribs; greater length than in any other breed from hip to stifle and from stifle to hock, so that the hind stroke may resemble that of a greyhound; and that whether the horse stands high behind on a straight hock like Persimmon, or has the more regular type, or has "sickle" hocks, or hocks right away from him. One way or another he must have *length*, and compensating balances of action will often enable the most oddly shaped animal to defeat what seems a more level built one. Conformation, however, is only the outward show. The real value of the British thoroughbred is the vital essence which does not appear on the surface. In this connection it need only be observed that some lines of blood are inferior in gameness and constitution. The Hermit line is conspicuously at fault here so far as tail male descent goes, but curiously enough this breed has a great aptitude for jumping and is in its element at National Hunt Meetings.

Briefly, it may be stated in conclusion that the British thoroughbred is the most perfect animal of any sort yet produced in the world; that his value in improving all other breeds of horses except those devoted to heavy draught work is simply inestimable; that without racing, however, he would never have been produced, and without the continuance of racing his individual soundness, courage, and constitution could never be discovered. These are facts which it is hardly possible to question, and, as there is every reason to suppose that the sport of racing in this and other countries will continue to flourish, we may be pretty sure that the thoroughbred horse will go on from strength to strength, as he is more and more carefully bred.

W. ALLISON.

HUNTERS—If the combination of means, opportunity, and no more than a moderate bodily weight enable a man to own a thoroughbred hunter, he can desire nothing better. The blood horse is at all times, and, in the writer's opinion, in every country, the pleasantest and, as often as not, the easiest to ride. He can skim over Leicestershire, surmount the formidable earthworks which divide field from field in Devon, and can prove himself quite a hunter in every intermediate kind of country. If, therefore, the man who can ride can mount himself on a thoroughbred horse, so much the better for him; but the novice may well content himself with a more ordinary animal until he has learned enough to be able to utilise to the full the advantages the blood horse offers to him who really means "going."

It is a wonder that more men do not attend the various bloodstock sales and pick up some of the cheaper yearlings and two-year-olds. Plenty of "rubbish" is bred annually; but a horse as "slow as a man in boots" for racing purposes is nevertheless a fast hunter, while an unfashionable pedigree does not matter for the hunting field. Of course these youngsters will require to be thrown by and forgotten for a year or two, and they would be out of place in the stable of any one who cannot himself make them into hunters or obtain the services of some one who can.

As, however, the thoroughbred hunter is not common, men must ride something else, and hunters vary in character as much as they do in size. In the field one sees every possible type, from the horse which only just misses being thoroughbred, the old "cocktail" in fact, down to something very nearly related to the carthorse; while in size they range from fourteen to seventeen hands, with an occasional specimen below and above these heights. Thus it is

LIGHT-WEIGHT HUNTER.

practically impossible to put forward any stamp of horse as the true type of hunter, except in the highest class of horses, horses fit to carry fourteen stone and upwards up to the tail of the hounds in a stiffly fenced country.

Just as the tyro at fiddling can do with a less valuable instrument than a "Strad" or a "Joseph," so the novice at hunting can enjoy a great deal of amusement on a very moderate priced mount. Yet even this cheap conveyance must possess certain attributes. He must, of course, be workably sound; and here let it be written down as a rule never to be broken that no one should, under any temptation of price, buy a roarer. In nine hundred and ninety-nine times out of a thousand the infirmity will grow worse with each succeeding season; while the noise is unpleasant both to the rider and other members of the field. Again, no horse with defective vision should ever be bought for hunting, purposes, nor should the purchase of a horse suffering from fever in the feet or navicular be entertained, for no humane man would find pleasure in riding a horse which is suffering from pain, not to mention the fact that a steed so affected would bring next to nothing if offered for sale. Opinions differ as to the risk in riding "nerved" horses; but the novice had better keep clear of them.

The hunter on which early experience is gained should be temperate and bold, that is to say, he should go at his fences only just quick enough to inspire his rider with confidence, and jump his places cleanly enough to show the beginner that a fence is not such a terrible affair after all. A lad or man who learns on a slow sticky jumper will be a very long time in acquiring the art of getting readily over a country; but as the beginner will not be in a position to sit down and ride with the best and boldest, it will be no harm if his early mounts be rather aged and show some amount of wear. They will know their business, and teach the learner his, while blemishes, of course, will not matter in the least. Make and shape, however, must not be left out of consideration, not merely because a nicely made horse is pleasant to look upon, but because without a certain conformation a horse is no good for use in the hunting field. A horse with bad shoulders is not comfortable to ride; he will never gallop freely, and is very likely to fall when going down hill. Good quarters and hocks are equally necessary, or he will never spread himself over his fences or get up hill; if he is somewhat long in the back it does not matter. It is a cardinal defect in the show ring; but except when a very heavy weight has to be carried it makes little difference in the hunting field.

The visitor to a fashionable country, such as the Quorn, Pytchley, Mr. Fernie's, the Cottesmore, and others will at once be struck by the number of fine horses to be seen at the covert side. A few may be home-bred, and a few picked up by chance at comparatively small sums; but the majority will have been bought from dealers at a high price. The dealers making hunters their chief line of business have agents all over the horse-breeding districts, and they themselves travel about to pick up all the horses which they deem saleable. They have to be transported home, in many cases schooled and brought into better condition; frequently credit has to be given; and accident, disease, and death have to be reckoned with, so that by the time a really good horse reaches the buyer's stable he has cost a good deal of money. Any one, however, who has once ridden a really perfect hunter will cease to wonder at the large sums of money given for horses of the right kind. The hunter which can gallop fast, will not turn his head from anything, wants no rousing and but little holding, one that skims over water, and can jump timber, that will walk through a gap, and so spread himself at his fences as easily to clear an unexpectedly wide ditch on the far side is not to be picked up every day, and when found must be paid for.

Still there are hundreds of men who cannot afford hunters costing from a hundred and fifty to four hundred guineas, and who have, of necessity, to put up with something cheaper, though it must not be supposed that a long price necessarily means a good horse; while, on the other hand, many a first-rate hunter is bought at quite a low figure, and it frequently happens that a horse regarded by his owner as being no more than middling is found, when the question is asked him, to possess galloping and jumping abilities of a high order. Nor must it be forgotten that much, very much, depends upon the man in the saddle, for some men could never show to advantage on the most brilliant hunter that ever looked through a bridle, while others will "shove along," to use an expressive hunting field phrase, on almost anything.

HUNTER.

The upstanding, weight-carrying hunter necessarily commands the most money, owing to his scarceness. He must show as much quality as possible, and be able to gallop and jump with the lighter horses; and hunters fit to carry men like the late Mr. Heywood-Lonsdale, Master of the Shropshire, or the late Mr. Bisset, for so many years Master of the Devon and Somerset Staghounds, can only be found now and then. No one at present has discovered how to breed these weight carriers to order, and they are entirely chance bred animals. Occasionally a thoroughbred horse gets a weight carrier from a mare which may not be of any great power; sometimes a cart stallion or a cart mare is responsible for a great strong horse in which cart blood is not observable, but it is seldom that two weight carriers are bred by the same parents in two successive years.

The light weight rider has a very wide field open to him from which to mount himself, as he can either ride weedy well bred, or thoroughbred horses, or can get along on smaller horses, horses, that is to say, which would bring good money were they but a little bigger; but, although people talk a good deal about the excellence of little horses, the almost universal feeling is in favour of horses from about 15 hands 3 inches to 16 hands 1 inch in height, and a horse standing less than 15 hands 2 inches must have a very grand reputation to realise a long price. Here then is the light weight's opportunity; he can afford to buy misfits of all kinds, while, if he be a good horseman, he can afford to disregard sundry little peculiarities of temper and temperament which would cause the horse to be rejected at once by any one ready to pay a good price for a hunter approximately perfect.

One hears a good deal at times of the horse for this country and the horse for that; but much of it is pure theory. One or two propositions certainly stand out prominently, one of them being that an indifferent horse is of no earthly use in the shires. If his rider does not want to jump he must at any rate gallop from gate to gate; but if a man "goes" on the grass he must have a good horse. But the horse for Leicestershire is also the best horse for everywhere else, and in no hunting country in England does the workman buy an indifferent hunter if he can afford a better. Mr. Charles Brindley, better known perhaps under his pseudonym "Harry Hieover," wrote in one of his books that a fifty pound hack was quite good enough for Surrey. Well, if any of the packs hunting over that county find a good fox on a good scenting day and get away on good terms with him, any one who thinks a common horse good enough for Surrey will learn the erroneousness of his opinion, especially if the line happen to lie in one of the Vales, the Godstone Vale, for instance. "Do you call the Blankshire a difficult country?" a young man is reported to have asked of a Nestor of the Chase. "My friend," was the reply, "all countries are difficult when hounds really run," and this should be kept in mind by horse buyers. In Essex, with its interminable plough, a stranger would scarcely imagine that there is ever much of the gaudy side of fox-hunting to be seen, but let him be out when scent lies and a stout fox is before the hounds, while the going is deep; the best horse in England will not then be found too good for the occasion.

It has often been said that you want nothing more than a cob in order to enjoy the sweets of hunting the wild stag on Exmoor or the Quantocks. There are many days on which a cob would suffice for Leicestershire or Northamptonshire; but the man on a cob who happened to be in a fine run which came off with the Devon and Somerset during September in the present year (1897) would have seen very little of it. Similarly, in the more wooded portions of Kent and Sussex, it will be found that the best horse procurable is better than an inferior conveyance.

So far as regards the physical characteristics of different countries, horses very soon grow accustomed to a change of fences. A Leicestershire horse would not be long in mastering the banks of the Blackmore Vale, or even the big banks to be found further west, but it is to be noted that, as a rule, a horse used to a flying country becomes clever in a cramped or banking country in less time than a horse accustomed to banks learns to jump freely in a flying country. Many Irish hunters, when they first come into the hands of English dealers, are by no means free jumpers, and take no little time to school before they perform in a manner which will commend itself to the buyer who desires to ride over a flying country; but a horse which may be regarded as somewhat rash over this description of country soon learns not to rush at banks, and quickly gives up attempting to fly them. Although, then, one can scarcely have too good a horse for any country, a man may have too good a horse for himself; that is to say, if a man does not jump, there is no necessity for him to go to the expense of buying a hunter fit to go anywhere. With respect to those good sportsmen who can afford small sums only for their horses, it may be asked where do the fifty and sixty pound horses—many seen in the field cost less—come from? They come from everywhere. A hunter out of an unknown stud sent to the hammer never realises much; a horse which will not go in harness or into a horse-box has a good deal of his value knocked off, while a tendency to pull or be light-hearted is amongst the causes which make hunters and other horses pass from hand to hand at little money.

And now just a word to the inexperienced on the subject of buying horses. Buying at auction is very dangerous, unless a man be a very good judge and know something about the horse he proposes to buy; nor should the novice rely upon his own judgment when buying privately.

There is no royal road to buying a hundred pound horse for half that sum, nor for obtaining a fifty pound horse for twenty-five pounds; so the beginner should at once abandon all idea of bargain hunting. Those who live in the country can generally hear of a horse by mentioning their wants to their friends, and when the time comes for selling the cub-hunters by auction a suitable mount can generally be obtained, or recourse can be had to a dealer who deals in the kind of horse required. It is a very common idea that every horse-dealer is a rogue, but there are just as many honest men in that calling as in any other, and if the beginner go to a respectable dealer, tell him what he wants, and the price to which he is prepared to go, he will probably not have reason to repent his line of action.

W. C. A. Blew.

Glossary.

Arm—The upper part of the fore-leg, from just below the *withers* (*q.v.*) down to just above the elbow. Generally called **shoulder.**

Bars of the Foot—Portions of the wall or crust of the foot, which turn inwards and upwards at the base of the foot near the heel, and then run nearly parallel to the sides of the *frog* (*q.v.*).

Bars of the Mouth—The intervals in a horse's jaws between the tushes or canine teeth and the grinders. Upon this smooth interval, which occurs just at the angle of the lips, the bit is placed.

Bay—A reddish nut-brown colour. Usually the term is applied to dark horses, but when a light bay is spoken of, a horse of yellow sunlight colour is intended. Bay is apparently the original colour of the Arab horse, probably with black points.

Bishoping—The practice of artificially modifying the appearance of horses in order to improve their price, usually by making them appear younger. The especial point worked upon is the teeth.

Blaze—A stripe of white down a horse's face.

Blue Roan—[*See* Roan].

Brisket—The lower part of a horse's chest, just behind the fore-legs.

Buck Knee—A knee joint which recedes from the front, instead of presenting a straight line from forearm to fetlock.

Calf Knee—A knee that bends sideways towards its fellow; similar to knock-knees in man.

Calkin or **Calk**—A spur projecting downward from a horse's shoe in order to prevent it from falling in slippery weather.

Cannon Bone or **Canon Bone**—The bone uniting knee joint and fetlock in the fore-leg, hock and fetlock in the hind. Also called **shank.**

Castors—Horny excrescences growing on the inside of each leg, just above the knees and below the hocks. Also called **chesnuts** and sometimes **ergots.**

Chanting—Originally, singing unjustified praises of a horse for sale, hence any form of swindling with unsound horses.

Chesnut—(1) *See* Castor; (2) A reddish colour, similar to bay, but usually lighter.

Chin Groove—The depression behind the horse's lower jaw in which the curb-chain fits.

Clicking—A defect in a horse's paces, which causes him to knock his feet against one another when he is trotting or galloping. Also called **forging.**

Cob—Any compact, short-legged horse.

Coffin Bone—The bone in the centre of the hoof.

Commissure—The natural clefts of a horse's foot. They are three in number, one down the centre of the frog, the others between the bars and the crust.

Coper—Any dealer in horses whose integrity is uncertain.

Coronet or **Coronary Process**—The bony fringe, partly consisting of an enlargement of the lower end of the small pastern, which surrounds the top of the hoof.

Cow-hock—A hock that approaches sideways to its fellow, thereby bringing the shanks of the hind-leg unduly close.

Croup—The upper part of the body forward from the insertion of the tail to the lumbar vertebræ, which constitute the **loins.**

Crust of the Feet—The horny outer portion of the hoof.

Dappled—Epithet of a coat more or less plentifully sprinkled with rings or spots of a darker colour.

Dishing—A peculiarity in a horse's action which causes him to throw out his feet sideways as he brings them up in a trot. (This action is admired in Spanish horses.)

Dock—(1) The stump from which the hairs of a horse's tail depend; (2) *Verb*: to cut this stump to a shorter length with the idea of improving the horse's appearance.

Dun—A dull dark brown. Horses of this hue have generally black extremities, and a black line down the back. Another authority says that "dun" means yellowish-sandy. This is probably the original colour of the wild horse of Northern Asia.

Elbow—The backward bony projection from a horse's fore-leg just below the junction of leg and body.

Ergot—The horny excrescence just at the fetlock joint, from which the fetlock itself depends. Sometimes applied to the castors or chesnuts higher up the leg.

Ewe Neck—A thin, hollow neck.

Fetlock—A lock of hair, usually short, depending from the back of the fetlock joint, which is itself the junction of the pastern and the shank or cannon bone.

Flank—That part of the horse's side which is free from bone, *i.e.*, between the ribs and the hip.

Fleabitten—A white coat plentifully marked with small red or dark spots. A favourite Arab colour, but indicative generally of age, as the spots seldom appear before the eighth year, often much later.

Forearm—That part of the fore-leg which lies between the knee and the junction of the leg with the body.

Forehand—The shoulders, arm, and forearm of a horse.

Frog—The triangular protuberance which forms in the centre of the bottom of a horse's foot.

Gaskin—That part of a horse's hind-leg between the hock and the junction of the leg with the body. Also specifically called the leg, and sometimes the thigh, or the *false thigh.*

Goose-rumped—A horse with buttocks that fall away sharply from the croup; tail set low. Common in Barbs or Spaniards.

Grey—The colour of coats that are composed of a mixture of black and white hairs, varying in proportion as the horse is dark or light grey, the coat growing lighter with age.

Haunches—The fleshy part of a horse's back at the junction of body and hips.

Hip—The top joint of the hind-leg, at the junction with the pelvis.

Hock—The backward-bending joint on the hind-legs, formed by the junction of the shank, or cannon bone, and the bone of the upper leg, or tibia.

Hoof—The horny box which encloses the extremities of fore- and hind-legs.

Infundibulum—[*See* Mark.]

Knee—The forward-bending joint of the fore-legs, formed by the junction of the shank, or cannon bone, and the bone of the forearm, or radius.

Loins—That part of a horse's body between the ribs and the pelvis and hips.

Mark—The hollow upon the top of a young horse's teeth which wears down with years, and is, therefore, valuable as an indication of age. Also called *infundibulum.*

Over at the Knee—Descriptive of a horse whose knees, either from congenital defects or from overwork, project forward.

Pastern—The bone joining hoof and fetlock joint.

Piebald—Strictly, the colour of a coat which consists of patches of white and black, but often used for a horse of any two colours. [*See also* Skewbald.]

Points—Those qualities of shape, action, and constitution, which determine a horse's value or worthlessness.

Ragged Hips—Hips that stand well away from the backbone.

Rat-tailed—Descriptive of a horse that has lost all, or nearly all, his tail hairs.

Red Roan—[*See* Roan.]

Roach Back—A back which slopes downward from shoulder to croup, owing to undue convexity. Usually accompanied by flat sides and a narrow chest.

Roan—The colour of a coat chiefly of a red or blue character, but closely flecked with grey hairs. According to the ground colour it will be blue roan, red roan, or strawberry roan.

Roughing—The turning up of *calkins* (*q.v.*) on a horse's shoe when cold has made roads slippery.

Shank—[*See* CANNON BONE].

Shoe—A loop of iron nailed on to horses' feet to preserve them from the rough wear of the roads.

Shoulder—The upper part of the fore-leg, from its junction with the body to the shoulder joint. Also called the *Arm*.

Sickle Hocks—Hocks that bend unduly backward.

Skewbald—The colour of a coat which consists of patches of any two colours except white and black. Such horses are properly called *Piebald*. Supposed to be an original wild colour in Eastern Asia. It is the favourite colour among the Gauchos of South America.

Snip—A small patch of white upon a horse's nose.

Sorrel—The colour of a coat which consists of yellowish- or reddish-brown hairs.

Splint Bones—Small bones running from hock or knee to fetlock parallel with shank bone.

Star—A square patch of white upon a horse's forehead.

Stifle—The joint at the junction of the hind-leg and the body, between the gaskin and the thigh proper.

Thigh—The upper part of the hind-leg, bounded beneath by the stifle, and above by the croup.

Wall of the Foot—[*See* CRUST].

Well ribbed up—Descriptive of a horse in which the lower ribs curve well back towards the hind-quarters, and do not leave too much flank exposed.

White Stocking—Descriptive of a horse otherwise dark or brightly coloured, which has the lower portion of one or more legs white. Three white stockings, the off fore-leg being dark, is the favourite arrangement of colour among the Bedouins of Arabia.

Withers—The highest point of a horse's back, just behind the neck.

[For diseases *See* VETERINARY WORK.]

HOUND BREEDING—Within the last thirty years the facilities for breeding fox-hounds of high class have been greatly increased. Before the *Fox-hound Kennel Stud Book* was published, the task of the M.F.H. who wished to study the pedigrees of the inmates of other kennels was an arduous one, for unless he could obtain access to the kennel-books of the leading establishments, he had to content himself with the meagre hound lists that appeared from time to time in the sporting magazines.

Stud Books—Mr. Cornelius Tongue, perhaps better known as "Cecil," in his preface to the *Stud Book*, published in 1866, complained of the difficulties that he had met with in procuring reliable information from some kennels, but the publication is fairly accurate, and, if the time occupied in tracing a pedigree in his *Stud Book* compares unfavourably with the ease with which reference can be made to the recent volumes, compiled with such admirable care, yet no lovers of well-bred fox-hounds should forget the boon which Mr. Tongue has conferred upon them.

To quote from his preface, "The principles observed by successful breeders of race-horses in the selection of sires and dams that have distinguished themselves on the turf and in the stud, are identical with those laws of nature which govern the pro-creation of fox-hounds. It will invariably be found that those animals are most to be depended upon for the perpetuation of their species whose genealogy can be traced in the greatest number of direct lines to great celebrities of olden times; the most valuable strains of blood may be readily recognised by reference to the *Kennel Stud Book*, and they will be found to be most copiously diffused throughout those packs which are in the greatest renown. It is the peculiar faculty of a highly bred and highly endowed animal to convey his type to posterity. An inferior bred hound may evince great superiority in his work, but the qualities of his progeny will be very uncertain. Hence the importance of accurate records of pedigrees."

In the *Stud Book* which follows, lists are given of fifty-three packs of hounds, with an appendix of the most important sales between 1851 and 1865; in addition to these the appendix contains several interesting pedigrees of famous hounds of the day, including the great "Furrier," known as Mr. Osbaldeston's, which was, however, bred at Belvoir in 1820.

In the succeeding volume of the *Fox-hound Kennel Stud Book*, which covers from 1865 to 1885, it is to be regretted that no hound sales are chronicled; but the book itself is far better arranged in other respects than its predecessor for easy reference, whilst in the volumes published in 1891 and 1896, valuable appendices are to be found containing particulars of sales.

Literature of the Fox-hound—In 1854, Mr. Tongue enriched the literature of sport by his *Records of the Chase*, in which students of hound lore will find much interesting matter; whilst other volumes more easily obtainable and of the greatest value are Beckford's *Thoughts upon Hunting*, Vyner's *Notitia Venatica*, and the *Diary of a Huntsman* by Thomas Smith (Craven Smith). In the last-named work, published in 1838, Chapter V. (on fox-hounds) is considered by many to be the best of all expositions on the subject; indeed, in its excellent pages the whole question of hound breeding is summed up.

"A mute hound is unpardonable; if he should be in every other respect perfect, so much the greater reason for drafting him," and "the two great points to attend to in breeding are stoutness and nose." If the hound breeder of to-day would treasure these, and, indeed, all other sentences in this admirable chapter, trite as some may seem to be, bad hounds would be scarce.

Another book containing most valuable information with regard to hounds is the *Noble Science*, by F. P. Delmé Radcliffe, who was Master of the Hertfordshire Hounds from 1836 to 1839. In this work, Chapter III. deals entirely with the fox-hound, and what he should be in the opinion of the author and others. This chapter is headed by an engraving of the stamp of hound which Mr. Radcliffe considered to be best suited to his country, and it is evident that he much admires the description of the hound by Somervile a century before. He advocates:

"A hound of middle size, active and strong," though he qualifies the poet's desideratum, a "round cat foot," by stating his experience of hounds thus endowed getting "toes down" sooner than others. It is doubtful if many modern lovers of hounds agree with Mr. Radcliffe in his fondness for "arched loins, or wheel backs with an inclination to drooping quarters," which he fancies are better adapted to hills. In this chapter, too, is mentioned an experiment of crossing a blood-hound with a fox-hound bitch with a view to improving the nose of the fox-hound; this, it appears, was not attained. The whole of Mr. Radcliffe's book is the work of a scholar and a sportsman.

Besides the works above alluded to, after a perusal of the writings of the "Druid" and "Scrutator," together with the books and contributions to magazines by "Nimrod," and the volume on "Hunting" from the *Badminton Library*, the student of fox-hound pedigrees will find in the Stud-books an absorbing interest.

Size—There is to be found, in the various books on hunting, a great difference of opinion as to the proper size of a fox-hound. Mr. Meynell's dictum is recorded that the *height* of a hound has nothing to do with his *size*; while Mr. Assheton Smith, according to the "Druid," changed his opinion on the subject during his Mastership of the Quorn. At first he swore by small hounds, and there was hardly a dog-hound at Quorn above 23 inches; but, on his hounds happening to clash with Lord Lonsdale's pack, and six couple of the latter being counted first away from Launde Wood, it struck him that the smaller hounds were at a disadvantage in jumping over the briars, and he set to work raising his standard until his dog-hounds were as near 25 inches as possible, and the bitches as much over 23 as they could be got.

Much has been said of different stamps of hounds for different countries, but there seems to be little doubt that by breeding from the very best blood only, and "avoiding lumber in any shape," as Mr. Radcliffe puts it, a pack of hounds can be obtained that can carry a good head over rough moorland, cold ploughs, and pastures equally well. "Quickness in working and catching for a scent" is all important; and here it is that blood tells.

Pedigrees—A glance at the list of packs in the Volume (V.) of the *Stud Book* published in 1896, will show that Ireland and Scotland are only represented by two packs each; whilst in England the south-west may be said to be the most benighted. West of the Cattestock, the list of one pack only, the Dartmoor, is found to be worthy of insertion; whereas, in the book of 1866, Devon and Cornwall enrolled four packs between them. With the exception of this district, the inaccessibility of good fox-hound blood can be no excuse for a deteriorating kennel nowadays, while the number of spectators at the Peterborough Hound Show speaks for itself. On an examination of the pedigrees of the prize-winners at Peterborough one will, in nearly every case, be taken back to some, if not all, of the great strains of blood, these being, in addition to those with which the regular attendant at Peterborough is familiar, the Belvoir, Fitzwilliam (or Milton), Bramham Moor, Grove (Lord Galway's), Lord Fitzhardinge's Grafton, Wynnstay, and Badminton. Other packs that have been broken up, but are frequently to be met with in classical pedigrees, are the Blankney, Burton, Mr. Parry's (Puckeridge), Lord Poltimore's, and the Croome (Lord Coventry's). Lord Portsmouth's and the Brocklesby dog pack have changed hands; so that when one adds the kennels from which hounds are shown almost every year, it is plain that the best blood is widely disseminated. In a good pedigree of a hound, however, as of every animal, judicious in-breeding is almost invariably to be found.

This can be seen in the pedigrees that are subjoined of three stallion hounds, the Belvoir Nominal, Warwickshire Tancred, and Oakley Dancer; the figures attached to the hounds' names denote the year in which they were entered.

The Belvoir Nominal and Gambler have been, perhaps, more sought after by hound-breeders than anything of late years. In nearly every pedigree of well-known hounds the Belvoir Senator's name appears, and he is represented twice in both the sire and dam of Nominal. It will be observed that Nominal is in-bred to the Senator blood on the dam's side, as Needful is his granddam, and also dam of his grandsire: the Milton blood is also to the fore in this pedigree.

BELVOIR NOMINAL, 1888				
	Gambler, 1884	Weather-gauge, 1876	Warrior, 1870	Wonder, 1864.
				Susan, 1867.
			Royalty, 1871	Rambler, 1868, by Senator 1862.
				Bella, 1861, by Milton Rasselas, 1855.
		Gratitude, 1880	Gallant, 1874	General, 1867, by Milton Gambler, 1863.
				Nimbler, 1869.
			Snowdrop, 1875	Ruler, 1867.
				Stella, 1871, by Senator 1862.
	Needy, 1884	Syntax, 1880	Grafton Silence, 1875	Grafton Statesman, 1871, by Senator, 1864.
				Their Garland, 1869, by Bramham Gainer, 1860.
			Needful, 1877	
		Needful, 1877	Fallible, 1874	Milton Furrier, 1869, by Forester, 1860.
				Prophetess, 1872, by Rallywood, 1868.
			Needless, 1870	Contest, 1864.
				Novelty, 1866, by Senator, 1862.

The Oakley Dancer is a beautifully-bred hound; though by a Grafton sire, he goes back on this side to the Oakley Flasher and Driver; the blood of the Oakley Flasher is also to be found on the side of Dancer's dam, Flourish being an own sister. Strains of the Grove,

Milton, Burton (Lord H. Bentinck's), Belvoir, and Lord Poltimore's are also in evidence.

Oakley Dancer, 1888.

- Grafton Dancer, 1883
  - Grafton Dashwood, 1880.
    - Driver, 1873
      - Oakley Driver, 1868, by Burton Dorimont, 1860.
      - Bountiful, 1868, by Boniface, 1864.
    - Starlight, 1877
      - Silence, 1875
        - Statesman, 1871.
        - Garland, 1869.
      - Flourish, 1874
        - Milton Finder, 1869, by Forester.
        - Speedwell, 1868, by Belvoir, 1862, Senator.
  - Their Fallacy, 1880
    - Oakley Flasher, 1874
      - Milton Furrier, 1869, by Forester, 1860.
      - Oakley Dabchick, 1868, by Burton Dorimont, 1860.
    - Watchful, 1875
      - Wildair, 1872, by Lord Poltimore's Whipster.
      - Seemly, 1870, by Senator, 1864.
- Redcap, 1883
  - Regent, 1879
    - Grove Richmond, 1873
      - Belvoir Rallywood, 1868, by Senator, 1862.
      - Rarity, 1869, by Furrier, 1862.
    - Spinster, 1876
      - Skirmisher, 1868, by Belvoir Senator, 1862.
      - Liberty, 1872, by Lounger, 1865.
  - Ruby, 1877
    - Milton Rutland, 1872
      - Milton Roman, 1868.
      - Their Audrey, 1867, by Forester, 1860.
    - Flourish, 1874
      - Milton Furrier, 1869.
      - Dabchick, 1868.

In the pedigree of the Warwickshire Tancred, the blood of the Burton Regulus is especially noticeable. In the Warwickshire entry of 1877 were Rosy, Ransom, Rival, and Ruin, of one litter, by Lord Coventry's Rambler. Rambler was by Lord Fitzhardinge's Collier out of Lord Coventry's Ransom; the latter was by the Burton Regulus out of Petulant, entered in 1865 by Mr. Chaplin, who had in 1864 purchased Lord Henry Bentinck's pack. In the pedigree of Warwickshire Tancred's sire, the Burton blood is also to be traced in the dam of Rifleman (1871), and also in Rallywood's (1877) dam. Burton Regulus was also grandsire of the Milton Rutland, 1872.

Warwickshire Tancred, 1895.

- Wildboy, 1889
  - Pytchley Prompter, 1885
    - Blankney Rallywood, 1877.
      - Rifleman, 1871, by Burton Regulus, 1861.
      - Fretful, 1872, by Guardian, 1867.
    - Pytchley Priestess, 1881
      - Milton Rhymer, 1877, by Brusher, 1870.
      - Precious, 1877, by Milton Rutland, 1870.
  - Wary, 1886
    - Whynot, 1882
      - Belvoir Weathergauge, 1876.
      - Ruin, 1877.
    - Facile, 1882
      - Archibald, 1879
        - Quorn Alfred, 1872.
        - Rival, 1877.
      - Fanciful, 1879, by Belvoir Fallible, 1874.
- Traitress,
  - Furley, 1883
    - Belvoir Fencer, 1880
      - Belvoir Brusher, 1874, by Saffron, 1870.
      - Their Furious, 1876, by Fallible, 1874.
    - Ransom, 1877
      - Lord Coventry's Rambler, 1873.
      - Charity, 1870.
  - Trusty, 1887
    - Brocklesby Tapster, 1882
      - Blankney Tapster, 1879, by Belvoir Whynot, 1869.
      - Brocklesby Rantipole, 1880, by Milton Reveller, 1876.
    - Roundelay, 1879
      - Belvoir Fallible, 1874.
      - Rosy, 1877.

Defects in Hounds—Under the present conditions of hound breeding, and with the lists of eighty-six packs in the *Stud Book*, there should be no obstacles to Masters of Hounds breeding back to the best blood. Of the necessity of obtaining good walks for the puppies, and of the annual encounter with the dread distemper, it is superfluous to speak here. As for the offences of muteness, babbling, skirting, &c., no hound guilty of these should be kept in a pack, much less be used for breeding In the mating of hounds that have bad feet, or fail in bone below the knee, the greatest care should be exercised; when once these faults become general in a kennel it is with the greatest difficulty that they are stamped out.

Another fault in hounds which is unfortunately to be met with frequently, is that of being "pig-mouthed," or, as some say, "swine-chopped" or "hog-jawed," *i.e.*, when the lower jaw is shorter than the upper one. Though in some kennels hounds with this defect are freely used for breeding, it should be borne in mind that most judges at puppy shows consider it a grave blemish, if not an absolute disqualification, for honours; thus it is very hard on puppy walkers to send them young hounds so handicapped. The fault is hereditary; and it sometimes comes out in the second generation, even when the sire and dam of the young hound are free from it. As for the fault of being "underhung," when the lower jaw protrudes beyond the upper, it is worse still.

Walking Puppies—If one thinks of the many perils that beset a foxhound's puppies at walk, it seems a marvel that more are not sent back to the kennel from quarters in a crippled state; still, some are sure to be disabled, and it is surely more humane to put them out of their misery than to keep them on in the hopes of their recovering sufficiently to be sent away with the draft. Some young hounds may come in afflicted with the mange, which is apt to give great trouble, maybe in vain. Other casualties to which the young fox-hound is liable need not be further enumerated; suffice it to say that if a hound breeder can, before the commencement of cub-hunting, show 33 per cent. or (if he can afford to be very particular about height, colour, &c.), 25 per cent. of young hounds sent out from kennel the year before, he should by no means consider himself unlucky. Much is to be said on behalf of the plan, which a few Masters have adopted, of having all the young hounds brought in on an appointed day in early spring, and having them judged on the spot, instead of pursuing the usual course of holding the puppy show after they have been some months in kennel. The great point is that the prizes are most likely to go where they have been best deserved, though it is hard on late puppies.

Care of the Bitch—With regard to putting the bitches to the dog in October or November, it may be suggested that a kennel must be very strong in hounds if the services in the field of good workers can be so early dispensed with; on the other hand, if a bitch valuable for breeding comes early in season, to miss such a chance is surely unwise. It is far better, even at the risk of having to hunt a rather short pack in the spring, to put all the best bitches to, than to be obliged to bring up more whelps than the bitches can manage; few bitches should suckle more than four whelps, and, if their whelping has been severe, it is preferable to let them bring up three whelps, or in some cases even two, properly, than to find, when the time comes to send the puppies out to quarters, that they are weedy and sickly.

The anxieties which devolve upon the huntsman are considerable; the bitches must have liberty both before and after whelping, the numerous risks thus entailed being better than the almost certain disasters which result from shutting them up. Should a bitch slip her puppies, to be on the safe side it is advisable to separate her at once from the other matrons of the kennel. However heavy a bitch may be, her skin should be loose; when it is tight there is trouble in store for her. In short, one shrinks from rehearsing at length all the dangers that attend the rearing of fox-hounds; they are familiar to all kennelmen who know their business, and without such men, breeding hounds is an impossibility.

Welsh Blood—During the last ten years there have been found many advocates for an infusion of the Welsh fox-hound blood into the English kennels. The excellence of the sport which this breed of hounds afford in wild and wooded districts is admitted, and there are many who hold that by crossing the English and Welsh strains the nose and tongue of the former would be improved. As to the value of the cross the opinions of those who have tried it are conflicting; nor is this surprising when one considers the variety of the circumstances under which the experiments must have been made. Though an inspection of the most recent volume of the *Stud Book* shows that the only pack in England into which the Welsh blood has been freely introduced is the Blackmore Vale, it is to be met with in many other kennels not included in the book; and, when a new departure in crossing strains of any breed has been made, it is as well, if possible, to see the result of other people's experiments.

Harriers—In some parts of England there are packs which hunt the fox, but cannot be said to be pure fox-hounds, being crossed with "harriers," though, after the voluminous correspondences that have been carried on as to "What is a harrier?" the word can hardly be written without misgiving; perhaps the breed alluded to may be better defined as that with which the hare was usually hunted before dwarf fox-hounds were generally adopted for the purpose. As for the hare-hound of the present day, from the old Southern hound to the draft from the fashionable pack of fox-hounds, the variety of stamp is so great that the so-called scientific system of breeding is in many cases not feasible. If the action of promoters of the "Harrier" Show at Peterborough, which follows that of the fox-hounds, in directing that the exhibits should be judged purely on fox-hound points has been criticised unfavourably by some old-fashioned hare hunters, it cannot be gainsaid that the emulation which the Show itself provokes is beneficial, so long as working qualities are not lost sight of thereby.

L. J. BATHURST.

HUNTING—FOX, was looked upon by Mr. Beckford as an art, and it may be considered to afford greater pleasure to all the classes of society which are accustomed to participate in it than any other field sport. Dr. Paley has said that he never met with any sportsman who could define or state correctly the principle of sport, but nevertheless the allurements of the chase are stronger now than they have ever been, and attract larger fields of followers every year. It has often been said that a man cannot hunt from a bad motive, and the justice of the observation is generally acknowledged.

Authorities differ with regard to the date in which foxhunting first became an amusement in England, but we may take it that it was not at all generally followed until about the middle of the last century; though the Charlton, afterwards the Goodwood, were in existence in the reign of William III., and the Bridgewater hounds very soon afterwards, besides others. We read, indeed, that King James in the year 1603, was accustomed to hunt as a pastime in the course of the long journeys which were undertaken at that period. The writer tells us that "live hares in baskets being carried to the Heath made excellent sport for his Majesty, Sir John Harington's hounds with good mouths following the game, the King taking great leisure and pleasure in the same." Gervase Markham, writing in the time of James I., praises the chase, and lays it down that "of all the field pleasures wherewith old time and men's invention hath blest the houres of our recreation there is none to excelle the delight of hunting"; but in those days, it must be remembered, the term included the pursuit of fox, hare, or stag. The followers and admirers of the Staintondale hounds, in Yorkshire, claim for this pack that they were formed 200 years ago, and they are trencher-fed. The Sinnington can also boast of considerable antiquity, but these hounds are now kennelled, as are the Bilsdale now (1897) for the first time. Squire Draper commenced operations in 1726, for the purpose of exterminating or reducing the number of foxes in Yorkshire, which had developed lamb-killing propensities. One of the earliest packs of foxhounds in the western part of England was established by Mr. Thomas Fownes, of Stapleton, in Dorsetshire, about the year 1730, and it appears that these hounds were subsequently sold to Mr. Bowes, of Streatlam, in Yorkshire. The Dukes of Beaufort and Rutland, the Earls of Yarborough and Fitzwilliam, were amongst the earliest owners of celebrated packs, whose reputation has been jealously maintained ever since they were first established. It has been stated that there are 354 packs of hounds in England and Ireland, but Mr. Sargent, who has been at great trouble in compiling an accurate list, allows for "hunts not returned," and estimates the total number at 360. In these days, foxhunting establishments are often conducted on a scale of lavish expenditure which is not only unreasonable, but which deters many promising young country gentlemen from becoming masters, and it is on this account that, at the end of the season, we frequently hear that well-known countries are vacant, and afterwards that the mastership has been offered to and accepted by a stranger, who has no interest beyond the chase in the land over which he hunts. Owners and occupiers of land will preserve foxes more readily for one born and bred in the country than they will for a stranger, however greatly they may appreciate his public spirit in coming forward to take the hounds.

Melton Mowbray may be considered as the metropolis of the foxhunting world, for Leicestershire, rich in glorious grazing grounds, has for a century been looked upon as the premier country; but the agricultural features of the provinces, which were formerly derided and looked down upon as being realms of heavy ploughed land, have undergone a considerable improvement, from a hunting point of view, during the last twelve years. The low price of wheat has effectually hindered the progress of the plough, and the land on which the crop formerly flourished has been laid or fallen down to grass.

Although the wave of agricultural depression which has swept over England and remained with us for so long a period, has had the effect of diminishing the attendance of owners and occupiers of land at the meets, they still give their loyal allegiance to a sport they love to encourage. In many provincial countries the subscriptions, for the same reason, have become seriously reduced.

Although there is no statute book of laws which governs the rights of country, there is an unwritten law in such matters which is perfectly well understood and respected. Thus, every master knows that he may not dig a fox which has found a sanctuary in an earth or drain in a neighbouring country; he may use a terrier, or employ almost any other means which ingenuity can suggest, but the soil must not be broken. It is greatly to the credit of all concerned that foxhunting disputes in regard to rights, limitation of country, or otherwise, so seldom arise; when they do, they are referred to the Master of Foxhounds Committee, which formerly held its sittings at Boodle's Club, but which now meets at Tattersall's once a year to hear appeals and administer justice. Nearly every master is jealous of any encroachment on his country, and huntsmen, who are generally anxious to conform to etiquette, will never allow their hounds to enter a neighbour's covert, unless they can carry and speak to a line into it. The ultimate decision of any vexed question must rest with the landowners and occupiers of land, but in case they are not unanimous it is found necessary to refer the dispute to arbitration, as indicated above. Although an owner of coverts may prevent hounds from drawing them if he chooses to do so, he cannot transfer this privilege to any neighbouring pack, unless with the consent and sanction of the master of the country in which they are situated.

It is difficult to lay down any rule, or, indeed, even to provide an estimate of the expenses which will probably be incurred in hunting a country; these will depend very much upon good management. Circumstances vary, and no two years will be found alike, for the price of oatmeal, oats, beans, hay and straw, is constantly changing, and this variation will often make a considerable difference in the cost. Mr. Delmé Radcliffe, writing in the year 1838, put his expenses for hunting three days a week, or seven days a fortnight, in Herts (exclusive, of course, of his own personal expenses) at £1,885 per annum; and he lays it down that a provincial country, such as Hertfordshire, may be well hunted for the sum of £2,000 per annum. To hunt four days a week it will be necessary to keep fifty couple of hounds, and for two days twenty-five couples will be found a sufficient number. Three days will require as many hounds to be kept as would suffice for four days.

Foxhunting is deserving of support and encouragement, because it not only provides employment for large numbers, but also gives a valuable impetus to our noble breed of horses; while the manly nature of the sport undoubtedly has a marked influence upon our national character. "No higher testimony to its practical utility," says Mr. Delmé Radcliffe, "in a national point of view can be required than that of as brave a hero as ever drew a sword. The gallant Lord Lynedoch, he whom Napoleon characterised as 'that daring old man,' has often affirmed that he should not have been the soldier he is had he not been bred a foxhunter." Colonel Cook remarks that what chiefly contributes to make foxhunting so very far superior to other sports "is the wildness of the animal you hunt, and the difficulty in catching him."

Cubhunting usually commences about the

first week in September, though the date will vary in accordance with the state of harvest and condition of the ground. In plough countries it is better to wait until the great bulk of the corn is carried, but in grass countries and in woodlands there is nothing to hinder the master from beginning as soon as weather permits. It is undertaken for the purpose of blooding and entering the young hounds, and may be regarded as the rehearsal of the more serious business in November. This schooling of the young hounds in the woodlands is a necessary performance, which is very interesting work for the establishment, whose care it will be to get the pack steady before the regular season comes round. The meets are fixed at an early hour, in the first place, because the fewer there are out, the better will the work be performed. Noise of any kind viz. hallooing, cracking of whips, and viewing over the rides is not wanted, and the huntsman's cheer is the only voice which should be heard. Nothing should be allowed to distract the attention of the young hounds from the work on hand into which they are being initiated, and every sportsman should remember this, and repress any inclination to halloo, for in so doing he will support the wishes of the huntsman and assist him in his endeavour to maintain silence. It will be well to select a good scenting covert, where there is known to be a strong litter of cubs, for the first morning; it should be a fair-sized wood, say of 80 or 100 acres, and, if there is no ride in it, so much the better. The hounds should not be allowed to go away, and if, after a good morning's work, a cub or a brace of cubs can be brought to hand, the young entry will go home victorious, and they will not easily forget their first impressions. During the month of September, at least, the scene of operations should be confined to the big woods, and young hounds should never be allowed to run over the open country until they have learned how to use their noses. If this precaution is not rigidly adhered to, and if the young master is not sufficiently strong-minded to resist the temptation of following a fox over a nice line of country, the result will be that the young hounds will be left behind, ridden over, and, moreover, they will pick up all sorts of bad habits, which will cling to them through their career. As the autumn advances, however, and when October comes in, and it is necessary to visit and disturb the litters of cubs in the smaller coverts, the entry will in all probability be handy enough, from the drilling they will have received in the woodland, to justify the master in letting them go.

An occasional gallop in the open after a cub will not only be an enjoyable relaxation after all the hard work endured in covert, but it will also afford an opportunity to the huntsman of seeing how they run together. Great care should be taken to avoid killing in a small covert; if this unfortunately happens, it will not hold again until after Christmas, and, indeed, it is often a moot point whether or not the pet places, which are very small, but yet favourite resorts, should be drawn at all during the cub-hunting season. If a fox should be unluckily killed in one, the chances are there will be no find in it for three or four months afterwards; and yet, if a strong litter of cubs should have made it their headquarters, it is a pity they should not be roused and taught to fly.

To the master who is fond of hounds, cub-hunting is the most enjoyable part of the season. In the fresh morning air he revels in the glorious crash of melody when hounds run for the first ten minutes, as they only can run at this time of year; he watches the entry with the keenest interest, and sees bewilderment gradually giving place to the dash and drive which are the conspicuous attributes of a foxhound.

The writer has always preferred a dry cub-hunting season to a wet one, when the coverts are dank and soaked by heavy rain, for in such conditions there is seldom much scent.

Dry seasons are an indication of settled weather, which is usually favourable for scent in covert and outside. It is an unsatisfactory thing to break off cub-hunting for a spell, which huntsmen often think they are compelled to do, when the ground becomes hard from continued drought; it is better to keep steadily on, confining hounds as much as possible to covert, or the entry will forget what they have learned. Colonel Cook, writing in 1826, says that he always considered the cub-hunting season the time when a master of hounds never ought to be absent, whether he hunts them himself or not; and to a real sportsman it is a great pleasure to see his young hounds enter. "At all events," he says, in addressing a young master, "you should never leave your hounds from the first day of cub-hunting until the end of the season. . . . Cub-hunting is very necessary for many reasons; you will gain by it a thorough knowledge of your pack; and they will know you, obey you, and, when you want them, will also carry you through many difficulties they otherwise would not." This is excellent doctrine, which will commend itself to all those who have been privileged to fill the post of master of foxhounds.

The Master—The master of foxhounds should be chosen, if possible, from the residents in the country in which the pack is established, for obvious reasons. Owners and occupiers of land will give their support more readily to one who lives in their midst than to a stranger; and as we know that hunting depends on the sufferance of these great men, and entirely upon their good-will for its maintenance, it is necessary to conform to their wishes. "To hunt a country and make the most of it, so as to give general satisfaction, requires some consideration. Supposing you have a thorough knowledge of it, use your own judgment and never be led by others, for you will find they most commonly have some selfish motives, and will often mislead you." These words of Colonel Cook will be generally endorsed.

The master should make himself thoroughly acquainted with the country he is taking over, and he should endeavour to obtain accurate information with regard to old customs and hunting rights—where these exist. Perhaps there are coverts which are neutral with another hunt, and in that case great care should be exercised in ascertaining the correct usage of them. For the summer months it will be a congenial task to ride about the country with the hounds at exercise in the morning, and obtain local knowledge. In this way the master will be enabled to make friends with the farmers and keepers, and discover any little details which may be useful when the regular season begins. He will find out where there are litters of cubs, and keep a record of any matter of importance which may strike him during his rides. When the time arrives for sending out the fixtures, these should be made judiciously and without favour or affection. The good and bad parts of the country should be hunted fairly and in their turn, and it will be found that this arrangement will also be the most conducive to sport. If you are continually calling upon the small coverts in the best part of the country, foxes will be difficult to find, and they will lie at earth. The master will keep a diary, which will contain a record of each day's sport, meet, coverts drawn, finds, and any incident likely to prove of interest. In most countries keepers receive a remuneration of 10*s.* for each find, and as they regard this gift as a perquisite, it is very necessary that a strict account should be kept. Colonel Cook dwells upon the advantage which is often taken of a master's good nature by followers of his pack to persuade him to draw some particular covert which may happen to suit their convenience, and recommends him to rely upon his own judgment in such cases.

The master will find plenty of work, in undertaking the management of a four days a week country, to occupy his attention both in the summer and winter months. If he should hunt his own pack, it will be found necessary to appoint a field master, who will maintain the discipline which is essential to success, and who will restrain the unruly spirits, a few of whom are to be found in every hunt, from spoiling their own sport and that of others by heading foxes and pressing upon hounds in their work. He will do his best to prevent injury to the farmers, and in this endeavour he will be loyally assisted by all true sportsmen.

The Huntsman—There is no better class of servant to be found in England than the huntsman to a pack of foxhounds; and the explanation of this assertion, with which it is not improbable that we shall most of us agree, is not very difficult to find. He has undoubtedly been selected for the post because he possesses qualities which would adorn the character of a man in almost any station of life. He should be well-conducted, sober, of strict integrity and even temper, and it is needless to say a good rider to hounds; moreover, as he is placed in a position of responsibility and trust, and is often obliged to act upon emergencies and to take upon himself to decide matters the consideration of which would more properly devolve upon his master, were he present, he should be possessed of intelligence and sagacity above the common order of mankind. Beckford, in describing the characteristics of an ideal huntsman, says: "he should have an eye so quick as to perceive which of his hounds carries the scent when all are running, and should have so excellent an ear as to always be able to distinguish the foremost hounds when he does not see them; he should be quiet, patient, and without conceit." It may be added to this description of essential qualifications, that he should be impervious to criticism, doing his duty and handling his hounds in the way which seems best to himself and his master, to whom alone he is responsible. The writer lays stress upon the fact that he must be impervious to criticism, because the veriest tiro who comes out hunting thinks himself capable of passing judgment on a cast.

In the words of Mr. Jorrocks, "a fish-fag's ware isn't more perishable than a huntsman's fame; his skill is within the judgment of every one—cleverest fellow alive—biggest fool going." And again, "a huntsman's fame rises and falls with the sport he shows." Tom Smith, a late master of the Craven Hounds, thus hits off the character of an ideal huntsman: "To be perfect a huntsman should possess the following qualifications: health, memory, decision, temper and patience, voice and sight, courage and spirits, perseverance, activity, and with these he will soon make a bad pack a good one. If quick, he will make a slow pack quick; if slow, he will make a quick pack slow."

All this is very sensible doctrine which must commend itself to every one, and, if a master can obtain the services of one who has all these gifts of excellence, he is a fortunate man. To my mind the conclusion of the whole matter, and the keynote of success in the field, is well summed up by Beckford thus: "he should let his hounds alone whilst they can hunt, and he should have genius to assist them when they cannot." The management of the kennel is perhaps the most important duty the huntsman has to perform; for if hounds are not brought out thoroughly fit to go, in good condition and steady, the chances of sport and a successful season are indeed reduced to a minimum. To keep hounds healthy, it is necessary that they should have the best food of its kind which it is possible to procure, and authorities agree that oatmeal of good quality is not only the best food for a foxhound, but also the most suitable for sustaining him in the long days and hard work he has to perform in all sorts of weathers and in all sorts of countries. Barley meal is heating, and meat or fish biscuits, in the opinion of experts, are generally considered unwholesome, for no one can say what they are composed of. When biscuits are used for a change in the summer season, ship biscuits are decidedly the best and most wholesome. Exercise, and plenty of it, is essential to the good health of a pack of hounds, and there is no greater mistake than to allow hounds in the summer to put on too much flesh.

Of the huntsman's duties in the field a more categorical description will be given later, and it will only be necessary at this point to state that in choosing a huntsman it will be well to ascertain if he has been brought up in a good school, and if he has been learning his business under a capable mentor. He should be a reliable servant who is willing to allow his hounds to do their share of the work without obtruding himself upon every opportunity. Nothing can be more distressing to a sportsman than to find himself associated with a huntsman who is always interfering with his hounds, who rides in front instead of behind them, and who, in short, wants to do all the work himself. Such an one will soon ruin any hounds, and convert them into a slack, disheartened, and unenterprising pack. "It is always great impertinence of a huntsman," says Beckford, "to pretend to make a cast himself before the hounds have made theirs." There is a depth of wisdom in this doctrine, which all sportsmen will at once acknowledge; and this good piece of advice is worthy of being printed, framed, and hung up in every boiling house. The writer's first impressions of a huntsman were derived from observation of the methods and practice of two remarkable men in their line, who inspired the veneration conceived by youth for those who have distinguished themselves in the world of sport. Jem Hills and Harry Ayris, then in their prime, carried the horn in the Heythrop and Berkeley countries, and each one of these well-known men had acquired a reputation for showing sport, handling hounds and accounting for a fox, which was not confined alone to the country in which his operations were conducted. Jem Hills was huntsman of the Heythrop hounds, but he was a native of Surrey, and came of a family well known in the foxhunting world, since it has turned out many capable huntsmen in days gone by. He was above the middle height, with a fine intelligent countenance and pleasant manner, and he possessed a fund of anecdotes which made him a favourite with all the country side; more especially was he beloved by the Oxford undergraduates, to many of whom he supplied lessons, inculcated by the observation of his practice in the field, which have never been forgotten. He was a good man to hounds in his particular way, going through rather than over a country, but he had a great aversion to jumping water, which often caused him to make some divergence from the line, though he always turned up as if by magic when it was supposed by the thrusters that they had left him far behind. His knowledge of the country and the run of the foxes stood him in good stead, and enabled him to take liberties with his hounds by lifting them in a failing scent. The art of doing this successfully seemed peculiar to him, though the writer has often seen others attempt to carry out the system, but nearly always with unsatisfactory results. When the fox appeared to have run us out of scent altogether, when there was no friendly holloa to guide and no beacon to steer for, and when it really seemed that there was nothing for it but to go home in the dumps, old Jem would catch hold of his hounds with his cheery "here-a-way, here-a-way," gallop off for a mile or so, when he would suddenly stop. "Yere-lert," down would go their noses; as if by magic they would hit the line, with a thrill of delight at the pleasure of once more getting on terms. Jem had the rare gift of being able to do all this without exciting hounds or getting their heads up. On the contrary, when he stopped, they would drop their noses at once, and settle to the line as if nothing out of the ordinary course had happened. But then it must be borne in mind that he always went with his hounds; he didn't gallop, screeching or blowing his horn half a field a-head, with the whippers-in rating and putting them on to him, but he kept his head, and so the hounds kept theirs.

Harry Ayris, who was huntsman to Lord Fitzhardinge, was an excellent servant, a capital rider, and one who was always ready to seize upon any advantage during the chase. Both of these celebrities hunted in a partly stone wall country, which certainly gives a huntsman a splendid opportunity of estimating the value of his hounds. In the first place he has an uninterrupted view of their work; whilst the chance of detecting skirters, mute hounds, babblers, unsteady ones given to riot, and those which cannot run up, becomes a certainty in the open country. Some of the faults enumerated in the above list may, and very often will, escape notice in a woodland country for a considerable time.

Let us follow a huntsman who knows his business into the field on a hunting morning. Let us suppose that he has received orders to draw first a wood of some sixty or eighty acres with a thick undergrowth of blackthorn. He will first consider from which quarter he may best approach this covert so as to give his hounds the wind. When he is about a hundred yards off, he will give his hounds a signal, and they will spread out like a fan, seeking meuses through the wood hedge; he will then himself proceed down the nearest ride, encouraging his hounds to draw with his voice. He will do this in leisurely fashion, taking care to keep behind rather than in front of his hounds whilst they are drawing. If he were to hurry them at all now, they would certainly slip out into the rides, for a foxhound dislikes nothing so much as to be left behind; and if the huntsman has not the full confidence of his hounds, they will become uneasy and shirk their work in covert. Some huntsmen will occasionally touch the horn whilst drawing, with the view, I suppose, of rousing the fox; but I cannot think this at all a necessary practice, for in my opinion the horn should be used as little as possible, and then only on occasions when it is really needed. But hark! old "*Traveller*" challenges. "*Have at him, Traveller!*" Every hound strains his very best to reach the veteran; the fox is unkennelled —we know that a fox well found is half killed—the glorious crash of music which follows fills the huntsman with ecstatic delight; he keeps as near to his hounds as the rides will permit, whilst they force the fox through the cover in such a determined fashion as will make him "fly or die." They are nearing the outside fence, in another second they pour over it like a cataract, and forcing his horse through a blind gap, our huntsman is behind them in the twinkling of an eye. A peculiar note of his horn, well known to "Dick" and "Joe," one screech, and, sitting down in his saddle, he runs his eye over the pack and gets a count. They are all there; and with a mind at ease he has time to look about him, and speculate on the probable point for which the fox is making. Hounds are meanwhile running over old pasture land, carrying a great head in the mute ecstasy of pace, and the huntsman riding behind them —a place of distinction which the master and he alone of all the field are privileged to hold. After twenty minutes, hounds check for the first time; and the huntsman, pulling up short, sits motionless like a statue, following them with rapt attention as they swing round and make their own cast, as it turns out unsuccessfully. Then, having done all they could without avail, they come back cheerfully to the huntsman to seek his aid. The cause of the trouble is easily perceived. Hounds have been revelling in the glorious scent peculiar to old grazing grounds, and they have now to work their way over the arable in the shape of a field of roots recently fed off by sheep. Naturally enough they cannot understand the difference in the scent, and they are disinclined to trouble themselves to work it out. The huntsman quietly holds them over the field, encouraging them to try; an old hound drops his nose; he shows a line; his companions follow his lead, soon they understand and settle to changed conditions, and, though they cannot trust themselves to race, they gradually surmount the difficulty, clustering like bees round old "*Traveller*," with their noses glued to the ground. Soon they come to grass again, and heads up and sterns down is once more the order of the day. A big woodland appears in view, and this is the point for which the fox has been making. He has entered it; but, to the intense joy of the huntsman, soon slips out into a ride, for, distressed as he is, he cannot make headway through the thick blackthorn covert. So the fox runs the rides, which is a certain indication that he has had enough, and the only fear is that a fresh one, disturbed from his kennel, should cross the line. There is but little chance of such a catastrophe, for there is no cry except a whimper or so as the leading hound snatches for the scent at the corners, and the huntsman knows better than to make any noise himself. By many signs he is well aware that the fox is close in front: the jays are blackguarding him, and show the way he goes. Now he slips out of cover and runs up the hedge side. Hounds catch a view, and straining their hardest, bowl him over with a snap and a worry. Fifty minutes, and every hound up. *Finis coronat opus.*

Whipper-in—The first whipper-in should be a light-weight, must be a good horseman, and, if he is to be a success, must make up his mind from the beginning to support the huntsman constantly and loyally. He must stop hounds and turn them to the huntsman's horn, even when he feels convinced they are right. In short, he must never attempt to take a leading part unless exceptional circumstances—such as an accident to the huntsman—should arise. Too much value should not be attached to the viewing of foxes in the early part of the chase; on the contrary, the whipper-in should rather be in attendance on the huntsman, ready to assist him as occasion requires; but when a fox has been on foot for forty minutes, and is beginning to run short, then is the time for the whipper-in to exercise his genius by getting forward for a view, stopping the fox from running his foil in cover and taking care that no fresh fox should allure hounds from the line. He should count his hounds upon every opportunity. The second whipper-in must also be a light-weight, and it is his duty to bring on any tail hounds, and to stop such as may have divided from the pack. He also should count hounds on every opportunity. In going to covert, the place of the first whipper-in is in front of the hounds, and that of the second some distance behind the huntsman; and he should take care to give hounds plenty of room to pick their way through muddy lanes and bridle-roads. When hounds are running riot, the whipper-in should get to the head of hounds before rating or attempting to stop them. Then the stinging lash should be applied to the ringleader, and he should be rated by name. In the case of hardened offenders, they may be taken up and flogged; but if it is found necessary to inflict this punishment, it should be done at the time, and not, as is sometimes the case, on the return of the hounds to the pack after a considerable interval of time has elapsed.

After all, hounds can only be made steady by constantly exercising them amidst din and riot of all kinds, and by judicious handling on the part of the huntsman. In windy weather hounds are often wild, and Vyner tells a story of a pack which one day broke away and commenced running the crows, which often skim along close to the ground in windy weather; and the old kennelman gave it as his opinion that they never would have been stopped at all if, "by the blessing of God, they had not changed to a jackass." Beckford thus recapitulates the qualifications of a whipper-in: "If your whipper-in be bold and active, be a good and careful horseman, have a good ear and a clear voice—if, as I said, he be a very Mungo, here, there and everywhere, having at the same time judgment to distinguish where he can be of most use; if joined to these, he be above the foolish conceit of killing a fox without the huntsman, but, on the contrary be disposed to assist him all he can, he then is a perfect whipper-in."

The necessity of counting hounds whenever it is possible to do so, has been insisted on, and as an illustration of the value of the practice, the following anecdote may be related. The writer, when he hunted the Croome country, found a fox in a large covert called Tiddesley Wood and hounds were not long in getting away. As they left I was able to count the pack, and discovered we were short of a hound. After a capital run the fox was killed the other side of Spatchley in the Worcestershire country and, on running them over, it appeared they still wanted a hound, and that hound was "Rambler." "Rambler" was never away before, and the writer, remembering that a hound was lost when they left Tiddesley Wood, told Fred, the second whipper-in, to ride back to that covert, many miles off, and see if he could hear anything of him. Fred accordingly rode through the boggy rides in the wood calling the hound's name and just as he was coming out in despair and giving it up as a bad job he heard a whimper. So getting off his horse and fighting his way through the blackthorn, he found poor old "Rambler" fast in a wire, set no doubt by some poacher for a fox, since it was almost strong enough to hold a man. If the master had not been able to count the hounds away from Tiddesley old "Rambler" would undoubtedly have perished miserably.

The Earth Stopper—In old times the "earth stopper" used to be part and parcel of a hunting establishment, and, mounted on a rough pony, with a spade over his shoulder, and carrying a lantern, it was his duty to proceed to the earths situated in the country which was to be drawn the following day, and carefully to stop them with earth or faggots about the hour of midnight. The fox, who feeds at night, upon returning at dawn, finds the access to his quarters barred, and so makes a kennel for himself in some snug place in the neighbouring covert. Now, however, it is generally left to the gamekeepers to undertake this duty in their respective beats, and it is questionable if they all of them perform this part of their work conscientiously and at the proper hour of night; many will content themselves by "putting to" the earths in the morning; but, where a country is frequently disturbed, foxes are shy and repair to their earths to lie with the first dawn of day, and so a blank draw is often the consequence of a piece of laziness on the part of the keeper. At the end of the season it is customary for the master to give an "earth stoppers'" feast, which is much looked forward to by those who are entitled to an invitation, and are accustomed to draw the pay which they are to receive. At this entertainment the tables are usually presided over by the huntsman, and a jolly evening is spent. These gatherings do much to encourage goodwill and promote the popularity of fox-hunting.

Kennels—All who have studied the questions involved in selecting the site of kennels, and who may therefore be regarded as authorities, agree that their position should be high and dry,—

> Its courts, wide opening to receive
> The sun's all-cheering beams when mild he shines
> And gilds the mountain tops,
> Upon some little eminence erect,
> And fronting to the ruddy dawn.

And when we reflect that our sport depends in so great a measure upon the health and condition of the hounds, it is not surprising that the construction and convenience of kennels is considered as a matter of the very first importance. The most essential qualification of a kennel is that it should be dry; for, if it is damp or insufficiently drained, or cold, you will always have lame hounds. Beckford's observations upon these points are so excellent that they should be followed in every particular; and, while he recommends economy, and condemns in sensible language the useless extravagance one sometimes finds in the architecture or building of kennels, he strongly advises that they should be of sufficient dimensions in the first place, for the simple reason that it is always difficult to make alterations when once the building has been completed.[1]

The floors of the lodging-rooms should be bricked and sloped on both sides, so as to carry off the water from the centre, and the yards which are attached to the lodging-rooms should be similarly constructed. The posts of the doors through which the hounds pass should always be rounded, otherwise these will be constantly causing injury to their stifles. The sleeping benches should be made of deal, and these should be open—that is, there should be a space of at least an inch between them, for reasons which are obvious—whilst they should be attached to the wall of the lodging-room by hinges, so that they may be folded up when the kennel is cleaned out. The benches should be low, in order that hounds may be prevented from creeping underneath, and also to enable them to jump upon them easily when they have come in tired from a long day's hunting. In some kennels the walls are heated by flues, and though this may be desirable enough in low and damp situations, it is hardly necessary when the building is on sound and high ground and not overshadowed by trees. Warm lodging, however, is absolutely indispensable for the comfort and well-doing of the pack, and must be secured at any cost, and, where dampness is found to exist the floor should be taken up and a layer of ashes and finely-broken stones put underneath. But, even with all these precautions, there will be occasional cases of rheumatic lameness in most kennels. Kennel lameness is, indeed, a dreadful calamity, which causes more uneasiness in the minds of huntsmen than any other affliction, because it is the most difficult to treat successfully. The only cure, as far as my experience goes, is to be found in a change of quarters. When a hound belonging to the writer was struck down with this scourge he was accustomed to send him to the kennels of a good friend who lived at some distance off, and he was invariably sent back sound in the course of a few weeks. Still, hounds which have once been troubled with it are, as a rule, always liable to a return of the malady, and are never to be depended upon. An old friend of mine, who was a master of foxhounds of considerable standing, used to say laughingly that in his belief the real origin of kennel lameness proceeded from bad shoulders, and it is certainly true that the disease is more frequently to be found in hounds with this defect than with those of perfect conformation.

AN OLD-TIME EARTH STOPPER.

The boiling-house is usually placed at the back of the building, with well-seasoned elm boards fastened to the wall to receive the

[1] It is said that the construction of the kennels at Goodwood cost £19,000.

pudding when it is taken out of the boiler. There should be two boilers made of cast iron, one for cooking flesh and the other for meal. The water-tanks in the yard should be made of slate, which is more readily kept clean than iron or wooden troughs, and care should be taken to enforce the regular cleaning and filling of them. It is unnecessary to add that there should always be an unfailing supply of pure water, since a very large quantity of this fluid is required for washing down the courts and dormitories. Nothing can equal good old Irish or Scotch oatmeal as food for foxhounds, and it is better always to have at least six months' supply in hand, for not only does it improve with age, but it also goes further by keeping. Great care should be taken to secure good meal, for in this, as in other food, there is often a considerable amount of adulteration. The flesh-house should be at some distance, since the smell which proceeds from it is neither pleasant nor conducive to health. To every kennel there should be attached a large walled-in yard, some three or four acres in extent, in which the young hounds just brought in from quarters should be allowed to exercise themselves during the greater part of the day. The number of hounds to be kept will regulate the size of the kennel, which need not be a very expensive structure.

Distemper is a disease which almost invariably attacks young hounds on coming into kennel, and which carries off a large proportion of the sufferers. It often appears in a variety of forms, which are all difficult to treat; but, when the yellows, or jaundice, accompanies distemper, the combination in ninety-nine cases out of a hundred proves fatal.

Distemper, for the most part, affects hounds in the same way as the visitation of influenza in human beings; for it generally attacks the head and is accompanied by a virulent discharge from the eyes and nostrils. The disease is felt in the brain and back, and it often happens that, when young hounds appear to have recovered, a twitching of the limbs remains behind; and when they are afflicted in this way, it is better to knock them on the head at once, for they will never prove capable of service in the field. When hounds come in from quarters where they have been well done and are full of flesh, the disease will generally attack the lungs and liver, and calomel is the best remedy which can be employed. Every huntsman has a nostrum of his own, which he thinks a specific cure for the malady; but, in spite of all this knowledge, the disease carries off large numbers of young hounds every year, and, of course, the weather has great influence in retarding the cure if it be wet or cold. Warm and dry quarters, with generous living, when the virulence of the disease is passing away, are the best remedies which can be employed. Some use Turkish baths, and this treatment is discussed in the paragraph which deals with jaundice.

Yellows, a disease corresponding with jaundice in the human frame, is often produced by excessively good feeding, and, at the same time, insufficient exercise. The sufferer must be kept in a warm place; but the complaint is very seldom successfully treated, and never when it is allied with distemper. A friend of the writer attached great value to the curative properties of the Turkish bath in cases of yellows; and he was accustomed to put his sick hounds in the bath, at the same time giving them as much water as they would lap, which he declared expelled the bile from the system; but, as I have never seen this treatment employed, I cannot speak of it with the confidence engendered by personal experience of the application of the remedy.

The Rounding of young hounds, which should not be performed till they are well over the distemper, is a painful operation, but one which it is supposed will save hounds from suffering from the wounds and laceration inflicted by drawing strong blackthorn coverts, if the ears are allowed to retain their long tips. A butcher's block with a smooth surface must be obtained, and upon this the ear is stretched, then a half-moon iron, laid on the tip, is struck with a mallet, and the operation is completed. A little oil will soon heal the sores, and in a very few days hounds will be able to go out. In several kennels the operation of rounding has been abolished.

Great stress should be laid upon the order that rounding should not be performed until young hounds are over distemper and have quite recovered their strength and spirits, for, if they are at all lower in condition, the loss of blood consequent upon the operation will pull them back and perhaps cause them to miss a part of the early education of cub hunting.

Drafts of old and and young hounds are made annually from every kennel, and the reasons for which the old ones are drafted are unsoundness in limb or constitution; for being rogues, that is wide runners, or skirters; for running mute; or for being noisy, that is babbling or speaking where no fox has been; for throwing their tongue when going to cry, or hanging on the line: because all of these vicious propensities would be likely to contaminate by their evil example the rest of the pack; then young hounds are got rid of because they are not "sorty," that is that they will not match the others in size or colour, or because they do not appear to have robust constitutions. Drafts were formerly considered to be the perquisite of the huntsman, but of late years gentlemen have found it desirable to take the management in this direction entirely in their own hands. The price for the old and young draft is usually fixed at three guineas a couple; but for the second draft of young hounds, which is often not made until just before the season for cub-hunting commences, five guineas a couple is not uncommonly demanded.

Coverts—The biggest woods will always hold the best foxes; big woods are the real preserves for good foxes; those found in gorse and stick coverts are often short runners. Foxes prefer natural coverts, which lie high; if these are warm and thick at the bottom, with plenty of shelter from the different quarters of the wind, they will seldom be drawn blank. The large woods and blackthorn brakes will prove a favourite resort, and, if the foxes are let alone, will always hold. We must, however, occasionally make artifical coverts; but these, like artificial earths are seldom satisfactory, and if great care is not taken to make the latter in a dry situation, it is not at all improbable that they will be the means of introducing mange into the country. However, it is often desirable to plant coverts in certain portions of a country where none exist, and also to establish a connecting link between woodlands and the more open portions of the country. The subject of making these coverts must be carefully considered, and only those planted which are likely to flourish, and suit the soil in which they are found. Thus in a strong, heavy, clay district gorse will never really succeed; and it will be much better to plant blackthorn, than which nothing in this description of land is more likely to grow kindly. Moreover, it is no joke to attempt to force your way through a strong blackthorn covert; and for this reason alone it may be cultivated, for it will be more likely to lie quiet. After all, the great secret of attraction to foxes is complete tranquillity. But in certain countries gorse is indigenous to the soil, and then there can be no better covert. If it is decided to plant a gorse, a piece of sound ground should be chosen and drained if necessary, and the land should be summer fallowed, well cleaned and manured as if for swedes. About three pounds of seed to the acre should be drilled in the month of April, and this should be treated in every respect the same as a crop of swedes, and well hoed until the gorse has out-grown the weeds. Rabbits are very fond of gorse, and they must be kept down in the earlier stages of its growth. Every fifth year a patch of the gorse, which by this time will probably have become hollow and weak, should be cut or burnt, and perhaps the latter plan is the better of the two. Privet, rhododendrons and laurels are sometimes planted, but they can never make such satisfactory covers as gorse or blackthorn, but the writer has known Jerusalem artichokes a certain find. Osier beds are a favourite resort for foxes, partly because they are grown on land which has been thrown up, and which is, in consequence of this treatment, high and dry, and partly because they are usually grown near brooks or rivers, where the water-rats are a great attraction. The writer recollects a small covert belonging to a staunch sportsman, which was drawn by hounds on an average once every three weeks during the season. It was not more than three or four acres in extent, and yet it never failed to produce a fox, and even if one was killed from it after a run, another one took his place and was always forthcoming when the hounds came. Some supposed that the old sportsman had some method of attracting the foxes, and the neighbours used to say that he was accustomed to trail a rat as a drag from several points to the copse, in which he always took care there should be a plentiful supply of dead rats. When you want to make some coverts which will hold at once, stick covers and faggot covers are often found to produce the desired result. A quantity of long ash poles should be felled, and should rest upon some forks stuck firmly in the ground, about two feet high. These should be roofed as it were with the loppings of young fir-trees, and hedge trimmings thrown all over, and if these small places, which need not be more than a couple of acres in extent, are securely fenced round and in quiet, foxes will soon lie in them; or you can fence a certain quantity of land and set up ordinary faggots not very far apart, and in the course of a summer's growth brambles, thorns, and long grass will twine themselves over the interstices, and make an impenetrable covert.

Scent—That no uncertainty in the world is greater than that of scent is the conclusion I have arrived at after close observation extending over more than forty years; and I should be sorry to take upon myself to lay down any rule with regard to it, knowing, as I do, that it has always been a puzzle to the best recognised authorities in many generations. Mr. Jorrocks remarks that scent is a "weary, incomprehensible, incontrollable phenomenon, constant only in its inconstancy;" and he adds that "nothing is so queer as scent except a woman." Somervile believed scent to depend upon the air alone.

> "Then on the air
> Depend the hunter's hopes."

But in this conjecture we know he was wrong, since we are all aware that some varieties of soil carry scent better than others; that when the land picks up, as it will do when a white frost yields to the influence of the sun, hounds can scarcely carry on the line over the sticky fallows; and, when the leaf falls in October, we know there will be no scent in cover until it is rotted by the heavy rains of November. These reasons are sufficient, in my opinion, to dispel the accuracy of Somervile's theory that scent is in the air only. Beckford says that scent depends chiefly on two things, "the condition the ground is in, and the temperature of the air;" and I am inclined to think a better definition cannot be found, and that when this happy combination occurs the prospects of sport are almost reduced to a certainty. "Scrutator" believed that there were two kinds of scent, one proceeding or exuding from the body and breath of the animal when in motion, and the other that left by the foot or pad. There are certain mystical signs or symbols indicative of the probabilities of a good scent or otherwise which must not be despised. Thus when hounds roll upon the grass, when they eat grass going to the meet, when they lash their sterns in drawing so as to stain them with blood, when gossamer floats, and cobwebs lie on the grass, when hurtling storms sweep over, and when the barometer falls and rainbows are seen in the sky,[1] —all these may be taken as indications of a bad scent; yet, as no one can possibly affirm it will be so, a sportsman will never give way to despair nor relax his efforts to show sport even in such untoward circumstances. Most huntsmen have their own ideas on the prospects of the day. Jem Hills could never "abear them nasty blue mists;" Harry Ayris held "a cold wind from the south" in equal abhorrence; whilst of Will Todd it is said that he was accustomed to remark on a propitious morning, "He must fly or die to-day, gentlemen."

When hounds exhibit unusual keenness on their road to the meet, when they smell strong coming out of kennel, when paving-stones sweat, when the barometer rises, when the atmosphere is so clear that you can almost count the thorns upon the hedges,—all these are favourable signs which are often found to denote a scent. Wind is always regarded as being most antagonistic to sport, and Beckford says, "Never take out your hounds on a windy day." There are, however, exceptions to every rule, and I can well remember a capital run in very windy weather. In February, 1867, the North Cotswold Hounds, of which the writer was then master, met at the Fish Inn. It blew a gale when we started, which increased in force until it was a regular hurricane when we left the meet. We drew Armley Bank, and it was dangerous work to ride in covert, for the wind snapped off some of the larch trees half way up, and they were falling about in all directions. We found a fox, however, and killed him after a good run at Stanway, a capital point, and it is worthy of remark that the fox *ran up-wind all the way*. In heathy countries in certain conditions there is a good scent; on a large tract of common land, known as Defford Common, in the Croome country, hounds will run hard even if a fox is half an hour or more ahead of them, because the fox brushes against the ant-hills, &c., with which it is covered. When hounds, getting well away with their fox, drive him up the wind at a rattling pace for fifteen or twenty minutes, if he turns down the wind, as he is almost certain to do, he is not unfrequently lost, for the reason that the hounds, all aglow with dash and fire after revelling in a burning scent, are most unwilling to stoop and hunt a colder line. It is at this critical juncture that the science and skill of a clever huntsman are called forth. Sitting like a statue on his horse, and motioning the field to do the same, he will encourage his hounds to drop their noses; he knows full well that any movement of his may upset their mercurial temperament and make them still more unwilling to descend to the drudgery of working out the line after the splendid fling in which they have been indulged; and his patience is indeed well and amply rewarded when old "Prudence," pushing her way through the pack, which with heads up are standing around uncertain and unsettled after the excitement of the burst, shows the line at a canter down the furrow, and, with a note sweeter to the ear of the huntsman than the most entrancing music, rings the knell of the doomed fox. Getting together and clustering round her, hounds settle like bees upon the line, which they will now never leave until the varmint is accounted for. When a fox runs the road it is often a long time before hounds will drop their noses and work out the line; but in every pack there is always one old road-hunter to be depended on, which comes to the rescue on these occasions, and when once he shows the way others take up the line with a determination and at a pace which leads one to wonder why on earth there ever should have been the slightest difficulty in hitting it off at once. A huntsman cannot give hounds too much time in reason upon a road, and he must be careful also to give them plenty of room and see that his followers do the same. When a frost is in the air and coming on at night hounds will almost always run with a burning scent.

When sheep cross the line of the fox during chase, a check invariably ensues, but no description of stock foils the scent so badly as colts. On these occasions the judgment and patience of the huntsman are called into requisition, and the services of a line hunter to guide the pack through their temporary difficulties are of inestimable value; for, when hounds have been running hard and are settled to the line it is a great mistake, in my opinion, to take them off their noses and rely upon lifting, unless there is no help for such a proceeding. In these circumstances patience is needed and a huntsman who knows his hounds will make them hunt the line, however indisposed they may have been in the first instance to work it out. In making a cast a huntsman should always have at least three-fourths of the pack in front of his horse.

Hounds—A hundred and fifty years ago there were two tribes of hounds, namely, the Southern and Northern. The former variety was chiefly used by those who were accustomed

[1] "When the dew hangs on the thorn,
The huntsman may put up his horn."

to follow the chase on foot; but the Northern breed possessed pace, and dash, and drive, so that their pursuers were obliged to ride to keep up with them. Gradually, however, these distinctive breeds disappeared, and, early in the present century, it would seem that a fixed type of merit was settled, and speed, beauty, stoutness, and nose became the ruling characteristics of the more modern breed. A foxhound should be 23½ inches high; his legs should be straight, his bone well carried down, his feet round, his neck clean, his shoulders well placed, and sufficiently strong and deep; his back broad, his stern not coarse, but set on so that he carries it well; his thighs muscular, his head rather large than small, and his conformation symmetrical throughout. When hounds stand over at the knee and are out of elbows, their shoulders will not always bear a strict scrutiny, and when they are light below the knee, and back at the knees, it sometimes happens that they are flat-sided, and generally wanting in muscle.

To form and establish a pack of hounds is a serious consideration indeed, and one who achieves success in an undertaking of the kind must be possessed of knowledge, energy, and judgment. A young master will do well if he can see his way to buy a pack which has been together for some years, otherwise the task of formation must be accomplished by purchasing drafts from the best kennels. Having these he will be unlucky if he cannot add supplementary assistance in the shape of some few couple of reliable working hounds, which he may have been able to beg or buy in the course of the summer. It will be advisable to put on a strong lot of young hounds in the first season, and with care and attention, in three or four years' time he should be able to get together a respectable pack of hounds. In breeding, the best kennels should be resorted to, and the best stallion hounds used. If good walks are plentiful, advantage should be taken of this piece of good fortune to breed as largely as possible, which is the certain road to obtain a good pack. The bitches should litter in the spring; that is to say, in the months of February, March, and April. Late puppies seldom thrive. The pedigrees will of course be strictly kept, and the puppies should be named before they are sent out to walk, and also branded on the side with a letter, denoting the name of the owner or country.

A great many sportsmen are prejudiced in regard to the colour of their hounds, and the Belvoir tan is generally admired and preferred to any other. No doubt uniformity in this respect makes the pack much more sorty, and adds to the beauty of their appearance. No sensible breeder will, however, use a stallion hound only because he excels in beauty of colour and conformation, and he will, in the first place, require to know from some trustworthy source whether the hound bears a good character in his work before he decides to avail himself of his services. It is the dash and high courage of a foxhound which is his chief distinguishing merit, and, if his eagerness should lead him to overrun the line with a twisting fox, yet this impetuosity is atoned for by the brilliant way in which he will do his work when scent serves.

The speed of hounds appears to have been a matter which excited great interest among sportsmen of the past, and we read that Mr. Meynell and Mr. Smith-Barry made a match for 500 guineas to run each a couple of hounds over the Beacon Course at Newmarket—4 miles 1 furlong and 177 yards. Mr. Barry's hounds were Bluecap, four years, and Wanton, three years; and Will Crane commenced training them on August 1st, teaching them to run keenly on a drag, and feeding them on oatmeal and milk and sheep's trotters. It is stated that Mr. Meynell's hounds were fed during the time of training with legs of mutton. The match was run on September 30th, 1762, and the drag from the Rubbing House on the Old Cambridgeshire Course, Newmarket Town End, to the Rubbing House at the starting post of the Beacon Course. The hounds were laid on the scent, and accomplished the distance in a few seconds more than eight minutes. Mr. Barry's Bluecap came in first, his Wanton (very close to Bluecap) second. Mr. Meynell's Richmond was beaten by 100 yards, and his bitch, the second string, never came in at all. The betting was seven to four on Mr. Meynell's hounds. Threescore horses started with the hounds, but of these twelve only were up at the finish, and the mare which carried Cooper, Mr. Barry's huntsman, who was first up, became quite blind. Merlin, a bitch bred by Col. Thornhill, was very speedy, and it is recorded of her that she ran a trial of four miles in seven minutes and half a second. This bitch, we read, was eventually sold for four hogsheads of claret, and the seller to have two couples of her whelps. The horses appear to have cut a poor figure in the trial over the Beacon Course, and this probably led to the frequent discussions which took place with regard to the relative speed of hounds and horses.

About thirty-five years ago, if the writer's memory is correct, a match was made between the Duke of Beaufort and Lord Glasgow, in which the former undertook to run his hounds against horses named by the latter over the Beacon Course at Newmarket. The match gave rise to a good deal of speculation at the time, and each side had its champions, but for some reason or other it was abandoned. The general opinion at the time was in favour of the horses, and considerable odds were betted that they would prove victorious.

Hound shows, which were held at Yarm, York, Cheltenham, and other places, have finally found a resting place at Peterborough, where they are annually held in the month of July.

The advantages of comparison are generally acknowledged, and without doubt these shows have done much to improve the breed and awake fresh interest in the noble science. No one would think of sending a crooked hound for exhibition; and masters and huntsmen from north and south and friends of the chase, make a point of being present; for the meeting at Peterborough is a sort of hunting parliament where changes are discussed and views ascertained and given on intricate cases, where any difference of opinion exists.

Mr. Vyner, writing in 1841 in *Notitia Venatica*, foreshadowed the good work of hound shows, and remarked that nothing would be more likely to improve the breed of foxhounds. He pointed out that the awarding of prizes to the best breeders and feeders of cattle had been attended with the most beneficial results, and could see no reason why improvement in the breed of the foxhound should not be promoted by the same means; and he further observed that, a few years before, three celebrated masters of hounds—Mr. Hodgson, Mr. Wickstead, and Mr. Foljambe—made a practice of showing a few couples of their new entry for a prize, which was most appropriate—namely, a piece of scarlet cloth to be made up into hunting-coats.

COVENTRY.

[*See also* DOGS and HOUND BREEDING.]

DRAG—Lowest, perhaps, in the scale of hunting comes the drag, though lowest only in the sense of not needing a wild or semi-wild animal for its object of pursuit. In strictly orthodox circles a drag hunt is always mentioned with somewhat bated breath, but at the same time it is by no means an amusement to be despised. Its followers do not claim for it that it is a high form of sport, while it is an excellent school for riding, and does not make so great demands on the forbearance of farmers or occupiers of land as either stag, fox, or hare hunting. The line of route can lie just where the master pleases; the horses need never enter a corn or clover field, or where there are root crops; and if a man objects to his land being ridden over, his wish can be respected without difficulty. To those who go out for the sake of a gallop a drag hunt is of short duration and makes but small inroads on the day's business.

The drag, however, is by no means a modern institution, for there is every reason to believe that in the times of the Stuarts trail scents were very common, and, as we know from Mr. Hoare's *History of Newmarket*, there was in Charles II.'s reign "a plate at Woodstock given to hounds running a trail scent over four miles," for which any gentleman might put in a hound; while at the same place in 1682 there was a buck and trail scent for hounds. The famous match between the hounds of Mr. Meynell, who then hunted the Quorn country, and Mr. Smith Barry, the Master of the Cheshire, shows that in the middle of the last century drag hunting took place. In its origin the trail scent was a race for hounds, but in course of time men began to ride to the hounds, and then a plan was hit upon for running a drag for the sole purpose of having a gallop.

A good many people say that the drag is not a sport, but at the same time even the most orthodox are loudest in their praise of hunting when the run after stag, fox, or hare most nearly assimilates to the drag, that is to say, when hounds go as hard as they can from start to finish. The foxhound must be regarded as an animal which can adapt itself to various circumstances, for he will run not only the usual beasts of the chase, but the otter and the drag as well, and when he has gone at his best pace for something like half-an-hour or forty minutes, he finds his reward in the paunch which awaits him when the drag hunt is over.

The *modus operandi* of running a drag is tolerably well known. Various masters have their own *recipe* for a drag, but perhaps the most common way is to keep a tame fox in the kennel, and then on hunting days to put the litter into a net, or it is sometimes put into a hare's skin. This is trailed over the ground, and every five minutes or so a few drops of oil of aniseed, or occasionally turpentine, are added, and after a little practice the hounds will stoop to this scent as readily as to that of the stag or fox. Generally speaking, the drag is laid by a man who runs the line on foot, but sometimes he is mounted. The former plan is, however, preferable, since the drag will not jump about so much as when it is trailed behind a horseman.

It is easy to arrange whether the line shall be stiff or not, and it should be understood that the drag is not laid over any trappy fences. The hounds need not of course be very valuable specimens, though in well-maintained packs, like that, for instance, kept at Windsor, a process of heading and tailing goes on, until they all go much of a pace. The usual plan is to have a check half-way through the run, when second horses are mounted, and after a few minutes the run begins again. A properly laid drag will leave a good scent behind it for about an hour after the runner has gone along, and even then the hounds go at a great pace. As before mentioned, the drag has taught many a man to ride. The fences may be big, and brooks may come in the way, but there is some sort of guarantee that a man will not find himself jumping into a quarry or on to a plough, as may be the case when hunting. Since, of course, every man who goes out with a drag hunts to ride, there is always more rivalry than is the case in other forms of hunting. A fast bold horse is necessary, and so long as he be a good jumper he need not be the most valuable animal in the stable, for he has not to make a long day.

It is rather surprising, perhaps, that so few packs of drag hounds exist. There are but eight, namely the Birkenhead, Cambridge University, Dublin County, Greenford, Household Brigade, Middlesex Farmers, Royal Artillery, and Staff College; and of these the most noteworthy are the Windsor and the Woolwich Drags, the former being kept by the Guards and the latter by the Artillery. In former days both Oxford and Cambridge Universities had each their drags, but the Oxford institution has now fallen into desuetude. At Cambridge, however, it flourishes greatly, the reason probably being that around that city the hunting is not so good as around Oxford, so the Cantabs make up for natural disadvantages by a drag laid over the best of the country.

In one respect a good many hunting men might learn from the drag hunts, since there is perhaps more good feeling between the farmers and the followers of the drag than in any other form of hunting. Hospitalities are not unknown, while in various other ways the kindness of the farmer in allowing his land to be ridden over is readily acknowledged by those who ride after what is sometimes called the "red herring."

W. C. A. BLEW.

HARE—Let it be granted that a harrier is a hound that hunts the hare chiefly by scent, and we need waste neither time nor space in endeavouring to ascertain *unde derivatur*, for indeed it is of little importance what the harrier formerly was, whether he was descended from the talbot or southern hound, or whether his remote ancestors were those "Castoreans," or hybrids between hare- and fox-hounds, which Xenophon declared to be the only two sorts used for this purpose. What really concerns the modern sportsman is to understand how and with what equipage one of the most ancient and fascinating of pursuits is now conducted.

Packs—There are, at the present moment, according to the Rural Almanack, 119 packs of harriers in England, 2 in Scotland, and 28 in Ireland, making a total of 149 for the United Kingdom; and there are 48 packs of beagles. In 1879 there were 97 packs in England, 2 in Scotland, and 43 in Ireland, with 18 packs of beagles. In 1880, 99 packs in England, in Scotland none recorded, and in Ireland 40—beagle packs being 20. In 1881, 97 packs in England, none again in Scotland, 44 in Ireland, and of beagles 21. The curious feature of these statistics, and the reason of their being quoted is that as far as they concern England they are almost the contrary of what we should have expected.

Sir W. Harcourt's Act "For the better protection of occupiers of land against injury to their crops from ground game," or, to give the well-known short title, "The Hares and Rabbits Bill," was passed in 1880; and everybody knows the enormous destruction of hares which took place as soon as that Act came into operation; in many places, indeed, they became practically extinct, and it would naturally be inferred that the effect of such destruction would have been to diminish the number of packs of harriers. It is indeed a fact that several packs were given up during the eighties on account of the number of blank days they experienced; but as there are twenty more harrier establishments now than there were in 1880, we must conclude that the disappearance of the hare in some places was counterbalanced by his diminution in others to such reasonable quantity, that it became possible to hunt where before it was out of the question on account of the constant changing, which is a greater annoyance to the huntsman and does far more injury to his pack than an occasional blank day.

Formation of Pack—The number of hounds wherewith to take the field must needs vary according to the fancy or pocket of the Master. There is no reason why five or six couple of real good-nosed ones should not kill a hare, but they would take a long time about it, not being enough to cover sufficient ground in their casts. On the other hand, more than eighteen couple at the very outside get in each other's way, and tumble over and distract each other, for there frequently occur moments in every chase when the problem of a hare's passage over two or three feet of ground is considered of vital importance by the whole pack. They literally lay their heads together over it, coming back to this particular spot time after time, as their one reliable point of departure, and it is easy to see that on such occasions the less jostling there is the better.

To say that ten or twelve couple should be taken out, of course means that a larger number must be kept. Harriers are almost always worked in mixed packs, and as bitches go to heat usually at the most inconvenient periods of the season, allowance must be made for their seclusion as well as for absence on sick leave from accidents and other causes. But if a man has twenty-five couple of good working hounds in his kennel—and he ought to keep no other—he need never fear being unable to bring to the meet a sufficient pack for all purposes of true sport. How to get together that number of trustworthy harriers is a matter which will occupy his most serious attention, unless he is one of those to whom money is of no object. In that case, the best thing he can do is to wait till some real good pack comes into the market; it is seldom that a year passes by without such being the case, and the prospective Master may well occupy some months in going about studying the manners and customs of hare hunters in various parts of the country. He will learn something everywhere, and be all the better equipped with knowledge by the time he makes his own start. If he can tempt the owner of any pack which specially pleases him to part with it privately, he had better not haggle overmuch about terms—it is impossible to lay down any rule as to what the cost should be, but speaking very broadly, about £100 will often buy the lot if he takes them old and young *en bloc*. Many and many a right down good old established pack has been thus sold for £25. In the case of the aspirant preferring to buy at auction, he must of course take his chance in that notoriously uncertain market. But five or six guineas a couple is a very high price, though instances do occur where they run into really large figures, *e.g.*, Major Wickham, who sold a celebrated and beautiful pack in the spring of 1897, realised in several instances as much as thirty-five guineas a couple, and a total of 500 guineas. Though a Master of Harriers must lay his foundation on purchased hounds, whether he buys a ready-made pack, or goes through the misery of making one for himself out of drafts picked up at random all over the country, the sooner he begins to breed for himself the better —no small part of the amusement of keeping hounds consists in watching the development of the young ones born and reared at home, and noting how far they emulate the virtues and vices of their parents; the latter will probably predominate, since it is far easier to reproduce evil than good; all the greater on that account is the pleasure when, as is not infrequently the case, the offspring is even straighter, truer, and stauncher than sire or dam. And once the Master has started breeding on his own account, let him, except in case of dire necessity, such as an outbreak of hydrophobia in the kennel, or his pack being over-ridden by a railway train, at once and for ever abjure having anything to do with drafts, beyond selling his own if his good luck or repute should bring him a customer. It is a true saying that the only certainty about a draft is that it consists of animals of which the owner, doubtless for some good reason, is anxious to be rid, and as the only reason which at all commends itself to the buyer is that of size, it is always because they are too big or too small that they are weeded. With puppies this may be a valid excuse, and puppies are the safest to buy, if buy you must. A present of a hound should never be even considered. Why should a man give away what is good? Or why should another accept what is bad? Even in the case of stallion hounds it is better to decline a gift. If an owner breeds, as nowadays most people do, from pure foxhound, there is no difficulty in getting a choice of small doghounds, and the fee, if anything is charged beyond a tip to the kennel huntsman, is but trifling. As the less is, or can be, contained in the greater, a brief sketch of an establishment where things are really done in first-class style without unnecessary display or profusion, may be useful to those whose ambition soars somewhat higher than the possession of a scratch pack—a mere agglomeration of dogs such as one often sees working under the name of harriers. Be it remembered too that in many respects it is quite as cheap to have things smartly as slovenly done, for instance in the matter of cleanliness! If a man is kept to sweep and wash the kennel and prepare the food, he will require just as much pay for being careless, dirty, and unpunctual, as he will for having everything in apple-pie order and ready to the minute. See therefore that he earns his wages.

Accommodation—Let us suppose then that our Master has got a pack together strong enough to hunt three days a week, and that, having obtained a roving commission to pursue the hare over a wide tract of country, he must lay his account to have now and then long distances to come home, besides an occasional 15 miles to covert. For this purpose he will have provided at least 25 couple, standing as nearly as possible 21 inches; that is, if he hunts a mixed pack, as most likely will be his choice. If, however, he chooses to divide the dogs and bitches, he will take the latter at 19 to 20 inches average, and run anything over that standard with the dog pack. For the accommodation of this number of hounds, he will require 2 yards with sleeping rooms attached, each yard to be about 22 by 18 feet, paved according to the fancy of the proprietor. (We are supposing always that our M.H. is starting everything *ab ovo*, and can have what he wants in the way of building.) There is nothing better than asphalte, scored and slightly inclined so as to facilitate washing; it wears far better than flagstones, which are sometimes very difficult to procure, is cheaper than brick, and is so easy to patch and mend when chipped. The lodging-houses should be thatched with straw inside, by far the best way of keeping a good mean temperature in summer and winter; and, if the sides are tiled half-way up, the rooms not only look more cheerful but are easier to clean. The beds should be raised a foot or so from the floor, and there is no need for much space per hound; they like to lie close and keep each other warm in cold weather; when it is very hot, the door may be left open and they can go outside. It is well also to have a third smaller yard where sick hounds and bitches at heat can be left, but it is evident that the farther the latter are removed from their comrades the better. Where there is no lack of elbow-room, it may be a good plan to have in addition a good-sized gravel yard, where occasionally the whole pack can run together, but when forces are thus joined, it is highly advisable for the feeder or some one whom they know to be within hearing, as a quarrel may arise at any moment amongst hounds. In fact it takes very few to get up a wrangle, which, if not promptly suppressed, nearly always results in serious mischief, when the best hounds are usually the victims, perhaps because the real good ones are often a little bit queer in their tempers. One of the best ways of preventing these outbreaks is absolutely to forbid the presence of terriers within the kennel walls on any pretext whatever; they are the very dragon's teeth of discord.

A boiler house for cooking the food will be required, and as this will open into its own small yard, there is no necessity for a feeding-room unless such be the whim of the paymaster.

The whole of these buildings should be surrounded with a high wall with coping stones projecting on the inside. Iron railed doors and gates are best; if wood is used, they must be covered with iron or zinc as far as hounds can reach. It is astonishing how soon they can gnaw through woodwork, and how much pleasure they apparently find in the employment.

The water supply will have to depend on the possibilities of the place. Anyhow, fresh water must be kept in troughs both in the yards and lodging-houses; the ideal plan, of course, is to have a stream constantly running through them, that being the only way of preventing hounds fouling the water; it makes, moreover, the sluicing down of the kennels a matter of ease and therefore of tolerable certainty; but there is not always a water company or a reservoir within reach, so the best must be made of the existing situation—always insisting that drinking water shall be accessible, and the places kept scrupulously clean.

Feeding—The food for such a pack will be the same as if they were engaged in their birthright pursuit of the fox. The best oatmeal and clean horseflesh must be their portion, with greenstuff boiled up occasionally, especially in the spring months. It is true that up to a certain point harriers will work well on Indian meal, which costs far less than oatmeal, and is indeed as cheap a feeding stuff as can be found; but the certain point means that they must be given neither long days nor long distances. You could hardly get a maize-fed pack home at all if they had an 18 mile trot at the end of the day's work, whereas those nourished on oatmeal would jog along round the huntsman's horse with their sterns over their backs.

Spratt's fish biscuits make a capital change from flesh during the non-hunting season, and are perhaps to be preferred in hot weather, and it is said that Hobman's dog cakes are equally good, but a pack of harriers which—not being dependent on the casual attentions of servants with other occupations—is properly exercised in and out of season, can stand a very liberal diet. As to time of feeding, the system may slightly vary in different kennels, but it may be laid down as a good general rule never to feed till one hour after returning from the chase. Hounds eat better than if given their food at once, and the interval may be occupied by having them sluiced over with warm water and then sprinkled with good broth; as is well known, hounds soon lick each other clean when this has been done. In summer, after horse exercise, they should never be fed till evening, no matter how long they have to wait; they sleep better after the late meal.

The hounds that have hunted should always lodge together, those that have not been out are restless, jealous, quarrelsome, and apt in consequence to disturb the rest of their tired companions. There is no reason why dogs and bitches should not sleep together, if care is taken that none of the latter are at heat or near it.

Staff—Presuming always that the Master hunts his own hounds, or at any rate that there is a gentleman-huntsman, the staff for such a pack need consist only of two men—a whipper-in and kennelman. The latter will never go hunting; he will find plenty to do looking after the hounds left at home, and having all ready for the return of the day's workers. The whipper-in will take the pack to covert, assisted by the groom, who takes on the Master's hunter, and who can remain out with hack or cart to help on the home journey should the M.H. be disinclined for the job. It takes a very short time to make hounds acquiesce in being thus handed over to the servants by the beloved provider of sport; indeed, I am not sure that they do not go home all the more steadily for such a signal that the business of the day is concluded. With a pack of this standard, in good condition, there will never be any necessity for vanning, always an expensive and inconvenient process which makes hounds lazy and dependent. "Where are your hounds?" said a fond Master to his colleague-huntsman whom he met in company with but a few couples. "Those that are not eating sausages are looking for the van," was the reply; the moral of which is that to do real work a pack should never be petted or spoilt like children.

Cost of Establishment—The following is a rough estimate of what such an establishment as has been here described would cost. The figures are supplied by a gentleman who has quite lately given up the cares of Mastership, and may therefore be taken as up-to-date. He puts whipper-in's book at £250. This included the man's wages, those of the feeder and flesh. Meal and biscuit bill, £140; rent of house for head man £16; keep of horse and a half £80 at least; liveries £20; dinner to farmers who walked puppies £20; in fact he arrives at a total of between £600 and £700 a year, and does not think that any one could keep twenty-five couples of hounds properly for less—an estimate which would surely frighten away the majority of aspirants, unless they bear in mind that the establishment above described is one conducted on the best and most liberal style consistent with absence of pomp or swagger, and that it is quite possible to have an immense deal of sport two days a week (three is an unusual number for harriers), at a third or even less of this outlay. Otherwise there would be very little hare-hunting in England in these days of general retrenchment in the agricultural counties.

A man may get together a cry of dogs for a comparatively moderate sum, more especially if he goes in for that most doubtfully bred animal called the genuine harrier. He will get some queer-shaped and some very rough-coated ones—two defects which even by careful breeding he may never be able to eliminate, the mixed ancestry being wont to reassert itself; but with perseverance he will get plenty of nose, plenty of music, and quite pace enough for the sort of horse best suited for his purpose. Great jumping power rather than speed in his mount is the hare-hunter's requisite; he will kill a lot of hares by steady hunting and show much sport to his field in the process. Fifteen or sixteen couples will suffice for this modest turn-out, and of these, with fair luck, an average of twelve couples should be able to show at the meet. Nineteen inches is, in the opinion of many good judges, a sufficient maximum height, and they are content with bitches on a smaller scale. It is certain that in countries where foxhounds are kept, harriers of this standard are much less likely to kill an outlying fox even on a good scenting day—and friction between the red and green coats is thus avoided. A small pack again, naturally eats less than a large one, and though, as already stated, harriers cannot do hard work and long distances without oatmeal, yet the Indian meal may well be used where six or eight miles is an outside distance to covert, and the day's hunting does not last more than four or five hours. It is better to have two servants for the kennel, but the work can be, and often is, done by one man, for whom however some assistant *must* be found to help take the pack to covert; otherwise they soon find out their attendant's helplessness, are all over the place, and perhaps have had a run and a kill before arriving at the fixture. A smart boy can easily be drilled into performing this service on foot if the master rides his hunter on.

The combined whipper-in and feeder will have the evening meal prepared before starting, and will only have to warm up on his return. The hounds left at home must look after themselves, which, as they will be but few, they can do very well. The M.H. must either come home with hounds himself, or get one of his field to do so. One horse will be quite sufficient for the whipper-in if he rides quietly; if he does not, he should be dismissed. Harriers will stand very little rating and less whipping-in. Some further economy may be practised in the kennel. It is evident from the figures quoted that in our ideal establishment the hides and bones were the perquisite of the servants; the former at least the Master may well claim as his own. He will give about £1 for each horse that comes for slaughter, and the skin will fetch nearly that sum. No dead animal should ever be accepted at the kennel unless it has died from the effect of some accident, and the history of the death is satisfactory and well authenticated; otherwise poisonous carrion will find its way to the larder —dangerous to the hounds that eat it, and still more so to the men who have to cut up and handle it. Servants are terribly careless in such matters, and unless there is absolute prohibition of foul flesh they will run insane risks of blood-poisoning.

The whipper-in's wages will be £1 to 25*s.* a week—clothes when necessary—not a regular allowance of livery, which often leads to a more or less dishonest arrangement between the man and the tailor, and his cottage must be given, unless there happen to be spare rooms at the stables which he can occupy.

For the summer horse exercise, which is most important, he can have the assistance of a groom, while, if his hounds are fond of him, as they certainly will be if he is worth keeping, he should be able to walk them about by himself in some paddock where they can roll and eat grass—the oftener he does this the better. By doing things in this comparatively humble style, it will be seen that great saving may be effected on the previous estimate.

For most of the many years during which I kept harriers their food cost me about a penny a day per hound, but their solitary attendant was a curious old-fashioned retainer with unusual notions of thrift. A second horseman whipped in, and a horse had to be reserved for this express purpose.

For the sake of illustration I have taken the accounts for 1888, 1889, 1890, when 15½ couples cost £114 10*s.* per annum. This sum was made up as follows: Keep of hounds, kennel-man's wages, medicine, and other incidental expenses, £83. The keep of horse for 21 weeks (he was only debited to the pack during the hunting season) at one guinea per week, £22 1*s.* The allocated portion of groom's wages for same time at 9*s.* per week, £9 9*s.* This was the lad who whipped in.

Things were roughly, perhaps very roughly, done, but we had capital fun for all that.

Sending puppies out to walk is just as necessary with harriers as with foxhounds, and I have here made no allowance for expense on that score. The farmers on my estate, or on that of my colleague, Colonel Estcourt, were most obliging in the matter, as indeed they are in all countries, and rarely, if ever, sent in a bill for damages. Sometimes, when puppies become intolerable to the farmer's wife, they are returned to kennel rather sooner than wanted, in which case the only thing to be done is to give them as much liberty as possible at home.

of the hunt bring his hound with him; it looks sportsmanlike and encourages healthy rivalry.

Harriers housed, fed, and exercised, on the lines above laid down, should be capable of doing great things if properly handled, and though he who pays the piper has every right to call the tune, and each M.H. may hunt hares after his own fashion, yet there is a right and a wrong way of doing everything. A few remarks therefore as to field management may be of use to beginners.

Field Management—The system of our forefathers of rising at cockcrow and hunting up to the hare in her form has been long and wisely abandoned; it must have been a slow

TYPES OF HARRIERS.

Beagles—The pursuit with beagles is no doubt a form of hare *hunting*, and a very prolonged method too. There is but seldom any hare *catching*. If beagles are small enough to give their field any chance of living with them, they will want a rare scenting day and a long one to effect a kill. If the pack is not of the miniature size, a man may easily do serious injury to heart or lungs without seeing much of what happens in the chase. It is absurd to ride to the little fellows, a horse is wasted on them, so why not have rather more size and a pace that will kill the pursued instead of the pursuer?

Still, beagles are better than nothing, and can be kept cheaply enough; it is not a bad plan to make a trencher-fed pack, and let each member

process, and they were as likely to spend an hour in puzzling out the line of a fox as of their proper quarry. Half-past eleven or midday is now the favourite hour for the green-coats to assemble; even in the short days they have thus plenty of time for their purpose, and if hares are not too scarce and adopt their usual circular tactics, the farmers of the locality may have had rather more than enough of trespass on their land. Their permission will, as a matter of course, have been first obtained, and their convenience consulted as to the day of fixture. The immense majority of them are most good-natured and liberal in this respect, and very many are exceedingly fond of a day with the hare dogs, but all are annoyed and disgusted if a heedless Master announces his meet on the day of a neighbouring market. He must never forget, too, that as every farmer has the right of shooting hares on his own holding, leave to hunt them is a very material concession.

Harriers should be allowed to spread about at will in drawing. Hares are often very difficult to move, and a hound who will take trouble in looking for his game is of much value. Their usual indifference to this part of the business may be attributable to the fact that they appear unable either to wind or see a squatting hare. Hares are well aware of this, and when beaten will let hounds run over them. It often requires a prod from a stick or the flick of a whip to stir them up. If the boys of the village school are about, they will start a hare if there is one in the country--but their ceaseless yelling, as long as the pack is within sight or hearing, more than counteracts the advantage of a quick find.

It is impossible to say where a hare may not be lying; they are not particularly fond of hedgerows when the leaf is falling, but it is hardly safe to assume they may not be sitting there. They like dry ground beneath them, but are very indifferent as to shelter; it is a common thing to see a hare squatting on the side of a hill with the wind blowing into her fur. In this respect she is far less luxurious than the fox.

If she jumps up in view of the pack, they must and will race after her, but when she is moved out of their sight the less said the better.

It is idle to hope that the viewer will hold up his hat and hold his tongue, but in the rare cases when he does so, and the huntsman is allowed to draw his hounds quietly across the line, a much better beginning will be made than with a view. Hounds will have their noses down at once, and keep them there unless interfered with. Harriers soon get to look out for holloas; there is so much of it, as somebody is always seeing a hare and shrieking as if he had never seen one before. It is invariably the hunted hare, too, even though the fresh form is steaming under their eyes. It is far easier to get harriers' heads up than to get them down again—indeed, it is no exaggeration to say that were it possible to collect a field exclusively composed of the dumb, hardly a single hare would escape a decent pack on days when there was an atom of scent.

The huntsman must of course carry a horn, and so must the Master where one man does not double the parts; it is the best and quietest means of signalling to each other and to the pack, who moreover are not so excited by its sound as by the voice, and become perfectly indifferent to it when blown with the unnecessary frequency of a beginner. On the whole there is not much harm done with the horn. The same cannot be said of the whip, which is a most potent instrument of evil in bad hands. To most whippers-in the word "Put 'em to me," is the signal for a frantic charge, cutting and slashing at every poor animal within reach. The Master will do well to forbid his servant ever to strike a hound at all, the whirling and crack of the lash is quite sufficient; even pure-bred foxhounds will sometimes sulk under punishment, but the so-called true harrier, *i.e.*, one descended from several generations of ancestors exclusively employed in hare hunting, is likely enough to fly to the heels of the huntsman's horse for protection, and there remain for the rest of the day. Sometimes he may go home, which is neither seemly nor conducive to sport. It is therefore obvious that volunteer whipping-in should be as much as possible discouraged, though, as it is often well and kindly meant, it is not easy or wise too sharply to rebuke the offenders. Any usurpation of the huntsman's authority, however, must at all risk be put down with the high hand at once.

"Let 'em alone" is the maxim by which, with a good many exceptions, the huntsman will be guided, and on all occasions he must leave the pack to make their own casts on coming to a check before he takes them in hand, when he must trust to luck, which he may call good guidance, in the event of hitting off the line. It is impossible to say what a hare may or may not have done, so manifold are her wiles, and to the true hare-hunter the chief pleasure of the game is to watch his hounds unravel a knotty problem and then dash off in the delight of a well substantiated scent, or in view of their prey at last aroused from her lurking place.

Old hounds often get very cunning knowledge of whether a hare has squatted or "clapt" as it is often called. They have an indescribable way about them which says as plainly as possible to an expert "In our opinion she is down." Then, as in cases where a fox is supposed to have gone to ground, the huntsman may make his all-round cast at once, and return if it fails, to search for the recumbent one—but he should leave some one to watch lest she should sneak away unseen, as she will probably try to do when she thinks all backs are turned.

On account of the hare's many twists and doublings, it is even worse to press on harriers than on foxhounds. Moreover, what is called the true harrier will not stand being ridden over. He can easily be driven two or three fields beyond the line, and when "harked back" is apt to be wild and unsteady, and will not settle down to work again till too late. For this, amongst other reasons, it is important that, if the Master is huntsman, he should have an accredited deputy to keep his field in order, not only when hounds are running, but also when drawing or casting—for he must do his utmost to prevent unnecessary damage to the land, otherwise, as the same ground may be traversed a dozen times in the course of the day, the nuisance will become more than the most sporting farmers can bear, and those who merely tolerate the amusement will be apt to send curt requests that they may be troubled no more with the hare dogs.

Unless the pack is a subscription one, there is no need to advertise. Cards can be sent to those who ought to know—plenty of those whose room is preferable to their company will be sure to find out—but a good deal may be done with care to limit the number of followers.

Of all the devices adopted by the hare to baffle her pursuers, running the roads is perhaps the most effective. She will go a couple of miles along the macadam if she meets nothing. There is seldom any scent, and hounds get flashy and jealous, trying to pick it up in the straight conducting line. The huntsman is then at his wits' end to know what to do; and, unless he possesses that pearl of great price, a hound with a road nose, he more often than not loses his hare. The only thing he *can* do is to trot very slowly along, and try every gateway and likely-looking spot where she may have turned off or lain down, but it is a mere matter of luck unless he has the real road hunter.

Not on the hard high road, but on the old fosse way which runs as straight as an arrow for miles through part of Wiltshire and Glo'stershire I was once witness of an absurd spectacle.

A hare which we had hunted for some time jumped up in full view and at once betook herself to the fosse, along which she went as hard as tired legs would let her. In a very short time there was a long tail; the leading hounds were never far from her, but she took advantage of a dip in the ground to jump on one side and squat in the ditch. On went the leaders full of confidence and dash, but some slow old hounds, toiling along in the rear, poked her up, and she actually overtook and raced past the foremost pursuers, who, once more seeing her, were very much confirmed in their good opinion of themselves, though of course they deserved to lose her.

SHE SQUATTED IN THE DITCH.

Provided always that the walls are fairly negotiable, a stone-wall country is first-rate harrier ground, until it gets dry in the early spring. In those large open fields one would suppose that a hare might fall a readier prey than elsewhere, but she is fully equal to the occasion, and, to the manner born, baffles her enemies quite as often here as in the fenced enclosures. It is said, and I quite believe it, that she will run the tops of the walls for considerable distances and squat on them, but I have never actually seen her do this, though I have often lost her in a mysterious manner that suggested some such method of escape.

It is a great, though not uncommon, mistake to suppose that hares have a dislike to water. Those at any rate who have been bred near the banks of a river take to it like otters, nor do they care how often they cross and recross, and the advantage of pure foxhound blood is very apparent on such occasions. The hounds dash across while the more plebeian harrier is thinking about it; indeed, it is not uncommon for some of the latter to stay lamenting their hard fate on the hither bank with unseemly outcries; when this happens, the hangers back should be kicked or thrown into the stream without loss of time. I can only remember two instances of hares drowning, and in each case they were dead beat.

Harriers require blood, now and again, at least; it is difficult to imagine how Sir Roger de Coverley's pack could have continued to take any interest in what to them must have been a most insipid occupation; anyhow, the modern hound would become slack were he never allowed to kill, but, though huntsmen do not like to be beaten and at times become very bloodthirsty, the impartial observer must fain confess that the kill is the worst part of the performance. One cannot help feeling that "poor is the triumph o'er the timid hare"—so pitiful is her appearance in her last moments. Nevertheless, it is fair to remember that even the shyest of birds and beasts, which are always on the alert and ready to fly in apparently abject terror on the most groundless alarm, cannot possibly suffer the agonies of fear with which we are wont to credit them; or, instead of waxing fat and hearty, enjoying life as they obviously do, they would be shrunken abject creatures destitute alike of health and beauty.

When the "who-whoop" has sounded, the paunch will be sufficient reward for the pack, except on very great occasions after an unusually severe run. They will moreover often enough secure for themselves the whole carcase by tearing it before it can be rescued. The disembowelling process has of course to be performed by the whipper-in, and a very disagreeable duty it is; the quicker he is about it the better: hounds should never be kept baying and waiting; give them what they have earned and be off, whether it be for home or a fresh draw. The ears of the hare must be retained for a trophy to nail up in kennel or stable, and the body should be the perquisite of the farmer on whose ground it was originally found.

If it be decided to draw again, try to get on to "pastures new" for the farmer's sake as well as for the greater chance of sport on unfoiled land. It is, however, nonsense to suppose that a hare can be prevented from running in the direction she pleases. "Start her with her head towards the good country" is often the request of the ignorant when she is seen sitting. You might as well place before her a chart of the line she is required to take. She will have her own way in the most literal sense of the term, and it is but rarely that she is so bustled up that she loses her head, and gets out of her knowledge. When this does happen the run that sometimes ensues would do credit to a dog-fox.

One of these red-letter days may also occur now and then in pursuit of an old Jack in March, when hares are scarce, with the difference that he knows what he is about and is returning to the home he quitted when on pleasure bent, and he will very likely get there with a whole skin, especially if he can bring a fallow or two into his line.

Save for the chance of a good point, March is certainly the worst of the hare-hunting months, and February is generally reckoned the best. Some people prefer November and December, but hares then are usually weaker than they are later on in the season.

Those who care to play at cub-hunting do so by going out early in September and October, though it is difficult to see the advantage of the proceeding; they can hardly want to kill leverets, and the puppies, if they have been properly exercised during the summer, will know their comrades and pack readily enough when business begins in November, though of course only a portion of the new entry will go out each day; the presence of a few neophytes is good-naturedly tolerated by the old hounds, who yet are amazed and disgusted by the vagaries of too many of the rising generation.

As to the manner in which a man shall ride to his own harriers, purposely but little has been said. He must please himself, and there is certainly as much scope for individual taste in that respect as in the more arduous pursuit of the fox. For him who likes being perpetually in the air, unrivalled opportunities are afforded by a hare-hunt in any enclosed country. He may be led into more queer corners and find himself negotiating more lonely places in the course of a couple of hours after a stout cunning old hare, than might come in his way during the greater part of a season of the "Nobler Science"; he will also in all probability have the advantage of testing the feasibility of these fences from either side. The most perfectly trained hunter that can be found is the mount on which to follow a sharp pack of harriers, though it does not in the least signify if he is somewhat deficient in speed. On the other hand, should a man restrict himself entirely to gates as a means of access from field to field, he will unquestionably be able to see a very large proportion of the sport. He will even see an immense deal if he chooses to sit still and "wait till they come round again."

At the same time, though the "let 'em alone" system cannot be too highly commended, there is no doubt that the huntsman, whether on foot or horseback (for this remark applies quite as much to beagles as to harriers), ought to be in a position to see exactly when and where his hounds throw up, unless he has a trusty companion on the accuracy of whose observation he can implicitly rely. When obliged to make a cast it is as well to have some data on which to act.

Whether a man ride hard or little, or not at all, if he is really fond of hunting for hunting's sake—and no other should encumber himself with the cares of an M.H.—he will find the chase of the hare a most fascinating sport, and in these days of enormous fields with foxhounds, when it is impossible without doing mischief to obtain much insight into their or their huntsman's work and tactics, there are no better lessons in the science of Venery than those afforded by the "Merry Harriers."

SUFFOLK AND BERKSHIRE.

BEAGLING—There are two ways of employing the beagle in the field sports, in hunting and in shooting. Several couples are sometimes used in coverts for rabbit-shooting: with this form of sport we are not now concerned, but with the hunting of the hare with beagles. As canoeing and small boat sailing are to yachting, so is running with beagles to the more expensive forms of the chase. That foot beagles are every year becoming more popular cannot for a moment be doubted, and beagles now take their place at Peterborough. The rapid growth of athletics may have had something to do with it, and the love of hunting which is in so many of us, a good deal more; but, whatever the reason, packs of beagles have increased in number.

When compared with foxhunting, harehunting may appear a tame sport. There are no fine horses and red coats to be seen, no crowd, and no premium on hard riding. In short, the credit of maintaining a good place and jumping hedges and ditches is due to the runner's pace, stamina and activity, instead of the powers of a horse. Farmers, again, are not averse to beagles crossing their land, except here and there. There is nothing like a large field, and men on foot are more careful of crops than those on horseback, while, as they are not so keen to jump as the mounted division, they generally do but little damage to fences, and they need not do any at all. The farmer, moreover, can have his day on foot at absolutely no loss to himself, while, in common with harriers, beagles do the foxhunting fraternity a good turn by disturbing outlying foxes and causing them to return to coverts where they will be more easily found by the hounds.

Hunting the hare with beagles is especially the poor man's hunting, and a hunting establishment can be maintained at comparatively small cost. There are many packs in which a kennelman is the only paid assistant, and he sometimes discharges some other duty in connection with stable, garden or shooting kennel. The number of hounds taken into the field may be from six to ten couples; no horses have to be bought and foraged, and there are no hunt uniforms, save perhaps an inexpensive jacket when some distinguishing dress is deemed advisable. In return for a small outlay, and, in some cases, a small subscription, one sees a great deal of interesting hunting and enjoys plenty of exercise, and this, to a busy man who cannot afford more costly sport, means a good deal.

At Peterborough Show the maximum height for a beagle is sixteen inches, and at the show this year (1897) all the exhibits but about two or three ran the limit very closely. Sixteen inches is possibly too big for beagles which are to be hunted on foot, because on favourable days they can get away from the huntsman and whippers-in. That they should not do so is obviously a matter of great importance, because they might follow their hare into coverts, disturb them, and possibly upset sundry shooting or foxhunting arrangements. In that event the wrath of some one would be aroused, and on the performance being repeated, a proposal to abolish the beagles might be made. Indeed, it is no bad plan to have some one out sufficiently well mounted to be able to get on and stop the beagles if from any reason they should get away from the officials, but, save in the case of this person, and any aged or infirm supporter of the pack, the use of horses or ponies in the field should be rigorously forbidden. It needs but a very little pressing on the part of a few horsemen to make beagles go faster than they otherwise would, and then they are necessarily less under the control of the huntsman, when half the charm of hunting beagles vanishes. From thirteen to fifteen inches is quite big enough for a beagle, and, taken all round, fourteen inches may be set down as the ideal size, as they will then be big enough to kill a certain number of hares, but not big enough to get far away, save perhaps on very good scenting days, from their followers. Just as the harrier has been largely crossed with the foxhound, so has harrier blood been mingled with that of the beagle, with the result that the pure breed is not always easy to find. Still, if hounds sufficiently small can be acquired to suit the master's purpose, the exact strain may not matter so far as sport is concerned, at any rate at the outset, and when once the pack is started the master can breed to his own ideas.

Reference has already been made to the question of riding to beagles, or rather to the necessary exclusion of all but the official horse and perhaps one or two more from the field; but it often happens that farmers, before granting permission for beagles to hunt over their land, make it an express stipulation that no horses or ponies shall be allowed. It is sometimes the case that beagles hunt over a district, or part of it, which is already covered by staghounds, foxhounds and harriers, in which event the farmer sustains his full share of whatever damage may be attendant upon the visits of the different hunts; so, when application is made for permission to run beagles, it is not surprising that as a condition precedent farmers should stipulate that the field shall consist exclusively of pedestrians. In any case, however, it may be as well to point out to the farmer that it may be advisable to have one mounted person out to prevent hounds from running into coverts, as before mentioned.

Then again, the masters of other packs have to be thought of. Before taking any steps to establish a pack of beagles, every master likely to be affected should be consulted, as hunting of every kind exists only on sufferance. So far as the law of the land is concerned, nothing more is required than to obtain the consent of landowners or occupiers so that the master and his friends shall not be trespassers, and strictly speaking the owner of land and coverts in one country may warn off the pack in whose country his estate is, and invite some other master. The acceptance of any offer of the kind is, however, quite another matter, and no one worthy of the name of a sportsman would do otherwise than observe, both in letter and spirit, the unwritten law of hunting. Any one, therefore, proposing to establish a pack of beagles should at once consult any master of foxhounds or harriers who already hunts over the same ground. It is not in disparagement of foot beagles that one must place it among the minor forms of the chase, not because it is the least interesting, but because it is the cheapest. A vast amount of money is expended on foxhunting, and it therefore naturally takes precedence of all other forms of hunting, while, as horses have to be found for harriers, they come next. Still, among masters and would-be masters, there is as a rule a kind of freemasonry which prompts them to do the best they can for one another, though, at the same time, there may be reasons why another pack should not be started. When once an understanding has been arrived at, it need hardly be said that the master of beagles should do his utmost not to interfere with the sport of others, and should so arrange his fixtures as not to interfere with those of any already established pack, even though his own amusement may, on occasions, be curtailed.

The beagle kennel need not be an extensive or expensive affair, though, if the occupants are to be kept in a state of health, sanitary precautions must be observed; in fact, the beagle establishment should be a foxhound or harrier kennel in miniature, with, of course, conveniences for breeding if the master makes up his mind to breed, as he probably would. The general treatment of beagles is, allowing for altered circumstances, much the same as that for foxhounds and harriers. There is, indeed, if possible, even more need for condition than in the case of larger hounds, because beagles, being comparatively slow, must work at their best all the time. The process of conditioning should therefore be begun early, in order that by the first hunting day they may be as fit as possible. In the main, too, the manner of hunting the hare is the same as in the case of harriers, but the huntsman of beagles may be less particular about cutting off a corner than he who hunts a fleeter pack; but casting must not be performed in a hurried manner, lest the hounds head the gallop, and those who are acquainted with other forms of hunting will know that those hounds hunt the best which are not too much interfered with.

In first forming a pack of beagles care and judgment are required. If a little pack which has been carefully bred be in the market so much the better; but should the new master have to depend on drafts he will find that he has no easy task before him, and he will learn, probably for the first time, how many faults a hound can have. When all preliminaries are arranged, the pack should be started as early in the season as possible, and the first dozen days at any rate should be strictly private, for the staff will in all likelihood have more than enough to do to keep order. Some of the pack will be too fat, some too slow, some too big, and all this will want attending to. At the outset there is no need to be too particular about appearances. If good looks can be had, well and good, but working qualities are the first consideration, and as the resources increase the ungainly ones can be drafted; but let a young master beware of too hastily getting rid of a real good hunter.

After several undress and dress rehearsals the master may venture to ask a field to meet him, and if he is his own huntsman he will speedily find that there is ample scope for all the observations and cleverness he possesses. A knowledge of the habits of the hare is naturally of great value, for hares do not have their forms in the same field all the year round, and as a rule they do not sit where they feed. When the hedges and trees are pretty well bare of leaf, hares come out into the fallows, where, as in September and October, they affect turnips and other covert, and when drawing turnips there is no harm in making a little noise or even in having some of the field in advance of the hounds, for a hare is somewhat easily chopped in turnips, as they seem to lose their heads. In drawing ploughed lands the huntsman should walk across the furrows, as he will then be able to see up and down each; and as beagles are not possessed of great pace they should view their hare at the start as often as possible. The inexperienced master will do well to miss no opportunity of conversing with practised hare hunters, for there are many wrinkles to be picked up. A huntsman for instance ought to know a hunted from a fresh hare, while at a check it is nearly always safe to cast in the same direction as that in which the hare has been running. For instance, if she has been more or less circling from left to right, the cast should be to the right.

The beagle kennel, like every other, will be visited by illness, and when the master comes to breed his own hounds distemper will have to be reckoned with. There are, however, plenty of books treating of dogs in health and disease, and the young master of beagles cannot do better than master the contents of some of them.

W. C. A. Blew.

OTTER—To the enthusiastic lover of hounds there is no more fascinating sport than the pursuit of the otter. Coming as it does at a period of the year when the foxhound is confined to his kennel, the hunter to his loose box or paddock, and when the voice of the harrier is no more heard in the land, it is doubly welcome, and doubly sweet to the true sportsman. Besides such merits as these, it has the recommendation that it requires no costly outfit, no expensive stud of hunters to enable its lovers to partake of the sport. A good physique, sufficient activity, and a strong pair of boots are all that are needed in order to see to its end the best possible day's hunting. And although packs of otterhounds are in these days migratory, and "lay out" for a fortnight at a time, covering during that period a wide stretch of country, yet the resting places selected are no costly caravanserais, but rather the old-fashioned riverside fishing inns, loved of old Izaak Walton and his fellows, where a man may rest peacefully without apprehension of the score that is to be presented to him on his departure. And if there be anywhere better companions than those who track the otter up and down the lovely streams of England and Wales, we have yet to hear of them. A man may do worse than spend a fortnight among such scenes and in such company.

"Countries"—The otter-hunter in these times is a very peripatetic philosopher. "Countries" belong to various packs, and the jealousy among them is great, if even the head waters of some river belonging to one pack are disturbed by a raid on the part of some other establishment. They are described as consisting of certain rivers, some in one county, some in another. A Devonshire pack will exercise the privilege of hunting rivers in Hampshire or Dorsetshire, or a Durham establishment take its fortnight or so across the Border into Scotland, but all have countries, as clearly defined as if the boundaries were laid down on some map. A list of the packs now hunting in the United Kingdom is appended, but owing to the wanderings abroad of each establishment, a very wide circle must be drawn around the kennel to include all the country hunted by the pack.

Otterhounds—The true otterhound is in our opinion one of the genuine ancient types of dog, viz., the rough or broken-haired hound, hunting by scent alone, the bloodhound being the prototype of the smooth variety. In the same way the Scotch deerhound and the English greyhound are the types, rough and smooth, of the gazehound.

The otterhound is a very strong, short-legged dog, not, as a rule, over 22 inches high. Shaggy and rough in his coat, with very pendant ears, a high "peak" somewhat like that of a bloodhound, and a very musical deep voice. He should have straight legs, fine shoulders, without which there can be no activity, and especially he should have a strong back and powerful loins, which are essential to assist him in scrambling in and out of the water, up and down steep and slippery banks. In colour he is frequently black and tan, red, sandy, or black and white, with the usual hound markings. Some packs of hounds, especially in the north of England, have kept their strains pure for many generations, and possibly owing to in-breeding, size has been somewhat lost. Some years ago the late Hon. G. R. C. Hill, who was most careful to keep his pack as one of genuine otterhounds, crossed a bitch with a foxhound and put the progeny again to the pure otter-hound, and thereby produced several hounds of the very highest class. They threw back in appearance to the original pure breed—the otterhound; a pure breed will always assert itself. They were very rough and with good tongue, but retained the size and the fine shape of the foxhound, without in any way deteriorating from the character of a pack of pure otter-hounds.

Many sportsmen of great experience eschew the otterhound altogether for this chase, and use the pure-bred foxhound—an animal that, like the well-bred hunter, cannot be put "out of his place." With these packs some of the best sport obtainable has been shown. Mr. Collier, for fifty years master of the Culmstock Otter-hounds, and one of the most skilful and popular masters of hounds that ever sounded the horn, stated to the writer, only a few years before his retirement, that "in all his experience of otter hunting he had never seen an otterhound," and that he yet hoped to have a day with one of the more northern packs in order to see what they were like. Mr. Collier had probably killed more otters than any man of his time, except the Hon. G. R. C. Hill, but during all his life he had used either harriers with a very strong dash of foxhound blood in them, or, latterly, pure-bred foxhounds. Many of his hounds were drafts from the Devon and Somerset Stag-hounds—giants from half the kennels in England—that could no longer run up in that arduous chase, and consequently he took the field with a pack of very large-sized hounds, all of pure foxhound breed. With them he generally had running two or three Welsh foxhounds, or harriers, rough hounds, most excellent in their work, but inclined to be untrustworthy where riot is concerned. The Carlisle pack is one of true otterhounds, and very beautiful specimens of the breed do they occasionally send to the benches of one or other of the big shows. Mr. Wilkinson, of Neasham, whose sport is second to none, arrives at it with a pack of mixed breed.

On the whole the rough hound stands long swimming in cold water better than the smooth. He is also a lower-scented hound, and more free with his tongue; hence the drag of an otter can frequently be hunted two or three hours later in the day with a pack of otterhounds than would be possible with foxhounds. These latter are most excellent when the otter is found, especially in streams where very long continued swimming is not required, but many will not speak at all to a drag, and few to a cold one. It is easier to find the otter with otterhounds, and that is a very great point—but foxhounds will often kill him better than the smaller rough hounds, when once they have found him.

Besides a good pack of hounds, two or three terriers, and good ones too, are absolutely necessary to accompany the pack. These are not very easily procured. They must be short on the leg and small, for an otter in a natural holt—not a drain—will often get into a very small hole. And he is a most formidable beast to tackle, for, although at first he bolts readily, he is not always so easy to move after he has had a glimpse of the hounds and put back again into his stronghold. A good dog otter will weigh 24 lbs. (some have much exceeded that weight), and no terrier that is over 14 lbs. will be of much service, owing to his bulk. Thus in meeting an otter of this kind he is at a great disadvantage as to weight, while as to muscular strength there is no comparison between them, the otter being for its inches one of the most powerful animals living. Gameness, then, is most essential, yet not the gameness of the bulldog, but the courage of the true terrier that will lay at his otter, and keep his tongue going well while he harasses and drives him, without fear, yet without uselessly rushing into close quarters. With plenty of tongue, his whereabouts can be ascertained, and with the help of the spade assistance is soon at hand; while those listening can tell by the sound of his tongue the moment the otter moves, and though he makes his exit invisibly and under the water, where the terrier cannot follow him, there is no doubt about what happens when a good dog is at work, and the welcome cry of "Look out below" will soon be confirmed by a "Tally-ho" at the lower shallow.

Wire-haired fox-terriers, chosen for their shortness of leg, are most in use. They have power and activity to stand a long day's work with the hounds, and yet are able to get to ground in most places. Scotch or Highland terriers are very good, especially where they can be assisted by a wheeled conveyance, but they do not travel quite so well as the fox-terrier. Yet so many qualities are needed in the terriers, and they are so important a part of the pack that breed and appearance are often disregarded when the other requisites are found not to be lacking.

Otters—As regards the habits of the otter there is a great deal that is unknown, but still sufficient information has been arrived at by experts to enable the animal to be hunted with success. There has been much controversy as to the period of the year when the bitch lays down her cubs. The Hon. G. R. C. Hill frequently stated to the writer that they bred in any and in every month of the year, and that he had found cubs when hunting of such ages as to bear out this theory. We believe that it is, in the main, a correct one, but that the early months of the year, from January to April, see more cubs laid down than any other period. The litter generally consists of three or four—five is exceptional—and is laid down underground, generally in a "holt" or "hover" by the banks of the stream, under the roots of some ancient alder, with an access to it both under water and on dry land. For the first two months of their existence they will use this home alone, and the wanderings of the mother will only extend to such a distance as will enable her to provide food for herself and her family.

The injury that otters do to fishing interests is a good deal exaggerated. That they will kill good trout and small salmon is of course indisputable, but these swift fish are not by any means the chief staple of their diet. Coarse fish come more readily to hand, and thus are far more frequently taken. Eels are the most favoured food of all, and next to them perhaps frogs—especially for the young otters.

As soon as the young cubs can travel and have lost their milk teeth, they begin to fish for themselves, and deserting their old home, commence to lead the wandering life so characteristic of the otter. It has been asserted by more than one competent authority that the full-grown otter never, except when breeding, lies twice consecutively in the same bed. His habits are entirely nocturnal. Emerging from his holt at dusk, he will fish and travel over many miles of river, laying up at sunrise in some other regularly used holt many miles away. Oftentimes the hunter, unravelling the mazes of these nocturnal wanderings, is led by some tiny tributary up to and over the watershed, and commences his hunt by marking his otter in some river miles away from the stream he intended to hunt; and again the "drag" or "trail" will sometimes lead him to the seashore itself, along which the otter may have travelled on his way to the mouth of some other river known to him.

In the famous trail hunt with Mr. Collier's hounds in the New Forest, which is recorded in the "Badminton" volume on hunting, the line led up to the source of the river on which the meet was held, over the water-shed, and down to another small river, along the course of which it was held for several miles; then, diverging on to a tributary stream, it followed the water nearly to its source, when the otter was found and almost instantly killed, lying above ground on the bed it had formed in the early morning hours. The distance traversed by the hounds was fully twelve miles, the whole of which was upon the scent left by the night's wanderings of the animal pursued. The otter was a small bitch.

Hunting—From these details it will be seen that the chiefest part of the otter-hunter's task is that of finding his wandering quarry. Otters may be stumbled upon by chance by trying some well known holt or drain, but this is not otter-hunting. What has to be done is to strike the "trail" or "drag" of the midnight wanderer at some point on the river along which his travels extend, and then, having found the scent of his line, to unravel it until the hounds arrive at the actual spot where he is then couched. Obviously, it is no easy matter to determine whether the course followed by the hounds is the same as that taken by the otter, for, since the line of scent is one that is many hours old, there is nothing which can guide the hounds as to whether they are actually following their prey or taking a line "heel way," that is, leading them further and further apart. Fortunately there are in most streams regular landing places, adopted by reason of the force of the current—just as salmon always are to be found one after the other under the lee of some big stone—or by the slope of the bank, and with a little care it ought before long to be ascertainable whether the "seal" or footmark of the travelling otter points up or downwards.

Dress—As to the dress of the otter-hunter, it should consist mainly of flannel; the colour varies with different hunts—with some the coat is scarlet, in others blue or green. The well-known costume of the Hawkstone Hunt, blue Welsh flannel coat and knickerbockers with scarlet cap, waistcoat and stockings, was perhaps the prettiest and most workmanlike of any. But whatever the colour, wool and all wool should be the material. Shoes carry less water about than boots; a stout pole about seven feet long is an invaluable assistance to serve as a leaping pole, to assist in crossing or standing in a rocky rapid stream, or to help its owner in scrambling up and down banks or over fences. They also come in very handily when an otter is floating and concealing itself "out of mark" in deep overhanging banks that touch the water, but are hollow underneath. The thrust of a pole anywhere near him will move and keep him moving when nothing else succeeds. Poles are generally made of ash, but some of the best we have seen have been made of bamboo—especially male bamboo, and some very neat ones are made of the best of hazel shoots. All poles require to be properly shod with steel, and a spike at the end is needed to make the support a reliable one. Where very mountainous rocky streams are hunted, it is an excellent plan to have a V-shaped spike inserted, as it gives a far better hold on slippery rocks than the simple tip.

Spears—In former days a spear was used on the end of the pole, and the otter was killed at the first opportunity by this unsportsmanlike contrivance. The barbarous usage has now quite died out, and the otter-spear is to the modern otter-hunter a relic of the past like the chain armour or portcullis of his ancestors.

The Hunt—An early hour is usually chosen for otter hunting, partly because it is a sport belonging to the summer months, and one therefore to be followed before the extreme heat of the day sets in, partly also in order to obtain the scent of the otter's night travels when it is as fresh as possible. Yet so strong is this scent that hounds will run it freely many hours after the otter has passed—especially in damp water meadows, through lush grass, or in shady coverts under the shelter of such tussocks as are usually found in bogs. In places such as these the scent will lie nearly the whole day, but more in the open it dies away much sooner. Hence the earlier the hunter is afoot the more certain he is of being able to mark his otter. This is more particularly the case where pure foxhounds are used, for these hounds are not so good at hunting the drag as the otterhound, nor will they hunt so low a scent. But, as a rule, seven or eight o'clock is soon enough except in very hot weather, and in September or later August, when days are cooler, and there are heavy dews which lie long on the ground, we have seen days of excellent sport when the hounds did not meet till ten or even eleven o'clock. At times it is necessary to be afoot very early, as where an otter fishes up some stream where he can be hunted, but drops down in the early morning to some large river where his stronghold is impregnable, or into tidal waters where he vanishes altogether. In such cases as these, a good hunt may be obtained by meeting very early indeed at the junction of the two streams and by working up the smaller one. The otter may be cut off before he reaches the strong water, and so kept in the stream where it is possible to hunt him. No half measures will do in such matters—the pack must be at the fixture before daylight, and the master must throw off as soon as it is light enough to count his hounds. On approaching the river, a whipper-in or an active member of the hunt should get well in advance of the pack and keep there if he can do so; he will be very useful in checking such hounds as are riotous or inclined to get too far ahead. Moreover, directly the drag is struck he will be able to examine the various places where the otter lands, before the hounds get there and efface the "seal" which the otter has left. In this way he will be able to get early intelligence as to whether the otter was travelling up or downwards. Often the otter has worked both up and down, or there are two on the same stream travelling different ways, as for instance when a dog otter has journeyed a long way to find a bitch which has very likely come down the stream to meet him, and afterwards returned to her holt on the upper river, while he has dropped down to stronger water and security. In these cases there is nothing for it but to work on and trust to luck. It is a wise precaution to have a whip thus in advance on either side of the river. Sometimes the drag is so hot that the hounds will run clean away from whips, field and all, but of course as soon as they mark or find their otter they are readily overtaken. The danger, however, in these hot drags, and indeed at all times, is that of passing the otter, or running over or past the holt where he is laid up, and carrying the drag right through to its end, while the quarry is left behind. Not infrequently the otter will work a certain distance above and also below his holt—here the drag is as strong in one direction as in the other, and the river must be tried yard by yard to mark the holt. Again, it is the usual habit of the otter, when travelling up stream, to work the river for a little distance above the holt where he lays up, and then, dropping into the water, to float down to the resting place, leaving no scent by the way. Whether this proceeding is an ingenious artifice or is a mere accident suiting the convenience of the animal we cannot say, but it will be clear to the reader that the drag or line of the otter when once struck cannot, however hot it may lie, be relied upon to take the pack direct to the holt where the otter is laid up, without a little assistance from the huntsman and the service of his experience and knowledge. Especially in the case of a hot drag leading up stream will hounds be apt to pass the otter. They will race along the bank and bed of the stream at a great pace, tearing across the bends of the river on land and striking the line again and again as they drive upwards. The field pants eagerly after them, many a novice fearing that the otter will be found, hunted and killed before ever he gets to the spot. Gradually the pace moderates a little, though the scent is still hot in places. Old hounds hang back, or try the banks and are not so eager to "go to cry" as they were, when the line is struck further up stream. Slowly but surely the scent waxes cold, and at last all the hounds have checked and are out on the bank, each of the old ones trying to get back again to where they came from. The otter has been passed—possibly some miles back. The day is no longer young, the first freshness is gone both from hounds and field, and the drag is foiled by the passage of the whole of the pack and the accompanying field with all their camp followers and attendant crew. Yet there is nothing for the huntsman to do but to retrace his steps ruefully, and with care and trouble to search out every yard of the river banks in the hope that there may yet be left scent enough for him to mark his otter and to find him after all. May luck attend him, for up to this point skill has failed him.

On the other hand, the careful otter-hunter and old hand, whose hounds first struck the drag and began to race ahead on it, would take careful note of the character of the stream he was hunting. Should there be open, level banks with no "holding" he may let his pack drive merrily and tunefully forwards. But if the stream be sinuous with many holts or coverts, it will not be long ere the notes of his horn signal to the whips, who are ahead of the pack (or by taking short cuts may get there), that the pack is to stop. Round they come to the master, who steadily holds them back down the stream, and along every yard of it that they have missed as they raced across the levels from bank to bank, till he knows for certain that not a place where an otter can lie has been missed by his hounds. It may seem to the stranger a peculiar and a slow proceeding to check hounds on a hot scent and cast them backward for no reason that he can perceive, but the old hand will thankfully hail the strategy and will well understand that never was time less wasted than that which is spent in making good, as he goes, every yard of stream, instead of leaving it to be done on the return journey. Especially where any tributary enters the river, or where the stream divides, will a cast backward be made. Often the otter has used both streams as he fished during the dark hours, and consequently the line may lead along both currents. One or other must be worked to its end, and, line or no line, a long cast up the tributary should be made lest the otter may have worked up the main stream for a short way and then, crossing the land, take to the tributary, on the lower part of which he has, of course, left no scent. When this has been worked out or made good, we may proceed up the main stream. Progress may seem slow with these irritating checks, but it will be much slower and less sure if all this has to be done on the return journey with a hot run and a cold scent. But if all goes well the drag will get hotter and hotter. The huntsman's care has assured us that it is hardly possible for our otter to be laid up behind us—and at last, at some old tree root or drain, we hear the welcome "mark" as the hounds bay and tear at the entrance to the holt. Yet all is not certain yet. Not a sound should be spoken as the huntsman keenly watches his hounds—it is by them and by his knowledge of them that the issue must be determined. Possibly the otter has only been there for a time, and may be lying yet further ahead. A hound that is a really reliable marker is worth his weight in gold. One or two such there should be in every pack. Many a hound will bay keenly at a holt where the scent of the otter is lying. So far he is right, but when a really good marker speaks, and if, after being drawn away with the pack to try further, he speaks again with decision on his return to the spot, there should be no more doubt. The otter himself is there, not the mere stale scent of his often-used lair. Once the mark is certain, the next task is that of bolting the otter, and here of course the terriers we have spoken of are indispensable. In the case of a drain, an opening far up in the field can be made, and the terrier introduced behind the otter. With deep water in front of him, he will generally bolt readily enough, but where an ancient tree root, washed hollow by successive floods, is the fortress, the matter is not so easy. If no hole can be found above water by which to introduce a terrier, an iron bar is very useful to sink holes here and there. If one of these penetrates into his subterranean galleries the otter will often bolt at once. Frequently he may be moved by a party of hunters jumping in unison on the top of the bank—their joint weight shakes the overhanging mass of earth and the otter will bolt as he feels it. And very often, where hounds have marked well at the door of his castle, he will move and show himself if they and the field are taken right away, and only a watcher left to report progress. This plan should always be tried in cases where the terriers cannot at once get to the otter and where long protracted digging seems likely to be required. During the progress of all these methods of attack, the nearest shallows or "stickles" must be manned, and a careful watch kept, lest the otter make his escape under water to some adjacent reach of the river and so on down stream, leaving no scent, till it becomes hopeless to hunt him. When he bolts it will be under water, for he has invariably a sub-aqueous access to his home, and, let there be never so many men and hounds all around his holt, the chances are that he will glide unperceived between their legs, and a "tally" from the shallow above or below will be the first intimation that their efforts to dislodge him have been successful.

When once the otter has stirred, a careful watch must be set at shallows both above and below, and through these lines of sentries the otter must not pass, at any rate unperceived. To many sportsmen this proceeding savours of mobbing and seems unfair. The answer is that without such a method the otter cannot be killed at all, and to forbid it is merely quixotic.

Of course, in small streams, there is no need to stop an otter anywhere, and the true sportsman will let him go where he likes, but even there he will find it essential to have sentries above and below to signal the departure of the otter from reach to reach, even though he is not to be interfered with. Although water carries scent to a certain extent and for a short time, it must never be forgotten that the scent flows downwards with the water, and is no criterion therefore of the direction taken by the animal which left it, or of his whereabouts at the time. Assistance therefore is necessary to the hounds, which are hunting, in an element foreign to their nature, an animal which is perfectly at home in it and has an immeasurable advantage of them. If then the water is at all deep or wide, with much holding on the banks, and there is no line of sentries above and below to confine the otter to a certain space, we can confidently say that the hounds may as well be taken home at once as allowed to weary and chill themselves by seeking to hunt an animal that can evade them by means of its native element just as it pleases.

Even with this assistance a good pack of hounds will find it hard enough to bring an old otter to book. Holt after holt he tries, and has to be re-found, marked, and dislodged either by the terriers or by other means. For a long period he will float, leaving only the tip of his nose above water. There is scent down the river in plenty, but the watchers of the ford will swear he has not passed them. At last a welcome "tally" shows his whereabouts, and the pack again get to close quarters. Finally, hotly pressed, he tries the land and makes his point to another reach full of stronger holding. After him fly the field—fresh fords must quickly be found and manned, and the hunt resumed with a fresh venue. But, tough as an otter may be, he cannot hold out for ever. His dives get shorter, he shows himself more often to the frantic crowd, and at last, as he makes a bold dash to force the guard holding the lower stickle, he is picked up or "tailed" by one of them, or the pack, catching a view, run into him ere he can regain deep water. Let them worry him all they can, they will make no hole in his skin, and those that were first to attack him will bear to their graves the marks of the gallant beast's last stand against them.

Hunting the otter varies much according to the county in which it is pursued. A chase in the rocky pools of Westmorland varies naturally from one in the water meadows of Hampshire, and there are intermediate scenes where hunts of widely different character may take place. Each has its charm—each its particular difficulties and need for special wood-craft. Yet speaking generally there is no more scientific, more arduous, and more "genuine" form of hunting—one more devoid of every suspicion of artificial treatment or cockneyism, or more worthy the attention of the true sportsman and lover of hounds, than the chase of this wiliest and toughest of British wild animals.

LIST OF PACKS OF OTTERHOUNDS NOW HUNTING IN THE UNITED KINGDOM.

Pack.	*Master.*	*Kennel.*
Brookfield (Cork)	Mr. T. Jennings	Brookfield, Co. Cork.
Buckley's, Mr. E.	Mr. E. Buckley	Mitford Hall, Newtown, N. Wales.
Bucks	Mr. W. F. Uthwatt	Great Linford, Newport Pagnell.
Carlisle	Mr. G. Mounsey Heysham	Canal Bank, Carlisle.
Cheriton's, Mr. W.	Mr. J. Cheriton	Ellicombe, South Molton Rd. Station, N. Devon.
Courtenay-Tracy's, Mr.	Mr. Courtenay-Tracy	Wilton, Salisbury.
Culmstock, The	Mr. F. Collier	Nicholashayne, Wellington, Somerset.
Cumberland, West	Mr. J. H. Jefferson	Little Mill, Cockermouth.
Dartmoor		Glazebrook, South Brent, S. Devon.
Dumfriesshire	Mr. D. J. Bell-Irving	Annan.
Hawkestone Otter Hunt	Mr. H. P. Wardell	Bromfield, Ludlow, Salop.
Kendal, The	Sir Henry Bromley	Dallam Tower, Milnthorpe.
Pembroke and Carmarthen	Mr. John Evans	Honeys Park, Milton, Pembroke.
The Rug	Hon. C. H. Wynn	Rug, Corwen, N. Wales.
Wilkinson's, Mr.	Mr. T. Wilkinson	Neasham Abbey, Darlington.
Ynysfor, The	Mr. John Jones	Ynysfor, Penrhyn, Dendraeth, Merionethshire.

GERALD LASCELLES.

STAG—By staghunting we here imply the chase of the deer with a pack of hounds on horseback, or, as it was formerly called, "hunting at force," as distinguished from the earlier form of sport, in which the horse and hound were used only as subsidiary to the hunter's main object, which was either the killing of the deer with a weapon—a form of staghunting which dates back into the mists of Egyptian history—or, to quote a mediæval writer, one Christopher Ware, gentleman, "the forestalling him with nets and engines."

History of the Hunt—There is no doubt that hunting at force existed at a very early period in Britain, and it is difficult to trace its exact origin or account for its partial desuetude in the fifteenth and sixteenth centuries. William of Malmesbury states of Edward the Confessor that he delighted "to follow a pack of swift hounds in pursuit of game, and to cheer them with his voice"; upon the other hand, Mr. Hore, in his *History of the Buckhounds*, gives Edward III. the credit of being the first Plantagenet who rode to his hounds and thus hunted at force.

As the history of the royal hounds is to some extent the history of staghunting in this country, Mr. Burrows' interesting introduction to my own book may here be cited. From this we learn that the earliest record of a regular establishment of the buckhounds is the grant to Hamon le Venour in 1216 of certain lands in Rockingham Forest known under the Edwards as "Hunters' Manor," to which for many centuries the hereditary mastership of the royal buckhounds was attached. The traces of this establishment, broken up on the permanent establishment of the Court at Windsor, are to be found in local names and ruins still existing in the woodland Pytchley country. These lands were held by the Lovels and De Borhuntes in consideration of their office, by the conditions of which they were bound to keep up a certain nnmber (varying from fifteen to twenty-four) of "canes currentes" (buckhounds), two "berners" (keepers), a "veutrer" or huntsman, and whippers-in, partly at their own and partly at the royal expense. Towards the end of the fourteenth century, by the marriage of Sir Bernard Brocas with Mary De Borhunte, the hereditary mastership came into the Brocas family, who held it until 1633.

Under Henry VIII. a new institution—the privy Buckhounds—had arisen, more suited than the old feudal system to the ideas of that liberal age, of which the mastership was to be held during the king's pleasure. The first master of the privy pack was the ill-fated George Boleyn, Viscount Rochford, who thus heads the rôle of Masters of the Buckhounds as we understand the office in these days. The two packs were jealous rivals; but eventually the hereditary mastership was sold by Sir L. Watson, a ruined cavalier, and the office became obsolete. So much for the past, now for the present.

A Meet.

The Deer Cart—Until evolution or some other process demolishes the proposition that the greater includes the less, precedence justly belongs to the deer cart. Without a deer cart there could clearly be no staghunting; but this solid engine of the chase claims our early attention upon higher grounds, inasmuch as the popular character of modern staghunting—in the widest sense of the word "popular";

witness, for instance, a turn-out at Salt Hill or Maidenhead Thicket—may largely be ascribed to its exciting influence.

In the course of my reading I have not been able to establish the date of the first deer cart, or discover its talented inventor. George III., however, acquired the freehold of Swinley paddocks in 1782 and started the hunting herd there about that time. Although deer may have been carted about previously to this for the royal chase, from that time onwards the deer cart may be said to have become the centre and pivot of modern staghunting.

A few words may be said here upon the causes which led to the introduction of the deer cart.

George III. at his own pace and convenience hunted the Berkshire side of the Thames and the Hampshire heathland very much in the same way as it is hunted now. He liked long runs, strong deer, the open country as against Windsor Great Park, and a field as against a court.

The deer cart and artificially conditioned deer were the only means to these ends. But the new system, as a system, was an innovation, not a revolution. Owing partly to the countless Enclosure Acts of the two previous reigns, the spread of agriculture, and the growing taste for high farming and reclamation, the area of staghunting in the environs of Windsor and all over the country was rapidly disappearing. As a matter of fact the red deer had long ceased to be the first "beast of venery" in England.

We should have to go back several hundred years to find in this country any such "astonishing extent" of forest as Colonel Thornton remarks upon in his sporting tour to France in 1805. Parks and fallow deer abounded in the year 1530. According to Manwood there were upwards of a hundred parks in the counties of Essex and Kent alone; and the best French writers upon venery of the sixteenth and early seventeenth centuries (an Augustan period of this sort of literature) held English staghunters in doubtful esteem, because their experience was limited to parks, and to fallow buck hunting as against staghunting.

In short, by the end of the last century, setting aside the gaunt and unvisited Highlands of Scotland, wild herds of red deer were only to be found upon Exmoor and Dartmoor, in the New Forest and in Wolmer Forest.[1]

It is true that a Swinley deer is recorded as having afforded a record run into Oxfordshire to the Duke of York and his suite, but I question whether this was a wild deer in the Exmoor sense of the word "wild." The red deer, saving the stately remnant who still enjoy the high privileges and ancient distinction of their race on Exmoor, has no such abiding city in England as he appears to hold and to keep in France. But perhaps whatever the "tall deer" may have lost in prescription he has gained in popularity. Upon the "greatest happiness" principle the carted deer may be congratulated upon rendering services to his generations which would have delighted Bentham, and upon playing a part, especially in the Ascot and Windsor districts, which merits the attention of the economist and the gratitude of the Inland Revenue.

The deer cart in use at the royal kennels, which, as the result of a century's experience, may be taken as typical of the species, consists of a rectangular wooden van on four wheels, giving the interior dimensions of 5 feet 9 inches by 3 feet 4 inches and 4 feet 1 inch high. There is a longitudinal division made in two parts and to slide, which divides the cart into two compartments, each compartment having a door. When the deer are carted in the morning,

DEER CART.

this sliding partition is so arranged as to allow the first deer to enter on the left and turn past the inner end of the partition into the right-hand compartment. The deer thus faces the right-hand wing of the double door in readiness for the turn-out. The second deer remains in the left-hand compartment in case the first does not afford a good run. The floor of the deer cart should be 3 feet 3 inches from the ground, and battened to prevent slipping; it should never be scrubbed, but merely brushed out, leaving some manure in order to improve the scent for hunting. The double doors are ventilated in the upper part on the Venetian blind principle, with two windows near the top that the deer may not be dazzled when first freed. The interior walls are padded and covered with strong cocoanut matting. Under the driving box is a place for lame hounds, 2 feet 2 inches × 3 feet 4 inches × 2 feet 6 inches. A deer cart of this type, and all of the best, costs about £120.

The best is the cheapest, for a deer cart has

[1] *Vide Rural Sports*, Rev. J. Daniel (1805); and for a description of the Wolmer deer, White's *Selborne*.

to stand exposure to much wind and weather and the wear and tear of all sorts of country roads. Initial solidity is an essential, and unfortunately solidity means weight. The approximate weight of the Ascot van, which has been in use since 1874, with its freight of two men and two deer, is about 23 cwts., which involves a strain of something like 16 cwts. upon the horses.

In these resourceful days it seems strange that something less cumbersome has not been discovered: pending the invention of a motor deer van, any suggestion for lightening the burden should be welcome. Mr. Kemsley, of the Royal Hotel, Ascot, who has horsed and driven the deer cart by contract for some years past, to whom I am indebted for the foregoing particulars, advises as an improvement the use of a cranked axle, which would lower the body six inches and render the van more practical for loading: and he would add higher front wheels and closer couplings, and make the body six inches shorter. This would materially decrease the weight. It has always seemed to me that a further lightening might possibly be effected by the substitution of a strong wicker roof, instead of the present wooden one, made waterproof by a covering of strong tarpaulin, on the principle and in the style of that important factor in every day life, the lady's travelling dress trunk.

Mr. Kemsley tells me that he reckons the average day's journey at forty miles. I know, speaking from my own experience, that this is within the mark. But an instance occurred last season when seventy miles had to be covered by the deer cart, which got back to the paddocks at about three in the morning. Mr. Kemsley reserves four horses solely for this work, each pair doing one journey a week. He likes a short-legged horse with plenty of bone, not over 15.3 and not under seven years. They must be well seasoned and fairly bred, in order to stand the long miles and face the weight.

The master of a pack of staghounds is exempt from the cares of earth stopping, but the efficiency and staunchness of the deer cart are heavy items in his budget and serious considerations.

Let us glance for a moment at some of these considerations: a well-horsed deer cart can even on woolly roads manage a steady six or seven miles an hour. As most staghounds do not meet till twelve, a very early start is seldom necessary. At the meet the deer van attracts as much attention as the Trojan horse might; upon its being driven into the field selected for the turn-out, popular enthusiasm knows no bounds, the excitement being kept up by conflicting suggestions as to the position it should occupy and several elaborate changes of front. But after the uncarting, the deer cart repairs to some central point. Among free-born Englishmen this always means a public-house—and here we come to a question of morals. The well-ordered number of these bulwarks of civilisation, coupled with long hours, stress of weather, agreeable company and personal popularity, mean that the driver and his comrade must unite the self-discipline of a St. Simeon Stylites to the hardihood of a Nansen.

"They also serve who only stand and wait"—in the circumstances a difficult thing to do without a glass of beer; but it is not all waiting. Possibly the first deer is taken or disgraces himself in half an hour, and the second deer is quickly wanted. A messenger arrives on the spur, and the deer van is expected to exhibit all the dash and alacrity of a London fire engine in getting to the scene of action. If, on the other hand, no orders have arrived by the time agreed upon, the whole caravan gets under its ponderous way, and follows to the best of its ability the line of hounds: depending upon the reckless information of passers-by or the vague accounts of discouraged sportsmen who have lost a shoe, lamed their horses, or had enough of it. This may go on for hours, and it will be admitted that a good deer cart driver is a valuable servant. The safe carting of the deer, its comfort in transit, and the soundness and welfare of the horses depend upon his care and competence. In a well-managed establishment the driver should always have a man with him who should be a good stableman, and if possible accustomed to the ways of deer.

Unless your men, your horses and your deer cart are all of the best, recognise their responsibilities and work harmoniously together, your troubles will not be to seek.

It may here be remarked that the van-driver and his comrade should be suitably but not too soberly dressed. The green plush coats and gold lace of the Royal Hunt give the deer cart a very classical appearance. In Utopia, I think, these officials would wear heavily furred white beavers, and a gaily attired postillion might be added. But in any case the rather prison-van-like appearance of the conveyance should be relieved somehow by colour and character.

The Carted Deer—The managing partner of a staghunting company next claims my attention.

Successful staghunting, by which a staghunter means a good run, in which little or nothing is seen of the deer, until he is taken safely and artistically, depends upon several things.

There is the mood and temperament of the deer; there is the weather, for though deer run well in under bright skies and a hot spring sun, I have seldom seen them run up to their form in muggy hazy weather; there is the country, that is the line taken by the deer, a matter of prime importance in such a riding pastime as staghunting. But, with the exception of the weather, all these largely depend upon the deer's condition—condition in the sense we mean when we speak of a Persimmon or a Slavin being trained to a day. In the case of a deer this training is the test and result of the paddock management. It will be good or bad in the same ratio as this is good or bad.

The number of deer in the paddocks depends upon purse, space, and the number of days a week the pack hunts. The hardest running deer are always the soundest, and very seldom get themselves into any trouble. Thus a crack deer will come out six or seven times in an open season; but three days a season is the most you can reckon upon with an average animal, and to hunt a two-days-a-week country properly, *i.e.*, assuming two deer are taken out daily, this may be taken as the basis of calculation.

At Swinley, the Royal Deer Paddocks, things were done on a liberal scale, but it is much better to have rather too many than rather too few deer. Deer easily get stale; like human beings, they have their days, and to my mind it is both foolish and wrong to hunt a weak or unwilling deer. The whole *raison d'être* of staghunting is the run. Thus a deer should not and must not be hunted as we hunt a fox. To press home even legitimate advantages with a deer involves the risk of bewildering him or even killing him. In the former case your run is spoiled and your field is disappointed. In the latter you are guilty of the cardinal sin of staghunting. Thus the most difficult thing for persons in authority out staghunting is to determine when to stop hounds and when to press a deer. It is a matter of intuition, with a dash of luck.

As the Swinley Paddocks are the oldest existing establishment of their kind, I cannot do better than give the following details of their disposition, for which I am indebted to Mr. F. Simmonds, of the Woods and Forests Department.

The Swinley Paddocks occupy an area of about 12 acres, divided into five separate paddocks, averaging rather over 2 acres each. The whole is fenced with an oak fence standing 8 feet out of the ground, of which the upper 3 feet are open palisade, and the rest close paling; at the point where these two parts meet, an iron sheet about 3 inches wide is laid along the fence; and at the bottom of the fence an iron ground sheet is let about 9 inches into the ground; the average cost of this (including banking) is £3 12*s.* 6*d.* per rod. The paddocks are treated as permanent pasture and never meadowed, a certain acreage being manured, harrowed, and rolled every year, and the deer are shifted about from one paddock to another, according to circumstances. This extra manuring and manual labour are necessary, in order to prevent the herbage going back, for deer are wasteful feeders, and will only graze the very best herbage, leaving the rougher parts untouched. If anything, the Swinley Paddocks are a little over shut in by trees, but shade and water are essential. At Swinley the latter is supplied from a stream flowing out of a neighbouring pond, small bays being made for its reception and storage.

The present Swinley herd consists of stags, hinds and haviers, and one or two polled haviers. As the difference between a havier and a polled havier is not always understood even by staghunters, it may here be pointed out that a polled havier never throws any horns, having been castrated very soon after he is dropped—whereas a havier is a stag castrated when full grown and at his best—that is, from four to seven years old. A havier's horns will grow again almost as usual the first spring after the operation. They are then taken off

IN THE PADDOCKS.

again, and after that velvet will grow on the brow antlers, but a havier never grows a head again. The hunting career of a stag should not begin before he is four years old.

A deer taken up into paddocks, say in September, if wanted for that season, should be at least four years old, and should not be hunted much before Christmas.

It is difficult to say whether stags, haviers or hinds afford the best sport. The great long-distance runs on record have almost invariably been after stags or haviers; but towards the end of the season, when the country dries up, hinds run the roads less than stags or haviers. One of the best deer I had in my time with the Queen's Hounds was a lop-eared polled havier.

The deer selected for hunting should be taken up into a deer stable on the afternoon of the preceding day, and should fare lightly. As soon as possible after he is taken he should be given some forage and water. The food of paddock deer of course largely depends on the time of year. During the summer they can and should live almost entirely upon grass. In the autumn and winter the average diet for a single deer may be taken as about a quart of the very best old beans and about one-fifth of a truss of second-crop clover hay daily, according to the weather and their keep in the paddocks. This menu is varied occasionally with carrots and pulped swedes or turnips, to the amount of, say, one-third of a bushel per day. Care should be taken to secure the best quality of forage. Given plenty of space and favourable conditions of every day life, there seems no reason why deer should not be bred in the paddocks for hunting purposes, but it has never been tried on any large scale to my knowledge. If at all lame, owing to road work and flints, the feet of a hunted deer require careful attention, and an experienced deer-keeper will have a liniment of his own, prepared from some recipe which wild horses would not induce him to divulge. It takes about four men to throw and examine a deer safely.

As a rule a deer tells you all about himself the first time you hunt him in an open country; but as staghunting is a pursuit peculiarly uncongenial to rules and formulas, he should always be given a second or even a third chance of winning the affection of the establishment and the esteem of the public. I have known instances of capital runs after very poor and even ridiculous starts. You never know what deer are going to do; they will run up and down the first fence, stand in the corner of a field looking at you, trot back down a road to meet the pack, or even pursue its quick retreat, and then all of a sudden settle down to run you out of daylight, or into the next county but one.

The best deer run to points, and I think concern themselves little about wind, although they are said to prefer to run on a side wind; but it is as well to uncart them with their heads up wind, and give them plenty of time to make up their mind. In some well-managed packs of staghounds it is customary for the first whip to ride the deer for a few hundred yards, with the object of edging him into the right country.

This was the plan of the celebrated Charles Davis, who held it desirable to point his deer on turning him out towards a conspicuous hill. As an example of this habit of running to points, the "Druid" relates of the Miller, a noted stag in Davis' time, that if he got two or three hundred yards out of his old line, he would take the greatest pains to right himself, and would then set-to in earnest. In one instance in my recollection, the polled havier I have just commended was left out after a 12-mile point. He was harboured in a big wood of Lord Downshire's; we found him a fortnight later, and he ran the last six or seven miles almost gap for gap on his old line the reverse way, being taken in an outhouse in the next field to the one in which he had been originally turned out.

The "Take"—It is related of the fifth Duke of Richmond that he was quite afraid to meet a certain butcher when he had not killed his fox. The butcher would never accept any excuses nor admit the possibility of a good run without blood. But it is just the other way staghunting. A master of staghounds who has killed his deer, keeps it to himself, if he does not wish to advertise his incompetence. In this connection it was remarked with justice by an apologist of the last century that whereas in every other kind of hunting everybody strives to be in at the death, out staghunting the exertion of all is to save the deer's life. This then is the grand test of a huntsman's skill and success: season after season old names and old friends in the paddocks.

To my mind the artificial conditions and high feeding of paddock life are not alone sufficient to put a deer in wind for the deep and holding country over which he is often hunted. Deer should therefore be exercised. As an example of how this may be done, I may say that in the Swinley Paddocks we formerly had a bob-tailed lurcher to whom this duty was confided. He performed it admirably. The deer and he thoroughly understood each other, and nothing would have induced him to turn into earnest the play which both parties thoroughly enjoyed. It is only fair to say, however, that the contrary opinion is held by many who are conversant with the subject as to the desirableness of this artificial exercise.

The "Druid," in one of his books, endeavours to point a distinction between the hunting aptitudes of different breeds of deer, the Woburn deer, for instance, being superior to the Chillingham, and so on. In my opinion, the question is not so much one of strain, which has little bearing on the question of a deer running well or ill, as of local antecedent conditions. It is a great point that the deer destined for hunting should have been bred in large, rough parks, where they have had plenty of range and wild life.

Country—I spoke just now of country as a condition of successful staghunting. In my opinion the prime requisites are extent and variety. From the riding point of view—a very material one—nothing can be imagined better than the Elysian fields of the Aylesbury Vale and the emerald provinces of the Ward Union. At the same time, if only some magician could do away with the wire, restore the Harrow country, obliterate many villas and an occasional village, and, perhaps, whilst he was in the humour, abolish the Thames, the Queen's county would be an ideal staghunting county. There is country of all kinds, and, above all, lots of room, and the value of the bold sweep of forest and heath lands cannot be over-rated. Staghounds should not meet in a systematically wired country, and they should always be stopped in water meadows or low-lying riverside lands. The best mounted and most resolute hunt servants cannot be counted upon to keep with hounds in these circumstances.

"The Lord of the Valley stands proudly to bay."

Like every other line of Whyte Melville's appreciative verses, this is absolutely true. Besides, habit is ten times nature, and the pack are so accustomed to bay round their deer in a lusty "Freischütz" chorus, but at a respectful distance, that so long as he is on his legs, it does not occur to them to do anything else. But the carrier of a water meadow, or the ooze of a withy bed, has a fatal attraction for deer, which they seem powerless to resist; they seem to abandon themselves to a sort of Nirvana. With the loss of the advantage of ground, there is the more serious loss of prestige,—and then it is soon all over.

The Staghound—The Rev. J. Daniel and other writers of authority in the first years of this century speak with disparagement of the slowness and heavy outline of the royal staghound. But a very few years after the publication of Mr. Daniel's *Rural Sports* in 1806, the old staghound type was extinct, at all events in the royal kennel. Both George IV.'s and Lord Derby's staghounds were pure bred foxhounds, and the good ground gained in the first quarter of the century has been more than held.

Nothing could be more different from the old Georgian staghound or the Massy buckhounds—a celebrated pack of curiously bred Talbots in Tipperary—than the type a Master of the Buckhounds or of the Ward Union sets before him and works up to to-day. Horses and men want to go faster and faster, and so must the hounds. Moreover, nothing is to be gained by the majestic size and massive bulk still honourably associated with these Vieille Roche aristocrats. A racing foxhound pack of the highest breeding—24 ins. at the very outside, 23 ins., in my opinion, is better—with the Blankney necks and shoulders, above all with the tirelessness which Lord Henry Bentinck and Mr. Tom Smith set such store by, are what the present conceptions of hunting and of riding to hounds require. To some extent, too, a staghound's is a thankless service; *bon sang ne peut mentir*, and only a foxhound of high degree will go on doing his very best in the face of the moral, and often practical, rebuffs which are his only meed when once it becomes a question of a deer's safety.

As the tendency of staghounds is to string, and as the drive and speed of your hounds are

HUNTSMAN AND HOUNDS

the first things to think about, a pack should be drafted hard up to high standards of pace and dash. In a pack of twelve couple—quite enough, in my opinion, to have out with a large field of eager and courageous horsemen—every hound should be fast enough to get to the front and determined enough to do his utmost to stay there. Nose is hardly the first consideration in a staghound, for, as Charles Davis used to say, the scent of a deer lies so high and sweet. It may be an impossible ideal, but a master of staghounds should not rest content till, in Beckford's phrase, he sees his hounds topping their fences "like the horses of the sun, all abreast," or, to quote another high authority, "spreading like a rocket," in a difficulty.

It is difficult to establish the exact origin of the old staghound, bred, as he was, with care and patience for the express purpose of staghunting. Perhaps the old Devon and Somerset pack, rather than George III.'s hounds, may be taken as the best of the sort. In height they ran from 26 to 28 ins.; in colour they were hare and badger pied, yellow and white, and black and white with long ears, colossal throats, deep chests and slab sides. Even when running hard, these hounds gave plenty of sonorous music; comparative silence is the price we have had to pay for pace. But a modern staghunter on a grass-country horse, with the Vale of Aylesbury unfolding itself in front of him, will cheerfully bear the loss of the melodious operations of the past.

Horses—Little need be said with regard to horses. The best is not too good for staghunting; "thoroughbred horses make the best hunters; I never heard of a great thing yet but it was done by a thoroughbred horse," said Dick Christian. I believe he was quite right, especially for staghunting. Dick Christian goes on to say that he likes them with lots of action and to see all four feet at once. It is not very clear what this means, though it gives one an almost uncomfortable idea of action; but in buying a staghunter bear in mind that road work, and fast road work, is inevitable, and that a noisy hackney-actioned horse knocks his legs to pieces in no time. Send him a quarter of a mile away, listen to him gallop down a road towards you, and if he recalls to you Virgil's hexameter, don't buy him. Of course a staghunter must go fast. A slow or underbred horse, if not outpaced by staghounds, soon gets blown by the persistence of the pace; for if the deer is really in the humour, a horse has few opportunities for getting his wind, and it is but seldom his rider can save him by riding cunning and getting a nick. In view of the long hours and the ever lengthening miles home, which stout deer usually mean, it is an economy to send out two horses for all the hunt servants; thus you want more horses than you would in a foxhunting stable. Unfortunately, too, the second horses do not often mean any great saving to the first. They can seldom get to points or make short cuts; and when they do arrive, have had to come along a pretty good pace and jump a few fences. Three days a fortnight is quite as much as a hunt horse can manage, and even then he must be seasoned, full of condition, and fairly ridden. But, given these desiderata and a capable stud groom, the effect of the most severe day's staghunting soon passes off.

It may here be remarked that the whippers-in should be quite as well mounted as the huntsmen, and on really bold horses. They should be "emergency" horsemen; by this I mean men who will jump a really big place at a critical moment.

The Past and Present of Staghunting—Since 1857, the first year the *Field* published its annual list of hunting establishments in the United Kingdom, the number of staghunting packs has steadily increased from six to sixteen in 1897, the highest figure recorded in this period. I have not got the figures for Ireland. But it is not an industry which has suffered from over production, and this increase bears no proportion to the remarkable increase of foxhunting establishments. As exhibited and practised by the Queen's, the Surrey, Lord Rothschild's, and other well-known packs, staghunting has never been more popular than at present; yet it continues to be, as it always has been, a localised form of the chase. For all but a century there have been staghounds in the home counties, in Hampshire and in Norfolk; but, as far as

I know, this sport has never taken root in the midland and northern counties; and whilst there are several packs of high reputation in Ireland, staghunting has made no way either in Scotland or in Wales.

As a good deal has been urged at one time or another to the depreciation of staghunting as compared with foxhunting, I may be excused for briefly noticing here some of the advantages which our good-humoured and democratic pastime affords. It is claimed, for example, that staghunting lacks much of the uncertainty which certainly distinguishes fox- and hare-hunting; but this very feature is in itself from some aspects commendable. To begin with, unless the deer cart has got lost, you are sure to find; and there is always scent enough to hunt a deer when hounds could not own to a fox. Then there are conditions attached to staghunting which make it an eminently suitable amusement and exercise for busy men who like a ride. Several of the most notable staghound packs are, thanks to our benevolent railways, within easy reach of London. In a good country, with a fast pack and a straight deer, a run of an hour, or at the most an hour and a half, should satisfy most people. Staghounds meet late, and nine times out of ten the best of the run is over early. Then we trouble ourselves less about conventions than foxhunters. If anything, staghunting is too liberal a school of morals; there are no canons of dress, and very few of behaviour. Lastly, from a master's point of view, our profession is absolved from many of the anxieties which take up a good deal of the time of a master of foxhounds. Your master of staghounds is spared, for example, all heart searchings as to the soundness of Mr. Jones' views on foxes; he need not upset all his arrangements owing to Lord Hawkeye's big shoot, or answer letters about massacres of poultry and game. If only he can keep his field in order—who are as a rule not good judges of seeds and meadow land—the damage done to land by staghounds should compare favourably with that caused by foxhounds in a fashionable country; a good deer runs over a long stretch of country, he runs straight, and does not, if he is worth his salt, dodge and twist about, like a bad fox on a poor scenting day, dragging a large and impatient field backwards and forwards over a few hundred acres of affectionately farmed land. If he does, a wise master leaves him to his own devices, and sends for the deer cart and the second deer.

Ethics naturally bring us to a freely debated aspect of staghunting, the humanitarian. A discussion of the "cruelty" question would be outside the scope of this article; besides, I have said all I have to say in the chapter on this subject in my *Staghunting Recollections.* Perhaps a rather closer acquaintance with our manners and customs may mitigate the asperities of our opponents; and if my book should have any such effect I should indeed be pleased; but on the broad issue I would recommend to their notice the discussion between Mr. Fox and Mr. Wakefield (the editor of *Lucretius*), given in Lord John Russell's *Memorials and Correspondence of Charles James Fox* (Vol. IV.), and in the words of Mr. Wakefield, "I wish that any dispute of the kind would terminate as amicably and after such gentle litigation" as theirs did.

Literature—The literature of carted deer hunting, though adequate, is not large: Mr. Beckford declined to include us in his *Thoughts*, Mr. Daniel only just admits it to his *Rural Sports*. "Nimrod" touches upon our pastime with occasional condescension, but his heart is far from us. In Scott and Sebright the "Druid" devotes a vivid chapter to the staghunting of his own and the preceding generation. Then we can see a fine run with the Baron in the pages of *Satanella*, and laugh at ourselves with the late Mr. Higgins in the Harrow country (*Wild Sports of Middlesex*), or with Mr. Surtees and John Leech when the Benicia Boy electrifies Miss Birch's establishment. Starting from Edward III., Mr. Hore in his *History of the Royal Buckhounds* traces the fortunes and investigates the budgets of the royal pack under successive sovereigns. Of my own book I will only say that its facts, experiences and recollections are the result of three years' close association with deer, staghounds, and staghunting.

RIBBLESDALE.

LIST OF PACKS.

1857.

Her Majesty's.	Devon and Somerset.	
East Berks.	Heathcote's.	
Cheltenham.	Baron Rothschild's.	6

1862.

Her Majesty's.	Mr. Heathcote's.	
Burton Constable.	Hon. F. Petre's.	
Devon and Somerset.	Baron Rothschild's.	6

1865.

Her Majesty's.	Mr. Nevill's (Winchester, given up).	
Sir C. Constable's (Yorks).	Hon. F. Petre's (now the Essex).	
Devon and Somerset.	Baron Rothschild's.	7
Mr. Heathcote's (now the Surrey).		

1871.

Same as above, except Sir C. Constable dropped out; but two new names appeared—the Easingwold in Yorks and the Berkhampstead in Herts. 8

1875.

Her Majesty's.	Hon. F. Petre's.	
Mr. Angerstein's.	Baron Rothschild's.	
Berkhampstead.	Surrey.	
Colchester.	Mr. Farnell Watson's.	
Devon and Somerset.	Waveney (Norfolk).	
Easingwold.	Lord Wolverton's (Dorset)	
Mr. Nevill's.		13

1880.

Her Majesty's.	Mid Kent.
Berkhampstead.	Norfolk and Suffolk.
Lord Carrington's.	Hon. F. Petre's.
Colline Dale. (He bought Lord Wolverton's and Mr. Nevill's.)	Sir N. de Rothschild's.
	Surrey.
	Mr. Farnell Watson's. 11
Devon and Somerset.	

1885.

Her Majesty's.	Hon. F. Petre's.
Berkhampstead.	Sir N. de Rothschild's.
Devon and Somerset.	Surrey.
Lady Meux's (Wilts).	Warnham.
Mid Kent.	4th Hussars.
New Forest.	11

1891.

Her Majesty's.	Lord Rothschild's.
Berkhampstead.	Surrey.
Devon and Somerset.	Surrey Farmers'.
Enfield Chase.	Warnham.
Essex (late Petre's).	8th Hussars. This is a regimental pack at Norwich, and the hunt is transferred from regiment to regiment. 14
Mr. Giles's (Herefordshire).	
Mr. Greene's (Suffolk).	
Mid Kent.	
New Forest.	

1895.

Her Majesty's.	New.
Berkhampstead.	Oxenholme.
Devon and Somerset.	Lord Rothschild's.
Enfield Chase.	Savernake.
Essex.	Surrey.
Hon. R. Gerard.	West Surrey (Farmers').
Mr. Greene's.	Warnham.
Mid Kent.	7th Dragoon Guards. 16

WILD RED DEER ON EXMOOR—If any one branch of hunting can be said to be especially popular with the readers of sporting magazines and other periodicals of the present day, surely that department of sport with which the Devon and Somerset Staghounds are associated may lay undisputed claim to the distinction. Yet the hunt has had its days of adversity, and many staunch supporters thereof, who have not yet left their middle age behind them, can well remember the days when the future of the chase of the wild red deer seemed more than doubtful.

Turning first to the **History of the Hunt**, it seems probable that deer were first hunted by the rangers of the forest of Exmoor from a very early date, apparently the thirteenth century, but it was not until 1775 that a pack of hounds was hunted there by a private gentleman. From that time to 1818 the hunt was prosperously carried on by various magnates of the district; then until 1825 the sport would seem to have languished, and from Vol. XV. of the *Sporting Magazine*, published in that year, it is obvious that the "North Devon" Stag Hunt was in a moribund state. In the volume above referred to is included a lengthy article by "Nimrod," which appeared in the November number, 1826, and describes the experiences of the author on a sporting tour in the West. His description of the hound is of interest, "the North Devon hounds appear to be, with one or two exceptions, thorough-bred staghounds, having all the peculiarities of the breed. They are heavy —or perhaps I should say strong—in their shoulders; short in their necks; slack in their loins; rather deep-flewed; heads long; ears fine and pendulous; noses somewhat flat and wide; tongues deep and sonorous; very good legs and feet; and from 24 to 26 inches high. The prevailing colours are yellow, badger, and hare-pie—not one black and white hound among them. They carry their heads high with a good scent, but will stoop to a low one; and are all line-hunters—a flinging stag-hound being seldom met with."

Nimrod, however, does not seem to have seen any sport on the occasion of his visit, and the heavy rains which prevailed were little to his taste.

In the February number, 1825, there is a piteous letter on the subject of the decline of the hunt, which, the writer avers, had received its death-warrant; and, in fact, at the end of that season the hounds were sold by auction in London to a German baron.

From 1825 to 1855 there was more than one interregnum, but in the latter year began a new era, on Mr. Fenwick Bisset coming forward as Master of the pack. How that gentleman faced difficulties of every kind unflinchingly, and how, thanks to his efforts, the sport has prospered, all interested in the annals of the Chase must know. He retired from the Mastership after twenty-six seasons of good sport, and his successors have all maintained the standard of excellence to which the management of the Hunt had been brought.

Literature of the Sport—Following this brief summary of the history of the "Devon and Somerset Staghounds," allusion must be made to two works, in which the seeker for information on this subject will find ample matter of interest; though it must be mentioned that both books are comparatively rare. The first of these is Dr. C. P. Collyns' *Notes on the Chase of the Wild Red Deer*, published in 1862. It deals very fully with the sport which the writer loved so well, and consists of eight chapters, besides an appendix of upwards of 80 pages "descriptive of remarkable runs and incidents connected with the Chase from the year 1780 to the year 1860." The book is, moreover, profusely illustrated and contains a map of the district.

The second work is entitled *Records of Stag-Hunting on Exmoor*, by the Hon. John Fortescue, published in 1887, and contains many illustrations, besides a map of the stag-hunting country, the extent of which is described in the opening chapter. Three appendices are subjoined, in which are to be found a "Record of the most notable Chases from 1855 to 1885," and a "Tabulated History of the North Devon and Devon and Somerset Staghounds," which is followed by a list of the ear-marked stags killed between 1855 and 1885.

Though the above two volumes stand out as those in which the best of information is given by writers well qualified for their task, there was published in 1849 a book entitled *Exmoor; or the Footsteps of St. Hubert in the West*, by Herbert Byng Hall, Esq., with illustrations which, however, can hardly be said to deal entirely with sporting subjects, nor indeed is the book itself confined to Exmoor. Mr. Hall's work is not easily obtained, but there are accounts in it of several runs which are of interest.

As for the Red Deer, in Dr. Collyns' book the noble beast of the forest is fully described in Chapters II. and III.: the author cites Manwood to show cause why the hart and the hind are both mentioned as beasts of forest in the book *Antiquitatis Britanniæ*, which dates from before the Conquest. Even at that early date "the hart hath his season in summer, and the season of the hart doth end." The reader is then inducted into the distinguishing names of deer at different ages; since Dr. Collyns' day some of the more purely technical terms of distinction have fallen out of use; *e.g.*, one does not hear a deer in his third year called a "spire or pricket," or a four year old a "staggart,"—nowadays they are generally called "three" or "four year olds," whilst a "knobber, or knobbler, or brocket" is called a "male deer" simply. Similarly, the term of "hearst" for a hind in a second year is seldom used. To continue observations on Chapter II. of Dr. Collyns' book, his notes on the size and character of stags' horns at various ages are not to be surpassed; it is a topic on which unanimity of opinion cannot always be expected, but the age of the stag can, as a rule, be distinguished up to a certain point, when the stag's head is said to be "going back" or—as Dr. Collyns called a deer in such a state—a "bater" or "backer." The deer in the Devon and Somerset country do not differ from the Scotch deer in any respect; the size of "beam" is generally a question of the quality of food accessible.

The author of the *Chase of the Wild Red Deer* is, in the matter of enthusiasm for the noble beast of venerie, hard pressed by one Richard Blome, to whom we are indebted for the *Gentleman's Recreation* published in 1686, in which the modern sportsman will find much instruction and not a little amusement. The book was intended, it appears, to be a general storehouse of sporting knowledge in its widest sense. Amongst "Profits and Advantages of the Stag," one learns that "the Horns are said to be Antidotes against Poyson, being little inferiour to those of the Unicorn, if there be any such Beast." But the sportsman and lover of Nature will read, perhaps, with greatest pleasure Richard Jefferies' *Red Deer*, the first edition of which work was published in 1884. Though a born naturalist, the author, when he first visited Exmoor, knew little or nothing about hunting, but it must be admitted that, during the short time that he was collecting materials for this book, he learnt his woodcraft with marvellous thoroughness. If Dr. Collyns' book is hard to obtain, this cannot be said of Jefferies' *Red Deer*, for an excellent edition of it is obtainable at a small price. In its ten chapters there are many passages descriptive of the beauties of red-deer land, whilst from a sporting point of view Chapter VI., on "Tracking Deer by Slot" or "Harbouring," is most instructive.

Harbouring—This branch of venerie is probably so familiar (in print) nowadays that it seems almost superfluous to write down that it is the duty of the "harbourer" to report at the meet of the staghounds where a "warrantable" stag, *i.e.*, one over four years old, has made his bed or lair. To ascertain this, the "harbourer's" movements are guided by the "slot" or footprint, which varies with the age of the deer in size, length and shape; the greatest care being exercised by the harbourer during his investigations not to disturb the deer, who are particularly shy in the early hours.

Hunting—Arrived at the meet, the Master directs the huntsman to kennel the pack in any farm buildings, &c., that may be convenient, and the huntsman forthwith starts off with a few hounds (the number varying according to the place where the stag is reported to be lying) to rouse the deer. These hounds or "tufters" seldom exceed in number four couples; that they should have good tongue is most necessary, though, if a stag is lying out on the moor, a couple or so of particularly fast hounds may be selected. This tufting is frequently a long process; the deer may have moved after the harbourer has duly satisfied himself as to his work being done, and many untoward accidents may bring this about.

Then, with the deer fairly found by the tufters, hinds, or young deer, may distract hounds' attention; indeed, a cunning old stag will do his best to put up other deer. But as a rule the patience and experience of his pursuers will be too much for him in the end, and he is forced to fly. The first opportunity is seized for stopping the tufters, and the field, most of which is waiting at the farm where the pack is kennelled, is set in commotion by the sound of the horn, giving the signal that the time has come for the "lay on." Though it may be half an hour or more before the pack is brought to the spot where the tufters have been stopped, the scent of the deer generally serves well enough, and to the lover of hounds at work perhaps laying on the pack is the prettiest sight of the day's hunting, for there is a crash of music and hounds "drive" along. This drive does not often last for long; the deer leaves behind so good a scent that hounds do not fling for it as they would after a fox, and they settle in their places, striding along at a good pace nevertheless. So the chase goes on; if the deer is a very heavy one, and he has been found near the sea, it will not take long to drive him down the cliffs, and he will swim out into the Bristol Channel; thence to be brought back by boatmen, and despatched on the beach. It is more often in the rivers and streams that abound in the district that the finish of the run takes place, the stag standing to bay in the water; when once he has been brought to bay, he fights for his life, and should a beaten stag break from bay, and jump into a road full of horses, the riders lose no time in dispersing, for he would stop at nothing in his desperate case. In some streams it is occasionally a matter of considerable difficulty to give the stag the *coup de grâce*, and he will run up and down the water until he can be lassoed, or seized by the horns from behind. It is not often that a stag is killed on dry land, though a notable case was that of the gallant stag killed on October 9th, 1889; he was found in the Bratton coverts sixteen miles from Luckham, where the kill took place, but instead of being brought to bay in the Horner Water, he still ran on, and finally jumped the high wall that surrounds the rectory garden, hounds rolling him over on the lawn. Cases such as this are dangerous; and this is evidently the opinion of the aforesaid Richard Blome, whose advice "as to the Land Bay" is "If the Hart be frayed and burnished then the place is well to be considered of; for if it be in a Hedge side or thicket, then whilst he is stareing on the Hounds you may come covertly amongst the bushes behind him and so kill him, but if you miss and he turn Head upon you it is convenient to take refuge behind some tree."

The excellence of this advice is beyond dispute; other words of counsel from the same source of authority, perhaps more rarely acted upon, tell us that "it hapneth very often that through some accident or other the Hart escapeth. Now for the recovering of the Chase the next day let there be some Mark set where the Chase is left off."

A CUNNING OLD STAG.

The Deer Country—As to the nature of the country over which the red deer are suffered to roam unmolested save by hounds, their territory is bounded on the north by the Bristol Channel, fringed with steep cliffs and strong woodlands for the most part as far as Minehead; east of this, the country lies lower and consequently is more enclosed until the range of Quantock Hills is reached. These heather-clad hills, and the large coverts that surround them, abound in deer, and, as this district lies wide of the Exford kennels, the hounds are kennelled at Bagborough for a week or fortnight at a time when the Quantocks are to be hunted. Some distance west of this are the Brendon Hills and the Haddon Woods, which afford shelter to deer galore. To the south of Haddon Hill and Skilgate Common runs the Devon and Somerset Railway, beyond which the territory of the staghounds does not extend, though recently the liberality of a gentleman and the sporting instincts of the inhabitants have led to an auxiliary pack being formed to hunt the deer south of the line. Close to Dulverton the river Exe is joined by the Barle, and both these rivers, the latter especially, run for miles down deeply wooded valleys. The part of the country in this district that is free from woods is strongly enclosed, though on Winsford Hill and its environing commons good galloping ground is frequently to be met with. West again of the Barle valley, Anstey and Molland commons stretch away to the Molland Woods, whilst some distance further west come the Bray coverts; the latter, with the Bratton Woods, though immediately surrounded by a rather impracticable country, are generally reckoned as most likely to provide a good deer that will boldly face the moor. When Yard Down is the meet, a stag will often set his head straight for Moles Chamber and the Forest, perhaps not touching another covert until the Horner woodlands, on the north-eastern extremity of the moor, are reached. Similarly, from a fixture at Friendship Inn, a Bratton deer worthy of the name climbs the ascent to Chapman's Barrows, and affords a fine run to the same fastnesses, should he have strength to reach them. Exmoor Forest itself, *i.e.*, the Simonsbath side of the moor, is almost free from heather; sedge grass here prevails, and in many parts the moor is intersected with narrow drains, which, being covered with thick grass in the stag-hunting season, are responsible for many an empty saddle. The commons of Brendon, Badgworthy, and practically all the moors east of the Badgworthy Water, are covered thickly with heather: over these moors the riding is good enough. On the Forest side the going is soft, in places very much so, and the dictum of a well-known deer preserver and follower of the hounds that there is no such thing on Exmoor as a bog has not met with universal assent.

Season—The staghunting season begins about August 10th, Cloutsham being always the fixture, followed a few days later by Hawkcombe Head; both these meets are in the Porlock or northern district. For the former meet, the Horner Woods, composed principally of oak scrub, may be relied upon to furnish a warrantable deer; Hawkcombe Head is more likely to mean a moorland gallop, though with so many coverts adjoining the rendezvous the starting point of the run from this fixture depends on circumstances.

The stag-hunting season usually comes to an end about the 10th of October, after which the hind-hunting season commences, and is continued until the end of April, that is, when the deer are plentiful, as is now the case. Towards the end of September a visible change comes over the male deer, for the rutting season is approaching; the stags' necks begin to swell, and they "bell" in search of the hinds. In the old days an interval was usual between the stag-hunting and the hind-hunting, but nowadays the vast area over which the large herd of deer are hunted makes any prolonged cessation of duty on the part of the Devon and Somerset Hunt establishment impossible. Thus the season for hounds and horses is a long one. Hind-hunting is productive of more hard days than the chase of the stag, for a hind will generally stand before hounds for three hours or more, and much trouble is caused if the pack gets among a herd of deer. The hind-hunting meets are not often very largely attended.

Hounds—The Devon and Somerset hounds are out, as a rule, three days a week, and the arduous nature and duration of their work are a severe strain on them; perhaps what tries hounds more than anything is the work that they have to do in the water; and hounds drafted from the Exford kennels often turn out to be valuable otter hounds. The pack is entirely composed of dog-hounds, and the average height is 25 inches; owing to the wear and tear of the kennel being heavy, a large entry is annually put on, consisting of hounds drafted from fox-hound kennels owing to their height. The very best of blood is to be found—and those to whom a good-looking hound is an attraction much appreciate an inspection of the Devon and Somerset kennels.

The hunting experiences of Dr. Johnson are reported to have led him to aver that "the dogs had less sagacity than he could have prevailed upon himself to suppose," and "that it was very strange and very melancholy that the paucity of human pleasures should persuade us to call hunting one of them."

But as we gather from the biographer who mentions these *obiter dicta* that the great man's observations on the chase were solely derived from the Brighton Downs, it may be suggested that after a few days with the Devon and Somerset Staghounds he might have qualified these aspersions on the Sport of Kings.

L. J. BATHURST.

GLOSSARY—FOX.

Away—(Of a fox), left the covert.

Babbler—A noisy hound; one which gives tongue when not on to line.

Bagman—A fox released when required; the term had its origin in the practice of some owners of estates allowing their keepers to kill foxes, and then to buy one when hounds were expected. He was commonly taken to the covert in a sack, and shaken out.

Balk—Of a horse, to refuse a leap.

Billet—The droppings of the fox.

Blank—A covert is blank or drawn blank when it holds no fox.

Blooding—Giving the fox to the hounds.

Breast-high—*See* SCENT.

Brush—The tail of the fox.

Bullfinch—A hedge too high to leap; riders have to bore through it.

Burning scent—*See* SCENT.

Burst—The first part of the run if the hounds get away close to their fox.

Burst him—(Of a fox) killed in the burst.

Carries—Of the ground, when it sticks to the fox's pads after frost.

Carry a good head—Of the hounds, to run and keep well together on a good scent.

Cast—To spread out, in search of the scent. Hounds either cast themselves or are cast by the huntsman.

Catch hold—A huntsman is said to do this when he, at a check, takes his hounds forward, either to a holloa or for some reason of his own.

Challenge—The first hound which speaks on hitting off the line "challenges."

Change—To leave the line of one fox for another.

Check—An interruption to the run, the scent being lost—**thrown-out.**

Chopped—Killed as soon as found.

Counter—To follow the scent from the fox, instead of following him.

Covert—A place where the fox is sheltered, whether wood, thicket, or gorse, &c. Such places have various local names, such as holts, roughs, coppices, or copses, spinneys, shaws, &c. Artificial coverts are often planted, gorse, laurel, withies, hawthorn, &c., being used. Temporary coverts are also made of dead wood and bushes, and are called stick, faggot, or dead coverts.

Covert-hack—A horse used for riding to the place of meeting.

Covert-hoick—The huntsman's cry, meaning "into cover."

Covert-lad—*See* PAD-GROOM.

Crash—When the pack all give tongue together on finding a fox.

Crop—The whip used in hunting, with a loop, called a keeper, at the top of the crop for the attachment of the thong.

Cub—The young of the fox.

Cub-hunting—Takes place before fox-hunting begins, and generally early in the morning. Its principal object is to train the hounds and teach cubs to go away at once.

Currant-jelly—The scent of a hare crossing that of the fox, and disturbing the hounds.

Dog-fox—The male fox.

Double—To turn back on one's course.

Draft—To remove hounds from a kennel, or pack.

Drag—(1) The scent left by the fox on his return to his lair. (2) An artificial scent, followed by drag-hounds.

Drag up to—To follow the scent of a fox up to his kennel.

Drain—Any underground passage for water, to which the fox may run.

Draw,—Draw a covert—To search for a fox in a covert.

Draw blank—An unsuccessful draw.

Dwelling—Not responding to the huntsman's call; lingering too long on the line.

Earth—The lair or burrow of the fox.

Earth-stopper—A person employed to stop earths. It is done while the fox is abroad at night, and on his return he finds himself stopped out. All earths are stopped in the district in which hounds are expected to be on any hunting day.

Enter—Young hounds when first put into the pack are said to be "entered."

Eye to hounds—The art of watching the leading hounds, and so following them by the shortest line.

Feathering—Moving the stern from side to side, an act which indicates that the hound recognises the scent, but not to a sufficient extent to speak to it.

Feeder—He is really the kennel cook. He prepares the meat and meal for the hounds and washes out the kennels.

Flash—(Of hounds), to overrun the scent.

Flighty—Uncertain and changeable, applied both to hound and scent.

Fling—To drive on the scent at the least semblance of a check.

Foil,—Foils—To run. To run over the same track.

Foiled—A term applied to ground which has been much traversed by hounds and horses.

Fox—*Canis vulpes*, order Carnivora. The object of Fox-hunting. It is said there were two varieties of fox in this country, the greyhound and the bull-dog; the latter distinguished by its wider head and darker colour; but they have almost disappeared since about 1830, being supplanted by the French fox, which is smaller than either, and of reddish hue.

Full cry—Originally alluding to the chorus of music from the pack, is now understood to mean the hounds going fast on a good scent.

Gone away—Left the covert.

Gone to Ground—Gone to a drain, earth, rabbit-hole, or other shelter underground.

Headed—(Of the fox), made to turn back.

Headed to death—Killed unfairly, when headed.

Heel—*See* SCENT.

Hold hard—The warning to riders not to press too closely on the hounds.

Hold them forrard—To take the hounds on, in search of a lost line.

Holding scent—*See* SCENT.

Hunt foil—Run foil.

Huntsman—The person who hunts the hounds. The Master (M.F.H.) frequently assumes this office, and then the official who feeds the hounds and sees after them generally in kennel is called the kennel huntsman. The first whipper-in usually discharges this duty.

Kennel—(1) The fox's lair. (2) The old word used for the hounds; now "Pack," formerly confined to harriers, is often used.

Kennels—The place where the hounds are kept.

Kennel huntsman—*See* HUNTSMAN.

Lift—To take the hounds from a lost scent, with a view to hitting the line further on.

Line hunter—A hound which keeps close to the scent.

Main earth—The fox's own lair and breeding place.

Mask—The fox's head. Also PATE.

Meet—The rendezvous of those about to take part in the chase.

M.F.H.—Master of Fox Hounds.

Mob—To surround and kill a fox, without giving him the chance of a run.

Mute—Silent, the hounds going too fast to speak. Some hounds are naturally mute.

Noisy—Speaking without a scent.

Over it—*See* SCENT.

Owning—*See* SCENT.

Oxer,—Ox-fence,—Ox-rail—A strong hedge with a wide ditch, and a single rail about one yard in front of it. A double oxer has a rail on each side.

Pack—The hounds employed in hunting. [*See* KENNEL.]

Pad—The foot of the fox.

Pad-groom—The groom who rides the hunter to cover, and brings back the hack. Also COVERT-LAD.

Pate—The fox's head. Also MASK.

Pink—The scarlet coat worn by fox-hunters.

Point-to-point—A straight run. Most hunts now have point-to-point races during the season. The course is not flagged, and the competitors take their own line.

Point-rider—One who does not ride as the fox and hounds go, but to points at which he hopes to pick up the hounds.

Rabbit-earth—A burrow, to which a fox often goes for shelter.

Rack—A way through a hedge.

Recovered—*See* SCENT.

Ringing-fox—One that runs in circles instead of going right away.

Roach-back—A round-backed hound.

Road-hunter—A hound which possesses the rare gift of being able to hunt a fox or hare on a road.

Riot—*See* RUN.

Run—(1) The chase of the fox from finding to the death. To run counter, foil, or heel [*see* COUNTER, &c.]. To run to earth [*see* EARTH]. To run to ground [*see* GROUND]. To run riot: to follow a wrong scent.

Scent—The odour given off by the fox, by which he is found and followed by the hounds. It is *burning*, if very good or strong; *breast-high*, if so good that the hounds do not stoop to it; *moving*, if it is so *fresh* that it must be recent, and not a *drag* (*q.v.*); *flighty* or *catchy*, if variable; *holding*, if good enough, but not very strong; *recovered*, if lost, and found again. When hounds speak on a scent, they *own* to it; when they go beyond it, they are *over* it; when they follow it the reverse way, it is *heel*, *counter*, or *foil* [*see* RUN]; when they remain on it without following it, they *dwell* on it; when they first perceive it, they *feel* it, or *hit* it, and *hit it off* when it has been lost; if they hunt any other animal than that which is their proper game, they *run riot*; when they lose it, they *throw-up* (*i.e.*, their heads).

Scoring—Hounds "score" when the whole pack speak to a strong scent.

Sinking—(Of a fox), nearly beaten.

Skirter—A hound which runs wide of the pack.

Speak—Of a hound, to cry, showing he is on the scent.

Spout—Rabbit-earth (*q.v.*).

Stained—Injured as regards scent by the previous passage of hounds, horses, or of cattle, &c.

Stern—The tail of a hound.

Stooping—(Of hounds), putting their noses to the ground. [*See* SCENT.] A hound is said to stoop to a scent when he has once taken to speaking to it.

Streaming—Going across open country, spread out.

Stub-bred,—Stump-bred—Foxes which, in certain districts, make their lairs in bushes or stumps instead of underground; stubbed was the old term.

Tailing—Hounds are said to tail when they run in almost Indian file. To tail is the opposite of carrying a good head.

Throw off—To start the hunt by putting the hounds into a covert.

Throw up—*See* SCENT.

Thrown-out—Checked. [*See* CHECK.]

Timber—A wooden fence, rail, stile, or gate.

View halloo—The cry when the fox is seen.

Vixen—The female fox.

Ware riot—The cry to the hounds, when running riot (*q.v.*).

Well clawed,—Well knit up—With strong claws, adapted for running.

Whelp—A very young puppy.

Whipper-in—The huntsman's help in controlling the hounds.

Worried—Killed by the hounds.

OTTER.

Bolt—To put the otter out of his holt or couch.

Chain—The series of air-bubbles sent by the otter to the surface of the water when he breathes during his dives.

Couch—[*See* HOLT].

Drag—The scent left by an otter, by which he is hunted up to.

Foil—(1) Used of spectators or huntsmen: to spoil the scent by disturbing the ground. (2) Used of the otter: to return on its own track.

Gaze—To view the otter.

Holt—The lair of the otter, and the various refuges to which he flies when pursued, or when driven from home by rising floods. It is a burrow excavated in the bank, generally overshadowed by a bush or tree, with an entrance beneath the water. There is generally also a *Vent-hole* of small size above water level, at which the otter may be winded. Other names for holt are *Couch*, *Hover*, *Kennel*, and *Lodge*.

Some authorities prefer to use "couch" and "kennel" for the permanent home, and "holt" and "hover" only for the temporary refuge.

Hover—[*See* HOLT].

Kennel—[*See* HOLT].

Litter—A family of young otters varying from three to five in number, and very occasionally six. They are generally brought forth in spring or early summer.

Lodges—[*See* HOLT].

Look below—The man stationed at the shallow beneath the pool where an otter is found in order to turn him back should he attempt to pass, or at any rate to give notice of his departure.

Otter—*Lutra vulgaris* or *Mustela lutra* (*Linnæus*). The otter is a member of the family *Mustelidæ*, to which belong the weasels, stoats, pole cats, martens, &c. It has beautiful fur of a brownish-grey colour covering the whole body. The limbs are short and provided with webbed feet; the tail is long and powerful, gradually tapering to a point.

The usual length of the body is about 2 feet, and of the tail about 15 or 16 inches. The male weighs from 18 to 26 lbs., the female from 13 to 22 lbs. upon the average, but one dog otter was caught in a net measuring 4 feet 10 inches, and weighing 40 lbs.

The otter is not only an extremely expert swimmer and diver, but can run swiftly overland, often escaping hounds in this way.

Otterhounds—The Otterhound is a perfectly pure and ancient breed of rough hound. Foxhounds are also used for otter hunting.

Otter-pole—The pole which most sportsmen use to assist them in wading and climbing banks, &c.

Put the Otter down—To drive him from his holt.

Seal—The track of the otter upon the bank; easily recognised by the mark of the five toes, the ball in the centre of the foot, and the absence of a heel.

Shoal—Verb: to drive the otter down to the shallows.

Spur—Rarely used for *Seal* (*q.v.*).

Spraint—The excrement of the otter; also called *Wedging*.

Stickle—West country term for a shallow.

Trail—[*See* DRAG].

Unkennel—To dislodge the otter from his holt.

Vent—(1) Of the otter: to come up to the surface to breathe; (2) the spot at which the otter comes up for air.

Vent-hole—The upper surface of the *Holt* (*q.v.*)

Wedging—[*See* SPRAINT].

STAG.

Antler—Originally the first branch of a deer's horns; now used for any of the branches or tines, and even for the whole growth of horn. *See* BROW, BAY, and TRAY.

Backer—A deer that has passed maturity, and has begun to diminish in size of body and horn as old age comes on. Also called BATER.

Bay—(1) The second tine or branch upon a deer's horns, counting from the head upwards. Also called BEY.

(2) The stag is "at bay" when he turns to face the hounds, either too much exhausted to run further, or having found a strong position of defence. The hounds in their turn are said to "bay" or "bring to bay" a deer in such a position.

Beam—The main stem of a deer's horns from which the branches proceed.

Bell—The challenge of the stag during the rutting season.

Blanch—To head, *i.e.*, turn the hunted deer from making his point.

Break soil—*See* SOIL.

Brocket—A two-year-old stag; also called *Knobber* or *Knobbler*. (Several of the old terms for deer at various ages are now never used.)

Brow—The lowest and forward projecting branch of a deer's horns.

Burr—The rounded swelling at the base of a deer's horns, just above the skull. Also called the CORONET.

Calf—A red deer of either sex in its first year.

Coronet—*See* BURR.

Crockets—The points upon the top of a deer's horns.

Foil—The trail of the pursued game.

Fraying stock—The stump of wood or stone which the stags use to rub off the *velvet* (*q. v.*) from their horns.

Harbour—(1) of the deer; to take up a settled abode in some covert.

(2) Of the harbourer; to track the deer to its favourite covert, and to make sure that it remains there.

Harling—The old Devonshire practice of taking a pack to covert roped together in couples.

Havier—A castrated deer.

Hearst—A two-year-old hind.

Hind—The female of the red deer.

Hoop-headed—Epithet of a deer whose horns, in place of spreading, tend to come together at the top.

Knobber. *See* BROCKET.

Layer—The spot at which the deer intended for pursuit couched over night.

Lay on—To put a pack upon the trail of a stag after the tufters have driven him from cover.

Mewing—Old term for the shedding of a deer's horns.

Nott—Of stags; hornless.

Pearls—The bony swellings that form a ring around the burr (*q. v.*) of a deer's horns.

Pricket—A three-year old stag. Also called SPIRE.

Rack—A gap in a hedge or fence through which a deer has passed.

Rights—The "rights" of a stag are his brow, bay, and tray antlers.

Rouse—To put a deer out of cover.

Run-up—A deer is said to be "run-up" when exhausted by the chase.

Set up—Of the hounds; to bring the deer to bay.

Single—The tail of the red deer.

Slot—(1) The footmark of the deer. (2) The foot itself. (3) Verb; to trace a deer by his footprints.

Soil—Of the deer; to take to water. Hence the place to which he goes is called his soiling place, or shortly, his "soil." When he leaves it he is said to "break soil."

Spire—*See* PRICKET.

Staggart—A stag in his fourth year.

Take—The successful conclusion of a run is always called the "take," whether the deer be killed or not.

Tine—A branch of the antlers.

Tray—The third projecting branch of a deer's horns, counting upwards from the head.

Tufters—Selected and steady hounds put into covert in order to separate the deer intended for pursuit from the rest of the herd, and to put him out from cover.

Velvet—The network of arteries that covers and nourishes the growing horns. It is extremely tender, and bleeds freely if touched.

Warrantable stag—A stag fit for hunting, *i.e.*, in his fifth year or upwards.

Yeld—Of the hind; barren.

Bibliography—[The following modern works may be found useful.] Lieut.-Col. J. Babington, *Records of the Fife Foxhounds* (Blackwoods, 1883); Duke of Beaufort and Mowbray Morris, *Badminton Library* (Longmans, 1886, 10*s.* 6*d.*); Peter Beckford, *Thoughts upon Hunting* (Toovey, 1881, new edition); Castor, *Century of Foxhunting with the Warwickshire Hounds* (J. Potts, Banbury, 1891); C. P. Collyns, *Notes on the Chase of the Wild Rea Deer in Devon and Somerset* (1861, scarce); Col. John Cook, *Observations on Foxhunting* (1826); H. H. Dixon ("The Druid"), *Silk and Scarlet* (Scott and Sebright), *Saddle and Sirloin* (F. Warne and Co., 1895); Capt. E. Pennell Elmhirst, *The Hunting Countries of Great Britain* (Horace Cox, 1883, six parts, 2*s.* 6*d.* per part); Hon. J. Fortescue, *Staghunting on Exmoor* (Chapman and Hall, 1887, 10*s.*); G.; I. H., *Hound and Horn, or, Recollections of George Carter* (Simpkin, Marshall, 1885); T. Gilbey and R. F. Ball, *The Essex Foxhounds* (A. H. Bailey and Co., 1896); W. Gomersall, *Hunting in Craven* (published at Skipton, 1889); J. P. Hore, *History of the Royal Buckhounds* (Remington, 1893); K. W. Horlock, *Science of Foxhunting* (1868); R. Jefferies, *Red Deer* (Longmans, 1884); Hon. F. Lawley, *Life and Times of the "Druid"* (F. Warne and Co., 1895); Sir C. Mordaunt and Hon. and Rev. H. R. Verney, *Annals of the Warwickshire Hunt* (1896); H. O. Nethercote, *The Pytchley Hunt, Past and Present* (Sampson Low, 1888, 8*s.* 6*d.*); "Nimrod" (C. Apperley), *Condition of Hunters* (Whittaker, 1855, 3*s.* 6*d.*), *Hunting Tours, Northern Tours*, and *Life of John Mytton, Esq.*, 1871); A. E. Pease, *Cleveland Hounds as a Trencher-fed Pack* (Longmans, 1887, 16*s.*); Sir R. D. G. Price ("Borderer"), *Hunting Notes in the West Midlands* (A. H. Bailey and Co., 1886); F. P. Delmé Radcliffe, *Ideas on Fox-hunting* (Nimmo, 1893, 21*s.*); Thomas Smith, *Life of a Fox, and Extracts from the Diary of a Huntsman* (Arnold, Sportsman's Library, 1896); "Tantara" (Master of Harriers), *Hare Hunting* (H. Cox, 1893); Cornelius Tongue ("Cecil"), *Records of the Chase* (Routledge, 1877), and *Hunting Tours* (1864); R. F. Vyner, *Notitia Venatica* (J. C. Nimmo, 1892, 21*s.*); W. H. A. Wharton (Master of the Cleveland), *Hints on the Hunting Field* (Simpkin and Marshall, 1897).

HUNTING DOG—The Cape hunting dog (*Lycaon pictus*), the *Wilde Hond* of the Boers, stands slightly under two feet at the shoulder, drooping somewhat at the quarters, and has an extreme length—from snout to tip of tail—of about four feet or a trifle over. The body is slight, the muzzle pointed, while the skull is like that of a wolf, but shorter and wider. The general body colour is yellowish red, blotched with irregular markings of black, white, and yellow. The face, nose, and muzzle are black; the ears large and erect. The tail is bushy and foxlike, separated towards the middle by a black ring. Above this ring the colour is yellowish, below white. The hunting dog runs in packs, ranging in number between a dozen and forty or fifty. It possesses great pace and staying power, and few antelopes in Africa can stand before the savage and relentless pursuit of these fierce and dangerous animals. The packs hunt in a systematic and organised manner, often driving their prey in a circle, so that relays of fresh hounds take up the pursuit. Mr. F. C. Selous has witnessed a single Cape hunting dog running down, single-handed, so strong and formidable an animal as the sable antelope. In the actual chase, the hounds, as they press their game, dash forward in turn and take snaps at the flank and under parts of the beast pursued. These animals are plentiful in many parts of the interior. In Cape Colony and the more settled regions of South Africa packs of hunting dogs, although being gradually exterminated, still exist and do enormous damage to flocks. Numbers of sheep and goats are destroyed in a single night by these dangerous marauders. On these occasions the hunting dogs, apparently from the mere savage delight of slaughter, rip and tear far more than the number of animals required for their supply of food. The hunting dog seems to have little fear of man. I have seen a pack in the interior, while in full chase after a koodoo, suddenly stop at sight of our hunting wagons and coolly indulge in a prolonged stare, after which they took up the pursuit again. Gordon Cumming, while shooting by night at a pool of water, once sustained a great fright from a large pack of these wild hounds, and had some difficulty in driving them off.

H. A. BRYDEN.

HYÆNA—There are three species of true hyænas: the **striped hyæna** (*H. striata*), found in India, South-western Asia, and the North and East of Africa; the **spotted hyæna** (*H. crocuta*), found only in South Africa; and the **brown hyæna** (*H. brunnea*), which is, perhaps, commonest in South Africa, but is known northward in Angola on the west, and as far as Kilimanjaro on the east of the continent. Another animal, not distantly connected with the hyænas, is the curious **Aard-wolf** of the Cape Dutch colonists, known to scientists as *Proteles cristatus*. This singular animal looks like a small striped hyæna, but has a more pointed nose and longer ears, five toes instead fo four upon the fore feet, while its teeth are, compared with those of the other hyænas, singularly poor and feeble. The aard-wolf has the honour of being set apart as a family unto itself, called by naturalists *Proteleidæ*. Hyænas are always miscalled wolves by the Boers of South Africa; the spotted hyæna being known as the "tiger-wolf," its pied coat resembling distantly that of the leopard, always called "tiger" by the Cape Dutch; the brown hyæna is called "strand-wolf," from its supposed partiality for the sea-shore; while the aard-wolf, "earth-wolf," takes its colonial name from its burrowing propensities.

All the true hyænas are fierce and ravenous, yet extremely cowardly brutes. They are essentially nocturnal beasts, and seldom or never have the hardihood to face mankind boldly and openly. The most formidable is undoubtedly the spotted hyæna of South Africa, the largest of the true hyænas, which will carry off young children, and in remote native districts even attacks sleeping adults. Not a few natives of South Africa have lost a cheek, or some other fleshy part of their person, from the cowardly nocturnal assault of a "tiger-wolf," made upon them while asleep in the open, or even in an unclosed hut. Where these ravenous brutes have not been killed off, their devastations upon flocks and herds are very great. Sheep and goats fall a ready prey to them, and they will easily master calves, and even cows and weak or ailing cattle. The teeth of all three of the true hyænas are immensely powerful, and with their highly-developed jaw muscles enable them to crack and devour bones that would offer great difficulties to any others of the Carnivora. The spotted hyæna stands some 2 feet 6 inches to 2 feet 8 inches at the shoulder; the striped and brown hyænas are rather less in size. The skins of the true hyænas are, from the carrion-eating propensities of the animals, usually very malodorous and are little sought after.

The coat of the aard-wolf is, however, very handsome, and not very offensive. In colour it is of a yellowish-brown, neatly marked with black stripes, and having a thick mane and bushy tail. This animal is trapped and hunted for its skin a good deal by the Bechuana natives, and the pelt is often to be seen at traders' stores up country. The aard-wolf

SPOTTED HYÆNA.

Measurements—Length from head to tip of tail, 5 ft. Weight of adult, 74 lbs.

is a good deal smaller than its congeners the true hyænas, and resembles somewhat a large, leggy, and high-shouldered fox—if such a beast could be imagined. The aard-wolf feeds occasionally on carrion, but the contents of its stomach indicate that more often than not its dietary consists of white ants, grubs, and other insects. The appetite of the true hyænas is well-nigh immeasurable. Like the vultures they gorge at a dead carcase until they can literally fill themselves no more, and a spotted hyæna, shot at early morning, as it is retiring from its disgusting banquet, will be found to be almost bursting with repletion. Against any animal that they can master, hyænas are murderously savage, and the poor beast, whether sheep, calf, goat, cow, or antelope, is torn to pieces and devoured with marvellous celerity.

In Cape Colony the spotted and brown hyænas have been shot, trapped, and poisoned off by the farmers until few now remain. Beyond the Orange River, however, they are, with the aard-wolf, still abundant in many places. It cannot be said that any of these creatures are good sporting animals; their habits are too nocturnal, and only at very early morning, when retreating to their earths and resting-places, do they offer a fair shot to the rifle. The Cape Colonists, long since recognising these difficulties, have achieved the downfall of the spotted and brown hyænas largely by aid of strychnine pills inserted into dead carcases. The "tiger-wolf," too, with his tremendous jaws and teeth, is a formidable beast for any but the very largest and fiercest dogs to tackle. The up country Boers used occasionally to capture one of these brutes in log traps, slit the hind legs just above the hocks, and insert between the sinew and bone an iron chain. Thus fastened up, the hyæna was suffered to break his teeth in the vain attempt to gnaw through his fetters. He was then considered a fit subject for the dogs to bait and kill. This extremely cruel sport was supposed among the old-fashioned Boers to be a capital training for young hounds.

In the hunting veldt, hyænas are often extremely troublesome round the camp at night. One of the simplest and most effective ways of dealing with them—known as the gun trap, or *stell* of the Dutch farmers—is still commonly practised. A loaded gun is firmly lashed in a horizontal position, at about the height of the hyæna's head, to two stout saplings, or strong poles, driven into the ground. A short piece of wood, which acts as lever, is tied to the side of the gun stock in such a way as to move slightly backwards and forwards. A piece of string connects the trigger with the lower part of the lever. Another piece of strong cord is then fastened to the upper part of the lever, the other end being firmly tied to a large piece of flesh secured over the muzzle of the gun. A small fence round the gun is then made, with an aperture in front, so that the hyæna can only seize the meat while facing the muzzle of the gun. Drags or trails of flesh or carrion, conducting to the trap, are then usually laid. If the affair comes off successfully, the hyæna seizes the bait, pulls the trigger, and the contents of the gun are lodged in its skull, or the head itself is blown to pieces.

It is a curious fact that the young of hyænas, if taken quite in infancy, can be so tamed as to become attached to human beings. Thus tamed, they will even make friends with dogs, usually their inveterate enemies.

H. A. BRYDEN.

SOMALILAND—The spotted hyæna of Somaliland is not hunted systematically, but it is killed as vermin whenever met. There are generally a dozen or so about each kraal; they prowl about at night outside the zeribas, or thorn fences, within which the sheep and goats are penned at night. They carry off children, and often molest men and women while asleep, generally attacking the face, and tearing off the cheek. Many are the Somali men and women to be seen with their faces horribly disfigured, without eyes or nose, the work of the Waràba, or spotted hyæna. They tear off cows' udders and camels' tails. Half a dozen of them will attack and kill a haltered camel in a few minutes. Old people are occasionally killed by hyænas.

Round the sportsman's camp they are nightly visitors, attracted by the scraps of meat scattered about; and I have, at different times, shot in all some two dozen from the tent door, and several while I was watching over water. On one occasion, at a well, I found the bodies of seven spotted hyænas, killed by natives by the simple expedient of putting poison in one of the troughs of puddled clay which stand at the mouth of every well where water is left after the cattle have drunk. The wells are deep and difficult to climb into, and wild animals often have to drink from these troughs left by the herdsmen.

The spotted hyæna of Somaliland, which is commoner there than the striped variety, should give a glorious run in suitable country, for they are very numerous round Berbera, Bulhar and Zeyla on the Somali Coast, and at Harar, when cholera was raging about 1892, they were said to come in thousands at sunset to drag away the dead bodies of the victims.

The cry of the spotted hyæna is a peculiarly mournful howl—a long drawn note ending with a high one, or two low notes with a high one in the middle. When breaking up a carcase, the hyæna emits curious low chuckles.

Striped hyænas are not often shot in Somàliland; they live more in the bush, and do not prowl so much round the kraals; they are also rarer. The skin of this variety is often very handsome, with a bushy tail.

There is no difficulty in shooting either kind of hyæna, and there is very little sport in it; but the spotted variety affords the very best practice in night-shooting. My own custom was to paste a long strip of white paper down the rib of the rifle, and, when shooting at night, to take a quick aim with the muzzle slightly raised, then to lower it, and pull the trigger as the white line disappeared from view. So fired, the rifle carries high, and the eyes should be fixed about six inches below the object at short range.

H. G. C. SWAYNE.

INDIA—The only variety in India is the striped (*Hyæna striata*). It is somewhat smaller than the African spotted variety, but appears bigger owing to the large mane or crest which hangs over on either side of the neck to a little below the withers. Its appearance is ungainly, as its front legs are higher than the hind, the stripes, resembling the hoops of a barrel, extending downwards on to the legs.

It stands about 2 feet 6 inches at the shoulder, and is about 5 feet 8 inches in length, including the tail, which is about 15 inches long and bushy, the snout moderately long but blunt. It has immensely powerful jaws, and can crack even a horse's thigh-bone with ease. The great longitudinal ridge on the top of the skull is far larger than even in the lion or tiger, and to this ridge are attached the great cheek muscles which close the jaw. The large grinding teeth have great conical crowns, the base of the cone being belted by a strong ridge which defends the subjacent gum, but the canines are proportionally smaller than in the felidæ, and the outermost incisor—that nearest the canine—is much larger than in the cats. The total number of teeth is thirty-four.

It is a cowardly animal as a rule, but occasionally shows pluck, as I shall presently show.

STRIPED HYÆNA.
Measurements—Max. length from head to tip of tail, 5 ft. 10 in.; Av. height at shoulder, 2 ft. 6 in.

It generally confines its attacks to the maimed, and carries off infants, and usually feeds on any carrion or offal it can find. These animals are very noisy at night, only inferior in that respect to the jackal. It is not of much account as a beast of the chase in India, but when one is found on a ridable plain, it is always a feather in a hunter's cap to run down on horseback and spear a hyæna. I have had a strong shaft—a solid male bamboo—of a spear that had survived many a boar hunt severed in two by a hyæna, after I had thrust it right through him. They not only possess considerable speed, but double like hares.

A friend of mine when chasing one of these beasts, after spearing him had the misfortune to fall with his horse almost on the top of the hyæna. The brute turned round, gave a snap, and bit the horse's leg almost in two just above the pastern, and then gave up the ghost. The horse had to be destroyed, of course.

The natives catch them by baiting a kid over a pit-fall on a small platform, which gives way when the hyæna springs, as it has to do, for there is a gap left all round.

When I was a mere griff beating some ravines, within 50 yards of me rose, only to disappear almost instantaneously, three striped bodies. My heart palpitated considerably faster than its wont, for I took the unclean brutes for tigers, and I was on foot in rather heavy jungle, but my disgust may be imagined when three striped hyænas trotted past my post within 10 yards, but in revenge for my disappointment I laid two of them low. If a dog hyæna, with his consort, come across a solitary dog they will muster up courage to attack it and make a speedy ending of him, but an officer of my regiment had a Poligar dog that fairly beat off a couple. How the fight might have ended had my friend not come to his dog's assistance I do not know, but he had the best of the fight up to then.

The hyæna is nocturnal in its habits, and will now and then carry off sheep and goats. As the hyæna desecrates graves, it is detested by the natives of India, and when one is killed the body is treated with every mark of indignity and finally burnt.

F. T. POLLOK.

IBEX—*Capra sibirica*, Blyth, *Cat.* 543; *Capra sakeen* and *Ibex himalayana*, Blyth; *Capra pallasii*, Schintz; but now universally, *Capra sibirica*.

Native names—*Keyl*, in Kashmir; *Skyn*, in Ladak; *Danmo*, in Tibet; *Buz*, in the Upper Sutlej; *Tangrol*, in Kulu.

The other varieties of this group are:—*Capra ibex*, the Alpine ibex or steinbok, now almost extinct, except in the royal preserves of the King of Italy, on the southern side of the Alps; *Capra pyrenaica*, the Bouquetin of the Pyrenees, the Sierra Nevada, and other ranges in Spain, also becoming rare; *Capra caucasia*, from the Caucasus; *Capra ægagrus*, Asia Minor generally, Persia and Afghanistan; *Capra nubiana*, or *sinaitica*, from both sides of the Red Sea; and *Capra wali*, founded on a single specimen from Abyssinia. Of all these varieties the most vigorous and typical animal is the Himalayan ibex.

Habitat—The Himalayan ibex may be said to be found generally on the highest ground throughout the Central Asian and Himalayan region from Gilgit to Nepaul. It is best known to sportsmen from the large number of fine heads which are killed year by year in the happy hunting grounds of Kashmir and Baltistan. Though it will be many years before the Kashmir ibex is killed out, there is no doubt that the modern rifle, and the modern shikari too, are gradually reducing the numbers of ibex in the best known and most available parts of Kashmir. Nullahs which, twenty and thirty years ago, were full of fine heads, are now hardly worth a visit, and to secure good heads the sportsman must push on to the further grounds of Baltistan, Shigar, Chilas, Gilgit, and others.

It is not found on the south-western side of the Vale of Kashmir—though good heads have come from the Hazara country, and the Gilgit district is said to be full of ibex and markhor. South-eastward the ibex extends from Kashmir and Baltistan through Ladak, Lahoul, Spiti, Koonawar, and Chumba, as far as the borders of Nepaul.

It is found on the higher ground in the Pamir region, in the Tian Shan, and in the mountains of the head waters of the Irtish; and no doubt

HIMALAYAN IBEX.

Measurements—Av. height at shoulder, 40 *in.*; *max. horn meas.*, 54⅜ *in.*; *av. horn meas.*, 35 *in.*

in many parts of Central Asia, wherever the ground is suitable to its habits.

Description—The general appearance of the ibex is well known. Of a somewhat stout and cobby appearance, it is nevertheless extremely active, and possesses very sharp eyes and nose. A good buck ibex will stand some ten hands at the shoulder, and with his massive, curving horns, and long, shaggy, black beard, he is a noble beast to observe or to stalk. The horns have been known to reach a length of 54 inches and a girth of 12 inches. But such heads are rare. Anything over 40 inches may be considered a good head, and one of 45 is a prize that does not fall to every shikari.

Of course the measuring tape is laid along the outside curve of the horn, but not run into the hollows between the knobs.

The female is an insignificant animal, with weak little horns of 9 or 12 inches in length. She has, however, a pair of eyes sharper, if possible, than the buck; and exhibits an exasperating patience in sitting for hours on some commanding crag from whence she may command the only approach accessible to the human enemy.

Ibex vary a good deal in colour and in character of head, and upon these insufficient data naturalists have sometimes founded impossible varieties.

Thus Mr. Delmar Morgan, in a footnote to his translation of Prejvalski's *From Kuldja across the Tian Shan to Lob Nor*, says:—"In all probability this is *Capra skyn*, not *Capra sibirica*, the horns approaching at the tips and turning inwards." This refers to an ibex obtained near the Yulduz valley.

Now, if the name *Sibirica* is to be used at all to distinguish between these two species, it ought surely to be given to the ibex of the Siberian range of the Tian Shan, in distinction from the ibex of the Himalayas, and not *vice versa*. Moreover, the word *Skyn* is the local name for ibex in Ladak, where the ibex of course belongs to the Himalayan variety—if any variety exists. Further, in the anteroom of a mess at Lucknow, the present writer saw an ibex head whose horns curved inwards and the points actually met and crossed. This head certainly did not come from Siberia, and almost certainly did come from the Himalayas.

Another so-called difference is founded on colour. Gordon mentions black ibex on the Pamirs; the writer was shown blue ibex in Ladak. This difference may be accounted for partly by the different seasons at which animals have been observed, and partly by the tendency to accommodation in colour of the coats of many wild animals—especially fish and birds—to the ground they habitually occupy.

One of the most striking characteristics of the ibex is his smell. The writer has several heads killed in 1883 and 1884, and they are to-day quite strong in the unmistakable aroma. In stalking ibex this quality is often of considerable assistance to the shikari. In the still, pure air of the high mountains there is no mistake about the proximity of ibex if the wind be in the right direction.

Stalking—Ibex stalking in Kashmir in the months of May and early June is most fascinating work. An ibex nullah generally combines the finest features of mountain scenery. Wild and picturesque groups of fir and birch surround the rocky torrent in the valley bottom. Here and there a green patch provides a camping-ground. Right and left rise rugged cliffs and masses of rock and shale and snow, while at the head of the valley gleams the dazzling whiteness of some mighty bulk of snow and ice. This is the home of the ibex, and if the sportsman is content to work hard and exercise self-control, he will sooner or later come to terms with some fine old bucks. "Make sure of the easy chances" is a maxim for stalkers in general. But in no case is it of such constant application as in that of ibex stalking. Ibex stick very hard to the same feeding grounds. The sportsman should, therefore, refrain from firing at doubtful chances and so disturbing the herd. Left to themselves they will be found again with tolerable certainty near the same spot, and in time they will be sure to take up a position where a tolerably certain approach may be made. Ibex, when alarmed, prefer to move upwards, and by remembering this fact several shots may be obtained before they get out of range.

Ibex are not tough beasts to kill, and a bullet in the ribs generally brings them to bag. When wounded an ibex almost always works up-hill 'till he dies, when his position is pretty surely indicated by a number of lammergeyers and other birds wheeling constantly above the spot.

April, May, and early June are the months when most of the ibex are killed in Kashmir. After that date the higher ground is open to them, and they are difficult to follow. In the rutting season at the end of October and in November they have been hunted with success.

S. H. WHITBREAD.

KASHMIR—Srinagar, the Kashmir capital, is reached by tonga in three days from Rawul Pindi, the nearest railway terminus. At Srinagar, with the help of a "banker" or agent, leather kiltas or coolie baskets, grass-shoes, sandals, snow spectacles, ice-axe, and cheap "puttoo" suits are obtained; rifles, telescope and field-glass, tents, and perhaps tinned stores, being brought from India.

Engaging a shikari and about twenty coolies, the sportsman must walk for some well-known ibex nullah, say ten to thirty marches from Srinagar. If starting late, say after April 1st, to secure a good nullah he must make two or even three ordinary marches, perhaps as much as thirty-two miles, in a day.

A nullah is any valley or gorge, not a main valley; and the rule generally accepted, and recognised by the Kashmir authorities, is that the first comer (sending on the tent will not do) has the right to the shooting, to the exclusion of other men.

The best nullahs are those rising gradually to the watershed of a range, winding perhaps for thirty or forty miles, before their source is reached in one of the great groups of peaks untrodden by human foot. Such a nullah, by its length, enables the sportsman, having disturbed one locality by shots, to shift camp further up to fresh ground; and in such a nullah he will probably be fairly near the haunts of the ibex, entailing but a short daily climb to the shooting-ground; for in May and June, the best time, it is at the edge of the melting snows, where the young grass is springing up, that the ibex are to be found.

A steep nullah, rising in two or three miles to the snows, is bad for sport, for a shot or two will disturb the whole, involving a search for another nullah just at a time when men are crowding into the country; and in such a nullah it may be nearly a day's climb to ibex ground and back, leaving little time for stalking.

The writer's first few days at ibex will give a fair idea of the sport.

We reached our ground, in Baltistan, and some twenty marches from Srinagar, early in May. The main valley, for which we had been making, contained four good nullahs, already

HIMALAYAN IBEX.

occupied for periods of one or two months; and there were two small gorges, each rising so abruptly to the snows that to carry the camp two miles from its mouth necessitated an arduous climb. We did this, however, on the evening of our arrival, and next day we could see the snows some twelve hundred feet above us, the sides of the gorge falling to the camp in rugged precipices.

With the shikari, local guide, and luncheon coolie, we climbed three-quarters of a mile further up the nullah, to within two hundred feet of the snow; and after spying through the glass for a long time, there appeared, just opposite and fifteen hundred yards distant across the gorge, a herd of nine ibex, scattered over the rocks. They were threading their way among the *débris* at the foot of a perpendicular sheet of rock, the face broken by ledges sloping at a gentle angle down to the moraine below.

Along one of these ledges they turned, going leisurely in Indian file, and one by one they stopped to lie down, or to feed about on the scanty herbage in the crevices.

Those acting as sentries lay with head looking out over the valley, nearly as motionless and colourless as the rocks themselves.

For four hours we sat and watched them through the glass, trying to discover a "shootable" buck; but when towards three o'clock they one by one rose and fed slowly down, and then crossed a snow-filled gully, not a pair of horns could we see larger than thirty inches.

Blinding snow and sleet coming on, we now made for home.

Arrived at camp, the servants pointed out two buck ibex, with fair horns, on the cliff directly over and 800 feet above us, looking down from a narrow ledge; but it was too late to attempt anything, and we watched them as they scrambled away up hill.

Next day, after a very cold night, we scaled this precipice by a deep rift, there being two bad places; and at last, emerging at the top among ragged points of rock, we saw a herd of ibex some two hundred yards away, across a chasm, on another mass of rocky pinnacles.

They were already alarmed and making off, but the last buck, while rounding a corner into safety, received a ·577 express bullet, "telling" loudly, but rather too far back behind the shoulder; and he disappeared after the others.

We gave up all attempt at recovering the wounded buck that day, as the ground was too bad to risk the chance of being caught by the snow and sleet which came on every afternoon; but our guide, knowing the ground, went after it with some villagers next morning, and found it dead near the spot where it had been hit, and brought the head into camp.

The nullah having now been disturbed, we moved camp to a village at its mouth, and slept there; and next day, after a tedious delay while the villagers were bridging a torrent, we crossed the main valley and ascended the bed of the other small nullah opposite.

Here, after watching a herd of twelve ibex daily for four days, we were able to get near enough (about three hundred yards) to pick off two bucks with a Lee-Metford rifle, using "service" bullets. The horns of these measured $37\frac{1}{2}$ and $36\frac{1}{2}$ inches respectively, those of the buck shot in the other nullah only $35\frac{1}{2}$ inches.

The question, what is a "shootable" head, has been much discussed, but it is generally considered that an ibex trophy of thirty inches is not worth having, one of between 40 and 45 inches is a head to be proud of, and heads of over 45 inches are very rare. There are still plenty of ibex, but near the Vale of Kashmir itself the heads, through constant shooting, are becoming very small.

H. G. C. SWAYNE

BEST AUTHORITIES ON KASHMIR IBEX.—Kinloch's, *Large Game Shooting* (*Thibet and North-west*); MacIntyre's *Hindu-Koh*; Badminton Library, *Big Game Shooting*, vol. ii.; Ward's "Sportsman's Handbook" in *Kashmir*.

SPAIN (*Capra hispanica*)—This splendid beast is seldom the object of the English sportsman's pursuit, yet Europe can show few finer trophies than the bearded head and massive horns of an old ibex ram. Such lack of attention may be accounted for in many ways, expense being perhaps the main obstacle. Apart from this, however, to carry out a trip satisfactorily, a certain knowledge of Spanish, good lungs and indomitable perseverance are essential to success. The game is not numerous, and the man is lucky indeed who succeeds in bagging an ibex without several days—indeed weeks—of arduous labour.

Habitat—The ibex, in Spain, is confined to four or five points, all in the highest mountain ranges, the two best known, or rather least unknown to the Englishman, being the Pyrenees, and the Sierra lying along the Mediterranean coast, not far from Gibraltar. Their haunts in other sierras, and more especially in Gredos, have never, I believe, been visited by an English party except ourselves. In the majority of cases, the goats live exclusively among the barren rock-summits and crags (*riscos*) at elevations of 6,000 to 10,000 feet, only descending to lower levels under the stress of severe winters. There are, however, ibex in isolated Sierras of lesser altitudes, when they are found frequenting scrub and even forest. In all cases their habits are nocturnal, the day being spent either basking in the sun, or sheltering from its rays in some cave or crevice amid crags and precipices.

Description—The Spanish ibex is peculiar to the Peninsula, differing from its Alpine congener in the form of the horns, which in the latter are scimitar-shaped, with annular knobs, while the Spanish goat's horns show a spiral form, diverging outwards, then recurved backwards and upwards; with the rings (one for every year) following the oblique course of the spiral curve.

A head of 24 inches must be regarded as more than a respectable trophy. The photograph represents an ibex ram whose horns exceeded 29 inches, but few (if any) such now survive in the Cordilleras of Central Spain.

The ibex ram is at his prime when ten years of age, but the horns continue to add extra rings for two or three years. The total weight of a ram (clean) is about nine to ten stone; the females are at least a third less in size, and have only rudimentary horns of some six or eight inches in length. The young are born in April and May, one, or more rarely two in number, and follow from the first with surprising agility. When alarmed, the ibex emits a shrill whistle, sometimes repeated several times. The rutting season begins in November, the rams congregating during the preceding month, when (barring the possibility of early snow-falls) they often afford a favourable opportunity to the stalker.

Shooting—The Risco Mansor, the highest point in the Sierra de Gredos, is the real home of the goats, towering on three sides over the Laguna de Gredos, a gloomy little lake of unknown depth, by whose stony margin we had

SPANISH IBEX.
Measurements—Av. height at shoulder, 26 in.; av. horn meas., 22 in.; max. horn meas., 31 in.

pitched our camp in August and September, 1896, after many hours of stiff climbing. As we could not go where the natives went without breaking our necks, we had recourse to drives, each "*monteria*" taking a whole day; the guns were placed in the small passes (*portillas*) of the giant ridges, dividing one valley from the next, and the beaters then brought up the whole country before them, the gun highest up having the best chance, as the goats when disturbed always make for the highest ground.

To our idea, however, too little attention was paid to wind, and indeed this negligence at a later date lost us a nice chance at a big ram. It was quite as much as we could do to reach these passes, for the distance we could travel in an hour was covered by the native in ten minutes, and by the ibex in thirty seconds. Yet perseverance was rewarded, and after a week's hard work we had got three ibex between the two of us, one a very good one, and one of our beaters had shot a small one-year-old male. We were lucky in having fine weather, as the lightning is terrible on these heights, and existence in our isolated position would have been unbearable in rainy weather, as there was absolutely no shelter. At night all the water in the camp froze solid, while at mid-day the heat reflected from the rocks was almost unbearable, yet we suffered no harm from the changes of temperature beyond the peeling of skin from our faces.

We had twenty mountaineers with us from the tiny village beneath, some over sixty years of age, splendid specimens of agility and grace combined with strength, and in perfect condition. Curiously enough, only two or three of them had ever seen an ibex before; these exceptions being the professional hunters. The flesh is much esteemed and fetches a good price in the valley below. These men are continually after the ibex, and as they shoot male and female alike, are gradually exterminating them; indeed, only twenty years ago, there were large numbers, where now they have ceased to exist. All our beaters (among whom was the Alcalde of the village) wore hempen-soled shoes studded with nails with shilling-sized heads, which gave a perfect grip on the rock, though every evening they required renewing.

The striking peculiarity of the ibex-haunted crags was their extremely irregular outline and broken nature, rising against the deep-blue sky, clear cut in saw-like ridges, or in monster pinnacles and spires like a cathedral; again, the line would be broken by deep rifts and dark crevasses. Below, by the lake, though not adjoining, were green grassy slopes, where our tent was pitched.

BERTRAM F. BUCK.

ICE YACHTING—[*See* YACHTING].

ICELAND, SPORT IN—Iceland is most easily reached by the Icelandic Government's Steam Navigation s.s. *Vesta*, which leaves Leith in the first week in June (agents, La Cour and Watson, Leith). The voyage takes only three days, as the *Vesta* goes direct to Reyjkwick, the capital of Iceland. The Danish Royal Mail boats, National Line (English agents, George Turnbull and Co., Leith), leave Leith every fortnight from the first week in April to the last in October. The run by these boats takes seven days, as they call at the Faroe and Westerman Islands. The return fare is £8, food not included, and the ticket is available to return by any boat of the above companies.

Clothes and kit to take—The same clothes are required as would be used in Scotland in the autumn. Long high boots, waterproof coat and hat, two pairs of shooting boots, a sweater (for the voyage and cold days), a pair of wading trousers and waders, and necessaries for repairing them, brogues with leather soles and nails clenched on the inside (the rocks are so sharp that felt soles are no use). The high boots are indispensable, as you have to ride through rivers and arms of the sea on your pony; and the macintosh must be your inseparable companion, as Iceland is a terrible country for sleet and rain showers. The most useful coat, adapted for riding, shooting, and fishing, is the "Buckland," made by Anderson, Anderson, and Anderson. A compass and a good map should be taken, also a "Jaeger" sleeping bag, for it is very cold at night. Take also a thick great coat. It is advisable to take gloves and nets, to keep off the black flies, gnats, and midges. A collapsible boat is absolutely necessary if you are going to fish on the lakes, as they are without exception boatless. The best boat is the Douglas, which measures 8 ft., weighs 40 lbs., and costs £6. Above everything, take two tents. The farmhouses are the dirtiest places on earth, and sleep with Esquimos is preferable to a night passed with an Icelander's family. A pair of Edgington's Whymper tents, weighing 18 lbs., made of Willesden canvas, are the very best (one for yourself and the other for your servant). These cost £4 each, and measure 8 ft. by 8 ft. by 6 ft. The floor and sides of these tents are all in one. For stores, I should advise a good supply of oatmeal for porridge, biscuits, tinned fruits, tea, sugar, coffee, &c. These should be packed in cases about 2 ft. long by 18 in. wide by 1 ft. high. You can get excellent mutton (a sheep will cost you 8*s.*), and it is policy to buy from a farmer if you are shooting or fishing on his land. Provide yourself with a couple of petroleum oil-stoves, such as are supplied by the Military Stores and Equipment Co., for cooking, since no fuel is to be got except dried cow-dung. Petroleum can be got in Reyjkwick. English tobacco and Scotch whisky are both cheap in the same town. Choose either a Lee-Metford rifle and Tweedy bullets or a 12-bore Paradox for bear and deer. Take also two 16 ft. fishing rods, and one 14 ft., wooden, not cane, as broken wood can be mended, but cane cannot. A heavy trout rod should be taken. Do not omit a bucket canteen, a camp-bed, a folding chair and table, but hire in Reyjkwick any boxes that may be wanted for carrying clothes on pony back.

Of course, it is much more comfortable to take an English servant, since natives make idle and dirty attendants, and you will have to do pretty well everything for yourself if you depend on them. A guide who can speak English can be engaged at Reyjkwick without difficulty at 4 kroners (about 4*s.* 6*d.*) a day. Gunnlanger, and his brother Johannis Peterson, I can personally recommend

As regards sport—Salmon fishing is, *par excellence*, the sport of Iceland. Near Reyjkwick and other towns the farmers are getting to know the value of their rivers, and ask for payment, but at any of the distant rivers and lakes you can get splendid sport *free.* It is customary to give the farmer living on the banks a small tip and some of the fish you catch, or else employ him during your stay on the river as your local guide; then you will be allowed to fish and shoot as much as you like on his land. The best rivers are those of the North and West coast. The East is poor and the South useless, because the rivers are all glacier streams. If the sportsman wishes to hire a river, he should do so some time before the beginning of the season —June 1st. Any information as regards rivers to let can be obtained from Mr. Paterson, the English Consul at Reyjkwick. The Elidao, a small river within three miles of Reyjkwick —the lower and best portion of which is owned by Mr. H. A. Thompson, of Copenhagen —is without exception the best river in Iceland, though the salmon are all small, averaging 5 and 6 lbs. There is enough fishing in Mr. Thompson's water for two rods. The sea trout in this river are also small, few being above 3 lbs. As many as twenty salmon have been caught in this river in a day by one rod. The Tvera and Grimsa, both a day and a half from Reyjkwick, are both good rivers. The upper reaches of the Tvera are two and a half days from the town. Here the salmon and sea trout run heavier, a few salmon having been taken up to 20 lbs., and sea trout up to 8 lbs. The Reynivellia Laxa—one day from Reyjkwick—is also a capital river, where most of the fish are caught in a pool below the falls. Any one intending to take a river should expressly stipulate that he is to have the exclusive right of fishing, and that no fish should be netted before he arrives, otherwise he may find that these things have been done up to the very day of his coming. In the Sog river, one day from Reyjkwick, permission to fish is granted for the asking; and here very fine char, brown trout, and salmo fario are to be got in plenty. Some of these fish weigh 10 lbs. The best inland places in the north are the Myvatn lake (Eng. fly lake), and the rivers draining it, and the rivers falling into the Hunafloi. In the west the Fiskvotn (Eng. fish lakes) and the rivers running from them, and all the big rivers falling into the Faxafjordr. On the south-west the streams running south from Tinc-valla lake, the Sog, Hvita, and Mima laxa, also the Pjorsa. The north-east is unknown as a fishing ground, and is full of grand rivers and lakes; but they are so hard to reach, and so far from Reyjkwick, that I know of no one who has tried them yet; in fact, I believe them to be virgin water up to the present date.

Salmon flies should be tied on single hooks, Nos. 1·0·2/0. The best patterns are the Silver-grey, Butcher, Durham Ranger, Jock Scott, or any other gaudy fly with plenty of silver tinsel. For trout, Zulus are extra-deadly, also the Big Red Spinner, Marchbrown, and a green Mayfly. The lake fish like Blackgnat, Alder, and Coachman. Take also a few prawns. The Devon and Phantom minnows are of little use. Certainly the most deadly bait for salmon is the despised worm, and these can always be got from the nearest farm. A good stock of worm-hooks should be taken, Nos. 0 and 2/0, tied on thick single gut. Strong single casts should always be used, as light casts are of little use, the rivers being rapid and the currents running between large, sharp boulders. If you mean to fish for char, take some spinning rods. They are a grand fish, which run to 10 lbs. or more, but you must spin deep for them. Lines of about 100 yards are long enough for the rivers, which are not very big. Excellent sea-fishing is to be got free all round the coast in a boat. Ordinary extra-strong sea tackle must be used because of the large halibut.

Whaling is much pursued on the north-west coast, and permission can generally be got to accompany a whaler on application to the owners.

Reindeer are to be found in the desert mountains of the east and north-east. They are hard to stalk, but carry magnificent heads, beating the Norwegian and Spitzbergen deer. No license or permission is necessary to stalk them, but there is a close season.

About a dozen Polar bears are got in the year, in January and February, when the Polar pack ice comes down and rests on the north coast. By wintering in the north one would be sure to get shots at one or two.

Blue foxes are fairly plentiful all over the island, but they are trapped and poisoned in the winter, as the Government gives 10s. to any one who kills a fox, on account of the depredations these animals commit among the Eider-duck.

There are enormous quantities of Willow-grouse, which may be shot without license from August 1st to February 1st. Permission to shoot these should be asked from the farmer on whose land you are, which he will readily grant for a few kroners.

Wild Duck are to be found on all rivers and lakes—very plentiful. In August the bogs swarm with Golden Plover, and there is always a fine sprinkling of Snipe.

The Eiders are not allowed to be shot under a heavy penalty and confiscation of the gun.

Divers, Loons, Puffins, Gulls, &c., swarm in clouds round the rocky coast, while most of the lochs have a pair of Great Northern Divers on them. Curlew abound all over the interior, and are grand eating.

The shooting season for Wild Fowl commences on July 20th. Cartridges and powder should be taken from England.

English is understood in the towns, but not in the country. Danish, Norse, and German are spoken at all the trading stations. Icelandic is rather hard to learn, but is not necessary if you have a guide.

An English sovereign or banknote is much appreciated in Iceland. The local money chiefly consists of ore, a hundred of which go to the kroner (Eng. 1/1½). No dogs are allowed to be imported.

Two things to be avoided are: First, sleeping in a farm in a native's bed, as leprosy and other bad skin diseases are very common in Iceland. Second, never stroke or pat a native dog, as they almost invariably suffer from a disease called *kist*, which is most contagious to man. Over 10 per cent. of the natives die of this. Shoot any dog that comes near your tent.

ERNEST L. S. ANNE.

INDIAN GAZELLE—The **Chickara, Chinkara, Ravine Deer,** or **Indian Gazelle** (*G. bennettii*), is found throughout the plains of India, with the exception of some parts of Lower Bengal and the Malabar District, and while preferring low rocky hills intersected by ravines, and clothed with scrub jungle, or tracts of the medium forest type containing glades, or open savannahs suitable for grazing, it is also numerous on some of the large plains of Southern and Central India, and on the confines of the sandy deserts of Rajputana and Scinde.

The buck is about 28 inches in height; colour above, deep fawn, white on the sides, buttocks, and lower parts generally; tail 8 inches long and black in colour; horns 10 to 13 inches according to locality. They occur in herds of from six to twenty individuals, but solitary bucks are not uncommon. Whether standing or moving they have a habit of wagging their tails vigorously, the movement often betraying their presence, when they would otherwise escape notice. Being small and active they are difficult to hit; the vital spot moreover is but a few square inches in size, and for this reason I preferred a small Express rifle fitted with telescopic sights, which facilitated accuracy of aim up to 180 yards, whereas with the ordinary bead-foresight the body would be greatly obscured at half that distance. The Chickara can exist for more than two days without water, being in this respect only equalled by the Nilgai.

On the verge of the Bikaneer desert the country is sandy, flat and devoid of cover, and although both Blackbuck and Chickara are abundant, they are almost unapproachable.

In the month of February, small patches of *Chenna* (pulse) are dotted here and there, near which one may sight an occasional herd, numbering some fifteen or twenty animals. Dismounting from his camel, and keeping close to it, the sportsman should direct the driver to shape his course so as to pass diagonally ahead of the herd, on the chance of their massing as is their custom, and giving a broadside shot at a good buck. On gaining any suitable cover the sportsman halts out of sight of the herd, directing the camel-man to move on circling gradually.

I recollect on one occasion getting in this way within 150 yards of a herd, which moved off, watching the camel intently, without giving the chance of a shot. The best buck was always on the move. I managed to gain the cover of a large bunch of weeds and peeped through the leaves.

The camel was 500 yards away, circling

INDIAN GAZELLE.

Height at shoulder, 28 in.; Av. horn measurement, 11 in.; Max. horn measurement, 14¼ in.

slowly round, and about midway between us were some does—the rear-guard of the herd—conforming to the camel's movements, but watching it suspiciously the while. Thus I was the centre of a circle on the diameter of which moved the Chickara, and utilising the principle of interior lines, I soon gained a position within a short distance of their probable line of retreat. Manœuvring in this manner, I soon saw an old doe within 80 yards pioneering a big buck straight towards me, but they vanished in a fold of the ground not 50 yards distant, without giving a favourable opportunity for a shot. Being uncertain whether they might not reappear at any moment and discover me, I decided not to stir. Immediately afterwards another doe suddenly appeared on some open ground to the left and would have seen me had I moved. She was the leader of the herd, and was followed by several does and a young buck, moving in file across the open, about 90 yards distant. I began to wonder what had become of the big buck, when he suddenly dashed forward and routed the youngster by butting him in the haunches, and while he stood triumphant I pressed the trigger. He trotted forward 20 yards wagging his tail furiously, then wheeling round, galloped back a few paces, halted for a second, and fell dead. The bullet had grazed the heart. His horns measured 13 inches, the best I ever got. The morning's sport was not yet over, for I shot another buck on the way to camp, but while occupied in stalking a flock of eight bustards, a wandering camel-man found my Chickara, annexed it, and ran like the wind towards a village nearly a mile away, where pursuit would have been useless.

[*Note.*—The name Chickara or Chinkara is also erroneously applied to the **Four-horn** (*Tetraceros quadricornis*), an Indian water-loving antelope (see **Antelopes**).]

ARTHUR POLLOCK.

IRISH SPORT—In Ireland to-day, and indeed at all times, the sports are sufficiently characteristic of our people to mark them as distinctly Irish and national. In spite of this it is surprising to find in every day experience that persons otherwise well informed in matters of sport, are astonished and incredulous when they learn for the first time that Ireland possesses such a thing as a national pastime.

It must certainly be as new, as surprising, to such persons to be told on the authority of Gaelic scholars, that long before Cæsar came to Britain the royal game of hurling was a feature of Irish daily life, and was patronised, and practised, among others, by King Lugh Lamhfhada at the famous fair of "Tailtin" in the year of the world "3370." This, the royal road to excellence in other exercises, was practised by Cahir Mor, Cormac MacArt, the redoubtable Finn MacCool and his son Ossian, and others, up to the evil days of Roderick O'Connor, Ireland's last High King, in 1183. Though dark and troublous days followed the reign of Roderick, the fostering and encouraging of the national game were never lost sight of. The O'Connors, Kings of Corcomroe, in the County Clare, next became its patrons, and by the establishment of a fair in the vicinity of Mount Callen and subsequently at Lahinch, the modern paradise of the golfer, handed down, almost to the present time, this unsurpassed recreation.

A game such as this, which traces its origin back through ages into the past, merits at least a sympathetic notice, if only for the sake of its antiquity.

Hurling or **Caman**, pronounced **Common**,

is an outdoor game, needing a field at least 140 yards long by 84 wide. At each end there is a goal with posts 21 feet apart and a crossbar 8 feet high. Twenty-one feet on each side of the goal posts stand the point posts, which must not be less than 16 feet high. Across the field are drawn at 21 yards, 50 yards, and half-way, lines which are parallel with the goal line. The next requisite is a hurley, which in shape approximates to that of the hockey stick, but may, however, assume almost any form which his playing or his fancy suggests to a player, provided always he does not violate first principles.

The **slitter** or ball, which is made of cork and woollen thread covered with leather, should never exceed 5 inches in diameter nor weigh more than 7 ozs. In such a ball as this there is a limpness and elasticity which free it from the maiming dangers of the cricket ball, and make playing even in the closest quarters absolutely safe.

To hurl with ease, grace, accuracy, and effect, in fact, to play the ball on both sides, it is necessary to hold the hurley in the orthodox manner, that is, placing the left hand below the right, contrary to hockey and cricket experience. In all matches seventeen players form a team, though by mutual agreement fourteen is allowable. In play the position which each man is to occupy is rigidly marked out for him.

After the toss for goal, the captains lead their men to the centre of the field where, forming two opposing lines with backs to respective goals, each player takes the end of his opponent's hurley. The referee appoints two goal umpires for each goal, who record the "goals" and "points" made, and also two sidesmen, who, whenever the ball passes over the side lines, throw it again into play. When the preliminaries are completed, the referee throws the ball on the ground, between the two lines of players. The immediate play is taken up by those players whose places are in the vicinity of the centre of the field, the others hurrying in all directions to take up their positions.

In hurling we are not permitted, under penalty, to take the ball off the ground with the hand, a privilege extended to the goal-keeper only when he is returning it into play after it has crossed the goal line, or after a "goal" or a "point" has been made. When hurleys become crossed, or otherwise barred from playing a ball, as for instance in a scrimmage, it is considered in such cases legitimate play to use the foot to obtain it, but a too generous use of this privilege is decidedly bad form. In scrimmages too, when a ball is in tight quarters, wild or reckless striking at it is not only foolish and frequently ineffectual, but positively dangerous to all concerned. It is only when a ball is in the open and is the common property of the "field" that we may hope to witness the finesse and finish of the practised hurler.

To an onlooker the game may appear commonplace and destitute of skill, but practice readily shatters such an idea. To become a good hurler requires great physical activity, a sober judgment, nerves and muscles as responsive as thought, and an eye that can readily and with unerring instinct measure the ever varying paces of a ball.

In playing, one of the most telling strokes is that obtained by meeting a ball, travelling towards an opponent's goal, either in the air or on the ground, with a swinging hurley, and, for adding pace to a ball, this stroke corresponds to the hit to "long-on" in cricket. Meeting the ball on the hop, as it comes from an opponent, is an easier and more playable stroke if the pace

HURLING.

be not too severe to set to it. Raising the ball with the "boss" or point of a hurley, and striking it while in mid-air, is a graceful and telling stroke, though a sore trial to a novice. This is a very fascinating stroke, which should rarely be attempted in matches, and then only in the most favourable circumstances by experienced players.

Some players, by gently tapping a dying or a dead ball against the ground, make it rebound, when they meet it with a swinging stroke and send it whistling through the air. Taking the ball into the hand by means of the hurley, or catching it when it is in the air, or on the hop, is good smart play, but it must be struck off at once, otherwise a penalty is incurred. In the progress of any match there may be witnessed at least a dozen other methods of playing a ball the treatment of which, while giving large scope for individuality, marks the finished player.

In hurling, as in other games, the commission of certain acts would be a source of endless discomfort to players, if tolerated, and would mar the pleasure of true sport. Tripping, holding, catching, or jumping, &c., &c., are penalised at the discretion of the referee, who may for every offence grant a "free puck" or stroke, which must be taken either by striking the ball off the ground, or raising it by the boss of the hurley into the air and striking as it descends.

The purpose of the game is to drive the ball through the goal posts, when a "goal" is recorded, or between the "point" posts or over the cross bar, when a "point" is registered.

A LONG THROW.

A game such as I have cursorily glanced at, a game fast yet not fatiguing, playable by all, free from irritating scientific niceties, suitable for summer and winter playing, free from danger and full of "divarshuns" should, if widely and sufficiently well known, become a ready favourite with all who desire to find an exercise, which contains in itself all the elements of a physical education, and is at the same time a veritable compendium of sport.

Except with the Dublin University, Dublin and county, and a few of the northern counties, the playing of Rugby or Association Football has very few practical friends. Irish indifference or opposition is directed not so much to football as to the form it takes. This attitude towards a sport would be as unreasonable as it would be unwarrantable if maintained in the case of **Gaelic Football**, which, unfortunately for its reputation, has never had a fair opportunity of displaying its virtues before an English gathering.

Like hurling, it may be played both in summer and winter, and though it cannot boast of having yet conquered that conservatism which attaches many to Rugby and Association, it may feel some pride, for so short an existence, in possessing more than a dozen clubs and a County Board in London, as well as several others in the provinces.

The field necessary for Gaelic Football is in measurement and detail similar to that needed for hurling, the number of players in both games being seventeen a side.

The ball, which is of the Association pattern, must not be less than 27 nor more than 29 ins. in circumference, and must be between 13 and 15 ozs. in weight.

In Association and Rugby each team, at commencement of play, occupies positions behind the centre of the field, but in Gaelic each side extends from goal to goal: an arrangement obviating long and distressing runs, which render play for any time fatiguing if not absolutely impossible.

In this game there are no "scrimmages," no "hands," and no passing except by means of the feet or a blow from the hands; and as no player, except he be in possession of some very decided advantage with the ball, plays beyond his position in the field, the game is necessarily a fast one. Hands are freely used either to strike or catch a ball, which when caught must be struck or kicked off at once.

The ball, to begin the play (and also at half-time), is thrown up at the centre of the field by the referee, but after every "goal" or "point" scored, or after the passing of the ball over the goal line, it is kicked into play from the seven yards square in front of his goal by the goalkeeper.

Should the defending side drive the ball over their goal line, the opposite side have a free kick from the fifty yards line.

Should the ball go over the side lines it is thrown in, in any direction, by one of the side opposed to that which kicked it out—a method of penalising reckless and faulty playing.

Dodging in front of a player to prevent his getting the ball, as well as tripping, holding, butting, catching, &c., &c., are fouls, for which a free kick is given. Whenever a "free kick," or a fifty yards kick, is given, no player of the opposite side must approach nearer than fourteen yards until after the ball is delivered.

Enough has now been written to show that, as an outdoor game Gaelic football has strong and attractive claims to a sympathetic consideration.

Should it succeed in creating a favourable impression and become a feature of English daily life, practice will confirm players in the wisdom of their choice, and any effort to dislodge or rob us of so worthy a game would be stoutly and reasonably resisted.

Another game, the game of **Handball**, or Fives as it is called in England, or Caitch, the name by which it is known beyond the Tweed, is a very popular one in Ireland, and of all our games is that best adapted for the wet day or winter recreation.

Nearly every town in Ireland formerly possessed its "court" or "alley," the floor of which was about 60 feet long by 28 feet wide. At one end of the floor stands a high plain-surfaced wall, with two walls projecting at right angles to it.

About the centre of the floor a line is drawn, called the "short line," over which, and between which and the line at 60, or the "over line," every service ball must drop to be in play. Should the side walls not extend the entire length of the court, lines are drawn to the end, "boundary lines," or "side lines," over which, should a ball pass it, is counted a "hand out" or an "ace," as the case may be.

A game generally consists of fifteen aces, sometimes twenty-one, and is won by the side or player who first gets this number. The ball, which weighs about two ounces, is hard, and covered with sheepskin.

The winner of the "coin" "tosses" out the ball, that is to say, he hops it on the ground, then strikes it with his hand against the plain wall when, if it pass over the "short line" and is not returned by the other side, it counts as an "ace" to the server. Should it be returned however, and neither the server nor his partner play it, it is a "hand out." The other side now take the service, when the game goes on as in the first case, until both partners' "hands" are out, when the first players retake the service.

If a server "toss" out three consecutive "short" balls—that is, a ball which drops short of half-way line—or should he in serving strike his partner, either of the side walls, or himself, with the ball before it touches the front wall, it is a "hand out."

Though not completely suited for a town sport, the game known as **Bowling**, that is, throwing, after the manner of the underhand bowler in cricket, metals or shots, generally about 4 lbs. each in weight, along the country roads, is very popular in Ireland.

It has for some reason incurred the active hostility of the Royal Irish Constabulary, many of whom are its greatest exponents, and as a consequence it has to be surreptitiously practised on the little frequented roads of the western counties. This game may be played by two, four, or six players, and is decided in favour of the player, or players, who in a certain agreed upon number of throws or "bowls" put the shots farthest on the road.

The course over which the game extends varies, according to the number of players, from a quarter to half a mile. A line is drawn across the road from which the play is to begin, and over which the two first bowlers must not pass until they have thrown the shot. Having stripped, each player takes his shot, and having, by a rapid glance, measured all the inequalities of the road, its slope and the quality of its margining earth banks, he goes back some twenty yards, where, poising himself like a discobolus, he runs towards the line, and jumping some four yards behind it, discharges the shot as he touches the line. The dropping of the shot on that part of the road from which it shall travel onward in its career, meeting with the fewest impediments, has often a greater influence in determining success than wild and sluggish strength. After each side has thrown, that player, or side, whose shot is behind always throws off first until the finish of the game.

Before the year 1884, when the Gaelic Athletic Association was founded for the fostering and encouragement of Irish sport, a great tidal wave of apathy and indifference passed over our country and almost swept away our pastimes. Here and there throughout the land a voice was raised on behalf of the old games, but feeble and unsupported. Cast down, benumbed and spiritless as the new organisation found us, yet, by its indomitable faith in the manhood of Ireland, it to-day, through its members, occupies a unique position in the world of sport as the holder of fourteen world's records.

A most telling testimony to the success which it has achieved in its little more than a decade of existence is to be found in the following list:—

EVENT.	TIME.	
220 yds.	22$\frac{4}{5}$ secs.	A. Vigne.
Half mile	1 min. 58$\frac{1}{5}$ secs.	W. Slade.
One mile	4 min. 25$\frac{4}{5}$ secs.	J. J. Mullen.
Four miles	19 min. 44$\frac{2}{5}$ secs.	T. P. Conneff.
120 yds Hurdle	15$\frac{4}{5}$ secs.	D. D. Bulger.
Putting 16 lbs. shot	48 ft. 5 ins.	D. Horgan.
Pushing 28 lbs. shot	35 ft. 1 in.	W. Real.
Throwing 16 lbs. hammer	(7 ft. circle, no follow) 131 ft. 7 ins.	T. F. Kiely.
Throwing 16 lbs. hammer	(unlimited run and follow) 157 ft.	J. Flanagan.
Slinging 56 lbs. hammer	(no run or follow) 26 ft. 10$\frac{1}{2}$ in.	J. C. Daly.
Slinging 56 lbs. hammer	(between legs with follow) 27 ft. 10 ins.	J. Walsh
High jump	6 ft. 4$\frac{1}{2}$ ins.	J. M. Ryan.
Long jump	23 ft. 2 ins.	P. Davin.
Hop, step and jump	50 ft. $\frac{1}{2}$ in.	D. Shanahan.

From the foregoing it will be seen how successfully the G.A.A. of Ireland have stemmed the decay which was beginning to destroy Irish sporting life, and how it has, by its uphill labours, made sport more popular in Ireland than it has been for years.

T. WALSH.

JACKAL HUNTING—This sport is indulged in more by new comers or Griffins in India than by men of mature standing. On arrival in the East one finds night made hideous by the unearthly yelling of these unclean beasts, which sally forth at night and prey on any offal they can find. The Griff is startled by a cry of a "Dead Hindo!" "Where, where?" "Here, here!" and looks forward to their destruction, with pleasure. Jackals differ greatly in various districts. In Assam, where the cattle plague is always more or less prevalent, they get so fat and sleek they can barely trot along. But in India, where food is scarcer, they take a good deal of killing.

Life in many stations in India is dreary enough, and nobler sport is not to be obtained without obtaining leave, so a bobbery pack consisting of mongrels of all sorts is kept up and the jackal is hunted once or twice a week.

JACKAL.

Thursday, being the Subalterns' Sunday or holiday, is generally chosen, and the meet takes place soon after dawn. When a jackal is viewed the curs are laid on, and if the jackal is in good fettle he will give a run of a mile or more before being overtaken. Overtaken I say advisedly, being killed is quite another thing. If a cat has nine lives, a jackal has a dozen. I have seen one to all intents and purposes as dead as a door nail, yet, after the departure of the hunters and pack, he will open first one eye, then the other, get up quietly, and sneak away. They often run to earth if they come across one big enough to admit one, and often live in drains and other unseemly places. To hunt them with greyhounds is no sport, as they are overhauled at once. Spearing them is better fun, for they twist and double as well, if not better, than a hare, and seek refuge in any fissure or hollow big enough to hold them. It is better not to course them with valuable dogs. I have known more than once a dog's leg to be bitten and broken by a hunted jackal, and as they live on the most putrid flesh their bite is always dangerous, and a mad jackal is not a rarity.

Once when I was sleeping on the floor in an open verandah, a mad jackal made a grab at the junction of my neck and back, but only inflicted a slight wound. Two people he bit a few seconds later both died of hydrophobia. So I had a lucky escape. A pony bitten by him went mad six months after the occurrence, and had to be destroyed. He was killed by the men of my detachment the next day.

There is far greater sport in hunting and spearing the hyæna or the nilgai. Both require a horse to be in good training to overhaul them. The hyæna is particularly difficult to spear, as he doubles like a hare, and has considerable pace and wind. To spear a wolf is almost impossible, but I have known it done two or three times by Tom Prendergast, off a thoroughbred English hunter, and off a very valuable Cape horse. A few instances are known of the black buck having been run down and speared. Nightingale, of the Nizam's Cavalry, speared many bears, twenty-six in a month. A few others under his auspices have killed a few, but he was the only man I ever heard of who made of it a regular pastime.

In old sporting books there is often mentioned a jackal with a peculiar cry which is called the Pheeal. Some have asserted that it is made by a different variety of jackal from the ordinary one whose cry I have before mentioned. The Pheeal is not often heard; but there is no doubt that the peculiar cry is uttered by the common jackal when suddenly frightened. As the yelping of a cur when chastised or alarmed differs from its ordinary bark, so the cry of the Pheeal is only heard when the jackal is alarmed. Twice have I heard it: once when a leopard sprang at a jackal which was helping itself to the remains of a goat slain by the former, and once when a tiger put in a sudden appearance under similar circumstances; and again when General Blake was watching over a cow killed by a tiger, with a Mr. Barry, a tiger trotted up and interfered with the proceedings of the jackal, which went off with its tail between its legs, uttering the cry of the Pheeal.

F. T. POLLOK.

JACKAL COURSING—The jackal leaves scent enough for fox-hounds, but where none are kept it can be coursed in the same way as the fox. Only it never doubles, so more dogs may be used, and they are necessary for killing it, as it is the stronger animal. When overtaken, he will sometimes fight savagely, sometimes pretend to be dead, and only by touching the eyeball with the finger can it be ascertained whether it is feigning or is dead. If feigning, it will lie still till the hounds are at a safe distance before stealing away.

JAGUAR (*Felis onca*)—The **Jaguar** inhabits certain portions of the American continent extending from the Southern States of North America through Mexico, Central America, and Brazil to Paraguay. It is a fierce, untamable beast, somewhat resembling the panther, but larger. The spots or rosettes are also larger, and more symmetrically arranged, each group consisting of a ring of well-defined spots enclosing a space somewhat darker in tint than the ground colour, in which the lesser spots often occur.

Melanoids exist, but are not very common; those that live in gloomy forests being far darker than those found in more open country.

The favourite haunt of the tiger in the hot season is a cool sheltered portion of a bheel, and the jaguar not only delights in water, but actually, when hard pressed for food, will wade into streams and with a dexterous pat will eject passing fish on to the bank and devour them at leisure. It is to a great extent arboreal in habit, and an adept at climbing, and by means of the claws alone will run up the smooth bark of a tree devoid of branches to a considerable height. When hunted it takes refuge in trees, and this habit is well known to hunters, who pursue it with dogs and pot it when treed.

Some jaguars from Mexico have the small spots, which ordinarily constitute the rings, at a

JAGUAR.

Measurements—Max. length from head to tip of tail, 9 ft.; av. length, 7 ft.

considerable distance from one another, so that complete rings or rosettes of spots only occasionally appear.

The skull differs from that of other large cats in the presence of a well-marked tubercle near the middle of the inner side of the socket of the eye. The total average length of a jaguar is from $6\frac{1}{2}$ to $7\frac{1}{2}$ feet, of which the tail occupies about 2 feet 2 inches.

It is a noisy animal, roaring much by night, especially before bad weather. Like other cats, it delights to sharpen its claws on the bark of certain trees. It rears itself up and, pressing the breast against the trunk, it claws at the bark on either side. A common method of ascertaining if a jaguar is in the neighbourhood is to examine the trunks of the trees. This is also a usual habit of the tiger and leopard in India. The object of the practice is to tear off the ragged ends of the claws, and not, as is generally supposed, to sharpen them.

The jaguar is found even in the Pampas, a place totally unfitted to its ordinary habits; it has been tempted, by the abundance of mammalian prey, to colonise that cold, treeless, and comparatively barren desert.

The cry of the jaguar cannot be described as a roar; it is loud, deep, and hoarse, and has been compared to a series of repetitions of the syllables "pu, pu, pu." From two to four cubs are produced at a birth towards the end of the year.

The mode of hunting them differs in accordance with the seasons and the locality. During floods, especially along the banks of the Parana River, the hunters proceed in boats, searching for the claw marks, and as soon as they discover a forest which these cats inhabit, some watch, whilst others of the party make a circuit with a few dogs. When the animal is started, they follow in hot pursuit. If the ground is sufficiently open, they use the lasso; otherwise, they drive it up a tree and surround it with the dogs, whilst the hunters with the guns come up. Often the similarity of the markings between the foliage of the forest and the jaguar puzzles the huntsman, as the animal crouches along a branch heavily fringed with leaves. Even if shot dead, it often remains pendent for a considerable time. Now and then, if only slightly wounded, and at no great height, it drops down on to the men and dogs and dies fighting. When encountered in open and ridable ground, it has no chance, and is easily lassoed, and if once, so hunted, it manages to escape, its dread of the lasso is so great, that it has been known to prefer being suffocated by fire rather than face its enemies armed with that instrument.

It is generally affirmed that tigers are accompanied by jackals, and doubtless those unclean beasts follow for the sake of any offal they may collect off the remains of their larder, but they remain silent until their feast begins. Not so with the foxes that follow the jaguar; they annoy it by their constant yelping, and often give warning to its prey.

The cause of the enmity between the puma and the jaguar is a mystery. Where the capybara is plentiful, there is ample food for both; but, odd to say, though the puma is an animal considerably inferior in size and power, it is the persistent persecutor of the jaguar, following it about, and when an opportunity occurs, springing upon its back and inflicting terrible wounds with teeth and claws.

As there are man-eaters among leopards, panthers, and tigers, so there are man-eating jaguars; and when the country is flooded, and their food, in the choice of which they are not particular, difficult to procure, they often prey upon men, preferring the black to the European. They often kill more than they can eat, and out of a party of thirteen men which accompanied a friend of mine, three were killed in one night.

It is also curious that whilst the flesh of the puma is considered a delicacy, that of the jaguar is never eaten, except under dire necessity. The flesh of the puma tastes like veal; that of the jaguar is rank to a degree, yet both are carnivorous.

The following extracts from a journal in my possession may be interesting :—

"Later on in the day, as we passed a heavy bush, a jaguar sprang upon one of the men's horses, embracing him and fastening his jaws in the poor brute's windpipe; down came horse and man. I sprang down and was going to the man's assistance when our headman galloped past as hard as his horse could go, and, shortening his bola as he swept by, gave the jaguar a blow that could be heard a long way off. I thought the brute's head must have been broken in two, but after it had struggled for a moment on its back, and was just clear of the horse, the same man returned at full speed, cast the bola with unerring aim and had the jaguar entangled and helpless, and, in a few minutes, more than half strangled. Two men dismounting soon put an end to the struggling animal. The horse was dead in a few minutes, for his jugular had been severed. The jaguar measured 7 feet 3 inches in length. On another occasion I had just entered the forest from the river bank, and had not penetrated far when I saw a jaguar stalking some animal, so I stepped behind a tree and waited events. As the brute passed through some longish grass, I saw some animal spring on to the jaguar's back; over they rolled, and in a moment the assailant had cleared itself and disappeared. The jaguar rose foaming from the mouth, and, as nothing further was to be expected, I put a bullet through his head. My people hearing the shot hurried up, and, on examination, we found the beast's back badly scored and bitten. The men said at once that it had been done by a puma; but, though I searched everywhere, I failed to find it."

In parts of South America the Indians kill jaguars by means of a blowpipe and poisoned arrows. The poison used is the wourali. They kill even the tapir with these tiny darts. The poison does not affect the meat; the portion round the wound is cut off and the rest eaten. Death takes place in a quarter of an hour, but within a few minutes the animal becomes drowsy, seems to be in no pain, and expires quietly and gradually.

F. T. POLLOK.

JOCKEY CLUB—[*See* RACING].

KANGAROOS—When English attention was first drawn to the peculiar Flora and Fauna of Australasia, their novelty was the chief occasion for comment and curiosity. They were interesting because they were unlike anything in our previous experience. But science soon learnt to dwell on the real antiquity of much that seemed so new. Observers and inquirers were not long, for instance, in noting that the *Zamia spiralis*, still so frequent in the neighbourhood of Sydney, was closely akin to some of the earliest forms of fossil vegetation. The Port Jackson shark again, *Cestracion phillipi*, with its curious rasp-like rollers for crushing shell-fish, was found to claim near kindred with some of the earliest fossil fishes.

The Marsupiates of Australasia are so closely mixed up with modern pastoral interest, that I hold myself at liberty to speak of them only from the squatter's point of view. They are, in fact, formidable enemies to the vast wool-gathering interest which maintains, I think, something like forty sheep for every man, woman, and child in Australia. They have, moreover, been greatly favoured by local changes. The "black-fellows" who were clever in killing them, have become a pitiful remnant, unless in the extreme North West. The warrigals—those voracious wild dogs who helped to keep them as well as the sheep down—have become very scarce, baits seasoned with strychnine having disagreed with them. Perhaps, too, station life has become more purely a matter of business, and is less seasoned with sport than in the days when my long circuits were enlivened by an occasional halt at some hospitable mansion, where the kangaroo dogs were an institution. Quite apart from the question of keeping down the kangaroo population, the *chasse* is of peculiar interest and well worth witnessing. The speed attained by the quarry in a regular succession of bounds, which forms his mode of progress, is sometimes extraordinary, particularly when the lighter limbed female is the fugitive. I have known an "old man" cover 19 feet at each bound for full half a mile, but his pace was not particularly fast. Moreover, the male is somewhat pugnacious, and often, instead of doing his best to escape, is meditating reprisals on the dogs. If he reach a convenient water hole, especially one affording a tree against which he can lean his back, they may catch a Tartar. Short as are his fore legs, his hug is formidable, and if his position be such that he can keep his balance, while lifting up a muscular hind leg, his strong horny toe cuts like a knife, and goes near to bisect his enemy. The same thing often happens when an eager young dog catches and throws his game, but receives a kick which is almost equal to that of a horse. The flying doe, however, as the adult female is termed, has no purpose of showing fight, but only tries to escape by speed. I have never had the opportunity of measuring her successive bounds on sand, but believe they average full 20 feet. I remember pressing one very hard over level ground, when well mounted and with a brace of excellent dogs. I counted on a kill, but just when she seemed to be out-paced, she took from her pouch a "joey," about the size of a large cat, and tossed it away from her line of flight. From that moment she left dogs and horses behind, went straight away, and doubtless, after tiring out her pursuers, duly retrieved her bantling. Indeed, the number of kangaroos coursed and fairly run down cannot be great. A few are shot, a very light charge sufficing if they are hit along the course of the spine. But dogs and guns are merely palliatives to a great evil.

When we consider that there are something like a hundred and ten millions of sheep in British Australasia, an army of rival grazers must be dealt with wholesale. And this is done by a grand drive, generally, I think, in the direction of Port Fairy, lying to the extreme south of Victoria at the end of an extensive range of valuable sheep pasture. A long double line of fencing opening to a great width inland, but converging as it nears the coast, is constructed to receive the driven kangaroos. The principle is the same as that adopted by the Indian Government in the construction of the keddah for the capture of wild elephants. A sort of funnel of fencing is, in fact, erected, wide open inland, but narrowing gradually as it approaches the spot fixed for the final capture. It will, however, be seen from the immense numbers of the game to be enclosed, that the scale of this kangaroo-trap is vastly greater than anything that can be required in the taking of elephants. There is another difference very distressing, if we must not say cruel, to the

KANGAROO.

driven kangaroos. The enclosure in which the elephants are finally secured is made strong, that there may be no risk of the captives breaking out, and a mighty barrier of timber is opposed to their attempts at escape, backed by a show of fire wherever a sally appears to be threatened, and by the trained manœuvres of tame elephants, who mingle with the wild ones, and subdue them one by one, by the joint action of force and guile. But the enclosure into which the kangaroos find themselves finally driven is formed, not to capture and subdue, but simply to destroy them. They descend in their thousands, down a treacherous slope into a deep hollow, from which, as from the lion's den in the fable, there are no backward tracks. They are there simply to be killed. One would like to know what provision, if any, is made for utilising the carcases of the victims. Kangaroo skins make excellent leather, and I remember "in my hot youth when George the Fourth was king," fancying that boots made of it were elegant as well as comfortable. Then there is a great amount of human food available where kangaroos are slaughtered by the thousands. The tails alone, sometimes very heavy, supply a soup equal to ox-tail, and ought to sell well among tinned meats. A half-grown kangaroo also supplies excellent cutlets taken lengthwise from the large muscle on each side of the spine, quite equal to those sliced from blue hares after shooting a Highland hill.

I must mention that I recognise three large species of kangaroo on the continent of Australia as specially worthy of the sportsman's notice. First there is the Great Red Forester, which I am sure I have seen sitting erect not less than 7 feet high. Next in size comes the Grey or "Blue" species; more particular, I think, about its pasture, and thus a worse enemy to the sheep owner. Thirdly there is the Wallaroo, a dark-coloured, rough-haired inhabitant of craggy hills, heavier in the arms and shoulders than the other two, and rather like a bear when seen erect against a background of rock. I have toiled to get a specimen, but was always baffled by the cunning "old men." Once I succeeded in shooting a doe, but only recognised her species on the authority of a highly scientific naturalist. She was a smooth, blue creature, weighing only some 12 or 13 lbs. In fact, throughout the kangaroo tribe the male has an immense superiority in bulk and strength though decidedly inferior in speed, even allowing for the combative temper which often inclines him to imprudent resistance. I knew a case near Wagga Wagga where a heavy "old man" turned on two mounted pursuers, and leapt up successively behind their saddles, tearing their coats nearly off their backs, and utterly scaring their horses, who, like Gilpin's, "never in such sort had handled been before."

I must invert rational order to remark finally that Halmaturus, "tail-jumper," is an absurd scientific misnomer for these leaping quadrupeds. The kangaroo, when grazing, may be said to walk with his powerful tail, which he bends under him as a lever to lift his hind quarters gently forward. But when it comes to a question of jumping, he keeps it carefully off the ground, flourishing it aloft with an effect which in a large mob looks highly comical. I believe, however, that this flourish has some useful result in steering his course. Be that as it may, he is most careful when hunted to keep it high and dry; if once draggled, it shortens his stride and cripples his pace. It was my ill fortune to be travelling on duty during the heaviest rain I ever encountered even in Australia. A fall of fifteen inches within three days had laid the grand level expanse of the "Old Man Plain" under water, and I saw before me a drive of more than twenty miles through an inland sea. On the last slope of the higher pasture-land which I was reluctantly leaving I saw a huge male kangaroo in utterly helpless plight, crawling rather than hopping, while his tail dragged piteously through the wet grass like a rope trailed behind a vessel to check her speed. A lady's lap-dog could have overtaken him. Thus, when I claim for the kangaroo—and especially for the stately Red Forester—a wonderful "turn of speed," I do so "with proviso and exception" on several grounds. He—or rather she, for the ladies are the fast sex—must not be called on to cross a wet meadow, or to scale a rocky slope, or even to travel at high speed across a level thickly strewn with loose stones, where the troop make much clatter but small way. From one hindrance or another, kangaroos seldom run "their level best," and can seldom stand long before dogs of the right breed, wire-haired, hard-footed, long in the stride, and in all essentials identical with the noble Scotch deer-hound. Indeed, I should like to see them hunted at less headlong speed, and with the classical accompaniment of a "musical pack."

H. R. FRANCIS.

KANGAROO-SHOOTING—The kangaroos and wallabies, which, if not perhaps the typical, are at any rate the most widely known of the great marsupial sub-class to which they belong, are, however interesting they may be to the student of the mammalia, familiar to the colonial chiefly as a plague to the stock-owner. The larger kinds, those in particular which frequent the plains, move so rapidly from place to place, and are so insatiable in their appetite, that they quickly over-run whole districts, their scissors-like front teeth cropping the herbage so close as to leave no meal for anything superior to a rat.

To cope with this evil, farmers in those parts organise drives on a generous scale, in which the flying beasts are done to death in their thousands, either hunted with kangaroo-dogs in the more sporting fashion described above by Mr. Francis, or driven in dense masses into enclosed stockades and there butchered with anything that comes handy—shot so long as the cartridges hold out, clubbed with the butt afterwards.

The visitor, however, who seeks in the course of his colonial experiences as much sport as can be got out of the pursuit of such timorous, inoffensive game, will elect some less wholesale means of finding his kangaroos, and, if he does not object to penetrating as far as the back blocks—the vast flocks of other days have long since deserted the neighbourhood of the populous centres—there is the choice of stalking most of the larger kinds in the plains (no easy performance for any one out of condition), or seeking the red kangaroo and smaller wallabies among the rocky boulders that, to the wonderment of the new arrival from England, strew the landscape in every direction.

Rock Kangaroos and Wallabies—The shooting of these animals among the rocks is a simple matter, and may be dismissed in few words. It is scarcely necessary for purposes of the present article to enumerate the dozen or more species found in such rocky country, beasts ranging in weight from 200 lbs. down to 20, their measurement from nose to root of tail varying between 60 inches and 30. What chiefly concerns those who would find them is the marvellous protective colouring with which, without exception, they are endowed. So closely indeed do the tints of many harmonise with their surroundings that I have more than once, when stalking one herd upwind, all but trodden on the outposts of another squatting motionless among the rocks. This similarity of colouring to the background is not perhaps shared, to quite the same degree, by the kangaroos of the plains, though there is at first some little difficulty in descrying them at even a short range on the sand, no unusual framing in that parched continent.

With the cover afforded by the rocks, there should be, where the beasts are at any rate plentiful, no great difficulty in bagging them; and it is amusing to take note of the strange miscellany of fire-arms that are taken out for the purpose. Shooting is a far more rough and ready affair in the Australian colonies than at home, subject to no restrictions and hedged by few etiquettes. Neither gun- nor game-licenses trammel the sportsman, or neither were at any rate enforced when I was there, in consequence of which only those were prevented from shooting who could not muster some kind of gun. These were few indeed, and the members of the party usually turned up with as many kinds of weapon, from the newly imported ·303 Magazine rifle (the weapon I would above all counsel for the work) down to the duck-gun and even the "converted rifle," a formidable article which I believe the Government sold for a few shillings, and which threw a good foot to the right or left when fired. Owing largely, no doubt, to the antiquity of some of the battery, as well as the carelessness with which they were handled, there was invariably a competition for last place in the file.

The procedure depended upon whether we were shooting over dogs—by far the most enjoyable, as also the most productive, style. Without dogs, every one crept away on his own beat and blazed at everything that came within range. If there were dogs, however, each gun was allotted a position near some high rock, and the hounds were sent on ahead by a circuitous route and then drove the frightened beasts back past the guns. It depended on the nature of the country whether the rifle or shotgun had the better time of it: in the general way, the chances lay with the former, but when, as occasionally happened, the rocks were very close together, the shot-gun got a hurried shot at a flying wallaby close at hand and a few pellets brought it down. No beasts of the same size, few, indeed, irrespective of size, take less killing, and a blow from the handle of a stockwhip is sufficient to kill a doe of the largest dimensions. As the wallabies are keen-sighted, all that is necessary, when waiting for the dogs to drive them past, is to remain motionless and in readiness to take a pot-shot at the shortest notice, for these creatures are as silent in their

WALLABY.

movements as they are swift, and only at the moment of their coming within close range are the rhythmic beats of their hind feet audible.

Stalking in the Plains—Without the aid of the cover of rocks, and, as often as not, in the full glare of a sun that can, even in midwinter, make itself felt to the European at an early hour of the morning, the pursuit of the kangaroo, in which there is no danger to attract and but the very poorest skin by way of trophy, is not likely to recommend itself except for the one trial necessary to all new experiences. A moment's contemplation of the larger kangaroos, even in captivity or the museum, will suffice to convince the visitor that such creatures, tall, with large eyes and sensitive ears to acquaint them with all that is going on around, without any means of defence (except the powerful hind nail) to encourage indifference to danger, and with a rapid amd eccentric mode of progression by leaps that in the larger species cover twenty feet at the least, are by no means the easiest to stalk, nor does the afore-mentioned resemblance of their colouring to that of the sandy earth make matters simpler. Even when there is a strong wind blowing, there are often unforeseen complications, not the least among which is the sudden change in its direction so characteristic of at all events the North Queensland plains, where I have followed these beasts by the hour, or maybe the abrupt appearance of a morass, the result of an overnight downpour, that either causes a sudden disturbance and the consequent warning of the kangaroo, or a *détour* of such a nature as to make it impossible to keep the game to windward. As they take the scent as quickly as most browsing animals, a moment is fatal, and in a few leaps they once more put between them and their pursuers as much ground as was gained in the previous half hour's stalk.

So much has already been written in these pages on the subject of stalking deer and other game, that it is only necessary in the present article to lay stress on the necessity for a thorough acquaintance with the ground to be gone over, more particularly in the immediate neighbourhood of rivers, beside which, for example, when their steamer is taking in cargo, those who visit the colonies have most of their opportunities for kangaroo shooting.

The islands that a prolonged drought unites to the mainland are excellent kangaroo ground, but, on the other hand, their soil is most treacherous, and, as already mentioned, a single tropical rain of only a few hours' duration is sufficient to convert a plain as hard as iron to a quicksand capable of swallowing, or at any rate detaining, both the kangaroos and their pursuers.

The shrieking ibis, which are flushed at every dozen yards, especially in the late summer, are also a great nuisance to the stalker, though, mercifully, the kangaroo sometimes pays no attention to their warning cries.

The ·303 Magazine rifle has already been recommended for the work, and it would, in fact, be hard to beat.

On the natural history of the kangaroos and wallabies, of unequalled interest among mammals to the biologist, it is unnecessary to dwell in any detail. The earlier fables in respect of their reproduction have long since been refuted; and we now know that the young one is born a month or two after Christmas, after a very short period of gestation (and without any pre-natal connection with the dam) in a perfectly helpless condition; is conveyed by its mother to her pouch immediately after birth, and is there nourished, the milk being pumped down its throat, until able to shift for itself, which it does in the course of ten months.

The kangaroos, indeed the marsupials generally, are the most primitive type of mammals, Nature's earlier attempts at fashioning the now predominant class. They cannot, however, be said to furnish sport of a very high order, although those who visit the colonies will scarcely miss an opportunity of experiencing the novelty of shooting at quadrupeds that leap more after the fashion of frogs than of any other living creature.

F. G. AFLALO.

KNURR AND SPELL—This game is scarcely known in the southern counties, but has some share of popularity in the north. It is not difficult to acquire, as any one possessing a good eye and a ready hand can soon become a proficient. It consists of a man striking a ball in a given number of strokes as far as possible.

The requisites for the game are a bat, a trap, and a ball. The ball, which should be about one and a half inches in diameter, is made either of wood or porcelain. The bat is made of a piece of good hard wood, like a pint bottle split in two longitudinally, attached to a long handle of stout cane, which varies in length from four to five feet, to suit the height of the player, who, holding the bat by the extremity of the handle in both hands, releases the trigger of the trap and catches the ball, if possible, in the centre of his bat, and drives it as far as he can. The spot where the ball pitches is marked, and its distance from the trap measured. His opponent then tries his hand, and so on, to any number of players, until the agreed number of strokes have been made. The number of feet each has covered are then totalled, and he who has aggregated the most is the winner. There is a great deal of acquired knack in this game, but he who hits high will send the ball further than he who drives it horizontally. Hit the ball at an angle of 45 degrees with the plane of the horizon. This may be roughly done thus. Stretch out the arm at right angles to the body, then lift it straight above the head, then let it drop to a position midway between these two positions and you will have the angle required. Hit well up and you will get as much as it is possible to do each time.

F. T. POLLOK.

KOODOO—The **Koodoo** (*Strepsiceros kudu*), though surpassed in size of body by the eland, may fairly be regarded as the handsomest of all the antelope family. Its great spiral horns form a trophy of which every hunter, who has the chance, desires to become possessed. So keenly is this noble animal pursued, that there is, in the writer's opinion, danger of its ultimate extinction unless the great Powers who are colonising Africa are mindful of their obligations in this respect, and provide sanctuaries for its preservation, or make stringent rules against the excessive slaughter of the bulls by sportsmen. The females very rarely carry horns, and therefore, except for meat, do not offer the same temptation as the males. The northern limit of the koodoo is the river Atbara in the Italian Abyssinian colony. From this point southward it is found throughout East Africa as far as the Transvaal, wherever the nature of the ground is suited to its habits. It almost invariably frequents dense thorny scrub, and it generally affects the sides of ravines, or steep and lofty mountains, so long as these are not barren. Living in such jungle, the koodoo relies chiefly on the acuteness of its hearing for protection, Consequently it is endowed with immense ears. comparable to those of the elk in the northern hemisphere, which is an animal similarly protected, and for the same reason. In searching for the koodoo it is these large leaf-like ears, fully ten inches in length, which first catch the eye, and which, together with the handsome fringe of hair on the throat, helped to give it its air of distinction and intelligence. The colour of the skin resembles that of the pale dun breed of Jersey cows, but white vertical stripes on its flanks, and crescent marks between the eyes, in imitation of the lines and patches of light in a thicket, help to break up and render invisible the expanse of grey hide. The animal, which is as large as a fourteen-hand horse, would otherwise be too readily discovered by its enemies.

From Ward's horn measurements it would appear that the longest heads have all been brought from south of the Equator. The horns gradually diminish in size as more northern latitudes are reached. The writer obtained a bull in Somaliland whose horns taped fifty-two inches following the curve, and forty inches from tip to tip, and these measurements have rarely been exceeded in that country, whereas many heads of sixty inches have been obtained in South Africa, and one of sixty-three inches. On the other hand no recorded heads from Abyssinia reach fifty inches.

Unlike many of the African antelopes, the koodoo is a tolerably frequent drinker, and, except in the rainy season, when his food contains abundance of moisture, must be sought within a few miles of water.

It aims at escaping by concealment, rather than by fleetness of foot, and it is said that a koodoo desiring to escape observation will lie almost as close as a rabbit when it knows itself to be well hidden, and will allow a man to pass within a few yards without moving. The alarm note is a "bark," somewhat like that emitted by a red hind, but louder. It is generally the females who give the warning signal. A thin-skinned and tender animal, the koodoo does not, like the oryx, carry away much lead. The first bull I saw offered a long running shot, and I consequently hit him far back. Finding the blood spoor, I insisted, much to my Somali's disgust, on giving him time, always the most prudent course in such circumstances. When we did ultimately take up the line, we found that he had not travelled more than 150 yards after receiving the shot. Almost any other antelope with such a wound would have got clean away.. My largest bull, above referred to, fell instantly to a single ·256 Mannlicher bullet. But I must not be understood to recommend that weapon, admirable as it is in the open, for an animal which may require to be tracked in thicket and over strong ground. In such a case, where the blood track

KOODOO.

Av. height at shoulder, 52 *in.*; *Av. horn measurement*, 45 *in.*; *Max. horn measurement*, 63 *in.*

is all important, a rifle which will inflict a larger wound should be used.

No description in words can convey an impression of this animal, its habits and surroundings, so vivid as Mr. Millais' admirable drawings in *A Breath from the Veldt*. To those who have the good fortune to possess that work, I commend the careful study of the pictures in pen and pencil of that close observer and good sportsman. I may sum up his impressions of the koodoo in his own words. "The sable will stand and stare at you, quite close sometimes, as much as to say, 'Who the devil are you?' The koodoo will creep under the shadow of a bush and hope to goodness gracious you won't notice him, but the roan will say 'good-morning' as soon as he sees you." Mr. Selous' works should also be consulted on the habits of this animal and the conditions for hunting it successfully.

For koodoo hunting in Somaliland, the chapter in Captain Swayne's work dealing with this subject is full of suggestive observation. He remarks that the hunter who secures one good head in a fortnight's hard work in the mountains may consider himself fortunate. It must be remembered that the best koodoo ground in that country, namely the Golis range and Gadabursi Mountains, is now comprised within the limits of the area reserved for the use of the Aden garrison. Some information with regard to the animal in Abyssinia may be derived from Baker's *Nile Tributaries*, and *Life with the Hamran Arabs*, by Myers.

THE LESSER KOODOO (*Strepsiceros imberbis*) is almost identical in appearance with the greater animal of the same name, but is on a far smaller scale, its size being less than that of a fallow deer. Its dorsal and flank stripes are more sharply defined, and it has two crescent marks on the throat, which are wanting in the typical species. The white, semi-transparent points of the dark horns are another special characteristic. This antelope has the most refined and high-bred air of all African animals, and a well-mounted head is a trophy to be coveted for its intrinsic beauty.

This koodoo has a much more restricted habitat than its larger congener. Unlike the latter, in my experience, it avoids steep ground, and is to be found in valleys or flat plains at the base of mountains, but always in thick covert. Wherever the low, pointed aloe abounds, or the green fleshy-leaved *ergin*, there may the *Godir*, to quote the native name, be sought, with good hope of success, always provided that it is not too far removed from water. The hunter who desires success must be gifted with great keenness of vision and quickness of hand and eye, for it is generally a question of a snap shot or none at all. The writer, who is deficient in the above qualities, allowed several good males to escape him, either by failing to see them in time, or by egregious bad shooting, before he annexed a fair specimen. This koodoo seems to have the instinct to stand or feed always in the shadow. Once aroused, there is one flashing bound over a bush, his white tail waving a parting flick, and, unless this brief opportunity be seized, he is not likely to afford another chance. Notwithstanding the difficulties attending the chase of this watchful beast, large numbers are killed by Midgans, or low caste Somalis, who use only a bow and poisoned arrows, but are expert and patient hunters.

E. N. Buxton.

LACROSSE—History of the Game—Catlin, and other early travellers amongst the North American Indians, found the game a firmly established institution; and the seriousness with which preparations for a great game between tribe and tribe would be undertaken, and the fierceness with which the play was conducted, were second only to actual warfare. Large stakes in kind were risked upon the issue of a game, and the women were privileged to urge their husbands on to increased exertions by the application of switches to their backs. The game bore a different name in the language of each tribe, and the implements used for carrying and throwing the ball also varied materially in shape. As the Indians became tame, and sought the shelter of towns, they brought their game with them. The white population were not slow to take to lacrosse; and it is on record that some Canadian boys introduced crosses into a school at Reading about 1865. In 1867 a team of Indians was brought to England for speculative purposes, and played at various centres. Their crosses were very unlike those in use at the present day, and no effective throwing could be done, but the game proved attractive and a serious attempt was made to start it. Matters progressed as far as the formation of an association; but the crosses that were made in England were altogether impossible, and the effort died out.

Implements of the Game—Lacrosse is a decidedly difficult game to learn, and this fact will always militate against a widespread popularity. The *crosse* (La Croix, the Bishop's

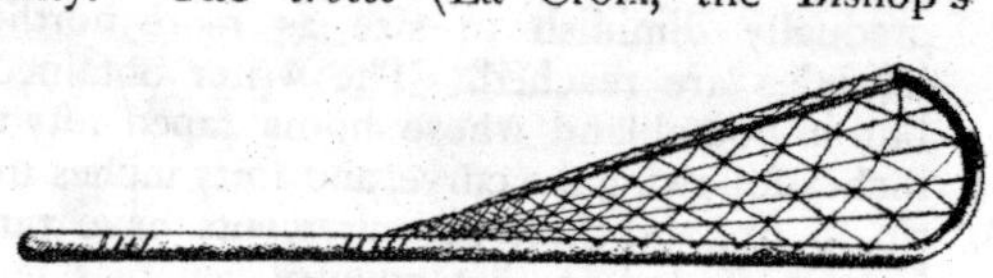

The Crosse.

crozier, is the origin of the title) is formed of a piece of wood, hickory for choice, having one end rounded and the other flattened. The flattened end is curved to form a bow (the *bend*) some 8 or 9 inches across, and from the top of the curve to the other end (the *butt*) is about 4 feet 3 inches. A strong piece of gut, the *leading string*, is tied from the extreme end of the curve, the *tip*, down to a point eighteen inches or more from the butt, called the *collar*. The space intervening between the leading string and the back of the crosse, which is cut with a perfectly straight face on the inside, is meshed with gut. The leading string is then joined to the *face* of the gut by means of other pieces of gut, and the crosse is complete. The *ball* used is of india-rubber sponge, specially constructed to eliminate danger as far as is possible, measuring between 8 inches and $8\frac{1}{4}$ inches in circumference, and weighing between $4\frac{1}{4}$ ounces and $4\frac{1}{2}$ ounces. The object of a side is to throw, or otherwise pass the ball through the adversaries' *goal* by means of the crosse, and goals are the only points that score. Each goal is six feet square. Formerly it consisted of two uprights merely, it being thought impossible to use a cross-bar because of the hindrance it would cause to the goal-keeper's crosse; but English players discovered that it was quite feasible, and now matches are played with the cross-bars from pole to pole, whilst a net is spread behind. Thus it is very difficult for any error in umpiring to occur, and the frequency with which the cross-bar is hit shows how often a doubtful goal might be given by an umpire. The goal stands in a *goal-crease* 12 feet square, into which no opponent may enter unless the ball be there.

The Players—Twelve players make a full team, and they are divided roughly into *attack* and *defence*. There is no off-side, but the ball

PLAN OF LACROSSE FIELD.

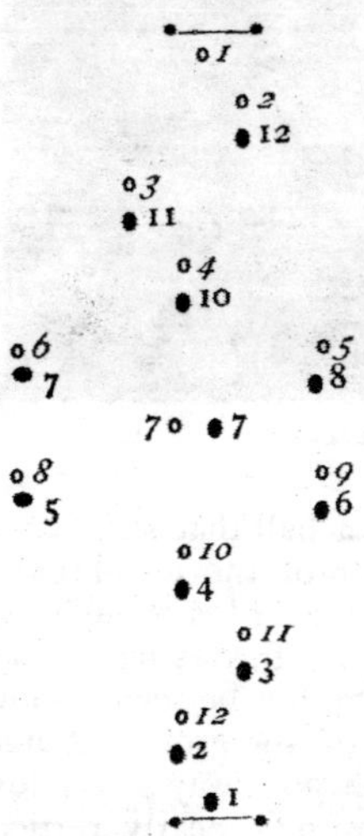

1, 1, Goal.
2, 2, Point.
3, 3, Coverpoint.
4, 4, Third man.
5, 5, Left defence field.
6, 6, Right defence field.
7, 7, Centre.
8, 8, Right attack field.
9, 9, Left attack field.
10, 10, Third home.
11, 11, Second home.
12, 12, First home.

may not be handled by a hand not upon the crosse. The players distribute themselves all over the field after a fashion which experience has shown to be the best, though slight variations are indulged in. One attack player, *First Home*, is placed near the opponents' goal in a position from which he may reasonably hope to shoot a goal should the ball reach him. A little farther out, and to one side, is *Second Home*, and still farther out and again on the other side, *Third Home*. The positions of these players, when the attack waxes brisk, are practically interchangeable, especially as play goes on behind the goal as well as in front of it. The three *Homes* must be adepts in taking short and hard catches with absolute certainty, and getting in their shot at goal without the least delay. Forty yards or fifty yards away from the goal, and wide on either wing, stand the two *Attack Fields*, and in the middle of the ground is the *Centre*. Then, in corresponding positions on the other side of Centre, come the two *Defence Fields*, whose duty it is to check the opposing Attack Fields, after which, nearing the goal, come *Third Man*, checking Third Home, *Cover-point*, checking Second Home, and *Point*, checking First Home. In either goal-crease stands the *Goal-keeper*.

Hints on Play—Properly held, the crosse is grasped by the butt in either hand, according as the player plays from the right or left side. With the ball on the ground, the player runs towards it, lowering the bend of the crosse as the ball is reached. The momentum causes the ball to run up on the netting, and the knack of controlling it there is one of the preliminaries that have to be learned. Next come *throwing* and *catching*. Throwing is executed by a swing, or sweep of the crosse, modified according to the desired magnitude of the throw. It is most easily done sideways or three-quarter face to the player, and correct throws are made along the back of the crosse. When the throw is thus made, the ball will infallibly travel in the direction in which the crosse is pointing when arrested at the completion of the throw. In catching, the *face* of the netting must be presented as much at right angles to the line of flight of the ball as circumstances will permit. As the ball comes at all sorts of angles and often at a high rate of speed, herein lies the difficulty of catching. Very high flying balls are best stopped in their flight, and caught on a horizontal crosse as they fall. One difficulty that has always raised great trouble has been the tendency of the ball to run up the netting and out of the crosse *via* the narrow part, the *angle*. In September last the Unions of England and Ireland sanctioned the use of a piece of gut, the *cross-string*, tied tight across the angle, so as effectually to prevent the ball running any farther. A properly made crosse of ten years ago did not need this, but manufacturers have continually altered the fashion of the netting, with the object of making the game easier, and the adoption of the cross-string has become unavoidable. It materially facilitates *dodging*, as the crosse can be held in a nearly perpendicular position without the ball being lost. Dodging, though strongly to be deprecated when carried to excess, is a necessary feature of the game. In its simplest form the crosse, with ball upon it and held horizontally, is waved from side to side, as the player endeavours to pass an opponent, by dashing from right to left, or *vice versa*. Opponents are allowed to strike at the crosse with the object of dislodging the ball, and the best way of preventing this is to wave the crosse about. Sometimes an opponent may be dodged round, and to do this the player must make a complete turn upon his axis. To effect this and not lose the ball the butt hand must be lowered and the bend raised.

The act of a defence player in stopping the progress of an opponent or preventing his throw is known as *Checking*. When a player is dodging no notice should be taken of his crosse, the *Checker* simply taking care to place his body in the way of the dodger. This is known as the *body check*, and no force may be imparted to it, or it becomes a charge, which is forbidden. Body checking is of most use out of the field. Near goal the attacks will be trying for shots at goal, therefore their crosses must be attended to. It may be assumed that, if a *Home* is given but half a second in which to make his shot at close range, he will score, in spite of the *Goal-keeper*. The business of the three defence men nearest goal must, therefore, be to keep the *Homes* at a respectful distance. If this is done, their shots will come easily to the *Goal-keeper*, though it is doubtful if they will shoot at all at long range. If the *Homes* elect to stand close in, *Point*, *Cover-point*, and *Third Man* must attend to their crosses very closely, beating them down and letting the ball go on for *Goal-keeper* to gather. But *Second Home* and *Third Home* cannot stand in very close without destroying the unity of the team, each member of which must operate in a certain area. The greatest latitude is given to *Centre*, who must be an untiring player, for he acts alternately on defence and attack.

The game is started by the ball being placed on the ground in the exact centre of the field of play; the two *Centres* stoop down and place the backs of their crosses on either side of the ball, and at the word "play," or the blowing of a whistle, the crosses are drawn smartly towards

FACING.

the holders of them. The ball comes to one or the other, is pounced upon, and the game has begun. The essence of attack play is quick dashes in the proper direction, but not an inch farther than is necessary to get a player in a favourable position clear for a *pass*. Thus, a quick runner is of great use, provided he be not one who holds the ball too long. Making quick passes when the player is in rapid motion is not easy, and every variety of throw must be learnt. When the ball has been worked into a position favourable for a shot, the greatest

GOAL-KEEPER.

chance of scoring lies in a ball that strikes the ground a few feet in front of the goal-keeper. At very close range a shot over his shoulder is the most effective. Very fast throws have to be judged, for often the ball cannot be seen. Shots that come rather low and off the ground should be beaten down and then got away; very low shots should be *blocked* with a nearly vertical crosse, *bend* downwards.

Point, *Cover-point*, and *Third Man* should be good throwers, for though it is better to pass the ball down the field, this is by no means always feasible, and in this case the ball is best thrown down to reach *Third Home's* position. To throw farther is to throw too far. When an *Attack Field* or *Centre* runs up with the ball, *First* and *Second Home* should spread out somewhat, and so give him a clear run. Presently one of the defence must go to meet him, thus leaving a *Home* free for a pass. Only rarely should *Attack Fields* run far past the centre: *Point*, *Cover-point*, and *Third Man* never. If the game is going against a side, the tendency is to bunch on defence, but this should be fought against, for by giving way to the impulse all possible chance of scoring is removed. The only man who should go back at all is *Centre*, on the chance of the ball coming to him.

For a long time matches between England and Ireland and the North and South of England have been annual fixtures. The match between England and Ireland presents difficulties, because in England the game is played in the winter, owing to the popularity of cricket and other games, whilst in Ireland, as in Canada and the United States, summer is the playing season.

E. T. SACHS.

LAWS OF THE GAME.

(Copyright of English Lacrosse Union).

I. THE CROSSE.—Sec. 1.—The crosse may be of any length to suit the player, woven with raw hide or gut—not cord or soft leather. The netting must be flat when the ball is not on it. In its widest part the crosse shall not exceed one foot. A string must be brought through a hole at the side of the tip of the turn, to prevent the point of the stick catching an opponent's crosse. A leading string resting upon the top of the stick may be used, but must not be fastened, so as to form a pocket, lower down the stick than the end of the length-strings. The length-strings must be woven to within two inches of their termination, so that the ball cannot catch in the meshes.

Sec. 2.—No kind of metal, either in wire or sheet, screws, or nails, shall be allowed upon the crosse. Splices must be made with either string or gut.

II. THE BALL.—The ball must be of india-rubber sponge, not less than eight inches and not more than eight-and-a-quarter inches in circumference. It must weigh not less than four-and-a quarter ounces, and not more than four-and-a-half ounces. In matches it must be furnished by the home club.

III. THE GOALS.—The goals shall be placed not less than 100 yards and not more than 150 yards apart, unless otherwise arranged, and in any position agreeable to the captains of both sides. The posts must be six feet apart, and the tops thereof, including any ornament, must be six feet above the ground. In matches they must be furnished by the home club. Goal nets may be used if agreed to by both captains.

IV. THE BOUNDARIES.—The boundaries of the field of play shall be agreed upon by the captains before the commencement of the match. Should the ball be thrown out of bounds, the referee shall call "stand," and the ball shall then be "faced" by the two nearest players not less than four yards within the bounds at the point where the ball went out.

V. THE UMPIRES.—Sec. 1.—There must be only one umpire at each goal, who shall be agreed to by both captains before the commencement of the match. They shall not be changed during the progress of a match without the consent of both captains. They shall not change goals during a match.

Sec. 2.—No umpire shall, directly or indirectly, be interested in any bet upon the result of the match. No person shall be allowed to speak to the umpires, or in any way distract their attention.

Sec. 3.—The umpire shall stand behind the posts. In the event of "goal" being claimed, he shall at once decide whether or not the ball has fairly passed through the goal-space, his decision being simply "goal" or "no goal." His decision shall be final, without appeal, and he shall not be required to give a reason.

Sec. 4.—In the absence of a referee, the umpires shall assume his functions, as set down in Law VI., each over his own half of the field. One only shall act as time-keeper and starter failing a referee, and this to be decided by tossing.

VI. THE REFEREE.—Sec. 1.—The referee shall be selected by the officers of the competing teams at any time prior to the match. He shall be a disinterested person.

Sec. 2.—Before the match begins he shall see that umpires have been properly chosen.

Sec. 3.—He shall draw up the players in lines, and see that the regulations respecting the crosses, ball, goals, and spiked shoes, &c., are adhered to. He shall ascertain the length of time the match shall last, directly from both captains, and he shall be sole time-keeper and starter.

Sec. 4.—If the referee observes any infringement of the rules, or when a "foul" claimed by any player has been allowed, or in case of injury or accident (Law VIII., Secs. 2 and 3), the referee shall immediately call "stand." If the ball enter goal after "stand" has been called by the referee, it shall not count; or if a foul be claimed by one side and their opponents score a goal immediately afterwards, the referee shall first give a decision on the foul, which, if allowed, shall nullify the goal. If the foul, however, be claimed by the scoring party, whether the claim be allowed or not, a goal scored before the referee has called "stand" shall count.

Sec. 5.—The infliction of penalties (Law XII.) shall be in the province of the referee, without appeal, and any side rejecting his decision or refusing to continue the match shall be declared the losers.

Sec. 6.—The referee shall arbitrate in all disputes between the captains, and his decision shall be final.

Sec. 7.—At the commencement of each game, and after "stand" has been called, the referee shall see that the ball is properly "faced," or otherwise dealt with according to the Laws. No "face" shall take place within 10 yards of the centre of goal when it is caused by the action of an attacking player.

VII. CAPTAINS.—Sec. 1.—A captain shall be appointed by each side previously to the commencement of a match. He shall be a member of the club by whom he is appointed. He may or may not be a player in a match; if not, he shall not carry a crosse, nor appear in lacrosse uniform. He shall be the mouthpiece of his team in all disputes, in which he may be assisted by one player selected by himself, and shall report any infringement of these Laws during a match to the referee.

Sec. 2.—Captains shall arrange, previous to a match, the length of time it shall last, and shall toss for choice of goals.

Sec. 3.—Nothing in this Law shall prevent a player appealing direct to the referee in case of rough or foul play.

VIII. THE TEAMS.—Sec. 1.—*Number.*—Twelve players shall constitute a full team. They must be regular members of the club they represent. Should one side be deficient in numbers at the time fixed for starting the match, their opponents may either limit their own numbers to equalise the sides, or compel them to play with as many as they have.

Sec. 2.—*Injury.*—Should a player be incapacitated from playing through wilful injury or rough play from an opponent during a match, his side shall be at liberty to replace such injured player or compel the other side to take off the offending player to equalise the sides. No change of players may be made after a match has commenced, except in cases of injury during the game.

Sec. 3.—*Accidents.*—Should an accident occur to any player, which, in the opinion of the referee, incapacitates him for playing, the other side *must* put off a man during his absence.

Sec. 4.—*Spiked Soles.*—No player may wear spiked soles under any circumstances. The soles must in every case be india-rubber, if boots or shoes are worn.

Sec. 5.—The players on each side shall be designated as follows:—

1—Goal-keeper.	7—Centre.
2—Point.	8—Right attack.
3—Cover-point.	9—Left attack.
4—Third man.	10—Third home.
5—Right defence.	11—Second home.
6—Left defence.	12—First home.

IX. THE GAME.—Sec. 1.—Each game shall be started by the centres facing at the centre mark, and when both sides are ready the referee shall call "play."

Sec. 2.—A match shall be decided by a majority of goals taken within a specified time. A goal shall be scored by the ball passing through the goal-space from the front not being propelled with any part of the foot or leg.

Sec. 3.—Should the ball be accidentally put through either goal-space by one of the players defending it, by whatsoever means, it shall be counted a goal to the opposite side. Should it be put through by anyone not actually a player, it shall not count.

Sec. 4.—In the event of a goal-post being knocked down during a match, and the ball put through what would be the goal if the post were standing, it shall count a goal for the attacking side.

Sec. 5.—When goal has been claimed and allowed, the ball shall be again faced in mid-field.

Sec. 6.—Ends shall be changed at "half-time," when either side may claim not more than ten minutes' rest; such rest not being counted as occupied in play.

Sec. 7.—The goal-keeper, while defending goal within the goal-crease, may put the ball away with his foot or hand (but not throw it), or block it in any manner with his crosse or body.

Sec. 8.—Any player is "out of play" if he drop his crosse during a game, and may not touch the ball or impede an opponent in any way until he recovers his own crosse.

Sec. 9.—Any player is at liberty to propel the ball with his foot or leg.

Sec. 10.—A match is ended by the referee calling "time."

X. FOULS.—Sec. 1.—No attacking player shall stand within the goal-crease, or check the goal-keeper within it, until the ball has passed within the bounds of the goal-crease. This shall not prevent a player from running through or across a corner of the goal-crease to field a wide ball. Each umpire at his own goal shall decide these points.

Sec. 2.—No player shall interfere in any way with another who is in pursuit of an opponent.

Sec. 3.—No player, except the goal-keeper (under Law IX., Sec. 7), shall wilfully touch the ball with his hand, save as provided in Section 4 of this Law; nor shall he wilfully fall and cover the ball with his body.

Sec. 4.—When the ball lodges in a place inaccessible to his crosse, or about his clothing, the player must at once remove it and "face" with his nearest opponent, all other players standing in the positions they may then occupy.

Sec. 5.—Should the ball catch in the netting, the crosse must immediately be struck on the ground and the ball dislodged.

Sec. 6.—No player shall grasp an opponent's crosse with his hands, hold it with his arms or between his legs or under his feet, or kick it.

XI. ROUGH PLAY.—Sec. 1.—No player, with his crosse or otherwise, shall hold or trip another, nor push with the hand; nor shall any player deliberately charge or shoulder an opponent, nor wrestle with the legs entwined, so as to throw an opponent. This does not prevent the use of the "body check," provided the same be strictly as defined (Law XIII.), nor the pushing an opponent with the shoulder in ground-scuffles.

Sec. 2.—No player shall deliberately strike another, or threaten to do so under any circumstances, and anyone considering himself purposely injured during play, must report to the referee.

Sec. 3.—The check commonly known as the "square" or "crosse" check, which consists of one player *charging* into another with both hands on the crosse, so as to make the stick meet the body of an opponent, is strictly forbidden.

Sec. 4.—No player shall throw his crosse under any circumstances.

XII. PENALTIES.—Sec. 1.—For breach of Law X., Secs. 1, 2, 3, 5, and 6, the referee may either order a "face" or order a "free position" at the place where the foul occurred, but the "free position" must not take place within ten yards of the centre of goal. The ten yards distance shall be measured in a straight line from the centre of goal through the place where the foul occurred.

Sec. 2.—Claiming "fouls" on trivial grounds, as when, in the opinion of the referee, no foul was intended, cannot be tolerated, and the referee shall first caution a player so offending, and, if persisted in, shall disqualify him until a goal is scored. Should the captain (non-playing) so offend, the same penalty shall be inflicted upon him as though he were a player.

Sec. 3.—For rough play (Law XI., Secs. 1, 2, 3, and 4), the penalty shall be either:—

(*a*) A "free position" for the side offended against; or
(*b*) Suspension of the offending player until a goal is scored; or
(*c*) Suspension of the offending player for the remainder of the match.

XIII. Definition of Terms.—*Goal* is the space contained between the two posts.

Goal-crease shall be a marked line twelve feet square, and the goal posts shall be placed six feet from the front and back lines, and three feet from the side lines. If not marked it shall be left to the umpire to decide.

Goal Nets shall be as follows:—From a point six feet behind the centre of a line along the ground from post to post, nets shall be taken to each post, and to a bar placed across the top of the posts.

Face.—The ball shall be placed upon the ground between the crosses of two opponents, and each of them shall have his left side towards the goal he is attacking. They shall not move till "play" has been called, but must then immediately draw their crosses apart (towards them) before removing them from the ground.

Tripping is the use of the legs, feet, or crosse to throw an opponent.

Holding shall mean clutching with the hand or arm, or detaining an opponent between the two arms and the crosse, or placing the crosse against his body so as to impede his movements.

Body-check is the placing one's body in the way of an approaching opponent, so that the latter is simply impeded. No checker shall use force in the body-check.

Striking means the giving a deliberate blow with either crosse or hand.

Charging or *Shouldering* implies motion and unnecessary force in checking, and is forbidden, because the object should be to play the ball and not the man.

Stand.—The ball is dead when the referee calls "stand," and no player shall move until the referee calls "play."

Free Position.—The players shall "stand," except the goal-keeper, who may resume his place and the player to whom the referee awards the "free position;" and no player may be nearer than five yards to the last mentioned. If anyone be within the prescribed distance, he must retire to the satisfaction of the referee. The player awarded the "free position" shall then take the ball on his crosse in front of him, and at the word "play" from the referee the game shall proceed.

LAPWING—[*See* Peewit].

LAWN FOOTBALL—The idea of a lawn game with a football first occurred to A. Tebbutt and G. H. Du Boulay, of Winchester, some years ago. It was, however, crystallised into a proper game by W. Pickford and J. A. Nethercote, of Bournemouth, in 1895.

A Lawn Football Association has been formed, of which W. Pickford, of Bournemouth, is hon. secretary. Two courts, 25 feet long and 20 feet wide, are marked out, and divided by a wooden bar 3 feet 6 inches above the ground. Nearly in the centre of each court is a 5 foot circle. The object of the game is to kick or head the ball backwards and forwards over the bar into the opposite court without using the hand or arm, and each failure to return the ball counts a point to the opponent. The game consists of five sets of five points each.

The ball used is an ordinary Association football. To commence the game, one player, standing in his own circle, throws the ball underhand into his opponent's circle, and it may be returned on the first bounce; but afterwards it may also be returned before it has bounced. Each player may play the ball in his own court so as to get into a good position to return it, but it must not touch the ground twice without being played.

In other respects the rules are generally the same as at Lawn Tennis.

Two a side makes the best game, and rubber shoes should be worn.

Lawn Football will generally be enjoyed by men who are, or have been, football players; it will be found good practice for Association football (more especially a half-back's play), as it teaches players to have great command over the ball, and, with practice, great skill is obtained in its management.

Play does not cut up and spoil a lawn; but it is not necessary for the lawn to be so smooth or level as for the games of tennis and croquet.

Arnold Tebbutt.

Laws of the Game.

1. The size of the field of play to be 50 ft. by 20 ft., divided into two equal courts by a bar 3 ft. high. The

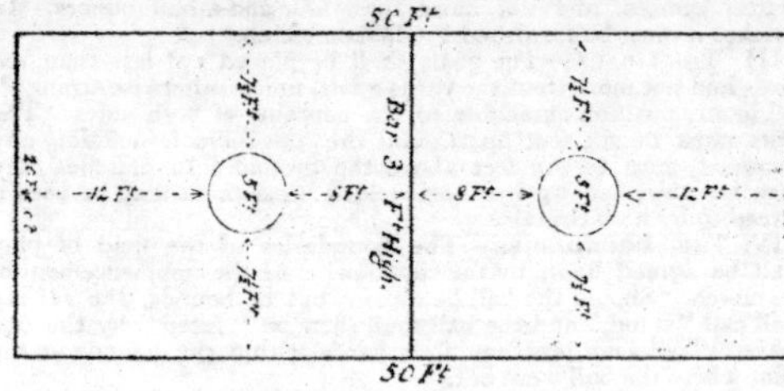

Plan of Lawn.

ground must be marked out, as in the diagram, with a circle 5 ft. in diameter in each court, 8 ft. from the bar, and equidistant from the sides.

2. The ball to be an Association football, match size. (It is advisable not to have it very tightly inflated).

3. Winner of toss to have choice of court or serve.

4. The player serving shall stand in his own circle and commence the game by throwing the ball into his opponent's circle. Should he fail to do so twice in succession, a point shall be scored by his opponent. The opponent must not play the ball until it has touched the ground within his own circle. He may then return it direct, over the bar, or, if he prefer, may play it within his own half, but it must not touch the ground twice without being played. Having eventually returned it over the bar, his opponent may do the same. Neither player must touch the ball with the hand or arm. Rubber shoes should be worn.

5. If either player fails to return the ball into the opponents' court, or touches the ball with his hand or arm, it shall count one point to the opponent, and the player reaching five points first shall score a set.

6. The players shall retain their courts until a second set has been scored, but the serving must be reversed.

7. The players shall then change ends and proceed as in the first two sets, if necessary, but the player scoring the majority out of the first 4 sets shall win the game.

8. In the case of a tie in sets at the end of the fourth set, a fifth set shall be played, and the players shall toss up for choice of ground or serve.

9. If the greater part of the ball when it touches the ground is inside the field of play, it is in play.

10. If the ball touch the ground in play and bounce out of the field of play in the air, it is not out of play until it has touched the ground outside the field of play.

11. The ball touching the bar and falling into the proper courts is to be in play.

12. The player serving must throw the ball underhand, with one hand, and without putting any twist or spin on it.

13. No player must encroach on his opponents' half of the field of play.

TWO-A-SIDE.

If two-a-side play the partners must serve, or take the *first* return, alternately, and the game then proceeds as above.

LAWN TENNIS—Although acknowledged to be the most modern of our national pastimes, lawn tennis in all probability had its origin in the ball games which were played in England and on the Continent some three or four hundred years ago. These have been variously known as hand-ball, longue-paumes, pallone and tennis, and, while some were played chiefly in enclosed and covered spaces, adaptations suitable foi out of door games were from time to time tried, with more or less successful results. In 1873, Major Wingfield endeavoured to obtain some order from the chaos of these numerous attempts by producing *Sphairistike*, a game which differs as much from the lawn tennis of the present day as it did from its numerous predecessors. Nevertheless, it was upon this foundation that our present popular summer pastime was built.

A meeting of lawn tennis players was held at Lord's Cricket Ground in 1875, and a new code of laws was promulgated by a committee then appointed. By these new rules it was provided that the net should be 5 feet high at the posts and 4 feet high at the centre, and the service lines were placed at 25 feet from the net. The scoring was by points, as at rackets, but instead of "setting" at "14 all," the deuce and the vantage from the tennis scoring was adopted. The M.C.C. Committee accepted the hour-glass-shaped court, and the balls were to be $2\frac{1}{4}$ inches in diameter and $1\frac{1}{2}$ ounces in weight. Plain rubber balls had been used until this time, but now the covered ball rapidly found favour. This was introduced by Mr. J. M. Heathcote, the famous tennis player, who, in a letter to the *Field*, stated that by covering the balls with white flannel they were more easily seen, and that the bound was greatly improved.

Rapid strides were made in the development of the game in 1875, among the earlier reformers being Mr. Henry Jones, better known as "Cavendish," and it was chiefly through the efforts of this gentleman that lawn tennis was introduced on the ground of the All-England Croquet Club at Wimbledon, where, in the same year, the first championship competition was held. The proprietors of the *Field* newspaper presented a challenge cup for competition, and Messrs. Henry Jones, Julian Marshall and C. G. Heathcote were appointed a committee to frame rules for the tournament. With commendable energy and sagacity these gentlemen set about their task, and the result was that the hour-glass court was replaced by a rectangular court 26 yards long by 9 yards wide. The height of the net was altered to 5 feet at the posts and 3 feet 3 inches at the centre. One fault was allowed to the server, whose position was fixed by law, inasmuch as he was bound to serve with one foot beyond the base line. It was then discovered that the server had a considerable advantage over the striker-out, and consequently the service line was placed 4 feet nearer the net, which was reduced in height to 4 feet 9 inches at the posts, and 3 feet at the centre. It was also provided that the double court should be 12 yards wide, thereby permitting the inclusion of the single court in it. Previously the double and single courts had to be laid out separately. These revised rules were mutually agreed upon by the M.C.C. and the All-England Club, although a difference of opinion as to

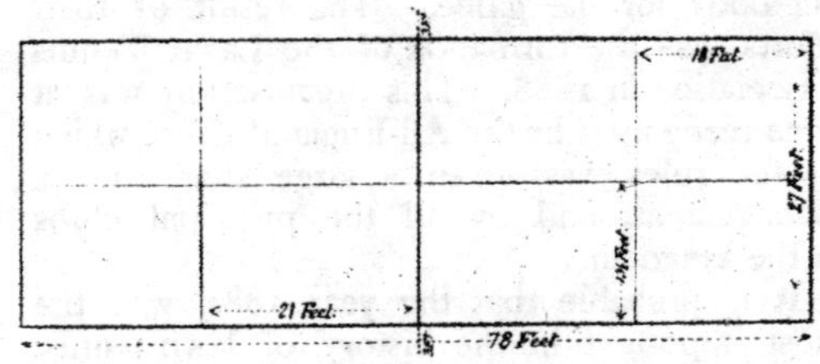

PLAN OF SINGLE COURT.

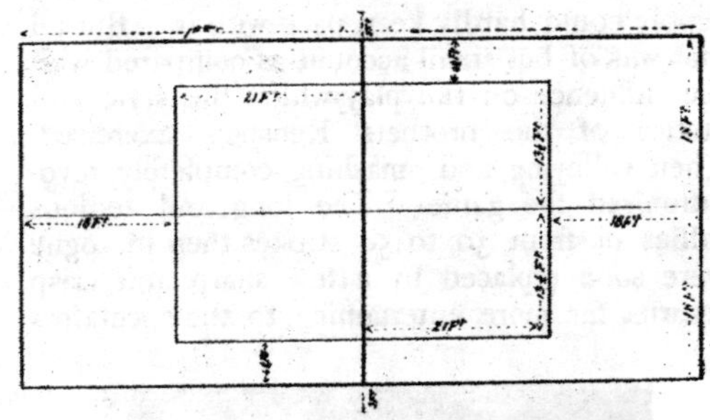

PLAN OF DOUBLE COURT.

whether the racket or tennis scoring should be adopted led to both being legal. The example of the All-England Club in using tennis scoring only was, however, soon generally adopted, and in 1883 the M.C.C. acquiesced in the omission of the racket scoring as an alternative system.

In 1879 the volleyer made his appearance, and, judging by the correspondence in the *Field* and other papers on the subject, party feeling ran very high, the anti-volleyers in particular disputing with great warmth. The result of this was a further amendment of the laws in 1880. The service line was brought a foot nearer the net (21 feet), and it was enacted that any player touching the net should lose the stroke. Subsequent alterations reduced the height of the net at the posts to 3 feet 6 inches, and also debarred a player from striking the ball until it had passed the net. The size of the ball was fixed at $2\frac{1}{2}$ to $2\frac{9}{16}$ inches in diameter, and the weight at $1\frac{7}{8}$ to 2 ounces. With these alterations the rules were practically completed;

and, except for one or two very slight amendments, they exist in the same form now.

For many years the All-England Club occupied a position in connection with lawn tennis very much akin to that held by the M.C.C. in cricket, but they did not exercise their authority with the same tact and discretion as the rulers at Lord's. So early as 1880 exception was taken to some of their actions, and in 1884 an attempt was made to organise a Lawn Tennis Association. This failed, chiefly owing to the apathy of the players themselves, and partly by reason of promises made by the All-England Executive. But such an association was bound to come, and in the autumn of 1887 Messrs. H. S. Scrivener and G. W. Hillyard, at the request of Mr. N. L. Jackson, decided to issue a circular with the object of instituting a governing body for the game. The result of their efforts was the formation of the Lawn Tennis Association in 1888. This organisation was at once recognised by the All-England Club, which by the rules was given a large share in its management, and by all the principal clubs in the kingdom.

It is probable that the year 1881 was the most important in the history of lawn tennis. The demand for rackets, balls, and other implements of the game was so great that the supply could hardly keep pace with it. But all that was of but small account as compared with the influence on the play which the style and tactics of the brothers Renshaw exercised. Their volleying and smashing completely revolutionised the game. The long and tedious rallies of from 30 to 50 strokes then in vogue were soon replaced by a few sharp and crisp returns, far more entertaining to the spectators

THE SERVICE.

and certainly less fatiguing to the players. Not that the new methods were accepted without protest. Many of the older players desired to forbid or penalise volleying, and for a long time any man who played at the net at a garden-party was accused of bad form, and was sometimes boycotted in consequence. Fortunately, common sense prevailed, and the new order of things gave place to the old, and soon became generally appreciated. The idea of volleying was not a new one, but hitherto the volleyers had stood close to the net, when they were easily beaten by a lob, even though a trifle short, or passed by a good return down the side line. The twins, recognising this, took their

VOLLEYING.

position for volleying near the service line. From this point of vantage they could volley or smash as well as they could at the net, and they could the more readily return to the base line for a lob, or get to the side line for a well-placed drive.

After a long and somewhat heated controversy on the question of "Volleyer *v.* Base-line player," it was decided, early in 1882, to lower the net at the posts to 3 feet 6 inches, so that from that time down to the present the arrangements of the court have remained unaltered. This alteration, slight though it appeared at the time to be, made an enormous difference to the game. The base-line players found that by hard and well-placed drives they could to a great extent defeat the machinations of the volleyer, and headed by the redoubtable H. F. Lawford, they set to work in earnest to achieve that much-desired end.

Thanks to the persistency of Mr. Lawford in maintaining that base-line play, if good enough, could hold its own with volleying, the interest in the various contests was enhanced during 1883. Taking advantage of the reduction in the height of the net at the sides, the back-court players cultivated hard driving down the side lines, but nearly all of them also adopted volleying to some extent. Mr. Lawford, in particular, proved that a combination of the two styles was the best, for although he did not run in to the service line and volley whenever an opportunity offered, he never failed to follow up a good length return, if it placed his opponent at a disadvantage.

Lawn tennis may be said to have reached the

zenith of its fame in 1884, for, although the entries at some of the tournaments were not so large as in subsequent years, the number of competitions and the enormous attendance of spectators forcibly demonstrated the important position which the game then occupied. Every week during the season saw two or three important meetings held, and the crack players who had the inclination and the leisure were able to take part in important competitions from the second week in May until the first week in September without a break.

Implements of the Game—Really to enjoy lawn tennis it is necessary that the accessories should be of the best. To obtain these, go to F. H. Ayres, Slazenger and Sons, Osmond (of Lee), or some other really first-class manufacturer. The posts should be easily removable, but perfectly rigid when in position. A strip of stout white canvas about 2 or 3 inches wide should run across the top of the net so as to be seen easily by the players, and the net should be stout and strong. A flexible centre stay, to keep the net at the right height in the middle, is preferable, but a metal one is frequently used, and this does not present any great disadvantage. Side posts for use when a single game is played on a double court should also be provided, and these should be placed at a distance of 18 inches from the outside line of the double court and 3 feet from the side line of the single court. Stop netting to prevent the balls from travelling too far away is a necessity, unless the court is enclosed. This should be placed about 21 feet behind each base line and should extend for about 54 feet. The netting should then be continued diagonally, but almost parallel with the side lines for another 30 feet on each side. It is as well to have the netting about 7 feet high. It can be placed on movable posts, and the whole can be removed and packed away in ten minutes. The balls should be of the authorised size and weight. Ayres' "Championship" are the standard balls, and Slazenger's are equally reliable, but both of these firms supply a cheaper article which complies with the regulations and is good enough for ordinary practice.

The Racket—So much depends upon the fancy of the player in adopting a racket to suit him or her that it is difficult to give any reliable advice, but as the game developed fancy shapes and eccentric ideas gave place to a straight-faced racket with an octagonal handle. The weight should be from $14\frac{1}{4}$ to $14\frac{3}{4}$ ozs. for a man, and about an ounce and a half less for a lady. The racket should balance when the finger is placed under the screw below the head; but in this players differ somewhat, as a base line player often prefers a little more weight in the head, while a confirmed volleyer prefers the heavier part in his hand. For a beginner, however, it is better to have a well-balanced racket made by one of the best makers. Avoid lop-sided or small-faced rackets, and see that the grain in the frame runs equally round the face. It should be tightly strung, so that when the gut is smartly struck it will emit a musical sound. Be careful not to select a small handle. All the best players use large handles, and nearly all have a rim of leather at the end of the handle to prevent it slipping through the fingers. The racket should not be gripped too tightly, and it should be held in such a way that the forehand and backhand strokes can be played alternately without shifting the fingers. Dr. Dwight, the first player to publish his views of the game, gives the following excellent advice with reference to holding a racket:—"Lay the racket on a table with the smooth side up. Open the hand with the thumb nearly at right angles with the fingers, and then clasp the handle in such a way as to make its upper right edge (or what would be its right edge if it were cut square) fit into the hollow of the joint between the thumb

BASE-LINE PLAY.

and forefinger. In closing the fingers on the handle do not put them directly round it, but with the first joint of each finger slanting up the handle, which will cause the top joints to slant down the other way. The first two fingers should be a little separated from the other fingers and from each other. The end of the handle should be well within the hand, with the little finger round the leather rim. The thumb should not go round across the fingers, but should slope upwards across the upper side of the handle." Nearly every player has a natural way of holding a racket, and this it would be difficult to overcome; but by learning to copy the orthodox style a beginner is more likely to play in good form.

The Strokes—First of all, a player should become thoroughly accustomed to handling his racket, and should practise the motions of hitting, driving, serving, and smashing, both forehand and backhand. It is also a good thing to knock a ball against a wall, returning it sometimes after it has bounded on the ground and at others as it comes direct from the wall. The player should remember that when making a forehand stroke his left foot should be in front and his body turned very slightly to the right. For a backhand stroke the body should almost face the left side line, towards which the toe of the left foot should point, while the right leg should be in front, and also inclining towards the left side line. Of course for a left-handed player these instructions must be reversed. Be careful not to commence the movements for a stroke until the latest moment possible. One of the greatest errors among beginners is their anxiety to get to the ball too quickly, instead of waiting for the ball to come to them. Always remember to strike the ball on its downward course and never as it is bounding up from the ground. Only the most expert players are able properly to play a rising ball.

The Service—There are two generally adopted methods of serving, one the overhand, for which the ball is thrown in the air and struck by the racket at a point almost as high as the player can reach; the other, chiefly adopted by ladies, the underhand service, for which the ball is dropped towards the ground and struck when within 18 inches or 2 feet of it. There are, however, many other ways of serving; and the usefulness of mastering these has been shown by many good players, notably by Dr. Dwight, Mr. E. G. Meers, and the Messrs. Renshaw. For the ordinary overhand service the ball should be thrown up in line with the right ear and slightly backwards. It should be struck by the racket just as it reaches its greatest height. If the service is intended to be a fast one, the racket should be used with a full face to the ball, but for a slower service with some cut on it the face should be diagonal, and drawn across the ball at the moment of striking. By the same rule a great deal of cut can be imparted to the underhand service by moving the racket sharply from left to right, or *vice versa*, when in the act of striking. As a rule, however, these fancy services are not of much use. A good hard service, *well placed*, so as to make the striker-out (*i.e.* the server's opponent) move from the position he has taken up, is the most reliable. Remember that at the moment of serving the body should be thrown well forward.

The Return of the Service—Many players who have become proficient in most of the strokes are unable to make their knowledge useful because they have never mastered the true methods of returning the service. This, indeed, is the most important stroke in the game. Should it be well made the striker at once assumes the advantage, but should it be weak or badly placed the server is almost sure to win the stroke. If the service is a very fast one the striker out must be content to return the ball into his opponent's court, doing this with as much force as possible; but should the service not be severe, then the ball should be returned straight down the side line or diagonally into the furthest corner of the court. Be sure to keep a good length, that is, to return the ball as near your opponent's base line as possible.

Base Line Play—Novices should devote themselves entirely to learning the base line play until they are fairly proficient at it. The volleying can soon be picked up afterwards. The base line strokes may be divided into two classes, the underhand and the horizontal. On a hard court, the latter should be adopted, but under other conditions the former is the best. For the horizontal stroke, the racket must be held at right angles with the body, the head being slightly higher than the hand. The ball should be struck just as it is at the top of the bound, or is beginning to drop, and the stroke should be made from the elbow, the arm being straightened as the ball is struck. For the underhand stroke, which is preferable to the other when practicable, the racket is held perpendicularly. The ball is struck when it is a little to the right front of the right foot, and the head of the racket should, at the moment of striking, be a little behind the hand, so that the wrist may be used in completing the stroke. The direction, too, should be imparted by the wrist, a slight turn of the racket to one side or the other effecting this. It is because of the direction being given at the last moment that this stroke is so useful, for the opponent is not able to get into position before. The cardinal point, however, in this and in all strokes, except when a lot of cut is required, is to remember to send the racket after the ball. Do not make a sharp, choppy stroke, but let the racket swing straight through even long after the ball has left it.

The Volley—No player can attain to any great degree of proficiency without learning to volley. There are more varieties of strokes in volleying than in any other method. There are forehand and backhand volleys, high volleys and low volleys, straight volleys and dropping volleys, and the "smash." The racket must hit the ball and not be held for the ball to rebound off it. It will be found advantageous to take a step with the foot furthest from the ball just before the moment of striking. Here again Dr. Dwight's sound advice cannot be improved upon. "As an example," he writes, "take the ordinary forehand volley at about the height of the shoulder (a very common stroke). The elbow should be away from the body and not down by the side, the wrist a little bent upward and the head of the racket above the hand. In striking, the weight is thrown forward on to the left foot, which is brought out with a good step in front of the right foot and a little across it. There is no preliminary swing of the racket backwards. The head of the racket should be brought forward on to the ball with a sharp bend of the wrist, and the arm should be straightened to nearly its full length. The racket should not be checked suddenly after striking the ball, but should swing well forward. The elbow, shoulder and wrist should all be left free, and not held stiff, while the stroke is made. The backhand volley is made in much the same way. The elbow should be raised and away from the body, the head of the racket should be just on the left shoulder, and the stroke should be made by stepping forward with the right foot, straightening the forearm, and bringing the head of the racket sharply forward by bending the wrist. It is this turn of the wrist at the last moment of the stroke that gives sharpness and character to all volleys." The low volley is a much more difficult stroke, but it should be cultivated, because it saves time and returns the ball quicker than your opponent expects, and before he has time to correct his position. The "smash" is made from a slowly dropping ball, usually after a bad stroke by one's opponent. In this all the joints are left free, the only object being to hit the ball as hard as possible into the opponent's court. Mr. William Renshaw once gave the writer a terse but perfect illustration of how to smash. "Do it," he said, "just as if you were going to hit someone over the head with a stick." The motions are really identical. When possible, a volley should be placed as carefully as a ground stroke, and only a smash should be made without regard to position.

The Half-Volley—This is a stroke which should only be used in an emergency. A few players, notably Mr. E. W. Lewis, have so mastered it as to use it offensively, but as a rule a return from a half-volley is easily dealt with by an opponent, and therefore it should be avoided. It is a pretty stroke to watch, and occasionally saves time. It is made by striking the ball directly it rises from the ground, and, as the player cannot watch the ball when striking it, this can only be properly done by accurate timing. The racket should be held nearly vertical, having a slight forward inclination; and a sharp lift, or upward jerk, from the elbow, should be made as the ball is struck.

The Lob—Lobbing is a stroke useful only to gain time or to drive a volleyer from the net. The ball should be tossed high into the air and should fall as near the base line as possible. If the opponent is close to the net a low lob, just out of his reach, should be made, because the ball will drop quickly; possibly before he can return to play it. To gain time, the higher the ball goes the better, particularly as it drops straight from a high lob and is therefore more difficult to volley. The forehand lob is much easier than the backhand. The ball should be taken well in front and the wrist should be held fairly stiff, the direction being given by the elbow.

General Principles—Let the ball be returned as hard and as near the net as possible. Chiefly rely upon base line play, and never run up to volley until the opposing player is placed at a disadvantage. Serve hard for the first service, but for the second run no risks. A double fault is inexcusable. Learn to place the strokes as accurately as possible. To be able to do this, get a lad to throw balls to you, and let your object be to return them into a given space. Let this space from time to time be moved to different parts of the court. Try to ascertain your opponent's strong points and his weak ones. Avoid the former and pound away at the latter. Be sure to keep a good length; for, whether playing against a volleyer or a base line player, the further back he is kept, the longer is the time allowed you to see his strokes and to get to the ball. Keep well away from the pitch of the ball, and do not commence your stroke until the ball rises. You can then see if the ball has bounded truly or has "broken" (as cricketers term it) to the one side or the other, owing to cut or to inequalities in the ground. Be sure to make yourself perfectly conversant with the laws of the game before playing it. Always keep your eye on the ball, watch it as intently as a cat does a mouse, and your hand will follow the more accurately. After going to the side of the court or towards its service line to return a ball, quickly return to the centre close to the base line. Do not attempt too much; one point gained by a brilliant shot will not compensate for two or three lost through showy play. Never use bad balls. Always place the head of the racket in the left hand when not in the act of striking, and thus relieve the right hand of the constant strain it would otherwise be subjected to.

N. L. JACKSON.

CARE OF COURTS.

Grass Courts—These can be made in three ways, viz.: (1) By improving an existing stretch of turf until it is level and smooth enough; (2) by levelling the ground, preparing the soil and growing grass seeds; and (3) by laying fresh turf. Of these the former is, of course, the simplest, but as the requisite piece of grass land is rarely available, particulars for preparing it are seldom required. In improving such a piece of turf care should be taken to remove all weeds or coarse grasses, and freely to use the spirit-level. To raise hollow places the turf should be cut out, lifted, and fine soil placed underneath until the proper height has been obtained, when the turf should be replaced and well beaten down with the flat side of a spade. On the other hand, small mounds should be removed by taking the soil away from under the grass, some fine mould being placed underneath the turf before it is replaced. To prepare a court for sowing seeds the same instructions may be followed as for making a turf-laid one, except that the seeds will be sown instead of the turfs laid. Take care that the seed is good by purchasing from a first-class seedsman, and, when ordering, it will be well to state what sort of soil is to be sown. By far the larger number of courts are made by laying fresh turfs.

When preparing the ground for a court, it is desirable to level a portion measuring 100 ft. by 50 ft., which allows an ample margin, but for the playing portion itself only 78 ft. by 36 ft. is necessary. If economy must be strictly considered, only the latter need be carefully prepared, but it is better to have the whole done if possible. In making the preliminary arrangements much depends upon the subsoil. If this is very light, a little clay should be worked in with it, but if very heavy, a better court may be made by excavating to the depth of three or four inches and filling in with gravel and mould. In every case a thin layer of fine mould, which has been sifted through a sieve with a ⅜-in. mesh, should be laid to the depth of an inch or so, and on this layer the turfs should be placed. Before this thin layer is put on, the ground should be rolled with a very heavy roller, so as to ensure its being thoroughly levelled. The superficial measurement of each turf is 3 ft. by 1 ft., and these can be obtained at prices varying from 6*s.* to 11*s.* per 100, according to the locality. For the court only about ten hundreds are necessary, but if the margin is relaid, twenty-four hundreds will be used. If the selected ground is covered with good turf, but is uneven, the turfs can be cut and taken off and relaid after the ground has been prepared as directed. The cost of the turfs can easily be ascertained, or can be estimated from the particulars given above. The amount of labour required varies according to the nature of the soil; but, roughly speaking, it would take three men four or five days to prepare the ground and cut and relay the turfs. If, however, there is some excavating to be done, the cost will be increased by the value of another four days' labour. Therefore, under favourable circumstances, with the turf already provided, the cost of a good grass court, with full-sized margin, would be from £13 to £15. If the turfs have to be purchased the cost would be about £23, and if, in addition, it is necessary to excavate and relay the soil, a further amount of £4 must be expended.

Care of Grass Courts—The incessant wear and tear to which lawn-tennis courts are subjected necessitates their receiving constant attention. By the end of a season a court is often so worn as to be almost bare. The best way to repair bare ground is to strip it and to lay fresh turf, and this should be done as soon as possible, so as to leave plenty of time for rolling and cutting during the early spring. Good tough turf, laid in February, or before the end of March, will be quite fit for use during the following season. Some of the finest turf for toughness and hard wear is to be found in the south and west of London. In the north-east the turf is upon clay, and is, consequently, poor and thin. Turf off the Downs is the toughest of all, but it is seldom that people will go to the expense of moving it any distance on account of the heavy railway carriage.

Sowing grass seeds is a less satisfactory method of repairing bare patches. Seed sown in March or April will give a nice-looking crop of grass by June, but there will be little or no wear in it, and it should not be played upon until the following year. On margins, however, and places which are not likely to be much worn, or on courts which will not be played upon until late in the season, grass seeds may be sown. A light covering of rich compost spread over the grass seeds will help them to take hold. Grass thus raised should not be cut with a machine for a while, as it will be so easily pulled up by the roots. It is best to use the scythe. The cheap grass seeds sold by most retail seedsmen are not good enough for tennis grounds. It is advisable to get a special mixture. Grasses for permanent lawns should include the Meadow Fescue (*Festuca pratensis*) and one or two other Festucas, Evergreen Meadow grass (*Poa sempervirens*), and the Cocksfoot (*Dactylis glomerata*). No clover seeds should be used if the ground is intended for very hard wear. Clovers look nice, but they are detrimental to good turf, and not only discolour the ball but greatly affect its bound.

Another point to which careful attention should be given is manuring. In the early spring grass roots may be greatly benefited by a good dressing of manure well worked in, but ordinary manuring is best done before winter. A good top dressing on turf helps to shelter the roots of the grass, and gives them something fresh to work into. Artificial manures, containing a high percentage of phosphate of lime, are useful to stimulate the growths, but do not thicken the turf much.

Worm casts, besides being a nuisance, are always a great eyesore. The best plan is to sweep them off, or spread them about every morning with a birch broom. Where it is thought advisable to destroy the worms, it will be a good plan to buy a special fluid for that purpose, and to follow carefully the directions given with it. Upon pleasure grounds and at private residences, which are surrounded by shady overhanging trees on the margin of the lawn, the rough bare spots beneath the trees are generally objectionable. These may be made to look nice by turfing them afresh each spring; the cost is but trifling, and the improvement will well repay the trouble.

A few days before any important event, such as a tournament, it is a good plan to select and mark off the special ground for the purpose. If the weather be dry, the ground should have a thorough soaking with water, which should be sprinkled gently from a rose watering can, not thrown on with a hose. Two days after, skim over with a mowing machine. Rest the ground for, say a week, then roll and sweep, and give another heavy soaking of water in the evening. Two days after that the lawn, if made of good turf, will be ready and fit for use.

Hard Courts—For winter or wet weather play it is necessary to find a substitute for grass courts, and many materials have been tried with the object of ascertaining which is the best. The variety of these is great. There are gravel, cinder, rubble, concrete, cement, tar paving and asphalt. Of these the last is the best, but it is also much the most expensive, and therefore less likely to be used. Concrete and cement courts rarely withstand the effects of a severe frost. Tar-paving is cheap and useful. Cinders are dry but dirty. Gravel is the best for ordinary wear and tear, but only if the proper sort of gravel is used. A good gravel court can be played on immediately after a heavy rain, for it dries quickly. It is pleasant in colour, and does not discolour the balls so rapidly as most of the other materials used for hard courts. The only occasion on which it cannot be used is when a thaw succeeds a sharp frost, and then it must be untrodden, or the gravel will come away in patches.

Gravel Courts—The ground, for a space of 80ft. by 36ft., should be excavated to a depth of seven inches. This completed, put in a layer of brick rubbish, in pieces about one and a half inch cube, to the depth of four inches. This must be thoroughly well beaten down, levelled and rolled with a heavy roller before the gravel is put on. The drainage will be improved by laying 4-in. drain pipes about 12ft. apart in this layer of brick rubbish. Immediately before laying the gravel the lower level should be thoroughly soaked with water, and then the coarser gravel, to the depth of about two inches, should be placed on it. The finer stuff should be laid on the top, and the whole well watered and rolled during the whole time it is being laid. Water, from a watering-pot or other contrivance, should be poured on to the roller while it is being used. It does not matter if the gravel gets "squashy," it will be firm and well bound when it has dried. The surface should be slightly inclined (a fall of two or three inches will do) from the ends to the centre, and an open drain should be laid underneath where the net will be placed, to carry off the water after a heavy rain. This may be covered with open tiles or light iron gratings to keep the balls from rolling in. After the top surface has been laid and well watered and rolled, it should not be trodden on until the whole is thoroughly dry. During hot or dry weather these courts should be watered and rolled every morning or evening—the latter for choice. The cost of gravel courts naturally varies considerably, according to the accessibility of the gravel pits. Croydon gravel is considered the best for the purpose; but there are many places where a good, hard, close-binding material can be obtained. The price of the gravel depends greatly upon the cartage required, but to enable an estimate to be made it will be sufficient to state that, in the southern suburbs of London, Croydon gravel can be obtained for about 8*s.* 6*d.* per square yard. If only the court itself—*i.e.*, a space 78ft. by 36ft.—be laid, twenty-six loads will be necessary, but if the margin be similarly laid (as it should be), the area will be 99ft. by 48ft., and sixty-seven loads of gravel will be required. For the smaller space thirty-five, and for the larger ninety loads of brick rubbish would be wanted. The labour required—exclusive of the carrying or cartage—would not be very expensive. Five men would do the excavation, levelling and filling-in, in six days for the smaller space, and in eight or nine days for the larger area. Approximately, the total cost for the court only should not exceed £25, and for the court and margin £48. Rubble courts are made very much in the same way as gravel. They are less expensive and less durable, and are not generally as satisfactory.

Cinder Courts—Cinder or ash courts are easily made, and cause little trouble to keep in order. To make them, a space of 100ft. by 50ft. in extent should be excavated to a depth of 8½in. A main drain, with 3-in. pipes, should be laid, with a fall of 2ft. in the whole length, and into this should run five branches of 2-in. pipes. Agricultural drain pipes, and not the glazed and jointed, must be used. About 5in. of brick rubbish should form the bottom layer, and this must be watered, rolled, and levelled. Next lay about 3in. of clinkers, or the rough scouring of ashes, which must be well watered and rolled, and then add the finishing layer of the finest screened household ashes. This must be put on in very thin layers, each layer being well watered and rolled, for if it is put on thickly it will not bind. The court when finished will soon dry, and afterwards a daily watering and rolling is all that is required. The fine cinders should cost about 5*s.* a load, and the brick rubbish and clinkers not more than 2*s.*, and the cost, including labour, would be about £50 or £60.

Asphalt Courts—None but skilled workmen can make a proper asphalt court, and it is not, therefore, necessary to give details of its construction. The cost may be roughly stated at from £100 to £130. Concrete or cement courts are expensive, although they do not cost so much as asphalt, but they give nothing like the satisfaction which the latter affords. They are very liable to crack, especially in frosty weather, and when this occurs their surface soon loses its evenness.

N. L. JACKSON.

LAWN TENNIS IN SWITZERLAND.

LADIES' LAWN TENNIS—People have very frequently asked me if I consider lawn tennis an athletic game, a question that has always amused me very much. I presume my questioners have never witnessed a hard five set match between two first-class men, played under a broiling sun. It is doubtful if any game is a severer test of endurance. For ladies, too, it is decidedly a very athletic exercise, always supposing that they go in for it heartily, and do not merely frivol at garden parties; and no game, in my opinion, is so eminently suitable for them, or so wholly delightful in every way. In spite of prognostications that it would die out entirely, which have persistently been made for the last twelve years, it still more than holds its own, and though it is not the fashionable craze now that it once was, and is not played as much at garden-parties, there are still a vast number of enthusiastic adherents, and it is wonderful how many tournaments take place every year. If ladies really want to become first-class players, they must of necessity enter for tournaments, as the practice they afford is invaluable in every way.

Ladies' dress is always more or less of a trial when taking exercise, and the blessings of our sex would be heaped upon any one who could invent a practical, comfortable, and withal becoming costume. It *must* be becoming, or very few of us would care to wear it. As the skirt must be endured, it is important to have it made somewhat short, reaching to the ankles, and equal in length. That is, seemingly equal; but in reality a lawn tennis skirt should be cut half an inch or an inch shorter at the back than the front. It will then appear uniform in length all round, and will not trip you up when you run backwards in volleying, say, a high lob, which skirts, as ordinarily made, are much inclined to do. It should be about three yards wide. If less, it would be rather apt to catch, when one makes sudden springs from side to side, as in volleying; and if wider, the wind blows it about and perhaps it hits the racket when we fondly imagine we are going to drive the ball.

Women certainly dress far more suitably nowadays when taking violent exertion than they used to do, and it would be impossible in these days to see a competitor in a large open tournament sallying forth to play a single on a broiling June morning, dressed in black velvet with long black kid gloves! But the spirit moved one of my opponents (years ago) thus to attire herself.

Novices nearly always get too near to the ball, and rush forward to strike it directly after the bound. It is a fatal mistake to get so close, as you lose freedom. Rather should you keep the ball at arm's length, taking care, however, not to be forced to stretch uncomfortably. There is a tendency now amongst good players to strike the ball somewhat higher from the ground than formerly, because the stroke is quicker, and allows the opponent less time to recover herself if she has lost a good position in court.

Ladies should practise volleying more. It is exceptional to find any who have a first-rate idea of it. The exertion, in playing a single, of running up to the service-line persistently, is very considerable, and probably for this reason the great majority elect to play from the base-line. As the size of the court stands at present, it is almost too large for a lady to cover comfortably from the service-line, and it is very disheartening to be easily passed after taking the trouble to puff and pant up to that coign of vantage! But it is invaluable to be able to follow up a good return and make a crisp volley across the court. It is excellent practice for volleying to stand at the service-line with some one on the opposite service-line and try to keep the ball going (all volleys) as long as ever one can. Particular attention should be paid to the position of the feet, and the body should be turned rather sideways to the net, right foot advanced for a back-hand stroke and left for a fore-hand, and one must be continually on the move and alert to get into the best possible position before hitting the ball. It is a fatal mistake to try and reach balls merely by stretching for them, as the balance of the body is then in quite the wrong place, and one cannot control the return or put any force into it.

Another important rule is that connected with "following through." Do not stop your racket at the moment of contact with the ball. Let the force which you put into the beginning of the shot expend itself naturally, otherwise it is apt to become jerky and stiff. And do not forget to watch your adversary closely and endeavour to see where she is going to place her return. How often we see a player standing still watching the effect of a fine stroke that she has made, and then giving a start of surprise when it is unexpectedly sent back! Instead of that she should immediately have returned to a safe position in the middle of the court and made every preparation to receive the return warmly. By the middle of the court I do not, of course, include that space half way between the base and service-lines, which is a very favourite spot for the novice to place herself at. It is one of the weakest positions in the court, as you can't volley a ball effectively so far from the net, and if you wait for it to bounce it necessitates running back a few paces most likely, with the alternative of making a risky half volley, which the novice almost invariably supposes to be a stroke worthy of much cultivation, but which, on the contrary, should only be used in emergencies. A good player will take a quick step forward to volley a ball which the beginner half volleys in an undecided way, and probably makes an easy shot for the opponent to jump upon. There is no reason why ladies should not become adept volleyers if they only take pains to practise enough, and it makes the game twice as enjoyable. It is quite pitiful sometimes to watch a ladies' double and to see those interminable rallies from the back of the court, and the poor umpire's head wagging mechanically from side to side, reminding one of the wee Chinese dollies, who move their heads, however, the other way—up and down. You long for one of the players to go up and volley the return smartly across the court. It adds enormously to the strength of a mixed double if the lady can go up and volley, and men always prefer a partner who can do so. If she stays back, there is always an opening through which the ball can be returned to her, whereas, if she is at the service-line, there is none. The best lady players are learning to volley more and more, but there is still great room for improvement, particularly as regards the pace with which they all hit their volleys. It is very little use merely to interpose the racket in the line of the ball's flight. The arms must be swung back boldly, and the ball must be distinctly hit. It is a revelation to have a really first-rate player for an opponent.

Overhand serving has been adopted very much more of late years by ladies, though it is doubtful if they gain much thereby. It is decidedly much more fatiguing, and is difficult to follow up to the service-line quickly, as it takes a moment or two to recover from the effort which it has caused. An underhand service however is generally much feebler, and it is well nigh impossible to help it being so. In playing a mixed double it is a moot point whether it pays better for the lady to serve underhand and then run up quickly to the service-line (where she *must* be in position before return is made) or to deliver a (we will hope) swift overhand ball, staying back to receive the return, which may also fall into the clutches of her watchful partner at the net. It is most important to serve a good length second service, a stroke much neglected by everybody. And we should strive not to make foot-faults! It is appalling how casual people are about them. Watch any ordinary game, and some of the players are certain to transgress that small rule, and are sure to be much put out, if they chance to play a match, when the umpire reminds them of the fact.

In golf, one is always told above all things "to keep one's eye on the ball." Now nobody seems to mention that particularly to lawn tennis players, yet I always think it is almost equally important, and have endeavoured to glue my own eyes as hard as possible on the approaching ball, particularly when in the act of striking.

A good player seems intuitively to divine where the ball is coming, and moves quickly into the best position for returning it. Novices very often have no idea where it is coming. It is simply a matter of practice and experience; there is no thought-reading about it. It is rather amusing to watch the eyes of your antagonist, as she will sometimes take a hasty glance at the spot in your court where she contemplates despatching the ball.

Those who have never gone in thoroughly for lawn tennis can form no idea of the infinite possibilities of the game. It has always, like golf, been much underrated by non-players, as it looks so absurdly easy. One finds garden-party folk ignorant of half the beautiful little delicate strokes which can be cultivated, and if any one happens to dare drop a ball short over the net, there are immediately cries of "Oh! how mean!"

It has always been a reproach against women that they never care to keep strictly to the rules of whatsoever game it pleases them to play. That may have been so in the past, when ladies were but novices in the pursuit of athletics, and had not had time to imbibe the true spirit of games, which men had done for generations. Still, it makes it only the more important for us all to strive so to model our behaviour that we may truthfully be called, in more senses than one, the ***fair*** sex!

L. DOD.

LAWN TENNIS IN AMERICA—Boston is responsible for the introduction of lawn tennis to America, and has continued its most sympathetic supporter. Beyond the few, and their friends, identified with its earliest history, not many know that lawn tennis was played in and around Boston for five or six years before it attracted general sporting attention in America. Yet it is perfectly true that a Boston man in 1874 purchased in England a set of nets, balls, rackets, &c., brought them to his country place, and there in August of the same year the first American lawn tennis court was laid out and played upon. This was at Nahant, a fashionable suburban residence section within a few miles of Boston.

The implements of that first game were crude, despite their being English. The net was 5 ft. in height, the rackets light in weight and poor of shape, and the balls, of the uncovered rubber variety, such as those with which children play. Dr. James Dwight and Mr. F. R. Sears, jun., may be set down as the pioneers of the game, for they first expounded the law and the practice of it, on this first court. Sears was an elder brother of R. D. Sears, who subsequently became so famous in the American annals of the game. Dr. Dwight is well known to English tennis of about twelve years ago; indeed, so is R. D. Sears, both having played in a number of British tournaments, though neither succeeded in bringing home a championship.

F. R. Sears abandoned the game before it attained much popularity, and even Dr. Dwight, although an active devotee in the latter seventies, during which time he was invincible, had practically retired from single play by 1884. He was decisively beaten by Sears in 1883, and on his other and last appearance in the championship single tournament in 1886 he was defeated in straight sets by H. A. Taylor. In the doubles championship, however, Dr. Dwight and R. D. Sears played from 1881 to 1887 with marked success; then they finally retired, Sears as an unbeaten singles champion, having won the title from 1881 to 1887 inclusive; and the pair with the doubles championship to their credit from 1882 to 1887 inclusive.

Play at Nahant naturally attracted attention, and the year following the importation of the pioneer set, another was brought over and the game started at Newport, R.I., in the early summer of 1875. Both this court and the one at Nahant were laid out on private grounds, and, of course, only open to a few intimates of the property's owners.

The honour of first adding lawn tennis to the list of club sports belongs to the Staten Island Cricket and Baseball Club, which laid out a court and got over from England the necessary paraphernalia in 1875. Staten Island was particularly well favoured as a sporting nursery; it was not over half an hour from New York, it had a number of young Englishmen in residence, and among the club members was so tireless an enthusiast as Mr. E. H. Outerbridge, who, more than any other single individual, set the lawn tennis ball a-rolling on Staten Island.

During these two years undoubtedly numerous matches were played, but the first tournament to be held in this country was, appropriately enough, given at Nahant in 1876.

The first open tournament held in the United States was given by the Staten Island Cricket and Baseball Club in 1880. The singles were won by O. E. Woodhouse, an Englishman in temporary residence, and the doubles by Wood and Maning over Dwight and Sears. But the chief end served by this tournament was to show the need of codified rules, universally observed.

Finally a call was issued in the name of the following: The Staten Island Cricket and Baseball Club; the All Philadelphia Lawn Tennis Committee; and the Beacon Park Athletic Association of Boston. Thirty-three clubs responded and the United States National Lawn Tennis Association was organised in New York, May 21st, 1881, with R. S. Oliver, of the Albany Club, as its President. A Constitution and Bye-laws were adopted, and the rules of the Marylebone Cricket Club and All England Lawn Tennis Club were adopted. It may be said that the Association has always, in its rule making, followed closely the English standard, except where an obvious improvement would result to the American game by departure from it. At that meeting it was also decided to hold an annual championship tournament in singles and doubles, at Newport, R.I.

With the organisation of the National Association, lawn tennis took one of those booms peculiar to this pulsing land of ours. Throughout the eighties the game waxed wonderfully in strength and popularity. It spread throughout the United States, the increase of clubs leading to sectional championships, although always under the rules and auspices of the National Association. Until three years ago there had been no abatement in lawn tennis interest—since that time the conquest of America by golf, and the slow development of worthy successors to replace the retiring first class, have lessened somewhat the recruiting field and lowered the general play in the last rounds of our best tournaments—notably the championship at Newport.

This condition is only true of Eastern United States; in the Middle, West, and far West, interest is by no means lessened. It is greater than ever it was.

In 1881, after having won the United States Championship, R. D. Sears was beaten by J. J. Cairnes, an Englishman, for a special trophy. In 1884 the Association ruled to bar the champion out of the All-Comers' Tournament, requiring him to defend his title against the All-Comers' winner immediately on conclusion of that tournament. In 1885, R. D. Sears, who had been playing in England, gave America its first view of that drop stroke—the Lawford, so-called. In 1886 it was decided to make all championship matches three out of five sets, instead of two out of three, as had been the previous custom.

In 1889, E. G. Meers, an Englishman reported to be ranked among the first ten of Great Britain, was defeated in the fourth round of the All-Comers' by O. S. Campbell, a boy of twenty. Campbell was defeated that year for the All-Comers' by Q. A. Shaw, jun., who in turn was beaten for the championship by H. W. Slocum, jun. But the next year Campbell defeated Slocum for the national honour, which he successfully defended in 1891 and 1892 by beating Hobart and Hovey. Campbell defaulted in 1893 to R. D. Wrenn, the present champion.

The period of Campbell's activity may be said to represent the heyday of American tennis. He showed the first perfected net game, which was subsequently adopted by the cleverest players we have; and during his time the general average of play at Newport was higher than it has been since. The men who then made all the rounds interesting have to a great extent retired, and there are none of equal skill to replace them. Men were ranked among the first ten last year who would not have had even a look in three years ago.

The year 1894 was notable in American lawn tennis because of the playing of M. F. Goodbody, an Englishman, in our championships. Goodbody beat, in successive rounds, F. H. Hovey, Clarence Hobart, and W. A. Larned (three of our best four players), and won the All-Comers'. But Wrenn defended the championship against Goodbody, beating him three sets to one. Wrenn lost the championship to Hovey in 1895, but won it back again last year (1896).

Several Americans at different times have played in British tournaments—Dwight, Sears, Campbell and Larned being the most prominent, but no one has yet been notably successful, certainly not to the extent of Mr. Goodbody's exploit in America. When Messrs. Pim and Mahoney visited Boston in 1895 they were fairly successful in singles, Pim beating Hovey, Larned and Chace, and Mahoney beating Hovey and Chace; but Hobart and Hovey beat them in doubles, and Hobart won a great match from Pim.

The performances in America of Englishmen, and the progress in English tournaments of Americans, prove conclusively that the English game, if not in occasional individuals, at least in general, is a harder game than the American average. Unless it be R. D. Wrenn, our present champion, there is not a native playing tennis in America to-day who could successfully go through the English champion tournament. There are probably several Englishmen, any one of whom could win the All-Comers' cup at Newport this year.

The superiority of, say, the first English ten over the first American ten is easily accounted for. Age, experience and opportunities for practice. Our first-class "men" are mere boys, who, as a rule, play but a year or two after graduation from college. Just as their play is maturing and strengthening they retire from the game. The contrary is the case in England.

The English game is less brilliant, but more forceful. The American plays a distinctively offensive game—striving to win every point by supreme exertion—and he is apt to be erratic. The Englishman is first of all a superb getter; he gets everything back, giving his opponent as many chances as possible to beat himself, and is almost certain to be steady. Englishmen hit the ball harder, and do not miss the comparative easy shots, as we see our cracks do in their hit or miss slashing style. When an English player gets a point, it is on his own winning stroke, and not on his opponent's poor play. Englishmen are provident of their strength and chances; the American uses both in great prodigality, and to his undoing, if he be opposed to one of the opposite sort. In short, the Englishman is the tortoise and the American the hare of lawn tennis.

However, it is true that although our first ten are not this year as good as a few years ago, the average of general play throughout the country is being greatly improved and steadied by the various inter-scholastic, inter-collegiate, and inter-state and other tournaments on an interminable list, which continues to grow, despite golf.

Meantime, however, it cannot yet be denied that Englishmen know more lawn tennis than do we.

CASPAR WHITNEY.

GLOSSARY.

Advantage—The next stroke won by either player when the score is *deuce* (*q.v.*).

Advantage-game—The odd game one, if both sides have previously scored an equal number of games over and including five games all.

Back-hander, Back-handed stroke—A stroke in which the ball is hit with the reverse side of the racquet.

Ball—[*See* LAW 2].

Bisque—A method of handicapping, now obsolete. It was one stroke which could be claimed at any time.

Deuce—The score when both players or sides have won three strokes (=40 all).

Deuce-game—The game won, which makes the score in games level when each side has won more than five.

Doubles—A game with two players on each side.

Drop-stroke—A stroke by which the ball is made to drop dead, just clearing the net.

Fault—[*See* LAWS 9–12, and 33].

Fifteen—The score for either player on winning his first stroke.

Forty—The score for either player winning his third stroke. [*See* DEUCE.]

Forty-all—[*See* DEUCE].

Games-all—If both players win five games, the score becomes games-all. [*See* LAW 22.]

Half-volley—A stroke made the moment the ball leaves the ground.

Hang—A method of service by which the ball comes up slowly or irregularly from the ground.

Let—A service, which for reasons defined in Law 16, is not counted.

Lob—A ball returned high in the air, usually to avoid a player at the net.

Love—Nothing scored.

Love set—A set won in six consecutive games.

Place—To direct the ball to a desired part of the opponents' court.

Poach—To take a ball that should be taken by one's partner.

Rally—A series of strokes, beginning with the service and ending with a failure to return the ball.

Rough side of Racket—The side of the racket from which the twisted gut projects.

Serve—The delivery of the ball from the back line at the commencement of the game, and after the scoring of each point.

Single—A game with one player only on each side.

Smooth side of racket—The side from which the twisted gut does not project.

Sudden death—A term used when it has been agreed to decide the set by the best of eleven games without playing *deuce* and *vantage* games.

Tennis-elbow—An injury to the arm, attributed to excessive strain in overhand service.

Thirty—The score for a player on winning his second stroke.

Twist—A movement imparted to the ball, causing it to swerve on rising from the ground.

Volley—Returning the ball before it reaches the ground.

LAWS OF THE GAME.

The Single-handed Game.

1. For the single-handed game, the court is 27 ft. in width, and 78 ft. in length. It is divided across the middle by a net, the ends of which are attached to the tops of two posts, which stand 3 ft. outside the court on each side. The height of the net is 3 ft. 6 in. at the posts, and 3 ft. at the centre. At each end of the court, parallel with the net, and at a distance of 39 ft. from it, are drawn the *base-lines*, the extremities of which are connected by the *side-lines*. Half-way between the side-lines, and parallel with them, is drawn the *half-court line*, dividing the space on each side of the net into two equal parts, called the *right and left courts*. On each side of the net, at a distance of 21 ft. from it, and parallel with it, are drawn the *service-lines*.

2. The balls shall not be less than $2\frac{1}{2}$ in., nor more than $2\frac{9}{16}$ in. in diameter; and not less than $1\frac{7}{8}$ oz., nor more than 2 oz., in weight.

3. In matches where umpires are appointed, their decision shall be final; but where a referee is appointed, an appeal shall lie to him from the decision of an umpire on a question of law.

4. The choice of sides and the right of serving during the first games shall be decided by toss; provided that, if the winner of the toss choose the right to serve, the other player shall have the choice of sides, and

vice versa; and provided that the winner of the toss may, if he prefer it, require the other player to make the first choice.

5. The players shall stand on opposite sides of the net; the player who first delivers the ball shall be called the *server*, the other the *striker-out*.

6. At the end of the first game the striker-out shall become server, and the server shall become striker-out; and so on alternately in the subsequent games of the set.

7. The server shall stand with one foot beyond (*i.e.*, further from the net than) the base line, and with the other foot upon the base line, and shall deliver the service from the right and left courts alternately, beginning from the right.

8. The ball served must drop within the service-line, half-court-line, and side-line of the court which is diagonally opposite to that from which it was served, or upon any such line.

9. It is a *fault* if the service be delivered from the wrong court, or if the server do not stand as directed in Law 7, or if the ball served drop in the net or beyond the service-line, or if it drop out of court or in the wrong court; it is not a *fault* if the server's foot, which is beyond the base-line, do not touch the ground at the moment at which the service is delivered.

10. A fault may not be taken.

11. After a fault, the server shall serve again from the same court from which he served that fault, unless it was a fault because served from the wrong court.

12. A fault may not be claimed after the next service has been delivered.

13. The service may not be *volleyed*, *i.e.*, taken before it touches the ground.

14. The server shall not serve until the striker-out is ready. If the latter attempt to return the service, he shall be deemed to be ready.

15. A ball is *in-play* from the moment at which it is delivered in service (unless a fault) until it has been volleyed by the striker-out in his first stroke, or has dropped in the net or out of court, or has touched either of the players or anything that he wears or carries, except his racket in the act of striking, or has been struck by either of the players with his racket more than once consecutively, or has been volleyed before it has passed over the net, or has failed to pass over the net before its first bound (except as provided in Law 17), or has touched the ground twice consecutively on either side of the net, though the second time may be out of court.

16. It is a *let* if the ball served touch the net, provided the service be otherwise good; or if a service or fault be delivered when the striker-out is not ready; or if either player be prevented by an accident beyond his control from serving or returning the ball in play. In case of a let, the service or stroke counts for nothing, and the server shall serve again.

17. It is a good return although the ball touch the net, or, having passed outside either post, drop on or within any of the lines which bound the court into which it is returned.

18. The server wins a stroke if the striker-out volley the service, or fail to return the service or the ball in-play (except in the case of a let), or return the service or ball in play so that it drop outside any of the lines which bound his opponent's court, or otherwise lose a stroke, as provided by Law 20.

19. The striker-out wins a stroke if the server serve two consecutive faults, or fail to return the ball in-play (except in the case of a let), or return the ball in-play so that it drop outside any of the lines which bound his opponent's court, or otherwise lose a stroke, as provided by Law 20.

20. Either player loses a stroke if the ball in-play touch him or anything that he wears or carries, except his racket in the act of striking; or if he touch or strike the ball in-play with his racket more than once consecutively; or if he touch the net or any of its supports while the ball is in-play; or if he volley the ball before it has passed the net.

21. On either player winning his first stroke, the score is called 15 for that player; on either player winning his second stroke, the score is called 30 for that player; on either player winning his third stroke, the score is called 40 for that player; and the fourth stroke won by either player is scored game for that player; except as below:—

If both players have won three strokes, the score is called deuce; and the next stroke won by either player is scored advantage for that player. If the same player win the next stroke, he wins the game; if he lose the next stroke, the score is again called deuce: and so on until either player win the two strokes immediately following the score at deuce, when the game is scored for that player.

22. The player who first wins six games wins a set; except as below:—

If both players win five games, the score is called games-all; and the next game won by either player is scored advantage-game for that player. If the same player win the next game, he wins the set; if he lose the next game, the score is again called games-all; and so on until either player win the two games immediately following the score of games-all, when he wins the set.

NOTE.—Players may agree not to play advantage-sets, but to decide the set by one game after arriving at the score of games-all.

23. The players shall change sides at the end of every set, but the umpire, on appeal from either party, before the toss for choice, shall direct the players to change sides at the end of the *first, third, and every subsequent alternate game of each set*, provided that in such event the players shall not change sides at the end of a set if the number of games in such set be even; but if the appeal be made after a match has been begun, the umpire shall only direct the players to change sides at the end of the *first, third, and every subsequent alternate game of the odd and concluding set.*

24. When a series of sets is played, the player who was server in the last game of one set shall be striker-out in the first game of the next.

ODDS.

25. In the case of received odds:—

a. One-sixth of fifteen is one stroke given in every six games of a set in the position shown by the annexed table.

b. Similarly, two-sixths, three-sixths, four-sixths, and five-sixths of fifteen are respectively two, three, four, and five strokes given in every six games of a set in the position shown by the table.

	1st Game.	2nd Game.	3rd Game.	4th Game.	5th Game.	6th Game.
$\frac{1}{6}$ of 15	0	15	0	0	0	0
$\frac{2}{6}$ of 15	0	15	0	15	0	0
$\frac{3}{6}$ of 15	0	15	0	15	0	15
$\frac{4}{6}$ of 15	0	15	0	15	15	15
$\frac{5}{6}$ of 15	0	15	15	15	15	15

EXAMPLE.—A player receiving four-sixths of fifteen receives nothing in the first and third games, and fifteen in the second, fourth, fifth, and sixth games of a set.

NOTE.—The table is not carried beyond the sixth game, as in the next and every succeeding six games the odds recur in the same positions.

c. The above odds may be given in augmentation of other receiving odds.

d. Fifteen is one stroke given at the beginning of every game of a set.

e. Thirty is two strokes given at the beginning of every game of a set.

f. Forty is three strokes given at the beginning of every game of a set.

26. In the case of owed odds:

a. One-sixth of fifteen is one stroke owed in every six games of a set in the position shown by the annexed table.

b. Similarly, two-sixths, three-sixths, four-sixths, and five-sixths of fifteen are respectively two, three, four, and five strokes owed in every six games of a set in the position shown by the following table:

	1st Game.	2nd Game.	3rd Game.	4th Game.	5th Game.	6th Game.
$\frac{1}{6}$ of 15	15	0	0	0	0	0
$\frac{2}{6}$ of 15	15	0	15	0	0	0
$\frac{3}{6}$ of 15	15	0	15	0	15	0
$\frac{4}{6}$ of 15	15	0	15	0	15	15
$\frac{5}{6}$ of 15	15	0	15	15	15	15

EXAMPLE.—A player owing two-sixths of fifteen would owe fifteen in the first and third games, and nothing in the second, fourth, fifth, and sixth games.

NOTE.—The table is not carried beyond the sixth game, as in the next and every succeeding six games the odds recur in the same positions.

c. The above odds may be owed in augmentation of other owed odds.

d. Fifteen is one stroke owed at the beginning of every game of a set.

e. Thirty is two strokes owed at the beginning of every game of a set.

f. Forty is three strokes owed at the beginning of every game of a set.

THE THREE-HANDED AND FOUR-HANDED GAMES.

27. The above laws shall apply to the three-handed and four-handed games, except as below.

28. For the three-handed and four-handed games, the court is 36 ft. in width. Within the side-lines, at a distance of 4½ ft. from them, and parallel with them, are drawn the service-side-lines. In other respects the court is similar to that which is described in Law 1.

29. In the three-handed game, the single player shall serve in every alternate game.

30. In the four-handed game, the pair who have the right to serve in the first game may decide which partner shall do so, and the opposing pair may decide similarly for the second game. The partner of the player who served in the first game shall serve in the third; and the partner of the player who served in the second game shall serve in the fourth, and so on in the same order in all the subsequent games of a set.

31. The players shall take the service alternately throughout each game: no player shall receive or return a service delivered to his partner; and the order of service and of striking out, once arranged, shall not be altered, nor shall the striker-out change courts to receive the service before the end of the set.

32. The ball served must drop within the service-line, half-court-line, and service-side-line of the court, which is diagonally opposite to that from which it was served, or upon any such line.

33. It is a *fault* if the ball do not drop as provided in Law 32, or if it touch the server's partner, or anything that he wears or carries.

34. If a player serve out of his turn, the umpire, as soon as the mistake is discovered by himself or by one of the players, shall direct the player to serve who ought to have served; but all strokes scored, and any fault served before such discovery, shall be reckoned. If a game shall have been completed before such discovery, then the service in the next alternate game shall be delivered by the partner of the player who served out of his turn; and so on in regular rotation.

KNOTTY POINTS.

ADDENDA TO THE LAWS OF THE GAME.

(*Revised and approved by the Council of the Lawn Tennis Association.*)

1. In no case may the striker-out volley the service, not even if the ball is clearly outside the service court.

2. A player who is struck by, or strikes a ball *in play* (unless he thereby makes a good return) loses the stroke, no matter whether he is standing within the limits of the court or outside them. (For definition of "in play" see Law 15.)

3. If the service is delivered before the striker-out is ready, and he tries to return it, but fails, he loses the stroke.

4. If the striker-out cries "not ready" after the service has been delivered, but before the ball touches the ground, he may not claim a fault because the ball ultimately drops outside the service court.

5. If the server, in attempting to serve, misses the ball altogether, it does not count as a fault, but if the ball is touched, no matter how slightly, by the racket, a service is thereby delivered and the rules governing the service at once apply.

6. If a ball, served or returned, drops into the proper court and screws or is blown back over the net, the player whose turn it is to strike may reach over the net and play the ball, provided that neither he nor any part of his clothes or racket touch the net. If he fails to play the ball, the stroke of course scores to his opponent, notwithstanding that the ball has gone back over the net.

7. If a player throws his racket at the ball and so returns the ball into the proper court, he loses the stroke.

8. If a player catches the ball on his racket, walks with it to the net, and, reaching over, drops it into court, he loses the stroke, as such a proceeding cannot be defined as an "act of striking" (*vide* Law 15).

9. If a player's racket passes over the net after he has returned the ball, he does not lose the stroke, providing the ball has passed over the net before being played, and has been properly returned.

10. If a player or his racket touches the posts or supports of the net or posts while the ball is in-play, he loses the stroke. (For definition of "in-play" see Law 15.)

11. If a player's racket slips out of his hand and touches the net while the ball is in-play, he loses the stroke.

12. If a player, to avoid touching the net, jumps over it while the ball is in play, he loses the stroke.

13. If a ball is returned outside the posts, either above or below the level of the top of the net, and drops into court, it is a good return.

14. If a player succeeds in returning a ball served or in-play which strikes a ball lying in the court, it is a good return.

15. If a spectator impedes, or in any way interferes with, a player, a "let" may be allowed under Law 16.

16. A "let" does not annul a previous fault.

17. The service always commences from the right-hand court, even though odds are given or owed, and the service always continues alternately from the right and left courts.

18. If an umpire erroneously calls "fault" and at once corrects himself and cries "play," and the striker-out fails to return the ball, a "let" must be allowed.

19. If the ball in play (other than a service) strikes any part of the net or its supports, or the centre stay, no

matter how low down (provided it does not touch the ground), and eventually goes over into the proper court, it is a good return.

20. If in a double game the server's service strikes *either* of his opponents, he wins the stroke.

21. If a match is postponed on account of rain or darkness coming on, or for any similar reason, and is continued on the subsequent day, the match shall be resumed from the point where it was discontinued on the previous day. An entirely new commencement may only be made with the consent of the referee.

22. If two players in a handicap play at the wrong odds, the match stands, unless they have been wrongly instructed by the referee, or any person or persons acting under his instructions, in which case the loser may claim to have the match replayed, unless the mistake in the odds has been in his favour. Such claim must be made within a reasonable time.

23. A similar decision must be given if two players neglect to play advantage sets when one of the conditions of the event in which they are competing is that advantage sets should be played.

LAZOING—Though the "lazo" has been known from very early times both in Europe and Asia, yet it was, perhaps, never brought either to such general use or perfection in usage as it has been since the horses of Diego de Mendoza in South America, and those of Cortés and Alvarado in North America, spread over the prairies and pampas, multiplied in vast numbers and became wild.

Probably more misconception exists as to the use and capabilities of the lazo than in regard to any other equally well-known implement in the whole field of sport. Though the dispeller of popular errors is as unpopular an individual as the proverbial peacemaker, it may not be without use to give a slight account of the lazo, its management and capabilities.

In the Argentine Republic, in Southern Brazil, and in the Republic of Uruguay, lazos are made of raw hide plaited in four strands. In Chile they are of raw hide, twisted into a three-strand rope. Their length, in all four countries, ranges from sixty to eighty, or, at the outside, ninety feet. In general they are about the thickness of the little finger of a man's hand. In Chile they are a little thicker, owing to the looser method of construction. In the above mentioned countries (with the exception of Chile) at the extreme end of the lazo is spliced a ring of about two ounces in weight. At the end retained in the hand, is a button formed like a Turk's head knot, and a strap of raw hide serving as a button-hole. This button is fastened into a strong iron ring placed just behind the rider's thigh in the circingle, which forms the girth of the South American saddle, called "*recado*" in the Pampas and "*enjalma*" in Chile.

In the latter country no ring is used, but at both ends there is a button and strap. The length of the lazo determines the extent of the throw, and as an ordinary lazo is about sixty-six feet in length, it follows that eighteen, or, at the most, twenty yards, is the outside limit at which an animal can be caught by it, and that only when thrown from a horse galloping. On foot, twelve to fifteen yards is considered a good throw. To throw the lazo it is necessary to make a noose at one end of the rope, from two to five yards in circumference. The iron ring should be allowed to hang about five feet from the hand. Then, gathering the slack of the rope into small coils, the lazoer swings the lazo round his head several times, taking care that the noose in circling round his head keeps open, and lets it go when the right hand is just over the right ear. No strength is required in throwing when on horseback, and much less when on foot than a spectator might imagine.

When the lazo has settled over the horns of the animal (if a bullock) or round the neck (if a horse), care must be taken to keep the animal lazoed always on the off side of your horse. On no account should it be allowed to cross to the near side, nor should the lazo be allowed to touch the horse ridden, either in throwing or in "working" the lazoed animal. Neglect of this precaution has cost many a man his life, as even a tame horse when touched by the lazo, and still more when entangled in it, is apt to buck or throw himself down. The lazo should be kept taut, which is accomplished by keeping your horse always bearing to the near side. There is no danger of being pulled over, as the weight of the horse, plus the rider and saddle, exceeds that of any bullock to be found in prairies or pampas.

On foot, the lazo is used to catch the feet of animals or to catch animals in a corral. It can be used with great accuracy to catch the two fore feet of a running animal or to catch a fore or hind foot, or in many other ways.

Lazos in South America are kept soft and pliable by frequent greasing.

In Mexico and South America lazos are made either of horsehair or of the fibres of the aloe and other plants, and in Texas and California of hemp. In no case in these countries is a ring used. Mexicans generally use a button and strap, and Texans and Californians merely tie a bow-line on a bight, and pass the other end of the rope through the bight to form the noose. The lazo used in Mexico and North America seldom exceeds sixty feet in length and is often shorter. It is made fast to the high pommel of the Mexican saddle, and, being thus in front of the rider, can be thrown on the "near" as well as on the "off" side, or, if the lazoed animal crosses, the lazo can be shifted over the horse's head with little danger.

Mexicans and Texans are probably not so skilful on horseback as the South Americans, but more dexterous than they in the use of the lazo on foot. Technically speaking, the lazo is hardly a sport, as it is rarely used for amusement, but it is a difficult, a dangerous, and a

picturesque exercise, and to acquire its use in perfection a man must be a skilful horseman, possessed above all of good hands, and must have practised from his earliest youth.

In guerilla warfare the lazo is a useful weapon, and can be used, moreover, to drag a gun or wagon out of mud or through a river, for, by attaching the lazo to the gun carriage or wagon, four or five men can instantly add the strength of their horses to that of the team. The Spaniards say of the guitar that it requires no science, but only strength in the wrists and perseverance; and the same may be said of the lazo, if we add judgment, a cool head, a firm seat, and a horse that can turn upon a Mexican's "*poblano*" hat.

R. B. Cunninghame Graham.

LEOPARDS AND PANTHERS—DISTRIBUTION OF—In spite of the great difference in size between the animals popularly known as the Leopard and Panther, both are now generally included by zoologists in the single species *Felis pardus*, of which, however, there are several local races. This species is characterised by the ground-colour of the fur being generally some shade of yellow, and by the black rosettes having no black spot in the central area. Its range includes the greater part of Africa, Asia Minor, Persia, Baluchistan, India, Assam, Ceylon, Burma, the Malay Peninsula, Sumatra, Java, and China. Apparently the name **Panther** properly belongs to the African race (*F. pardus typicus*), in which the spots are generally small and a large number of them are solid. In the Albany district of South Africa occurs a dark variety in which there is often a distinct black stripe down the middle of the back, and the spots elsewhere are much broken up and very numerous. Whether this form indicates a distinct race, or only a dark variety, is uncertain. In India and the Malayan countries there are a large and small variety, the former generally known as the Panther, and the latter as the Leopard. Both have the spots larger than in the African race, and with a greater tendency to form rosettes; and both must be regarded as constituting a single race. To this race must likewise be referred the **Asiatic Black Leopard**, most frequently met with in elevated districts in Southern India and the Malay Peninsula. It is not a distinct race, but merely a black, or "melanistic" variety, the spots clearly showing in certain lights.

Much more distinct is the **Persian Leopard** (*F. pardus tulliana*), distinguished by its light colour, the large size of the spots, the length of the fur, and the great thickness of the tail. In all these respects this race forms a transition towards the Snow-Leopard. A fourth very distinct race is the **Chinese Leopard** (*F. pardus fontanieri*) from Northern China, a mounted specimen of which is now exhibited in the British Museum. This is a large, stoutly-built animal, characterised by the long light-coloured fur, the moderately thick tail, and the confluence of the spots to form large jet black rosettes, differing from those of the Jaguar mainly by the absence of the black centre. The muzzle, too, is shorter than in the Indian Leopard, and the entire animal has a massive appearance, very similar to that of the Manchurian Tiger, northern races of widely spread species very generally exhibiting the same peculiarity. This race is mainly known by flattened trade-skins, which are imported in considerable numbers from China; its exact geographical limits are unknown, but it certainly inhabits Manchuria, and not improbably, further south, gradually passes into the ordinary Indian race.

The **Ounce**, or **Snow-Leopard** (*Felis uncia*), although showing some resemblance to the Persian Leopard, is classed as a distinct species, characterised by the long thick fur, the white ground-colour, the large size of the spots, which, with the exception of those on the head, are somewhat ill-defined, and the great thickness and length of the tail, which scarcely tapers from root to tip, and is nearly three-quarters the total length of the head and body. Other distinctive features are afforded by the skull; the large yellowish spot on the otherwise black ears is also a characteristic mark of the species. The Snow-Leopard is an inhabitant of all the higher ranges of Central Asia, including the inner Himalaya, the Altai, and the Thian Shan. Its distributional area thus extends from Gilgit and Hunza through Baltistan, Zanskar, and Ladak to Turkestan, Tibet, Trans-Baikalia, Amurland, and North-Western China. How far its southern limits extend is not precisely known; but it certainly occurs in the Pangi district of the upper Chinab valley. Whereas in the greater part of the Himalaya it does not descend below 9,000 ft. above the sea level, and ranges up to 16,000 and 20,000, in Gilgit it has been found in winter as low as 6,000 ft., and further north it doubtless occurs at still lower elevations.

The third and fourth specific representatives of the Leopard group are the **Jaguar** (*F. onca*) and the **Puma** (*F. concolor*), both of which are American. Since each has a separate article, it will suffice to state that the former is distinguished from both the Asiatic species by the presence of a black centre to the rosettes, and that in the latter the spots have practically disappeared, although frequently visible in certain lights. The numerous species of Puma recently named by Dr. Merriam must be regarded merely as local races. The last member of the group is the **Clouded Leopard** (*F. nebulosa*), distinguished by the long tail and the broad black-bordered markings on the fur of the body. It occurs at elevations up to 7,000 ft. in the south-eastern Himalaya and Assam, and extends thence to the hilly districts of Burma, Siam, the Malay Peninsula, Java and Borneo. In Formosa it is represented by a shorter-tailed race (*F. nebulosa brachyurus*). The **Hunting-Leopard**, or **Cheetah** (*q.v.*), has, of course, nothing to do with the true Leopard, but represents by itself the genus *Cynælurus*.

R. LYDEKKER.

LEOPARD, AFRICA (*Felis pardus*)—**Nomenclature**—The greatest possible confusion has long prevailed concerning the nomenclature of the various spotted cats—the panther, leopard, cheetah, puma, and jaguar, having from time to time been mixed up in the minds of writers upon the subject.

In North America the uniformly-coloured puma is often styled "panther," the term applied by Buffon to the jaguar of South America; in India "panther" is the name given to the large, and "leopard" to the smaller, variety of *Felis pardus*.

Sir J. E. Tennent tells us that in Ceylon the leopard is frequently called *cheetah*—the latter word, I believe, merely meaning "spotted." I think it quite likely that the term "leopard"—lion-panther—was originally applied to the cheetah by the ancients, the panther-like *tout ensemble*, combined with the maned neck of the cheetah, being sufficient to account for this application of the term.

In South Africa the Boers and many colonists still call the cheetah "luipard."

However, it is now generally admitted that there is but one true species of large spotted cats in Africa, viz., the leopard (the cheetah being of course placed in a different group). Notwithstanding the apparently wide difference in size, coloration, and habits between the large and small varieties, the frequent occurrence of forms intermediate between them establishes the identity of species.

The **Hill** or **Kloof Leopard** is common on the mountain ranges in all parts of Africa in which I have hunted, and amongst the Kloofs and Krantzes of the foot-hills, practically wherever it can obtain plenty of cover, water, and food.

It preys principally upon the small game which abound in such localities—bush-buck, bush-pig, drinkers, and klipspringers, and at a pinch even the little hyrax affords it a meal. Monkeys are occasionally caught, while, if there are any farms about on the terrace-lands, foals, donkeys, goats, sheep, and dogs are amongst the leopard's victims.

The average total length of the male hill leopard is 6 ft. 5 ins. or 6 ft. 6 ins. (though this length I have often seen much exceeded), the tail being usually about 2 ft. 10 ins., shoulder height 2 ft. 5 ins., girth of forearm, 12 to 13½ ins. His girth and muscular development are immense, the head somewhat long and narrow. The average length of the leopardess is 6 ft. 2—3 ins. The fur is long, the ground-colour usually a rich, dark orange buff, paling on flanks and inner portions of limbs; the chest and belly are pure white. Bases of ears black. The spots are dark brown or black, arranged in the form of open rosettes around a centre of ground colour darker than elsewhere.

These open rosettes occur only on the back, sides, and upper portions of hind limbs, those on the chest, forearm, flanks, belly and thighs being solid and of large size, while on the face, head, neck and lower limbs the spots are very small. The most typical forms of this variety can be recognised at once by the manner in which the spots on the back run into one another, forming more or less broken stripes, long, broad, and dark, continued down the tail, the tip of which is always black; both the rosettes and solid spots all over the body are very close-set.

The **Low Country Leopard** is at first sight a very different beast, higher on the legs, longer in body, less muscular, and of gaunt appearance. He inhabits the dense cover of reeds, grass, or thorn-thickets along the banks of the principal streams, and is often found in low stony hills, covered with brush, adjacent to water.

He has far wider choice in the matter of food and less trouble to secure it, as in the Low Country game, both big and small, is plentiful.

This fact accounts for the marked difference in outward appearance between him and his congener; the latter attains great muscular development from the necessity of constantly climbing hills, krantzes, kloofs, and even trees in pursuit of its prey; the former, on the contrary, takes life more easily, usually seizing its prey when it comes to the water, and is altogether a lazier animal.

Average length 6 ft. 10 ins. to 7 ft., the tail occupying 2 ft. 6 ins., shoulder height 2 ft. 7 ins. or 8 ins. Fur short, close and sleek; head short, round and heavy; limbs long, and less muscular than those of the hill leopard. Ground colour pale fulvous, but subject to much variation. In the typical animal the spots, though of a similar nature to those of the hill leopard, *never* run into bars or lines, but are always *widely set* one from another. In the intermediate forms, however, found commonly amongst the lowest foot-hills and throughout all the Low Country, so variable are the markings and measurements that in most cases it is impossible to determine to which variety any particular one belongs. All are, in fact, but modifications of one widely distributed type.

Tracking.—As an object of sport I consider the leopard has seldom had fair play. They are extremely difficult to find, but once this is accomplished, their pluck and savage nature will fully reward the sportsman. Good dogs, I consider, are almost an absolute necessity, especially in the hill country. The best for use in this country is a cross between the rough "Boerdog" and a greyhound. He will be plucky, strong, with good staying power, a keen nose, and will have a turn of speed. Very large dogs are quite useless, for they cannot get through the under-wood and dense thorny thickets which abound in the kloofs, and into which leopards invariably retreat. Dogs that show too eager a desire to run forward contrary to orders should be promptly checked, and if disobedient, should either be led by a boy or drafted out of one's "leopard-pack." Such dogs are apt to come to close quarters with the leopard too soon and unsupported, and may either get killed or permit the leopard to escape before the sportsman can get up.

In the summer months, *i.e.* during the rainy season, December to April, leopards are difficult to find, whether in the hills or on the plains, owing to the length of the grass and denseness of the vegetation; but during the dry season, more especially when the grass is burnt off, it only requires patience and perseverance to bring them to bag. In the hill country, wherever leopards are of frequent occurrence, they will often be met with in the early mornings, and until the sun is an hour or more up, on the edges of kloofs and forest tracks, and on the long open grassy spurs so common to the broken country at the foot of a mountain range.

They delight in sunning themselves on the rocks, and playing about in the cool dewy grass under the genial rays of the early sun. In the Low Country, also, the banks of rivers and small watercourses in the early morning are the most likely places in which to look for them.

Watching at Kills.—As a rule, however, leopards, like lions, are found by means of their "kills," a careful examination of which will soon tell the sportsman whether they are the work of a lion, leopard, hyæna, or cheetah. If the spoor can be made out, that will of course decide it at once;[1] otherwise the carcase itself must be examined. With the exception of the hyæna, all these animals drag their prey some distance from the spot where it was killed,—the hyæna *only drags portions*, when dismembered. The hyæna also eats meat, bones, skin, entrails, in fact everything indiscriminately; the other three disembowel their kill, and tear off large portions of skin with their teeth before eating. The cheetah disembowels in a rough, dirty fashion, *frequently eating some of the entrails*, *never* burying them; after devouring the viscera, he tackles the head, biting off the ears and nose, and lacerating the throat. The lion and leopard disembowel *neatly*, and bury the entrails; both then devour the viscera, but whereas the lion then sets to work upon the buttocks or inside of the hind legs, the leopard invariably tackles the breastbone, brisket, and soft ends of the ribbones. The hill-leopard very seldom returns to its kill if once actually disturbed thereat, otherwise, provided the kill has not been unduly tampered with, it may be expected to return on the following night. The Low Country leopard, on the contrary—possibly because it fears man less, not having so frequently come in contact with him—displays the utmost audacity in returning again to its kill, no matter how much it may have been interfered with. In Central Africa the hill-leopards are equally bold and audacious; a good deal depends upon how much or how little reason they may have had to fear man.

[1] Both hyæna and cheetah leave the imprints of their nails on the ground, the former deeply, the latter slightly. A full-grown male leopard's spoor is 4 in. in diameter, front feet—hind feet 3¼ in. in diameter.

In all cases, however, I advise the *utmost* caution and skill in dealing with these creatures, for they are beyond question the wariest brutes in the world. Supposing the leopard's kill has been found early in the morning, say any time before the dew is dry upon the grass; the sportsman then has two alternatives before him: he can either follow up the leopard at once with the help of his dogs, or he can set to work and construct a "*scherm*" (shelter of branches) from which to watch for the leopard at night on its return to the kill.

In the first event he should lose no time in getting his dogs together, and obtaining the assistance of two good native spoorers. I consider the latter invaluable, even though a man may have had so many years' experience amongst wild game as to have become as proficient in this branch of forest-craft as nine out of ten natives themselves.

The sportsman is too heavily handicapped if forced to keep his eyes constantly on the spoor; he requires to be free to keep a sharp look-out for the game, and to use his rifle instantly. Four good dogs such as I have described are better than a whole pack of doubtful ones; if they know their work they will lose no time in getting on the spoor, and with their aid and that of the natives, good progress can be made.

If the dew is on the grass, so much the better; it will then be easier to spoor the game across the open stretches of long grass and scrub.

When by the excited action of the dogs it becomes evident the game is near (usually, if his drinking place is found, it is safe to expect a leopard to lie up within a few hundred yards of it) three of them should be taken in hand and led, unless they are sufficiently trained to keep close up or go "to heel" when ordered. The steadiest dog still keeps the spoor, and the sportsman must now be all eyes, examining critically every heap of rocks, every ravine crossed, every thorn-thicket, and the lower limbs of the larger trees. If the approach has been—as it should be—silent and cautious, the leopard will jump up at close quarters, and the dogs must be instantly released. They will then quickly bring him to bay, or if he bolts, will follow him up and "tree him." It is well to provide each dog with a broad and somewhat tightly-fitting leather collar; it may save them from an ugly mauling.

Should the sportsman decide to watch by night (by moonlight, of course, from choice) he must study the prevailing wind, and also note carefully the direction taken by the leopard when leaving its kill, as from that direction it will surely return. These points noted, he can erect his screen—a $2\frac{1}{2}$ feet breast-work of interlaced branches is sufficient—which should be about 20 to 25 feet distant from the kill; the latter must be handled as little as possible, and firmly lashed *by the neck* to a tree by means of a light chain or strong *riem*. It can, with advantage, be hung up about 5 feet from the ground, while another good plan, especially if the night is dark, and there seems but a poor chance of obtaining a shot, is to lash it to a log of wood about 8 feet in length and 4 inches in diameter. If the leopard seizes the kill, unseen by the watcher, he drags it away, log and all, but thereby leaves a spoor which can be followed *at earliest dawn*, when the animal can often be shot at the carcase. Under any circumstances, there is great risk of the leopard winding one, for as a rule, before approaching its kill, it makes a complete circuit round the spot, to test the wind. If, however, the watcher gets his chance he must keep cool, seize his *first* good opportunity, and *fire low*.

When the nature of the ground is such as to permit of the "scherm" being erected on *higher ground* than that where the kill lies, such as on the bank of a creek, top of an ant heap or a pile of rocks, then the sportsman's chances of success are at least doubled. Watching from any height in a tree is almost useless; it is difficult to see an animal on the ground, and besides, a leopard, unlike a lion, always *examines the trees* when approaching a kill, far more critically than he does objects on the ground.

A yet more certain plan, and in fact the only one to be adopted in case the leopard fails to revisit its kill on the first night, is to hang the latter well up in a tree, and then tether a goat on the spot, tying a piece of string to one ear, the other end of the string being led into the "scherm"; an occasional pull on this will cause the goat to bleat "to order"—a temptation few leopards can resist. On the leopard's approach, the goat tugs and strains at its tether, usually bleating loudly at first; then, standing stiffly at the end of the rope and staring hard in the direction from which the leopard is approaching, it becomes quite silent. The shot is best taken after the goat is seized, but sometimes a leopard gives a good chance when creeping in on its victim. On this account the ground should be cleared as much as possible round the bait; on no account should the latter be tethered less than 30 ft. distant from any heavy cover. Judgment and caution must be exercised from first to last; the branches for the "scherm" must be cut quite 100 yards from where the bait is to be placed, and in fact every endeavour must be made to retain the former natural appearance of the spot, even to artfully concealing the "scherm" by throwing branches loosely in front of it.

I have frequently used Brock's blue lights for shooting on dark nights, with fair measure of success, the plan adopted being to fasten one or more of the lights to a bush or tree, behind and above my right shoulder, pointing in the direction from which the game is expected. Thus placed, the light when struck shows up the rifle sights well, as also any object in front for a distance of 25 to 30 yards, so that if lit up when the leopard is eating at the carcase, there is ample time, if one is quick, to put a bullet in the brute's chest as he springs to his feet and stares at the unwonted glare. Of course, they do not always stand thus, frequently bolting precipitately, but one must take the chance of it.

Following a wounded leopard is most risky work, he will hide anywhere, for scarcely any cover is so small and insignificant but he will make himself invisible in it. Leopards seldom give any warning of their proximity in such a case, as does a lion, but will fly out at dogs or man with implacable fury and lightning speed; one must be smart with the rifle then or stand by for a mauling.

A smooth bore, loaded with AAA shot, should stop any leopard in its charge at close quarters, but I consider the use of such a weapon quite unsportsmanlike. A wounded leopard, unless closely pursued by dogs, never takes to a tree but if not too badly hit, will travel a great distance before lying up. One should get quickly on the spoor, and even then, without dogs, there will be many checks, as the loosely set skin frequently covers up the bullet hole and prevents external bleeding.

The same general rules apply to hunting the Low Country leopard, but the latter are usually more difficult to spoor from a kill, not only because if found in fly country one seldom has any dogs in camp, but also owing to the nature of the ground traversed. A leopard scarcely leaves any trace of his passage either through long grass, reeds, or over the short stiff "wire-grass" and strong rubble of many of the Low Country ridges; whereas spoor is fairly easy to follow over the damp, soft soil of the kloofs. The Low Country leopard, however, seldom travels far from its kill, especially if water is handy; and a systematic search through all the most likely and unlikely cover within a radius of 300 yards from the kill usually proves successful; in fact it is not at all an unusual thing to find this animal lying at his kill throughout the day.

Rifle and Ammunition—Any light, accurately-sighted double rifle with a slightly hollowed conical lead projectile of *not less* than 360 grains, will account for a leopard.

I have on most occasions used a Gibb's Metford. It is a perfect weapon for leopard shooting; but in kloofs and dense bush I often use a double 12 rifle, a wound from which leaves a good blood spoor. Owing to the weight of its projectile the shock to the animal is great, and prevents its going any great distance after being hit. The ·303 rifle should be a deadly weapon for leopards, if a reliable expanding bullet is used.

Aim should always be taken for the shoulder, if the animal is broadside on, and for the centre of the chest or the junction of neck and shoulder if facing or quarter face on.

Although I invariably use ivory bead foresights I do not consider them "quite the thing" for bush shooting. A small enamel bead-sight, which if necessary can be made to slip over the ordinary sight, is more opaque and therefore gives better results; for moonlight nights these enamel sights are excellent.

For work in dense and thorny bush, no material will be found to answer so well or to wear so long as gabardine, which is practically thorn proof. A close-fitting cloth cap is the best head-gear; a broad-brimmed felt hat or a helmet is knocked off too easily by the twigs.

FRED. V. KIRBY.

SOMALILAND—Leopards and panthers are so cunning, so stealthy in their habits, so easily concealed, and they live in such broken and intricate ground, that they can seldom be systematically hunted like other kinds of large game. Moreover, they live chiefly in stony hills, where tracking their light footsteps is next to impossible. Leopards are seen now and then by daylight when the sportsman is in pursuit of other game, but they generally disappear before a shot can be fired. They turn up at the most unexpected times and places, but are most often heard of in the hunting countries of North East Africa, in the neighbourhood of the grazing grounds of the flocks of the nomads, when the kraals are pitched at the foot of the rugged hills or on the edge of broken country intersected by ravines. In the afternoons, and about an hour before sunset, as the flocks are being driven homewards, the leopards sneak out from their rocky hiding places to strike down any lagging sheep or goat.

There are exceptions, however, and a kill may occur at any time when the flocks are about, and attacks by night are bold and frequent, the victims being dragged out through the thorn fences of the kraals.

If darkness is setting in when the kill occurs, by the time the news gets to the sportsman's camp it is too late to do anything. But if a kill takes place early in the afternoon, a not uncommon occurrence, there is time to erect a small screen of brushwood down wind and within a few yards of the carcase, behind which the sportsman can hide. The leopard will almost surely return to such a kill at sunset, and can be easily shot. In a case of this kind it is important not to touch the carcase or even approach it too closely, as the human taint hanging about would be quite enough to excite suspicion of a trap. The attacks of leopards are very varied in character. On one occasion the writer, when following a wounded antelope, found that a leopard had taken up the chase, leaving its tracks over those of the antelope; and when a little later the antelope was discovered lying dead, a leopard, which had been drinking its blood, bounded away. This occurring at about 4 p.m., the writer sat in the shade of a bush thirty yards from the carcase for an hour, at the end of which time the leopard returned boldly to the kill and was shot, being soon afterwards packed on a camel along with its victim and sent to camp.

On occasions leopards were shot by watching over a goat tied up as a living bait at night. A screen was erected if possible down wind, and a little above the bait, the latter being tied to a heavy log of wood; it is a mistake to tie it to a stake fixed in the ground, as unless the leopard can drag his kill a little way he will suspect a trap and bound off. The best time to shoot is when the leopard is lying on the victim drinking its blood, or is dragging it slowly along. A half-grown kid, which will bleat loudly, is the best.

The writer found it a good plan to take post just as the men were finishing work on the screen. They had instructions when going away to make plenty of noise, talking loudly, so as to give the impression that no one remained behind. On one occasion when this ruse was practised, the men having only just walked away, and while they were still only two hundred yards distant, the leopard walked boldly up, and was shot by the writer, who had remained in ambush.

On another occasion he sat behind a screen of brush-wood, watching a pool of water before sunset, at a time when most of the other streams and pools in the neighbourhood were dry. The animal came to drink while it was still twilight, and was shot, stumbling away to die in a ravine close by, where he was found half-an-hour later by the aid of a lantern.

Leopards are very bold and enterprising when

they have made up their minds to attack, and it is well known that in civilised neighbourhoods they will enter houses; and many a time has the writer's camp been attacked and a goat killed within the thorn fence, in spite of the presence of an armed sentry. On one occasion the brute was seen to creep under the outer fly of a "Cabul" tent within a few yards of where the writer was standing, and springing over a circle of sleeping men, seize a goat which had been tethered close to the camp fire. An approach was made on another night along the branch of a tree overhanging camp, followed by a perpendicular drop on the goat, which, however, it had no time to kill before it was driven away.

The leopard will charge against any odds when wounded. Once when following one by the light of a faint moon, accompanied by a dozen natives armed with rifles, the writer was charged by a leopard, which sprang on the next man to him. This man held down his assailant by the throat till it could be shot. This animal had first attracted attention two evenings before by prowling round camp, emitting at intervals the peculiar rasping growl, something like the sound of sawing of wood, which is so often heard echoing through the hills, even in the day-time, where leopards are common. It can be heard at a great distance. In this case, a goat was tied up on the first night, but on springing, the leopard caught sight of the ambushed sportsman, promptly let go the hold on the goat's neck, and bounded away. The same tactics were resorted to on the second night, but the writer, forewarned, fired a snap-shot at the beast while in its spring and disembowelled it. It crawled, however, into a bushy hill and died fighting, as above described. Moonlight tracking is not recommended, where dangerous game is concerned; the lights and shadows are uncertain, and accurate aim is difficult; in the case related it was only resorted to in order to prevent the valuable skin from being spoilt by hyænas.

Examples are numerous in the experience of most sportsmen of leopards turning up at unexpected times and places. The writer once came upon one lying on its side asleep at three on a hot afternoon in full view, on the open level sand of a river-bed, where a recent freshet had left the surface damp, and a high overhanging bank cast a cool shadow. Sometimes they were sighted for a moment in forest country, to bound away without giving a shot, and once a leopard was found asleep in the shade cast by the body of a dead elephant, just as a party with axes arrived to cut out the ivory. On another occasion a shot at one of a herd of gazelles was spoilt by the charge of three leopards, which scattered them. Once when the sportsman's caravan was on the march, the man driving the milch goats happening to lag behind, the head of a leopard, which had evidently been following, was seen over a bush, and on finding itself observed it sprang away.

When a leopard or panther has carried off a goat and can be traced to one of the boulder-strewn hills in which they live, there are two ways of bringing it to bag.

One plan is to follow the tracks, if possible, or the trail where the carcase has been dragged along, till the leopard's cave is discovered. Very likely the remains of the meat will be found at the cave mouth. Then choose a convenient spot not far away at the foot of the hill, erect a zeriba or utilise a bush as a screen, and watch over a live goat for half an hour before sunset. It is not worth while waiting long after sunset, as by that time any leopard about will probably have gone further afield to prowl round the kraals.

Another way is for the sportsman, having found the cave, to post himself early in the afternoon on a pinnacle of rock above it and watch on the chance of catching a glimpse of the animal when he comes out for his afternoon ramble, after the sleep he will probably have taken during the heat of the day. Several men may be posted on the tops of the largest boulders in spots commanding the whole of the broken ground, so that if he is on the move he will probably be seen; and when seen his progress can be followed by signals passed along by the men; then with judgment and good wind on the part of the sportsman a shot may be obtained. It involves a good deal of jumping from rock to rock where a fall would be disastrous, and rubber tennis shoes are the best in dry weather.

Somalis sometimes kill leopards, as well as hyænas, at the wells, by leaving poison in the rough clay troughs which still contain a little muddy liquid after the flocks have been watered. Wild animals, being unable to climb down to drink from the deeper wells, seem often to depend on these troughs, which are situated at the surface of the ground.

The range of the leopard, in North-east Africa at any rate, is not confined to any locality; it is most common in Somaliland, in the Golis Mountains, and their continuations east and west. It is rather rare on the flat stoneless interior plateau, and possibly altogether absent on the open treeless grass prairies. It is common everywhere where broken ground, intersected by ravines, is combined with the presence of goat and sheep kraals. It is seldom seen in the Maritime plain, though common in the interior plains behind the low Maritime ranges. It is, as before pointed out, so unexpectedly found that the only methods of hunting it, promising substantial probability of success, are by watching over water, over a kill, or over a living bait.

When driven by a line of beaters it is said often to escape observation by crouching or taking to the branches of a tree till they have passed; and it must be remembered that a platform in a tree is little protection against such a good climber, and in India many a sportsman has been pulled out of a tree.

When it offers a good chance, a leopard, being a small and thin-skinned animal, can be killed with comparative ease, and a double ·450 express rifle should be a good weapon; some writers recommend a double 12 bore gun, with S.S.G. shot, for use at close quarters. Being savage, vindictive, and fearless above almost any other game animal, they require straight and quick shooting. There are many occasions on record where a good knife, or a double ·577 pistol, would have been useful carried in the belt, for in a charge the rifle may be knocked out of the sportsman's hand, and a leopard is not too powerful an animal to be met in this way as a last resort.

The Somalis call all leopards "*shabel*," but they affect to believe in the existence of a large kind, rare and inhabiting the highest hills, possessing supernatural powers, and the ability to change itself into a human being at will. This animal, if we strip it from exaggeration and superstition, is probably the larger heavily built leopard, which would be called a panther in India. These fine hill specimens sometimes take to man-eating, and when they do they are most destructive, one upon the Golis range in Somaliland having been credited, by native report, with a hundred human victims.

It appears not to be very clear among naturalists what the difference between a panther and leopard really is, the chief points being the size and build and the formation of the spots; but the writer is unable to throw any special light on this subject.

H. G. C. SWAYNE.

INDIA—It is proposed under this name to treat of the animal (*Felis pardus*) called by sportsmen in India panther, leopard, and cheetah. The Hindoostani name is "*Tendwa*," but it is frequently called cheetah by the natives, though this latter name is more appropriately applied to the hunting leopard (*Felis jubata*), a totally different animal. There can be no doubt that there exist two varieties of the leopard in India, one much larger than the other; indeed, some zoologists hold that they are distinct species, but Jerdon considers them to be varieties only, and not distinct species. This seems the better opinion. Jerdon uses the term "panther" for the larger, and "leopard" for the smaller variety. The chief distinction between the two is in size, the leopard rarely, if ever, exceeding 6 feet in length from the nose to tip of the tail, while the panther measures from 6 feet to nearly 8 feet, more usually a few inches under or over 7 feet. The other points of difference are: (1) in the panther, the ground colour of the skin is of a light yellow, while the leopard is much darker, and the spots on the latter are closer together and smaller than those on the panther; (2) the skull of the leopard is rounder than that of the panther, and is said to want the bony ridge running along the occiput which characterises the panther's skull. This last observation, however, is, in the writer's opinion, not correct; the bony ridge referred to is found in all *old* animals of either variety, and is wanting in young specimens of both. The older the animal, the more developed is the bony ridge, and the surest sign of age in any of the cat tribe is the size of this bony ridge. Most authors also state that the panther is more slender in figure than the leopard, but this also is not in accordance with the experience of the writer. The habits of the two varieties are similar, though, as might be expected, the larger animal is able to kill a larger prey. Both varieties in the remainder of this article are included in the term panther.

The panther, then, is found throughout India wherever there is jungle of any extent, and it is particularly partial to rocky hills, its favourite haunts being in the cavities among the rocks, where it lies up during the day, issuing forth at evening in search of food. At night time it does not seem to mind the vicinity of man, and prowls close round the villages in search of any stray dog or goat. Panthers feed on cattle, goats, dogs, deer, pigs, monkeys, hares, peacocks, and any smaller bird or animal that they can get hold of. They are very fond of dogs, and many a good dog has been carried off by them. When sportsmen are tying out for tigers, panthers frequently take the bait intended for the larger animal. Many instances have occurred of a panther carrying the animal it has killed up into a tree and concealing it in the branches. They occasionally go up into trees to sit during the day, but this is exceptional, as they usually prefer to remain on the ground. In one well authenticated instance a panther was seen ascending a tree in the course of a beat to look about him; and it is well known that they have, when wounded, gone up the tree and pulled down their assailant sitting in it. Sometimes in a beat it is believed that panthers ascend a tree and remain there hidden until the beat has passed. They have also been observed treed by wild dogs. When wounded and followed on foot, they are, if their wound disinclines them to travel, almost certain to charge; they are very courageous under these circumstances, and will go at one man after another with astonishing rapidity.

The panther has a wonderful knack of concealing himself. The smallest depression of the ground and the shortest of grass suffice to render him invisible. Conspicuous as he is when walking, the moment he has crouched in the yellow grass and flickering shade it is impossible to see him before he makes his charge.

Of course, if he does not intend to charge, as he moves to go away you can shoot him easily enough. The wounds inflicted by the panther, though not so deep as those made by the larger *Felidæ*, are frequently fatal, blood-poisoning being a common sequel.

The usual mode of shooting is by driving them towards the gun by a number of beaters, but it is often impossible to induce the panther to leave his hole in the rocks, where he sits listening to the din. If there are no rocks, he is lying under a bush or in the grass in the shade of a tree; nevertheless, he sometimes manages in some wonderful way to slip away unseen, or what is not unlikely, sits close and lets the beat pass him by. Another way is to tie up a goat near the rocks where the panther is supposed to be. The goat bleats for his comrades, and the panther is attracted and comes out. From 3 P.M. to sunset is the best time. Or a goat can be tied just outside a village, where the tracks of a panther are seen, and about sunset, or shortly after, the panther may come. Another method is to sit over the carcase of a kill, and wait for the panther's return to it. Panthers are also occasionally seen and shot when out stalking, but it is not possible to track them up. It is mere chance, walking them up, and rarely occurs. They bring forth their young usually in April and May, and as a rule produce two cubs, which accompany the mother until nearly full grown. Man-eating panthers are not so common as man-eating tigers, but when they take to the habit they become a terrible scourge, entering the villages at night and seizing man, woman, or child as they lie asleep. One male panther, in the writer's own experience, in the Hyderabad districts, killed in less than a fortnight two women, two men and one boy, and had killed several others before. In every case the victim was seized by the throat when asleep. The panther's career ended in a trap; he was of the large variety, and in full vigour. It also transpired that he was accompanied by a female, whose tracks, however, had not on any previous occasion been observed. On the night of his capture, the female seized a man at the same village, who succumbed afterwards to his wounds, though they were of a trifling character. In the twelve months afterwards she only killed two persons, so there can be no doubt that the male was the chief offender. There are two ways of trapping panthers; one by a box-like cage with a falling floor, in one end of which a goat is placed for bait, and in this the panther is taken alive. In the other mode, a heavy triangular framework of wood, loaded with stones, is supported by an arrangement something like a "figure-of-four" trap. The ground beneath is excavated a few inches to the shape of the triangular frame, which fits into the excavation when it falls. In the centre a small hole is dug, in which a kid is placed with its legs tied; this is covered with a dry palm leaf; a string attached to the trigger which lets the erection fall is fastened inside the hole, and when the panther comes, he scrapes with his paw at the palm leaf, so as to get at the kid, and pulls the string, when the whole weight of the frame and stones descends and crushes him to the ground. If not killed by the fall, he is easily despatched, as he cannot move. The man-eater referred to was caught in a trap of this description placed in a shed in the middle of the village, and close to a hut from which he had taken a girl a week previously.

The track of the adult male is squarer and rounder than that of the female, the impression left by the foot of the latter being oval in shape. Black panthers are rare, and at one time it was supposed that they were a distinct variety, but the evidence rather points to their being the offspring of the ordinary panther. Sanderson mentions that a black female in the Zoological Society's Garden at Amsterdam had two cubs, one black and one of the ordinary colour, but nothing was known of the male parent. The converse case of an ordinary female with one black cub among others of ordinary hue has been seen, it is believed, in India, though chapter and verse for this statement cannot be given. There is a good specimen of the black panther stuffed at the Natural History Museum at South Kensington, the colour of which, however, appears to be turning rather rustier than it used to be. The Indian panther appears to be identical with the African leopard. The writer saw in Somaliland one of the smaller variety, and a skin of the larger variety, both undistinguishable from the Indian leopard.

J. D. INVERARITY.

LEOPARD SPEARING.— Spearing the common leopard (*Felis pardus*) is a sport to which some Rajahs are partial. The leopard is caught in the forest in a cage-like structure made of natural boughs, with an inner compartment baited with a live goat; and, being transferred to a smaller cage, is taken without delay, so that it may lose none of its courage or activity, to an open plain. It is there loosed with ample law, in the presence of sportsmen mounted, armed with boar spears. If it makes for the forest, it affords a spirited chase before it is speared; and if it crouches, awaiting the attack, it ordinarily makes good its spring on the first assailant, so that it is not speared without some danger to horse and man.

END OF VOL. II.